THE EUROPEAN UNION SERIES

General Editors: Neill Nugent, William E. Paterson, Vincent Wright

The European Union series provides an authoritative library on the European Union, ranging from general introductory texts to definitive assessments of key institutions and actors, issues, policies and policy processes, and the role of member states.

Books in the series are written by leading scholars in their fields and reflect the most up-to-date research and debate. Particular attention is paid to accessibility and clear presentation for a wide audience of students, practitioners, and interested general readers.

The series editors are **Neill Nugent**, Professor of Politics and Jean Monnet Professor of European Integration, Manchester Metropolitan University, and **William E. Paterson**, Director of the Institute of German Studies, University of Birmingham.

Their co-editor until his death in July 1999, **Vincent Wright**, was a Fellow of Nuffield College, Oxford University. He played an immensely valuable role in the founding and development of *The European Union Series* and is greatly missed.

Feedback on the series and book proposals are always welcome and should be sent to Steven Kennedy, Palgrave Macmillan, Houndmills, Basingstoke, Hampshire RG21 6XS, UK or by e-mail to s.kennedy@palgrave.com

General textbooks

Published

Desmond Dinan **Encyclopedia of the European Union** [Rights: Europe only]

Desmond Dinan **Europe Recast: a History of European Union** [Rights: Europe only]

Desmond Dinan **Ever Closer Union: An Introduction to European Integration (2nd edn)** [Rights: World excluding North and South America, Philippines and Japan]

Simon Hix **The Political System of the European Union (2nd edn)**

Paul Magnette **What is the European Union?: Its Nature and Prospects**

John McCormick **Understanding the European Union: A Concise Introduction (3rd edn)**

Brent F Nelsen and Alexander Stubb **The European Union: Readings on the Theory and Practice of European Integration (3rd edn)** [Rights: Europe only]

Neill Nugent (ed) **European Union Enlargement**

Neill Nugent **The Government and Politics of the European Union (5th edn)** [Rights: World excluding USA and dependencies and Canada]

John Peterson and Elizabeth Bomberg **Decision making in the European Union**

Ben Rosamond **Theories of European Integration**

Forthcoming

Laurie Buonanno and Neill Nugent **Policies and Policy Processes of the European Union**Mette

Mette Eilstrup Sangiovanni (ed) **Debates on European Integration: A Reader**

Philippa Sherrington **Understanding European Union Governance**

Also planned

The Political Economy of the European Union

Series Standing Order (outside North America only)
ISBN 0–333–71 [illegible] -7 hardcover
ISBN [illegible]

The major institutions and actors

Published

Renaud Dehousse **The European Court of Justice**
Justin Greenwood **Interest Representation in the European Union**
Fiona Hayes-Renshaw and Helen Wallace **The Council of Ministers**
Simon Hix and Christopher Lord **Political Parties in the European Union**
David Judge and David Earnshaw **The European Parliament**
Neill Nugent **The European Commission**
Anne Stevens with Handley Stevens **Brussels Bureaucrats?: The Administration of the European Union**

Forthcoming

Simon Bulmer and Wolfgang Wessels **The European Council**

The main areas of policy

Published

Michelle Cini and Lee McGowan **Competition Policy in the European Union**
Wyn Grant **The Common Agricultural Policy**
Martin Holland **The European Union and the Third World**
Brigid Laffan **The Finances of the European Union**
Malcolm Levitt and Christopher Lord **The Political Economy of Monetary Union**
Janne Haaland Matláry **Energy Policy in the European Union**
John McCormick **Environmental Policy in the European Union**
John Peterson and Margaret Sharp **Technology Policy in the European Union**
Handley Stevens **Transport Policy in the European Union**

Forthcoming

Bart Kerremans, David Allen and Geoffrey Edwards **The External Economic Relations of the European Union**

Laura Cram **Social Policy in the European Union**
Stephen Keukeleire and Jennifer MacNaughton **The Foreign Policy of the European Union**
James Mitchell and Paul McAleavey **Regionalism and Regional Policy in the European Union**
Jörg Monar **Justice and Home Affairs in the European Union**
John Vogler, Richard Whitman and Charlotte Bretherton **The External Policies of the European Union**

Also planned

Defence Policy in the European Union
Political Union

The member states and the Union

Published

Carlos Closa and Paul Heywood **Spain and the European Union**
Alain Guyomarch, Howard Machin and Ella Ritchie **France in the European Union**

Forthcoming

Simon Bulmer and William E. Paterson **Germany and the European Union**
Phil Daniels and Ella Ritchie **Britain and the European Union**
Brigid Laffan **The European Union and its Member States**
Luisa Perrotti **Italy and the European Union**
Baldur Thorhallson **Small States in the European Union**

Issues

Published

Derek Beach **The Dynamics of European Integration: Why and when EU institutions matter**

Forthcoming

Thomas Christiansen and Christine Reh **Constitutionalising the European Union**
Steven McGuire and Michael Smith **The USA and the European Union**

Also planned

Europeanization and National Politics

The Political System of the European Union

Second Edition

Simon Hix

palgrave
macmillan

First edition 1999
Second edition 2005

Published by
PALGRAVE MACMILLAN
Houndmills, Basingstoke, Hampshire RG21 6XS and
175 Fifth Avenue, New York, N.Y. 10010
Companies and representatives throughout the world

PALGRAVE MACMILLAN is the global academic imprint of the Palgrave Macmillan division of St. Martin's Press, LLC and of Palgrave Macmillan Ltd. Macmillan® is a registered trademark in the United States, United Kingdom and other countries. Palgrave is a registered trademark in the European Union and other countries.

ISBN-13: 9780333–96181–0   hardback
ISBN-10: 0333–96181–1   hardback
ISBN-13: 9780333–96182–7   paperback
ISBN-10: 0333–96182–X   paperback

This book is printed on paper suitable for recycling and made from fully managed and sustained forest sources.

A catalogue record for this book is available from the British Library.

Library of Congress Cataloging-in-Publication Data
Hix, Simon.
   The political system of European Union / Simon Hix. — 2nd ed.
     p. cm. — (The European Union series)
   Includes bibliographical references and index.
   ISBN 0-333–96181–1 (cloth) — ISBN 0–333–96182–X (pbk.)
    1. European Union. I. Title. II. Series.

JN30.H5 2005
341.242'2—dc22   2004056955

10 9 8 7 6 5 4 3 2 1
14 13 12 11 10 09 08 07 06 05

Printed and bound in China

For Ben and Ruth
citizens of the EU and the US

Contents

List of Tables and Figures

Tables

Figures

Preface to the Second Edition

When the first edition of this book was published, in 1999, it was still somewhat controversial to think of the EU as a political system. The situation is now quite different. With 25 EU states and the prospect of a codified 'Constitution' it now seems peculiar to think of the EU as just another international organization that can be understood as the amalgam of the preferences and actions of the 'big players' (namely Germany, France and the United Kingdom).

But, the development of the EU also made the task of revising the book much harder. As the EU has become increasingly complex, integrated and important, the volume of research on EU government, politics and policy-making has grown exponentially. As a result it has been impossible to read, digest and review all the major contributions to our knowledge about the EU that have been produced since the first edition of this book. In addition to updating empirical developments since 1999, I have tried to synthesize and communicate the ideas and findings of much of the new research. If I have excluded or given insufficient space to other research, this is more a reflection of time and space constraints than the quality of that research.

I would like to thank Damian Chalmers, Hae-Won Jun and Margaret McCown for commenting on various parts of the text, and Willie Paterson and Derek Beach for reading and suggesting improvements to the complete draft. Finally, two events have changed in my life since the first edition of this book – the arrival of my children Ben and Ruth, to whom I dedicate this work.

London   SIMON HIX

Preface to the First Edition

The idea for this book first came to me in 1991, while I was studying for an MSc in West European Politics in the Government Department at the London School of Economics and Political Science (LSE). The LSE is a rare institution in that it has separate departments of International Relations (IR) and Government. At the LSE, research and teaching on European Integration and the European Community (EC) institutions was traditionally the preserve of the IR department. But, in the early 1990s, with the single market and the new EC policy competences in the Single European Act and the Maastricht Treaty, the Government Department started to become interested in teaching and researching EC politics and government. At that time, however, there was not much theoretical literature from this perspective. 'Neofunctionalism' and 'intergovernmentalism' are theories of European integration, and are hence limited when applied to government and politics. Those interested in the day-to-day workings of the EC had to be content with mainly empirical and inductive literature, under the umbrella of 'EC studies'. As students of government, we desperately sought a theoretical text on the government, politics and policy-making of the emerging European-level political system.

Then, in 1994 I found myself in Washington, DC, working as a freelance consultant on European Union (EU) affairs while trying to finish my doctoral thesis for the European University Institute, in Florence. One of my most enjoyable assignments while in Washington was running a series of sessions on 'How the European Union Works' for some officials in the US State Department. I needed a book about the EU that could speak to people who were primarily interested in the policy-process of the EU, and were eager to compare it to the American system of government. Alberta Sbragia's edited book, from a project for the Brookings Institution, came the closest (Sbragia, 1992). However, I still felt that a monograph would be the best vehicle for achieving a coherent and comprehensive text.

I subsequently set about planning and writing the book when I returned to academia in 1996, first at Brunel University in West London, and then 'back home' in the Government Department at the LSE. This process turned out to be easier than I had feared. Since the early 1990s there had been a huge increase in the number of political scientists trying to approach the EU as an emerging 'political system'. The result was an explosion of theoretical and analytical literature on

EU government, politics and policy-making. This new research appeared for the first time in comparative politics journals (such as *Comparative Political Studies* and *West European Politics*) and general political science journals (such as the *European Journal of Political Research* and the *American Political Science Review*), as well as in the specialist EU studies publications (such as the *Journal of Common Market Studies* and the *Journal of European Public Policy*). I consequently decided that the task should be to provide an extensive review of this new research, while highlighting how these approaches are connected to general issues in political science.

The result, I hope, is that this book will satisfy several interests. First, it can be used as a teaching tool on EU government, politics and policy courses, particularly for advanced undergraduates or graduates. For introductory courses, the book may be used as a companion volume to an introductory text on the EU, such as Dinan (1994). Second, the book should be a guide for those involved in political science research on the EU, particularly within the fields of comparative politics and comparative public policy/public administration.

This book would not have been possible without the encouragement and support of friends, family and colleagues. I wish to thank my publisher, Steven Kennedy, and Vincent Wright, of Nuffield College, Oxford, who provided invaluable encouragement throughout the writing of this book. I would also like to thank my colleagues at the LSE who read and commented on various draft chapters: Damian Chalmers, Keith Dowding, Patrick Dunleavy and Christopher Hood. A special note of gratitude goes to Matt Gabel, who read almost the entire book and provided numerous suggestions for improving the text and ironing-out inconsistencies. I am thankful to my students at Brunel and the LSE, who have had to suffer my often strange and incomprehensible thoughts about the EU, and have given me invaluable feedback on my ideas for the book, particularly Jan Meyer-Sahling. Also, my ideas in this book have been shaped profoundly by my friends and 'fellow travellers' in the international political science community, particularly Karen Alter, Cees van der Eijk, Mark Franklin, Maria Green Cowles, Kris Deschouwer, David Farrell, Liesbet Hooghe, Hussein Kassim, Amie Kreppel, Chris Lord, Howard Machin, Giandomenico Majone, Peter Mair, Gary Marks, Anand Menon, Andrew Moravcsik, Mark Pollack, Herman Schmitt, Tapio Raunio, Alberta Sbragia, Roger Scully, Paul Taggart, George Tsebelis, Helen Wallace, William Wallace, Paul Webb, Antje Wiener and Steve Wolinetz. And, I would really like to thank the people in the EU institutions who have taught me so much about the EU, especially Pete Brown-Pappamikail, Richard Corbett, Francis Jacobs, Mike Shackleton and Martin Westlake.

Finally, I am deeply indebted to my parents, Godfrey and Maureen Hix, without whose emotional and financial support over the years I could never have been able to do the job of my dreams. However, the person who deserves the greatest thanks is my wife and best friend, Beth Ginsburg. She has been by my side since the beginning, enduring my single-mindedness and my self-doubts, and offering support and counsel at every stage. Beth, I dedicate this book to you.

London   SIMON HIX

List of Abbreviations

ALDE	Alliance of Liberals and Democrats for Europe
CAP	Common Agricultural Policy
CCP	Common Commercial Policy
CFSP	Common Foreign and Security Policy
COPA	Confederation of Professional Agricultural Organizations
CoR	Committee of the Regions
COREPER	Committee of Permanent Representatives
DG	directorate-general
EAGGF	European Agricultural Guidance and Guarantee Fund
EC	European Community
ECB	European Central Bank
ECHR	European Convention on Human Rights
ECJ	European Court of Justice
Ecofin	Council of Economic and Finance Ministers
ECSC	European Coal and Steel Community
EDD	Group for a Europe of Democracies and Diversity
EEC	European Economic Community
EFTA	European Free Trade Area
ELDR	European Liberal, Democrat and Reform Party
EMS	Economic and Monetary System
EMU	Economic and Monetary Union
EP	European Parliament
EPC	European Political Cooperation
EPP	European People's Party
ERDF	European Regional Development Fund
ERM	Exchange Rate Mechanism
ERT	European Round Table of Industrialists
ETUC	European Trade Union Federation
EU	European Union
EUL/NGL	European United Left/Nordic Green Left
GATT	General Agreement on Tariffs and Trade
G/EFA	Greens/European Free Alliance
IGC	intergovernmental conference
JHA	justice and home affairs
NATO	North Atlantic Treaty Organization
OCA	optimal currency area
OECD	Organisation for Economic Cooperation and Development

PES	Party of European Socialists
QMV	qualified-majority voting
UEN	Union for a Europe of Nations
UN	United Nations
UNICE	Union of Industrial and Employers' Confederations
WEU	West European Union
WTO	World Trade Organization

Chapter 1

Introduction: Explaining the EU Political System

The EU: a Political System but not a State
How the EU Political System Works
Actors, Institutions and Outcomes: the Basics of Modern Political Science
Theories of European Integration and EU Politics
Allocation of Policy Competences in the EU: a 'Constitutional Settlement'
Structure of the Book

The European Union (EU) is a remarkable achievement. It is the result of a process of voluntary economic and political integration between the nation-states of Europe. The EU began with six states, grew to 15 in the 1990s, enlarged to include a further 10 in 2004, and may eventually encompass another five or 10. The EU started out as a coal and steel community and has evolved into an economic, social and political union. European integration has also produced a set of governing institutions at the European level with significant authority over many areas of public policy.

But, this book is not about the history of 'European integration', as this story has been told at length elsewhere (for example Dedman, 1996; McAllister, 1997). Nor does it try to explain European integration and the major turning points in this process, as this too has been the focus of much political science research and theorizing (for example Moravcsik, 1998; Stone Sweet et al., 2001). Instead, the aim of this book is to understand how the EU works today. Who has ultimate executive power? Under what conditions can the Parliament influence legislation? Is the Court of Justice beyond political control? Why do some citizens support the central institutions while others oppose them? How important are political parties and elections in shaping political choices? Why are some social groups more able than others to influence the political agenda? Are the policies governing the single market deregulatory or reregulatory? Who are the winners and losers from expenditure policies? What are the political consequences of economic and monetary integration? Have policies extended and protected citizens' rights and freedoms? And, how far are the central institutions able to speak with a single voice on the world stage?

We could treat the EU as a unique experiment. However, the above questions could be asked of any democratic political system. Furthermore, the discipline of political science has developed a vast array of theoretical tools and analytical methods to answer exactly these sorts of question. Instead of a general theory of how political systems work, political science has a series of mid-level explanations of the main processes that are common to all political systems, such as public opinion, party competition, interest group mobilization, legislative bargaining, delegation to executive and bureaucratic agents, economic policy-making, citizen–state relations, and international political and economic relations. Consequently, the main argument of this book is that to help understand how the EU works, we should use the tools, methods and cross-systemic theories from the general study of government, politics and policy-making. In this way, teaching and research on the EU can be part of the political science mainstream.

This introductory chapter sets the general context for this task, explaining how the EU can be a 'political system' without also having to be a 'state'. It then introduces the key interests, institutions and processes in the EU political system and the connections between these elements. The chapter subsequently reviews some of the basic assumptions of modern political science, and discusses how these assumptions are applied in the three main theories of EU politics. Finally, the chapter describes the allocation of policy competences between the national and EU levels.

The EU: a Political System but not a State

Gabriel Almond (1956) and David Easton (1957) were the first to develop formal frameworks for defining and analyzing political systems. Most contemporary political scientists reject the functionalist assumptions and grand theoretical aims of these projects. Nonetheless, Almond and Easton's definitions have survived. Their essential characterizations of democratic political systems consists of four main elements:

1. There is a stable and clearly defined set of institutions for collective decision-making and a set of rules governing relations between and within these institutions.
2. Citizens and social groups seek to realize their political desires through the political system, either directly or through intermediary organizations such as interest groups and political parties.
3. Collective decisions in the political system have a significant impact on the distribution of economic resources and the allocation of social and political values across the whole system.
4. There is continuous interaction ('feedback') between these political outputs, new demands on the system, new decisions and so on.

The EU possesses all these elements. First, the degree of institutional stability and complexity in the EU is far greater than in any other international regime. The basic institutional quartet – the Commission, the Council, the European Parliament (EP) and the Court of Justice – was established in the 1950s. Successive treaties and treaty reforms – the Treaty of Paris in 1952 (establishing the European Coal and Steel Community), the Treaty of Rome in 1958 (establishing the European Economic Community and the European Atomic Energy Community), the Single European Act in 1987, the Maastricht Treaty in 1993 (the Treaty on European Union), the Amsterdam Treaty in 1999, the Nice Treaty in 2003 and the 'Constitutional Treaty' (signed in June 2004 but not yet ratified) – have given these institutions an ever-wider range of executive, legislative and judicial powers. Moreover the institutional reforms have produced a highly evolved system of rules and procedures governing how these powers are exercised by the EU institutions. In fact the EU probably has the most formalized and complex set of decision-making rules of any political system in the world.

Second, as the EU institutions have taken on these powers of government, an increasing number of groups attempt to make demands on the system – ranging from individual corporations and business associations to trade unions, environmental and consumer groups and political parties. The groups with the most powerful and institutionalized position in the EU system are the governments of the EU member states, and the political parties that make up these governments. At face value, the centrality of governments in the system makes the EU seem like other international organizations, such as the United Nations and the Organization for Security and Cooperation in Europe. But in the EU the member state governments do not have a monopoly on political demands. As in all democratic polities, demands in the EU arise from a complex network of public and private groups, each competing to influence the EU policy process to promote or protect their own interests and desires.

Third, EU decisions are highly significant and are felt throughout the EU. For example:

- EU policies cover virtually all areas of public policy, including market regulation, social policy, the environment, agriculture, regional policy, research and development, policing and law and order, citizenship, human rights, international trade, foreign policy, defence, consumer affairs, transport, public health, education and culture.
- In fact some scholars estimate that the EU sets over 80 per cent of the rules governing the production, distribution and exchange of goods, services and capital in the member states' markets (for example Majone, 1996).

- On average more than 100 pieces of legislation pass through the EU institutions every year – more than in most other democratic polities.
- Primary and secondary acts of the EU are part of the 'the law of the land' in the member states, and supranational EU law is supreme over national law.
- The EU budget may be small compared with the budgets of national governments, but several EU member states receive almost 5 per cent of their national gross domestic product from the EU budget.
- EU regulatory and monetary policies have a powerful indirect impact on the distribution of power and resources between individuals, groups and nations in Europe.
- The EU is gradually encroaching on the power of the domestic states to set their own course in the highly contentious areas of taxation, immigration, policing, foreign and defence policy.

In short, it is beyond doubt that EU outputs have a significant impact on the 'authoritative allocation of values' (Easton, 1957) and determine 'who gets what, when and how' in European society (Lasswell, 1936).

Finally, the political process of the EU political system is a permanent feature of political life in Europe. The quarterly meetings of the heads of government of the member states (in the European Council) may be the only feature of the system that is noticed by many citizens. This can give the impression that the EU mainly operates through periodic 'summitry', like other international organizations. However, the real essence of EU politics lies in the constant interactions within and between the EU institutions in Brussels, between national governments and Brussels, within the various departments in national governments, in bilateral meetings between governments, and between private interests and governmental officials in Brussels and at the national level. Hence unlike other international organizations, EU business is conducted in multiple settings on virtually every day of the year.

What is interesting, nevertheless, is that the EU does not have a 'monopoly on the legitimate use of coercion'. As a result, the EU is not a 'state' in the traditional Weberian meaning of the word. The power of coercion, through police and security forces, remains in the hands of the national governments of the EU member states. The early theorists of the political system believed that a political system could not exist without a state. As Almond (1956, p. 395) points out:

the employment of ultimate, comprehensive, and legitimate physical coercion is the monopoly of states, and the political system is uniquely concerned with the scope, direction, and conditions affecting the employment of this physical coercion.

However, many contemporary social theorists reject this conflation of the state and the political system. For example Badie and Birnbaum (1983, pp. 135–7) argue that

> the state should rather be understood as a unique phenomenon, an innovation developed within a specific geographical and cultural context. Hence, it is wrong to look upon the state as the only way of governing societies at all times and all places . . .

In this view, the state is simply a product of a particular structure of political, economic and social relations in Western Europe between the sixteenth and mid-twentieth centuries, when a high degree of centralization, differentiation, universality and institutionalization was necessary for government to be effective. In other words, in a different environment government and politics could be undertaken without the classic apparatus of a state.

This is precisely the situation in the twenty-first century in Europe. The EU political system is highly decentralized and atomized, is based on the voluntary commitment of the member states and its citizens, and relies on suborganizations (the existing nation-states) to administer coercion and other forms of state power.

In other words, European integration has produced a new and complex political system. This has certainly involved a redefinition of the role of the state in Europe. But, the EU can function as a full-blown political system without a complete transformation of the territorial organization of the state – unlike the evolution from the city-state to the nation-state in the early-modern period of European history.

How the EU Political System Works

Figure 1.1 shows the basic interests, institutions and processes in the EU political system (the arrows indicate the direction of connections: complete arrows indicate a strong/direct link, and non-continuous arrows indicate a weaker/non-direct connection). At the base of the system are the EU citizens – the nationals of the 25 member states. EU citizens make demands on the EU system through several channels. In national elections, citizens elect the members of their national parliaments, who in turn form (and scrutinize) the governments that are represented in the EU Council. In European elections, citizens elect the members of the EP. By joining political parties and interest groups, citizens provide resources for these intermediary organizations to be involved in EU politics. By taking legal actions in national courts and the Court of Justice, citizens influence the development and enforcement of EU law. And, as a result of these links, public office-holders in

Figure 1.1   *The EU political system*

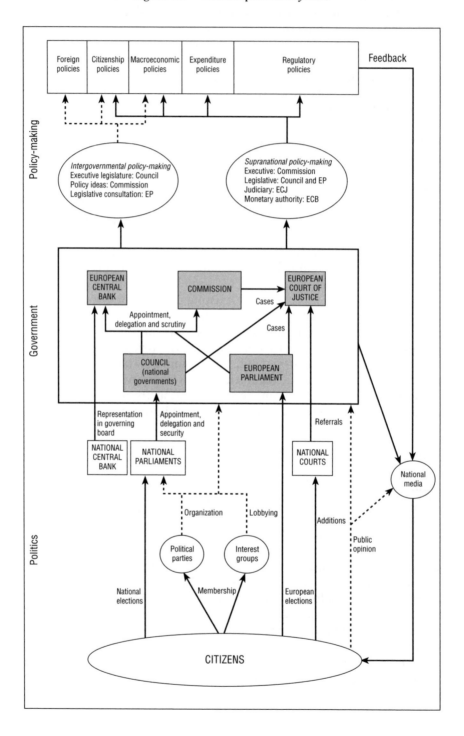

all the EU institutions take note of public opinion when defining their preferences and choosing actions in the EU policy-making process.

Two main types of intermediary associations connect the public to the EU policy process. First, political parties are the central political organizations in all modern democratic systems. Parties are organizations of like-minded political leaders, who join forces to promote a particular policy agenda, seek public support for this agenda, and capture political office in order to implement this agenda. Political parties have influence in each of the EU institutions. National parties compete for national governmental office, and the winners of this competition are represented in the Council. European commissioners are also partisan politicians: they have spent their careers in national party organizations, owe their positions to nomination by and the support of national party leaders, and usually seek to return to the party political fray. Members of the EP (MEPs) are elected on (national) party platforms and form 'party groups' in the EP, to structure political organization and competition in the Parliament. And, in the main party families, the party organizations in each member state and the EU institutions are linked through the transnational party federations.

Second, interest groups are voluntary associations of individual citizens, such as trade unions, business associations, consumer groups and environmental groups. These organizations are formed to promote or protect the interest of their members in the political process. This is the same in the EU as in any democratic system. National interest groups lobby national governments or approach the EU institutions directly, and like-minded interest groups from different member states join forces to lobby the Commission, Council working groups and MEPs. Interest groups also give funds to political parties to represent their views in national and EU politics. In each policy area, public office holders and representatives from interest groups form 'policy networks' to thrash out policy compromises. And, by taking legal actions to national courts and the Court of Justice, interest groups influence the application of EU law.

Next are the EU institutions, and the process of 'government' within and between these institutions. The Council brings together the governments of the member states, and is organized into several sectoral councils of national ministers (such as the Council of Agriculture Ministers). The Council undertakes both executive and legislative functions: it sets the medium and long-term policy agenda, and is the dominant chamber in the EU legislative process. The Council usually decides by unanimity, but uses a system of qualified-majority voting (QMV) on a number of important issues (where the votes of the member states are weighted according to their size and a large majority is needed for decisions to pass). Also, each government in the Council chooses its members of the Commission, and the governments collectively nominate the Commission president.

The other main representative institution in the EU is the European Parliament. The EP is composed of 732 MEPs, who are chosen in European-wide elections every five years. The EP has various powers of legislative consultation, amendment and veto under the EU's legislative procedures. The EP can also amend the EU budget. The EP scrutinizes the exercise of executive powers by the Commission and the Council, votes on the Council's nomination for the Commission president and the full Commission college (the investiture procedure), and has the power to throw out the Commission with a vote of censure.

The European Commission is composed of a political 'college' of 25 commissioners (one from each member state) and a bureaucracy of 36 directorates-general and other administrative services. The Commission is responsible for initiating policy proposals and monitoring the implementation of policies once they have been adopted, and is hence the main executive arm of the EU.

The highest judicial authority is the European Court of Justice (ECJ), which works closely with the national courts to oversee the implementation of EU law. The EU also has an independent monetary authority – the European System of Central Banks – which is composed of the European Central Bank (ECB) and the central banks of the member states in Economic and Monetary Union (EMU).

These institutions produce five types of policy:

- *Regulatory policies*: these are rules on the free movement of goods, services, capital and persons in the single market, and involve the harmonization of many national production standards, such as environmental and social policies, and common competition policies.
- *Expenditure policies*: these policies involve the transfer of resources through the EU budget, and include the Common Agricultural Policy, socioeconomic and regional cohesion policies, and research and development policies.
- *Macroeconomic policies*: these policies are pursued in EMU, where the ECB manages the money supply and interest rate policy, while the Council pursues exchange rate policy and the coordination and scrutiny of national tax and employment policies.
- *Citizen policies*: these are rules to extend and protect the economic, political and social rights of the EU citizens and include cooperation in the field of justice and home affairs, common asylum and immigration policies, police and judicial cooperation and the provisions for 'EU citizenship'.
- *Foreign policies*: these are aimed at ensuring that the EU speaks with a single voice on the world stage, and include trade policies, external

economic relations, the Common Foreign and Security Policy, and the European Security and Defence Policy.

There are two basic policy-making processes in the EU. First, most regulatory and expenditure policies and some citizen and macroeconomic policies are adopted through supranational (quasi-federal) processes: where the Commission is the executive (with a monopoly on policy initiative); legislation is adopted through a bicameral procedure between the Council and the EP (and the Council usually acts by QMV); and law is directly effective and supreme over national law and the ECJ has full powers of judicial review and legal adjudication.

Second, most macroeconomic, citizen and foreign policies are adopted through intergovernmental processes: where the Council is the main executive and legislative body (and the Council usually acts by unanimity); the Commission can generate policy ideas but its agenda-setting powers are limited; the EP only has the right to be consulted by the Council; and the ECJ's powers of judicial review are restricted.

Finally, there is 'feedback' between policy outputs from the EU system and new citizen demands on the system. However the feedback loop is relatively weak in the EU compared to other political systems. EU citizens gain most of their information about EU policies and the EU's governmental processes from national newspapers, radio and television, rather than from pan-European media channels. In addition, the national media tend to be focused on national government and politics rather than on European-level politics. Consequently, national elites are the main 'gatekeepers' of EU news: deciding which information is important, and how this should be 'spun' in the national setting. Only social groups who have direct contact with EU institutions, such as farmers and some business groups, are able to circumvent the filtering of EU information by national elites.

Table 1.1 provides some basic socioeconomic and political data on the EU member states and their representation in the EU institutions. As the data show, no member state is either physically, economically or political powerful enough to dominate the EU. In a sense, every member state is a minority in the EU political system.

Actors, Institutions and Outcomes: the Basics of Modern Political Science

Political science is the systematic study of the processes of government, politics and policy-making. The modern discipline dates from the end of the nineteenth century, when people such as Woodrow Wilson, Robert Michels, Knut Wicksell, Lord Bryce and Max Weber first developed tools and categories to analyze political institutions, including

Table 1.1 Basic data on current and prospective EU member states

Member state	Date joined	Socioeconomic data		Political data		Representation in the EU		
		Pop (2003) (mil.)	GDP/head (2004) (€, PPS)	Main political parties and votes in the last national parliamentary elections (%)	Territorial structure	Votes in the Council under QMV	Commissioners	MEPs (2004)
Austria	1995	8.1	27700	CD 42, SD 36	Federal	10	1	18
Belgium	1952	10.4	26570	SD 28, L 27, CD 19	Federal	12	1	24
Cyprus	2004	0.7	19690	RL 35, C 34	Unitary	4	1	6
Czech Republic	2004	10.2	15880	SD 30, C 25, RL 19	Unitary	12	1	24
Denmark	1973	5.4	27700	L 31, SD 29	Unitary	7	1	14
Estonia	2004	1.4	11020	Cen 25, C 25, L 18	Unitary	4	1	6
Finland	1995	5.2	24910	L 25, SD 23, C 19	Unitary	7	1	14
France	1952	59.6	25770	C 24, SD 24	Regional	29	1	78
Germany	1952	82.5	24940	SD 39, CD 39	Federal	29	1	99
Greece	1981	11.0	18,700	C 46, SD 41	Unitary	12	1	24
Hungary	2004	10.1	13970	SD 42, C 41	Unitary	12	1	24
Ireland	1973	4.0	30590	C 42, CD 23	Unitary	7	1	13
Italy	1952	57.3	23960	C 45, SD 35	Regional	29	1	78
Latvia	2004	2.3	9530	C 24, SD 19, L 17	Unitary	4	1	9
Lithuania	2004	3.5	10800	SD 31, Cen 20, L 17	Unitary	7	1	13
Luxembourg	1952	0.4	46560	CD 30, SD 24, L 22	Unitary	4	1	6
Malta	2004	0.4	17450	C 52, SD 48	Unitary	3	1	5
Netherlands	1952	16.2	26900	CD 29, SD 27, L 18	Unitary	13	1	27

Poland	2004	38.2	10920	SD 41, C 13	Regional	27	1	54
Portugal	1986	10.4	17100	C 40, SD 38	Unitary	12	1	24
Slovakia	2004	5.4	11970	N 20, C 15	Unitary	7	1	14
Slovenia	2004	2.0	17450	L 36, C 16	Unitary	4	1	7
Spain	1986	40.7	21770	SD 43, C 38	Regional	27	1	54
Sweden	1995	8.9	25700	SD 40, C 15	Unitary	10	1	19
United Kingdom	1973	59.3	27080	SD 41, C 32, L 18	Unitary/Regional	29	1	78
Bulgaria		7.8	7450	Cen 43, C 18, SD 18	Unitary	10	1	17
Romania		21.8	7460	SD 37, N 20	Unitary	14	1	33
EU15		379.4	25210			237	15	570
EU25		453.7	22940			345	25	732

Notes: RL = radical left, SD = social democrat, L = liberal, Cen. = centrist, CD = Christian democrat, C = conservative, N = nationalist.

Source: Eurostat; OECD; Elections Around the World (http://www.electionworld.org/election.htm).

bureaucracies, governments, parliaments and political parties. In the interwar period, a 'behavioural revolution' replaced this focus on the structural features of politics with 'methodological individualism' (Almond, 1996). The new method sought to explain political outcomes as the result of the interests, motives and actions of political actors (such as elites, bureaucrats, voters, political parties and interest groups) rather than as a consequence of the power of institutions and political structures (such as constitutions, decision-making rules and social norms). However in the 1980s and 1990s there was a return to interest in institutions under the label of 'new institutionalism', and since then many contemporary political scientists have integrated theories and assumptions about both actors and institutions in a single analytical framework (Shepsle, 1989; Thelen and Steinmo, 1992; Hall and Taylor, 1996).

Starting with actors, a common assumption in theories of politics is that political actors are 'rational' (see for example Dunleavy, 1990; Tsebelis, 1990). This means that actors have a clear set of 'preferences' about what outcomes they want from the political process. For example, party leaders want to be re-elected, bureaucrats want to increase their budgets or to maximize their independence from political interference, judges want to strengthen their powers of judicial review, and interest groups want to secure policies that increase the well-being of their members. Furthermore actors act upon these preferences in a rational way by pursuing the strategy that is most likely to produce the outcome they want. So party leaders will position themselves close to the key voters, bureaucrats will try to increase the size of the public sector, judges will make rulings that strengthen the rule of law, and interest groups will lobby those officeholders who are most likely to be decisive in the bargaining process.

But actors do not form their preferences and choose their strategies in isolation; they must take account of each other's interests and expected actions. 'Strong' rational choice theories assume that actors have perfect information about the preference ordering of the actors in the system, and therefore can accurately predict the result of a particular strategy. Nevertheless the perfect information assumption is often relaxed to allow for unintended consequences of actions and policy decisions. In either approach, political outcomes are seen as the result of strategic interaction between competing actors. Sometimes this interaction results in the best outcome for the actors involved – this is said to be an 'optimal' outcome. But very often actors are forced to pursue strategies that do not lead to the best outcome – as in the famous 'prisoners' dilemma' game (see Chapter 4). When this happens, the result is said to be 'suboptimal'.

Turning to institutions, these are the main constraints on actors' behaviour. Institutions can be 'formal', such as constitutions and rules of procedure, or 'informal', such as behavioural norms, shared beliefs and ideology (North, 1990). One example of a formal institution is the fixed term of office of a elected official, which restricts the office-holder to a particular 'time horizon', and hence leads the office-holder to disregard the possible long-term effects of strategies or outcomes. Institutions determine the likely payoffs from particular actions, and therefore the best strategy to achieve a particular goal. As a result, institutions can produce particular outcomes (equilibria) that would not occur if the institutions were absent or were changed (Riker, 1980). When this happens the outcome is said to be a 'structure-induced equilibrium' (Shepsle, 1979).

However institutions are not fixed. If an actor thinks he/she will be better off under a different set of institutions, he/she will seek to change the institutional arrangements. Thus actors have preferences about political institutions, and act upon these 'institutional preferences' in the same way as they do on their primary political goals. The process of institutional choice, therefore, is no different from strategic interaction over policy outcomes (North, 1990; Tsebelis, 1990). In political bargaining over policies and over institutions there is an existing structure of preferences and institutions. But in the institutional choice game the outcome is an 'institutional equilibrium' (Shepsle, 1986), which in turn might produce a different policy equilibrium as a result of a new set of rules governing policy bargaining.

In sum, the basic theoretical assumptions of modern political science can be expressed in the following 'fundamental equation of politics' (Hinich and Munger, 1997, p. 17):

preferences + institutions = outcomes

Preferences are the personal wants and desires of political actors; institutions are the formal and informal rules that determine how collective decisions are made; and outcomes (public policies and new institutional forms) result from the interaction between preferences and institutions. This simple equation illustrates two basic rules of politics:

- If preferences change, outcomes will change, even if institutions remain constant.
- If institutions change, outcomes will change, even if preferences remain constant.

Politics, then, is an ongoing process. Actors choose actions to maximize their preferences within a particular set of institutional constraints and a particular structure of strategic interests. But some actors change their preferences, for example when new politicians come to power. Or actors collectively decide to change the institutions. In either case, actors pursue new actions, which lead to new policy or institutional equilibria, which lead to new preferences relative to the existing policy status quo, and so on.

But once a particular institutional or policy equilibrium has been reached, these institutions and policies are often 'locked in'. First, despite the emergence of new actors or changes in actors' preferences, certain actors invariably have incentives to prevent any change from the new 'status quo'. These actors are said to be 'veto-players', and the more veto-players there are in a bargaining situation, the harder it is for policies or institutions to be changed (Tsebelis, 2002). Second, when new issues then emerge or the policy environment changes, policy options are now compared with the existing policy equilibrium rather than with the policy situation that prevailed when the equilibrium was first agreed. As a result, politics is often 'path dependent', whereby a particular institutional or policy design has long-term consequences that were not initially considered by the actors in the initial bargaining situation, for example because the actors had short time horizons or lacked information or knowledge about the long-term impact of their decisions (North, 1990; Pierson, 2000).

These assumptions can easily be applied to the EU. As discussed above, there are a number of actors in the EU system (national governments, the supranational institutions, political parties at the national and European level, bureaucrats in the national and EU administrations, interests groups, and individual voters), and the EU institutional and policy environment is complex. To explain how the EU works we must understand the interests of all these actors, their strategic relations *vis-à-vis* each other, the institutional constraints on their behaviour, their optimal policy strategies, and the institutional reforms they will seek to better secure their goals.

Theories of European Integration and EU Politics

Many contemporary scholars of the EU describe it as a political system (for example Attinà, 1992; Andersen and Eliassen, 1993; Quermonne, 1994; Leibfried and Pierson, 1995; Wessels, 1997a), and some early scholars of the European Community (EC) argued that European integration was creating a new 'polity' (for example Lindberg and Scheingold, 1970). However, few contemporary theorists try to set out a systematic conceptual framework for linking the study of the EU political system to the study of government, politics and policy-making in all political systems. The conceptual framework presented in this book does not constitute a single theoretical approach that explains everything about the EU. Thankfully, the 'grand theories' of the political system died in the 1960s, to be replaced by mid-level explanations of cross-systemic political processes. As discussed, an underlying argument in this book is that much can be learned if we simply apply these cross-systemic theories to the EU. This is a very different project from seeking grand theories of European integration. Nevertheless the 'integration theories' are the intellectual precursors of any theory of EU politics (cf. Hix, 1994, 1998a).

The first and most enduring grand theory of European integration is neofunctionalism (Haas, 1958, 1961; Lindberg, 1963; Lindberg and Scheingold, 1970, 1971). First developed by Ernst Haas the basic argument of neofunctionalism is that European integration is a deterministic process, whereby 'a given action, related to a specific goal, creates a situation in which the original goal can be assured only by taking further actions, which in turn create a further condition and a need for more, and so forth' (Lindberg, 1963, p. 9). As part of the wider 'liberal school' of international relations, neofunctionalists believe that the driving forces behind this 'spillover' process are non-state actors rather than sovereign nation states. Domestic social interests (such as business associations, trade unions and political parties) press for further policy integration to promote their economic or ideological interests, while the European institutions (particularly in the Commission) argue for the delegation of more powers to supranational institutions in order to increase their influence over policy outcomes.

Neofunctionalism's failure to explain the slowdown of European integration in the 1960s, and the subsequent strengthening of the intergovernmental elements of the EC, led to the emergence of a starkly opposing theory of European integration known as intergovernmentalism (for example Hoffmann, 1966, 1982; Taylor, 1982; Moravcsik, 1991). Derived from the 'realist school' of international relations, intergovernmentalism argues that European integration is driven by the interests and actions of the European nation states. In this interpretation the main aim of governments is to protect their geopolitical interests, such as national security and sovereignty. Decision-making at the European level is viewed as a zero-sum game, in which 'losses are not compensated by gains on other issues: nobody wants to be fooled' (Hoffmann, 1966, p. 882). Consequently, against the neofunctionalist 'logic of integration', intergovernmentalists see a 'logic of diversity [that] suggests that, in areas of key importance to the national interest, nations prefer the certainty, or the self-controlled uncertainty, of national self-reliance, to the uncontrolled uncertainty of the untested blunder' (ibid., p. 882).

These two approaches have been the two great monoliths at the gate of the study of European integration since the 1970s. Subsequent generations of researchers have been forced to learn the approaches virtually by rote, and to explain how their own theories relate to these dominant frameworks, usually by siding with one or the other. However three new theoretical constructs have emerged as the main new frameworks for understanding government, politics and policy-making in the EU.

First, Andrew Moravcsik has developed a theory he calls 'liberal-intergovernmentalism' (Moravcsik, 1993, 1998; Moravcsik and Nicolaïdis, 1999). Liberal-intergovernmentalism divides the EU decision process into two stages, each of which is grounded in one of the classic integration theories. In the first stage there is a 'demand' for EU policies from domestic economic and social actors – and, as in neo-functionalism and the liberal theory of international relations – these actors have economic interests and compete to have these interests promoted by national governments in EU decision-making. In the second stage EU policies are 'supplied' by intergovernmental bargains, such as treaty reforms and budgetary agreements. As in intergovernmentalism, states are treated as unitary actors and the supranational institutions have a limited impact on final outcomes. In contrast to the classic realist theory of international relations, however, Moravcsik argues that state preferences are driven by economic rather than geopolitical interests, that state preferences are not fixed (because different groups can win the domestic political contest), that states' preferences vary from issue to issue (so a member state may be in favour of EU intervention in one policy area but opposed in another), and that interstate bargaining can lead to positive-sum rather than simple zero-sum outcomes. Nevertheless in liberal-intergovernmentalism the EU governments remain the primary actors in the EU political system, and institutional reforms as well as day-to-day policy outcomes are the product of hard-won bargains and trade-offs between the interests of the member states.

Second, Gary Marks, Paul Pierson, Alec Stone Sweet, Markus Jachtenfuchs, Beate Kohler-Koch inter alia have developed an alternative set of explanations under the label of 'supranational governance' (Marks *et al.*, 1996; Pierson, 1996; Sandholtz and Stone Sweet, 1997; Kohler-Koch, 1999; Stone Sweet *at al.*, 2001; Jachtenfuchs, 2001; Hix, 2002). While there are considerable variations among the ideas of this group of scholars they share a common view of the EU as a complex institutional and policy environment, with multiple and ever-changing interests and actors, and limited information about the long-term implications of treaty reforms or day-to-day legislative or executive decisions. This leads to a common claim: that the member state governments are not in full control, and that the supranational institutions (the Commission, EP and ECJ) exert a significant independent influence on institutional and policy outcomes. For example Pierson (1996) explains the trajectory of European integration in three steps. At time T_0, the member state governments agree a set of institutional rules or policy decisions that delegate power to one or other of the EU institutions. At time T_1 a new bargaining environment emerges, with new preferences by the member states, new powers for and strategies by the supranational institutions, and new decision-making rules and policy competences at the EU level. Then at time T_2, a new policy or set of institutional rules is chosen. But as a result of the changes at T_1, and because of the strategic behaviour of the newly empowered supranational institutions, the decision taken by the member states at T_2 is very different from that which they would have taken if they had faced the same decision at T_0. In other words, at the first stage the member state governments were in control. Decisions by the governments produce particular 'path dependencies', that invariably result in the further delegation of policy competences and powers to the EU institutions.

Third, George Tsebelis, Geoff Garrett, Mark Pollack, Gerald Schneider, Fabio Franchino inter alia argue for a more explicitly 'rational choice institutionalist' perspective on EU politics (Schneider and Cederman, 1994; Tsebelis, 1994; Tsebelis and Garrett, 1996, 2001; Pollack, 1997a, 2003; Franchino, 2004; Jupille, 2004). These theorists start with formal (and often mathematical) models of a particular bargaining situation. From these models predictions are generated about the likely policy equilibrium, the degree of delegation to the supranational institutions, the amount of discretion the supranational institutions will have compared with the member states, and so on. Sometimes the models result in predictions that are similar to the liberal-intergovernmantalist view: for example that there are few short-term unintended consequences when the member state governments must decide by unanimity and have perfect information about each others' preferences and the preferences of the EU institutions (as in the reform of the EU treaties in Intergovernmental Conferences). However rational choice institutionalist models also produce explanations that are similar to the supranational governance view: for example that outcomes are controlled by the supranational institutions rather than by the member states when agenda setting is in the hands of the Commission, EP or ECJ, or when there is incomplete information in the policy process (Schneider and Cederman, 1994). In other words, rather than seeing EU politics as being controlled either by the member state governments or by the EU institutions, this approach tries to understand under precisely what conditions these two opposing outcomes are likely to occur.

The differences between the three contemporary theories of EU politics can easily be overemphasized (Aspinwall and Schneider, 2000; Pollack, 2001). All three approaches borrow assumptions and arguments from the general study of political science and political systems. All three share a common research method: the use of theoretical assumptions to generate propositions, which are then tested against the empirical reality. As a result, deciding which theory is 'right' is not a case of deciding which theory's assumptions about actors, institutions and information are closest to the reality. How good a theory is depends on how much and how efficiently it can explain a particular set of facts. However some theories are more efficient, some are more extensive, and all tend to be good at explaining different things. For example the liberal-intergovernmental theory uses some simple assumptions, and from these assumptions produces a rather persuasive explanation of the major history-making bargains. But, this theory seems less able to explain the more complex environment of day-to-day politics in the EU (cf. Rosamond, 2000; Peterson, 2001). The rational-choice institutionalist approach also aims for parsimony over extensiveness, with some simple assumptions being applied to a limited set of empirical cases, and it is good at predicting outcomes when the rules are fixed and information is complete. The supranational governance approach uses a more complex set of assumptions and is more able to explain a broader set of policy outcomes from the EU system and the long-term trajectory of the EU. Consequently the power of the different theories can only be judged where they produce clearly identifiable and opposing sets of predictions about the same empirical phenomenon. Unfortunately this is rare in EU politics, as it is in many areas of social science.

This may seem a rather arcane debate. However this overview of the main theoretical positions in EU politics is essential for understanding the intellectual foundations of the more empirically based research covered in the following chapters. The final building block is a basic knowledge of the allocation of policy competences in the EU system.

Allocation of Policy Competences in the EU: a 'Constitutional Settlement'

In the EU, as in all political systems, some policy competences are allocated to the central level of government while others are allocated to the state level. From a normative perspective, policies should be allocated to different levels to produce the best overall policy outcome. For example the abolition of internal trade barriers can only be tackled at the centre if an internal market is to be created. Also, policies where state decisions could have a negative impact on a neighbouring state (an 'externality'), such as environmental or product standards, are best dealt with at the centre. Policies where preferences are homogeneous across citizens in different localities, such as basic social and civil rights, could perhaps be dealt with at the centre (see Alesina *et al.*, 2002). And in the classic theory of 'fiscal federalism', the centre should be responsible for setting interest rates, as well as income distribution from rich to poor states, on the ground that central monetary policies inevitably constrain the tax and welfare policies of the states (Brown and Oates, 1987; Oates, 1999). But in the new theory of 'market-preserving federalism', the centre should provide hard budgetary constraints on state expenditure (to prevent high deficits) and regulatory and expenditure policies should be decentralized, to foster competition and innovation between different regimes (Weingast, 1995; Quin and Weingast, 1997).

From a positive perspective, in contrast, the allocation of competences is the result of a specific constitutional and political bargain and the way in which actors with different policy goals have behaved within this bargain (Riker, 1975; McKay, 1996, 2001). For example social democrats usually prefer regulatory and fiscal policies to be centralized (to allow for income redistribution and central value allocation), whereas economic liberals prefer strong checks and balances on the exercise of these policies by the central government. In addition, some constitutional allocations of competence are more rigid than others. For example, where the competences of the centre and the states are clearly specified and there is independent judicial review of competence disputes, the states are more protected against 'drift' to the centre. Alternatively, where competences are divided along functional rather than jurisdictional lines – with different roles for the centre and the states within each policy area (such as the setting of broad policy goals by the centre and of policy details by the states) – there are fewer constraints on the expansion of central authority. Nevertheless, under all constitutional designs the division of competences is never completely fixed, and the long-term trend in all multilevel political systems has been policy centralization.

Table 1.2 shows the evolution of competences in the EU and the US. This exercise is largely impressionist and uses a variety of secondary sources, and is hence not an exact science. Nevertheless several broad trends can be observed. First, both polities started with a low level of policy centralization. Second, policy centralization occurred remarkably quickly in the EU compared with the US, and in some areas faster than others. By the end of the 1990s most regulatory and monetary policies were decided predominantly at the EU level, while most expenditure policies, citizen policies, and foreign policies were controlled by the member states. In the US, in contrast, foreign policies were centralized before economic policies. Third, in the area of regulatory policies the harmonization of rules governing the production, distribution and exchange of goods, services and capital is now more extensive in the EU than in the US (Donohue and Pollack, 2001). For example in the field of social regulation, where there are few federal rules in the US, the EU has common standards for working hours, part-time and temporary workers' rights, worker consultation and so on. Also, after the

Table 1.2   Allocation of policy competences in the EU and US

	European Union					United States				
	1950	1957	1968	1993	2004	1790	1870	1940	1980	2004
Regulatory policies										
Movement of goods and services	1	2	3	4	4	1	3	4	4	4
Movement of capital	1	1	1	4	4	1	3	4	4	4
Movement of persons	1	2	3	4	4	1	3	4	4	4
Competition rules	1	2	3	4	4	1	1	4	4	4
Product standards	1	2	3	4	4	1	1	4	4	4
Environmental standards	1	2	2	3	3	-	-	3	4	3
Industrial health and safety standards	1	2	2	3	3	1	1	2	4	3
Labour market standards	1	1	1	3	3	1	1	2	3	2
Financial services regulation	1	1	1	3	4	1	1	2	3	3
Energy production and distribution	1	2	2	3	3	1	1	3	3	3
Expenditure policies										
Agricultural price support	1	1	4	4	4	1	2	4	4	4
Regional development	1	1	1	3	3	1	1	3	4	3
Research and development	1	1	2	2	2	1	1	2	3	2
Social welfare and pensions	1	1	1	2	2	1	1	3	4	3
Public healthcare	1	1	1	2	2	1	1	3	3	3
Public education	1	1	1	1	2	1	1	2	4	3
Public transport	1	1	1	1	1	1	1	2	3	2
Public housing	1	1	1	1	1	1	1	2	2	2

	EU 1950	EU 1957	EU 1968	EU 1993	US 1790	US 1870	US 1940	US 1980
Monetary and tax policies								
Setting of interest rates/credit	1	2	3	4	2	3	4	4
Issue of currency	1	1	1	4	1	4	4	4
Setting of sales and excise tax levels	1	1	4	4	2	2	2	3
Setting of income tax levels	1	1	1	1	1	1	3	3
Citizen policies								
Immigration and asylum	1	1	2	3	2	4	4	4
Civil rights protection	1	1	2	2	2	2	2	4
Policing and public order	1	1	2	2	1	2	3	3
Criminal justice	1	1	1	1	2	2	3	3
Foreign policies								
Trade negotiations	1	3	4	4	3	3	4	4
Diplomacy and IGO membership	1	1	2	3	3	3	4	4
Economic–military assistance	1	1	2	3	3	4	4	4
Defence and war	1	1	1	2	4	4	4	4
Humanitarian and development aid	1	1	3	3	4	4	4	4

Notes: 1 = all policy decisions at the state level (EU national/regional level; US state level); 2 = some policy decisions at the central level (EU level, or US federal level); 3 = policy decisions at both state and central level; 4 = most policy decisions at the central level. EU: 1950 – before any treaties, 1957 – EEC Treaty, 1968 – Merger Treaty, 1993 – Maastricht Treaty. US: 1790 – end of ratification of Constitution, 1870 – reconstruction era, 1940 – New Deal, 1980 – before Reagan.

Sources: Schmitter (1996); Donohue and Pollack (2001); Alesina *et al.* (2002).

high point of regulatory policy-making by Washington in 1980, the 1990s brought the deregulation of US federal regimes and increasing regulatory competition between the states (Ferejohn and Weingast, 1997). Fourth whereas the EU has harmonized sales tax, there are no EU rules governing the application of income tax. In the US, in contrast, there are few federal restrictions on the imposition of consumption taxes by the states, while income taxes are levied by both the states and the federal authorities.

These variations in the policy mix in the EU and US stem from their very different social, political and historical experiences (Elazar, 2001). Despite these differences there are remarkable similarities in the area of socioeconomic policies. A normative perspective would hold that market integration should be tackled by the centre. From a positive perspective, however, in both the EU and the US basic constitutional provisions guaranteeing the removal of barriers to the free movement of goods and services have been used by the central institutions to establish common standards in other areas, such as social rights, and the gradual integration of economic powers, such as a single currency, and constraints on fiscal policies. In the US this occurred between the late nineteenth century and the end of the 1970s. In the EU it took much less time: from the early 1980s to the early 1990s. In other words, whereas the US constitutional structure placed some constraints on the central authority, there have been few constraints on the ability of the member state governments and the EU institutions to centralize power in the name of completing the single market.

Nevertheless, Table 1.2 also shows that once the single market was completed and the EU was given the necessary policy competences to regulate this market, a new European 'constitutional settlement' had been established: whereby the European level of government is responsible for the creation and regulation of the market (and the related external trade policies); the domestic level of government is responsible for taxation and redistribution (within constraints agreed at the European level); and the domestic governments are collectively responsible for policies on internal security (justice and crime) and external security (defence and foreign). This settlement was already established by the Single European Act, with some minor amendments in the Maastricht Treaty. The subsequent reforms (in the Amsterdam and Nice Treaties and the proposed constitution agreed in June 2004) have not altered the settlement substantially. For example the proposed Constitution would set up a 'catalogue of competences' which would further constitutionalize the settlement: with a separation between exclusive competences of the EU (for the establishment the market); shared competences between the EU and the member states (mainly for the regulation of the market); 'coordination competences' (covering macro-economic policies, interior affairs, and foreign policies), and exclusive competences of the member states (in most areas of taxation and expenditure).

Hence despite the widely held perception that the EU is a 'moving target', with the permanent process of institutional reform, the opposite is in fact the case. The EU has not undertaken fundamental policy and institutional reforms because the settlement constitutes a very stable equilibrium. It would be much better if the member states would acknowledge the stability of the competence-allocation settlement and focus on the question of how to reform the central institutions to increase the efficiency and democratic accountability of the system as a whole. The EU political system has been established – the challenge now is to determine how it should work. This is exactly what happened in the negotiations on the proposed constitution, where the allocation of competences between the member states and the EU was settled within a few months of the start of the Convention on the Future of Europe in Autumn 2002, while the battles over the reform of the Council and the Commission derailed a planned agreement in December 2003, and were not resolved until June 2004.

Structure of the book

The rest of this book introduces and analyzes the various aspects of the EU political system. Part I looks at EU government: the structure and politics of the executive (Chapter 2), political organization and bargaining in the EU legislative process (Chapter 3), and judicial politics and the development of an EU constitution (Chapter 4). Part II turns to politics: public opinion (Chapter 5), the role of parties and elections and the question of the 'democratic deficit' (Chapter 6), and interest representation (Chapter 7). Part III focuses on policy-making: regulatory policies (Chapter 8), expenditure policies (Chapter 9), economic and monetary union (Chapter 10), citizens' rights and freedoms (Chapter 11), and the EU's foreign economic and security policies (Chapter 12). To create a link with the rest of the discipline, each chapter begins with a review of the general political science literature on the subject of that chapter. Finally, in Chapter 13 the underlying arguments and issues in the book are brought together in a short conclusion.

Government

Part I

Governments

Executive Politics

As the EU has evolved the governments of the member states have delegated significant powers of political leadership, policy implementation and regulation to the Commission. The result is a 'dual executive', where the Council and the Commission share the responsibilities of 'government'. This institutionalized separation can sometimes lead to deadlock, as in other dual executive systems (Blondel, 1984). However consensus and stability are secured through a division of labour, with the Council governing long-term matters and the Commission governing short-term ones, and through highly developed mechanisms to manage Commission discretion, such as comitology. To help understand how this division of labour came about and how it works we shall first explore some theories of executive power, delegation and discretion.

Theories of Executive Power, Delegation and Discretion

In the classic constitutional framework the legislature decides, the executive enacts and the judiciary adjudicates. However modern governments do more than simply implement law. They have two types of executive power: political power (leadership of society through proposals for policy and legislation), and administrative power (the implementation of law, the distribution of public revenues, and the passing of secondary and tertiary rules and regulations).

In some systems these powers are concentrated in the hands of one set of office holders. However in many systems, such as the EU, executive tasks are divided between different actors and bodies. One means of conceptualizing the relationships between different executive actors is 'principal–agent' analysis. In this approach the principals – the initial holders of executive power – decide to delegate certain powers to agents. Put another way, principals demand certain tasks that agents supply. The eventual division of power is located at the point where the demand for and supply of executive tasks meet. This framework was originally developed to analyze the relationship between the US Congress (the principal) and the US presidency and federal bureaucracy (agents), but a similar relationship exists between the EU member state governments and the EU Commission (Pollack, 1997a).

When delegating responsibilities to agents, principals usually require their agents to exercise their powers in a neutral fashion. However agents have their own interests and policy preferences, which derive from several sources. First, once a bureaucracy or a regulatory agency has gained a degree of autonomy it becomes the target of lobbying by private interest groups. Interest groups that are the subject of the bureaucratic actions of the agency have an incentive to 'capture' the agency (Lowi, 1969). Also the head of an agency may be tempted by inducements offered by interest groups, such as a well-paid job or senior position in the industry in question when his or her term of office expires.

Second, once established, agencies are interested in increasing their influence in the policy process. In classic public choice theory, public officials are 'budget maximizers' (Niskanen, 1971). They seek larger budgets to increase their own salaries, employ more staff, secure more patronage or raise their profile and reputation. In addition agents are in competition with each other to secure limited public resources, so they deliberately overestimate their budgetary needs and oversupply policy outputs (by spending as much as possible) to prevent downgrading relative to their competitors. The result is ever-larger demands by bureaucracies for public resources.

Third, an alternative view is that bureaux prefer to shape their own destiny (Dunleavy, 1990). Different bureaux have different budgetary needs: delivery agencies, which provide direct entitlements and subsidies, can distribute more benefits with larger budgets, whereas regulatory agencies only need to cover their personnel, research and administration costs. Also, within each agency senior and mid-level officials have different incentives. Mid-level officials usually seek more resources to distribute. Senior officials, on the other hand, gain few personal benefits from a larger budget, and a larger budget usually means more pressure. As a result, senior officials are primarily interested in securing policy influence, job security and freedom from direct line responsibilities. Rather than maximizing budgets, then, senior bureaucrats (particularly in regulatory agencies) will seek to maximize their independence from control and their opportunities to determine policy outcomes.

The implications of these theories are the same: agents wish to diverge from the principals' original policy intention. A key issue, then, is how agents are able to do this (cf. Weingast and Moran, 1983; Epstein and O'Halloran, 1999; Huber and Shipan, 2002). The problem for principals is that the delegation of power often results in 'bureaucratic drift' (or 'agency loss'), in which an agent is able to use its policy discretion to move final policy outcomes closer to its ideal position. This phenomenon is illustrated in Figure 2.1, which shows a two-dimensional policy space in which there are three governments with 'ideal policy preferences' (points *A*, *B*, and *C*). The Commission's ideal policy preference lies outside the 'core' of governmental preferences (depicted by the triangle). The governments and the Commission will each try to secure a policy that is as close as possible to their ideal point. The governments agree on a piece of legislation at position *X*. The Commission is responsible for implementing this legislation, and during the implementation it is able to shape the final outcome, thereby moving the policy away from *X* towards its ideal policy preference. In fact the Commission can move the final policy as far as position *Y*. Governments *A* and *B* prefer this policy to the original deal since *Y* is closer to their ideal preferences than *X*. Consequently, these governments have no incentive to introduce new legislation to overrule the Commission, and will oppose any attempt by government *C* to take such action. However governments *A* and *B* will block any moves further towards the Commission's ideal point, as any policy in this direction would be less attractive to these two governments than position *Y*. Hence the Commission has discretion to change the original policy outcome, but within the constraints of the preference structure of the legislators.

Figure 2.1   *Bureaucratic drift by the European Commission*

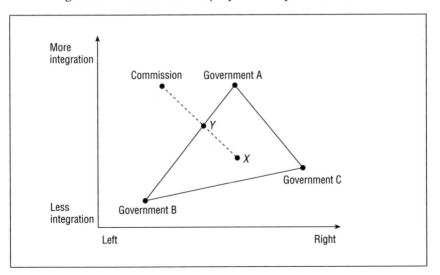

Nevertheless, principals can limit bureaucratic drift. First, they have several powers at their disposal to monitor the behaviour of agents (McCubbins and Schwartz, 1984). For example they can gather information on the performance of an agent and force the latter to disclose information in public hearings, a strategy known as 'police patrol' oversight. But the cost of information gathering can outweigh the benefits of delegating the responsibilities, so principals may use private and public interest groups to do the monitoring for them. Interest groups that are the subjects of an agent's actions possess special expertise and information on the actions of the agent, and if the agent is captured by a particular interest group, competing groups will inform the principals. Thus principals can simply sit back and wait for complaints before acting – this alternative strategy is known as 'fire-alarm' oversight.

Second, principals can design rules and procedures to minimize agents' discretion (Moe, 1989; Kiewiet and McCubbins, 1991; Horn, 1995; Huber and Shipan, 2002). For example rules can be established that specify what an agent must do before reaching a decision (such as listening to both sides of the debate), how the agent should relate to other administrative and political officials, and how the agent's deliberations should be reported to the media.

The result of such controls is a restriction of the ability of an agent to diverge from the original policy intention. This is illustrated in Figure 2.2. As in Figure 2.1, the governments agree on a piece of legislation at point X, but to limit the ability of the Commission to change the policy outcome, the governments introduce a set of procedures that define exactly how the Commission should go about its job. The result is some drift towards the Commission's ideal point, but only to Z instead of Y.

Figure 2.2   *Controlling bureaucratic drift by restricting discretion*

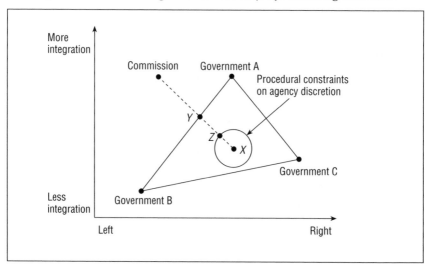

In sum, the degree of autonomy that executive agents are given by their principals depends on the nature of the tasks in question, the institutional rules under which they operate, the degree of conflict between the principals, and the amount and quality of information the principals have on the likely actions of the agents (Horn, 1995; Tsebelis, 1999, 2002; Huber and Shipan, 2002). All these elements are central to the relationship between the Council and the Commission in the EU (see especially Pollack, 1998; Moravcsik, 1999; Franchino, 2000a, 2000b, 2000c, 2004; Tallberg, 2000).

Government by the Council and the Member States

As discussed in Chapter 1, the Council is composed of ministers from the governments of the member states. Possessing both executive and legislative powers, the Council is the decision-making centre of the EU (Wessels, 1991). The organization and operation of the Council in exercising legislative power is discussed in the next chapter; in this section we shall focus on the Council's executive powers, which it exercises in four main ways:

- In treaty reforms, the Council sets the long-term policy goals of the EU and delegates powers to the Commission for the pursuit of these goals.
- The European Council (heads of government) sets the medium-term policy agenda of the EU and monitors the national macroeconomic policies of the member states through the 'open method of coordination'.
- The member states are responsible for implementing EU legislation through their own bureaucracies.
- The member state governments manage the day-to-day administration of EU policies in cooperation with the Commission through the comitology system (see below).

The first two of these relate to the political (leadership) aspect of executive power, and the third and fourth relate to its administrative (implementation) aspect.

When exercising these powers the general practice in the Council is to decide by consensus (as close to unanimity as possible) and any government can block an initiative that is against its interests. This is akin to the classic power-sharing arrangement, whereby stable government is secured in deeply divided societies through the participation and agreement of each societal group in executive decisions (Lijphart, 1977; Taylor, 1989; see also Chapter 5).

Treaties and treaty reforms: deliberate and unintended delegation

The signing of treaties and their subsequent reform are the result of careful bargaining and agreement among the member state governments in intergovernmental conferences (IGCs) (Moravcsik, 1998). The requirement of unanimity tends to produce 'lowest common denominator' treaty bargains. However the process of European integration has been able to proceed because different governments have placed different emphasis on different issues, and hence have been prepared to 'lose' on some issues in return for 'winning' on the issues that are more important to their national interests. The resulting package deals have gradually added new competences to the EU and delegated increasing executive powers to the Commission (cf. Christiansen *et al.*, 2002; Greve and Jørgensen, 2002).

For example the Treaty of Paris (signed in 1951 and entered into force in 1952), which established the European Coal and Steel Community (ECSC), was essentially a deal between France and Germany. In return for fostering German reconstruction and reindustrialization, France sought a framework for planned production and distribution in its own coal and steel industry. To secure these aims, the member state governments delegated certain powers to a new supranational body: the High Authority, the precursor of the Commission. Robert Schuman and Jean Monnet were the brains behind this idea. The common production and distribution of coal and steel could have been governed through meetings of ministers of the member governments, but Schuman and Monnet argued that such intergovernmental arenas would suffer from procrastination, indecision and disagreement, as each government would defend its own interests. Consequently they proposed that decision-making efficiency could only be guaranteed by delegating to a supranational body the responsibility for generating policy ideas and for the day-to-day management of policy (Haas, 1958, pp. 451–85; Monnet, 1978). This combination of intergovernmental decision-making with policy initiation and management by a supranational executive – the so-called 'Monnet method' – provided the model for future treaties (Rittberger, 2001; Parsons, 2002).

The Treaty of Rome (signed in 1957 and entered into force in 1958), established the European Economic Community (EEC) and the European Atomic Energy Community (Euratom). In the EEC, the bargain was between the German goal of a common market and the French goal of protection for agricultural products, through the Common Agricultural Policy (CAP) (Lindberg, 1963). Again, to achieve these aims the EEC treaty delegated policy initiation in the common market and administration of the CAP to the Commission. A further innovation of the Treaty of Rome was a legislative procedure that made it easier for the Council to accept a Commission proposal than to overturn it. This rule allowed the new supranational executive significant 'agenda-setting' powers in the establishment of rules governing the common market (see Chapter 3).

The package in the Single European Act (SEA) (signed in 1986 and entered into force in 1987) centred on the economic goal of establishing a 'single market' by 31 December 1992 in return for new social and environmental 'flanking policies' (cf. Hoffmann, 1989; Moravcsik, 1991; Garrett, 1992; Budden, 2002). This time, however, the Commission had played an important leadership role by detailing how the single market could be achieved and by preparing the treaty reforms (Sandholtz and Zysman, 1989; Dehousse and Majone, 1994; Christiansen, 2002). The reward was new responsibilities for the Commission: to initiate over 300 pieces of legislation to establish the single market; to propose and implement common environmental, health and safety, and social standards; to prepare the reform of the structural funds; and to draft a plan for economic and monetary union (EMU). Moreover, to enable the single market programme to be completed by the 1992 deadline, the decision-making rules of the European Community (EC) were amended to strengthen the agenda-setting powers of the Commission – through more qualified-majority voting in the Council and a new legislative procedure, the cooperation procedure (see Chapter 3). Finally, the SEA introduced provisions for intergovernmental cooperation in foreign policy, known as European Political Cooperation (EPC), but in this area the member state governments decided that executive authority should be held by the Council.

The Treaty on European Union (the Maastricht Treaty, agreed in 1991 and entered into force in 1993), institutionalized the Commission-brokered plan for EMU (see Chapter 10). In return, more funds were promised for cohesion policies, EU social policy was strengthened, new health, education, transport and consumer protection policies were added, and EU 'citizenship' was established (cf. Moravcsik, 1993; Sandholtz, 1993; Falkner, 2002). The Commission was again delegated the responsibility of initiating legislation and managing these policies. However, the Council refused to delegate executive powers to the Commission in two new 'pillars', which were separate from the main EC pillar: on justice and home affairs policy (JHA), to pursue the goal of the 'free movement of persons' between the EU member states; and common foreign and security policy (CFSP), which replaced EPC. The Maastricht Treaty also introduced a new legislative procedure, the co-decision procedure, which weakened the agenda-setting powers of the Commission (see Chapter 3).

The main policy innovation in the Amsterdam Treaty (signed in 1997 and entered into force in 1999), was the transfer of the provisions for establishing the free movement of persons to the EC part of the EU Treaty (McDonagh, 1998; Moravcsik and Nicolaïdis, 1998, 1999; Sverdrup, 2002). The member state governments accepted that the justice and home affairs (JHA) provisions in the Maastricht Treaty had failed, partly due to the lack of political leadership, and to resolve this the governments again agreed to delegate policy initiation rights in this area to the Commission (but also allowing policies to be initiated by the member states). However, similar arguments about the lack of development of CFSP did not result in new Commission powers in this field. Instead, the governments delegated responsibility for policy ideas and the monitoring of CFSP issues to a new 'task force' located in the Council secretariat. The Amsterdam Treaty also strengthened the legislative powers of the Parliament (see Chapter 3).

The Nice Treaty (signed in 2001 and entered into force in 2003) was mainly aimed at reforming the EU institutions in preparation for the accession of Central, Eastern and Southern European countries (Galloway, 2001). Nevertheless, there were some policy changes, particularly in the area of defence policy. Defence was formally established as an EU competence for the first time, as an integral part of the provisions on a European Security and Defence Policy (ESDP). As with the CFSP provisions, policy initiation, agenda-setting, decision-making and implementation in the area of defence were kept well away from the Commission.

Finally, the 'Treaty establishing an EU Constitution' (signed in 2004 but not yet ratified) would formalize the allocation of policy competences between the member states and the EU in a 'catalogue of competences'. The Constitution would also reform the decision-making rules within and between the institutions: such as the weighting of votes in the Council, two new leadership offices (a single 'Chair' of the European Council and an EU Foreign Minister), the number of Commissioners, and the power of the EP in the legislative and budgetary procedures.

In other words, the development of the EU treaties is a story of selective delegation of political and administrative powers by the governments to the Commission. Treaty reform is a blunt instrument. When signing treaties, governments cannot predict the precise implications of treaty provisions and new decision-making rules, or exactly how the Commission will behave when granted new powers. For example, few member states understood the implications of the new decision-making rules in the Treaty of Rome and the Single European Act (Tsebelis and Kreppel, 1998). Moreover, in the above discussion of the theories of executive power, once certain powers have been delegated through this mechanism, they are unlikely to be overturned in subsequent treaty reforms as at least one member state will feel that they benefit from Commission discretion. This leads to long term 'unintended consequences' of delegation by the member states and bureaucratic drift by the Commission (Pierson, 1996).

However, the history of treaty reform in the EU suggests that the member state governments learned from past mistakes. With the extensive delegation of agenda-setting to the Commission in the Single European Act, the member states experienced the day-to-day implications of these powers in the construction of the single market. As a result, in Maastricht, Amsterdam and Nice, the governments were more reluctant to hand over agenda-setting in new or highly sensitive policy areas, and reformed the legislative procedures to restrict the agenda-setting powers of the Commission in those areas where policy initiative had already been delegated to the Commission.

The European Council: EU policy leadership and the 'open method of coordination'

The main executive tasks of the European Council are to set guidelines and objectives for the Commission, to monitor the work of the Commission in implementing of these guidelines, to delegate short-term responsibilities to the Commission, to execute CFSP, JHA and EMU policies, and to adopt new policy competences for the EU (under Article 308). To highlight the contrast between the Council's executives and legislative powers, Hayes-Renshaw and Wallace (1997) describe these executive powers as 'political rather than legal decisions'.

At the top of the EU political system are the summits of the EU heads of government. These meetings have been held since the Paris and Rome Treaties, but formally became part of EU decision-making only in 1975 with the establishment of the European Council. European Councils are where final agreements and compromises are reached on treaty reforms. In addition, as laid down in Article 4 of the EU Treaty, 'The European Council shall provide the Union with the necessary impetus for its development and shall define the general political guidelines thereof'. Because of this Werts (1992) describes the European Council as the 'Provisional European Government' (cf. Bulmer and Wessels, 1987, pp. 132-46; Johnston, 1994). The European Council meets at least four times a year, usually in the middle and at the end of each presidency of the Council – the presidency of the Council rotates every six months between the member state governments (see Chapter 3). The proposed Constitution would replace the rotating presidency with a single chairperson of the European Council, with a renewable two and half year term of office.

The European Council takes a central political leadership role by guiding the work of the lower meetings of the Council, inviting the Commission to develop policy initiatives in particular areas, and monitoring the domestic policies of the member states. The variety of its remits can be illustrated by the results of the Gothenburg European Council, on 15–16 June 2001, at which the heads of government:

- Confirmed their commitment to the ratification of the Nice Treaty by the end of 2002, despite a negative vote in a referendum in Ireland in June 2001.
- Confirmed breakthroughs in the negotiations with 12 prospective member states in Central, Eastern and Southern Europe, and urged the candidate states and the Commission to complete the negotiation process as quickly as possible.
- Confirmed the EU's commitment to an open, rule-based multilateral trading system in the World Trade Organization (WTO), and urged all WTO members to reach agreement on further trade liberalization at the next WTO meeting.
- Reviewed developments that had taken place since the Stockholm Council (March 2001) on the economic policy guidelines for the member states.
- Adopted a 'strategy for sustainable development', which involved the monitoring of member states' environmental policies by the European Council and the coordination of environmental objectives in all internal and external EU policies by the General Affairs Council and the Commission.
- Agreed to discuss at the next European Council the question of where certain new EU agencies would be located.
- Urged the Council and the EP to resolve their differences over the directive on the information and consultation of workers and the legislative package relating to the liberalization of telecommunications.
- Urged the Council and the member states to accelerate their negotiations on a package of measures in the area of freedom, security and justice.
- Invited the incoming Belgian presidency of the Council and the secretary-general of the Council to work together to ensure that the European Security and Defence Policy would become operational as soon as possible (without waiting for ratification of the Nice Treaty).
- Welcomed the progress made at the EU–US summit on 14 June (attended by President George Bush) on greater transatlantic cooperation on trade and development issues, but warned of the dangers of EU–US disagreement over the Kyoto Protocol on global warming.
- Endorsed a number of decisions by the General Affairs Council and the Commission in the field of external relations, such as EU–Russia energy cooperation, and aid to Croatia, the Former Yugoslav Republic of Macedonia and Kosovo.

- Adopted a declaration on the prevention of proliferation of ballistic missiles.

None of these issues was really resolved at the level of heads of government. All were prepared and agreed in lower meetings of the Council and in the Committee of Permanent Representatives (COREPER) (see Chapter 3). Nevertheless the acknowledgements made by the European Council confirms the highest level of political commitment on all the issues.

One particular example of strategic planning by the European Council is the so-called 'open method of coordination'. This method, which was formally established by the Lisbon European Council in March 2000, involves the collective monitoring of the domestic policies of the member states. Coordination of each others' domestic policies, particularly in the area of economic policy, had been a key part of member state decision-making since the Treaty of Rome. However the Lisbon European Council formalized the breadth and operation of the open method: through the agreement on basic policy guidelines by heads of government, the presentation and monitoring of national policy plans, and provisions for the European Council and the Commission to warn member states if they deviated too far from the guidelines. By the end of 2002 the open method covered a wide range of policy areas, including macroeconomic, employment, research, social, enterprise, education and pension reform.

Some political scientists see this as a new mode of governance in the EU (for example Goetschy, 1999; Hodson and Maher, 2001; de la Porte and Pochet, 2002). The open method is viewed as a break from the traditional EU method of delegating agenda- setting and monitoring to the Commission, decision-making by lower meetings of the Council, and the possibility of formal sanctions by the European Court of Justice for breach of EU-level agreements. Under the open method, in contrast, decision-making is centralized in the European Council and the preparatory work is undertaken by prime ministers' personal offices, the secretariat of the Council and the relevant divisions of the Commission. Also, the policy guidelines are not binding and the watchwords of the open method are consensus, benchmarking and flexibility.

However the open method may not be so novel. For a start, it is really an extension of the existing treaty rules on EMU, covering macroeconomic policy coordination and a few other areas (see Chapter 10). Also, competition between the member states is as ferocious under the open method as in the traditional method. For example throughout 2000 and 2001, under the umbrella of the 'employment guidelines', at successive meeings of the European Council a battle raged between three prime ministers (Blair, Aznar and Berlusconi), who wanted to use the open method to encourage liberal labour market reforms, and most of the others (led by Jospin and Schröder), who wanted to resist such measures. Furthermore the sanction of 'naming and shaming' under the open method is not very effective if the voters in a particular member state are opposed to matters agreed in the European Council, for example the liberalization of labour markets. As a result, policy convergence at the domestic level is unlikely to occur without either collective interests or incentives or potential punishments for member states that do not share the common interest (Dimitrova and Steunenberg, 2000). Also, the final policy outcome in each member state – whether through the open method or the traditional method – is always shaped by its domestic institutional structure and the interests, power and resources of the political actors within this structure (see the discussion below on Europeanization).

Put this way, the open method may simply be 'cheap talk' by the member state governments. If they were serious about policy reform in a particular area then the classic EU method would probably be the most efficient way of achieving the policy goals. For example, in the area of labour market reform, the European Council could invite the Commission to propose a directive harmonizing national rules governing the hiring and firing of employees by small and medium-sized enterprises. The open method may in fact be a first step towards further policy coordination via the traditional method of delegation and decisions, as was the case with environmental policy and social policy before and after the Single European Act, and justice and home affairs before and after in the Maastricht and Amsterdam Treaties.

National coordination of EU policy: 'fusion' and 'Europeanization'

National administrations are responsible for the coordination of EU policy-making at both the European and the domestic level (see Kassim *et al.*, 2001a; Kassim *et al.*, 2001b; Wessels *et al.*, 2003). At the European level, the civil services of the member states play a central role in the pre- and post-legislative stages of EU policy-making. In the drafting of legislative initiatives, national officials are members of expert committees and consultative committees set up by the Commission, national civil servants are involved in scrutinizing Commission proposals in COREPER working groups. Then, following the adoption of legislation, national civil servants monitor the implementation of EU legislation in comitology committees (see below). In fact Wessels and Rometsch (1996) estimate that over 25000 national officials were involved in the EU policy process in 1994.

At the domestic level, national civil servants are at the front line of the implementation of EU legislation. Each national administration organizes its coordination and implementation of EU policy in a different way. For example in Germany a State Secretaries' European

Committee was set up in 1963 and the Cabinet Committee on European Policy in 1973 to coordinate the federal ministries' involvement in EU policy-making (Wessels, 1996). However the involvement of the EU in the policy competences of the German *Länder* governments has constrained the ability of Berlin to centrally control German responses in the EU policy process (Goetz, 1995). Also, the involvement of national administrations in both the initiation and implementation stages of the EU policy process and at the European and national levels creates coordination problems for national governments (Wright, 1996). The continuous nature of the EU policy process puts constant demands on national administrations, and responses at one level of the EU system or at one stage of the EU policy process are inherently linked to responses at another level and at a later or former stage. Sometimes, administrations can use this to their advantage. Governments can cite 'problems back home' when opposing a policy initiative or an implementation measure in comitology, while claiming that 'Brussels made us do it' when forcing unpopular measures on domestic constituencies. Nevertheless, the result tends to be a highly unsettled policy environment in most member states, with often inconsistent policy responses by national governments.

The growing interaction of national administrations in the day-to-day running of EU government led Wolfgang Wessels (1992, 1997a) to develop what he called a 'fusion thesis'. At an empirical level, European integration has led to a 'fusion' between administrative responsibilities at the European and domestic levels and between the member states. But, the fusion thesis is also a theory of European integration: national administrative elites have played a crucial role in promoting the development of the EU. European integration increases civil servants' inability to respond to societal transformation and globalization, and administrative elites have designed the EU system to give themselves powerful executive and legislative powers, beyond the control of national parliaments.

Furthermore, this constant interaction between public officials from different member states, together with the same policy pressures resulting from the EU level, has led many political scientists to point to a 'Europeanization' of national policy-making practices and styles. Europeanization in this context means convergence on a common policy style. This convergence is partly driven by adaptation to common regimes imposed from the European level, which inevitably favours some actors' interests and some policy practices over others. However, convergence is also driven by the common interests, preferences and values of senior officials in similar positions in different member states, who are able to use their specialist role in the EU policy process to promote their agendas 'back home' (cf. Hix and Goetz, 2000; Risse *et al.*, 2001; Knill, 2001).

Nevertheless, despite the growing evidence of Europeanization, there remains considerable variation in the degree of the effect of EU policies and the EU policy process on domestic administrative and policy processes. Most research points to two main factors explaining this variation: (1) the degree of policy and institutional compatibility between the member states and the EU (the amount of change required to bring domestic arrangements into line with EU rules or EU-level practices); and (2) the extent to which EU policies and EU-level opportunities change domestic opportunity structures and interest relations (see for example Albert-Roulhac, 1998; Knill, 1988; Knill and Lenschow, 1998; Börzel, 1999, 2002; Harmsen, 1999; Schmidt, 1999; Falkner, 2000a; Goetz, 2000; Haverland, 2000; Smith, 2000; Cole, 2001; Cowles and Risse, 2001; Héritier, 2001; Knill and Lehmkuhl, 2002).

In summary, member state governments, both in the Council and at the domestic level, possess key executive functions in the EU. Wessels (1997) describes this as a third way between pure intergovernmentalism, where no powers are delegated to supranational institutions, and pure federalism, where powers are concentrated in a separate federal executive. However, the EU could also be thought of as a form of 'executive federalism', in which the governments of the subunits play a dominant role in the political system, both in the initiation and adoption of legislation at the federal level, and in the coordination and implementation of federal policy at the lower level (see for example Frowein, 1986). Moreover, as in other executive-federal systems, the EU governments, and the senior officials in the public administrations of these governments, are in constant competition with the other holders of executive power at the EU level: the Commission.

Government by the Commission

The Commission has several responsibilities:

- To propose policy ideas for the medium-term development of the EU.
- To initiate legislation and arbitrate in the legislative process.
- To represent the EU in bilateral and multilateral trade negotiations.
- To issue rules and regulations, for example on competition policy.
- To manage the EU budget.
- To scrutinize the implementation of the primary treaty articles and secondary legislation.

To carry out these responsibilities the Commission is organized much like a domestic government, with a core executive (the College of

Commissioners) focusing on the political tasks (the first second and third items on the list), a bureaucracy (the directorates-general) undertaking legislative drafting, administrative work and some regulatory tasks (items two, four, five and six), and a network of quasi-autonomous agencies undertaking a variety of monitoring and regulatory tasks (especially item six).

A cabinet: the EU core executive

At the political level the EU commissioners form the College of Commissioners. Under the Treaty of Rome there were two commissioners from each of the large member states and one from each of the medium-sized and small states. So with 15 member states there were 20 commissioners: two each from Germany, the UK, France, Italy and Spain, and one from each of the other 10 states. Under the provisions of the Nice Treaty, however, and following the enlargement of the EU in May 2004, there is now only one commissioner per member state. Basically, the larger member states agreed to lose one of their commissioners in return for more votes in the Council in the legislative process (see Chapter 3).

The College of Commissioners meets at least once a week (usually on a Wednesday), and the meetings are chaired by the president of the Commission. As far as possible, College decisions are by consensus, but any commissioner may request a vote. When votes are taken, decisions require an absolute majority, with the Commission president casting the deciding vote in the event of a tie. This absolute majority rule means that abstentions and absentees are equivalent to negative votes. Voting is usually by show of hands (so not by secret ballot). The results of votes are confidential, but how each commissioner has voted is recorded in the College minutes, and on high-profile issues this information is often leaked to the press from somewhere in the Commission bureaucracy. Nonetheless, the commissioners are bound by the standard principle of 'collective responsibility' (a key norm in most cabinet government systems). This principle means that even if a commissioner was in a losing minority in a vote, he or she must toe the line of the majority in the outside world.

The political leadership of the Commission operates along the lines of cabinet government in several other ways. The first is the allocation of a portfolio to each commissioner, as shown in Table 2.1. The most high-profile portfolios are given to the Commission vice-presidents and those who were commissioners in previous administrations. In the Barroso Commission, for example, those commissioners who were in the previous Prodi administration all held key portfolios. Nevertheless any commissioner is capable of making a name for him- or herself through hard work and skilful manipulation of the media.

Table 2.1   *The Barroso Commission*

	Member state	Party	Portfolio
President:			
José Manuel Barroso	Portugal	CD	
Vice-presidents:			
Margot Wallström*	Sweden	SD	Institutional relations and communication strategy
Günter Verheugen*	Germany	SD	Enterprise and industry
Jacques Barrot*	France	Con.	Transport
Siim Kallas*	Estonia	Lib.	Administrative affairs, audit and anti-fraud
Franco Frattini	Italy	Con.	Justice, freedom and security
Members:			
Viviane Reding*	Luxembourg	CD	Information society and media
Stavros Dimas*	Greece	Con.	Environment
Joaquin Almunia*	Spain	SD	Economic and monetary affairs
Danuta Hübner*	Poland	Ind.	Regional policy
Joe Borg*	Malta	Con.	Fisheries and maritime affairs
Dalia Grybauskaite*	Lithuania	Ind.	Financial programming and budget
Janez Potočnik*	Slovenia	Ind.	Science and research
Ján Figel'*	Slovakia	CD	Education, training, culture, and multilingualism
Markos Kyptianou*	Cyprus	Lib.	Health and consumer protection
Olli Rehn*	Finland	Lib.	Enlargement
Louis Michel	Belgium	Lib.	Development and humanitarian aid
László Kovács	Hungary	SD	Taxation and customs union
Neelic Kroes-Smit	Netherlands	Lib.	Competition
Mariann Fischer Boel	Denmark	Lib~	Agriculture and rural development
Benita Ferrero-Waldner	Austria	CD	External relations, and European neighbourhood policy
Charlie McCreevy	Ireland	Con.	Internal market and services
Vladimir Špidla	Czech Republic	SD	Employment, social affairs and equal opportunities
Peter Mandelson	UK	SD	Trade
Andris Piebalgs	Latvia	Lib.	Energy

Notes:
* = Member of the previous Commission. CD = Christian Democrat, Con. = conservative, Lib. = liberal, SD = social democrat, Ind. = independent.

The Commission president is what Bagehot (1963 [1865]) called the 'first among equals'. The president sets the overall policy agenda of the Commission by preparing the annual work programme, sets the agenda and chairs the meetings of the College, and is in charge of the Secretariat General, which oversees the work of the directorates general). Under rules introduced by the Amsterdam Treaty, the president also decides which commissioner gets which portfolio, in consultation with the individual commissioners and the governments that nominated them. In practice the member state governments hold agenda-setting power in this relationship as they are responsible for nominating their commissioners in the first place. Nevertheless the Commission president can exert some pressure on national governments to propose more high-profile and competent figures (and sometimes more pro-European figures). The president can also ask individual commissioners to resign if they prove to be corrupt or incompetent.

The political impact of any 'first among equals' also depends on their personal characteristics and policy ideas (cf. Jones, 1991; Rhodes and Dunleavy, 1995). Of all the Commission presidents (Table 2.2), Walter Hallstein and Jacques Delors have probably been most influential (Ludlow, 1991). Both had a clear vision of the political development of the Commission, sought a high-profile role for the Commission, and were ready to withstand opposition by prominent European leaders to achieve their goals. For Hallstein the goal was a federal union, which was adamantly opposed by De Gaulle. For Delors the goal was economic and political union and a 'social Europe', which was adamantly opposed by Thatcher (Drake, 1995). Jacques Santer and Romano Prodi, in contrast, were deliberately selected by the member state governments because they were less ideological and duly promised that the Commission should do 'less but better'.

A further aspect of cabinet government is the system of the commissioners' *cabinets*. These are teams of political advisors who are hand-picked. The *cabinet* system was imported from the French government system, although it exists in a more or less formalized way in most collective-government systems. The *cabinets* have four main functions – that is, to serve as political antennae and filters for party and interest-group demands, as policy advisors to counterbalance the advice of civil servants in the directorates-general, as mechanisms for intercommissioner coordination and dispute resolution, and as supervisors and controllers of the work of the directorates-general responsible to the Commission (Donnelly and Ritchie, 1997). The *chefs des cabinets* meet together every week (usually on a Monday) to prepare the agenda for the weekly meeting of the College of Commissioners. They try to resolve most of the items on the weekly agenda of the Commission, leaving only the more controversial and political decisions to their political masters.

The workload of the *cabinets* has steadily increased as the volume of activity of the Commission has increased (Cini, 1996, pp. 111–15; Nugent, 2001, pp. 119–33). How efficiently the *cabinet* system functions can depend on the holders of the key positions. For example in the Delors administration, Delors' *chef de cabinet*, Pascal Lamy (who became a member of the Prodi Commission), was the mastermind behind the evolution of a coordinated and coherent policy framework for all the commissioners and their *cabinets* (Ross, 1994; Nugent, 2001, p. 77). Similarly, in the Prodi administration Stefano Manservisi, Prodi's *chef de cabinet*, and David O'Sullivan, the secretary-general of the Commission, were able to influence the policy direction of the Commission by reorganizing of the weekly *chefs des cabinets* meetings, for example by limiting the speaking time allotted to each *chef*, carefully preparing agendas and introducing strict deadlines for the completion of meetings.

Finally, as in national cabinets, commissioners are partisan actors. Article 213 of the EU Treaty proclaims that

> The Members of the Commission shall, in the general interests of the Community, be completely independent in the performance of their duties. . . They shall neither seek nor take instructions from any government or from any other body.

This principle of independence derives from Jean Monnet's vision of an apolitical functionalist bureaucracy to protect the collective interest of European citizens. Nevertheless, because of their previous occupations, peer contacts, future aims and national media scrutiny, all the commissioners tend to have significant links with partisan domestic constituents.

As Table 2.3 shows, commissioners are career politicians. Over 70 per cent of all commissioners have held at least one elected post before becoming a commissioner, and almost 25 per cent have held a senior cabinet office in a national government (either as prime minister, foreign minister, or finance minister). In the Barroso commission, moreover, almost 70 per cent have held a senior position in their political party (such as party leader or member of the party executive), only four members have not held elected political office (Hübner, Grybauskaite, Potočnik, and Ferrero-Waldner), and only two members have not held executive office of any kind (Reding and Rehn).

These partisan affiliations are important in determining the overall direction of the Commission. The Commission has always been a grand coalition of socialists, Christian democrats, liberals and conservatives (MacMullen, 1997). However its political agenda changes as the political colour of the president and the partisan make-up of the College changes. For example Delors' advocacy of a social dimension to the single market was clearly a social democratic agenda, and in the

Table 2.2   *The Commission presidents*

	Name	Member state	Party	Position before Commission
1958–67	Walter Hallstein	Germany	CD	Foreign minister
1968–69	Jean Rey	Belgium	Lib.	Economics/finance minister
1970–72	Franco Maria Malfatti	Italy	CD	Public works minister
1972	Sicco Mansholt	Netherlands	Lib.	Agriculture minister
1973–76	François-Xavier Ortoli	France	Con.	Economics/finance minister
1977–80	Roy Jenkins	UK	SD	Economics/finance minister
1981–84	Gaston Thorn	Luxembourg	Lib.	Prime minister
1985–94	Jacques Delors	France	SD	Economics/finance minister
1995–99	Jacques Santer	Luxembourg	CD	Prime minister
1999–04	Romano Prodi	Italy	CD/Lib.*	Prime minister
2005–	José Manuel Barroso	Portugal	CD	Prime minister

* For most of his political career, Romano Prodi was a member of the Italian Christian Democrats, but when the party split in the early 1990s he stayed with the wing of the party that joined the left-wing Olive Tree Alliance, and just before becoming Commission President he was a founder member of the Democrats party, which sits in the liberal group in the EP. CD = Christian Democrat, Con. = conservative, Lib. = liberal, SD = social democrat.

Prodi Commission there were divisions over several market regulation questions (such as deregulation of the car sales market) between the 11 socialists and greens and the nine more 'free market' Christian democrats, conservatives and liberals.

The partisan affiliation of commissioners also affects their choice of portfolios, as commissioners prefer to have portfolios that correspond with the personal ideological preferences. For example in the Barroso commission conservatives or Christian democrats are in charge of internal market and services, education, fisheries, external relations, and justice, freedom and security; liberals are in charge of competition, consumer protection, and fighting fraud; and social democrats are in charge of employment, industry, and social affairs and equal opportunities. However liberals are in charge of agriculture (which is usually held by a Christian democrat) and development aid (usually held by a social democrat), and a Christian democrat is in charge of the environment portfolio (which is usually held by a social democrat).

Table 2.3   *Political careers of commissioners*

Political offices held before enteringthe Commission	All Commissioners (1967–2009)		Current Commission (2005–09)	
	No.	Per cent	No.	Per cent
Governmental office				
Senior minister (PM, foreign min., or finance min.)	31	24.2	11	44.0
Other cabinet post	51	39.8	11	44.0
Junior government post	24	18.8	12	48.0
No ministerial office	35	27.3	2	8.0
Elected office				
Member of national parliament	90	70.3	21	84.0
Senior party position (e.g. executive)	43	33.6	17	68.0
Local government	30	23.4	7	28.0
Member of European Parliament	24	18.8	2	8.0
Regional assembly	7	5.5	0	0.0
No elected office	25	19.5	4	16.0
Total	128		25	

Sources: Page (1997); European Commission (2000b); Wonka (2004), Europa website.

Finally, partisan affiliations affect other parts of the Commission administration: the members of the *cabinets* are often recruited from partisan contacts, and senior appointments and promotions in the directorates-general are often determined by partisan affiliations and contacts.

A bureaucracy: the EU civil service

Below the College of Commissioners is the EU bureaucracy, composed of 36 directorates-general (DGs) and other services. The DGs are the organizational equivalent of government ministries in domestic administrations and they fulfil many of the same functions: policy development, preparation of legislation, distribution of revenues, monitoring of legislative implementation, and provision of advice and support to the political executive.

The DGs and other services in the Prodi administration are listed in Table 2.4. The number of DGs has increased as new competences have been delegated to the Commission (Fligstein and McNicholl, 1998). Also, each new College of Commissioners has reorganized the DGs to promote particular agendas. For example, as part of a drive to make the Commission more relevant to individual European citizens the Santer administration turned the Consumer Policy Service into the Consumer Protection DG. Under Prodi this became the Health and Consumer Protection DG through the addition of several divisions from other DGs that covered consumer protection issues, such as the food safety division in the Agriculture DG.

Each DG is responsible for policy initiation and management in a particular policy area, and the DGs are broadly aligned with the policy competences of the commissioners. However the division of competences between the DGs is at a lower-level of policy competence than in most national administrations. For example the competences of the Internal Market DG, Enterprise DG, Information Society DG and Research DG would be combined in a single Ministry of Industry in most domestic administrations, under the leadership of a single minister. This often leads to competing policy positions among the DGs under the same commissioner.

This lack of policy coherence is facilitated by the fact that most DGs have a particular administrative culture. For example the Employment and Social Affairs DG has a highly corporatist culture and on many issues formally involves the European peak associations for industry and labour (UNICE and ETUC), whereas the Information Society DG is more pluralist and focuses on technical expertise and ideas (Cram, 1994; cf. Cini, 1997). Different administrative cultures also stem from the predominance of different national groups in senior positions in each DG (Abélès *et al.*, 1993; Page, 1997). For example many senior officials in the Agriculture DG are French, German and Irish, whereas the Competition DG is dominated by British and Dutch.

The Commission employs approximately 28000 staff, but as Table 2.4 shows there is considerable variation in staffing levels among the DGs. Traditionally the agriculture DG was the largest, with well over 2000 staff (Cini, 1996, p. 105). However, with the removal of some of its divisions to other DGs under the Prodi administration it fell to eighth in the pecking order, although its budget remained the largest by a considerable margin.

There was some discontentment amongst officials in posts immediately below the political appointments (Spence, 1997), and in this regard one of the aims of the internal reform of the commission bureaucracy, under the direction of Neil Kinnock, was to end the system of national quotas at the senior level and to promote staff within each DG and across DGs on a more meritocratic basis. This was initially resisted by several member states, which feared losing key positions, and by the commission officials' staff trade union. However the reform was backed at the political level and was implemented in early 2002.

To investigate the political views of officials in the Commission, Liesbet Hooghe interviewed 137 senior officials in the DGs and sent written questionnaires to a further 106 (Hooghe, 1999a, 1999b, 2001). She found that their attitudes towards the role of the Commission, the process of integration and the policies of the EU were shaped more by their experiences outside the Commission than within it. Officials' party affiliation, member state, and prior work experience exerted a stronger influence than internal factors, irrespective of how long they

Table 2.4 *The Commission bureaucracy under the Prodi Commission*

Administrative division	Commissioner	Staff, 2002 responsible	Budget, 2002 (€m.)
Directorates-General:			
Press and Communication	Prodi	607	149.9
Personnel and Administration	Kinnock	5 707	1 248.0
Energy and Transport	de Palacio	929	1 022.4
Regional Policy	Barnier	514	21 807.8
Internal Market	Bolkestein	408	65.9
Taxation and Customs Union	Bolkestein	399	89.6
Research	Busquin	1 578	2 526.4
Joint Research Centre	Busquin	2 084	257.9
Health and Consumer Protection	Byrne	696	744.0
Employment and Social Affairs	Diamantopolou	669	9 738.3
Agriculture	Fischler	883	47 591.7
Fisheries	Fischler	277	1 093.8
Trade	Lamy	482	67.1
Enterprise	Liikanen	856	291.0
Information Society	Liikanen	1 022	1 071.3
Competition	Monti	595	73.9
Development	Nielson	2 095	1 119.1
Humanitarian Aid Office (ECHO)	Nielson	151	670.8
External Relations	Patten	2 999	3 270.3
Education and Culture	Reding	653	780.7
Budget	Schreyer	416	52.7
Financial Control	Schreyer	182	19.0
Economic and Financial Affairs	Solbes Mira	469	494.2
Enlargement	Verheugen	796	1 816.9
Justice and Home Affairs	Vitorino	240	147.0
Environment	Wallström	520	263.6
Other services:			
Secretariat-General	Prodi	1 208	195.8
Legal Service	Prodi		
Group of Policy Advisors	Prodi		
European Group on Ethics in Science and New Technologies	Prodi		
Joint Interpreting and Conference Service	Kinnock	*	*
Translation Service	Kinnock	*	*
Internal Audit Service	Kinnock	*	*
Office for Publications (EUR-OP)	Reding	*	*
European Anti-Fraud Office (OLAF)	Schreyer	335	48.2
Eurostat	Solbes Mira	701	117.6
Total		28 471	96 834.9

* Included in the figures for Personnel and Administration.

Source: Website of the European Commission.

had worked in the Commission or in which DG they worked. Moreover their attitudes were determined more by basic ideological preferences (which were causally related to party affiliations) than by their career ambitions or the policy interests of their DG. In other words, Hooghe found little evidence of socialized 'Eurocrats', who promoted the interests of the Commission at all costs, but instead found nationally- and party-affiliated officials who defended the interests of their member state and had ideological preferences about EU policies.

Regulators: the EU quangos

A common feature of executive power in representative government is the use of executive instruments to enforce legislation. These are sometimes called tertiary instruments as they follow primary constitutional (EU Treaty) articles and secondary legislation in the hierarchy of legal acts. The US and UK governments use orders or regulations, French governments use *ordonnances* and German governments use *Rechtsverordnungen*. Similarly the EU Commission can issue directives, regulations and decisions without recourse to the EU legislative process.

These executive instruments are a traditional feature of representative government for two reasons (Majone, 1991, 2001; Franchino, 2002; Gilardi, 2002). First, executives have the power to act as surrogate legislators in areas where the legislature has neither the time nor the ability to take action. For example executives are often allowed to act if a rapid response is needed, if technical knowledge is required or if the issue is insufficiently salient for the legislature to be involved. The Commission issues between 6000 and 7000 such instruments a year (mostly relating to the Common Agricultural Policy).

Second, some executive agencies have the power to prevent the involvement of parliamentary institutions in the making of rules and regulations. In certain circumstances it is often in the public interest for policy to be made by independent executive agencies as they have longer time horizons than elected parliaments and governments. These agencies can be independent competition regulators, such as competition authorities or the regulators of privatized utilities, or independent central banks. The delegation of regulatory policies to such quasi-autonomous nongovernmental organizations (quangos) is a classic feature of American government and has been growing at the domestic level in Europe (Majone, 1994; Thatcher, 2002b).

In some respects the Commission is such an agency (Majone, 1993b). For example it makes rulings under the competition and state aid sections of the treaty and the merger regulation (see Chapter 8). This is managed by the Competition DG, which operates like a European cartel office. The media like to refer to the commissioner in charge of the Competition DG as the EU's 'competition policy tsar'. Nevertheless, to protect competition policy from interference by national interests and the political aims of the Commission, many commentators advocate removing the Competition DG from the Commission bureaucracy and setting it up as a truly independent regulatory agency, along the lines of the German Federal Cartel Office (cf. Wilks and McGowan, 1995).

The Commission also oversees the work of a number of independent European agencies. These agencies, listed in Table 2.5, are set up by Council decisions on the basis of Commission proposals, and most had forerunners somewhere in the Commission bureaucracy. For example the European Agency for the Evaluation of Medicinal Products came from two comitology committees, the European Environment Agency came from one of the Commission's policy programmes (CORINE), and the European Food Safety Agency is composed of several divisions from the Health and Consumer Protection and Agriculture DGs. Others, such as the Office for Harmonization in the Internal Market and the European Police Office, were set up as part of new EU policy regimes (Kreher, 1997, pp. 232–3).

None of these agencies are full regulatory authorities with the power to adopt and implement policies. The responsibilities of the current agencies fall into four broad categories (cf. Majone, 2002a):

- Agencies that facilitate the operation of the single market by providing services to specific industrial sectors: the Office for Harmonization in the Internal Market, the Community Plant Variety Office, the European Agency for the Evaluation of Medicinal Products, the European Maritime Safety Agency, and the European Aviation Safety Agency.
- Agencies that gather and disseminate information in a particular policy area through a network of national partners: the European Environment Agency, the European Monitoring Centre for Drugs and Drug Addiction, the European Monitoring Centre on Racism and Xenophobia, the European Police Office, the European Union Satellite Centre, and the European Institute for Security Studies.
- Agencies that promote cooperation between industries and trade unions, with a view to reaching European wide collective agreements in a given area: the European Centre for the Development of Vocational Training, the European Foundation for the Improvement of Living and Working Conditions, and the European Agency for Safety and Health at Work.
- Agencies that execute specific programmes and tasks for the EU – the European Training Foundation, the Translation Centre for the Bodies of the EU, and the European Agency for Reconstruction.

As the reputations of the agencies develop, and through control of the collection and supply of information, some of the other EU agencies

Table 2.5   Autonomous executive agencies of the EU

Agency	Est.	Location	Staff, 2002	Budget, 2002 (€m.)
European Centre for the Development of Vocational Training (CEDEFOP)	1975	Thessaloniki	83	13.9
European Foundation for the Improvement of Living and Working Conditions (EUROFOUND)	1975	Dublin	88	16.5
European Environment Agency (EEA)	1990	Copenhagen	83	19.7
European Training Foundation (ETF)	1990	Turin	130	16.8
Office for Harmonization in the Internal Market (Trade Marks and Designs) (OHIM)	1993	Alicante	847	138.6
European Monitoring Centre for Drugs and Drug Addiction (EMCDDA)	1993	Lisbon	59	9.4
European Agency for the Evaluation of Medicinal Products (EMEA)	1993	London	251	64.9
Translation Centre for the Bodies of the European Union (CdT)	1994	Luxembourg	165	0.6
European Agency for Safety and Health at Work (EU-OSHA)	1994	Bilbao	31	9.2
Community Plant Variety Office (CPVO)	1994	Angers	33	8.7
European Monitoring Centre on Racism and Xenophobia (EUMC)	1997	Vienna	28	6.2
European Police Office (EUROPOL)	1995	The Hague	242	51.7
European Agency for Reconstruction (EAR)	2000	Thessaloniki	316	510.0
European Institute for Security Studies (ISS)	2001	Paris	–	–
European Union Satellite Centre (EUSC)	2001	Torrejon de Ardoz	–	–
European Aviation Safety Agency (EASA)	2002	Brussels*	–	–
European Maritime Safety Agency (EMSA)	2002	Brussels*	–	–
European Food Safety Agency (EFSA)	2002	Brussels*	–	–
European Justice Office (EUROJUST)	2002	The Hague	–	–
Total			2 356	866.2

* = provisional location.

Source: General Budget of the European Union for the Financial Year 2002, OJ L 29, 31.1.2002.

(such as the European Environment Agency) have begun to play a key role in the emerging European 'regulator networks', through which new rules are drafted and implemented (Dehousse, 1997; Majone, 1997, 2002a; Kelemen, 2002). For example the three new 'safety agencies' (EASA, EMSA and EFSA) monitor the implementation of existing EU-wide standards, and help to develop and set new common rules.

The traditional image of the Commission is that of a monolithic supranational bureaucracy, with no real executive powers and a single policy objective: to promote European integration (see for example Coombes, 1970). In this chapter a somewhat different picture has been painted: of an executive organization that fulfils many of the traditional tasks of government and that is politically and organizationally comparable to other public administrations. At the pinnacle there are partisan politicians in a classic cabinet government system, who pursue individual and collective political objectives. Beneath the politicians there is a highly developed bureaucracy and a growing network of regulatory agencies, where the various administrative organs have different policy and organizational interests and cultures.

Comitology: Interface of the EU Dual Executive

The Commission is not completely free to shape policy outcomes when implementing EU legislation. The Council has designed an elaborate system of committees composed of national government officials who scrutinize the Commission's implementing measures (Vos, 1997). This is known as 'comitology'. Under some procedures of the comitology system there is a separation of powers, whereby the legislators (the governments) can scrutinize the executive (the Commission). Under other procedures, however, comitology has created a fusion of powers, whereby the member governments enforce their wishes on the Commission, and hence exercise both legislative and executive authority.

The comitology system was established by a Council decision in July 1987 (1987/373/EEC) and reformed by a Council decision in June 1999 (1999/468/EC). The decisions established three types of committee – advisory, management and regulatory – and a set of rules governing their operation. In its report on the activities of the comitology committees in 2000 the Commission listed 224 separate committees (European Commission, 2002).

The membership of the committees depends on their role: committees composed of national civil servants monitor the implementation of legislation; temporary committees composed of representatives of private interest groups consider matters for which the Commission feels wider consultation is necessary; and committees composed of scientists and experts give advice on technical issues (ibid., p. 213).

The committee procedures

Table 2.6 shows how the comitology system works (in addition to the 1999 Council decision, the standard rules of procedure for the committees are set out in the *Official Journal*, OJ C38 6.2.2001). As the number of the procedure rises, the autonomy of the Commission from national governments declines. Under the advisory procedure (procedure I), the Commission has the greatest degree of freedom: although it must take 'the utmost account' of the opinion of the national experts, it can simply ignore their advice. This procedure is used in most areas of EU competition policy, such as Commission decisions on mergers and state aid to industry. The management procedure (II) is mostly used for the Common Agricultural Policy and most other areas of EU expenditure, such as regional policy, research, and development aid. The regulatory procedure (III) was developed by the Council in the late 1960s to cover areas outside agriculture where the member governments wanted more control over the Commission than they had under the advisory and management committee procedures (Docksey and Williams, 1997, pp. 136–7). This procedure is now used in such areas as animal, plant and food safety, environmental protection and transport.

Finally, the 1999 amendment of the 1987 comitology decision, established two other procedures, under which the Council has the final power of veto. First, the Commission can take safeguard measures to protect the interests of the EU or a member state, but must secure prior agreement from the Council. This procedure (IV) is usually used for issues that come under the Common Commercial Policy, such as signing association agreements with non-EU states. Second, in specific cases the Council has the right to exercise implementing powers itself (procedure V). These are used in highly sensitive areas, such as matters to do with financial institutions.

Table 2.7 shows the activities of the committees in 2000, from the Commission's first report after the introduction of the new procedures. With regard to the number of committees, one surprise in the report was that there were more committees in the area of environmental policy than in any other policy area. However, as could be expected the agriculture committees were most active, with 367 meetings in 2000. These took up 260 working days and tackled almost 2000 draft implementing measures. Almost 50 per cent of the 224 committees operated through regulatory procedures; only 12 per cent operated through the more permissive advisory procedure.

Interinstitutional conflict in the choice and operation of the procedures

The data in Table 2.7 show that the Commission's implementing measures are rarely overturned by the committees. In 2000, of the 4357

Table 2.6 *How comitology works*

Procedure	Operation of the procedure
Advisory (I)	1. The Commission submits a draft implementing measure to the relevant committee 2. The committee delivers its opinion on the draft measure, if necessary by a vote (either by simple majority, qualified majority vote (QMV) or unanimity, depending on the policy area) [the rules are unclear here!] 3. The Commission must take 'the utmost account' of the opinion of the committee, and must inform the committee of exactly how this has been done
Management (II)	1. The Commission submits a draft implementing measure to the relevant committee 2. The committee delivers its opinion on the draft measure (by QMV) 3. The Commission may adopt the measure immediately, regardless of the opinion of the committee 4. The Commission must inform the Council if the measure is not in accordance with the opinion of the committee, or may defer the measure for up to three months 5. Within the specified deferral period the Council may take a different decision (by QMV) to the committee or the Commission
Regulatory (III)	1. The Commission submits a draft implementing measure to the relevant committee 2. The committee delivers its opinion on the draft measure (by QMV) 3. If the committee approves the measure, the Commission adopts the measure 4. If the committee does not approve the measure or does not give an opinion, the Commission must submit the measure to the Council and inform the EP of this fact 5. If the legislation from which the measure derives was adopted under the co-decision procedure, the EP can give an opinion on whether it thinks the measure exceeds the implementing powers envisaged in the legislation 6. If the Council opposes the measure (by QMV) the Commission must re-examine the measure and either submit an amended measure to the Council, resubmit the measure to the Council or present a new draft legislative act relating to the issue

	7. If the Council adopts the measure (by QMV) or fails to act within the specified period, the Commission adopts the measure
Safeguard (IV)	1. The Commission must notify the member states of any decision on safeguard measures
	2. Any member state may refer the Commission's decision to the Council within the time limit specified in the original legislation
	3. The Council may confirm, amend or revoke the decision (by QMV)
	4. The Council may stipulate in the original legislation that if a decision is referred to the Council and the Council fails to act, then the decision is deemed to have been revoked
Council itself (V)	In special cases the Council has the right to exercise direct implementing powers
Role of the European Parliament	1. Under procedures I–III, the Commission must give the EP all committee agendas and minutes, draft measures (if related to legislation passed under the co-decision procedure), final decisions and lists of member state representatives (and their organizational affiliations)
	2. The Commission must also inform the EP when a decision is referred to the Council
	3. If a draft measure relates to legislation passed under the co-decision prodecure and the EP indicates that it thinks the measure exceeds the implementing powers provided for in the legislation, the Commission must re-examine the measure and either (a) submit a new draft measure, (b) continue with the existing measure or (c) submit a new legislative proposal to the EP and Council

Source: Council Decision on comitology, 28 June 1999 (1999/468/EC), OJ L184, 17.7.1999.

Table 2.7 Activities of the implementing committees

Policy area	No. of committees by type of procedure						Activity in 2000			
	I	II	III	IV	Operating under several procedures	Total	Meetings	Consultations	Unfavourable opinions	Referrals to Council
Environment	2	4	34		1	41	52	80	2	1
Enterprise	8	4	17		3	32	54	269	0	0
Agriculture		23	3		4	30	367	1889	0	1
Transport (incl. trans-European networks)	4		17	1	3	25	35	31	1	0
Health and consumer protection	4		7	4	11	22	122	449	0	4
Trade	1	3			3	11	28	135	0	0
Information society	1	1	5		3	10	30	36	0	0
Internal market	1	3	5		1	10	24	8	0	0
Taxation and customs union	1	2	4		2	9	110	512	0	0
Employment and social affairs	1	2	4		1	8	14	44	0	0
External relations	1	2	1		3	7	44	269	0	0
Research		6				6	32	83	0	0
Statistics		4			2	6	15	102	0	0
Education and culture					6	6	23	92	0	0
Development		2	2		1	5	19	19	0	0
Energy	1	1	2			4	10	12	1	0
Fisheries		2			1	3	10	41	0	0
Enlargement	1			1		2	7	121	0	0
Regional policy	1	1				2	16	87	0	0
Justice and home affairs			1		1	2	7	4	0	0
Humanitarian aid					1	1	7	28	0	0
Budget	1					1	5	46	0	0
Anti-Fraud Office			1			1	1	1	0	0
Total	26	61	103	6	48	224	1032	4358	4	6

Source: Calculated from data in European Commission (2002a).

proposed measures, only four unfavourable opinions were expressed by the committees of national experts (0.1 per cent), and only six referrals were made to the Council (0.1 per cent). Of the latter, four were in the area of health and consumer protection (1 per cent of total implementing measures in this field).

However these figures do not necessarily mean that the Commission gets its own way most of the time. With so many implementing measures under discussion, the Commission must have very good information about the opinions of every national expert on every committee. Consequently the Commission can probably predict exactly how each committee will react to each draft implementing measure, and therefore drafts each measure accordingly. It would perhaps be more surprising if there were a large number of negative opinions and referrals, indicating that the Commission had misjudged the mood of the committees on many occasions.

Given the different degrees of freedom the Commission has under each of the procedures, one would expect the Commission and the Council to be constantly in conflict over which procedure should be used for the enactment of each piece of legislation. However Dogan (1997, 2000) has found that this is not necessarily the case. For example 29 per cent of all comitology procedures proposed by the Commission between 1987 and 1995 were under procedures where the Commission was weak (such as procedure III), and contrary to the Commission's rhetoric about the Council's opposition to the advisory committee procedure, the Council accepted 40 per cent of the Commission's proposals for use of this procedure. Dogan consequently argues that 'the Commission is deeply implicated in the pattern of Council comitology preferment' (ibid., p. 45). However, as with the seemingly harmonious relationship between the Commission and the committees in the operation of comitology, the figures might reflect the fact that the Commission is strategic in its choice of comitology procedures, and hence only proposes the advisory procedure in cases where it thinks it has a reasonable chance of getting them past the Council.

The EP has been highly critical of comitology (Corbett *et al.*, 1995, p. 253; Bradley, 1997; Hix, 2001a). After the establishment of the system the EP argued it lacked transparency, due to the secretive nature of the committee proceedings. It also argued that by allowing the member state governments to scrutinize the executive powers of the Commission, the comitology system undermined the principle of the separation of powers between the legislative authority of the EU (the Council and the Commission) and the executive implementation authority (the Commission). Moreover it was critical of the fact that the procedures only allowed for issues to be referred back to one part of the EU legislature (the Council), rather than to both the Council and the European Parliament.

In 1988, under the so-called 'Plumb–Delors Agreement', the president of the Commission and the president of the EP agreed that the Commission would refer most implementing measures to the EP at the same time as they were forwarded to the comitology committee. However the EP was dissatisfied with the operation of the agreement, and in July 1994 rejected a directive (on open network provision in voice telephony) because the Council refused to change the proposed comitology procedure to a procedure more favourable to the Commission. Following this EP veto, the Council and the Commission agreed a *modus vivendi* with the EP, whereby the Commission would send all measures to the EP and inform the EP of decisions in comitology, and the Council would 'take due account of the EP's point of view'. The *modus vivendi* was reviewed by the intergovernmental conference that negotiated the Amsterdam Treaty, but no agreement was reached on the issue.

In June 1997 the Amsterdam European Council nevertheless instructed the Commission to draft a proposal for revising the 1987 comitology decision. The 1999 decision was a direct result of the interinstitutional *modus vivendi* and the Amsterdam European Council instruction. Several changes were made to the 1987 rules: the criteria for determining the choice of committee procedure were specified; the procedures were simplified (reducing the number of procedures from six to four); the system was made more transparent (the Commission would publish an annual report on the activities of the committees, and the same principles that applied to public access to internal Commission documents would be applied to comitology documents; and the EP would be involved more directly (by supplying the EP with all committee agendas and minutes, and specifying that measures deriving from legislation adopted under the co-decision procedure would be referred back to both the Council and the EP).

Overall, Joerges and Neyer (1997) argue that comitology is a unique political process, which the Commission and national experts work together to solve policy issues in a non-hierarchical and deliberative policy style, the technical nature of EU legislative and executive actions calls for a high degree of scientific expertise. The comitology system removes bureaucrats and experts from national settings, and promotes a collective identity in each policy community. However, contrary to the claim of uniqueness, the involvement of scientific experts and private interests in the process of policy implementation and regulation is a common feature of most public administration systems. And on high-profile policy issues, conflicts do arise between the Commission and the national experts, and between experts from different member states.

Democratic Control of the EU Executive

In most systems the political and administrative roles of the executive are legitimized in different ways. The political leadership role is usually legitimized by electoral competition for political office and control of the political agenda. In presidential systems the head of the executive is directly elected, whereas in parliamentary systems the executive is accountable to the parliamentary majority (Lijphart, 1992). In contrast the administrative role is usually disconnected from electoral and parliamentary majorities, which enables bureaucrats and regulators to serve the public interest rather than the interests of a particular political coalition (Majone, 1996, pp. 284–301; 2002b). Instead civil servants and regulators are usually held accountable through the principle of 'ministerial responsibility' (whereby ministers are accountable for the actions of the civil servants serving under them), and the right of public access to documents and information (for example through a freedom of information act).

Political accountability: selection and censure of the Commission

In the collective exercise of political leadership in the Council the member state governments can claim legitimacy via national general elections (see Chapter 7). However the legitimacy of the political leadership role of the Commission is more problematic. Until 1994 the president of the Commission was chosen by a collective agreement among the heads of government in the European Council. The Commission president was regarded as one post in a package deal between governments on the heads of a number of international agencies, such as the secretaries-general of the World Trade Organization and the North Atlantic Treaty Organization. This was more akin to selecting the head of an international organization than to choosing the 'first among equals' in a political cabinet.

However the Maastricht Treaty introduced a new procedure (Article 214), whereby the term of office of the Commission was aligned with the term of the EP. Also, the EP would now be consulted on the member state governments' nominee for Commission president, and the members of the full Commission would be subject to a vote of approval by the EP. However the EP interpreted 'consulted' as the right to vote on the nominee for Commission President (Hix, 2002a). Consequently in July 1994, in the first ever 'Commission president investiture vote' in the EP, Jacques Santer was approved by the EP as Commission president by a margin of only 12 votes (Hix and Lord, 1995). In addition, following the nomination of the individual commissioners, the EP introduced 'Commission hearings', where the nominees had to give evidence to the EP committee covering their portfolios (consciously modelled on US Senate hearings of the nominees for the US president's cabinet) (Westlake, 1998). Finally, once the committee hearings were complete the EP took a second vote on the Commission as a whole. The Amsterdam Treaty reformed Article 214 to formally institutionalize the EP's power to veto the nominated Commission President and team of commissioners. Subsequently the Nice Treaty introduced qualified-majority voting in the European Council for the nomination of the Commission president and the commission as a whole. The proposed constitution would only slightly amend this combination of qualified-majority voting in the European Council and veto by the EP by requiring that the European Council take account of the EP election results when nominating a Commission president.

Since the Treaty of Rome the EP has had the right to censure the Commission as a whole by a 'double majority': an absolute majority of MEPs and two thirds of the votes cast (Article 201). Motions of censure have been proposed on several occasions, but none has ever been carried. The EP tends to fear that throwing out the Commission would backfire, as governments and the public would accuse the EP of acting irresponsibly. Also, before the new investiture procedure there was nothing to prevent governments from reappointing the same commissioners. Above all, the EP is aware that the Commission, as a fellow supranational institution, is more often an ally against the Council than an enemy. In practice, then, the EP's right of censure is more like the right of the US Congress to impeach the US president than the right of a domestic parliament in Europe to withdraw majority support for a government, and therefore it can only be exercised in extreme circumstances – in instances of what the US constitution calls 'high crimes and misdemeanours'.

However in 1998 and 1999 the EP became more confident about using of the threat of censure. In 1998, with widespread public disapproval of the Commission's handling of the BSE crisis, the EP successfully threatened censure to force the Commission to reorganize its handling of food safety issues. In January 1999 the EP demanded that the Commission respond to the high-profile allegations of financial mismanagement, nepotism and cover-up (the Commission had sacked an official who had leaked a report on fraud and financial mismanagement). On the eve of the censure vote the president of the Commission promised that an independent committee would be set up to investigate the allegations, and that there would be a fundamental administrative reform of the Commission, including a new code of conduct, rules governing the appointment and work of the cabinets, and restrictions on 'parachuting' political appointees into top administrative jobs. As a result the censure motion was narrowly defeated, with 232 MEPs in favour of censure and 293 opposed (mostly from the Party of European Socialists and European People's Party groups).

In a separate motion passed in January 1999, however, the EP put the Commission on probation until the committee of independent experts set up by the EP reported on the allegations of fraud, corruption and nepotism. When the highly critical report was published in March 1999 a new motion of censure was tabled. On Sunday 14 March, the day before the vote, Pauline Green, the leader of the largest party group in the EP (the Party of European Socialists), informed Jacques Santer that because the majority in her group would be voting for censure, the motion would probably be carried. Santer promptly called an emergency meeting of the commissioners, who agreed they should resign *en masse*. Hence one can reasonably claim that the EP did in fact censure the Commission in March 1999, even though a vote was never taken – in much the same way as president Nixon was forced to resign in 1974 after a committee of the US House of Representatives had issued an opinion, and before an actual impeachment vote in either the House or the Senate was taken.

Because of the effective censure of the Santer Commission by the EP, the incoming Prodi Commission was much more sensitive to EP concerns. For example during their committee hearings, the prospective commissioners showed more respect for the opinions and questions of the MEPs than several of the members of the previous Commission had in their hearings. Also, during the debate on the investiture of the next commission, Romano Prodi promised to sack individual commissioners if the EP could prove allegations of corruption or gross incompetence. This effectively gave the EP the right to censure individual commissioners. However, counterintuitively, this could limit the influence of the EP over the Commission as a whole, as it might undermine the norm of collective responsibility in the Commission – a key weapon of any parliament over a government.

Consequently the procedures for selecting and deselecting the Commission have become a hybrid mix of the parliamentary and presidential models. The Maastricht and Amsterdam Treaties injected an element of parliamentary government by requiring the Commission to have the support of a majority in the EP before taking office, and the right of censure allows the EP to withdraw this support. Also, the introduction of qualified-majority voting in the European Council for nominating the Commission means that the same majority is now required for electing the executive and passing the legislative initiatives of the executive. Hence there is a fusion of the executive and legislative majorities, as in a parliamentary system.

However, in the process of selecting the Commission president the member state governments are the equivalent of a presidential electoral college, over which the EP can only exercise a veto. The EP cannot propose its own candidate. And once invested, the Commission does not really require a working majority in the EP. The right of censure is only a 'safety valve', to be released in the event of a serious political or administrative failure by the Commission.

This design reflects a conscious effort by the member state governments to maintain their grip on who holds executive office at the European level. The EP has gained a limited role in the investiture procedure because the governments had to address the 'democratic deficit' (see Chapter 6). During the Convention on the Future of Europe, which drafted the Constitution, a variety of alternative models were proposed. These included a classic parliamentary model, with a contest for the Commission president in EP elections and the translation of the electoral majority in the European Parliament into the formation of the Commission; and a presidential model, with some form of direct or indirect election of the Commission president. However, neither model was acceptable to the member state governments, which perceived that the value of the benefits of any alternative (democratic) model of electing the Commission would be considerably lower than the potential costs: the loss of their power to choose the members of the other branch of the EU executive, and the likely politicization of the Commission.

Administrative accountability: parliamentary scrutiny and transparency

The administrative and regulatory tasks of the Commission and the Council are subject to parliamentary scrutiny in much the same way as domestic bureaucracies and regulatory agencies are (cf. Rhinard, 2002). First, the president of the Commission presents the Commission's annual work programme to the EP. Second, commissioners and civil servants in the DGs regularly give evidence to EP committees, and certain EP committees have introduced a 'question time' for the commissioner responsible for the policy areas they oversee. Third, the president-in-office of the Council presents the Council's six-monthly work programme to the EP. Finally, government ministers from the member state that currently holds the presidency often appear before EP committees, and the president of the European Central Bank and the heads of the EU agencies appear before the EP committees on a regular basis.

The EP has a highly developed system of presenting oral and written questions to the Council and the Commission (Raunio, 1996). As in national parliaments, these questions enable MEPs to gain information, force the executive to make a formal statement about a specific action, defend their constituencies' interests, and inform the Commission and Council of problems with which they might be unfamiliar. Between 1994 and 1999 the EP put 21 096 questions to the Commission and 3 958 questions to the Council (Corbett *et al.*, 2000, p. 250). The full texts of the questions and the answers by the institutions are published in the EU *Official Journal.*

Unlike most national administrations, however, there is no system of ministerial responsibility in the EU. Individual commissioners are often blamed for inconsistencies in the DG in their charge, or for lack of action in the policy area they cover, but no procedure exists for forcing individual commissioners to resign. Moreover the Commission has not developed a culture in which a commissioner or a senior official would resign out of a sense of obligation, and the EP has no right to censure individual commissioners. Nonetheless in January 1999 the EP announced it would hold separate votes of no-confidence in two commissioners: Edith Cresson and Manuel Marín, who were in charge of administrative divisions where fraud and nepotism had been alleged. Although these motions would have no legal force, considerable pressure to resign was put on the two commissioners by the media and several governments if the EP passed the motions by a simple majority. In the event the motions were defeated.

Despite the above, since the early 1990s the Commission has been eager to promote transparency in its administrative operations. First, in February 1994 it unveiled a 'transparency package'. This included the publication of its annual work programme in October instead of January, which allows the EP and Council time to debate the draft before the final adoption of the full legislative programme in January. Second, in the initiation of legislation the Commission now makes more use of green and white papers, public hearings, information seminars and consultation exercises. Third, the Commission's new code of conduct commits it to make internal documents public, with the exception of minutes of its meetings, briefing notes, the personal opinions of its officials and documents containing information that might 'damage public or private interests' (Peterson, 1995b, pp. 478–81). Finally, the Commission submits draft legislation to national parliaments so that their committees on EU affairs can scrutinize the legislation before their government ministers address it in the Council. If ratified the proposed constitution would formalize this by means of a procedure that would require the Commission to reconsider the legislation if one third of the national parliaments think that the proposal is in breach of the separation of competences between the member states and the EU.

Officially the Council supports greater openness in EU decision-making, and in October 1993 it signed an interinstitutional 'Declaration on Democracy, Transparency and Subsidiarity'. However both the Commission and the EP have accused the Council of hypocrisy. First, the majority of member states (and thus the Council) have opposed the Commission's efforts to allow public access to EU documents – many member state governments are keen to prevent private interests and the media from learning more about what they sign up to in the EU legislative and executive processes. Second, the Council has proved reluctant to expose itself to public scrutiny. The Amsterdam Treaty (Article 207) specifies that:

> the Council shall define the cases in which it is to be regarded as acting in its legislative capacity, with a view to allowing greater access to documents in those cases. In any event, when the Council acts in its legislative capacity, the results of votes and explanations of vote as well as statements in the minutes shall be made public.

However this allows the Council to remain highly secretive about matters that come under its executive capacity, and also to define for itself when it is 'acting as a legislature'. The proposed constitution would change this slightly by defining that the Council acts as a legislature under the 'normal legislative procedure', and so require the Council to be more open in its legislative activities.

The activities of the governments in the Council are scrutinized by their national parliaments (Norton, 1996; Bergman, 1997; Raunio, 1999; Saalfeld, 2000). In every national parliament this is primarily conducted by a special EU affairs committee, which receives drafts of legislative initiatives by the Commission, and usually asks national government officials and ministers involved in EU affairs to give evidence and answer questions. Some national parliaments are more effective than others in this role. For example the EU affairs committee in the Danish *Folketing*, which was set up in 1972, issues voting instructions to Danish government ministers prior to meetings of the Council. In contrast the Select Committee on European Legislation at the British House of Commons has very little control over the activities of British ministers in the Council.

As European integration has progressed, and governments have delegated more powers to the EU institutions, several scholars have detected a decline in the ability of national parliaments to scrutinize the executive branch of their national governments effectively (e.g. Andersen and Burns, 1996). For example, Moravcsik (1993, p. 515) argues:

> by according governmental policy initiatives greater domestic legitimacy and by granting greater domestic agenda-setting power . . . the institutional structure of the EC strengthens the initiative and influence of national governments by insulating the policy process and generating domestic agenda-setting power for national politicians. National governments are able to take initiatives and reach bargains in Council negotiations with relatively little constraints.

However, since the mid 1990s national parliaments have fought to retrieve at least some of the powers they have lost to the executive as a result of EU integration (Raunio and Hix, 2000). By 1995 all the national parliaments had set up EU affairs committees to scrutinize their governments' activities at the EU level, and developed procedures requiring ministers and national bureaucracies to provide detailed information on new EU legislation and how EU decisions would be implemented in the domestic arena.

Explaining the Organization of Executive Power in the EU

How can this division of executive responsibilities between the Council and the Commission be explained? One answer is that the level and types of delegation to the Commission are at the point where the demand by the member state governments for independent executive powers meets the supply of political leadership, administration and regulation by the Commission.

Demand for EU government: selective delegation by the member states

Having created the single market, the member state governments have been faced with the problem of how and by whom the single market should be governed. They could undertake these tasks themselves, by drafting and passing laws through intergovernmental arrangements and cooperation between national regulators. However, it is in the collective interests of the governments to delegate governing responsibilities to the Commission for a number of reasons.

First, they need someone to formulate legislative ideas (cf. Moravcsik, 1993, pp. 511–12; Pollack, 1997a, pp. 104–5). Governing a market of 450 million consumers and harmonizing/replacing the 25 existing regulatory regimes requires legislative specialization. Each government could specialize in a particular area, just as national legislators specialize in parliamentary committees. However this would enable each government to promote its particular economic and sectoral interests and only supply limited information on alternative options to the others. To avoid this each government could come up with separate proposals for every piece of legislation, but this would be extremely costly. Alternatively, the responsibility for initiating legislation could be delegated to an independent authority, which would be required to take account of the diverse national and sectoral interests when drafting legislation and would also be charged with promoting the collective European interests. This would significantly reduce the transactions costs of initiating legislation.

Second, the governments also need an independent agent to execute and administer legislation once it has been adopted (cf. Moravcsik, 1993, pp. 512–14, 1999; Majone, 1996, pp. 72–4; Pollack, 1997a, pp. 102–4). Again, they could undertake these tasks through intergovernmental means, with each government promising to implement legislation in its own system. However there would be an incentive to free-ride. For example if a government implemented an EU environment directive or opened part of its market to European competition, another government would benefit without having to enforce the legislation in its own system. It would also be difficult for the member states to monitor each other's compliance with EU law. Hence, as long as the EU governments do not trust each other, it is also in their collective interest to delegate the monitoring of the transposition and implementation of EU legislation to the Commission.

Third, the delegation of certain initiative and implementation functions to a supranational agent is facilitated by the fact that the governments are primarily interested in being re-elected. A classic assumption of political science is that the main aim of political parties is to win and maintain government office (cf. Downs, 1957; see also Chapter 6). Consequently the member state governments constantly focus on the next general election, which at most is only a few years away. With such a short time horizon, they would be less concerned about the long-term implications of delegating powers to the Commission than about how immediate decisions would affect their electorate and supporting interest groups. When popular decisions were made by the Commission they could claim that they had 'brought home the bacon'. Conversely, delegating unpopular decisions to the Commission would enable them to insist that 'Brussels made me do it'. This has been a popular claim in relation to EU rules on state aids and the privatization of public monopolies (Smith, 1997b).

At the moment, delegation to the Commission by the Council and the degree of implementing discretion allowed by the Council are not uniform across policy areas. In the most sophisticated research in this area, Fabio Franchino (2000a, b, c, 2001, 2002, 2004) explains how variations in the amount of delegation and discretion result from two key factors: the level of policy disagreement between the member states, and the level of expert information required in a particular area. In policy areas where member states' preferences are homogeneous and where a high level of expertise is needed, the member state governments prefer to delegate to the Commission rather than to their own national administrations, and will give the Commission more leeway in the implementation of policies (for example by using the more permissive comitology procedures). In contrast, when the governments are divided or no specialist expertise is required, they prefer either to delegate implementation to their national administrations, or to delegate it to the Commission, but under the comitology procedures where the Commission's discretion is limited.

For example in the case of agricultural policy, where the governments have diverse policy preferences, the member states have delegated considerable implementing power to the Commission, but have chosen to use the restrictive comitology procedures to prevent too much Commission discretion in this area. In contrast, in the case of competition policy, where the governments' preferences are more uniform, the Commission has a greater degree of implementing discretion and significant power over the domestic administrations.

The governments have also changed the decision-making rules laid down in the treaty with a view to the likely behaviour of the Commission in the implementation of legislation (cf. Bräuninger *et al.*, 2001; Carrubba and Volden, 2001; Tsebelis, 2002). The use of qualified-majority voting in a particular policy area increases the probability that the Council will be able to pass new legislation to overturn an unpopular implementing action by the Commission. Under unanimity voting, in contrast, even if only one member state will benefit from the implementing action, that state can vote against and thus overturn the introduction of new legislation. Hence the Commission has a greater degree of discretion over implementation when legislation is adopted by unanimity voting than by majority voting (see Tsebelis and Garrett, 2000b).

In summary, the member state governments would like to maintain a monopoly on the collective exercise of executive power in the EU, but there are a number of reasons to delegate certain executive responsibilities to the Commission in particular policy areas. However, to prevent 'bureaucratic drift' in the exercise of these functions the governments have recognized the need to police the work of the Commission, and hence the comitology system has been established as a means of 'patrolling' the executive powers of the Commission (Pollack, 1997a, pp. 108-21; Franchino, 2000c). The governments have also maintained a monopoly on the nomination of the Commission president and the selection of individual commissioners.

Supply of EU government: Commission preferences, entrepreneurship and capture

Just as the member states are selective about what and how they delegate to the Commission, the Commission is selective about what it supplies to the member states. First, the Commission has specific policy preferences: like any bureaucracy it has an incentive to promote its own power and organizational development. As discussed in the first section of this chapter, most bureaucracies try to maximize their budgets, but there are tight constraints on the ability of the

Commission to do so. The EU budget only amounts to 1.27 per cent of the total GDP of the member states, and the proportion of the budget spent on expenditure policies (such as agricultural and cohesion policies) is set by the member states (see Chapter 9). As a result the Commission is prevented from expanding its budgetary capacity. But this has not prevented the Commission from developing its executive powers.

For example, during the creation of the single market the proportion of the EU budget spent on administration increased from 4.35 per cent of the total budget in 1985 to 4.8 per cent in 1994. Meanwhile, in the same period, the volume of legislation proposed by the Commission and the number of direct executive instruments it issued increased dramatically. This was because the Commission was more interested in expanding its responsibilities and shaping its own organizational design than in increasing its budget (Dunleavy, 1997; Dunleavy and O'Duffy, 1998). The Commission is not a 'delivery agency' that provides public services such as health and education. Instead, the Commission's administration is composed of a variety of regulatory agencies (which make rules for private actors), control agencies (which pass on their budgets to other public bodies, as under the EU cohesion policies), transfer agencies (which pass on their budgets to the private sector, as under the development aid policies) and contract agencies (which spend their budgets on private corporations, as under the research and development policies). These agencies are not particularly interested in increasing their budgets. Rather they are interested in increasing their control over the policy agenda, and the staff in the agencies are keen to raise their profile within their own policy community (for example through more contact with the private sector). As a result the Commission does not press for greater EU expenditure, but does seek more regulatory policies and greater involvement of private sector actors in the policy process. Majone (1996, p. 65) consequently concludes that 'the utility function of the Commission is positively related to the *scope* of its competences rather than to the *scale* of the services provided or to the size of its budget'.

Second, and linked to its preference structure, the Commission is a 'policy entrepreneur' an actor that can set the policy agenda under certain circumstances (Majone, 1996, pp. 74–7; Pollack, 1997a, 1997c; Cram, 1997; Moravcsik, 1999). Policy entrepreneurs are particularly influential when there are information asymmetries and a large variety of actors across time and space, and when the preferences of the actors are underdetermined (Kingdon, 1984). The Commission does not have a monopoly on information and expertise. However if the circumstances are right – such as when the Council is divided, or when the Council is in desperate need of new information or policy ideas – the Commission can shape the policy agenda by manipulating the asymmetries between the member states, joining forces with private interests to influence the member states' positions, or bringing new policy ideas to the table (cf. Smyrl, 1998; Moravcsik, 1999). The Commission can also use its implementing powers indirectly to influence bargaining in the Council (Schmidt, 1998, 2000, 2001; Tallberg, 2000). By taking particular implementing measures in a given area, or by taking action against particular member states, the Commission can influence the position of key member state governments *vis-à-vis* the *status quo*. This leads to new policies being adopted in the Council, as member states have less of an incentive to block EU-wide measures once they have enacted domestic policy changes in response to implementing and monitoring actions by the Commission (see Schmidt, 2000).

Third, like any agency the Commission is susceptible to 'capture' by private interests. In an ideal world, when drafting policies and promoting issues the Commission would simply be a neutral arbiter between competing private interests. Inevitably, though, some interest groups are more able to organize to influence the Commission than others, and the targets of EU policies and regulations (such as private firms) have a particular incentive to mobilize to influence the policy process (see Chapter 7). For example farmers have a vested interest in lobbying the Agriculture DG to prevent reform of the Common Agricultural Policy. Similarly multinational firms have a vested interest in securing the deregulation of social and environmental policies as part of the completion of the single market programme. The Commission can promote the involvement of public interests in EU decision-making, such as consumer and environmental groups. However private firms have considerable resources at their disposal and can offer particular inducements to Commission staff, such as lucrative jobs outside the EU bureaucracy. The Commission also relies on public and private interest groups to provide information and expertise, but interest groups can be selective about the type of information they provide to policy makers.

Conclusion: the Politics of a Dual Executive

The power to set the policy agenda and implement EU policies is shared between the EU governments (in the Council) and the Commission. Basically, the Council sets the long- and medium-term agendas, by reforming the EU Treaty and delegating political and administrative tasks to the Commission. In the areas where executive powers have been delegated, the Commission has a significant political leadership role and is responsible for distributing the EU budget, monitoring policy implementation by the member states, and making rules and regulations. This separation of powers has evolved through an interaction between the strategies of the Council and the Commission.

On the one hand, the member state governments have delegated powers to the Commission to overcome collective action problems, reduce transaction costs and produce policy credibility. However they have been selective in this delegation. For example they have limited the Commission to certain regulatory matters, such as competition and agricultural policies. They have also retained control of key executive powers; such as treaty reform, policy-making under the JHA and CFSP, front-line implementation of EU legislation, long-term agenda-setting and the coordination of national macroeconomic policies in the European Council. In addition, the governments have limited the Commission's discretion through the comitology system and retained their monopoly over the nomination of the Commission president and the selection of the commissioners.

On the other hand, the Commission has developed many of the characteristics of a supranational 'government'. At the political level, the College of Commissioners operates along the lines of cabinet government, with collective responsibility and the Commission president acting as the first among equals. Also the commissioners are partisan career politicians and pursue their own ideological objectives in the EU policy process. At the administrative level, the Commission directorates-general are quasi ministries, and the Commission is at the heart of an emerging network of European regulatory agencies. Also, like national administrations each service in this Euro-bureaucracy has its own administrative culture, institutional interests, policy objectives and supporting societal groups. As a result the Commission has powerful incentives and significant political and administrative resources to pursue an agenda independently from the member state governments.

The member state governments have tried to tilt the balance of power in this dual-executive relationship back to themselves. For example, following the activism by Delors they were careful to choose Commission presidents (Santer and Prodi) who they felt were more sensitive to member state interests. Moreover they have tried to use the European Council to set the medium- and short-term policy agenda, and thereby take away some of the Commission's policy-initiation power. Finally, since the resignation of the Santer Commission the Commission administration has gone through a period of self-investigation and internal reform, which has bred further insecurity *vis-à-vis* the member state governments.

The result is a system with strengths and weaknesses. The main strength is that the dual character of the EU executive facilitates extensive deliberation and compromise in the adoption and implementation of EU policies. This is a significant achievement for an emerging political system, and it reduces the likelihood of system breakdown.

However there are two important weaknesses. First, the flip side of compromise is a lack of overall political leadership (cf. Christiansen, 2001), and dual-executive systems tend to be characterized by policy immobilism. Second, and linked to this issue, there is the problem of democratic accountability. There is no single chief executive, whom the European public can 'throw out'. The consequence is a political system that seems remote to most European citizens, as we shall see in Chapter 5.

Chapter 3

Legislative Politics

Theories of Legislative Coalitions and Organization
Development of the Legislative System of the EU
Legislative Politics in the Council
Legislative Politics in the European Parliament
Legislative Bargaining Between the Council and the EP
Conclusion: Complex but Familiar Politics

The EU has a classic two-chamber legislature in which the Council represents the 'states', and the European Parliament (EP) represents the 'citizens'. In contrast to many other legislatures, however, the Council is more powerful than the EP. Nevertheless, under the so-called co-decision procedure the EP and the Council are genuine colegislators. Finally, despite the fact that the main actors in the Council are governments and those in the EP are political parties, internal politics and political organization in the two chambers are very similar. To understand how this system works we shall first look at some theories of legislative behaviour and organization.

Theories of Legislative Coalitions and Organization

Contemporary scholars of legislatures are less interested in their functions than in explaining the working of legislative bargaining, coalition formation and organization. One of the first such approaches was Riker's (1962) theory of 'minimum-winning coalitions'. According to Riker, legislators aim to have as much influence as possible in a winning coalition. As a result coalitions are unlikely to include any group that is not necessary to reach a majority. Fewer coalition partners means fewer interests to appease in the distribution of benefits. But if a party is decisive in turning a minimum-winning coalition into a majority-winning coalition it can demand a high price for participating in a coalition. Hence the more likely an actor is to be decisive (pivotal) the more 'power' it will have in coalition bargaining (Shapley and Shubik, 1954; Banzhaf, 1965).

An alternative view is that political actors do not form coalitions with just anyone. Coalitions are easier to hold together if they are between actors with similar policy preferences. Hence Axelrod (1970) predicts 'minimum-*connected*-winning' coalitions between legislators who are next to each other on a policy dimension. Whereas Riker's theory of coalition formation in legislative bargaining is 'policy blind', Axelrod's theory is 'policy driven'.

When studying legislative behaviour in the US Congress, Mayhew (1974) adopted a similar policy-driven assumption. He argues that the primary goal of legislators is to gain reelection, but to achieve this they must secure policy benefits for their constituents. To secure this end they try to exchange votes with other legislators to form winning majorities. For example legislators from agricultural constituencies will agree to back a proposal by legislators with manufacturing constituencies in return for their support in a future vote on an agricultural issue. This legislative exchange is often called 'logrolling' or 'pork-barrel' politics because the result is usually a new policy initiative and/or increased public expenditure.

One theoretical problem with policy-driven approaches is that vote trading between legislators is inherently unstable. This is illustrated in Figure 3.1, where three legislators (A, B and C) have different ideal policy positions on the pro-/anti-Europe and left–right dimensions, and try to achieve policy outcomes on each dimension that are as close as possible to this ideal. The current policy situation, the *status quo* (*SQ*), is between the three legislators. Each legislator prefers a policy to *SQ* if it is closer to his or her ideal policy. So the circles passing through *SQ* are the 'indifference curves' for each legislator: whereby any policy on these curves is equally far from the ideal policy of the legislator. Any policy in the shaded areas (the 'win-set' of *SQ*) is preferred to *SQ* by a majority of legislators. Consequently legislator A can propose policy X, which A and C prefer to *SQ*. But legislator C can then propose policy Y, which both B and C prefer to X. If this happens legislator B can then propose *SQ*, which both A and B will support to beat Y, and so on *ad infinitum*. The result is chaos: there is no stable policy (equilibrium) that is preferred by a legislative majority in two or more policy dimensions (McKelvey, 1976).

This is a problem for majoritarian democracy. Thankfully, however, vote-cycling rarely occurs in practice. This is usually because institutions in the legislative process produce a 'structure-induced equilibrium' (Shepsle, 1979; Riker, 1980), as discussed in Chapter 1.

First, the rules that govern who is the agenda-setter and who can exercise a veto change the dynamics of legislative bargaining (see Romer and Rosenthal, 1978; Baron and Ferejohn, 1989; McCarthy, 2000). In Figure 3.1, if A is the agenda-setter and B and C are not allowed to make counterproposals, then A can make a 'take it or leave it' bid to the other two actors. In this situation A can propose any policy in the areas indicated by Z, which will be supported by a majority of A and either B or C. As the agenda-setter, then, A can

Figure 3.1   *Legislative instability in a two-dimensional policy space*

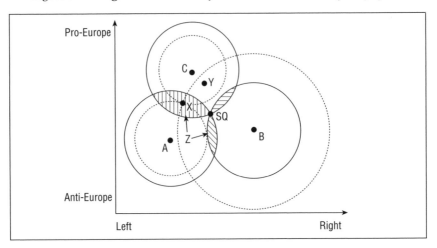

secure an outcome that is closer to its ideal point than is the *status quo*.

Now add a rule that C is the veto-player, meaning that no policy can be adopted without C's support, regardless of the actions of B. Knowing this, A will only propose a policy that is closer to C's ideal policy than *SQ*, otherwise C will veto. In this situation the policy outcome will be in the shaded area where policy X is located: the set of policies that both A (the agenda-setter) and C (the veto-player) prefer to *SQ*. A casual observer witnessing the fact that no veto is exercised might assume that all the power resides with the agenda-setter. In reality the agenda-setter will have taken account of a potential veto and proposed a new policy accordingly (cf. Cameron, 2000).

Nevertheless, in general it is better to be the agenda setter than the veto-player, since by definition, all policies will be closer to the agenda-setter's ideal point than is *SQ*. If the veto-player were to oppose such a change the agenda-setter would not propose any policy choice. In other words, either a policy change will be better for the agenda-setter or there will be no policy change. Nevertheless the higher the number of veto-players the harder it will be for the agenda-setter to find a new policy that defeats the *status quo* (Tsebelis, 1995c, 2000, 2002). For example in Figure 3.1, if everyone is a veto-player (a unanimity rule) then no policy change can occur as any move from *SQ* will make at least one of the actors worse off (cf. Colomer, 1999).

Second, if each policy dimensions is tackled separately (the 'germaneness rule'), stable legislative majorities can be constructed on each dimension. For example legislators A and B form a stable majority that beats *SQ* on the pro-/anti-EU dimension, and legislators A and C form a stable majority that beats *SQ* on the left–right dimension. This effect can be established through legislative specialization, for example in parliamentary committees. If each specialist committee 'controls the gates' on a particular policy issue the committee can preclude consideration of its policy issue when another issue is being discussed, and consequently prevent the issue linkage that might result (Shepsle and Weingast, 1987). Krehbiel (1991) offers an alternative explanation of legislative specialization. He argues that although legislators try to get policies as close to their ideal position as possible, they are not certain of the precise relationship between legislative instruments and final policy outcomes. Hence there is an incentive for all legislators to foster policy expertise through legislative specialization. From this perspective, legislative organization results from the need to acquire and disseminate information.

Third, political parties facilitate legislative stability. Cohesive political parties exist when politicians have incentives to act together to control and influence executive power, as in parliamentary systems (Cox, 1987; Huber, 1996a, 1996b). But, in the US Congress and the EP the legislative majority does not form a government. Even in these assemblies, however, parties enable individual legislators to overcome collective action problems (see for example Aldrich, 1995). Each legislator is unlikely to obtain his or her policy objectives by acting alone. Legislators could cooperate spontaneously, but each coalition would have to be negotiated separately. Hence by establishing formal relationships that bind individuals together the transaction costs of coalition formation are reduced (Cox and McCubbins, 1993). Parties also help to overcome information gaps (Kiewiet and McCubbins, 1991). With uncertainty about other legislators' preferences and the impact of legislative decision, legislators with similar policy preferences benefit from institutional arrangements that divide information-gathering and policy expertise amongst themselves. The result is a delegation of tasks: backbench MPs provide labour and capital, and party leaders distribute committee and party offices and determine the party line on complex legislative issues. Once these organizational arrangements have been set up the costs of leaving a legislative party are high.

Fourth, legislative stability is also facilitated by bicameralism: the existence of two legislative chambers. With two chambers, two different majorities have to be in favour of a proposal before it can become law, which restricts the set of possible policy choices and therefore simplifies legislative bargaining (Riker, 1992; Tsebelis and Money, 1997). However, depending on how the legislative procedures are designed – which determines which chamber is the agenda-setter and which is the veto-player – one chamber may have more influence over policy outcomes than the other. But if disagreement between the chambers leads to the convening of a special intercameral committee (such as a conciliation committee), then both houses will be able to propose amendments and veto any final deal.

In summary, there have been three generations of institutional rational choice research on legislative behaviour and organization (Shepsle and Weingast, 1994). The first generation, which included Riker and Mayhew, focused on the motives of individual legislators and the formation of coalitions in an institution-free environment. The second generation, including Shepsle, introduced institutions to explain why legislative outcomes are stable, and the third generation which includes Cox, Krehbiel, Tsebelis and Huber, explain where these institutions came from. Together these theories help us to understand how the EU legislative process works: what coalitions are likely to form, why the internal Council and EP rules are organized in the way they are, and who is most powerful under the EU's legislative procedures.

Development of the Legislative System of the EU

Despite its complexity the EU legislative system is highly effective in developing, amending and passing laws. As Figure 3.2 shows, in the 1990s on average the EU produced more than 120 pieces of legislation each year (counting only directives and regulations, and excluding decisions). The peak of legislative activity was in the early 1990s. Between 1987 and 1993 over 300 pieces of legislation relating to the completion of the single market were adopted (see Chapter 8). Of the three main procedures for adopting legislation – consultation, cooperation and co-decision (see below) – the bulk of legislation has been adopted via the consultation procedure, where the powers of the EP are limited compared with those of the Council. Many of the regulations adopted under the consultation procedure have been technical measures for implementing the Common Agricultural Policy (there were 14 such measures in 2000 and 17 in 2001). As a result, in 2000 and 2001 the majority of non-agricultural legislation was adopted using the co-decision procedure, under which the EP has equal power with the Council.

The rules of the EU legislative process have evolved considerably since the Treaty of Rome established that legislation would be adopted through interaction between the Council of national governments, the Commission and the EP. The treaty did not set out a single procedure to govern this interaction; instead the procedure to be used was specified in each individual article (see the Appendix for the decision making rules under the current treaty articles). Each article specified what voting rule would be used in the Council – whether the Council should decide by unanimity or qualified-majority voting (QMV, a system of weighted voting) – and whether or not the EP should be consulted by the Council.

The right of the Council to make decisions by QMV was challenged

Figure 3.2   *Annual EU law production, by legislative procedure*

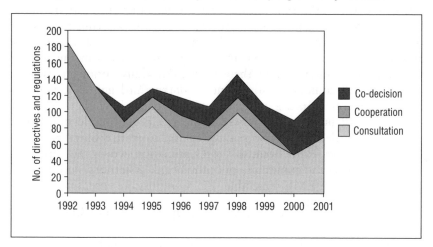

Sources: Data collected from General Reports on the Activities of the European Community/Union.

in the mid 1960s, when President Charles de Gaulle of France, objected to the idea of majority voting being used in a number of important areas. De Gaulle insisted that every member state should be allowed to veto legislation, even when the treaty specified that QMV could be used, and in 1965 he provoked a crisis by withdrawing French representatives from the EC – the famous 'empty chair' policy. The crisis was resolved in January 1966 by the so-called 'Luxembourg compromise', which established the principle that if a member state declared that a vital national interest was at stake the Council should make every effort to reach a unanimous agreement.

The Luxembourg compromise was not legally binding, as it was not laid down in the treaties, but it ushered in nearly two decades of 'intergovernmental' bargaining. Any member state faced with being outvoted on a key issue could simply invoke the Luxembourg compromise and halt proceedings. For example, although the Treaty of Rome specified that after 1966 the liberalization of capital movements would be decided by QMV, the Commission did not initiate any proposals as it expected that at least one member state would claim the right to veto a directive (Teasdale, 1993, p. 570).

Nevertheless, by the mid 1990s the EU legislative system had developed into something much closer to a traditional bicameral model. The first major development was the 1980 'isoglucose' ruling by the European Court of Justice (ECJ). The first direct elections to the EP had been held in June 1979, and between the dissolution of the EP before the elections and the reconvening of the new EP the Council had adopted a piece of legislation without consulting the EP. In its ruling the ECJ annulled the legislation on the grounds that the treaty required the Council to consult the EP, and the Council should not have acted before the EP had issued an opinion to the Council. The ECJ argued that consultation with the EP was 'an essential factor in the institutional balance intended by the Treaty'. This did not mean that in future the EP could force its opinions on the Council, as a national parliament could on an upper house. But backed by the isoglucose ruling the EP now had a 'power of delay'. For example in 1989 it threatened to delay a Commission proposal to start the first phase of EMU on 1 July 1990 because the Commission would not accept a stronger role for the committee of central bank governors. Anxious not to jeopardize the EMU timetable, the Commission accepted the relevant EP amendments.

The powers of the EP were substantially increased by three subsequent treaty reforms. First, in 1987 the Single European Act (SEA) introduced a new legislative procedure: the cooperation procedure. This was the first procedure to be set out in a separate treaty article (Article 252), to which other treaty articles referred. The procedure allowed the EP a second reading, after the Council had adopted a common position, and reduced the ability of the Council to overturn EP amendments made in the second reading. The SEA applied this procedure to only 10 treaty articles, but these included most areas of the single market programme, specific research programmes, certain decisions relating to the structural funds and some social and environmental policy issues. Together these constituted approximately one third of all legislation. The SEA also introduced an 'assent procedure', whereby the approval of the EP was required before the Council could act. This applied to association agreements with non-EC states and the accession of new member states.

Second, in 1993 the Maastricht Treaty extended the assent procedure and introduced a fourth legislative procedure, the co-decision procedure, which was also set out in a separate treaty article (Article 251). This procedure introduced the rule that if the EP and Council disagreed on a piece of legislation a conciliation committee should be convened, consisting of an equal number of representatives of the EP and the Council. After a conciliation committee had reached an agreement the EP could reject the legislation outright. The co-decision procedure originally applied to most areas of internal market legislation that had previously been covered by the cooperation procedure, and several new areas introduced by the Maastricht Treaty, such as public health, consumer protection, education and culture.

Third, in 1999 the Amsterdam Treaty reformed and extended the co-decision procedure. The reforms increased the power of the EP within the procedure and extended the procedure to most areas previously covered by the cooperation procedure. The co-decision procedure established by the Maastricht Treaty is often referred to as 'co-decision I' in order to distinguish it from the reformed procedure under the Amsterdam Treaty, which is called 'co-decision II'. In 2003 the Nice Treaty extended the co-decision procedure into a number of additional areas. The proposed constitution, if ratified, would establish the Amsterdam version of the co-decision procedure as the 'normal legislative procedure' and significantly extend this procedure to almost all areas of EU law.

Since the signing of the Nice Treaty most areas of regulation of the EU single market – such as environment policy, health and safety, social policy and the harmonization of standards – have been covered by the co-decision procedure. One anomaly is that unanimity is still required under the co-decision procedure on social security for migrant workers and rules governing the professions. The cooperation procedure is now almost moribund, being restricted to some limited provisions relating to EMU. The consultation procedure, on the other hand, still exists in a wide range of areas, while the assent procedure is mainly used for international agreements. There are still several issues where legislation can be agreed by the Council without EP involvement, such as matters relating to the Common Commercial Policy.

Research has shown that despite the complexity of the rules, and despite the expanding legislative agenda and volume of legislation, the EU legislative system has adapted well. For example in an analysis of the time taken between the initial proposal and the final legislation in the period 1984–94, Schulz and König (2000) found that although the EP's increased involvement had slowed down decision making (due to the need for several readings in the EP), this had been more than compensated by the increased efficiency that had resulted from the extension of qualified-majority voting in the Council (cf. Golub, 1999; Jordan *et al.*, 1999).

The other reason for the efficiency and effectiveness of the EU legislative system is that both the Council and the EP have developed sophisticated rules to improve their scrutiny, amendment and adoption of legislation, and sophisticated strategies to maximize their influence *vis-à-vis* each other in the various stages of bicameral bargaining.

Legislative Politics in the Council

As discussed in the previous chapter, the Council is composed of ministers from the governments of the EU member states – that is, agriculture ministers in the Council of Agriculture Ministers, economic and finance ministers in the Council of Economic and Finance Ministers (EcoFin) and so on.

Ministers in the Council are like legislators in any parliament in that they weigh potential benefits to the whole of society (the EU) against potential losses to their constituents. This can lead to conflicts of interest between different ministers from the same country. First, in coalition governments (which is the case in most member states) ministers from different parties have different core electorates, and consequently a policy proposal before the Council might benefit the supporters of one governing party but threaten the supporters of another. This leads to pressure for different ministers to take opposing positions in different Council meetings. Second, different ministerial portfolios have different functional support groups and fiscal interests. For example, whereas ministers in EcoFin have an interest in constraining public spending, ministers in the Social Affairs Council, the Regional Affairs Council and/or the Employment Council have an interest in increasing public spending on their social programmes.

Agenda organization: the presidency, sectoral councils and committees

The Council has developed several mechanisms to improve the coordination of the EU legislative agenda. First, the presidency of the Council has evolved since the 1970s into the central coordinating mechanism. The presidency rotates every six months among the member governments in a prearranged system. The rotation was originally in alphabetical order, but the order was changed in 1998 to achieve a balance between large and small states. The rules of procedure of the Council set out the main tasks of the presidency as follows (cf. Westlake, 1995, pp. 45–6; Hayes-Renshaw and Wallace, 1997, pp. 136–9):

• To convene Council meetings and announce the dates of the meetings seven months in advance.
• To draw up the provisional agenda for each meeting and to indicate which items any government or the Commission may request a vote.
• To chair the meetings of the Council and the meetings of the Committee of Permanent Representatives.
• To submit a six-month work programme.
• To sign the minutes of meetings and all decisions.
• To represent the Council to the EP, the Commission and the outside world.

As can be seen, the government that holds the presidency has considerable control of the legislative agenda inside the Council. Each government takes over the presidency with a particular list of policies it would like to see adopted. These form a central part of the presidency's work programme and will be on the agenda of all the key

Council meetings. However the presidency can only act on these issues if legislation is proposed by the Commission. Conversely if the presidency does not like a Commission proposal it can simply refuse to put it on the Council agenda.

In general member states treat their term of office as an opportunity to pursue their own policy objectives. The result is the rolling addition to the Council agenda of specific national policy issues (Bulmer and Wessels, 1987; Kirchner, 1992). However member states also like to be seen as having held 'good' presidencies, and not all member states are able to manipulate the agenda to the same extent. The member states that are most capable of this are those with ministries that are well adapted to dealing with European issues and have sufficient administrative capacity. This is often not the case with the smaller member states, but the larger member states also have problems as their presidential terms tend to be taken up with domestic political developments and attempts to promote their own national agendas at the expense of the overall Council agenda (O'Nuallain, 1985; Kirchner, 1992). Consequently Hayes-Renshaw and Wallace (1995, p. 571) conclude that where the presidency is concerned '"medium-sized" member governments probably have a comparative advantage'.

The proposed constitution would replace the rotating presidency with a single 'chair' of the European Council, with a renewable term of two and a half years. Lower formations of the Council would be able to choose their own chairs. This represents a compromise between the larger member states, which wanted a more permanent leadership structure in the Council, and the smaller member states, which wanted to maintain an element of rotation between large and small states, for example in a 'team presidency'. While the large states have secured a permanent, single president of the European Council, the smaller member states expect the chairs of the lower Councils to reflect a balance between large and small states and to rotate between the member states.

Second, the existence of sectoral councils means that the Council agenda has become increasingly specialized. As Table 3.1 shows, until the mid 1980s the General Affairs Council (of foreign ministers) and the Agriculture Council accounted for almost half of all council meetings. But in the 1990s – with the rise of EcoFin, the various councils dedicated to regulation of the single market, and the new activities of the justice and home affairs ministers, this figure fell to less than one in three. Formally the General Affairs Council is still at the pinnacle of the hierarchy, and issues are referred to it if agreement cannot be reached at a lower level. However the increased legislative volume and the constant pressure of foreign policy and security issues on the agenda of EU foreign ministers have limited the ability of the General Affairs Council to control decisions in lower meetings. Also, with the

Table 3.1   *Frequency of sectoral council meetings, 1980–2000*

	1980	1985	1990	1995	2000
General Affairs	13	14	13	14	14
EcoFin	9	7	10	9	13
Agriculture	14	14	16	10	10
Social Affairs	2	2	3	4	6
Justice and Home Affairs	1	0	1	4	6
Environment	2	3	5	4	5
Transport	2	3	4	4	5
Internal Market	0	5	7	2	4
Fisheries	7	3	3	4	3
Culture	0	2	2	3	3
Development	1	2	4	2	3
Telecommunications	0	0	2	2	3
Industry	0	6	4	3	2
Research	0	2	4	3	2
Budget	3	5	2	2	2
Health	0	0	2	2	2
Education	1	1	2	2	2
Energy	2	3	3	2	1
Consumer Affairs	0	1	2	2	1
Other	3	0	1	1	0
Total	**60**	**73**	**90**	**79**	**87**

Source: Annual Reports on the Activities of the Council of the European Union.

development of EMU and the new 'open method of coordination' (see Chapter 2), EcoFin and the European Council (of prime ministers) have usurped some of the coordinating functions of the General Affairs Council on economic issues.

In terms of the organization of the EU legislative agenda, sectoral councils are the functional equivalent of parliamentary committees, with each having a specific policy domain. By delegating issues to meetings of ministers with shared functional and fiscal interests, and often with an established *esprit de corps* (as in EcoFin), the potential for trading agreements between different policy sectors is increased. For example to overcome a deadlock in the adoption of the single market programme, an agreement between internal market ministers on market liberalization can be traded-off with an agreement between social affairs ministers on minimum health and safety standards. The inevitable result is a 'logrolling' of the EU towards further integration.

Third, to facilitate prelegislative agreement there is a network of council committees, working groups and the Council secretariat. The

Committee of Permanent Representatives (COREPER) is the real engine for much of the work of the Council, and it is where the majority of issues are decided before legislation is seen at the ministerial level (Zwaan, 1995; Schendelen, 1996; Lewis, 1998). COREPER meets each week at the level of member states' ambassadors to the EU (COREPER II) and their deputies (COREPER I). Hayes-Renshaw and Wallace (1995, p. 562) estimate that approximately 70 per cent of Council business is agreed in working groups consisting of national officials below COREPER II. The EU permanent representatives then tackle about 15–20 per cent of business, which they pass on to Council meetings as 'A points' – issues that have already been resolved, and therefore only require formal ministerial approval. This enables the Council to focus on the 10–15 per cent of 'B points' that still need to be resolved.

Under COREPER there are various sectoral committees of specialist civil servants, such as the Special Committee on Agriculture (SCA), the Political and Security Committee (covering Common Foreign and Security Policy), the Article 133 Committee (dealing with the Common Commercial Policy) and the Article 36 Committee (on police and judicial cooperation). Supporting these committees is the Council secretariat, with a staff of approximately 2000 and a network of over 170 working groups. Every day, between 300 and 400 officials from national bureaucracies attend meetings in the Council building (Hayes-Renshaw and Wallace, 1997, p. 70).

Traditionally, the Council is regarded by many scholars of the EU as the central intergovernmental institution, where civil servants and ministers work tireless to promote and defend their national interests. However research on the internal operation of the Council and the nature of the interactions between the various officials has revealed significant supranational behaviour, such as a willingness to compromise a particular national position in order to promote the collective interests of the EU as a whole (Beyers, 1998; Beyers and Dierickx, 1998; Lewis, 1998). But is this reflected in high-level political bargaining in the Council: in the voting and coalition behaviour of the ministers?

Voting and Coalition Politics in the Council

There are two basic voting rules in the Council:

- Unanimity, where each member state has one vote and legislation cannot be passed if one or more member states vote against the legislation.
- Qualified-majority voting (QMV), where the votes are weighted according to the size of a member state's population and an 'oversized majority' is required for legislation to be passed (258 of the 345 votes in the current EU of 25 member states).

However there is a quirk in the Council's voting rules in the case of abstention. Article 205(3) of the Treaty states that 'Abstentions . . . shall not prevent the adoption by the Council of acts which require unanimity.' In other words, under unanimity an abstention is equivalent to support for a proposal (although an abstaining government can argue to its voters that it did not support the legislation). Under QMV, in contrast, an abstention is equivalent to voting against a proposal, as 258 votes are still required to carry the legislation. Consequently as one of the Council's own publications points out:

> This sometimes results in the paradoxical situation where a decision for which a qualified-majority cannot be reached . . . is taken more easily unanimously as a result of abstention by certain members of the Council who do not wish to vote in favour but who do not want to prevent the Act concerned from going through. (Council of the European Communities, 1990, p. 41)

Table 3.2 shows the number of votes each government has under the Council voting rules before and after the 2004 enlargement. Under unanimity every member has an equal chance of being 'pivotal', that is, to determine whether a coalition wins or loses. Under QMV, although the larger member states have more votes the system of weighting over-represents the number of citizens in the smaller EU member states (cf. Felsenthal and Machover, 1997). Nevertheless the larger member states are more than twice as likely to be part of a winning coalition than the smaller ones (cf. Brams and Affuso, 1985; Hosli, 1995b; Lane and Maeland, 1995; Widgrén, 1995).

The member governments are acutely aware that changes to their voting strengths or the QMV threshold will affect their relative power. For example the level of the new QMV threshold was a key issue in the enlargement of the EU to include Austria, Finland and Sweden in 1995 (Johnston, 1995, 1996; Garrett *et al.*, 1995; Morriss, 1996; Garrett and McLean, 1996). Some member states argued that the 'blocking minority' as a proportion of all votes should be extrapolated from the old threshold of approximately 30 per cent of the total votes. However the UK, Spain and Italy argued that the addition of three small northern member states would alter the type of coalition needed to achieve a qualified-majority. As a result, in the Ioninna Declaration of March 1994 the member states agreed to 26 votes as the blocking minority (30 per cent of all votes), but stipulated that 'if members of the Council representing a total of 23 to 25 votes indicate their intention to oppose [an Act] ... the Council will do all in its power to reach ... a satisfactory solution that could be adopted by at least 65 votes' (cf. Westlake, 1995, pp. 93–4).

A similar argument arose during the negotiations on voting weights

Table 3.2   *Voting weights and voting power in the Council*

-	Pop. (mil.)	Unanimity Votes	Unanimity Power[1]	Qualified-Majority EU15 (Rome rules) Votes[2]	Qualified-Majority EU15 (Rome rules) Power[1]	Qualified-Majority EU27 (Nice rules) Votes[2]	Qualified-Majority EU27 (Nice rules) Power[1]
Germany	82.5	1	100.0	10	11.7	29	8.7
France	59.6	1	100.0	10	11.7	29	8.7
United Kingdom	59.3	1	100.0	10	11.7	29	8.7
Italy	57.3	1	100.0	10	11.7	29	8.7
Spain	40.7	1	100.0	8	9.6	27	8.0
Poland	38.2	1	100.0	–	–	27	8.0
Romania	22.5	1	100.0	–	–	14	4.0
Netherlands	16.2	1	100.0	5	5.5	13	3.7
Greece	11.0	1	100.0	5	5.5	12	3.4
Belgium	10.4	1	100.0	5	5.5	12	3.4
Portugal	10.4	1	100.0	5	5.5	12	3.4
Czech Republic	10.2	1	100.0	–	–	12	3.4
Hungary	10.1	1	100.0	–	–	12	3.4
Sweden	8.9	1	100.0	4	4.5	10	2.8
Bulgaria	8.2	1	100.0	–	–	10	2.8
Austria	8.1	1	100.0	4	4.5	10	2.8
Denmark	5.4	1	100.0	3	3.5	7	2.0
Slovakia	5.4	1	100.0	–	–	7	2.0
Finland	5.2	1	100.0	3	3.5	7	2.0
Ireland	4.0	1	100.0	3	3.5	7	2.0
Lithuania	3.5	1	100.0	–	–	7	2.0
Latvia	2.3	1	100.0	–	–	4	1.1
Slovenia	2.0	1	100.0	–	–	4	1.1
Estonia	1.4	1	100.0	–	–	4	1.1
Cyprus	0.7	1	100.0	–	–	4	1.1
Luxembourg	0.4	1	100.0	2	2.1	4	1.1
Malta	0.4	1	100.0	–	–	3	0.8
Total votes		15/27		87		345	
Required to adopt		15/27		62	(71.3%)	258[3]	(74.8%)
Required to block		1		26	(29.9%)	88	(25.5%)

Notes:
1. Power = proportion of times a member state is pivotal (the Shapley–Shubik index is used for qualified-majority voting; the IOP 2.0.2 program, developed by Bräuninger and König (2001), has been used to calculate the Shapley–Shubik indices).
2. The voting weights are as set out in the Amsterdam Treaty for the EU15 and the Nice Treaty for the EU27.
3. Under the rules of the Nice Treaty a 'triple majority' is required: 258 out of 345 for 27 member states, a majority of member states, and 62 per cent of the population of the member states.

in the Nice Treaty. The larger member states were concerned that their power in the Council would be reduced after the proposed accession of a large member state (Poland) and eleven smaller ones. France was also eager to maintain parity with Germany. The result was a rather messy compromise. First, the total number of votes for each member state was increased, allowing each to claim that its votes had gone up. Second, the balance of weights between the member states was altered to increase the weights of the larger member states against the smaller ones (as Table 3.2 shows). Third, the qualified-majority threshold after EU enlargement was increased from 71 per cent to 75 per cent, while the blocking-minority threshold was reduced from 30 per cent to 26 per cent. Fourth, a 'triple majority' requirement was established, so that legislation could only be passed if it was supported by a qualified-majority of votes and a majority of member states, and only if these member states contained at least 62 per cent of the population of the EU.

Compared with the original rules in the Rome Treaty and the weights that existed after the 1995 enlargement, under the voting rules established by the Nice Treaty the larger and smaller member states are better off, the medium-sized ones are worse off, and legislation is significantly less likely to be passed (Felsenthal and Machover, 2001; Baldwin *et al.*, 2001b; Aleskerov *et al.*, 2002; Moberg, 2002; Tsebelis and Yataganas, 2002; cf. Raunio and Wiberg, 1998; Sutter, 2000).

The agreement on voting weights in the Nice Treaty almost derailed an agreement on the constitution. The Convention on the Future of Europe, which prepared a draft constitution for the governments to consider, proposed replacing the Nice rules with a simple 'double majority', whereby legislation would require the support of a majority of member states representing 60 per cent of the population of the EU. However this system would significantly reduce the voting power of Spain and Poland. Whereas under the Nice Treaty, Spain and Poland had almost as many votes as Germany, France, Italy and the United Kingdom (27 votes compared with 29), the introduction of a double majority would mean that these states would only have approximately 50 per cent of the influence of Germany (with double the population of Spain and Poland) and two thirds of the influence of France, Italy and the United Kingdom (with 50 per cent more people than Spain and Poland). The Spanish and Polish prime ministers refused to support the simple double majority in December 2003, but settled on a compromise deal in June 2004, whereby legislation would require 55 per cent of the member states representing 65 per cent of the population, and a blocking minority would have to consist of at least four member states, thus increasing the ability of Spain or Poland to block agreements in the Council compared to original draft of the constitution.

These calculations of relative power based on the absolute number of votes for each member state assume that all types of coalition are equally as likely, which is clearly not the case (Garrett and Tsebelis, 1999; cf. Lane and Berg, 1999; Holler and Widgrén, 1999). Coalitions are likely to form between governments with similar policy goals and interests. For example a Franco-German coalition – the so-called Paris-Bonn–Axis – has been at the heart of Council decision- making since the 1950s. The Benelux states are more economically and politically integrated than any other grouping in the EU. The less prosperous member states – Greece, Ireland, Portugal and Spain (a 'cohesion bloc') – often vote together to protect their interests in the single market and under the EU structural funds. Denmark, Sweden and Finland (the 'Nordic bloc') have close economic and political ties and similar cultural and economic structures. The new member states in Central and Eastern Europe (the 'eastern alliance') have similar economic and social structures relative to the other member states. Hosli (1996) calculates that the Franco-German coalition and the cohesion bloc are each pivotal in 25 per cent of cases, the Benelux Countries are pivotal in 15 per cent of cases, and the Nordic bloc is pivotal in 11 per cent of cases. In the enlarged EU, the eastern alliance could command 29 per cent of the votes in the Council (cf. Winkler, 1998).

Nonetheless there is an underlying culture of consensus in the Council that ensures that the Council hardly ever acts by QMV even when it is allowed to under the provisions of the treaty (Hayes-Renshaw and Wallace, 1997). For example Mattila and Lane (2001) found that between 1994 and 1998, 79 per cent of decisions in the Council were taken by unanimous vote, that one or more member state voted against a proposal in only 16 per cent of cases, and that three or more member states voted against a proposal in only 2 per cent of cases (cf. Mattila, 2004). The largest percentage of negative votes was for agricultural issues, followed by internal market matters and there were very few negative votes on social and environmental policies.

The fact that national governments are involved in adopting EU legislation and have to implement the legislation once it has been passed causes real problems of compliance under QMV. If a member state is in a minority in a vote it may not only be under pressure from domestic interests to oppose the legislation but may also be subjected to pressure not to implement the legislation. The problem of compliance may in fact become more acute as voting records in the Council become more transparent (Hayes-Renshaw and Wallace, 1995, p. 575). It is unsurprising, then, that in most cases the Council would rather see no legislation being adopted than risk undermining a delicate consensus. Nevertheless it might also be the case that the voting rules have an implicit impact on decision making. For example if a qualified-majority is in favour of a proposal there is pressure on the minority governments to concede in order to maintain consensus. As the Council admits, 'the relatively small number of decisions actually taken by a qualified-majority does not fully show the part played by qualified-majority voting as a factor for efficiency in the implementation of Community policies' (Council of the European Union, 1995, p. 11).

Despite the incentives for consensus, how each government has voted (exercised a negative vote or abstained) in relation to the other governments allows us to plot the voting patterns in the Council. The results shown in Figure 3.3 – in which the distance between any two governments is a reflection of how often these two governments voted the same way or differently – suggest that policy preferences do have an impact. In the period 1995–98 Sweden, Denmark and the Netherlands tended to vote together against the natural majority in the Council, as did Italy and Spain. Also, Germany and the UK voted against the majority but on opposite sides – with Germany being the most isolated government in this period (casting a negative vote on 11 per cent of occasions). This was probably due to the British and German governments' positions on the reform of the internal market, with the British government being most in favour of deregulatory policies and the

Figure 3.3 *Voting patterns in the Council, 1995–8*

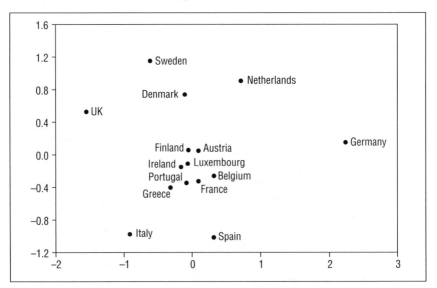

Note: This is a 'multi-dimensional scaling' plot of all roll-call votes in the Council between 1995 and 1998.

Source: Mattila and Lane (2001). Reprinted by permission of Sage Publications Ltd, from *European Union Politics*, Vol. 2, No. 1 © Sage Publications 2001.

German government being most opposed. Once data have been collected for the 1999–2004 period we shall be able to see whether the shift from the left to the right in the Council led to even greater isolation for the German government.

Legislative politics in the European Parliament

Unlike the Council, the EP does not have a fixed seat. It holds most of its plenary sessions in Strasbourg, the official seat of the EP secretariat is in Luxembourg and the bulk of the work of the EP is in Brussels, where an increasing number of plenary sessions are held, the party groups and committees meet and the offices of the MEPs and the party group and committee secretariats are based. Despite this handicap, the EP operates like any other parliament: organizing and mobilizing to influence EU legislation and the EU executive.

The institutional design of the EU – the separation of executive and legislative powers – means that the EP is more like the US Congress than most domestic parliaments in Europe. The Commission does not require the permanent support of a majority in the EP to govern: the censure procedure in the EU is more akin to the impeachment of the executive in a presidential system than a parliamentary majority withdrawing its support for the government in a parliamentary system (see Chapter 2). In return, though, there is no EU government to enforce its wishes on a supporting majority in the EP. So the EP is a relatively independent legislative body, and is free to amend legislation proposed by the Commission and agreed by the Council.

MEP behaviour: reelection versus promotion and policies

Since 1979, MEPs have been elected in EU-wide contests every five years. Public opinion surveys repeatedly show that less than 60 per cent of EU citizens know anything about the EP, and less than 5 per cent have an informed impression of what MEPs do. Also, European elections are not fought on European issues; the campaigns are by national parties and on national issues (see Chapter 6). Hence an MEP's chance of re-election is not dependent upon his or her performance in the EP, but is determined by the popularity of his or her national party. Moreover most member states use list-PR systems in EP elections, whereby the national party leadership determine the order of MEPs on the list. Consequently for most MEPs the chance of standing as a candidate and being reselected is determined not by his or her party group in the EP but by his or her national party leadership (Bowler and Farrell, 1993; Norris and Franklin, 1997).

Traditionally, a career in the EP was considered either as a training ground for a job in national politics or as a 'retirement home' at the end of a national career. However the 1994, 1999 and 2004 elections brought an increasing number of MEPs who planned to stay for at least two terms or to pursue a career in another EU institution or European-level organization (approximately 30 per cent of all MEPs and approximately 60 per cent of British and German MEPs) (cf. Scarrow, 1997).

MEPs intent on making a career in the EP have two types of goal: office goals, such as promotion to party leadership, a senior position in the EP (for example EP president) or the chairmanship of an EP committee; and policy goals, the pursuit of ideological views or the interests of their constituents through the influence of the EP on the EU legislative and executive processes. Whereas re-election is usually not dependent on parliamentary performance, the ability to achieve these goals is dependent upon gaining promotion within the EP committees and the groups, and on being able to form coalitions with other legislators to secure common policy aims.

In other words MEPs face a dilemma: to secure reselection and re-election they must cater to national party interests; but to secure both promotion within the EP and policy outputs from the EP they must cater to the interests of EP committees and party leaderships.

Agenda organization: leaderships, parties and committees

Like most national parliaments the EP determines its own organization and writes its own rules. It prefers to use formal rules of procedure rather than informal conventions and norms (probably because the EP is multilingual and formal rules reduce miscommunication and linguistic confusion). Through the rules of procedure the EP has set up three main organizational structures to facilitate agenda control.

The first of these is the parliamentary leadership. The most senior offices in the EP are the president and the 14 vice-presidents. There are also three leadership bodies: the Bureau of the Parliament (consisting of the president and vice-presidents), the Conference of Presidents (consisting of the EP president, the leaders of the EP parties and the chairman of the Conference of Committee Chairmen), and the Conference of Committee Chairmen. Together these committees involve all the senior figures in the EP. The Bureau deals with internal organizational and administrative matters, but is increasingly active on political issues and meets almost every week. The Conference of Presidents is traditionally where most political issues are tackled, particular with regard to the relationship between the EP and the Commission and Council, and normally meets twice a month. The Conference of Committee Chairmen coordinates the committee agendas and tackles intercommittee demarcation disputes.

Second, the EP party groups are the central mechanisms for structuring debate and coalition formation in the EP legislative process (Hix and Lord, 1997; Raunio, 1997; Kreppel, 2002a; see also Chapter 6). Rule 29 of the rules of procedure set out how many MEPs are needed to form a party group: at least 19 MEPs from at least one fifth of the member states (thus five out of the current 25). The party groups have certain privileges, such as a significant secretarial and research staff and financial resources. Table 3.3 shows the seats of the party groups and their national memberships in July 2004, following the sixth direct elections to the EP in June 2004. The European People's Party-European Democrats (EPP-ED), on the centre-right, and the Party of European Socialists (PES), on the centre-left, are the two dominant groups and command two thirds of the seats between them. There are, however, several smaller groups that can have crucial influence on legislative behaviour.

The real relevance of the EP parties relates to the fact that their leaderships determine most of the vital political issues in the EP: the choice of the EP leadership, the allocation of committee positions and *rapporteur* assignments, the agenda of plenary sessions and the policy positions of the party groups. If a national political party is not a member of a party group it is unlikely to secure any office or policy goals for its MEPs. Also, national parties are more likely to secure these goals by belonging to the two larger groups than to one of the smaller ones. This has resulted in a reduction in the number of EP parties and consolidation of the EPP and PES. Although elections increase party group fragmentation (because of the national issues considered in the campaigns), the incentive structure within the EP reduces group fragmentation between elections (Bardi, 1996). For example in 1992 the European Democratic Group was disbanded after all its member parties (the British, Spanish and Danish conservatives) joined the EPP, in 1996 Forza Europa was disbanded after its members (the Italian Forza Italia and its allies) joined the Union for Europe (UPE), and in 1999 the European Democratic Alliance group was disbanded after the main national party in the group (the French Gaullists) joined the EPP. Similarly in 1992 the Italian ex-communists left the European United Left (EUL) to join the PES, and in 1994 and 1996, respectively, the French Parti Républicain and the Portuguese Partido Social Democrata left the European Liberal, Democrat and Reform Party (ELDR) to join the EPP.

The same factors ensure that individual MEPs avoid upsetting their party group leaderships. Individual MEP adherence to the group line in legislative voting is enforced through a 'whipping' system, in which votes are designated as 'one-line', 'two-line' and 'three-line' whips, according to the importance of the agenda item to the party group (based on the system in the British House of Commons). The result has been growing cohesion in the major party groups, to a level that is

Table 3.3   *Seats in the European Parliament, July 2004*

	EPP-ED	PES	ALDE	EUL/NGL	G/EFA	IND/DEM	UEN	na	Total seats
				Party group					Total seats
Austria	6	7		2				3	18
Belgium	6	7	6	2				3	24
Cyprus	3		1		2				6
Czech Republic	14	2		6		1		1	24
Denmark	1	5	4	1	1	1	1		14
Estonia	1	3	2						6
Finland	4	3	5	1	1				14
France	17	31	11	3	6	3		7	78
Germany	49	23	7	13	7				99
Greece	11	8			4	1			24
Hungary	13	9	2						24
Ireland	5	1	1		1	1	4		13
Italy	24	16	12	2	7	4	9	4	78
Latvia	3		1	1			4		9
Lithuania	2	2	7				2		13
Luxembourg	3	1	1	1					6
Malta	2	3							5
Netherlands	7	7	5	4	2	2			27
Poland	19	8	4			10	7	6	54
Portugal	9	12			3				24
Slovakia	8	3						3	14
Slovenia	4	1	2						7
Spain	23	24	2	3	1				54
Sweden	5	5	3	1	2	3			19
United Kingdom	28	19	12	5	1	11		2	78
Total	**268**	**200**	**88**	**42**	**41**	**37**	**27**	**29**	**732**
% of seats	36.6	27.3	12.0	5.7	5.6	5.1	3.7	4.0	100.0

Notes:

EPP-ED	= European People's Party-European Democrats (Christian democrat/ conservative).
PES	= Party of European Socialists (social democrat).
ALDE	= Alliance of Liberals and Democrats for Europe (liberal).
G/EFA	= Greens/European Free Alliance (green and regionalist).
EUL/NGL	= European United Left/Nordic Green Left (radical-left).
IND/DEM	= Group for Independence and Deomcracy (anti-European)
UEN	= Union for a Europe of Nations (nationalist-conservative).
na	= non-attached members (mostly extreme right).

almost as high as in some European national parliaments and certainly higher than in the US Congress (Hix *et al.*, 2005; see also Chapter 6).

Nevertheless within the party groups the national delegations have remained powerful, with the larger national delegations in each group dominating the key leadership positions. Also, because national parties control the selection of candidates in elections, when MEPs are torn between their national party and their EP party they almost always vote with their national party, and hence against their EP party (Hix, 2002b). This suggests that the strong cohesion in the EP parties is more a reflection of the high degree of policy agreement among the national parties that make up these groups than of the organizational power of the EP groups over the national parties (cf. Kreppel and Tsebelis, 1999).

Third, there are the EP committees. As Westlake (1974, p. 191) puts it, 'If the political groups are the Parliament's life blood, then its ... committees are its legislative backbone', and it is in the committees that the real scrutiny of EU legislation takes place. The committees propose amendments to legislation in the form of a report and a draft resolution, which are then submitted to the full EP plenary session in more or less a 'take it or leave it' form. Amendments to the proposed committee resolutions can be made in the full plenary, but without the backing of a committee and the EP party support that goes along with this, amendments are less likely to be adopted by the parliament. Thus in terms of the influence of committees on the legislative agenda, the EP is again more akin to the US Congress than to most European parliaments.

The jurisdictional organization of EP committees is based on the need to specialize in the legislative process. Table 3.4 shows the EP committee jurisdictions for the 1994–99 parliament. MEP membership of these committees is correlated more with the MEPs' interest-group affiliations and previous occupational experiences than with nationality or party affiliation (Bowler and Farrell, 1995). In fact many MEPs join committees with policy competences that are close to the interests of their constituents or supporting interest groups, which suggests legislative specialization to secure distributional benefits. Other MEPs join committees because of their previous occupational experience, which suggests legislation specialization to secure information and knowledge. Either way the design of EP committees facilitates logrolling and legislative agreement in the full plenary session.

The importance of the committees means that committee chairmanships are prized offices for MEPs, and this is particularly so in the case of committees with active roles in the EU legislative processes, such as agriculture, environmental and consumer affairs, and economic and monetary affairs. For example Ken Collins (PES, UK), who was chair of the environment committee between 1989 and 1999, was a key

Table 3.4 Work of the EP committees in the 1994-99 parliament

Committee name (acronym)	Chair 94-6/97-9	Number of reports by committee[1]									Total
		A	B	C	D	E	F	G	H	I	
Economic & Monetary Affairs (EMAC)	EPP	63	73	7	–	120	–	16	8	1	288
Environment, Public Health & Consumer Policy (ENVI)	PES	20	86	47	–	37	–	9	8	–	207
Transport & Tourism[2]	EPP/UFE	7	27	80	1	31	–	6	13	–	165
External Economic Relations[3]	ELDR/EUL	70	1	–	13	15	–	18	12	–	129
Foreign Affairs, Human Rights, Common Security & Defence Policy (AFET)	EPP	12	–	–	23	50	–	32	10	–	127
Legal Affairs & Internal Market (JURI)	EPP/ELDR	12	45	2	1	30	–	8	19	–	117
Agriculture & Rural Development (AGRI)	EDA/PES	85	3	–	–	11	–	7	9	–	115
Research & Energy[3]	FE/EPP	41	17	9	1	29	–	8	8	–	113
Fisheries (PECH)	EPP	86	–	–	2	11	–	8	5	–	112
Budgets (BUDG)	PES	28	2	2	–	7	58	6	1	–	104
Employment & Social Affairs (EMPL)	PES	14	12	13	–	40	–	8	11	1	99
Citizens' Freedoms & Rights, Justice & Home Affairs (LIBE)	PES	37	4	–	–	24	–	17	15	–	97
Budgetary Control (CONT)	EPP	22	2	–	–	15	37	8	–	–	84
Culture, Education, Youth, Media & Sport (CULT)	EUL/EPP	20	30	4	–	8	–	10	3	–	75
Development & Cooperation (DEVE)	PES	9	4	34	5	11	–	10	–	–	73
Regional Policy[2]	PES/EPP	6	2	–	4	43	–	6	9	–	70
Rules of Procedure[4]	PES	–	–	–	–	–	–	5	1	29	35
Women's Rights & Equal Opportunities (FEMM)	G	3	2	2	–	7	–	10	8	–	32
Institutional Affairs[4]	PES	3	–	–	–	10	–	10	1	–	24
Petitions (PETI)	PES/EPP	–	–	–	–	5	–	7	–	–	12
Temporary or Inquiry committees	–	–	–	–	–	–	–	6	–	–	6
Total 1994-99		538	310	200	50	504	95	215	141	31	2084

Notes:

1. A = consultation procedure, B = co-decision procedure, C = cooperation procedure, D = assent procedure, E = consultation on non-legislative issues, F = budgetary reports, G = committee 'own initiative' reports, H = reports on motions for resolution (tabled by individual MEPs), I = other issues, including legal base issues, reports on EP rules and petitions.

2. In 1999 the Regional Policy and Transport and Tourism committees were merged into the Regional Policy, Transport and Tourism (RETT) committee.

3. In 1999 the Research and Energy and External Economic Relations were merged into the Industry, External Trade, Research and Energy (ITRE) committee.

4. In 1999 the Institutional Affairs and Rules of Procedures committees were merged into the Constitutional Affairs (AFCO) committee.

Source: Calculated from data in Corbett *et al.* (2000).

player in determining the outcome of several important pieces of environmental legislation (Judge, 1993; Judge and Earnshaw, 1994).

The importance of the EP committees also provides an incentive for the EP party leaderships to influence committee assignments and agendas. At the beginning of each parliamentary term and again halfway through each term the committee chairmanships are reallocated, and the party groups have established a system of allocating these posts in proportional to each party group's seats (using the d'Hondt counting system, which is broadly proportional but favours the larger groups). The portfolios to be received by each party group are then subject to intergroup negotiation, and the complete package is presented to the EP. For example, as shown in Table 3.4 in the first half of the 1994–99 parliament the PES had nine committee chairs compared with the EPP's six (in the first half of the 1999–2004 parliament, the EPP took eight chairs to the PES's six). After this carve-up among the party groups, similar negotiations take place within the groups over how the party groups' prizes are distributed between the national delegations. The party groups have also developed a system for influencing committee agendas and coordinating party policy across committees. This is done through group coordinators in each committee, who meet regularly to discuss party group strategies.

Coalition formation

There is no permanent coalition in the EP, and without a government to support, legislative coalitions are formed for each vote (again like the US Congress). On many issues the EP behaves as if it were a single actor with a single interest (to promote its own powers and institutional interests), in opposition to the interest of the other legislative chamber of the EU (the Council) or the holders of executive power (the Council or the Commission).

However an informal 'grand coalition' between the PES and EPP is facilitated by the rules of the EU legislative process. In the adoption of opinions in the early stages of the legislative procedures when voting on 'own initiative' reports and when adopting amendments to resolutions on legislation the EP decides by a simple majority of those present at the vote. For the second reading in the co-decision procedure the EP is required to proposed amendments by an absolute majority of all MEPs, not just of those turning out to vote (see below). In the past this rule caused a problem for the EP as the average attendance for legislative votes was less than 65 per cent (cf. Scully, 1997a), and with a 65 per cent turnout a coalition of 77 per cent of all those voting was needed to carry legislation by an absolute majority. Consequently in 1998 the party group leaderships agreed to new rules on the reimbursement of MEPs' expenses. Henceforth, in addition to being present in Strasbourg for plenary sessions MEPs would have to participate in votes in order to claim their expenses. This led to a higher turnout. But, with still only an approximate turnout of 75 per cent a coalition of 67 per cent (two-thirds) of those voting is still needed to pass legislation. This encourages cooperation between the two largest groups.

Coalition politics in the EP, is therefore shaped by whether a simple or an absolute majority is required. Under a simple majority procedure the EPP and PES can form winning coalitions with various combinations of the smaller party groups. As Table 3.5 shows, although the PES and EPP have the most power (in terms of the proportion of times they are pivotal in the formation of a winning coalition), the smaller groups can sometimes be pivotal under simple majority rules. In contrast, when an absolute majority is required it is virtually impossible to construct a winning coalition without the EPP and PES. In this situation the PES and EPP are very powerful and the smaller groups are marginalized (Lane *et al.*, 1995; Hosli, 1997; Nurmi, 1997).

Since the EP voting records are more readily available than those for the Council, and because there are more 'roll-call' votes (whereby the way in which each legislator votes is recorded in the minutes) in the EP than in the Council, there has been more empirical research on voting behaviour and coalition patterns in the EP (see for example Kreppel and Tsebelis, 1999; Hix, 2001b; Kreppel, 2002a; Noury, 2002; Hix *et al.*, 2005). This research shows that MEPs vote more along transnational party lines than national lines, that different coalitions form on different issues, and that the EPP and PES do not always vote together. For example Kreppel (2000) has found that the EPP and PES are more

Table 3.5   *EP party voting power under simple and absolute majorities*

	Percentage of seats	Power under simple majority	Power under absolute majority
EPP-ED	36.6	38.7	51.5
PES	27.3	20.4	28.4
ALDE	12.0	16.2	4.6
EUL/NGL	5.7	5.7	3.9
G/EFA	5.6	5.5	3.6
IND/DEM	5.1	5.0	2.9
UEN	3.7	3.8	1.6
Non-attached MEPs	4.0	4.8	3.5
Percentage (No.) of seats to win		50.1 (367)	66.7 (488)

* Power is calculated as the proportion of times when a party group is pivotal (using the Shapley–Shubik index). The IOP 2.0.2 program, developed by Bräuninger and König (2001), has been used to calculate the Shapley–Shubik indices.

likely to coalesce in later rounds of the legislative process and for votes on whole proposals (as opposed to individual amendments), when there is a greater need for the EP to present a united front against the Council and Commission.

Figure 3.4 illustrates voting patterns in the first two years of the 1999–2004 parliament. Each of the symbols represents an individual MEP, and the distance between any two MEPs (parties) reflects how often these MEPs (parties) voted in the same way or differently. In the post-1999 parliament the ELDR group voted as much with the EPP as with the PES, despite the fact that the ELDR and EPP had struck a deal at the beginning of the new Parliament over the EP president – whereby Nicole Fontaine (France, EPP) would serve as EP president for the first half of the parliament and Pat Cox (Ireland, ELDR) for the second half. The gaps between these three groups and the other groups shows that the three main groups often vote together as a bloc against the smaller groups on the left (the Greens and EUL/NGL), the right (UEN) and the anti-Europeans (EDD). Hence the EPP, PES and ELDR can be thought of as the 'governing bloc': they are all strongly pro-European, incorporate almost all the governing parties in the EU, and

Figure 3.4   *Voting patterns in the EP, 1999-2001*

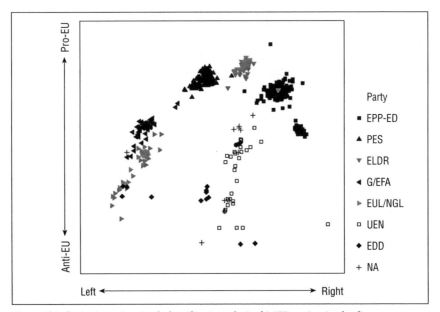

Note: This figure is an 'optimal-classification plot' of MEP voting in the first two years of the 1999–2004 parliament. Each symbol in the figure is an MEP, and the distance between any two MEPs is a reflection of the number of times these MEPs voted in the same way/differently. Hence if two MEPs were on different sides in every vote they will be located at the opposite extremes on both dimensions.

hence dominate the Council and Commission (with which most EP business is concerned).

In sum, an oligopolistic relationship between the two largest parties in the EP is reinforced by common EPP and PES policy positions on many issues (especially interinstitutional questions) and the absolute-majority requirement. However with the growing use of a simple majority in most rounds of the legislative process (see below), and with further consolidation of the size of the PES and EPP compared with the smaller groups, there is more scope for competition between these two groups. When this occurs, for example on issues that split the parties along left–right lines, it gives significant power to the ELDR as the 'king-maker' of a winning-coalition (Hix, 2001).

Legislative Bargaining Between the Council and the EP

Figure 3.5 provides details of the main EU legislative procedures: the consultation, cooperation and co-decision procedures (version II of the co-decision procedure, as amended by the Amsterdam Treaty, unless indicated otherwise). The first stage is the proposal of legislation by the Commission, which has the exclusive right to initiate legislation under most treaty articles (see the Appendix). The Commission submits the proposed legislation (a draft directive or regulation) to both the EP and the Council. In the first reading the EP (in full plenary) and the Council adopt positions on the legislation. The EP adopts an 'opinion', which normally involves a series of amendments to the Commission's text, prepared by the EP committee that has reported on the legislative proposal. The Commission then issues an opinion on the EP's amendments, in the form of a revised proposal, explaining which EP amendments it accepts and which it rejects.

The Council then examines the revised Commission proposal. Under the consultation procedure, the Council can either adopt the proposal as legislation (usually by QMV), amend it (by unanimity), or refuse to make a decision, in which case the legislation remains pending. Under the cooperation procedure the Council simply adopts a common position, confirming or amending the Commission's proposal. Under the co-decision procedure, if the EP adopts a proposal without amendment and the Council does the same, the legislation is passed at this stage. Also, if the Council accepts all the EP amendments (by QMV, except in a couple of exceptional cases, see the Appendix) the legislation is passed. If the Council does not accept all the EP's amendments it adopts a common position (by QMV) which sets out its position on the proposal in the form of a series of amendments to the Commission's revised text.

Under the cooperation and co-decision procedures the legislation

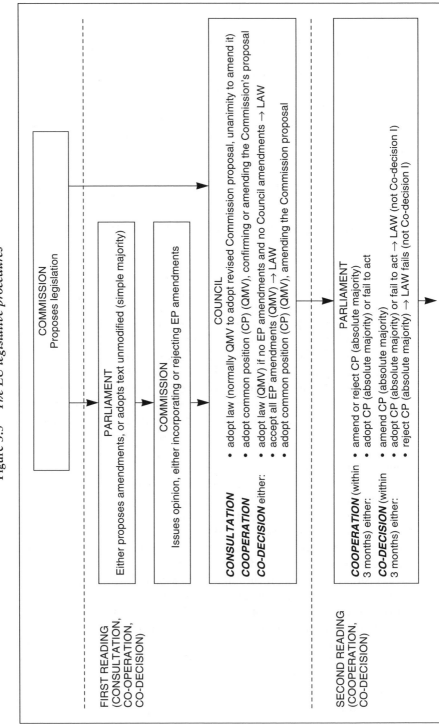

Figure 3.5   *The EU legislative procedures*

COMMISSION

COOPERATION either:
- after EP rejection, can withdraw legislation
- issue an opinion incorporating/rejecting EP amendments

CODECISION
- issue opinion, either incorporating or rejecting any new EP amendments

COUNCIL

COOPERATION (within 3 months) either:
- adopt law (QMV) if no EP amendments → LAW
- adopt EP amendments accepted by Commission (QMV) → LAW
- overturn EP rejection or reject EP amendments accepted by Com. (Unan.) → LAW

CODECISION (within 3 months) either:
- accept EP amendments (QMV for those accepted by Com., unanimity otherwise) → LAW
- fail to accept all EP amendments or fail to act → convene Conciliation Committee (within 6 weeks)

CONCILIATION (CO-DECISION only)

CONCILIATION COMMITTEE
(25 from Council, 25 from EP, 1 from Commission [with no right to vote])

(Within 6 weeks) either:
- adopt joint text (JT) (QMV of Council members/simple majority of EP members)
- fail to adopt JT or fail to act → law fails (law may not fail under Co-decision I – see below)

THIRD READING (CO-DECISION only)

COUNCIL

(Within 6 weeks) either:
- adopt JT (QMV)
- fail to adopt JT (QMV) or fail to act → law fails
  (or, in co-decision I, if no JT agreed then Council can reconfirm CP [QMV])

PARLIAMENT

(Within 6 weeks) either:
- adopt JT (simple majority) → law
- fail to adopt JT (simple majority) or fail to act → law fails
  (or, in co-decision I, if Council reconfirms CP then EP can reject CP [abs. maj.] → law fails)

Note: Unless stated otherwise the rules of co-decision are for the procedure as reformed by the Amsterdam Treaty (in other words co-decision II, in contrast with co-decision I from the Maastricht Treaty).

then goes to a second reading. Under the cooperation procedure the EP either amends, rejects or adopts the common position by an absolute majority. Under the co-decision procedure, if the EP accepts the common position unamended or fails to act the legislation is passed. Conversely if the EP rejects the common position the law falls (under the co-decision I version of the procedure, as established by the Maastricht Treaty, the EP had to declare an 'intention to reject', and the legislation was then passed back to the Council). If the EP decides to amend the common position the procedure continues. The Commission then decides whether to accept or reject the EP amendments before resubmitting the legislation to the Council.

Under the co-operation procedure the Commission could decide to withdraw the legislation if the EP had voted to reject it. In the Council second reading, under the co-operation procedure (acting by QMV) the Council could adopt the law if there were no EP amendments or accept the EP amendments approved by the Commission. Alternatively (acting by unanimity) the Council could overturn an EP rejection or reject the EP amendments accepted by the Commission. Under the co-decision procedure, if the Council accepts all the EP amendments (by QMV for those accepted by the Commission, and by unanimity for those rejected by the Commission), the legislation is passed. If it rejects any of the EP amendments or fails to make a decision a conciliation committee must be convened within six weeks.

Hence under the co-decision procedure, if the EP and the Council do not agree after two readings each a conciliation committee is convened, consisting of 25 members from the Council and 25 from the EP, plus one non-voting representative of the Commission. The conciliation committee has six weeks to adopt a 'joint text' by a qualified-majority of the Council representatives and a simple-majority of the EP representatives. If the conciliation committee fails to agree a joint text the legislation fails (under the co-decision I version of the procedure, if the conciliation committee failed to agree a joint text the procedure nonetheless continued to a third reading).

Finally, following the adoption of a joint text by the conciliation committee the legislation goes to a third reading in the Council and the EP. Within six weeks the Council must approve the joint text by QMV and the EP by a simple majority, otherwise the legislation falls.

This final stage of the procedure, as amended by the Amsterdam Treaty (co-decision II), constitutes a major change from the original version of the procedure in the Maastricht Treaty (co-decision I). Under co-decision I, if the conciliation committee failed to produce a joint text, in the third reading the Council could choose by QMV to reaffirm its common position (as adopted in the first reading). The Council's common position then became law unless the EP voted by an absolute majority to reject it.

Theoretical models of EU bicameralism

The above process sounds complex, but fortunately there are theoretical models that allow us to reduce it to some simple propositions. One of the best-known models was developed by George Tsebelis (Tsebelis, 1994, 1995b, 1996; Garrett, 1956; Tsebelis and Garrett, 1997a, 1997b; Tsebelis and Kreppel, 1998). Figure 3.6 is a simplified version of the Tsebelis model, which starts with a series of assumptions about the spatial orientation of the actors in the legislative process:

- For QMV, the Council is deemed to have seven members, and a winning qualified-majority is five out of seven (an approximation of the 71 per cent threshold).
- There is a single dimension of legislative bargaining – between 'more' or 'less' European integration.
- The actors have ideal policy preferences on this dimension and Euclidean preferences – they want outcomes that are as close as possible to their ideal policy, regardless of whether this is on the 'more' or 'less' integrationist side of their ideal policy, and they are indifferent between proposals that are at equal distance from their ideal position.
- The member states are aligned at different points along this single dimension (at positions 1, 2, 3, 4, 5, 6 and 7).
- The Commission and the EP are more pro-integration than most member states.
- The *status quo* (SQ) (if the legislation is not adopted) is less integrationist than any member state.

These simple assumptions predict rather different legislative outcomes under the different EU procedures (cf. Steunenberg, 1994; Crombez, 1996).

Under the consultation procedure the Council decides whether to accept the Commission's proposal by QMV or reject it by unanimity. Similarly, under the cooperation procedure the Council decides whether to accept EP amendments supported by the Commission by QMV or to reject the amendments by unanimity. For the Council to agree to a policy by unanimity the legislation must be supported by the least integrationist member state (at position 1). But the Commission and the EP (the agenda-setters under the two procedures) simply have to gain the support of member state 3 for the Council to support their proposal by QMV, as member state 3 is 'pivotal' in creating a winning coalition (of states 7, 6, 5, 4 and 3).

However if the Commission or the EP makes a proposal at position 5, the Council will be able to agree to a policy at position U by unanimity (which member state 3 will support as it is closer to its ideal

Figure 3.6   *The Tsebelis model of conditional agenda-setting*

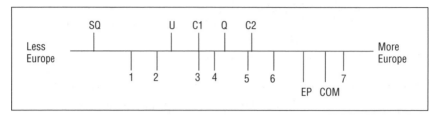

Notes: SQ = *status quo*, EP = European Parliament, COM = European Commission, U = outcome under unanimity in the Council under the consultation or cooperation procedure, Q = outcome under QMV in the Council under the consultation or cooperation procedure, C1 = outcome under the codecision I procedure, C2 = outcome under the codecision II procedure, SQ-1 = 1-U (the distance from SQ to 1 is equal to the distance from 1 to U), U-3 = 3-Q (the distance from U to 3 is equal to the distance from 3 to Q), 3-C2 = C2-EP (the distance from 3 to C2 is equal to the distance from C2 to EP).

point than position 5), and thus reject the Commission/EP's proposal. Hence the Commission or the EP can make a proposal at position Q, which member state 3 will support as it is indifferent between policies U and Q (since the distance from U to 3 is the same as the distance from 3 to Q).

Tsebelis and his coauthors consequently argue that the Commission (under the consultation procedure) and the EP (under the cooperation procedure) can influence policy outcomes by proposing amendments that are easier for the Council to accept than to reject. In other words the Commission and EP are 'conditional agenda-setters', the condition being that the Council must be split and the SQ must be located close enough to the position of the least integrationist member state for the pivotal member state (under QMV) to prefer a Commission/EP proposal to the likely alternative under unanimity.

These insights lead to rather counterintuitive conclusions about version I of the co-decision procedure under the Maastricht Treaty. At face value the EP has more power under co-decision I than under the consultation or cooperation procedures, since it enables the EP to veto the common position agreed in the Council. However the Tsebelis model predicts that under the co-decision procedure agenda-setting power will lie with the Council rather than the EP. In fact the Council has an incentive to engineer a breakdown of the conciliation committee so that it can reaffirm its original common position. In this situation the EP only has an unconditional veto: it must either accept the Council's common position or reject it and accept the *status quo*. As Figure 3.6 shows, however, if the EP is more integrationist than most member states, it will prefer any proposal by the Council to the *status quo*. Because the Council can adopt a common position by QMV, the common position is likely to be located at position 3: the pivotal actor under this decision rule. The Council can make this a 'take it or leave it' proposal to the EP, which the EP will invariably accept. The likely outcome under co-decision I (C1) is thus less integrationist than the likely outcome under cooperation (Q). Consequently Tsebelis argues that by introducing the co-decision procedure the Maastricht Treaty actually reduced rather than strengthened the power of the EP (Tsebelis, 1995b, 1996; Garrett, 1995b; Tsebelis and Garrett 1997a, 1997b).

However this model is not universally accepted. For example in the case of the consultation and cooperation procedures it downplays the role of the Commission, since the EP cannot submit a proposal to the Council without the Commission accepting it first (Steunenberg, 1994; Crombez, 1996; Moser, 1996). Crombez (1997b) also points out that since the Commission is appointed by the member states by unanimity (until the Nice Treaty) it is more realistic to assume that the Commission is close to the least integrationist member state in the Council, and so the Commission is unlikely to propose policies (or accept EP amendments) that would move the policy outcome in a too integrationist direction.

Moreover in the case of the co-decision procedure Crombez (1997a), Moser (1997, 2000) and Scully (1997b, 1997c, 1997d) argue that the EP has more power under co-decision I than the Tsebelis model predicts. In particular, if conciliation breaks down the Council's fall-back position (the common position) will have been adopted on the basis of a proposal from the Commission that contains EP amendments that are acceptable to the Commission. Hence in the worst case the EP will be able to secure the same policy that it could have achieved under the consultation or cooperation procedures.

Nevertheless there is almost unanimous agreement amongst theorists of the legislative procedures that the reform of the co-decision procedure in the Amsterdam Treaty fundamentally changed the power balance between the Council and the EP (Crombez, 2000, 2001; Tsebelis and Garrett, 2000a, 2000b; cf. Steunenberg, 1997a). The key change between co-decision I and co-decision II was that the Council's ability to act unilaterally after a break down of the conciliation committee was removed, thus preventing the Council from making a 'take it or leave it' proposal to the EP. This has effectively made the conciliation committee the final stage of the bicameral game, rather than the third reading in the EP.

This change means that no policy can be adopted without the support of the Council and the EP. For example, with the line-up of actors and the *status quo* in Figure 3.6, the Council and EP will probably agree to split the difference between the Concil's common position (CP, position 3) and the EP's ideal point, and adopt legislation at

C2 (the distance from CP to C2 being equal to the distance from C2 to EP). Hence under the co-decision II procedure the Council and EP have become genuine co-legislators.

The Nice Treaty has also had an impact on the relative power of the Council and the EP (Baldwin *et al.*, 2001b; Tsebelis and Yataganas, 2002). The Nice Treaty did not change the operation of the legislative procedures, but by making it more difficult to adopt legislation in the Council (under the reformed weighting of votes) the treaty has reduced the ability of the EP to propose amendments that are acceptable to the Council. Hence there has been a moderate increase in the veto power of the Council relative to that of the EP.

However the proposed constitution would establish the co-decision procedure as the 'normal legislative procedure' of the EU and extend the procedure to almost all areas of EU law, so further increase the legislative powers of the EP *vis-à-vis* the Council and the Commission.

Empirical evidence of EP power

The real test of these theoretical models is empirical. After the introduction of the cooperation procedure the EP had a significant influence on a number of important pieces of legislation (cf. Earnshaw and Judge, 1997). For example in the area of health and safety at work the Council accepted several significant EP amendments to the machine directive (89/392/EEC) and the display screen equipment directive (90/270/EEC) that would probably not have been accepted by the Council under the consultation procedure (Tsebelis, 1995a). Also, in the area of environmental policy the EP secured significant amendments to the regulation establishing the European Environment Agency (1210/90/EEC), the directive on genetically modified micro-organisms (90/219/EEC), the directive on the deliberate release of genetically-modified organisms (90/220/EEC) and the directive on car emissions (91/441/EEC) (Judge *et al.*, 1994; Hubschmid and Moser, 1997; Tsebelis and Kalandrakis, 1999, cf. König and Pöter, 2001). On all these issues, several member states were adamantly opposed to the EP proposals, which were generally aimed at strengthening EU regulation of national regimes. Nevertheless, as the Tsebelis model predicts, on these policy issues there was a qualified-majority in the Council who preferred to accept the EP proposals than to see no EU legislation passed. Also, under the cooperation procedure the EP tried to reject several directives, but these were overturned in the second reading by the Council.

The EP has also had an impact under the co-decision procedure (cf. Garman and Hilditch, 1998). In July 1994 the EP exercised its third-reading veto for the first time. On the draft directive on open network provision in voice telephony (ONP), the Council and the EP were unable to agree a joint text in the conciliation committee. The Council subsequently reaffirmed its common position, which was then rejected by an absolute majority in the EP. In March 1995 the EP exercised a third-reading veto on the draft directive on biotechnology inventions (Rittberger, 2000). However this time the situation was different as in the conciliation committee the EP leadership had agreed to a joint text with the Council. But following a lobbying campaign by the environmental movement, the rank-and-file MEPs (particularly in the PES group) rejected the EP leadership's recommendation and voted against the joint text in the third reading.

On other occasions the EP leadership would have liked to threaten rejection of a Council common position, but the EP leadership was not sure that it could guarantee a majority vote in the third reading (Jacobs, 1997). Indeed the veto of the ONP directive was a special case as the vote was held in the first session of the new EP following the June 1994 EP elections when there was a very high attendance of MEPs (Earnshaw and Judge, 1995). Miller (1995) estimates that of the first 26 joint texts agreed in conciliation committees, 12 (46 per cent) were effectively the same as the Council's common position, six (23 per cent) were closer to the EP's second reading position, and eight (31 per cent) were genuine joint texts. These figures seem to confirm Tsebelis's scepticism.

When looking at individual EP amendments, however, the EP has been more successful under the co-decision procedure than under the cooperation procedure. According to the EP's figures, in the 400 cooperation procedures completed between 1987 and 1997 and the 82 co-decision procedures completed between 1993 and 1997, approximately the same proportion of EP amendments (just over 40 per cent) were accepted by the Council in the first reading under both procedures. However the EP was much more successful in the second reading under the co-decision procedure than under the cooperation procedure (47 per cent compared with 21 per cent), and was even able to get several amendments (12 per cent) accepted in the third reading (European Parliament, 1997; Maurer, 1999).

In Tsebelis's own research on EP amendments under the cooperation and co-decision I procedures – in which a team of researchers looked at the result of over 5000 amendments by the EP on 230 pieces of legislation – he found that the key factor in determining the Council's acceptance of EP amendments was the behaviour of the Commission (Tsebelis *et al.*, 2001). Under the cooperation procedure, once the Commission had rejected an amendment by the EP the probability that it would also be rejected by the Council was 88 per cent, while if the Commission accepted an amendment the probability that it would be accepted by the Council (and become law) was 83 per cent. Meanwhile under the co-decision I procedure, 67 per cent of EP amendments rejected by the Commission were then rejected by the Council, and 73 per cent of EP amendments accepted by the Commission were accepted by the Council.

In a related study Amie Kreppel (1999, 2002b) found that the EP is more successful when proposing amendments that clarify a position taken by the Council or Commission than when proposing substantive policy changes. Also the EP is more likely to get amendments passed when it is united – in other words, when the two main EP parties vote together. In addition the EP is more able to get amendments passed in the first reading than the second reading. Kreppel concludes that this is because the EP tends to repropose amendments in the second reading that were rejected in the first reading.

Part of the explanation of the EP's success under the co-decision procedure is how it decided to work under the new decision-making rules (Shackleton, 2000; Hix, 2002a). In a conscious effort to undermine the ability of the Council to reaffirm its common position in the third reading the EP added a new rule to its rules of procedure (Rule 78). This rule stated that following the breakdown of the conciliation committee the EP would ask the Commission to withdraw the legislation, and if the Commission refused and the Council decided to reaffirm its common position, the EP leadership would automatically propose a motion to reject the Council's text at the next EP plenary session. This rule suggests that faced with a 'take it or leave it' proposal from the Council the EP leadership preferred to veto the legislation as a matter of principle, even if the Council's proposal was closer to the EP's policy position than the *status quo*. This was a credible threat as the EP leadership could argue to its members that the EP was involved in a long-term institutional game (to secure a further reform of the co-decision procedure) rather than a short-term policy bargain. The subsequent veto of a reaffirmed common position, in the case of the ONP directive, gave extra force to this threat. After the adoption of Rule 78 the Council did not force the EP to vote on a single reaffirmed common position. Hence the addition of Rule 78 implies that from the EP's point of view the co-decision procedure, as set out in the Maastricht Treaty, stopped with the conciliation committee.

The above theoretical arguments and the empirical evidence help explain why in the Amsterdam Treaty negotiations the EP proposed that the cooperation procedure be replaced by a reformed codecision procedure, and why the member states accepted this proposal (European Parliament, 1995a). From the point of view of the EP, it would be more able to secure amendments under the co-decision procedure than under the cooperation procedure, and the removal of the third reading of the co-decision procedure would strengthen the EP's power to bargain with the Council. From the member states' point of view there would be little risk in making these changes. As a result of the EP's Rule 78 the *de facto* operation of the old co-decision procedure was without the third reading. In this situation, the member states were indifferent between the old co-decision procedure and the proposal to delete the third reading, and so accepted the EP's proposal. Hence a clever strategic move by the EP in the operation of co-decision I led directly to the reform of the procedure, and made the EP and Council equal players in the EU legislative system.

Conclusion: Complex but Familiar Politics

The EU has developed a sophisticated and effective legislative system. The Council and the EP are able to cope with the highly technical task of regulating a single market of over 450 million consumers, as well as appease the various national, sectoral and societal interests that are threatened by the process of harmonizing the member states' markets. To meet these challenges the Council and the EP have evolved into highly organized and decentralized legislative chambers, and have tended to rule through consensus instead of by competition and division.

But this is functionalist logic: legislative complexity and a plurality of interests produces legislative specialization and consensus. Contemporary theories of legislative behaviour see the internal organization of the Council and the EP and the processes of bargaining and coalition formation as products of the rational self-interests of the EU legislators: the governments in the Council, and the MEPs and party groups in the EP. The governments set up the Council presidency and the MEPs established the EP leadership structures to promote agenda-setting. Similarly sectoral councils and EP committees enable EU legislators with similar interests and/or informational requirements to monopolize the legislative agenda in their area, and the party groups enable MEPs and national delegations with similar preferences to reduce the transaction costs of coalition formation and information gathering.

Likewise, consensus and oversized majorities in coalition formation in the Council and EP are less a response to diverse social interests than a consequence of the institutional rules and policy preferences of the actors. The informal PES–EPP grand coalition in the EP is fostered by the absolute-majority requirement in the second reading of the main legislative procedure and the similar policy preferences of the two parties on many issues in EU politics. Similarly, in the Council the requirement of unanimity and a fear of being isolated ensures consensus. Nevertheless certain member states, such as Germany and the UK, have tended to be more isolated than others, and between 1999 and 2002 the isolation of the centre-left German government was exacerbated by the rightward shift in the make-up of the Council.

Finally, the underlying structure of contestation and conflict, driven by institutional interests and policy preferences, is revealed in the bicameral interactions between the Council and the EP. Ever since the EP has been directly elected it has tried to maximize its influence in the legislative process: for example by threatening to veto any attempt by the Council to act unilaterally under the Maastricht version of the co-decision procedure. The EP has not always won, but compared with many national parliaments in Europe it has been quite successful in forcing the Council and the Commission to accept amendments to EU legislation and a gradual increase in the EP's powers.

As a result, in a relatively short space of time legislative politics in the EU has evolved into something that would be familiar to observers of two-chamber parliaments in other democratic political systems. As with all legislators, the EU governments and MEPs seek legislation that satisfies their voters and supporting groups, furthers their personal careers or promotes their ideological goals, and to achieve these goals they organize their institutions and compete/coalesce with each other in similar ways to those in other legislative systems.

Chapter 4

Judicial Politics

Political Theories of Constitutions and Courts
The EU Legal System and the European Court of Justice
Constitutionalization of the European Union
Penetration of EU Law into National Legal Systems
Explanations of EU Judicial Politics
Conclusion: Unknown Destination or Emerging Equilibrium?

No treaty, constitution, piece of legislation, or executive decision can account for all possible developments – they are always incomplete contracts. As a result, the actors responsible for enforcing these contracts in democratic polities – the courts – can often use their discretion and thereby shape policy outcomes beyond the intention of the legislators. This battle between the intentions of legislators and the discretion of courts is what political scientists call 'judicial politics'. Judicial politics is particularly interesting in the EU, where the flexible constitution of the EU and the nature of the EU's legal instruments allow the European Court of Justice (ECJ) and national courts a high degree of discretion. To help explain how judicial politics works in the EU we shall first look at some general theories of the role and power of courts.

Political Theories of Constitutions and Courts

A common argument in political science is that constitutions are created to resolve collective action problems (Buchanan and Tullock, 1962; Taylor, 1976; Ostrom, 1990). A simple way of illustrating why collective action is often problematic is the so-called prisoners' dilemma game (Luce and Raiffa, 1957; Hardin, 1971). A version of this game using the example of the EU is shown in Figure 4.1 (cf. Ordeshook, 1992, p. 166).

In this hypothetical example two states agree to establish a common market by removing their joint barriers to the free movement of goods and services – as in the Treaty of Rome. However in the absence of a constitution, the member states are free to decide whether or not to implement this agreement, and when making this decision each state calculates the costs and benefits of their available options. Suppose the

111

Figure 4.1   *A collective action problem in the establishment of a common market*

		Member State B	
		Don't implement common market (defect)	Implement common market (cooperate)
Member State A	**Don't implement common market (defect)**	**Cell I** A = €0 B = €0	**Cell II** A = + €7 B = – €3m
	Implement common market (co-operate)	**Cell III** A = – €3m B = + €7m	**Cell IV** A = + €4m B = + €4m

Notes: Cost of implementing a common market for each member state is €10 million. The benefit of one member state opening its markets is €7 million to all states. The benefit of two member states opening their markets is €14 million to all states.

cost to each state of implementing the common market will be €10 million; for example this could be administrative costs plus job losses in some domestic industries. Now suppose that if one state opens its markets each state will benefit by €7 million from the extra trade, economies of scale and market efficiencies. Hence if both states open up their markets, each will benefit by €4 million: $(7 \times 2) - 10$. This would be the best (optimal) collective solution as it would produce the greatest total benefit: €8 million (cell IV).

However this outcome is unlikely. Instead, each state is likely to decide that its best strategy is to not implement the agreement. For example, if state A chooses not to implement the agreement, either state B will implement the deal, in which case state A will gain €7 million (cell II), or state B will not implement the deal, in which case state A will lose nothing (cell I). Conversely, if state A implements the agreement, state B can simply choose not to implement it, gaining €7 million while member state A loses €3 million. To minimize the risk of losing and to prevent the other state from free riding, the only option for state A is not to implement the agreement. Consequently if each state pursues its best strategy, neither state will implement the common market. But this is a suboptimal outcome as the EU as a whole will miss out on the collective benefits of cooperation (cell IV). The prisoners' dilemma hence illustrates that in a constitution-free world, it may be in the collective interest to cooperate, but it is often in individuals' interests to defect.

This collective action problem can be overcome if the parties set up a rule of law. By establishing that agreements are binding on participants, and by creating mechanisms (courts) for punishing defection, cooperation can be enforced. In the case of the EU, in the presence of a rule of law (a quasi-constitution) a member state that does not implement the common market can be challenged before the ECJ. In this situation all states have an incentive to cooperate, which produces the optimal outcome.

Nevertheless, this solution requires that the enforcers of law (the courts) are independent from the legislative majority. If a legislative majority is able to determine whether or not there has been a breach of law, or can ignore a court's decision, the incentive for parties to abide by the law (to cooperate) is reduced (Moe, 1990). Hence for the rule of law to be credible it must be supported by a separation of powers between the judiciary and the legislative majority (Dicey, 1939 [1885]). As Madison, Hamilton and Jay (1987 [1788], pp. 438–9) extol:

> If it be said that the legislative body are themselves the constitutional judges of their own powers . . . the Constitution could . . . enable the representatives of the people to substitute their will to that of their constituents. It is far more rational to suppose that the courts were designed to be an intermediate body between the people and the legislature in order . . . to keep the latter within the limits assigned to their authority.

The assumption here is that the separation of powers works because judges are neutral political actors: they exercise judgement instead of will (ibid., p. 440). Put another way, the rule of law requires judges to follow the following formula: 'Rules × Facts = Decisions' (Frank, 1973).

But judges do have a will, and constitutions and laws are sufficiently flexible to enable them to exercise this will. As the judicial review of legislative acts has evolved, and as societies have become more litigious, judges have become increasingly involved in making choices between different ideological positions. Consequently judicial preferences, and the court judgements that result from these preferences, are crucial determinants of the final political outcome of the policy process (see for example Cohen, 1992). This realization has spawned a growing literature on the comparative study of judicial politics and judicial policy-making, of which research on the ECJ is part (for example Shapiro, 1981; Stone, 1992; Shapiro and Stone, 1994; Volcansek, 1993b; Shapiro and Stone Sweet, 2001).

To explain judicial policy-making, political scientists have developed models of the strategic interaction between legislators and courts (Miller and Hammond, 1989; McCubbins *et al.*, 1990; Eskridge, 1991; Gely and Spillar, 1992; Steunenberg, 1997b; Vanberg, 1998, 2001; Shipan, 2000; van Hees and Steunenberg, 2000; Rogers, 2001). One such model, based on the US system of government, is illustrated in Figure 4.2 (cf. Weingast, 1996, pp. 172–4). The model assumes that the legislature, the executive and the court are unitary actors in a uni-dimensional political space, with symmetrical and single-peaked preferences, and ideal policy positions at points *L*, *E* and *C* respectively (see Chapters 2 and 3 for explanations of spatial analysis). Legislation *X* is an agreement between the legislature and the executive. If the court is free to interpret the legislation when cases are brought before it, it will try to move the political outcome towards *C*. When the opportunity arises the court moves the policy outcome to point *Y*. This is as close to the ideal point of the executive as position *X*, so the executive is indifferent between the original piece of legislation and the new court interpretation. However if it is relatively costless for the executive to initiate new legislation it will propose legislation that amends the court's ruling, at position *E*. The legislature will then agree to this new legislation, as *E* is closer to *L* than *Y*. Hence because of the court's discretion and the executive's collusion with the court, the final policy outcome is *E* rather than *X*.

Figure 4.2   *Court discretion in a separation-of-powers system*

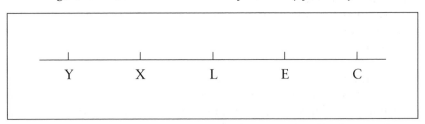

Note: L = position of the legislature, E = position of the executive, C = position of the court, X = position of a policy agreement between L and E, X-E = E-Y (i.e. the executive is 'indifferent' between X and Y).

An implication of this type of analysis is that a court's discretion varies inversely with the probability that new legislation can be introduced to repeal its decisions (Ferejohn and Weingast, 1992; Cooter and Ginsburg, 1997; Vanberg, 1998), and with the amount of information the legislators have about the court's preferences and the probability that it will receive cases that allow it to act on these preferences (Rogers, 2001; Rogers and Vanberg, 2002). As the ease of adopting new legislation and acquiring information about the likely action of the court goes up, the discretion of the court goes down. As a consequence the court has most potential power when there is little information about its likely actions, as at the birth of the European Community. Courts also have more freedom when there are many 'veto-players' who can block changes to its interpretations, such as multiple political parties, multiple legislative chambers or a separation of authority between the executive and the legislature (Tsebelis, 1995c, 2000, 2002). Hence in separation-of-powers systems (such as the US and the EU), and where legislation must be adopted by oversized and multiple legislative majorities (as in Germany and the EU), a court can reasonably assume that at least one actor will prefer the court's interpretation to the original legislative intention, and hence block a repeal of the court's decision.

Conversely, the discretion of courts is restricted under constitutional arrangements where there is a fusion of judicial and legislative powers. For example, in the UK there is no codified constitution and the doctrine of parliamentary sovereignty asserts that no legislative majority can introduce rules or laws that bind a future majority – as a result the parliament is free to overturn court rulings. Similarly in France the Constitutional Council is composed of ex-politicians who are highly partisan; consequently it is more like a third chamber of parliament than an independent 'supreme court' (Stone, 1993, p. 30). Nevertheless even in these systems the ability of judges to make policy has developed as the practice of judicial review has restrained the legislative authorities (Stone, 1992; Drewry, 1993; Steunenberg, 1997b; Vanberg, 2001; Stone Sweet, 2002).

In summary, at the heart of judicial politics there is a paradox. On the one hand constitutions, backed by the rule of law and independent courts, are necessary for free citizens to enforce collective agreements. On the other hand constitutions enable judges to make law rather than simply apply law. Legislative majorities could design constitutions to limit the power of judges or introduce new legislation to repeal court decisions, but this would undermine the ability of the legal system to preserve property rights and enforce contracts fairly.

The EU Legal System and the European Court of Justice

'EU law' (which here will be use as shorthand for the legal acts of the EC and EU) constitutes a separate legal system that is distinct from but closely integrated with international law and the legal systems of the EU member states, and which derives from three main sources (cf. Hartley, 2003).

First, there are the 'primary' acts between the governments of the EU member states. These include the Treaty of Paris, the Treaty of Rome, the Merger Treaty (establishing a single set of institutions), the Single

European Act, the Treaty on European Union (the Maastricht Treaty), the treaties reforming the European Union Treaty (the Amsterdam and Nice Treaties), the four Accession Treaties, the two Budgetary Treaties and the various other Conventions reforming the basic institutional structure of the EU.

Second, there are the 'secondary' legislative and executive acts of the Council, the European Parliament and the Commission, which derive from the articles in the treaties. Article 249 of the EU Treaty sets out five kinds of secondary act:

- *Regulations*, which have general application and are binding on both the EU and the member states.
- *Directives*, which are addressed to any number of member states, are binding in terms of the result to be achieved and must be transposed into law by the national authorities.
- *Decisions*, which are addressed to member states or private citizens (or legal entities such as firms) and are binding in their entirety.
- *Recommendations*, which can be addressed to any member state or citizen but which are not binding.
- *Opinions*, which have the same force as recommendations.

However these descriptions are somewhat misleading, particularly the distinction between regulations and directives. Directives are often so detailed that they leave little room for manoeuvre in the transposition of the legislation by the member states. Also, through a series of judgements the ECJ has made directives much more akin to regulations in terms of their ability to confer rights directly on private citizens.

Added to these two formal, written sources of EU law are the 'general principles of law'. As in all legal systems, primary and secondary sources of law are unable to resolve all legal issues. Article 220 of the EU Treaty instructs the ECJ to ensure that 'the law is observed', which the ECJ has interpreted to mean that when applying the primary and secondary acts it can apply general legal principles derived from the EU's basic principles (as expressed in other articles in the treaty, such as the preamble) and from the constitutions of the member states. There are four main types of principle:

- *Principles of administrative and legislative legality*, which are drawn from various member states' legal traditions, such as 'legal certainty' (laws cannot be applied retroactively, and litigants can have legitimate expectations about EU actions), 'proportionality' (the means to achieve an end should be appropriate) and 'procedural fairness' (such as the right to a hearing and the right of legal professional privilege).
- *Economic freedoms*, which are drawn from the EU Treaty and include the 'four freedoms' (freedom of movement of goods, ser-

vices, capital and persons), the freedom to trade, and the freedom of competition.

- *Fundamental human rights*, which are not defined in the EU Treaty but are set out in most member states' constitutions, in the European Convention on Human Rights (of the Council of Europe) and in the Charter of Fundamental Rights of the European Union.
- *Political rights*, which have been introduced in declarations by the member states and are referred to in the EU Treaties, such as 'transparency' (access to information) and subsidiarity (the EU can only act in policy areas not included in the Treaties if the policy aims cannot be achieved adequately at the national level).

Composition and operation of the European Court of Justice

To apply these sources of law the member states established the European Court of Justice in Luxembourg (not to be confused with the European Court of Human Rights in Strasbourg, which is the Court of the Council of Europe). The ECJ has one judge per member state, and eight advocates-general. The number of advocates-general can be increased by a unanimous decision by the Council, acting on a request by the ECJ. Article 223 of the treaty lays down how they should be appointed:

> The Judges and Advocates-General shall be chosen from persons whose independence is beyond doubt and who possess the qualifications required for appointment to the highest judicial offices in their respective countries . . . they shall be appointed by common accord of the governments of the Member States for a term of six years. Every three years there shall be a partial replacement of the Judges and Advocates-General . . . The Judges shall elect the President of the Court of Justice from among their number for a term of three years. He [*sic*] may be re-elected.

The staggered terms of office of the judges ensures continuity. The other elements of the article are somewhat misleading. In practice, 'by common accord of the member states' means that each member state proposes a judge, whose nomination is then ratified by the other member states. Also, by convention the large member states each appoint one advocate-general, with the remaining places rotating between the smaller member states. In addition the independence and qualifications of the judges are sometimes compromised. There is little evidence of explicitly political appointments to the ECJ, unlike the US Supreme Court. But, several member states have tended to appoint 'academic lawyers' instead of recruiting judges from the senior ranks of the judiciary.

When a case comes before the ECJ the court follows a carefully defined procedure:

- An advocate-general and a judge-rapporteur are appointed to gather information relating to the case and to hold the necessary preparatory oral and written enquiries.
- A public hearing is then held at which the lawyers of the parties involved present their views orally, and at which the judges and advocates-general question the lawyers.
- The advocate-general appointed to the case submits a report to the judge-rapporteur, outlining how the case fits with existing EU law and suggesting a judgement.
- On the basis of the advocate-general's report, the judge-rapporteur presents a draft decision to the court.
- Each judge expresses an opinion on the decision, and the final decision is then taken by a simple majority vote.

There is a specific order of voting, whereby the most junior judge (in terms of their order of precedence) votes first and the most senior last. Unlike in the US Supreme Court, there are no provisions for dissenting opinions to be recorded. In fact the judges on the ECJ swear an oath to preserve the secrecy of the vote.

The workload of the ECJ has increased dramatically. The number of cases brought before it rose from 79 in 1970, to 279 in 1980, 384 in 1990 and 543 in 1999. On 1 January 2000, 896 cases were pending. To cope with this increase the Court of First Instance (CFI) was created in 1989, but the CFI soon became as backlogged as the ECJ – for example on 1 January 2000, 732 cases were pending before the CFI.

The ECJ also established procedures to allow cases to be handled in a chamber of three or five judges instead of the full plenary. The Treaty of Nice extended this practice by formally reversing the precedence between the chamber system and the full court, whereby the ECJ now sits in chamber as the general rule, and the 'Grand Chamber' of eleven judges or the fully plenary of the court only meet on special occasions (Johnston, 2001, pp. 511–12). The Nice Treaty also introduced provisions for the establishment of specialized 'judicial panels' (by unanimity in the Council, following a proposal by the Commission of the ECJ, and after consultation with the EP). The reason for this new practice was the need far a new procedure to deal with EU staff-related cases. It is likely that these panels will also be used in many highly technical areas of EU law, such as intellectual property rights (ibid., pp. 513–14).

Another innovation by the ECJ was the US practice of 'docket control', whereby it could refuse to hear a case that it thought should be resolved by a national court. This was used on an informal basis. The Treaty of Nice introduced a new procedure, whereby the CFI had the right to reject referrals from national courts if they did not fall under the jurisdiction of Article 234. However the treaty left the wording of Article 234 (the preliminary reference procedure) untouched, thereby rejecting calls by several member states and some members of the ECJ to allow only the domestic courts of last instance to refer cases to the ECJ (see Court of Justice, 1999; Turner and Muñoz, 2000).

Justice via the ECJ is a long and drawn-out process, the average length of proceedings being 21 months for direct actions and 18 months for references for preliminary rulings. Various suggestions have been made for speeding up this process, such as creating 'circuit courts' modelled on the US federal legal system (cf. Weiler, 1993). However further reform would require a substantial overhaul of the EU court system and the national court referrals procedure, which to date the member state governments have refused to contemplate (cf. Craig, 2001).

Jurisdiction of the European Court of Justice

As defined in the EU Treaty, the ECJ has jurisdiction in three main areas (cf. Weatherill and Beaumont, 2004). First, it hears actions brought against member states for failure to comply with their obligations under the EU treaties and EU legislation. These actions, known as 'infringement proceedings', can either be brought by the Commission under Article 226, by another member state under Article 227, or in the area of state aid by either the Commission or a member state under Article 88. Article 228 also asserts that the member state concerned 'shall be required to take the necessary measures to comply with the judgement of the ECJ'. The ability of the ECJ to enforce rulings against the member states is limited. Until the Maastricht Treaty the Commission was only able to introduce new infringement proceedings against a state in an effort to embarrass it into submission. However, the Maastricht Treaty enabled the ECJ to impose financial sanctions on a member state if the Commission brought an additional action for failing to comply with the ECJ's original infringement judgement.

Second, like many national constitutional courts the ECJ has the power of judicial review of EU legislative and executive acts. Under Article 230 it can review the legality of acts (other than recommendations and opinions) adopted by the Council, the EP, the Commission and the European Central Bank, and EP acts intended to produce legal effects on third parties. Under this article any member state, the Council and the Commission can bring an action to the ECJ either on the ground of lack of competence, or because of an infringement of the treaty or a procedural requirement. In contrast the EP, the Court of Auditors and the European Central Bank can only bring actions to protect their own prerogatives. Finally, private citizens can bring actions against a decision by EU institutions that is of direct concern to them. A further aspect of the ECJ's power of judicial review is hearing actions against EU institutions for failing to act when they have been called upon to do so by the EU Treaty or a piece of secondary legislation (such as the delegation of powers to the Commission) under Article 232. These actions can be brought by any member state or EU institution.

Third, under Article 234 the ECJ has jurisdiction to give preliminary rulings on references by national courts. Under this procedure all national courts can ask the ECJ to issue a ruling on cases that relate to any aspect of EU law. The national courts then have some discretion in determining how they should use the ECJ ruling when making their judgement on the case in question. At face value this suggests that it is the national courts that give the final ruling on many cases of EU law, which was probably the intention of the drafters of the Treaty of Rome. In practice, however, the jurisdiction of the ECJ under this article has been far more significant for the development of EU law and the constitutionalization of the EU system than the ECJ's jurisdiction in any other area. The ECJ often interprets EU law in a manner that allows little discretion to be exercised by national courts when applying ECJ interpretations. Also, Article 234 rulings constitute the majority of all ECJ judgements. On the one hand this reveals a high penetration of EU law into the national legal systems (see below). On the other hand, by enabling national courts to enforce ECJ judgements, the preliminary references procedure has the effect of making national courts the lower tier of an integrated EU court system, and the ECJ the quasi-supreme court at its pinnacle.

The ECJ has jurisdiction over a number of other miscellaneous areas for which a small number of cases are heard each year. These include actions for damages against the EU institutions by a member state or a private individual (under Article 235), and employment disputes between the EU and the staff of the various EU institutions (under Article 236). Staff disputes account for about 8 per cent of all cases heard by the ECJ.

In sum, the Treaty of Rome created a new legal system and a powerful supranational court to enforce this system. Nevertheless when signing the treaty the founding fathers probably did not realize the potential long-term implication of their action: the gradual constitutionalization of the EU through the operation of the legal system and the judgements of the ECJ.

Constitutionalization of the European Union

In a now renowned statement, in a judgement in 1986 the ECJ described the founding treaties as a 'constitutional charter' (case 294/83, *Parti Ecologiste 'Les Verts'* v. *European Parliament* [1986], ECR 1339). This was the first time the court had used the term 'constitution' to describe the treaties, although academic lawyers had been pointing to the constitutional status of the treaties for some time (Green, 1969). Nevertheless the EU constitution lies less in the founding treaties than in the gradual constitutionalization of the EU legal system (Stein, 1981; Hartley, 1986; Mancini, 1989; Weiler, 1991, 1997a; Shapiro, 1992). The two central principles of this constitution are the direct effect and the supremacy of EU law, which are classic doctrines in federal legal systems.

Direct effect: EU law as the law of the land for national citizens

The direct effect of EU law means that individual citizens have rights under EU law that must be upheld by national courts. This makes EU law 'the law of the land' in the member states (Weiler, 1991, p. 2413). The ECJ first asserted the direct effect of EU law in a landmark judgement in 1963 (case 26/62, *Van Gend en Loos* v. *Nederlandse Administratie der Belastingen* [1963], ECR 1). In this case a private firm sought to invoke EC law against the Dutch customs authority in a Dutch court, and the Dutch court consulted the ECJ for a preliminary ruling on whether EC law applied. Four of the then six member states argued to the court that the specific article in the EC Treaty to which the case referred (Article 25) did not have direct effect. Despite the opposition of the majority of the signatories of the treaty the ECJ ruled that individuals did have the right to invoke EC law because 'the Community constitutes a new legal order . . . the subjects of which comprise not only member states but also their nationals'. This was accepted by the Dutch court. This ruling meant that direct effect applied to primary treaty articles, and in subsequent judgements the ECJ expanded the doctrine to all categories of legal acts of the EU.

However direct effect works differently for regulations and directives. Regulations have a vertical and a horizontal direct effect, meaning that citizens can defend their rights against both the state (vertical) and other individuals or legal entities (horizontal). But, in the case of directives the ECJ has taken the view (against the opinion of several advocates-general and academic commentators) that these only have a vertical direct effect because they must be transposed into national law by the member states (case 152/84, *Marshall I* [1986], ECR 723; case C-91/92, *Faccini Dori* [1994] ECR I-3325).

Nevertheless, to compensate for the lack of a horizontal direct effect of directives the ECJ has developed the doctrine of 'states' liability'. This implies that the state is liable for all infringements of EU directives. For example when an Italian firm became insolvent and failed to make redundancy payments to its employees, the ECJ ruled that the Italian state should foot the bill because it had not properly transposed Directive 80/987, which required the establishment of guarantee funds for redundancy compensation (cases C-6,9/90, *Francovich I* [1991], ECR 1-5357).

The central implication of direct effect is that EU law is more like domestic law than international law. The subjects of international law are states: if a state fails to abide by its obligations under an international convention, individuals cannot invoke the convention in their national courts unless the convention has been incorporated into domestic law. In contrast to international law, the subjects of domestic law and EU law are private citizens who can invoke their rights in domestic courts.

The establishment of the doctrine of direct effect led to a dramatic increase in the number of cases brought by individuals to national courts to defend their rights under EU law. The effect, as Weiler (1991, p. 2414) argues, was that 'individuals . . . became the "guardians" of the legal integrity of Community law within Europe similar to the way that individuals in the United States have been the principal actors in ensuring the vindication of the Bill of Rights and other federal law'.

Supremacy: EU law as the higher law of the land

Unlike the US constitution, the Treaty of Rome did not contain a 'supremacy clause' stating that in the event of a conflict between national and EC law, EC law would be supreme). However, shortly after the establishment of direct effect the ECJ asserted the supremacy of EC law, and like direct effect this doctrine was confirmed and reinforced in subsequent rulings.

The landmark judgement on this doctrine was in the case of *Costa* v. *ENEL* in 1964 (case 6/64 [1964], ECR 585). An Italian court asked the ECJ to give a preliminary ruling on a case in which there was a clear contradiction between Italian and EC law. The ECJ duly argued that:

> By creating a Community of unlimited duration, having its own institutions, its own personality, [and] its own legal capacity . . . the member states have limited their sovereign rights, albeit within limited fields, and have thus created a body of law which binds both their nationals and themselves. The integration into the laws of each member state of provisions which derive from the Community . . . make it impossible for the states, as a corollary, to accord precedence

to a unilateral and subsequent measure over a legal system accepted by them on a basis of reciprocity.

In other words the ECJ held that the doctrine of supremacy was implicit in the transfer of competences to the EC level and the direct effect of EC law.

Formally speaking, EU law takes superiority over national law only in those areas in which EU law applies. But as the competences of the EU have expanded into almost all areas of public policy, the application of supremacy no longer applies to the 'limited fields' to which the ECJ referred in 1964. Also, through successive judgements the ECJ has established that supremacy applies to all EU norms, be it an article in the treaties, a secondary act by the EU institutions (no matter how minor, such as administrative regulations of the Commission) or even a 'general principle of EU law', as defined by the ECJ.

As a result the supremacy doctrine has further distanced the EU legal system from international law. Direct effect is insufficient by itself to establish the EU legal system as a system of domestic law. When international conventions are incorporated into domestic law, individuals can invoke them in domestic courts. But if a domestic legislature subsequently adopts a national law that contravenes the international convention, the provisions of the international law no longer apply. With the supremacy of EU law, in contrast, national legislative majorities are permanently bound by the provisions of EU law. Weiler (1991, p. 2415) therefore concludes that 'parallels of this kind of constitutional order ... may be found only in the internal constitutional order of federal states'. By establishing the dual doctrines of direct effect and supremacy of EU law the ECJ has transformed the EU from an international organization to a quasifederal polity.

Integration through law, and economic constitutionalism

The application of these basic doctrines has enabled the ECJ to play a central role in the economic and political integration of the EU (cf. Weatherill and Beaumont, 2004). For example, in the area of economic freedoms Article 28 states simply that 'quantitative restrictions on imports and all measures having equivalent effect shall be prohibited between the member states'. While this article seems pretty innocuous, through a series of judgements the ECJ has transformed the EU's economic system on the basis of the article (Alter and Meunier-Aitsahalia, 1994).

In 1974, in the *Dassonville* decision (case 8/74 [1974], ECR 837), the ECJ declared illegal any national rule that was 'capable of hindering, actually or potentially, directly or indirectly, intra-Community trade'. Such hindrances included not only quotas and other restrictions on imports, but also internal rules that affected the competitive position of imported goods. The implication of this interpretation became clear with the *Cassis de Dijon* judgment in 1979 (case 120/78 [1979], ECR 837). In this decision the ECJ ruled that a German law specifying that a 'liquor' must have an alcohol content of at least 25 per cent could not prevent the marketing of the French drink *Cassis de Dijon* in Germany as a liquor, despite it having an alcohol content of less than 20 per cent. This is known as the principle of 'mutual recognition': that is, any product that can be legally sold in one member state can be legally sold anywhere in the EU. Mutual recognition subsequently became one of the basic principles in the establishment of the single market (see Chapter 8).

This interpretation of Article 30 is inherently deregulatory. It has obliged member states to delete numerous social and economic rules that in many cases were established as expressions of particular social, cultural and ideological preferences. The effect has been a specific type of 'economic constitution', whereby competition between different national regulatory regimes, has the potential of facilitating a 'race to the bottom' (cf. Joerges, 1994; Chalmers, 1995; Streit and Mussler, 1995; Ehlermann and Hancher, 1995; Maduro, 1997) (see Chapter 8).

State-like properties: external sovereignty and internal coercion

As discussed in Chapter 1, the EU is not a state. In particular it does not have external sovereignty in the international legal system in respect of acting independently and above the interests of the member states. Neither does it have a legitimate internal monopoly on the use of coercion to enforce its decisions. Nevertheless the ECJ has been instrumental in developing state-like properties for the EU in both these areas.

First, on the external side the EU has the formal power to make treaties with third parties under Article 133 (common commercial policy) and Article 310 (association agreements). Even in these limited fields most member states originally considered that the articles merely allowed the Commission to negotiate agreements on behalf of the member states, and that sovereignty remained with the member states. However, in 1971 the ECJ established the principle that when making agreements with third countries the EU would be sovereign over any existing or future acts between the individual member states and the third countries in question (case 22/70, *ERTA* [1971], ECR 263). In the same judgement the ECJ argued that the jurisdiction of the EU in the international sphere covered *all* areas of EU competence, not just those included in Articles 133 and 310. In other words, in one stroke the ECJ conferred new treaty-making powers to the EU and deprived the member states of their own independent powers relating to EU competences.

The ECJ's interpretation of the legal sovereignty of the EU in the international sphere was further expressed in two 'opinions' on the proposed European Economic Area (EEA) between the EU and the European Free Trade Area (EFTA) (Opinion 1/91, *EEA I* [1991], ECR I-6079; Opinion 1/92, *EEA II* [1992], ECR I-2821). The original proposal for the EEA, which had been approved by the EU and EFTA states, provided for the establishment of the EEA as a new type of legal order, partially merged with the EU but no longer under the sole judicial authority of the ECJ. However the ECJ rejected this idea out of hand. It again argued that the EU Treaty was a 'constitutional charter of a Community based on the rule of law', and consequently that the proposed EEA arrangement would compromise the independence and sovereignty of the EU. The ECJ approved a revised version of the EEA that gave jurisdiction over the EEA exclusively to the ECJ (even over the national courts of the EFTA states). What was remarkable about this episode was that the supposedly sovereign nation states of the EU accepted the ECJ's assertions and duly revised the international treaty. The proposed constitution would institutionalize the existing external sovereignty of the EU by formally establishing a 'legal personality' for the EU.

Second, on the internal side, Article 10 of the EC section of the EU Treaty instructs the member states to 'take all appropriate measures . . . to ensure the fulfilment of their obligations arising out of the Treaty'. Most member states originally assumed that this article took effect only in relation to the other treaty articles and EU law. However the ECJ used it as a substitute for the lack of direct enforcement powers in the EU system (cf. Shaw, 1996, pp. 208–13; Weatherill and Beaumont, 2004). For example it ruled that member states must adapt all relevant national rules to the requirements of EU law (cases 205-215/82, *Deutsche Milchkontor GmbH* v. *Germany* [1983], ECR 2633), and that Article 10 should be applied to all state organs at all levels of government (Case C-8/88, *Germany* v. *Commission* [1990], ECR I-2321).

Furthermore the ECJ broadened the definition of the types of action a member state must use to enforce EU law. For instance in 1997 it ruled that the French government should have used the state security forces more effectively to ensure the free movement of goods in the internal market (case C-265/95, *Commission* v. *France* [1997]). The court acknowledged that member states should 'retain exclusive competence as regards the maintenance of public order and the safeguarding of internal security', but it went on to argue that:

it falls to the Court . . . to verify . . . whether the member state concerned has adopted appropriate measures for ensuring the free movement of goods. . . . [In the present case] the French police were either not present or did not intervene . . . the actions in question were not always rapid . . . [and] only a very small number of persons has been identified and prosecuted.

In other words the EU did not need a police force of its own in order to exercise coercive power. According to the ECJ the member states were obliged to take all reasonable measures to enforce EU law, including the use of security forces.

Kompetenz-Kompetenz: judicial review of competence conflicts

A key weapon in the arsenal of supreme courts in any multilevel political system is the ability to police the boundary of competences between the states and central government: what German constitutional laws call *Kompetenz-Kompetenz*. The EU Treaty gives no formal powers to the ECJ to undertake this task (see Bogdandy and Bast, 2002). The treaty refers to the principle of subsidiarity: meaning that the EU can only act in areas that are not better tackled at the national level. The European Council has agreed a set of rules on how this principle should apply, for example the Commission must prove in the draft of any legislation that the legislation does not breach the principle of subsidiarity. However it is open to question whether the subsidiarity principle is justiciable before a national court or the ECJ. The treaty does not contain an explicit 'catalogue of competences', and under Article 308 the member state governments (acting by unanimity) can add any policy area to the competences of the EU without it being challenged in a national court or the ECJ.

Nevertheless the ECJ has gradually developed a power to police the vertical allocation of competences. Most significant in this respect was the ECJ's decision in 2000 to annul a directive on tobacco advertising and sponsorship (case 376/98, *Germany* v. *European Parliament and Council* [2000]). In 1998 the Council and EP had adopted this directive under Article 95 of the EC Treaty, covering the harmonization of laws for the completion of the single market. However the ECJ ruled that 'Article [95] should be available as a legal basis only in cases where obstacles to the exercise of fundamental freedoms and distortion of competition are considerable.' Thus a ban on tobacco advertising could only be adopted under Article 95 if it allowed products that circulated in the internal market (such as newspapers or magazines) to move more freely than if there were different national tobacco advertising rules. Since the proposed ban was more widespread than simply covering these goods, the ECJ pointed out that 'the national measures affected are to a large extent inspired by public health policy objectives'. However the public health competences in the treaty (Article

152) only allowed for the adoption of EU legislation on common safety standards in organizations, and hence did not extend to the harmonization of national public health standards more generally.

Some observers were surprised by the judgement to annul the directive as the ECJ had applied Article 95 quite broadly in the past (Hervey, 2001). However the ruling can be interpreted as a strategic signal by the ECJ to the governments that it could be trusted in competence-conflict decisions: in this case between the harmonization of rules in the single market (an exclusive EU competence) and public health standards (an exclusive competence of the member states). By ruling that the EU could only harmonize rules in the single market if there was a clear case of market distortion, the ECJ effectively defined a boundary between the federal powers of the EU and the rights of the member states.

This was particularly significant because the ECJ judges were aware that the Convention on the Future of Europe was about to begin, and that one of the key issues in the design of an EU constitution would be the policing of vertical competences. Several member states had already proposed a new quasijudicial body for this task: a special EU constitutional court composed either of national parliamentarians or judges from the highest courts in the member states. By ruling against the legislative majorities in the Council and EP, the judges demonstrated that they could be trusted to protect the rights of states that were on the losing side in the EU's legislative process.

The Convention subsequently proposed a catalogue of competences in the draft EU constitution, with areas defined as either exclusive competences of the EU, shared competences between the EU and the member states, areas for mutual cooperation between the governments, or exclusive competences of the member states. The Convention also proposed a mechanism for policing the boundaries between these categories: if a certain number of national parliaments were to protest against a legislative proposal, the matter should be referred to the ECJ. In other words, following the tobacco advertising ruling the Convention decided to grant exclusive *Kompetenz-Kompetenz* to the ECJ rather than to a new body. Irrespective of whether or not the constitution eventually enters into force, the agreement in the Convention suggests that the member state governments are content to allow the ECJ to become the main adjudicator of competence conflicts. Without the tobacco advertising judgement it is unlikely that the Convention would have been able to propose this important precedent.

Even if the proposed constitution, agreed in June 2004, is not ratified an EU 'constitution' exists in a 'formal legal' sense in terms of the rules governing the operation and powers of the EU institutions, the separation of competences between the EU and the member states, and the quasi-federal rights granted by the EU to individuals and member states (cf. Grimm, 1995; Habermas, 1995). An EU constitution also exists in a 'social' sense in terms of acceptance of the EU system and the doctrines established by the Court of Justice by national legal and constitutional authorities – to which we shall now turn.

Penetration of EU Law into National Legal Systems

The penetration of EU law into national legal systems has developed both quantitatively and qualitatively. On the quantitative side there has been a substantial increase in the use of the Article 234 procedure for requesting preliminary rulings from the ECJ by national courts, and on the qualitative side national courts have gradually accepted the existence and supremacy of the EU legal system over national law and constitutions.

Quantitative: national courts' use of ECJ preliminary rulings

Figure 4.3 shows the number of Article 234 references by all member state courts to the ECJ in 1958–97. During this period, while the EU grew from six member states to 15 the number of references to the ECJ rose from one or two a year in the early 1960s to over 250 a year in the late 1990s. The rapid rise in references in the 1970s followed the establishment of the doctrines of direct effect and supremacy, which encouraged national courts to use the references procedure to strengthen their position in the domestic political system, and encour-

Figure 4.3   *Growth of Article 234 references, 1961–97*

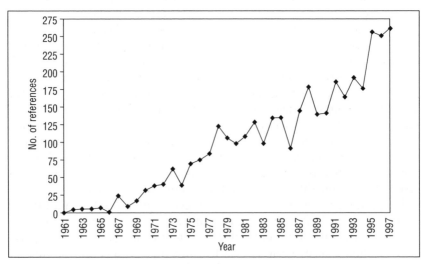

Source: Calculated from the Stone Sweet and Brunell (1999) dataset.

Table 4.1   *Number of Article 234 references, by member state*

	Average annual references in each period				
	1958–67	*1968–77*	*1978–87*	*1988–97*	*1958–97*
Germany	1.6	21.1	34.4	48.6	26.4
France	0.5	5.8	24.7	25.9	14.2
Austria	–	–	–	13.3	13.3
Italy	0.2	5.5	11.6	33.1	12.6
Netherlands	2.0	6.1	19.1	19.1	11.6
Belgium	0.5	6.3	12.3	19.9	9.8
United Kingdom	–	1.6	6.8	16.9	9.8
Spain	–	–	1.0	10.6	9.0
Sweden	–	–	–	6.3	6.3
Greece	–	–	2.7	3.0	2.9
Denmark	–	0.4	2.3	4.4	2.8
Finland	–	–	–	2.3	2.3
Portugal	–	–	0.0	2.4	2.0
Ireland	–	0.6	1.7	1.4	1.4
Luxembourg	0.2	0.4	1.5	1.8	1.0

Note: For each member state the total number of references in a period is divided by the number of years the member state was a member of the EU in that period, rather than by the number of years in which references were made.

Source: Calculated from the Stone Sweet and Brunell (1999) dataset.

aged private litigants to use the procedure to invoke their rights in the domestic courts.

However not all national courts used the references system to the same extent. As Table 4.1 shows, the number of references from each member state rose over time. The figures suggest a 'learning curve', with the original member states making more references in each period than the member states that joined later. Nevertheless there were several other factors cross-cutting this trend. First, within each wave of EU members, the larger states made more references than the smaller states: Germany, France and Italy made more references than The Netherlands, Belgium and Luxembourg; the UK made more than Denmark and Ireland; Spain made more than Portugal; and Austria and Sweden made more than Finland (Stone Sweet and Brunell, 2000). Second, despite the learning curve, British courts made fewer references in the early 1990s than did Dutch and Belgian courts, which perhaps reflects the sceptical attitude towards the EU among the public and the elite in the UK (Golub, 1996a). However the courts in Ireland, Portugal and Luxembourg, where the public and elites are strongly pro-European, also made few references to the ECJ. Nevertheless, Stone Sweet and Brunell (1998a, 1998b, 2000) argue that one of the

Table 4.2   *Proportion of Article 234 references by subject matter*

| Subject matter | Percentage of total references in each period | | | | |
	1958–67	1968–77	1978–87	1988–97	1958–97
Agriculture	9.8	36.1	26.0	12.8	20.3
Free movement of goods	14.8	19.7	18.5	16.3	17.5
Social security	34.4	12.6	7.5	8.4	9.0
Taxation	18.0	4.3	5.4	10.9	8.3
Competition	9.8	6.4	5.0	7.4	6.5
Establishment	1.6	2.8	3.7	8.3	6.0
Social provisions	0.0	0.6	2.5	7.3	4.7
Approximation of laws	1.6	1.2	3.3	5.9	4.4
Free movement of persons	0.0	3.1	3.5	4.4	3.8
External	0.0	2.4	2.5	1.8	2.1
Environment	0.0	0.0	1.1	2.4	1.6
Transport	0.0	1.2	1.3	1.8	1.5
Commercial policy	0.0	1.2	1.2	1.7	1.4
Other	9.8	8.4	18.5	10.5	12.9
Total references per period	61	675	1635	2547	4918
Percentage of all references in 1958–97	1.2	13.7	33.2	51.8	100.0

Source: Calculated from the Stone Sweet and Brunell (1999) dataset.

key factors explaining the variation in national use of the preliminary reference procedure is the combined size and openness of a member states' economy – in other words, the larger the market and the larger the volume of imports, the greater the incentive for importing firms to take cases to the ECJ to guarantee market access for their goods and services.

The subject matter of references to the ECJ by national courts has also changed significantly. As Table 4.2 shows, in the period 1968–97 most references related to the Common Agricultural Policy. However by the early 1990s, issues relating to the operation of the internal market – such as the free movement of goods, the free movement of workers, taxes, freedom of establishment and the approximation of national laws – comprised over half of all references. This reflects the fact that the majority of laws governing the regulation of the market were set at the European rather than the national level (see Chapter 8).

Finally, there was considerable national variation in the extent of compliance with EU law. Table 4.3 shows the average number of infringement cases brought before the ECJ in 1972–93. At face value these figures reinforce the conventional wisdom that the southern EU states (except Portugal) are generally less likely to enforce EU law as effectively as the northern states. However Mbaye (2001) has found

Table 4.3   *Non-compliance cases brought before the ECJ, 1972–93*

	Average number per year
Italy	7.0
Greece	4.3
Spain	3.4
Belgium	3.1
Germany	1.9
France	1.8
United Kingdom	1.5
Netherlands	1.2
Ireland	1.1
Denmark	0.6
Portugal	0.4

Note: These figures reflect the number of cases in which the ECJ declared that a failure to fulfil a treaty obligation had occurred, regardless of whether this was at the administrative or the judicial phase of an infringement proceeding.

Source: Calculated from the data in Mbaye (2001).

that in addition to the efficiency of the domestic bureaucracy (the southern effect), the greater political and economic power of northern member states in terms of their voting weight in the Council and importance to the European economy reduces the likelihood that they will be subject to infringement proceedings before the ECJ (cf. Börzel, 2001).

Qualitative: national courts' acceptance of the EU legal system

Not all national courts capitulated to the emerging constitutionalization of the EU at the same time (Mattli and Slaughter, 1998a, 1998b). The Benelux states accepted the direct effect and supremacy of EU law almost immediately upon the establishment of these doctrines: since the 1920s Belgian courts had accepted that international law was inherently part of Belgian law, and saw their role *vis-à-vis* the EU and the ECJ as a logical extension of this practice (Bribosia, 1998). Dutch courts applied a similar norm, and the 1983 reform of the Dutch constitution introduced provisions that explicitly referred to the supremacy of EU law over Dutch law (Claes and de Witte, 1998).

The German Constitutional Court (Bundesverfassungsgericht) at first acknowledged the ECJ's proclamation that the EU system constituted 'an autonomous legal order' (Kokott, 1998), and also accepted the supremacy of EU law, but in the narrow form of 'priority in application' rather than the more general 'priority of validity' (Alter, 2001, pp. 64–123). However it retreated from this position when in 1974 it ruled that when there was a conflict between national and EU law, the constitutional Court could decide the limits of the supremacy of EU law. The implication of this ruling became clear with the landmark *Brunner* judgement by the court in 1993 on the constitutionality of the Maastricht Treaty.

In the *Brunner* judgment the court ruled that the German Basic Law limited the transfer of powers to the EU, and argued that the EU was a *sui generis* organization and not a state based on democratic norms. The court claimed that because it was commanded by the German constitution to defend the basic rights and principles of democracy set out in the German Basic Law, it had the jurisdiction to declare acts of the EU *ultra vires* (beyond the legal authority of the EU) if they breached the Basic Law (but it would seek to cooperate with the ECJ if faced with such a prospect). Having said this, the court declared that the Maastricht Treaty could be ratified by Germany because the German parliament maintained the right to transfer (or withdraw) German government competences to the EU. The court warned, however, that the EU could only legitimately become a state if it were fully democratic, with the necessary institutions of parliamentary democracy, a clearly defined hierarchy of rights and a single *demos* (Weiler, 1995).

Acceptance of the direct effect and supremacy doctrines by the Italian courts was more problematic (Catabia, 1998; Laderchi, 1998). Direct effect was accepted in 1973, but the highest Italian court refused to accept the supremacy of EU law and did not make a preliminary reference to the ECJ for four years after the *Costa* v. *ENEL* judgment. The court justified this position by arguing that Italian and EU law were separate and parallel legal orders. However in 1984 highly conscious of its almost complete isolation from the other EU courts, the Italian Constitutional Court ruled that the EU did not have the power to repeal Italian law, but when EU law and national law applied in the same area, Italian judges should choose to apply EU law. This amounted to conditional acceptance of the supremacy of EU law. Laderchi (ibid., p. 166) points out that 'The Court was cheating when it said that the results of its new doctrines coincided with the requirements set by the ECJ'.

In the UK, the courts accepted direct effect immediately upon the country's accession to the EU in 1973. However it was difficult for the UK to accept the supremacy of EU law as this conflicted with the central constitutional concept of parliamentary sovereignty – that is, acts of parliament immediately overrode all existing law or legislation (Craig, 1998). However in 1990 the House of Lords found a way to reconcile parliamentary sovereignty and EU supremacy. On a reference from the House of Lords, the ECJ ruled that a 1988 parliamentary act was in breach of EU law, and the House of Lords accepted this judgement on the ground that in passing the 1972 act of accession to the EU the British parliament had voluntarily accepted the EU legal system, of which the supremacy of EU law was a central part. The House of Lords also argued that this did not compromise parliamentary sovereignty, as a future British parliament could repeal the act of accession, and thus withdraw the UK from the EU.

In France there was a marked difference between the Cour de Cassation (the highest civil court) and the Conseil d'Etat (the highest administrative court) in terms of how and when they accepted the EU legal system (Plötner, 1998; Alter, 2001, pp. 124–81). The French constitution combined a monist approach to international law with a philosophy of parliamentary sovereignty. Initially the French courts interpreted this combination to mean that EU law was supreme over acts of parliament prior to the Treaty of Rome, but that the French courts were free to determine whether subsequent acts were in breach of EU law. However in 1975 the Cour de Cassation accepted that in all cases EU law was superior to French national law. The Conseil d'Etat, on the other hand, did not reach the same conclusion until 1990, and even then it argued that EU legal supremacy only applied because all international treaties ratified by the French parliament were sovereign over French law. In other words the EU constitution was justified through the lens of national rather than European constitutional norms.

In Sweden there was dispute over whether the domestic constitution would have to be changed if Sweden became a member of the EU (Bernitz, 2001). The constitution had been amended in 1965 to allow for the conclusion of treaties with the then European Community. But most experts in Sweden took the view that because of the development of the EU and its competences in the 1980s and 1990s, this provision was not enough to allow for the substantial transfer of power that would result from accession. The new constitutional provision that was finally agreed upon by the *Riksdag* (the Swedish parliament) was significantly less extensive than many legal experts had proposed, stating that:

> The Parliament may transfer a right of decision-making to the European Communities so long as the Communities have protection for rights and freedoms corresponding to the protection provided under this Instrument of Government and the European Convention for the Protection of Human Rights and Fundamental Freedoms.

In other words, this amendment imposed constraints on EU law that flowed directly from the German *Brunner* judgement. If an EU law conflicted with a fundamental right that was protected by the national constitution and backed by a national democratic majority, a Swedish court would be forced to reject the EU law unless it was clear that the relevant right was sufficiently protected at the EU level by a European charter of fundamental rights.

In summary, EU law has been accepted as an integral part of national legal systems and as sovereign over national law. However in several member states the highest national courts maintain that this is conditional on national constitutional norms: for example that parliaments retain the right to revoke the supremacy of EU law by withdrawing the transfer of sovereignty to the EU (as in Germany, the UK and France). One could argue that this solution has been driven primarily by the desire of national courts not to renounce their previous positions on the EU, or to declare basic constitutional principles null and void (such as parliamentary sovereignty in the British case). Only in Germany did the Constitutional Court withdraw from its previously unconditional acceptance of supremacy, but this had profound effects on the other member states, as in the Swedish case, and forced the EU to address the protection of fundamental rights and the democratic accountability of the EU institutions. From this perspective, the decision in December 2001 to hold a Convention on the Future of Europe, and to charge this forum with proposing a codified constitution, resulted at least partly from the growing ambivalence of national judiciaries towards the EU's uncodified constitutional settlement.

Explanations of EU Judicial Politics

How was the ECJ able to promote legal integration and constitutionalization of the EU? Why was this process accepted by the member state governments and their national courts? Scholars of the EU have come up with five answers: (1) the 'formalism' of law, (2) the strategic behaviour of the European Court of Justice, (3) the strategic behaviour of national courts, (4) the interests of transnational private actors and (5) the strategic behaviour of national governments.

Legal formalism and legal cultures

Legal scholars of the EU have traditionally emphasized the internal logic of law and the legal process. As Weiler (1994, p. 525) explains 'The formalistic claim is that judicial process rests above or outside politics, a neutral arena in which courts scientifically interpret the meaning of policy decided by others'. In other words the ECJ simply applies EU law as set out in the EU treaties and in secondary legislation, without any conscious desire to promote its own power or institutional interests. An EU constitution has developed because the EU legal system had its own internal 'integrationist' logic. Without an explicit definition and separation of competences in the EU Treaty there was no clear hierarchy of norms. So, the EU had to apply the goal of 'ever closer union' as the ultimate norm of the EU polity, thus forcing the ECJ to develop the doctrines of direct effect and supremacy. Furthermore there was an *effect utile* in the legal workings of the EU (whereby the ECJ preferred to apply EU law in the most efficient and effective way), which compelled the ECJ to promote legal integration in order to prevent the EU political system from becoming ineffective and unworkable (Cappelletti *et al.*, 1986).

In the same vein, legal formalist explanations posit that national courts were eager to find ways to reconcile their previous jurisprudence with the emerging EU legal system. Through the preliminary references system, the ECJ provided national courts with the appropriate argumentation and rationale for them to absorb the new doctrines into their national legal systems (cf. Wincott, 1995). Variations in the use of the preliminary references system and the dates of acceptance of the ECJ doctrines can be explained by variations in national legal cultures and doctrines (Chalmers, 1997; de Witte, 1998; Mattli and Slaughter, 1998a, 1998b; Maher, 1998; Stone Sweet, 1998). On the cultural side, different systems of training judges, different promotion systems and different career paths had produced different patterns of behaviour and reasoning by judges – such as formal versus pragmatic, deductive versus inductive, or abstract versus consensual. Also, each system had a different relationship between administrative, constitutional and common law courts, and different rules, traditions and powers of judicial review. On the doctrinal side, the place of fundamental rights in domestic constitutions and how the concept of sovereignty was defined affected the relationship between national legal norms and the EU constitution.

These legal-formalist explanations have some important shortcomings. At the empirical level, the doctrines of supremacy and direct effect are not simply logical extensions of the EU Treaty: if federalization of the EU had been intended from the outset, the EU Treaty would have contained a supremacy clause as in other federal constitutions. Also many national courts were not immediately convinced of the ECJ's justification of direct effect and supremacy (cf. Alter, 1998a, pp. 230–4). From the general study of courts and judicial politics we know that the institutional interests of courts and the personal policy preferences of judges drive judges' actions. In a sense the structural and cultural logic of the law are simply another set of constraints within which courts and judges secure these aims. Consequently at the theoretical level, explanations of the emergence of the EU constitution must also take account of the institutional and policy incentives of EU and national judges, and the strategic motivations of other actors in the system.

Activism by the European Court of Justice

In direct contrast to the legal-formalist approach, an alternative explanation depicts the ECJ as an explicitly political actor (see for example Weiler, 1981, 1991; Rasmussen, 1986; Mancini, 1989; Volcansek, 1993a). The pioneer of this perspective was Eric Stein (1981, p. 1), who opened his ground-breaking article with an oft-cited passage:

> Tucked away in the fairyland Duchy of Luxembourg and blessed, until recently, with benign neglect by the powers that be and the mass media, the Court of Justice of the European Communities has fashioned a constitutional framework for a federal-type structure in Europe.

In this explanation the ECJ is a strategic actor with specific institutional interests and policy preferences that it has promoted and protected. In terms of institutional interests, the ECJ wants to strengthen its position *vis-à-vis* the other EU institutions, and therfore it has consciously sought to develop its powers of judicial review of Commission and Council actions. It has also used preliminary references by national courts to develop a policy-making role in areas where the treaty is vague or legislation is absent or incomplete, and it has sought to establish a jurisdiction for itself in determining the division of competences between the national and EU systems.

In terms of policy preferences, this theory argues that the ECJ has promoted European integration at every opportunity. The pursuit of this goal stems from the assumption that further economic and political integration will eventually turn the ECJ into an all-powerful supreme court – perhaps like the US Supreme Court. To this end the ECJ has asserted the autonomy of EU law from the very beginning, implying that the EU legal order is fundamentally different from international law. Also, the doctrines of direct effect and supremacy smack of an explicit federalist plan; similarly, when establishing the principle of mutual recognition the ECJ knew that the doctrine would be a powerful motor of economic integration (Alter and Meunier-Aitsahalia, 1994).

However this explanation also has its limitations. At an empirical level, activism by the ECJ has not been linear (Chalmers, 1997). Rather it has responded to the pace of the integration process, and has been sensitive to anti-ECJ feelings amongst certain national governments. And why did it take so long to establish the principle of mutual recognition? The strategic behaviour of the ECJ must be analyzed in terms of the opportunities and constraints it has faced, ranging from institutional and cultural factors of the EU system to the competing interests and preferences of the member state governments, national courts and private litigants.

Strategic national courts: judicial empowerment and intercourt competition

Related to this approach are explanations that depict the constitutional development of the EU as a product of the strategic behaviour of national courts in cooperation with the ECJ (Weiler, 1993, 1994; Alter, 1996, 2001). Unlike the ECJ, national courts are not interested in the emergence of an EU constitution to promote the goal of European integration. Instead they seek to use the EU legal system to secure their interests and policy preferences within their own national legal and political contexts. And national governments are unable to resist the penetration of EU law into domestic polities because of the special role of law in domestic democratic polities. In the words of Burley and Mattli (1993, pp. 72–3): 'Law ultimately proved impervious to political interference, not only due to "the mask" of technical discourse, but also "the shield" of domestic norms of rule of law and judicial independence.'

There are two main variants of this 'national courts approach'. First, several scholars argue that national courts have been empowered by the emergence of the EU constitution (see for example Weiler, 1991, 1994). In many domestic political systems the powers of judicial review are weak, parliaments are sovereign, and governments have substantial administrative and political resources at their disposal. Consequently national courts welcome the direct effect and supremacy of EU law and actively use the preliminary references system to strengthen their hand in the national policy process. At one extreme of this argument, the ECJ and its rulings are used as instruments by national courts to promote the rule of law, judicial review and the protection of individual rights against the domestic state. For example the ECJ has often been asked by national courts to make preliminary rulings on issues that are parochial national court obsessions (Volcansek, 1986). Alternatively, national courts are said to be in cahoots with the ECJ to strengthen the judicial system against national governments at both the European and national levels of the EU political system. In the other words the ECJ has consciously sought to appeal to national courts' self-interest (Mancini, 1989; Weiler, 1994).

Second, within each national legal system, lower and higher courts have different institutional incentives *vis-à-vis* the EU legal system. Alter (1996) contends that lower judges and courts use EU law to increase their prestige and power. Through the preliminary references procedure they are able to 'play higher courts and the ECJ off against each other to influence legal developments in the direction their prefer' (Alter, 1998a, p. 242). In all the member states but Luxembourg, either lower or intermediate courts have made more use of the preliminary references procedure than higher courts, and in seven member states both lower and intermediate courts have made more references than the higher courts (Stone Sweet and Brunell, 1998b). In other words, EU legal integration is an inadvertent product of this intercourt competition in the national arena.

At a theoretical level these explanations offer sophisticated conceptions of the interaction between courts' preferences and their domestic institutional and political environments. However at an empirical level they have some important shortcomings. For example, they do not explain why certain national courts accepted EU doctrines before others. Also, based on their data on the use of preliminary references, Stone Sweet and Brunell (1998b, p. 90) dispute the intercourt competition argument because they find that on average higher courts have been more active than lower courts in using the preliminary reference procedure.

Accepting these problems, later works from this perspective have moderated the earlier claims. For example Alter (2000, 2001), Golub (1996a) and Mattli and Slaughter (1998a, 1998b) accept that different national political and institutional settings affect the way in which national courts respond to EU law. For instance there are different degrees of public support for European integration, awareness of the ECJ, satisfaction with the ECJ and general satisfaction with courts and judges (Caldeira and Gibson, 1995; Gibson and Caldeira, 1995, 1998). If courts ignore these mass sentiments they risk provoking parliamentary challenges to their judicial autonomy and undermining public acceptance of courts and the judicial system. Also, each national system has a different structure of legal institutions, such as court procedures, powers of judicial review, cost of access for litigants, and legal training of judges (Alter, 2000). Hence variations in public support for the EU and the structure of legal systems go a significant way towards explaining national variations in the use of the preliminary references procedure, the acceptance of ECJ doctrines and the application of EU law in some areas more than others (Alter, 2000, 2001; cf. Craig, 1998; Chalmers, 2001).

Private interests: the other interlocutors of the ECJ

There are a number of other private interlocutors of the ECJ who have actively promoted the integration of the EU legal system (Weiler, 1993, 1994). Primary amongst these are private litigants. As noted earlier, the doctrine of direct effect enables individual citizens to invoke EU law in national courts, and this gave private citizens a stake in the EU legal system early in the integration process (Burley and Mattli, 1993, pp. 60–1).

Lisa Conant (2002, p. 3) goes even further:

Pressures for policy responses to innovative judicial interpretations consist of strategic litigation campaigns of copycat cases, the mass filing of parallel claims before bureaucracies, the systematic prosecution of parallel cases by enforcement agencies, and the lobbying of officials and elected representatives.

In her view, variations in the organization of private interests explain why EU law has developed in areas other than those of direct interest to the ECJ or national governments. 'Concentrated' interests (who potentially face large costs/benefits from EU law) tend to be better organized than 'diffuse' interests (who potentially face small costs/benefits from EU law) (see Chapter 6). But the relatively low cost of gaining access to the ECJ means that EU law has been a vehicle for the promotion of some interests that are underrepresented in several domestic systems of interest representation (Pollack, 1997b). For example women's groups, trade unions and consumer groups have forced national courts and the ECJ to develop and apply EU law in the area of gender equality, labour rights and consumer protection.

Second, Stone Sweet and Brunell (1998a, 1998b) argue that firms involved in the import and export of goods are the dominant private litigants in the EU legal system. These interests have a particular incentive to secure effective application of the free movement of goods and services, and have sufficient resources to take actions all the way through to the ECJ. In the view of Stone Sweet and Brunell the average annual volume of intra-EU trade – which they use as a proxy for the level of transnational economic interests in each member state – is the strongest predictor of the annual number of references by member states to the ECJ (cf. Golub, 1996d). Also, because these litigants have particular policy interests there is a significant relationship between the volume of intra-EU trade and preliminary references for matters relating to the operation and regulation of the internal market (Stone Sweet and Brunell, 1998a, p. 75).

Third, another set of transnational interests with a vested interest in the development of the EU legal system is the legal community outside the ECJ (Weiler, 1994). The process of European integration is primarily elite-driven, and this is as true in the legal field as in the political and social fields. Also, members of the legal community in Europe are highly integrated at both the economic and the social level, and have a vested interest in furthering the legal and political integration of Europe to support their activities. Stein (1981) argues that the list of actors that have played an active role in the promotion of EU law should include the Legal Service of the Commission, the Legal Counsel of the Council, lawyers in national ministries, attorneys appearing before national courts, legal scholars and writers, and the 'legal establishment' in political positions. Weiler (1994) also points out that academic lawyers, particularly in continental Europe, are often 'custodians of *La Doctrine*'. In several states this has enabled the law professorate to play a crucial part in the acceptance of EU legal norms, by supplying ideas and arguments to national courts to enable them to reconcile EU and national constitutional doctrines.

In other words this explanation is a logical extension of general theories of European integration that place emphasis on the role of transnational economic and social activities in promoting integration: such as neofunctionalism (for example Stone Sweet and Sandholtz, 1997; see also Chapter 1). However this explanation suffers from some of the same weaknesses as these general theories. In particular it overemphasizes the autonomy of supranational institutions and transnational interests in the promotion of EU legal integration. These scholars argue that once transnational activities and supranational institutions have been unleashed there is little that national governments can do to stop them (Pierson, 1996). However, national governments are the signatories of the treaties, and if provoked they can restrict the powers of the ECJ and redefine the nature of the EU constitution. That is, as with the ECJ and national courts, there are strategic constraints on the actions of transnational interests.

Strategic member state governments

Several scholars have argued that the development of the EU constitution has been a deliberate strategy by national governments (for example Garrett, 1992, 1995a; Garrett and Weingast, 1993; Cooter and Drexl, 1994; Garrett *et al.*, 1998; Kelemen, 2001). They claim that governments have consciously allowed the ECJ, national courts and transnational litigants to promote legal integration in the EU because it has been in the governments' political or economic interests. The flip side of this is that if the ECJ or a national court takes an action that is contrary to a government's interest it will simply ignore the ruling. High-profile clashes between national governments and the ECJ or national courts over EU legal issues are rare. But this does not mean that governments are powerless in the face of court activism. It simply suggests one of two things: either courts are careful not to make decisions that threaten government interests, or governments accept decisions that appear to be against them because they are in fact in their long-term interests.

On the first issue, Garrett and Weingast (1993, pp. 201–2) explain why courts exercise restraint:

> Embedding a legal system in a broader political structure places direct constraints on the discretion of a court, even one with as much constitutional independence as the United States Supreme Court ...

The reason is that political actors have a range of avenues through which they may alter or limit the role of courts ... the *possibility of such a reaction drives a court that wishes to preserve its independence and legitimacy to remain in the arena of acceptable latitude.*

If courts are strategic actors, then they are constrained by the possibility of government threats, such as reform of the EU Treaty or the passing of new legislation. For example, when faced with potential opposition by several national governments the ECJ has refused to establish that directives have horizontal direct effect, despite the opinions of several advocates-general and numerous academic lawyers.

On the second issue, Garrett (1995a) proposes a simple model to explain why governments often accept ECJ rulings against them. The model posits that governments take two main factors into account: the domestic political clout of the industry that is harmed by the ECJ decision, and the potential gains to the national economy as a whole. If the industry is domestically weak and the general economic gains will be large the government will accept the ECJ ruling and put up with complaints from the domestic industry. For example, with regard to the *Cassis de Dijon* judgment Garrett argues that the German government accepted a ruling that would damage its (relatively small) spirits industry because the rest of the German economy stood to benefit from the trade liberalization that would result from the principle of mutual recognition. Conversely if the industry in question is domestically powerful and the general economic gains will be small the government will engage in 'overt evasion' of the ECJ's decision. However this rarely occurs because the ECJ is careful to avoid such a showdown. The implication is that in the *Cassis de Dijon* case the ECJ waited for the right case to come along in order to establish the principle of mutual recognition (for a similar model of ECJ behaviour on international trade disputes see Kelemen, 2001).

By focusing on the centrality of national governments in the EU system and conceptualizing their actions as highly rational, these explanations have some of the same limitations as the intergovernmentalist explanations of European integration (see Chapter 1). At the empirical level there is substantial evidence that the ECJ and national courts have often taken decisions that governments have opposed, and which have had negative effects on the competitiveness of national economies in the single market (Mattli and Slaughter, 1995). At a theoretical level this can be explained by the fact that governments do not have perfect information about the likely outcome of delegating adjudication to the ECJ and national courts (see Alter, 2001, pp. 182–208; cf. Pierson, 1996). For example when the EU Treaty was signed few governments realized that the EU would establish the doctrines of direct effect and supremacy, or considered the potential impact of the Article 234 procedure (Alter, 1998b).

In a later work Garrett *et al.* (1998) accepted that governments are not completely free to ignore adverse rulings. For example in cases where the EU treaties are clear and the legal precedent is strong, the costs to a government of ignoring an adverse ruling (in terms of threatening the very foundations of the EU) will be high. In other words, although national governments behave strategically, there are long-term constraints on them as a result of their allowing the ECJ to develop its own legal precendents and norms. However the main thrust of Garrett *et al.*'s argument remains: the ECJ is heavily constrained if the potential costs to a powerful domestic constituency are high or if a large number of governments are likely to be adversely affected by an ECJ ruling. For example the *Barber* judgement on equal pension rights for men and women imposed substantial costs on all governments. In response the governments added a protocol to the treaty that prevented the retroactive application of the judgement, and susequently the ECJ moderated its activism in this area – although it extended its activities in other areas of pension rights (cf. Pollack, 2003, pp. 360–72).

Conclusion: Unknown Destination or Emerging Equilibrium?

The EU has a legal-constitutional framework that contains two of the basic doctrines of a federal legal system: the direct effect of EU law on individual citizens throughout the EU, and the supremacy of EU law over domestic law and constitutions. Also, in the ECJ the EU has a powerful constitutional and administrative body to oversee the implementation of EU law and keep the EU institutions in check.

How this came about is a matter of contention. The truth probably lies somewhere between the explanations discussed above. On the one hand political actors – national governments, the ECJ, national courts and transnational litigants – have particular interests and policy goals. On the other hand these actors are constrained by their cultural, institutional, political and informational contexts (environmental constraints), and by the interests of other actors in the system (strategic constraints). However in special 'windows of opportunity', actors can shape their environmental surroundings, for example by reforming institutional structures, establishing institutional norms or modifying national legal cultures.

As we saw in the discussion of general theories of judicial politics, courts have more discretion under certain institutional designs than others. The ECJ has substantial room for manoeuvre because there is only a small probability that the EU Treaty will be reformed to reduce the ECJ's powers or that new legislation will be passed to overturn one of its decisions. Because there are many veto-players in the EU system, at least one member state, the Commission, the European Parliament or a group of powerful transnational economic actors is likely to block a reduction of the ECJ's powers or the overturning of one of its decisions.

But the ECJ has imperfect information on how other actors will react to its decisions. Governments have shorter time horizons than courts because they face general elections every few years. This means that they are less interested in the long-term implications of delegating powers to the ECJ than in the immediate political salience of a decision. But it also means that the ECJ is uncertain about what issues will become politically salient in which states.

This judicial politics game has produced an incomplete constitution. For example the EU does not have a bill of rights, and who will have *Kompetenz-Kompetenz* will remain unclear until the proposed constitution is ratified and has been operating for some time. Weiler (1993) consequently argues that the EU has an 'unknown destination' (cf. Shonfield, 1973).

However the theoretical analysis in this chapter suggests that the current constitutional set-up already constitutes a relatively stable equilibrium: a balance between the discretion of the ECJ/national courts on the one hand, and the conscious decision by national governments to construct a rule of law to enable economic integration on the other. This goes hand in hand with the emerging equilibrium in the vertical allocation of competences (discussed in Chapter 1). Put this way, the constitutional settlement relating to the allocation of market regulation competences to the European level relies on a stable structure for the enforcement of contracts in these policy areas. Furthermore, the *de facto* existence of these parallel equilibria enabled the Convention on the Future of Europe and the 2003–4 intergovernmental conference to codify the main elements of the EU settlement in a single constitutional text without too much dispute (the conference was dominated by arguments over the design of the EU institutions, such as the weighting of votes in the Council, rather than the allocation and policing of competences between the EU and the member states).

Nevertheless this equilibrium could be upset by changes in public opinion, party competition and ideology, interest group politics and so on, which could push the EU towards a full federal constitutional arrangement or even result in a constitutional step backwards (as happened with the German Constitutional Court ruling on the Maastricht Treaty). It is to the political context of institutional politics that we turn in Part II of this book.

Politics

Public Opinion

Citizens' attitudes towards European integration and the EU institutions and policies are increasingly important. As the EU has become more integrated the publics have become more questioning. Europe's political leaders, at both the national and European levels, live in a new strategic environment where actions at the EU level are tightly constrained by voters' preferences. Hence understanding how citizens' preferences on European integration are formed is now essential to understand both the possibility of further integration and the lines of political conflict in EU policy-making.

Theories of the Social Bases of Politics

Each individual has a set of beliefs, opinions, values and interests in respect of the political process. These political preferences often derive from deep historical or cultural identities such as nationality, religion or language. Political preferences also stem from economic interests, such as whether a policy will increase a person's income. Inevitably, different individuals and social groups have different preferences and this produces conflicts in the political process.

The 'cleavage model' of politics posits that political divisions derive from 'critical junctures' in the development of a political system (Lipset and Rokkan, 1967). For example in Europe the democratic revolution in the eighteenth and early nineteenth centuries produced a conflict between church and state (between liberals and conservatives), and the industrial revolution of the nineteenth century divided workers and the owners of capital (between socialists and liberals/conservatives). Using the Lipset–Rokkan model to conceptualize the social bases of EU politics, two main cleavages in the EU can be identified: national–territorial and transnational–socioeconomic. First, the combination of a common territory, historical myths, mass culture, legal rights and duties, and a national economy constitute a powerful force for individual attachment to the nation-state (Smith, 1991, p. 14). The EU society is segmented along national lines: that is, between the EU member states, within which the bulk of individual social interactions and experiences take place and interests and identifications are formed (cf. Lijphart, 1977). This national–territorial cleavage emerges in EU politics when an issue on the agenda puts individuals from different nations on different sides of the debate, for example when one national group appears to gain at the expense of another.

Second, cross-cutting these national segments are 'latent' transnational divisions. On certain issues on the EU agenda a group of citizens in one nation-state may have more in common with a similar group in another nation-state than with the rest of society in their own nation-state. For example Dutch and Hungarian farmers have a common interest in defending the Common Agricultural Policy against the interests of Dutch and Hungarian consumers. Transnational cleavages can be mobilized around traditional social divisions, such as class, but can also emerge around newer 'issue divisions', such as postmaterialism, age, education and information. These transnational divisions tend to be less salient in EU politics than national divisions, but, they become increasingly important when the EU agenda shifts to questions of economic redistribution between functional rather than territorial groups (such as EU social policy) and questions of social and political values (such as EU environmental policy).

These ideas explain why different countries and social groups have different interests in EU politics, but they do not explain how these attitudes change over time. For this we can consider David Easton's (1965, 1975) theory of 'affective' and 'utilitarian' support for political institutions. Affective support is an ideological or non-material attachment to a political institution; while utilitarian support is the belief that the institution promotes an individual's economic or political interests. Rather than seeing these two types of support as competing or contradictory, Easton sees them as related. His idea was that a citizen's affective support for an institution provides a basic reservoir of good will. Some citizens have a high level of basic support, while others have a low level. If a citizen perceives that an institution is acting in support of (against) her interests, this basic level of support will go up (down). Hence utilitarian cost–benefit calculations determine whether the underlying level of support goes up or down over time.

This chapter looks first at the general pattern of support for European integration. It then considers various explanations of support for European integration (Europe right or wrong?), before turning to the issue of how the socioeconomic structure of European society shapes citizens' attitudes towards the direction of the EU policy agenda (Europe – right or left?) When the answers to these questions are combined, a two-dimensional map of EU politics emerges. This is the new environment for Europe's political elites, who must compete for voters' support for their policies towards and within the EU.

Public Support for the European Union: End of the Permissive Consensus

According to Lindberg and Scheingold (1970), in the 1950s and 1960s, following the signing of the Treaties of Paris and Rome, there was a 'permissive consensus' amongst European citizens in favour of European integration. This term came from V.O. Key (1961), who had used it to describe support by the American public for certain government actions, particularly in foreign affairs. The same phenomenon was apparent amongst the publics of the founding members of the European Communities. As Inglehart (1970b, p. 773) explained:

There was a favourable prevailing attitude toward the subject, but it was of low salience as a political issue – leaving national decision-makers free to take steps favourable to integration if they wished but also leaving them a wide liberty of choice.

In other words a large majority of the citizens of all member states were either not interested in European integration, and therefore had no opinion about their governments' actions on the issue, or generally supported their government's efforts to promote further integration.

However these claims could not be tested without survey data. Since 1973 the European Commission has commissioned Europe-wide public opinion polls every six months, conducted by private polling agencies in each member state and involving a sample of approximately 1000 interviewees in each country. These *'Eurobarometer'* surveys consequently provide a large dataset for the study of citizens' attitudes towards European integration. As with national governments and national opinion polls, the European Commission, the European Parliament, the EU Council and even the European Court of Justice study these polls carefully to gauge the level of support for or opposition towards further EU integration or specific EU policies.

Three questions that are asked in most *Eurobarometer* surveys are:

- *Membership* Generally speaking, do you think [your country's] membership of the Common Market/European Community/ European Union is a 'good thing', a 'bad thing', 'neither good nor bad', 'don't know'.

- *Benefit* Taking everything into consideration, would you say that [your country] has on balance benefited or not from being a member of the European Union? (Response: 'benefited', 'not benefited', 'don't know'.)
- *EP powers* Would you personally like the European Parliament to play a more or less important role than it does now? (Response: 'more', 'about the same', 'less', 'don't know'.)

The first and second questions may seem quite similar, but, they measure subtly different things. A person may not think that her country currently benefits from the EU, but she may still be in favour of EU membership for political reasons or because she expects to benefit in the future. Alternatively, a person could recognize the economic benefits of membership of the EU, but could nonetheless be opposed to membership of the EU because of concerns about further political integration or the lack of democratic accountability of the EU institutions. This is where the third question comes in, since more powers for the only directly elected EU institution is widely regarded as the best way to increase the accountability of the EU.

Figure 5.1 *Public support for European integration, 1973–2003 (per cent)*

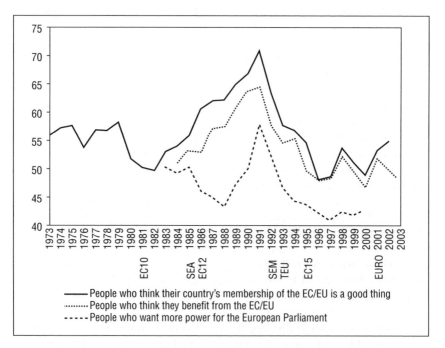

Notes: EC10, EC12, EU15 = enlargements of the EU to 10, 12 and 15 member states. SEA = Single European Act. SEM = Single European Market. TEU = Treaty on European Union. EURO = introduction of euro notes and coins.

As Figure 5.1 shows, in the early 1970s just over 50 per cent of EU citizens were in favour of their country's membership. Throughout the 1980s support for European integration rose steadily, perhaps as a result of public interest in the '1992 programme' – the project of completing the single market by the end of 1992 (Inglehart and Reif, 1991; see also Chapter 8). Support peaked in 1991, with 71 per cent being in favour of their country's membership of the EU and 65 per cent feeling that their country benefited from the EU. Enthusiasm for the granting of more powers to the EP started to pick up slightly later, but climbed rapidly after the third European elections in 1989. It peaked in 1991, when 58 per cent wanted more powers to be given to the EP. All three indicators then slumped and stayed at a lower level to this day, with some annual fluctuations.

Widespread opposition to the EU first emerged during the process of ratifying the Maastricht Treaty, in 1992–93, as manifest in referendums held in France, Denmark and Ireland, a series of votes in the British House of Commons, and a Constitutional Court challenge in Germany. This opposition continued in the form of votes for anti-European parties in the 1994 European elections, in the 1994 referendums in Austria, Finland, Sweden and Norway on EU enlargement, in the European elections in 1995 and 1996 in Austria, Sweden and Finland, in opinion polls in the build-up to the launch of EMU in 1999, and in the first EP elections in the enlarged EU in 2004.

If a permissive consensus did exist in the first few decades of European integration, it is no longer present (cf. Niedermayer, 1995a). As Franklin *et al.* (1994) elegantly put it, the anti-Europe 'bottle' has finally been 'uncorked'. Citizens are now much more aware of policies and events at the European level, and much less likely to follow blindly the positions of their governments (Franklin and Wlezien, 1997). So how can the decline in general support for integration be explained? Have all member states and social groups followed the same pattern? To answer these questions we need to consider how citizens' support for the EU varies across member states, social groups, and time.

More or Less Integration: Europe – Right or Wrong?

As with the development of many political systems at the national level (Rokkan, 1973), European integration has created a centre-periphery conflict between groups whose interests are threatened by economic and political integration and those whose interests are promoted by integration. In the EU the conflict has primarily been between national interests, but it has also mobilized transnational socioeconomic divisions, such as class interests and new social and value divisions. We shall first look at national interests and identities, before turning to economic interests and other transnational social and political divisions.

National divisions

In addition to the territorial boundaries between the nation-states, there are numerous interests and traditions that divide Europe's nations. For example:

- *Cultural differences*, such as weak versus strong national identities, Catholic versus Protestant, North versus South, East versus West, high-trust versus low-trust societies, and homogeneous versus multiethnic societies (Almond and Verba, 1963; Rokkan, 1973; Inglehart, 1991).
- *Economic differences*, including rich versus poor, urban versus rural, industrial versus agricultural, service-based versus manufacturing-based, centre versus periphery, high versus low unemployment, large versus small income inequalities, and energy producers versus energy consumers (see Gourevitch, 1989; Krugman, 1991; Cole and Cole, 1997).
- *Political differences*, for example large versus small populations, long versus short democratic traditions, majoritarian versus consensual, corporatist versus pluralist, liberal versus social/Christian democratic welfare states, Anglo-Saxon versus Rhineland models of capitalism (for example Lijphart, 1984; Esping-Anderson, 1990; Lange and Meadwell, 1991; Hall and Soskice, 2001).

These produce a complex pattern of national attitudes towards European integration.

Table 5.1 shows support for membership of the EC/EU by member states at three points in time: the early 1980s, the early 1990s and 2003. There is clearly considerably variation in the level of support for the EU across member states, with the public in Luxembourg, Ireland and the Netherlands being the most pro-EU and the public in Austria, Finland, Sweden, the UK and Denmark being the most consistently sceptical of EU membership. In 2003 support for the EU in the accession and candidate states was more than 10 per cent higher than in the 15 existing EU states. Interestingly, support was highest in the three states that were not able to join in 2004 (Romania, Bulgaria and Turkey). And, in referendums on EU membership large majorities voted in favour in all ten accession states, despite considerable scepticism amongst the citizens of many of these states.

In terms of variation over time, analysis of the changes between 1981 and 2003, and 1991 and 2003 reveals interesting patterns. Over the period 1981–2003 support for the EU changed most dramatically in

Table 5.1   *Nationality and European integration*

	Percentage who thought their country's membership of the EC/EU was (would be) a good thing			Percentage change	
	1981 (1986)	1991 (1995)	2003	1981/86–2003	1991/95–2003
Sweden	–	(38)	40	–	2
Austria	–	(39)	35	–	–4
Ireland	46	77	73	27	–4
Denmark	30	62	57	27	–5
Luxembourg	78	84	77	–1	–7
Finland	–	(50)	39	–	–11
Greece	42	76	62	20	–14
Spain	(62)	78	62	0	–16
Belgium	50	75	56	6	–19
Italy	73	79	58	–15	–21
Germany	49	70	46	–3	–24
Portugal	(60)	79	55	–5	–24
France	52	71	44	–8	–27
Netherlands	76	89	62	–14	–27
United Kingdom	24	57	28	4	–29
All EU	50	74	48	–2	–26
Romania	–	–	81	–	–
Bulgaria	–	–	73	–	–
Turkey	–	–	67	–	–
Cyprus	–	–	59	–	–
Slovakia	–	–	58	–	–
Hungary	–	–	56	–	–
Lithuania	–	–	55	–	–
Malta	–	–	55	–	–
Poland	–	–	52	–	–
Slovenia	–	–	50	–	–
Latvia	–	–	46	–	–
Czech Republic	–	–	44	–	–
Estonia	–	–	38	–	–
All accession and candidate states	–	–	62	–	–

Note: For Spain and Portugal the data for 1981 are from the first *Eurobarometer* poll in these countries in 1986, and for Austria, Finland and Sweden the data for 1991 are from the first poll in these countries in 1995.

Source: *Eurobarometer*, nos 15 (Spring 1981), 25 (Spring 1986), 35 (Spring 1991), 43 (Spring 1995), 60 (Autumn 2003), CEEC2003.4 (Autumn 2003).

Ireland, Denmark and Greece, rising from a very low level of support in the early 1980s to moderate to high levels in 2003. At the other extreme, over the same period support fell most in two of the founding member states: Italy and the Netherlands. Between 1991 and 2003 support declined in all member states but Sweden. While there was only a moderate decline in Austria, Ireland, Denmark and Luxembourg, support fell by more than 20 per cent in Italy, Germany, Portugal, France, the Netherlands and the UK. In 2003 a majority supported EU membership in only nine of the the 15 member states!

So, how can this pattern be explained by the differing national cultural, economic and political factors? Beginning with cultural factors, a key variable is the length of a country's membership of the EU. The citizens of the original member states were neither clearly pro- nor anti-European in the 1950s, but there was a high level of trust between these societies and a sense of community (Inglehart, 1991; Niedermayer, 1995b). These factors allowed the national elites to begin the process of integration. Building on this, the integration process had a socializing effect as the citizens grew used to the idea of integration and were more willing to accept its consequences. This led to a general increase in support for European integration over time (Anderson and Kaltenthaler, 1996; cf. Gabel, 1998b). Consequently the citizens of the states that joined first – Germany, France, Italy, Belgium, the Netherlands and Luxembourg – were on average more in favour of the EU in the 1980s and early 1990s than those which joined later – Ireland, Denmark, the UK (in 1973), Greece (in 1981), Spain and Portugal (in 1987) and Austria, Sweden and Finland (in 1995). However the effect of the length of membership seems to have worn off, as by 2003 the citizens of the states that founded the EU were no less likely to favour EU membership than the citizens of the member states that joined later.

At an aggregate level, the strength of national identity does not seem to be related to support for EU integration. For example France and UK have traditionally had strong national identities. But French nationalism has been reinforced by France's perceived leadership role and the tangible benefits it draws from the EU, while the opposite applies in the UK. Hence attachment to one's country may be positively or negatively related to support for the EU, depending on whether European integration is perceived to strengthen or weaken a country's national identity (Diez Medrano and Gutiérrez, 2001; Schild, 2001) or its national political or policy-making institutions (Martinotti and Stefanizzi, 1995; van Keesbergen, 2000). Nevertheless there is growing evidence that within each state, the stronger an individual's sense of national identity, the more they will perceive that European integration is a threat to their national identity, and the less supportive they will be of European integration as a result (Kaltenthaler and

Anderson, 2001; McLaren, 2002; Carey, 2002; Marks and Hooghe, 2003).

Turning to economic factors, as citizens have learnt more about the EU they have become aware of how much their national economy stands to gain or lose from European integration. One factor is whether a country has gained or lost under the EU budget, for example in terms of the structural funds and the CAP (Bosch and Newton, 1995; Carrubba, 1997; Whitten *et al.*, 1998; see also Chapter 9). Another issue is whether a national economy has gained or lost from trade liberalization through the EU single market (Eichenberg and Dalton, 1993; Gabel and Palmer, 1995; Anderson and Reichert, 1996; see also Chapter 8).

Put together, these economic factors explain much of the variation over time in the level of support for European integration amongst the original member states and the states that joined later (cf. Gabel and Whitten, 1997; Gabel, 1998a). For example, the German and Dutch economies benefit from the single market, but the citizens of Germany and the Netherlands have become increasingly aware that they are the major contributors to the EU budget. Conversely, between the early 1980s and early 1990s the citizens of Greece, Ireland, Portugal, Spain and Italy, whose national economies benefit from EU cohesion policies, increased their support for the EU (of 34 per cent, 31 per cent, 19 per cent, 16 per cent, and 6 per cent, respectively). However, with the prospect of a radical overhaul of the cohesion policies as a result of the 2004 enlargement of the EU, support for the EU has declined substantially in Italy, Spain, Portugal and Greece. There has been a less marked decline in support in Ireland, but this is probably due to the growth of the Irish economy in the 1990s, which many attribute to Ireland's relative attractiveness for business in the single market.

Finally, the political benefits of European integration have affected nation-states differently. For instance the human and physical devastation caused by the Second World War was greater in the founding member states than in those which joined later, so these states had more to gain politically from the peace dividend that was expected to result from economic and political integration in Europe (Gabel, 1998a). Similarly, in states without a long tradition of democratic capitalism, voters who desire this political end tend to be in favour of European integration as a means to promote it. In contrast, voters in states with stable democratic histories have no such incentive. These factors help explain the generally higher levels of support for the EU in Italy, Spain, Portugal and Greece than in the UK, Denmark and Sweden (ibid.) Related to this, concerns about a 'democratic deficit' at the European level have had a larger impact on support for the EU in countries with strong democratic institutions (Rohrschneider, 2002).

Citizens are generally uninformed about the EU: in 1996 only 16 per cent felt they were well-informed about the EU and only 32 per cent were able to answer correctly a series of basic questions about the EU (*Eurobarometer*, no. 44.2bis). This 'information deficit' ensures that citizens' opinions are strongly influenced by their domestic political contexts (see Anderson, 1998; Sánchez-Cuenca, 2000; Bruter, 2004). For example in Denmark the level of support for the EU is determined by the popularity of the government rather than the party a person supports. In other countries the party a person supports, and the position that party takes on European integration, has a strong influence on whether the person supports the EU. For example in the UK, the switch in the positions of the Labour Party and the Conservative Party in the mid 1980s affected the attitudes of the supporters of these parties, with Labour voters becoming more pro-European than Conservative voters for the first time (Carey, 2002a).

But in states where there have been vigorous public debates on membership of the EU, usually in connection with referendums on EMU or treaty reforms (as in Denmark, Sweden and Ireland), or where Europe has been a key issue in a national election (as in Austria), people are more informed about the EU. The active domestic debates on Europe may explain why these are the only four states in which support for EU membership declined by less than 5 per cent between 1991 and 2003. Across the EU, where support for the EU has generally declined, political context may become less important as citizens become more questioning of the generally pro-European views of their governmental or party leaders.

Other political factors specific to particular member states also seem to matter. In France and Germany, growing unease about the liberal direction of the EU's regulatory policies may have contributed to declining public support for the EU since the early 1990s (Brinegar *et al.*, 2002). Related to this, as the EU has expanded to 25 states, and as other member states (such as Italy, Spain, Poland and the Netherlands) have demanded more influence in Brussels, there is growing awareness in Germany and France that the interests of the traditional Franco-German axis no longer dominate the EU.

But what about the UK, whose citizens seem to be outliers on many issues related to Europe, with the lowest levels of support for EU membership, the largest decline in support over the last decade and the lowest level of knowledge about the EU? The UK joined the EU comparatively late, but so did many other states with higher levels of support for the EU. The UK has a long tradition of democracy and stable domestic government, but so too do Denmark, Sweden and the Netherlands. The UK does not gain as much as some states from the EU budget, but it does not pay out as much (as a percentage of GDP) as the Netherlands, Germany and Sweden. Also, since the mid 1980s the UK has won most of the economic policy debates in Brussels against France and Germany. There are several factors however that stand the UK apart from the rest of Europe: Britain's traditional cultural attachment to the English-speaking world, several vehemently anti-European newspapers (owned by openly Europhobic proprietors), and the combative style of Westminster politics, which seems to force party leaders to pander to deep-seated prejudices about the cultural and economic superiority of the UK compared with countries on the continent.

All the factors discussed above also help explain variations in support for the EU within and between the states that joined the EU in 2004 and the potential future candidate states. In cultural terms, the Czech Republic, Slovakia, Slovenia, Hungary and Poland may seem more part of the Western/Central-European cultural mainstream than the Baltic states and those in South-Eastern Europe (Romania, Bulgaria, Turkey, Cyprus). However these cultural factors may work in the opposite direction, with citizens of the states on the North-Eastern and South-Eastern European peripheries being more eager to be part of the European integration project than citizens in the traditional heart of Europe (Laitin, 2002). Also, cultural factors are easily outweighed by the economic and political impact of European integration in these states, and the nature of domestic political and economic contexts. For example in postcommunist states, citizens who support the free market, and consequently are 'winners' of the economic transition process, tend to be far more supportive of European integration than those who fear further economic transformations (Cichowski, 2000; Szczerbiak, 2001; Tucker *et al.*, 2002). Also, because of the poor availability of information about the EU in many of these states, the positions adopted by governmental and party leaders, and the extent to which these leaders are trusted by their citizens, tend to be stronger predictors of support for EU membership than individual socio-economic characteristics (Kucia, 1999; Cichowski, 2000; Ehin, 2001). This consequently enabled pro-European party and political elites to win over sceptical citizens in referendums in Poland, Latvia, Estonia and Slovakia.

Transnational conflicts: class interests

The process of economic integration in Europe affects individual citizens differently (Eichengreen and Frieden, 2001). In *Interests and Integration* (1998a) Matthew Gabel presents a theoretical framework for understanding how this works (cf. Anderson and Reichert, 1996; Gabel, 1998d).

First, the introduction of free movement of goods in the single market has presented opportunities for citizens connected with export-oriented manufacturing and service industries in the private sector.

Entrepreneurs, business owners and company directors can now market their products elsewhere in the EU, and reap economies of scale from a higher turnover. But trade liberalization has brought new competition for sectors that are either non-tradeable (such as the public sector), or cater to national markets (for example small businesses in the retail sector) or compete with imported goods (such as local manufacturers). Moreover, the EU's competition and state aid policies have presented new challenges to jobs in industries that rely on government subsidies or protectionist trade policies (cf. Frieden, 1991; Smith and Wanke, 1993).

Second, the free movement of capital and the single currency have created new investment opportunities for citizens with capital; in other words, with high personal incomes. Capital liberalization has also led to cross-border competition for investment: skilled workers attract investment by offering advanced skills, while manual workers attract investment by offering lower wages. Consequently, capital liberalization has increased the opportunity of low-wage manual workers to attract investment, but threatened manual workers in high-wage regions who might become victims of capital flight. Also, the fiscal policy rules of EMU force governments to restrict their public expenditure, thus threatening welfare programmes that support low-income citizens and the unemployed (see Chapter 10).

Third, the free movement of services and persons has increased competition for jobs in all sectors of the economy. Citizens with considerable human capital, such as a high level of education and employment in professional or management positions, are likely to see this as a chance to improve their status. Low-skilled manual workers, on the other hand, are likely to see it as threatening their jobs.

Fourth, the Common Agricultural Policy (CAP) is the only clearly distributive EU policy (see Chapter 9). The benefits of the CAP subsidies are concentrated on one specific economic group (farmers), whereas the costs are spread amongst EU taxpayers and consumers. However some farmers benefit from the CAP more than others. In general farmers with high incomes are likely to perceive that the CAP helps them to secure markets for their products and subsidizes their production, whereas farmers with low incomes are likely to perceive that the CAP does not benefit them.

This theoretical framework goes some way towards explaining the structure of socioeconomic attitudes towards European integration. Table 5.2 presents descriptive data on class support for the EU for broadly the same time periods as those used in our analysis of national support. The data show that individuals in higher occupational categories are much more favourable towards European integration than those in lower categories. Professionals (such as doctors, lawyers, accountants, architects and university professors!), with highly mobile

Table 5.2   *Social class and European integration*

	Percentage who thought their country's membership of the EC/EU was (would be) a good thing			Percentage change	
	1981	1991	1999	1981–99	1991–99
Employer/director/senior manager	71	88	73	2	–14
Professional	62	86	69	7	–17
White-collar employee	55	79	61	6	–19
Manual worker	41	64	44	3	–20
Farmer	56	72	50	–5	–21
Houseperson	47	71	51	4	–21
Small business owner	54	78	56	2	–22
Student	57	82	59	2	–23
Skilled worker	41	73	46	5	–26
Retired	47	71	45	–3	–26
Unemployed	44	69	41	–3	–28

Note: The 1981 survey made a distinction between unskilled and skilled workers, so the scores reported in the table in 1981 for these two social groups are the scores for all manual workers in that year.

Source: Eurobarometer, nos 15 (Spring 1981), 35 (Spring 1991), 51 (Spring 1999).

skills in the single market are most supportive of integration, as are company directors and senior managers with new profit opportunities. Support by these groups for integration underwent the smallest decline between 1991 and 1999.

White-collar employees (over 15 per cent of EU voters) are generally less supportive, but are more in favour than small business owners, who are predominantly in non-tradeable sectors. Farmers, surprisingly, are relatively sceptical. Farmers were relatively pro-European in the 1980s compared with some other social classes, but their support declined markedly after 1991, perhaps reflecting their concern about the ongoing reform of the CAP. Skilled workers (over 20 per cent of EU voters) are slightly more favourably disposed towards European integration than are manual workers, but their support for EU membership declined faster un 1991–99 than that of manual workers.

Of the social groups that are not active in the labour market, students are relatively supportive of integration, while the retired, unemployed and housepersons are relatively sceptical. In addition to students' immediate opportunity for subsidized education elsewhere in the EU, through such programmes as Erasmus and Socrates, in the future they are likely to enter the professions or take up senior management positions, and hence their attitudes are similar to those held by these groups. At the other end of the social spectrum, the unemployed are the least supportive of European integration; they may have lost their jobs as a result of competitive pressures in the single market or government cut-backs to meet the convergence criteria for EMU.

To test the framework further we need to discover whether varying levels of economic resources, human capital and comparative advantage alter the degree of support for the EU within these social groups. A good indicator of these variables is the level of an individual's income, where a higher income suggests:

- for employers/directors: more capital to invest.
- for professionals and skilled workers: more marketable skills in the single market.
- for white-collar employees: a greater likelihood of employment in the private rather than the public sector.
- for farmers: greater benefits from the CAP.
- for manual workers: better wage protection as a result of trade union organization and collective bargaining or minimum wage and other social legislation, but a comparative disadvantage in the competition to attract cross-border investment.

We should expect that as incomes rise within a social group, support for the EU will rise in all social groups except manual workers.

Based on data from the so-called 'mega-barometer' survey in 1996, in which more than 65000 people were interviewed (*Eurobarometer*, no. 44.2 bis), Figure 5.2 shows the impact of income on support for EU membership amongst the major social groups (these are linear regression lines). As incomes rise, support for the EU amongst professionals, employers/directors, white-collar employees, skilled workers and farmers also rises. with farmers showing the fastest rate of increase. This trend is clearly reversed for manual workers, where higher incomes reflect higher levels of wage protection rather than skills, which are threatened in the single market by the ability of firms to transfer production to less-protected and lower-wage manual workforces.

Overall, therefore, it can be said that transnational social class positions shape attitudes towards European integration. This suggests that there are incentives for individuals from the same social class in different member states to mobilize to promote their interests in the EU policy process, and consciously compete with national interests in the Council. For example organizations representing the professions, groups representing directors of large companies, and farmers' lobbies all have an incentive to protect the gains they have made from the single market (see Chapter 7). However, the working class is divided:

Figure 5.2 *Influence of class and income on support for the EU*

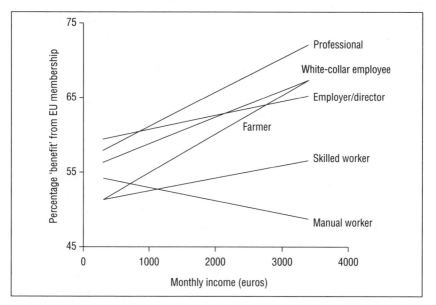

Note: The question read as follows: Taking everything into consideration, would you say that (your country) has on balance benefited from being a member of the European Union? Response: 'benefited', 'don't know', 'not benefited'. The graph shows the percentage of respondents who felt they had benefited .

Sources: Eurobarometer, no. 44.2bis (Autumn 1996); idea from Gabel (1998a).

whereas skilled workers and low-wage manual workers benefit from economic integration, high-wage (well-organized) manual workers are threatened by economic integration.

Other transnational divisions: age, education, gender, religion, and elite versus mass

Since the 1960s class has declined as an indicator of general political attitudes. For example 'class voting', whereby working classes vote for socialist parties and middle classes vote for liberal, Christian or conservative parties, has declined throughout Europe (Dalton, 1988; Franklin, 1992). Class identity has also eroded as different patterns of production, consumption, and educational life experiences have produced cross-cutting socioeconomic attitudes, interests and values (Dahrendorf, 1959; Bell, 1960; Giddens, 1973; Dunleavy, 1979). As a result, Ronald Inglehart (1977a) argued that a 'silent revolution' had taken place as a result of economic prosperity and peace: class-based materialist values of economic and political security were being replaced through generational-change by postmaterialist values, such as environmentalism, women's and minorities' rights, democratic participation and nuclear disarmament. At the same time two other divisions have emerged: a religious divide, and a gap between the elites and the masses.

Applying his theory of postmaterialism to the issue of European integration, Inglehart (1977b, p. 151) argued that:

> we would expect post-materialists to have a significantly less parochial and more cosmopolitan outlook than materialists. ... First, the post-materialists are less pre-occupied with immediate concrete needs than are materialists; other things being equal they should have more psychic energy to invest in relatively remote abstractions such as the European Community. Moreover ... the relative priority accorded to national security has fallen ... [hence] one of the key symbols of nationalism has lost much of its potency – especially among post-materialists.

Because younger age cohorts are more postmaterialist, Inglehart proposed that support for European integration should be stronger in younger groups (Inglehart, 1970b; 1977b; see also Wessels, 1995a). Inglehart also developed several other hypotheses about non-class-based attitudes towards Europe. For example he argued that individuals with greater cognitive skills are more able to understand the abstract process of European integration (Inglehart, 1970a; Inglehart and Rabier, 1978; Janssen, 1991), which suggests that individuals with higher levels of education are more likely to support European integration, as are individuals who are well-informed about the EU. These arguments are not self-evident, as one could argue the opposite: that greater understanding of and information about the EU will lead to greater awareness of its failings and limitations, such as its lack of democratic accountability, the secrecy of decision-making and corruption in the EU budget.

Gender is another transnational social division that might affect support for the EU. More women than men tend to be employed in low-paid jobs, public sector jobs, and part-time and temporary positions. Consequently women are disproportionately affected by downturns in the economy, and by job losses that result from the privatization of public utilities or cuts in the public sector and welfare state. Hence if the EU single market forces domestic states to liberalize their economies, and member states are forced to rein in public spending as a result of EMU, then women are likely to be less favourably disposed towards the EU than are men (Liebert, 2000; Nelson and Guth, 2000).

With regard to religion, Nelson and Guth (2003, p. 151) note that:

The very idea of a united Europe reaches back to early medieval conceptions of Christendom united under the spiritual and temporal authority of the Roman pontiff. Moreover, integration in the post-war period was largely a Christian Democratic project led by Catholic politicians – such as Konrad Adenauer, Robert Schuman and Alcide de Gaspari – who enjoyed unwavering support from the church hierarchy. On the other side of the Reformation divide, Protestant politicians in Britain and Scandinavia feared joining a European project dominated by 'wine-drinking Catholics'.

And what about the other major religions in Europe: the Orthodox Christianity, Islam and Judaism? In contrast to the 'national' churches of the Protestant faith, like Catholicism, these other faiths are based on transnational religious organizations and identities, and might even be considered to be anti-nationalist in their ideologies.

Table 5.3 contains data on variations in public support for EU membership based on these non-class transnational divisions. As Inglehart predicted, age seems to be negatively related to support for the EU: the older a person is, the less likely she is to support the EU. However the variation in support for the EU between the age groups below 65 is not large, and each age group underwent a similar decline in support between 1991 and 1999. Differing levels of education seem to have a much larger effect, with the more highly educated being significantly more in favour of the EU than people with lower levels of education, and the gap between these groups increased between 1991 and 1998.

In the 1970s Inglehart (1977b) concluded that his theory bode well for European integration, as successive generational changes and higher levels of education would lead to greater support for European integration. However the opposite has happened. Age does have a small influence on support for the EU, but this is not related to generational change. The data in Table 5.3 suggest that while younger people tend to support the EU, as they get older they become more critical.

The data confirm the suggestion that women are less pro-European than men. The attitudinal gap between men and women increased between 1991 and 1999 to more than 10 percentage points. Moreover this ten-point spread was either side of the divide, with a majority of men in favour of their country's membership of the EU and a majority of women opposed. This perhaps helps explains why the EU is not a topic of discussion at family dinner tables across Europe!

The data suggest that religion has a stronger influence on support for the EU than age or education (see also Nelson *et al.*, 2001): there are much larger variations across religious groups in terms of both the level of support for the EU and the extent of decline in support for the EU. Catholics are considerably more pro-European than Protestants, as are Orthodox Christians, Muslims and Jews. Atheists and agnostics are

Table 5.3   *Other transnational social divisions and European integration*

| | Percentage who thought their country's membership of the EC/EU was (would be) a good thing | | | Percentage change | |
	1981	1991	1999	1981 to 1998–99	1991 to 1998–99
Age					
15–24	51	77	55	4	–22
25–34	52	76	53	1	–23
35–44	52	76	52	0	–24
45–54	51	74	53	2	–21
55–64	49	72	50	1	–22
65+	44	69	44	0	–25
Education					
Up to age 15	43	68	46	3	–22
16–19	52	74	54	2	–20
20+	66	81	66	0	–16
Still studying	59	82	63	4	–20
Religion					
Catholic	60	77	60	0	–17
Protestant	48	68	49	1	–19
Orthodox	39	77	67	28	–10
Muslim	–	86	55	–	–31
Jewish	–	99	65	–	–34
No religious affiliation	49	74	51	2	–23
Gender					
Female	47	71	47	0	–24
Male	52	78	56	4	–22

Note: The number of Jewish and Muslim respondents was small: 13 and 18 in 1991, and 13 and 30 in 1998, respectively.

Source: *Eurobarometer*, nos 15 (Spring 1987), 16 (Autumn 1981), 35 (Spring 1991), 50 (Autumn 1998), 51 (Spring 1999).

more critical of the EU than all citizens who declare a religious affiliation, except Protestants. Nelson and Guth (2003) also find that the degree of devoutness of a person – for example as measured by how frequently the person attends a religious service – affects support for the EU in opposite ways for different faiths. More devout Catholics and Orthodox Christians are more pro-European than less devout Catholics, while more devout Protestants are less pro-European than less devout Protestants. But, Europe is an increasingly atheist or agnostic continent (compared with the US for example), and because

Table 5.4   *Comparison of elite and mass support for European integration*

	Membership (percentage in favour)		EMU (percentage in favour)		Average Elite–Mass Difference
	Elite	Mass	Elite	Mass	
Germany	98	39	90	39	55
Austria	86	31	78	35	49
Belgium	96	45	98	55	47
Sweden	84	27	65	32	45
Finland	88	39	68	29	44
Denmark	84	44	76	33	42
France	93	46	90	56	41
United Kingdom	86	36	60	31	40
Spain	97	51	95	65	38
Greece	92	57	92	63	32
Portugal	91	54	77	57	29
Luxembourg	93	73	93	66	24
Ireland	95	76	89	64	22
Netherlands	96	74	91	69	22
Italy	97	68	88	73	22
EU15	94	48	85	51	40
Range	14	49	38	44	–
Standard deviation	4.8	15.4	11.4	15.5	–

Notes: The question on EMU read as follows: Are you for or against the European Union having one European currency in all member states, including [your country]? That is, replacing the [name of national currency] by the European currency, the euro? Responses: 'very much for', 'somewhat for', 'somewhat against', 'very much against'. the table shows the percentage of 'very much for' and 'somewhat for' responses.

Sources: *Eurobarometer*, no. 46 (Autumn 1996); *Top Decision-Makers Survey* (Spring 1996).

less devout people and people of no religious faith are less likely to support the EU, declining religiosity may be one factor behind declining support for the EU, at least in the Catholic parts of Europe.

Finally, Europe's elites are more pro-European than are European citizens (cf. Slater, 1982; Katz, 2001). In February–May 1996, the Commission undertook the first survey of elite attitudes towards European integration – the so-called Top Decision-Makers Survey. In every member state, interviews were conducted with 200–500 senior elected politicians, senior civil servants, business and trade union leaders, leading media owners and editors, influential academics, and leading cultural and religious figures. Some of the results of this survey are presented in Table 5.4, and compared with the attitudes revealed in the *Eurobarometer* survey of the general population in October–November 1996.

The data reveal three things. First, in all member states elites are more in favour of European integration than is the public as a whole. For example 94 per cent of all elites see EU membership as a good thing, compared with only 48 per cent of the general public. Second, there is considerable variation in the elite–public gap in different member states. The gap is much larger in Germany, Austria, Belgium and Sweden than in Portugal, Luxembourg, Ireland, the Netherlands and Italy. Third, there is a higher degree of cohesion amongst elites from different nations than amongst the public – as indicated by the lower ranges and standard deviations for the elite scores. For example in all member states, a majority of the national elite supports the single currency.

The gap between elite and mass attitudes towards the EU explains why referendums on European integration have not always gone as the governmental and party elites have expected (see Chapter 6). It also explains why mass-based anti-European protest movements have emerged, with demonstrations being held on an almost weekly basis outside one or other of the EU institutions in Brussels, by citizens who feel that their domestic political leaders are not properly representing their views at the European level (Tarrow, 1995; Marks and McAdam, 1996; Imig and Tarrow, 2001; Imig, 2002).

Overall, national identities, class divisions and other transnational social and political divisions produce a complex mix of responses to the question of 'Europe right or wrong?' Typically, the most pro-European individual is an Irish, Italian or Benelux male who is a professional or a company director, younger than 55, highly educated, a practising Catholic and a member of the political or cultural elite. As the EU has become increasingly politicized, with winners and losers emerging as a result of EU policies, a pro- and anti-European cleavage has become manifest in EU politics. This cleavage produces national or transnational alliances on either side of the debate.

What the EU Should Do: Europe Right or Left?

The issue of more or less European integration, in terms of how far and fast the EU political system should be built, does not capture conflicts of interest and ideology over what the EU should do once it is set up. This question is associated with a more traditional dimension of politics, relating to the extent to which public institutions should constrain individual social, political and economic choices for the greater public good. At the domestic level these issues are collapsed into a single dimension of politics, the ubiquitous 'left–right', and when they are tackled by the EU, actors take up positions based on their location on the left–right spectrum.

The demise of the left–right as the main dimension of politics has been predicted since the 1950s (Bell, 1960; Giddens, 1994). However left and right have remained the dominant categories for political differentiation, voter orientation and party competition throughout Europe (Bartolini and Mair, 1990; Franklin *et al.*, 1992; Laver and Budge, 1992). On the cognitive level, the left–right enables individuals to differentiate themselves from each other in both a categorical (dichotomous) and a relative (continuous) sense. As a result, left and right are flexible concepts that have adapted over time as new issues have been put on the political agenda. For example in the early eighteenth century, left and right represented differences over the degree of individual political and social freedom from state power, with the left supporting liberty and the right supporting state authority. But with the coming of industrial society, left and right came to represent different degrees of individual economic freedom from state power, with the left supporting state intervention and the right supporting the free market.

Following the social changes that had occurred since the 1960s, the left–right dimension captures two sets of issues: liberty–authority issues, such as environmentalism and the demand for greater democratic accountability; and intervention–free market issues, such as welfare policies, unemployment and inflation (cf. Lijphart, 1981; Flanagan, 1987; Laver and Hunt, 1992). The left tends to favour equality of outcomes: intervention to promote equitable outcomes in the market, but liberty to promote social and political equality before the law. The right, on the other hand, tends to favour equality of opportunities but not outcomes, thus allowing the inequalities inherent in the free market and the privileges of authority and tradition to be protected (Bobbio, 1996). This does not preclude intermediate positions: intervention–authority (the traditional stance of Christian democrats), and *laissez-faire*–liberty (such as liberals). However these positions are less common in the 1990s than those of the oft-observed 'left-libertarians' (such as greens and social democrats) and 'right-authoritarians' (such as conservatives and contemporary Christian democrats) (cf. Finer, 1987; Dunleavy and O'Leary, 1987; Kitschelt, 1994, 1995).

In EU politics, therefore, we should expect individuals on the left to favour allocating policy competences to the EU level to tackle:

- *Economic 'intervention'*, such as an EU social policy, tax system, and unemployment policy, EU aid for poorer regions, and EU aid for the Third World; and
- *Sociopolitical 'liberties'*, such as an EU environmental policy, more

democratic accountability, citizenship rights, human rights, consumer rights, and sexual equality.

Conversely we should expect individuals on the right to favour allocating competences to the EU to:

- *Establish an economic free market,* such as the single market,
  deregulatory policies, and a single currency; and
- *Sociopolitical 'authority',* such as EU policies on drug trafficking,
  organized crime, immigration and asylum, and security and
  defence.

Table 5.5 shows what policies citizens at various locations on the
left–right axis thought should be allocated to the European level at two
different points in time: 1991 and 1999 (cf. Sinnott, 1995; De Winter
and Swyngedouw, 1999). The data reveal that the left and right had
different attitudes towards the range of policy competences that should
be held by the EU, and that these changed over time (Gabel and
Anderson, 2002). Those on the left were generally more in favour than
those on the right of allocating policy competences to the EU in all
policy areas. However as the ranges and standard deviations in the
rows reveal, in 1999 there was more disagreement across the political
spectrum on EU environment policy, immigration policy and security
and defence policy than on currency policy, employment policy and
health and welfare policy.

There was also considerable change in the structure of left–right attitudes towards EU competences over time. First, between 1991 and
1999 there was a considerable decline in support for EU competences
across the political spectrum for all policy areas except allocating currency powers to the EU. This was not surprising given the launch of
EMU in 1999, and is consistent with the logic of the political-economy
of federalism, which claims that there is a high level of preference
homogeneity across the political spectrum on currency policy and clear
negative externalities of separate monetary policies in a single market
(see Chapter 1).

Second, there were greater differences of opinion between the left
and right in most policy areas in 1999 than in 1991, including currency policy. For example in 1991 only 3 per cent more people on the
centre-left than people on the centre-right supported environmental
policy being handled at the European level. In 1999, the difference was
6 per cent. Interestingly, whereas those on the centre-right were more
in favour than those on the centre-left of an EU security and defence
policy in 1991, this was reversed in 1999.

In conclusion, irrespective of their pro- and anti-EU positions, EU
citizens are divided over what the EU should do. As we discussed in the

Table 5.5   *Left–right location and support for EU policy competences*

	Far Left	Centre Left	Centre	Centre Right	Far Right	Range	Std Dev.
1999							
Currency	62	66	64	65	58	8	2.9
Environment	56	60	56	54	49	11	3.9
Immigration	56	54	52	49	46	10	3.9
Fight unemployment	50	50	49	46	44	7	2.8
Security and defence	43	45	42	40	37	11	4.1
Health and welfare	29	28	28	24	26	5	2.3
Standard deviation	11.9	13.1	12.3	13.9	11.4		
Mean	49	51	49	46	43		
Range	33	38	36	41	32		
1991							
Currency	64	64	62	62	60	4	1.9
Environment	72	76	73	73	66	10	3.6
Immigration	58	60	58	52	50	10	4.6
Fight unemployment	48	50	50	46	44	6	2.8
Security and defence	52	51	53	53	48	5	2.2
Health and welfare	45	41	41	38	37	8	3.0
Standard deviation	10.3	12.3	11.0	12.2	10.6		
Mean	57	57	56	54	51		
Range	27	35	32	35	29		

Notes: Policy Competence Allocation. The question asked was: some people believed that certain areas of policy should be decided by the national governments, and that others should be decided jointly within the EU. Which of the following areas of policy do you think should be decided by the national government, and which should be decided jointly within the EU. The table shows the percentage 'jointly within the EU' responses for each policy area. With regard to Left–Right Self-Placement the question was: In political matters people talk of 'the left' and 'the right'. How would you place your views on a scale of 1–10? [1 Left, 10 Right]. The responses were then categorized as follows: 1 + 2 = left, 3 + 4 = centre left, 5 + 6 = centre, 7 + 8 = centre right, 9 + 10 = right.

Source: Eurobarometer, nos 35 (Spring 1991), 37 (Spring 1992) 51 (Spring 1999).

previous section, social groups with shared interests might join forces to lobby for an EU competence in a particular area: for example highly paid white-collar employees and highly skilled workers are likely to ally with employers/directors and professionals to promote economic integration. But once this has occurred, this pro-European alliance will divide into left and right positions, with the left supporting social and environmental regulation of the single market and the right supporting deregulatory policies (cf. Rhodes and van Apeldoorn, 1997; Hooghe and Marks, 1998; Hix, 1999; see also Chapter 8).

The Electoral Connection: Putting the Two Dimensions Together

With the collapse of the 'permissive consensus' in favour of European integration, Europe's political leaders must compete for public support within the new two-dimensional space of EU politics. Figure 5.3 shows the approximate location of the electorate in the EU issue space, where the centres of the circles mark the mean positions of the occupational groups in response to two questions in a *Eurobarometer* survey in 1999: (1) where they place themselves on the left–right dimension, and (2) whether they support their country's membership of the EU. The positions of the occupational groups illustrate that the EU political market is fragmented: intra-class alliances such as manual workers with skilled workers, white-collar workers with professionals, and employers with small business owners, may hold together on left–right issues (such as the degree of social regulation of the single market), but if the pro-/anti-EU dimension is salient such alliances are likely to break down.

This presents problems for political parties (see Chapter 6). For example, as the traditional constituency of social democratic parties (manual and skilled workers) has declined, these parties have built alliances with groups that are close to them on the left-right dimension (such as white-collar employees, students and members of the liberal professions) (Kitschelt, 1994). However, because of the differing attitudes of these groups towards European integration, the cross-class alliance cannot hold together on the pro-/anti-Europe dimension. On the other side, conservative parties and Christian democrats have traditionally attracted the support of farmers, employers, professionals and small businessmen, who are logically adjacent on the left–right dimension but far apart on the question of whether there should be more or less government by Europe.

As a result parties are forced to pursue one of two strategies to ensure that there is no party competition on this dimension of EU politics (Hix, 1999):

- *Parties* can refuse to differentiate themselves from each other on this dimension by taking up identical (usually moderately pro-Europe) positions.
- *Parties* can play down the differences between them on this dimension by refusing to address the question of European integration in domestic electoral contests.

Figure 5.3 *Location of classes in the two-dimensional EU political space*

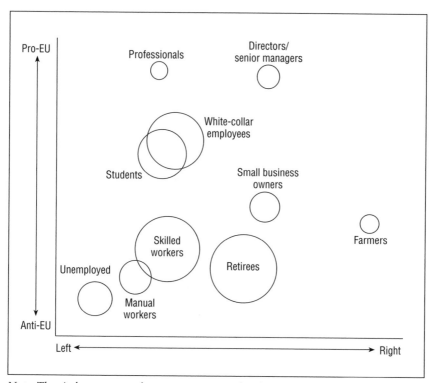

Note: The circles represent the mean responses of each occupational group to the EU membership and Left–Right questions and the size of each occupational group as a proportion of the total EU population.

Source: *Eurobarometer*, no. 51 (Spring 1999).

Either strategy reduces the saliency of the pro-/anti-Europe cleavage.

Figure 5.4 illustrates the relationship between the left–right and pro-/anti-European dimensions in each member state. It appears that three patterns of political competition in the EU issue space have emerged. First, the centre left and centre right are pro-European, whereas the far left and far right are anti-European. In these systems, parties on the moderate left and right can pursue the first strategy to minimize inter-party competition: that is converge on the question of Europe and allow extremist movements to advocate anti-European positions. This is the traditional model of political competition over European integration (Hix and Lord, 1997; Taggart, 1998; Aspinwall, 2002). However, only five states now fit clearly into this category: Ireland, the Netherlands, Portugal, Austria and Denmark.

Figure 5.4   *Three models of political competition in the EU*

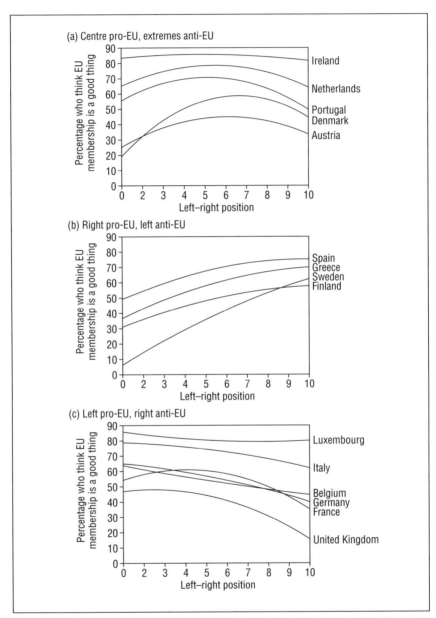

Note: The graphs are quadratic regression models, where the independent variable is the position of citizens on the left–right placement question and the dependent variable is the percentage of citizens at each point on the left–right spectrum who think that their country's membership of the EU is a good thing.

Source: Calculated from data in *Eurobarometer*, no. 51 (Spring 1999)

Second, in Spain, Greece, Sweden and Finland the right is more pro-European than the left. In Scandinavia, for example, European integration is seen as a threat to the national welfare states. Third, in Luxembourg, Italy, Belgium, Germany, France and the UK, the left is more pro-European than the right. For example in Italy and the UK, European integration is seen as a progressive force in domestic affairs, and in Germany and France it is viewed as a cosmopolitan, social-democratic project.

In the second and third models the question of Europe has the potential of becoming a cleavage in the domestic party system. Here party leaders face a dilemma between pressure for inter-party competition on the question of Europe and the difficulty of building a cross-class alliance that could sustain a coherent pro- or anti-European stance. In this situation the second strategy is likely to be adopted: to play down the significance of Europe in domestic party competition. The result, however, would probably be internal party fragmentation between the leaders and rank-and-file members, as has happened in many of the states in these two groups.

Conclusion: the EU as a Plural Society

> Social homogeneity and political consensus are regarded as prerequisites for, or factors strongly conducive to, stable democracy ... but it is not impossible to achieve and maintain stable democratic government in a plural society. In a consociational democracy, the centrifugal tendencies inherent in a plural society are counteracted by the co-operative attitudes and behaviour of the leaders of the different segments of the population. (Lijphart, 1977, p. 1)

The EU is a plural society divided between the multiple nation-states of Europe. Until the 1990s, however, the EU was a stable system of governance. This was essentially because of the elite behaviour prescribed in Lijphart's theory: that is, national elites had a shared interest in promoting European integration while preventing the erosion of national interests that provided their own legitimacy (cf. Taylor, 1991; Chryssochoou, 1994). The result was the so-called 'permissive consensus', whereby citizens were content to delegate responsibility to their leaders to tackle the European integration project.

However the permissive consensus has collapsed, resulting in a more complex pattern of social and political interaction. At the societal level, European integration no longer commands widespread support and new transnational socioeconomic and value-based divisions are shaping people's attitudes towards the EU. In different nation-states, people in the same social class share the same interests in the single market, and consequently share the same attitudes towards the EU. Similarly individuals in different nation-states from the same generation or educational group share similar political values that produce similar attitudes towards European integration.

But EU politics is not simply about how far and how fast the process of integration should proceed. For example, should the EU promote the free market or protect the welfare state? Should the EU promote civil rights and freedoms or protect European social and cultural traditions? On these questions the attitudes of EU citizens are determined less by national affiliation than by their position on the traditional left–right dimension of politics.

Consequently, in the post-consensus environment Europe's elites are faced with a dilemma. They can continue the practice of consensus politics, but this risks provoking even more public opposition to the EU. Alternatively they could abandon consensus politics and compete on the question of European integration, between nations: with different national elites taking up different pro- and anti-European positions. However this would result in the breakdown of the EU system. Or, they could compete on issues on the EU agenda in the same way as they do in the domestic arena, with left and right parties advocating different EU policy agendas. However this would provoke a breakdown of existing class–party alliances, as different groups within both the working class and the middle classes have different interests in the single market.

Chapter 6

Democracy, Parties and Elections

This chapter looks at how the two central processes of representative democracy – party competition and elections – operate in the EU. At the domestic level, parties and elections operate hand in hand in the 'competitive democratic government' model. There is also an emerging party system at the European level. European-wide elections are held every five years, and party organizations exist in the EP (the party groups) and between the national party leaders (the transnational party federations). But competitive democracy in the EU remains some way off.

Democracy: Choosing Parties, Leaders and Policies

Elections are the central mechanism of representative democracy and operate in two interlinked ways (King, 1981). First, elections allow voters to choose between rival agendas for public policy. These are presented by political parties or leaders, and the winning 'team' implements its agenda by taking control of the levers of public policy. Second, elections allow voters to choose between rival office holders: voters' choose between rival candidates for public office, as much on their personality as on their policy platform or party affiliation, and the winning candidate becomes the head of the executive branch of government. Elections consequently allow voters to 'throw the scoundrels out' if they flout their electoral promises, prove incompetent or become less popular than a rival group of elites. In other words democracy only really exists if there is a choice between competing policies and politicians, and if there is a reasonable chance of alternation in government (Schumpeter, 1943; Downs, 1957).

In most democratic systems, competition over policies and competition for public office are combined in a single model of 'competitive democratic government' (ibid.; Weber, 1946 [1919]; Schattschneider,

1942). In this model the leader of the party that wins the election becomes the head of the executive (the prime minister), and the party acts cohesively in the legislative arena to implement the policy agenda presented in the electoral manifesto. Meanwhile the losing opposition parties try to demonstrate the failings of the politicians in government. In this model voters exercise an indirect influence on policy outcomes.

Alternative models allow voters to exercise a direct choice over office holders or the policy agenda. First, in the presidential model, voters directly elect the head of the executive. Parties may play an important role selecting presidential candidates and running their campaigns, but presidential elections tend to be dominated by the policies and personality of the individual candidates rather than by the general manifestos of the parties. Also once elected the president is directly accountable to the voters, over the head of his or her political party.

Second, through referendums voters can choose policies directly. Again, parties play a role, advocating one side in a referendum, and the (un)popularity of the parties on each side of the debate (particularly those in government) will affect the way citizens vote in the referendum. Nevertheless, if a referendum outcome is binding, this has a direct impact on public policy in that parties will not be able to amend the policy by subsequent legislation. Thus in contrast to the competitive democratic government model, in the direct model cohesive political parties are not required, or do not interfere in, the translation of voters' choices into executive or legislative action.

So, which model is right for the EU? Following the logic of the competitive democratic government model, in the past most commentators on the EU's democratic deficit argued that (1) the EP should be directly elected and (2) it should be given greater powers in the EU legislative process and the selection of the EU executive (that is, the Commission). As a result, direct elections to the EP were introduced in 1979 and have been held at five-yearly intervals ever since, and in a series of institutional reforms the EP has been given a greater power in the EU legislative process *vis-à-vis* the Council and in the selection of the president of the Commission (see Chapter 3).

At face value, then, the democratic deficit has been overcome. However a genuine system of competitive party democracy cannot come about simply because the right rules are in place. The model also requires actors to behave in a certain way within these rules. In other words:

- Political parties should compete in EP elections over issues on the EU policy agenda and/or for EU political office.
- Voters should make a choice in EP elections on the basis of these rival policy platforms or candidates.
- The winning electoral choices should be translated into legislative

and executive action at the European level via cohesive political parties.

If this pattern of behaviour is absent the democratic deficit remains. Nevertheless, there is room for development within the current design of the EU, and further institutional mechanisms could be introduced to promote genuine competitive party democracy in the EU.

The 'Democratic Deficit' Debate

Articles on the so-called democratic deficit in the EU started to be published in academic journals in the mid to late 1980s. More widespread discussion of this issue in the media soon followed, in response to the collapse in support for the EU in the early 1990s (see Chapter 5). There is no single definition of the democratic-deficit in the EU. However Weiler *et al.* (1995) describe a 'standard version' of the democratic deficit, which is a set of widely-used arguments by academics, practitioners, media commentators and ordinary citizens. Adding some elements to Weiler's original definition, the current 'standard version' of the democratic-deficit involves five main claims (cf. Siedentop, 2000):

- *Increased executive power/decreased national parliamentary control.* EU decisions are made primarily by executive actors: the Commission and national ministers in the Council. This has meant a reduction of the power of national parliaments, as governments can ignore their parliaments when making decisions in Brussels or can be out-voted in the Council (where qualified-majority voting is used) (Andersen and Burns, 1996; Raunio, 1999).
- *The European Parliament is too weak.* Increases in the powers of the EP have not sufficiently compensated for the loss of national parliamentary control, since the Council still dominates the EP in the passing of legislation and adoption of the budget, and citizens are not as well connected to their MEPs as to their national parliamentarians (Williams, 1991; Lodge, 1994).
- *No 'European' elections.* Citizens are not able to vote on EU policies, except in periodic referendums on EU membership or treaty reforms. National elections are fought on domestic rather than European issues, and parties collude to keep the issue of Europe off the domestic agenda (Hix, 1999; Marks *et al.*, 2002). EP elections are also not about Europe either, as parties and the media treat them as mid-term national contests (Franklin *et al.*, 1996).
- *The EU is too distant.* Citizens cannot understand the EU. The Commission is neither a government nor a bureaucracy, and is

appointed through an obscure procedure rather than elected by the people or a parliament (cf. Magnette, 2001). The Council is the only legislature in the democratic world that makes decisions in secret. The EP is impenetrable because of the multilingual nature of the debates. And the policy process is technocratic rather than political (Wallace and Smith, 1995).

- *Policy drift.* As a result of all these factors, the EU adopts policies that are not supported by a majority of citizens in many (or even most) member states, such as a neoliberal regulatory framework for the single market, a monetarist framework for EMU and massive subsidies to farmers through the Common Agricultural Policy (Streeck and Schmitter, 1991; Scharpf, 1997a, 1999).

However these arguments are not universally accepted. In particular Giandomenico Majone and Andrew Moravcsik – two of the biggest names in the study of the EU – vehemently criticize these claims.

Majone argues that the EU is essentially a 'regulatory state' and therefore does not engage in redistributive or value-allocative policies (Majone, 1996, 1998a, 2000, 2002b, 2002c; see also Chapter 8). Because regulatory policies are pareto-efficient rather than redistributive (in other words, everyone benefits), EU policy-making should be isolated from the standard processes of majoritarian democratic politics, in the same way that courts should be independent of legislatures and executives, and central banks should be independent from the 'political business cycle'. From Majone's perspective, the problem for the EU is less a democratic deficit than a 'credibility crisis' or a 'legitimacy deficit'. The solution, he believes, is procedural rather than fundamental. What the EU needs is more transparent decision-making, *ex post* review by courts and ombudsmen, greater professionalism and technical expertise, rules that protect the rights of minority interests, and better scrutiny by private actors, the media and parliamentarians at both the EU and national levels. In this view an EU dominated by the EP or a directly elected Commission would politicize regulatory policy-making. Politicization would result in redistributive rather than pareto-efficient outcomes, and therefore undermine rather than increase the legitimacy of the EU (cf. Dehousse, 1995).

Moravcsik (2002a, 2003) goes even further and presents an extensive critique of all the main democratic-deficit claims. Against the argument that power has been centralized in the executive, Moravcsik points out that national governments are the most directly accountable politicians in Europe. Against the critique that the executives are beyond the control of representative institutions, he points out that the most significant institutional development in the EU in the past two decades has been the increased powers of the EP in the legislative process and in the selection of the Commission. Moravcsik also argues that EU policy-making is more transparent than most domestic policy-making, that the EU technocrats are forced to listen to numerous societal interests, that there is extensive judicial review of EU actions by both the European Court of Justice and national courts, and that the EP and national parliaments have increasing powers of scrutiny that they are not afraid to use (as illustrated by the EP's censure of the Santer Commission in May 1999). Finally, against the so-called 'social democratic critique' that EU policies are systematically biased against the median-voter, Moravcsik argues that the EU's elaborate system of checks and balances ensures that an overwhelming consensus is required for any policy to be agreed. As a result, free-market liberals are just as unhappy as social democrats with the centrist EU policy regime.

These arguments are logical extensions of Moravcsik's liberal-intergovernmental theory (see Chapter 1). Basically, because the member state governments run the EU and the Commission is simply an agent of these governments, there are no unintended consequences of intergovernmental bargains. Hence there is no gap between the preferences of the elected governments and final EU policy outcomes, and therefore the EU is not undemocratic.

In some respects, Majone and Moravcsik echo the critics of mass democracy in the nineteenth and early part of the twentieth centuries, who praised the virtues of 'enlightened' bureaucracy or despotism. For Majone, the technocrats in the Commission, the Council working groups and the EU agencies are more likely to protect citizens' interests than the majority in the EP or a hypothetical majority in an election of the president of the Commission. Similarly Moravcsik believes that there is no need for full electoral democracy if the design of the EU already guarantees that any policies that are passed are in the interests of the overwhelming majority of EU citizens.

But there are at least three reasons why democracy, in terms of competitive elections to choose policies and leaders, is better than enlightened technocracy. First, in both majoritarian or more consensual models of democracy, competitive elections guarantee that policies and elected officials respond to the preferences of citizens (Powell, 2000). Electoral contests provide incentives for elites to develop rival policy ideas and propose rival candidates for political office. They also allow citizens to punish politicians who fail to keep their electoral promises or are dishonest or corrupt (Fearon, 1999). Where the EU is concerned, policies might be in the interests of citizens when they are first agreed, but without electoral competition there are few incentives for the Commission or the member state governments to change these policies in response to changes in citizens' preferences.

Second, political competition is an essential vehicle for fostering political debate, which in turn promotes the formation of public opinion on different policy options. Without the policy debate that is an inherent by-product of electoral competition, voters would not be able to form their preferences on complex policy issues. An example of this in the EU is the debate on structural reform of the European economy. The EU has the legal instruments and powers to undertake fundamental reforms, but without a public debate citizens cannot form opinions about the options, and the EU institutions do not have the incentive or a legitimate mandate to undertake such reforms.

Third, elections have a powerful formative effect, promoting the gradual evolution of political identities. For example in the evolution of the American and European democracies, the replacement of local identities by national identities occurred through the process and operation of mass elections and party competition (Key, 1961; Rokkan, 1999). In the EU, rather than assuming that a European 'demos' is a prerequisite for genuine democracy, a European democratic identity can only be formed through the practice of democratic competition, whereby citizens accept being on the losing side in one particular contest in the expectation that they will be on the winning side in the not too distant future (Habermas, 1995).

In other words, even if one accepts most of the arguments of Majone and Moravcsik – for example about the need to isolate the implementers of some regulatory policies (such as competition policy) from democratic competition, or about the existing openness of the EU policy process – the EU polity can only really be considered democratic if competitive elections determine the direction of the EU policy agenda. Hence the rest of this chapter focuses on the electoral processes in EU politics, the behaviour of the main collective actors in these processes (political parties at the national and European levels) and why democracy in the EU does not exist in any standard sense.

Parties: Competition and Organization

EU politics is party politics. This may not seem obvious to a casual observer of the EU. But on closer inspection party organizations, labels, ideologies, policies, coalitions and interests take centre stage. All politicians at the domestic and European levels are party politicians who owe their current positions and future careers to the electoral success and policy positions of 'their' parties. Parties are the main actors in domestic elections, EP elections and referendums. They are the main organs connecting governments to parliaments and parliaments to voters. As a result, they provide vital links between the national and EU arenas and between the EU institutions themselves. To understand how EU politics work, then, we need to understand how parties compete and organize in the EU polity.

National parties and Europe

The relative electoral support for and policy positions of parties determine what coalitions are feasible in EU politics, how cohesive these alliances are, and how dominant they are likely to be. Table 6.1 shows the electoral strengths of the various party families in each member state in early 2004, and the total support for each family weighted by the number of seats each state has in the EP. As can be seen no single party family dominates the whole of the EU. The socialists are clearly dominant in the left bloc in all member states, whereas the mainstream right is split, with Christian democrats being the largest force in some states and conservatives the largest in others. Nevertheless, in terms of the main political blocs, the left and (mainstream) right are fairly balanced, commanding just over 40 per cent of the votes across the EU. The liberals hold a pivotal position between these two forces and are available to form coalitions with the left or the right.

With regard to the policy positions of parties in EU politics, at the domestic level most social divisions are summarised in the single ubiquitous left–right dimension. At the European level, in contrast, traditionally the dominant dimension of political competition has been between actors that favour further integration and those which favour the *status quo* or less integration: an integration–sovereignty cleavage (Garrett, 1992; Tsebelis and Garrett, 2000a). However as EU policy-making starts to encroach into traditional areas of domestic political competition, the left–right dimension can be expected to emerge at the European level (see Chapter 5). Hence, Figure 6.1 shows where the party families are located, and the extent to which they are internally divided on these two main dimensions of EU politics. The ovals illustrate the location and range of the national parties in each party family (cf. Hix and Lord, 1997, pp. 49–53; Ray, 1999). The locations of the families suggest several possible alliances in EU politics. The clearest natural allies are the Christian democrats, conservatives and liberals, all of whom are moderately centre right and pro-European. The socialists, in contrast, are faced with a choice: a potential alliance with these centre-right forces on a common pro-European platform, which could also include the regionalists; or an alliance with the greens and radical left in a common left-wing bloc. However the latter alliance would be divided on the question of more or less European integration. Similarly an opposing centre-right coalition that included the conservatives would be divided on European questions. By virtue of their isolation in the EU party system, the extreme right and anti-europeans are 'uncoalitionable'.

But, the shape of the ellipses (shorter on the left–right than on the anti/pro-EU dimension) reveals that most party families are internally divided on the question of Europe. Party families are historically

Table 6.1 Electoral strength of parties and political blocs

| | | | Pro-Europe | | | | Right | | | | |
| | | | Left | | | | | | | | |
	Radical left	Green	Social democrat	Left regionalist	Liberal	Right regionalist	Christian democrat	Pro-EU conservative	EU-critical conservative	Extreme right
Austria	1	10	37		1		42			10
Belgium	37	6	28	3	29		19			14
Cyprus		2	7		20			34		
Czech Rep.	19	2	30		3		2	39	13	2
Denmark	6	2	29		38		2	9	13	
Estonia			7	2	43		1	32	2	
Finland	10	8	23	1	30		5	19	3	
France	11	6	26		7			39		15
Germany	4	9	39				39			1
Greece	11		44					43		
Hungary	3		42		9			41	1	4
Ireland	8	4	11		7		25		42	
Italy	7	2	17	1	9	4	18	30	12	1
Latvia	9	10	17		5			34	18	5
Lithuania			32	4	47		4	9	4	1

Luxembourg	4	9	24		22		30		11	
Malta		1	47		22			52		
Netherlands	6	5	27		3		29	18	10	
Poland	10	1	41					40	19	18
Portugal	8		38		11		23	11	9	
Slovakia		1	17	1	41		9	31		27
Slovenia	6		12	5	3		2	47		4
Spain	8	5	34		19	3	9	15		
Sweden	1	1	40	3	19				1	
UK	1	4	41	1	11	1	12	20	33	2
EU total		4	32				42		9	5

43   77   42

Note: These are the percent of votes won by each party in the most recent national election prior to January 2004. EU-totals are calculated by multiplying the vote shares in each member state by the percent of MEPs from that member state.

Source: Calculated from data on the Elections Around the World website: http://www.electionworld.org.

Figure 6.1   *Party policy positions in EU politics*

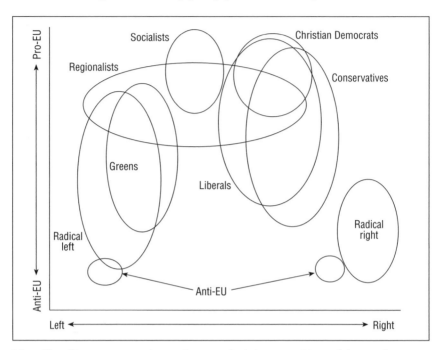

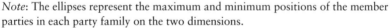

Note: The ellipses represent the maximum and minimum positions of the member parties in each party family on the two dimensions.

Source: Calculated from data in Marks *et al.* (2002).

defined in relation to the left–right dimension of politics in the domestic arena and not on the question of European integration. As a result parties in the same party family have similar policy preferences on left–right issues. But rather than change their domestic policy positions to adapt to the new reality of European integration, they prefer to couch the issue of European integration in terms of their existing ideological positions: supporting EU integration and EU policies if this furthers their domestic policy agenda, and opposing the EU if it undermines support for their party in the domestic arena (Marks and Wilson, 2000; Aspinwall, 2002; Marks *et al.*, 2002).

Also, because there is variation in the existing policy mix at the domestic left (with some policy regimes more to the left, as in Scandinavia, and some more to the right, as in the UK), parties in different domestic contexts will view the EU differently (cf. Sitter, 2001). As discussed in the previous chapter, in states with more right-wing policy mixes, left-wing voters favour European integration while right-wing voters are opposed, and the reverse is true in more left-wing policy regimes. This means that when the questions of more or less European integration emerges, most party families will not have united positions across all EU states, as different national parties faced with different domestic policy contexts will invariably see EU policies in different ways.

Only the regionalists and anti-Europeans do not fit this pattern, defining themselves, respectively, 'against' and 'for' the existing structure of the nation-state in Europe. Hence these families occupy coherent positions on the European integration issue dimension but not on the left–right dimension. The Christian democrats are somewhere between these two extremes, because support for European integration has always been part of the domestic policy portfolio of this party family; they are coherent on both left-right and European integration dimensions (Johansson, 2002; Hanley, 2002).

Put together, the electoral strengths and policy positions of the parties explain why in recent years EU politics has not been about two powerful political blocs competing for control of the EU agenda. Neither the left nor the right are strong enough to form a dominant coalition across the EU. And within these two blocs there are deep divisions on European integration both between party families and within them. This has forced the pro-European parties across the left–right divide to cooperate in order to construct large enough majorities to win key EU decisions: for example the elites of the mainstream parties on the left and the right, in government and opposition, mobilized together in Scandinavia on the issue of joining the single currency (Johansson and Raunio, 2001; Aylott, 2002), and in Central and Eastern Europe on joining the EU (Kopecky and Mudde, 2002; Hughes *et al.*, 2002).

Nevertheless, the dominance of this cross-left–right pro-EU alliance, which has effectively prevented the mainstream parties from competing on European issues in domestic electoral campaigns and parliamentary debates, means that anti-European positions amongst the electorate have not been articulated by national party systems (Mair, 2000). There is little evidence that the main national parties are disconnected from the majority of their supporters on the question of Europe (van der Eijk, Franklin and van der Burg, 2001; Carrubba, 2001). However within most parties there are significant minorities who are opposed to European integration, and there are parties to the left and right of this centrist/pro-European bloc that cannot challenge the dominance of this coalition. As a result anti-European voters express their frustration at this pro-European 'cartel' in electoral arenas where the normal structure of party competition is not so dominant: that is, in European elections and referendums on European questions (see below).

The need for a cross-party pro-European alliance may be particular to the late 1980s and early 1990s. In the 1970s the centre right was more coherently pro-European, and the centre left was more sceptical, seeing European integration as mainly a free market project against the social democratic project in the domestic arena. It was not until the mid-1980s that the elites in most social democratic parties started to support European integration, which allowed for a powerful cross-party, pro-European coalition to be built to support the single market programme and economic and monetary union. In the late 1990s the situation reversed somewhat. Most parties on the centre-left became strongly pro-European, whereas many of the conservatives (even in the more 'pro-EU' bloc) grew more critical of the EU, fearing overregulation by Brussels and interference in national macroeconomic decisions.

In other words a realignment in EU politics may be under way, with a less powerful cross-party pro-European coalition dominating the political agenda at the domestic and EU levels, and more competition between the left and right blocs over the direction of EU policies (Hooghe and Marks, 1998; Pennings, 2002; Gabel and Hix, 2003; Hooghe *et al.*, 2003).

Parties at the European level

There are two party organizational structures at the European level. The most prominent of these are the party groups that were first formed by national parties from the same party families in the old Assembly of the European Coal and Steel Community in 1953 – the precursor of the modern EP (van Oudenhave, 1965). In the period since this development, the parties in the EP have evolved into highly developed organizations, with their own budgets, leadership structures, administrative support staff, rules of procedure, offices, committees and working groups.

The second organizational structure consists of the so-called transnational party federations, which were formed in the run-up to the first direct elections in the mid 1970s. The Confederation of Socialists Parties of the EC was the first to be established, in April 1974, followed by the Federation of Liberal and Democratic Parties of the EC, in March 1976, and the European People's Party (EPP) of Christian democratic parties in April 1976. Despite their names, these were very loose organizations, did not have highly sophisticated organizations at the European level, and did not have a clear and coherent policy orientation, despite biannual European party conferences. Nevertheless, at the instigation of the three secretaries-general of the party federations the Maastricht Treaty introduced a new 'party article' (Article 191), which stated that:

Political parties at the European level are important as a factor for integration within the Union. They contribute to forming a European awareness and to expressing the will of the citizens of the Union.

Following this article, the socialist, liberal and Christian democrat party federations established new and more coherent organizations. The Party of European Socialists (PES) was launched in November 1992, the EPP adopted a set of new statutes in November 1992, a new European Federation of Green Parties (EFGP) was set up in June 1993 and the European Liberal, Democratic and Reform Party (ELDR) was established in December 1993. Moreover each of these organizations reinforced their links with the party groups in the EP, and with the representatives of these parties in the Commission, Council and European Council. Instead of being simple transnational umbrella organizations for fighting EP elections, the new 'Euro-parties' began to develop as extraparliamentary party organizations at the European level, much like the extraparliamentary central offices and central committees of parties in the domestic arena (Hix, 1995a).

As Table 6.2 shows, there have been some shifts in the party-political balance of power in the EU institutions since the early 1990s. In the EP the dominance of the left in the 1990–94 period has slowly eroded, with the EPP emerging as the largest party and the Liberals now in a pivotal position between the left and right. The reverse is true in the Council: with the majority switching from the right in 1990–94 to the left in 1995-99, and then back to the right in 1999–2004. Finally, the Commission gradually shifted from a right-dominated college in 1990–99 to a left-dominated college in 1999–2004. Because the dynamics in each of these three institutions have not followed the same pattern, no single party-political force has been able to dominate the EU as a whole. However the right had a clear advantage (although not a majority) in 1990–94 period, in 1994–99 the balance was more even, and in 1999–2004 the left had a slight majority. At the start of the 2004-9 period the right had a majority in all three EU institutions for the first time.

If the model of competitive party government works in the EU, these changes should produce a concomitant shift in the EU policy agenda away from market deregulation (of the single market programme) in the 1990–94 period to social protection and social expenditure in 1999–04, and then back to more liberal/free market policies in 2004–9. However, as discussed above, this translation from party strengths to policy outputs requires party actors in the same party family to cooperate, and winning coalitions to be constructed between different party families.

Research on voting by MEPs has revealed comparatively high and growing levels of voting cohesion between the EP parties (Attinà, 1990; Quanjel and Wolters, 1993; Brzinski, 1995; Hix *et al.*, 2005). Table 6.3 shows 'agreement index' scores for each party group in each of the five parliaments since the first direct elections in 1979. If all the members of a party group vote together in every vote in a particular parliament the party's score is one, and if a party group is split down

Table 6.2 *Strength of parties in the EU institutions*

Party family	Percentage of MEPs			Percentage of commissioners			Percentage of government ministers in the Council			Percentage in all EU institutions		
	1990–94	1995–99	1999–04	1990–94	1995–99	1999–04	1990–94	1995–99	1999–04	1990–94	1995–99	1999–04
Socialists	35	34	29	33	45	50	24	46	35	31	42	38
Greens + left-regionalists	9	9	8			5		2	3	3	3	5
Radical left	9	5	7					1		3	2	2
Total Left	50	44	44	33	45	55	24	49	38	36	46	45
Liberals	10	9	9	18	15	10	18	8	12	15	11	10
Chr.dems and cons in EPP	20	22	37	31	20	30	28	29	41	26	24	36
Non-EPP Conservatives	15	13	5	18	20	5	30	13	8	21	15	6
Total Right	35	35	42	49	40	35	58	42	49	47	39	42
Total pro-Europe	65	68	78	82	80	90	70	83	88	72	77	85
Extreme right	1	5	2					1	2		2	1
Anti-EU	1	3	3								1	1

Notes: As in Table 6.1, the pro-Europe bloc consists of the socialists, EPP, liberals and regionalists. The figures for the Council refer to the percentage of all national government ministries controlled by each party family, weighted by the percentage of votes a government has under qualified majority voting. The figures for 'all EU institutions' were calculated by adding the percentages in each of the institutions and dividing by three.

Sources: Corbett *et al.* (1995); Edwards and Spence (1997); Hix and Lord (1997).

Table 6.3 *Party cohesion in the European Parliament*

Party (left to right)	First parliament (1979–84)	Second parliament (1984–89)	Third parliament (1989–94)	Fourth parliament (1994–99)	Fifth parliament (1999–01)
Radical left	0.81	0.87	0.86	0.80	0.76
Greens and allies	–	0.81	0.85	0.91	0.91
PES	0.76	0.87	0.90	0.90	0.90
Regionalists	–	–	0.87	0.91	–
ELDR	0.85	0.85	0.85	0.86	0.91
EPP	0.90	0.93	0.91	0.90	0.86
Gaullists and allies	0.80	0.84	0.85	0.79	0.72
Conservatives	0.89	0.92	0.89	–	–
Radical right	–	0.93	0.88	–	–
Anti-EU	–	–	0.83	0.67	0.54

Note: The scores are 'agreement indices' (AI), which are calculated as follows for each vote:

$$AI_i = \frac{\max\{Y_i, N_i, A_i\} - \frac{1}{2}[(Y_i + N_i + A_i) - \max\{Y_i, N_i, A_i\}]}{(Y_i + N_i + A_i)}$$

where Y_i is the number of Yes votes by party i, N_i the number of No votes, and A_i the number of Abstain votes.

the middle in every vote (with a third voting 'yes', a third voting 'no', and a third voting to 'abstain') the party's score is zero. The party groups were already relatively cohesive in the first parliament (for the purpose of comparison, the Democrats and Republicans in the US Congress usually have agreement scores of between 0.80 and 0.85). Since then cohesion has continued to increase: for example the socialists' score rose from 0.76 in the first parliament to 0.90 in the fifth parliament. However the cohesion of the EPP has declined, but this is only a minor decline if one considers the expansion of the EPP and hence the greater national and ideological diversity of this group.

The explanation of this growing cohesion lies in the nature of the resources controlled by the EP parties, which encourages the MEPs to toe the party line. The EP parties control the nominations for the key offices of the EP, such as the EP president, the appointment of Committee chairpersons, offices within the groups, *rapporteurships* on EU legislation in the EP committees, and the agenda of the parliament as a whole (Raunio, 1996, pp. 44–86). As MEPs have learned that the likelihood of their playing an influential role in the EP is dependent upon the EP parties, there has been a strengthening of group cohesion in the legislative workings of the parliament. Also, as the two largest groups – the EPP and PES – have disproportionately more control over appointments than the smaller groups, MEPs in the smaller groups have gradually chosen to leave the smaller groups and join the two largest groups (Bardi, 1996).

However research has also shown that the EP parties are rarely able to prevent particular national delegations of MEPs from defecting in key votes (Gabel and Hix, 2002; Hix, 2002b). For example in the 1999–2004 parliament the British Conservative MEPs, who belonged to the EPP group, voted differently from the majority of their EP party about 30 per cent of the time. The EP parties may control rewards inside the parliament, but national parties control the selection of candidates for the European elections and hence whether MEPs will be reselected. As a result, if MEPs have conflicting voting instructions from their EP party and their national party, more often than not they will follow the instructions of their national party. MEPs from member states with candidate-centred electoral systems (such as open-list proportional representation or single transferable vote) or who are selected locally rather than centrally are freer to vote with their EP party groups when there is such a conflict (Hix, 2004). Overall though, the growing cohesion of the EP parties, despite the power of national parties over their MEPs, suggests that national parties rarely choose to instruct their MEPs to vote differently from their party groups, either because they share the same policy preferences as the EP parties, or because issues raised in the EP are not particularly salient in domestic politics.

Competition between the EP parties has also grown (Hix *et al.*, 2003; Hix *et al.*, 2005). Figure 6.2 shows the percentage of times the majority in each party group voted with the majority in another party group in a series of votes in the third parliament and in the first half of the fifth parliament. The data illustrate several key aspects of party competition in the EP. First, the main dimension of competition in the EP is the left–right: as the percentage of times a party group votes with another decreases as the group is further away on the left-right spectrum. The only case where this does not hold is for the Europe of Democracies and Diversities and the Union for a Europe of Nations groups. But this still fits into the two-dimensional picture of EU politics. Because these groups are aligned on the pro-/anti-Europe dimension of EU politics rather than the left–right dimension, they vote more with the European United Left (at the other end of the left–right spectrum) than the parties in the centre (which are pro-European).

Second, the data demonstrate that the 'grand coalition' between the

Figure 6.2   *Coalitions in the European Parliament*

a. Third parliament (1989–94)

						Green Group
					Left Unity	74
				Rainbow Group	74	73
			Party of European Socialists	77	76	54
		European Liberal, Democratic and Reform Party	70	65	61	57
		European People's Party	79	71	62	59	52
	European Democratic Alliance	73	72	63	60	58	50
Right Group	56	54	52	45	44	44	44

b. Fifth parliament (1999–01)

					European United Left
				Greens/European Free Alliance	76
			Party of European Socialists	72	65
		European Liberal, Democratic and Reform Party	74	63	54
	European People's Party	71	69	52	46
Union for a Europe of Nations	60	48	51	49	55
Europe of Democracies & Diversities	63	53	55	55	58	63

Note: The figures are the percentage of times the majority in one party group voted the same way as a majority in another party group in roll-call votes in each parliament.

EPP and PES dominated the third parliament, with the PES more likely to vote with the EPP than with the ELDR. There are two main reasons for this coalition. First, in many legislative votes an absolute majority of all MEPs is required, which means that at least 65 per cent of MEPs have to show up to vote. Second, in the case of most EP votes the EP sees itself as united against the Commission or, more often, against the member states in the Council (Kreppel, 2000). But, in the first half of the 1999–2004 parliament, grand coalitions between these groups were less prevalent. This new pattern of competition was partly because of the new ideological split between the EP and the other EU institutions in this period. The EPP was now the largest party in the EP, in 'opposition' to a centre-left-dominated Council and Commission. Against the EPP, the PES tended to back the initiatives of the Council and Commission, and therefore behaved like a minority 'governing' party.

The transnational party federations have also evolved substantially since their establishment in the 1970s (Hix and Lord, 1997). One of the most important changes has been the institutionalization of the party leaders' summits. These were initially informal meetings of the national party leaders, but in the late 1980s they became the central decision-making organs within each of the party federations. More significantly for the operation of the EU, these party leaders' meetings began to be organized around the agenda and dates of, and often in the same venue as, the European Council. For the first time in the history of the EU, national party leaders from the same party family now had an incentive to come together to try to agree a common platform before the EU heads of government met to set the medium- and long-term agenda of the EU.

This does not suggest that the party federations were able to exert a great influence on decisions in the European Council, although there were instances when this was the case (Hix and Lord, 1997, pp. 188–95). Nevertheless for the first time extraparliamentary party organizations at the European level had a high-level forum for coordinating their policies and strategies. For example party leaders' summits could potentially serve as vehicles for organizing the selection of candidates for the post of Commission president.

In summary, party organization at the European level is relatively underdeveloped compared with national party systems, and national parties remain the key actors in the European level party organizations. However the parties in the EP do behave like national parliamentary parties: MEPs vote increasingly along party lines and decreasingly along national lines, and party competition in the EP is driven by left–right policy positions. Also, the party federations – especially the PES and the EPP – are beginning to serve as essential interinstitutional links between the key party actors (the national party leaders) in the national and European arenas. But are voters able to choose between the policy platforms of these nascent Euro-parties in electoral contests related to Europe?

Elections: EP Elections and EU Referendums

There are two types of EU-specific electoral contest: European Parliament elections, and referendums on EU treaty reforms or other major changes to the EU. Whereas EP elections are held throughout the EU according to a fixed schedule, referendums on EU-related issues have only been held sporadically in some member states.

EP elections: national or European contests?

Direct and universal elections to the EP were first held in June 1979, and since then have been held every five years. In the run-up to the first elections many scholars argued (hoped) that elections to the EP would provide a new legitimacy for the EU (for example Fitzmaurice, 1978; Marquand, 1978; Pridham and Pridham, 1979). According to Walter Hallstein (1972, p. 74), a former president of the European Commission:

> Such a campaign would force those entitled to vote to look at and examine the questions and the various options on which the European Parliament would have to decide in the months and years ahead. It would give candidates who emerged victorious from such a campaign a truly European mandate from their electors; and it would encourage the emergence of truly European political parties.

After six elections it is clear that these optimistic predictions could not be further from the reality.

This is because EP elections are fought not as European elections but as 'second-order national contests'. As Reif and Schmitt (1980) first pointed out, EP elections tend to be about national political issues, national political parties and the fight for national government office. The main goal of national political parties is to win and retain national government office. Elections that decide who holds national executive office are therefore 'first-order contests', and political parties consequently treat all other elections – EP elections, regional and local elections, second chamber elections and elections to choose a ceremonial head of state – as beauty contests on the performance of the partyor parties that won the last first order election (Heath *et al.*, 1999).

The second-order nature of European elections has two effects. First, because second-order contests are less important than first-order elections, there is less incentive for people to vote in EP elections, and hence there is a lower turnout in these elections than in national elections. Second, because EP elections are really about the performance of national governments, the people who do vote will vote differently than if a national election were held at the same time. There are two reasons for this (Oppenhuis *et al.*, 1996). First, EP elections give citizens an opportunity to vote sincerely rather than strategically ('vote with the heart'), by voting for a (small) party that is closest to their preferences rather than a (large) party that is more likely to form a government. Second EP elections allow people to express their dissatisfaction with the party or parties in government ('put the boot in'), by voting for one or other of the opposition parties. Either way the consequence of such 'vote switching' is that large governing parties lose votes in EP elections while opposition parties and small parties gain votes.

These hypotheses are confirmed in analyses of EP election results (Reif, 1984; Irwin, 1995; van der Eijk and Franklin, 1996; Marsh,

1998). First, with regard to electoral turnout, the percentage of people voting in EP elections fell from 70 per cent in 1984 to 59 per cent in 1994, 49 per cent in 1999 and 45 per cent in 2004. Moreover, the difference between general election turnout and EP election turnout has increased. As Table 6.4 shows, apart from in member states where national elections have been held concurrently with EP elections (as in Ireland in 1989, Luxembourg in 1989, 1994 and 1999, and Belgium in 1999) or where voting is compulsory (Belgium, Greece and Luxembourg), the average difference in turnout between national and EP elections increased from 25 per cent in 1989 to 29 per cent in 1999.

Second, evidence from surveys held during the 1989 and 1994 elections confirms that people do vote for different parties in EP elections, especially if a national election is not being held at the same time. Approximately 20 per cent of voters switched their votes in the 1989 and 1994 European elections. This individual level analysis consequently confirms that the aggregate losses of government parties in EP elections cannot simply be explained by a fall in turnout, where government supporters actually do not bother to vote. What actually happens is that voters change their votes in European elections, particularly when they take place in the middle of a national election cycle.

The second-order model consequently suggests that lower turnout in EP elections and voting for different parties in these elections has nothing to do with 'Europe' *per se* (Franklin *et al.*, 1996). People do think that the EP is important. But survey evidence suggests that people who do not vote in EP elections perceive that these contests are not important to national politics. And those who do vote choose different parties in EP elections not because they particularly want divided government at the EU level, but because they wish to influence the result of, and the policy positions of the national parties in, the next national general election.

However the second-order election model is not universally accepted. First, with regard to turnout Franklin (2000) demonstrates that there has been virtually no real decline in turnout in EP elections if one controls for the reduction of compulsory voting, the parallel fall in turnout in national elections, the changing location of EP elections in national electoral cycles, and the enlargement of the EU to include states with lower levels of voter turnout than in the original six member states. Focusing on the motivations for voting, Blondel, Sinnott and Svensson (1997, 1998) find evidence that voters' attitudes towards Europe are not irrelevant: if individuals are opposed to their state's membership of the EU, have a negative attitude towards the EP or lack knowledge of the EP or the EU more generally, they are less likely to vote in EP elections.

Second, voters and parties' preferences on EU issues do have some impact on voters' choice of which party to support in EP elections. For example in some member states – such as Denmark (since 1979), France (in 1999) and the UK (in 2004) – a different party system exists in EP elections as a result of the emergence of European integration as a cleavage in the national party system, and anti-EU parties or parties with strong anti-European positions take votes away from the more

Table 6.4   *The 'second-order election' effect in European Parliament elections (per cent)*

	Voter turnout in European elections compared with the previous national election			Quasi-switching – number of voters in European elections who would have voted for a different party if it were a national election[1]	
	1989	1994	1999	1989	1994
Austria	–	–	–28	–	–
Belgium[2]	–3	–3	0[3]	13	19
Denmark	–39	–36	–37	35	43
Finland	–	–	–35	–	–
France	–17	–25	–21	27	41
Germany	–22	–18	–37	12	14
Greece[2]	–4	–9	–5	8	12
Ireland	–2[3]	–24	–15	29[3]	24
Italy	–10	–11	–12	20	21
Luxembourg[2]	–3[3]	0[3]	0[3]	15[3]	14[3]
The Netherlands	–39	–43	–43	12	20
Portugal	–22	–33	–22	10	13
Spain	–16	–18	–7	22	13
Sweden	–	–	–38	–	–
United Kingdom	–39	–41	–48	13	16
Average, all member states	–18	–22	–23	–	18	21
Average, EU12	–18	–22	–21	–	–	–
Average, excluding cases of concurrent national elections and compulsory voting	–25	–28	–29	–	–	–

Notes:
1. Data on quasi-switching in the 1999 European elections are not available.
2. Member states where voting is compulsory.
3. Cases where national elections and European elections were held concurrently.

Sources: Mackie and Rose (1991); Koole and Mair (1995); van der Eijk and Franklin (1996); Lodge (1996); Elections Around the World (http://www.electionworld.org).

mainstream national parties. Irwin (1995) argues that extremist parties do well in EP elections not only because they provide voters with an opportunity to protest against the mainstream parties (as the second-order election model predicts), but also because they present clear anti-European platforms against the collusive pro-EU policy positions of the mainstream parties. However Ferrara and Weishaupt (2004) demonstrate that what matters in EP elections is not whether a party is strongly pro- or anti-European, but whether it has a coherent policy towards the EU. Parties that do not present coherent policies towards the EU do badly in EP elections, all other things being equal.

Nevertheless the basic claims of the second-order theory of EP elections remain intact as these 'European' aspects of the elections only affect voting behaviour at the margins. This has consequences for the ability of EP elections to reduce the democratic deficit in the EU. Despite the increased powers of the EP in both the legislative arena (*vis-à-vis* the Council) and the executive arena (*vis-à-vis* the selection and accountability of the Commission), EP elections are still fought by national parties. From 1994 there was a possibility of connecting the EP elections to the process of selecting the president of the Commission, as a result of the Maastricht and Amsterdam Treaty reforms, which gave the EP the power to vote on the candidate for Commission President immediately after the EP elections. However even if different candidates for Commission President had been put forward in the 1994, 1999 and 2004 elections, the contest would still have been second-order. As Reif (1997, p. 221) explains, the national arena would still be the first-order political arena and the European arena a collective subsystem of the primary arena. Hence regardless of the ability of the EP elections to influence the make-up of the EU executive, EP elections are unlikely to ever allow Europe's voters to 'throw the scoundrels out' as long as national parties have an incentive to use the elections for their principal goal of national government office.

Referendums on EU membership and treaty reforms

So, do referendums on European issues do any better than EP elections in respect of enabling voters to express their preferences? As Table 6.5 shows, there have been 40 referendums on EU-related issues in 22 countries. Thirty per cent of these referendums have been in two states: Denmark and Ireland, which have had six referendums. While the pro-EU side tends to win these contests it has not done so well recently. For example, of the 10 referendums that were won by the anti-EU side, two were in the 1970s and 1980s, five in the 1990s and four in 2000–3. Finally, the turnout in these referendums has varied enormously, ranging from a low of 35 per cent in the first referendum in

Ireland on the Nice Treaty (2001) to a high of 91 per cent in the referendum in Malta on EU membership (March 2003).

So what explains voting in EU-related referendums? Based on an analysis of the results of referendums around the world, Butler and Ranney (1994) point out that referendums often produce results that are at odds with opinion polls held only a few months before the vote. This may be because opinions on complex issues are often 'soft' and therefore are influenced by arguments put forward in the final weeks of the campaigns, as voters respond to the 'cues' of parties or other interest groups.

However Franklin *et al.* (1994, 1995) propose that EU referendums work very much like EP elections. Looking at the Danish, Irish and French referendums on the Maastricht Treaty in 1992 and 1993 they find that the determining factor in all cases was not attitudes towards the EU but support for or opposition to the party or parties in government at the time of the referendums. For example in the case of the French referendum, polls showed overwhelming support for the EU, but voters used the referendum to punish the increasingly unpopular Mitterrand presidency. In the opposite direction, when the government changed in Denmark from a liberal-conservative coalition to a social democrats administration the new government was able to win the second referendum on the Maastricht Treaty because its popularity was high in the 'honeymoon period' that followed its general election victory. Siune and Svensson (1993) also find that an individual's level of knowledge about the EU had no effect on whether the individual participated or how he or she voted in the 1992 Danish referendum, thus supporting the notion that the referendum was less about Europe than domestic politics (cf. Franklin *et al.*, 1994).

Nevertheless there is evidence that attitudes towards the EU and the positions taken by various political actors towards Europe do play a part in referendum outcomes. For example, Siune *et al.* (1994) demonstrate that in the Danish case, parties that were opposed to the EU were more able to mobilize their voters against the Maastricht Treaty in the 1992 and 1993 referendums than the parties that were in favour of the EU. They also claim that the changing attitude of the media towards the EU following the compromise agreement at the Edinburgh European Council in December 1992 was crucial in persuading 47 000 voters to change their minds between the two polls. Downs (2001) offers a similar explanation of the Danish people's rejection of membership of the single currency in 2000. In this case the popularity of the prime minister, Paul Nyrup Rasmussen, did not affect the result. Instead the No campaign and the anti-European media framed the debate around the issue of protecting national sovereignty, thereby foiling the attempt by the government and the main opposition parties to focus on the alleged positive economic benefits of adopting the euro.

Table 6.5 Referendums on European integration, 1972–2003

Date	Member state	Topic	Result (% yes)	Turnout (%)
23 April 1972	France	Enlargement	68.3	60.2
10 May 1972	Ireland	Membership	83.1	70.9
24–25 September 1972	Norway	Membership	46.5	79.2
2 October 1972	Denmark	Membership	63.1	90.1
3 December 1972	Switzerland	Treaty (EC-EFTA)	72.5	52.0
5 June 1975	United Kingdom	Membership (continued)	67.2	64.0
23 February 1982	Greenland	Membership (continued)	46.0	74.9
26 February 1986	Denmark	Treaty (Single European Act)	56.2	75.4
6 May 1987	Ireland	Treaty (Single European Act)	69.6	44.0
18 June 1989	Italy	Mandate for Spinelli Treaty	88.1	85.4
3 June 1992	Denmark	Treaty I (Maastricht)	49.3	82.9
18 June 1992	Ireland	Treaty (Maastricht)	68.7	57.3
20 September 1992	France	Treaty (Maastricht)	51.1	69.7
6 December 1992	Switzerland	Treaty (EEA)	49.7	78.0
13 December 1992	Liechtenstein	Treaty (EEA)	55.8	87.0
18 May 1993	Denmark	Treaty II (Maastricht)	56.8	85.5
12 June 1994	Austria	Membership	66.6	82.4
16 October 1994	Finland	Membership	56.9	70.4
13 November 1994	Sweden	Membership	52.3	83.3
20 November 1994	Åland Islands	Membership	73.6	49.1

Date	Country	Subject		
28 November 1994	Norway	Membership	47.8	89.0
9 April 1995	Liechtenstein	Membership (EEA)	55.9	82.1
8 June 1997	Switzerland	Membership (open negotiations)	25.9	35.0
22 May 1998	Ireland	Treaty (Amsterdam)	61.7	56.3
27 May 1998	Denmark	Treaty (Amsterdam)	55.1	76.2
21 May 2000	Switzerland	Treaty (EU–Switzerland)	67.2	48.0
28 May 2000	Denmark	Membership of EMU	46.9	87.5
4 May 2001	Switzerland	Membership (resume negotiations)	23.2	55.0
7 June 2001	Ireland	Treaty I (Nice)	46.1	34.8
19 October 2002	Ireland	Treaty II (Nice)	62.9	49.5
9 March 2003	Malta	Membership	53.5	90.9
23 March 2003	Slovenia	Membership	89.6	60.2
12 April 2003	Hungary	Membership	83.8	45.6
10–11 May 2003	Lithuania	Membership	89.9	63.4
16–17 May 2003	Slovakia	Membership	92.5	52.2
7-8 June 2003	Poland	Membership	77.5	58.9
13–14 June 2003	Czech Republic	Membership	77.3	55.2
14 September 2003	Estonia	Membership	66.8	64.1
14 September 2003	Sweden	Membership of EMU	42.0	82.6
20 September 2003	Latvia	Membership	67.7	72.5

Sources: Hug (2002); IRI Initiative and Referendums Institute (http://www.iri-europe.org).

Similarly Saglie (2000) finds that voters' perceptions of the EU were crucial in how they voted in the Norwegian referendum on EU membership in 1994, but that these perceptions were only partially shaped by the positions of the parties on both sides of the debate. Finally, looking at the No vote in the first Irish referendum on the Nice Treaty in June 2001, Sinnott (2002) finds that despite overwhelming support for the EU amongst Irish voters, the No campaign was much more able to mobilize its supporters than the Yes campaign, despite a comparatively popular government and unity amongst the main parties in support of the treaty.

Hence EU referendums tend to be about domestic politics and EU politics. Schneider and Weitsman (1996) present a theory of why this is the case and under what conditions domestic politics will dominate in a campaign. Because voters cannot be certain about the consequences of a major constitutional change, such as a treaty reform or membership of the EU, how they vote will depend on how much they trust the protagonists on each side of a referendum campaign. If both sides are trusted the referendum is less likely to be purely about the popularity of the government. However if the government is not trusted the voters may decide to punish the government. In both cases, though, the voters may be torn between voting to punish/reward the government and voting sincerely on the issue before them.

Building on the work of Schneider and Weitsman, Simon Hug predicts how the institutional context of a referendum will determine whether voters act sincerely or strategically (Hug and Sciarini, 2000; Hug, 2002). First, a referendum is less likely to be a pure popularity contest between domestic parties and leaders if it is constitutionally required rather than initiated by a group of opposition parties, the media or a protest movement. From the perspective of the government, submitting an issue to the voters in a non-required referendum and suffering a defeat is more likely to damage the government irreparably than suffering a defeat in a required referendum. The latter may still be damaging, but it will not be the result of a serious miscalculation by the government. Second, a referendum is less likely to be about domestic parties and leaders if the result of the referendum is binding on the elites rather than simply consultative, whereby even a simple or oversized majority in parliament could overturn the referendum result. In a non-binding vote, citizens may vote against the government for one of two reasons: either to vote sincerely against the issue, or to signal protest against the government but nonetheless hope that the referendum outcome will be overturned by the parliament. Hence there is less opportunity for voters to use referendums strategically to punish the government in binding referendums than in non-binding referendums.

Finally, EU referendums affect national governments' and voters' attitudes towards the EU, and therefore have policy consequences for the EU as a whole. First, having to hold a referendum on an EU treaty reform increases the risk that the reform will be rejected. This strengthens the negotiating position of those member states which have to hold referendums and whose voters are more critical of the EU, compared with those member states in which treaty reforms only require a parliamentary vote and a single party controls a clear parliamentary majority (Hug, 1997, 2002; König and Hug, 2000).

Second, in terms of changing voters' attitudes towards the EU, referendums have a more powerful 'inducing effect' than do EP elections (Christin and Hug, 2002; Hug, 2002). Holding a referendum on the EU forces the elites to debate the associated issues in public and to explain the EU institutions and complex treaty reforms to their citizens. As a result, citizens in member states that have had referendums tend to be significantly better informed about the EU than citizens in member states that have never had a referendum, or only had referendums twenty years ago. Furthermore EU referendums affect the level of support for European integration by increasing public acceptance of government decisions related to the EU, and hence the legitimacy of the EU. For example, the four states that had the smallest decline in support for their country's membership of the EU between 1991 and 1999 – Sweden, Austria, Ireland and Denmark – had at least one EU-related referendum in this period (see Chapter 5).

Overall the existing electoral contests related to Europe do not allow citizens to express their preferences on European integration in a clear way or to choose between particular policy packages for the EU. Despite the increasing powers of the EP to influence EU policy outcomes, there are few incentives against national parties using EP elections as mid-term polls on the performance of national government. EU referendums give voters more of an opportunity to express their views on the EU, most institutional and political contexts encourage them to vote strategically (against or in favour of particular domestic parties) rather than to express their sincere views on EU matters. Also, EU referendums are about big constitutional issues rather than whether the EU policy agenda should move to the left or the right. Interestingly, EP elections have been less 'second-order' in member states that have had closely-fought referendums as the success of anti-European movements has spilled over into the subsequent EP election.

Nevertheless, there is some hope. As van der Eijk, Franklin and Oppenhuis (1996, p. 365) explain:

> The lack of European content in European elections cannot be attributed to inherent limitations of European voters... When it comes to voting choice only differences in political context are at issue. If such differences were removed, this would also remove the differences we

observe in the manner in which party choices are made. The answer to the question 'one electorate or many?' when interpreted in these terms is unequivocally in the singular.

In other words, given a genuinely European contest, fought between rival EU-wide movements instead of national parties on issues such as who should hold European executive office or the nature of the European legislative agenda, all voters in all member states will behave in the same way in such contests. The challenge, therefore, is to provide incentives for parties to compete and voters to choose on the basis of EU issues, rather than on the basis of national policy positions and personalities. This will require further reform of the EU institutions.

Towards a More Democratic EU?

The EU has been in a permanent state of reform since the mid 1980s. At the start of most reform negotiations EU leaders declare that this time they will address the question of the accountability of the EU – as did the European Council in the Laeken Declaration (December 2001) on convening a Convention on the Future. However this concern is soon relegated to a distant second place and governmental negotiators instead focus on the policy competences of the EU, the efficiency of the EU (its ability to make decisions) and which member states will be winners or losers under the proposed reforms. Nevertheless two areas of reform have potentially altered the incentives for voters and parties, and hence affected the democratic accountability of the EU: the powers of the European Parliament, and the way in which the Commission is elected.

A more majoritarian and/or powerful parliament

The power of the EP to influence EU policy outcomes has increased substantially since the 1980s (see Chapter 3). As discussed earlier, the evidence from MEP voting shows that as the EP's powers have increased, the EP parties have become more cohesive and more competitive. These are related: with more at stake in the EP there is a greater incentive to organize a division of labour within the EP and to compete to shape policy outcomes. This has led to increased media coverage, for example of the battle in March 1999 over the censure of the Santer Commission and the EP's rejection of the Takeover Directive in July 2001. However, the impact of these developments on the policy direction of the EU as a whole has been relatively limited because of the inherent checks and balances in the EU system. Therefore, who wins or loses EP elections has only a minor influence on the policy direction of the EU. Hence, the increasing powers of the EP have not forced national governments to worry too much about the outcome of EP elections.

However this could change. First, even without further treaty reforms the result of EP elections would matter more if the EP was organized differently. The EP parties control the key parliamentary positions, but these resources are allocated on a broadly proportional basis: for example each party wins committee chairs and *rapporteurships* in proportion to the number of seats it won in the last EP election. If resources and powers inside the EP were distributed on a winner-takes-all or even a winner-takes-most basis – for example if the largest party could choose the first five committee chairs – then the largest party group would have much more control over the EP policy agenda. As a result much more would be at stake in EP elections, as parties in government would start to fear being in a marginalized party group in the EP.

Second, further increases in the powers of the EP would also raise the stakes in EP elections. For example the proposed constitution would extend the co-decision procedure to all areas of EU law and give the EP majority the right to amend all areas of the EU budget (rather than simply those budgetary items that come under the heading 'non-compulsory expenditure'). With more powers for the EP, especially over the budget, the policy impact of the party-political make-up of the EP would be much more visible to national governments, the media and the EU citizens. For example a liberal–socialist–green coalition in the EP would be able to force the member state governments to accept fundamental changes to the Common Agricultural Policy (CAP). At present the EP cannot touch the CAP as agricultural spending is included in the 'compulsory expenditure' part of the budget.

Basically, parties and voters will only treat EP elections as opportunities to influence EU politics and policies if the result of these elections has more than a marginal impact on policy-making in the EU. This will require either fundamental changes to the internal workings of the EP or a dramatic step-change in the powers of the EP relative to those of the Council and the Commission. Another possible way of doing this would be to link the results of EP elections to the make-up of the Commission.

Election of the Commission: parliamentary or presidential?

The main electoral contest in all democratic polities is the battle for the head of the executive – the person who has most influence in setting the policy agenda, which in the case of the EU is the president of the Commission. As discussed in Chapter 2, traditionally, the s/election of the Commission President, by unanimous agreement among the heads of government, has been more akin to the selection of the head of an international agency than to the election of a head of government. The Maastricht and Amsterdam Treaties started to move the Commission President election procedure closer to a more traditional parliamentary model by giving the EP the right to veto the governments' nominee for Commission president. However, even under this new procedure the choice made by the governments has been easy to impose on the EP (Hix and Lord, 1995; Gabel and Hix, 2002).

However, the Nice Treaty introduced qualified-majority voting in the European Council for the selection of the Commission president. Superficially this might seem a minor step. However, this reform might fundamentally change the way the Commission president is elected by opening the door – or at least pushing it ajar – to more partisan competition for the most powerful position in EU politics. Without the prospect of having to build a large coalition, more politicians may be willing to put forward their name (as was the case in June 2004). Also it will be less easy for a small majority in the European Council to force their nominee on a reluctant EP.

Above all the Nice Treaty has changed the incentives for national parties, and made it more likely that the choice of the Commission president will be connected to the results of the EP elections. Political parties that are likely to be on the losing side in the nomination vote in the Council will have an incentive to propose a candidate before EP elections, in an attempt to take the political initiative away from the other side. And once one party federation has endorsed a candidate, the others will feel pressure to do the same. Then, with a number of names on the table, national parties would be forced to take sides in the EP election, and to maintain their positions in the subsequent bargaining in the European Council and EP. After the election the party that emerges as the largest group in the newly elected Parliament would refuse to support any other candidate in the European Council, or at least vote against a nominee from a party group that did not win the EP elections.

This could occur without any changes to the treaty. However, if adopted the proposed constitution would establish a more explicit link between EP elections and the choice of the Commission president. Article I-26 of the constitution states that when nominating a candidate the European Council must 'take into account the elections to the European Parliament'. Although the European Council would not be forced to follow the results of the elections, the wording of the article would make it difficult for the European Council to propose a candidate who is not the choice of one of the largest groups in the newly elected parliament. Other reformers wanted to take this even further by allowing the Commission president to be nominated by a majority in the EP, and then ratified by a qualified-majority in the Council.

Nevertheless, giving the EP the power to elect the Commission president would not be the same as allowing a government to be formed from the majority in a national parliament. Because the member state governments would still control the selection of the other commissioners, the Commission would remain a multiparty coalition. Also, despite some increases in the power of the Commission president to shape the allocation of portfolios, she or he would not have the same 'hire and fire' power as a national prime minister over her or his 'cabinet'. Hence even if EP elections were to determine who is the Commission president, this might not be enough to force national parties to stop treating these elections as second-order national contests.

Hence, one alternative would be to accept that the possibility of transforming EP elections via a quasi-parliamentary model of government for the EU is limited, and instead to introduce a presidential model of government: with a separate election for the Commission president (cf. Bogdanor, 1986; Decker, 2002). For example a direct election for the Commission president could be introduced, whereby candidates are selected by a certain number of MPs and MEPs in a certain number of member states, and then put before the electorate in a two-round contest, as in the French presidential election (Laver *et al.*, 1995). Alternatively the Commission president could be indirectly elected via an 'electoral college' of national MPs, or of MPs and MEPs (Hix, 1998b; 2002c). One advantage of the indirect method is that it would overcome the problem of an electorate not being motivated to vote in a contest for the Commission president. Then, if citizens in different member states demand that their parliamentary vote be replaced by a direct election, a direct election of the Commission president could gradually evolve in response to voters' demands, rather than being imposed from above.

The EU would look very different if there was a contest for the post of Commission president and real competition between parties for control of the EU policy agenda. The 'winning team' in these contests would be backed by a clearly identifiable group of supporters and would have a clear policy platform. If this platform failed the supporters would be held responsible. Moreover the losers of the contest would have an incentive to fight every proposal, to cultivate a president 'in waiting', and to try to construct a coalition large enough to support this candidate at the next election. This is how normal democratic politics works at the domestic level, and there is no reason why it should not also work at the European level.

There is some scope for parties to link the outcome of EP elections to policy-making and power inside the EP, and to the choice of Commission president. However if national parties continue to treat these elections as mid-term national contests, then the introduction of a new electoral contest (for the Commission president), with new powers at stake, may be the only way of breaking the hold of national parties and national governments over EU politics.

But, a directly elected Commission president would be inherently more powerful than is the case today, with a new legitimacy and a mandate to speak for all of the EU. This would reduce the ability of the Commission to act as an impartial broker in the EU legislative and regulatory processes. Moreover, it would be a giant step towards a more integrated Europe, which Europe's voters may neither support nor be prepared for. Also, because it would reduce their relative power in the EU system, the member state governments would no doubt resist such a move tooth and nail.

Conclusion: Towards Democratic EU Government?

The EU is not a very democratic system of government. We certainly elect our governments, who negotiate on our behalf in Brussels and decide who forms the EU executive. However, national government elections are about *national* issues, fought by *national* parties, and about who controls *national* government office. EP elections, moreover, are by-products of these national electoral contests: fought on domestic issues rather than the EU policy agenda or executive office-holders at the European level. In no sense, therefore, can Europe's voters choose between rival policy programmes for the EU or 'throw out' those who exercise political power at the European level.

The political consequences of this indirect system of representation and elections are not all bad. Voters have a distant impact on EU policies via national elections, and have increasingly used referendums on EU issues to constrain their governments' actions at the European level. Also, because EP elections tend to be lost by parties in government and won by parties in opposition, 'divided government' is the norm in the EU. As a result, no single political majority can dominate the EU policy process.

The problem, however, is that without a more directly democratic system there are few incentives for Europe's leaders to tackle some of the fundamental problems facing Europe: such as structural economic reforms, the place of the EU in the world, and how to deal with Europe's multiethnic society. In the current system the EU's elites have no incentive to tackle these issues, as any decision would alienate large sections of the public, and thus undermine the legitimacy of the EU. In a fully democratic polity, in contrast, tough policy decisions are resolved through the process of competitive elections, which forces elites to debate issues and allows voters to form opinions in response to this debate.

Given the opportunity, EU's voters and the nascent European level party organizations would be up to the challenge of EU democracy. In EP elections, the same factors explain the behaviour of EU voters in every member state. Politics in the EP is very much like politics in the member states, with cohesive parties competing on traditional left–right lines. Also, there are opportunities within the current institutional design of the EU for party-political contests to influence the policy process and the election of the president of the Commission.

However a real contest over the direction of the EU may only come about through more fundamental reforms. And since the battle for control of the policy agenda is the crucial contest in all democratic systems, how the Commission president is elected and the political fallout of a contest for this office on the workings of the EU will probably determine the viability of a more directly democratic system of government at the European level.

Because the power of the member state governments to run the EU would be significantly reduced by either a more powerful EP or an elected president of the Commission, it is unlikely that the governments will introduce the necessary reforms any time soon. However the point may be reached in the not too distant future when governments are punished by their voters for failing to take key decisions at the European level and the very existence of the EU will be threatened. Only then might governments consider more dramatic reform options that transform the EU into a more competitive model of democracy. Until such time it will be rational for EU citizens to be sceptical of the European integration process, and therefore not bother to vote in EP elections.

Chapter 7

Interest Representation

Theories of Interest Group Politics
Lobbying Europe: Interest Groups and EU Policy-Making
National Interests and the Consociational Cartel
Explaining the Pattern of Interest Representation
Conclusion: a Mix of Representational Styles

This chapter looks at the representation of societal interests at the European level. Interest groups play a central role in all democratic political systems, where private organizations represent 'civil society' in the policy-making process. Whereas political society at the European level, in terms of transnational political parties, is comparatively weak (as we saw in the previous chapter), civil society in Brussels is more developed, dense and complex than in most national capitals in Europe. In a sense Brussels is more like Washington, DC than Paris, London, Warsaw, Berlin or Prague. But is EU policy-making open to some of the popular criticisms of American pluralism – in which the best organized and funded special interests seem to reap the biggest rewards? Or is the EU more like national European polities, where policy-makers take an active role in balancing private and public interests?

Theories of Interest Group Politics

Pluralism is the classic model of interest group politics in democratic systems. The central idea in this model is that open access to policy-makers enables interest groups to provide checks and balances against powerful state officials and special interest groups (Truman, 1951). The main assumption is that for every group pressing on one side of a debate, another group will present the opposing view. If there are cross-cutting (rather than reinforcing) social divisions there will be 'multiple oppositions', and no single interest will ever be able to monopolize the political process (Lipset, 1959). In other words there is always a 'countervailing power', which will lead to social equilibrium (Bentley, 1967). A central requirement of the pluralist model, therefore, is that opposing interests have equal access to the political process. For example, environmentalist groups should have equal influence on government officials as the industrial lobby. If this is the case, to promote the 'public interest', governmental officials need only act as neutral referees of the interest group game.

But pluralists naïvely assumed that opposing groups have equal access to power (Galbraith, 1953; Schattschneider, 1960). Mancur Olson (1965, pp. 127–8) provided a powerful explanation of why:

> Since relatively small groups will frequently be able voluntarily to organize and act in support of their common interests, and since large groups normally will not be able to do so, the outcome of the political struggle among the various groups in society will not be symmetrical ... The small oligopolistic industry seeking a tariff or a tax loophole will sometimes attain its objective even if the vast majority of the population loses as a result. The smaller groups ... can often defeat the larger groups – which are normally supposed to prevail in a democracy. The privileged and intermediate groups often triumph over the numerically superior forces in the latent or large groups because the former are generally organized and active while the latter are normally unorganised and inactive.

The reason, Olson argued, was a 'logic of collective action': where there are high incentives to join a group that seeks benefits only for the members of the group (private interests), and low incentives to join a group that seeks benefits for all of society (public interests). With public interests people can simply 'free ride': reap the benefits of higher environmental protection, for example, without helping an environmentalist group to lobby the government. Similarly 'concentrated interests', representing particular producer interests, are more able to organize than 'diffuse interests' that represent the interests of society as a whole. The result is unequal access to political power, the capture of state officials by groups with the most resources, and outputs that benefit special interests at the expense of society as a whole (Wilson, 1980).

To overcome the biased outcomes inherent in the pluralist model, three alternative models of interest group intermediation have emerged. In each of these models the state actively promotes a particular structure of interest group politics, with the aim of producing more balanced representation and policy outcomes.

First, in the corporatist model the state assumes that the main division in society is between capitalists/business and workers/labour (Schmitter 1974; Schmitter and Lehmbruch, 1979). To promote an equal balance of power between these two forces the state recognizes, licenses and grants representational monopolies to the two sides of the class divide: the 'social partners'. Instead of open policy networks, the leaders of the business community and the trade union movement participate in closed tripartite meetings with state officials. If agreement can be brokered in these meetings, the assumption is that policy outcomes will reflect a broad social consensus.

Second, whereas corporatism privileges class interests, a consociational system of interest intermediation privileges cultural divisions, such as language, religion and nationality (Lijphart, 1968, 1977). Consociationalism is usually thought of as a set of formal constitutional practices – for example coalition government and proportional representation – to promote social harmony in culturally fragmented societies. But because the practices of equal participation, representation and veto for each cultural/linguistic group are extended into the bureaucracy, the policy-making process and the allocation of public funds, consociationalism can also be viewed as a system of interest intermediation (cf. Lehmbruch, 1967). For example, this is the dominant model of interest articulation in Belgium and Switzerland, and it is particularly relevant for the EU context, where the main social division is between the nation-states of Europe (see Chapter 5).

Third, neopluralists argue that the inherent biases in pluralism can be overcome if state officials simply cease to be neutral arbiters (Dunleavy and O'Leary, 1987; Petracca, 1994). In this model bureaucrats deliberately seek out, subsidize and give access to underrepresented public interests (Lindblom, 1977). Unlike corporatism and consociationalism, neo-pluralism does not involve privileging a particular set of social interests. Instead, on each policy issue the state promotes the group that represents the particular public interest at stake. So environmental groups would be asked to give evidence on industrial standards, consumer groups to look at product standards, women's groups to speak on gender equality legislation, trade unions to provide information on labour market policies, and so on.

However each of these models has its problems. First, corporatist and consociational systems arbitrarily privilege particular social groups while excluding others. As societies have changed, new social movements have emerged – such as environmental groups, women's groups and consumer groups – outside the traditional representational structures of labour and business (Dalton *et al.*, 1990). Second, in the corporatist system big business and industrial labour share similar 'producer interests' and hence promote these interests at the expense of the 'diffuse interests' of consumers and taxpayers. Third, requiring consent from both sides of industry, or from all cultural/national interests, reduces the ability of policy-makers to undertake policy change. Fourth, even in neo-pluralism, providing state funds to public interest groups introduces a perverse incentive for groups to organize for the purpose of securing state subsidies for their organizations rather than to promote the policy views of their members.

Nevertheless Olson's (1965) critique of pluralism may be overblown.

For example Becker (1983) argues that as the level of policy supplied to a concentrated interest rises, the incentives for the losing group to organize to oppose these policies will also rise. As a result, an equilibrium balance of interests will exist, and this will prevent policy-makers from supplying unlimited benefits to concentrated interests. In addition, considering the supply of access by policy-makers, information provided by interest groups is valuable for making good policy, and information from a group that has incurred high costs to gather and provide information is probably more credible than information from a group that has found it cheap to provide. Hence policy-makers are more likely to use information from groups that represent diffuse interests than groups that represent concentrated interests (Austen-Smith, 1993; cf. Lohmann, 1998). And, on the demand for interest group access, Austen-Smith and Wright (1994) argue that because groups will secure greater returns from lobbying policy-makers who have opposing policy views than from policy-makers with similar views, there are greater incentives for 'counteractive lobbying' than is often assumed in the classic critiques of pluralism (cf. Baumgartner and Leech, 1996).

In other words a perfect model of interest group representation does not exist, and what explains the structure of interest group politics in a policy area is the nature of the incentives and the interests of interest groups and policy-makers in that particular policy area. Hence more interesting questions for our purpose are which model of interest intermediation exists in which area of EU policy-making, and why? And how does the structure of interest representation in Brussels affect the policy outcomes, operation and legitimacy of the EU?

Lobbying Europe: Interest Groups and EU Policy-Making

The number of private individuals and groups seeking to influence the EU policy process has increased dramatically since the 1980s (Greenwood *et al.*, 1992; Mazey and Richardson, 1993; Pedlar and Van Schendelen, 1994; Wessels, 1997b; Greenwood and Aspinwall, 1998; Pedlar, 2002). Until the mid 1980s there were up to 500 interest groups with offices in Brussels (Butt Philip, 1985), but this number had trebled by the mid 1990s (Greenwood, 1997). Table 7.1 shows the number and types of interest group seeking to influence the EU policy process in 2001, as calculated by Greenwood (2003) from a variety of sources. Other scholars quote much higher figures, even as high as 5000 groups (Marks and McAdam, 1999), but, these estimates tend to be based on educated guesses rather than the Greenwood's careful counting from reliable sources.

Table 7.1   *Types and numbers of interest groups at the European level,
c. 2001*

Types of interest group	Number
Formal European level interest groups representing:	
Business	950
Public interests (e.g. NGOs)	285
Professions	158
Trade unions	43
Public sector	14
Individual companies in Brussels (with public affairs offices geared towards the EU)	250
Offices of member states' regions in Brussels	171
National interest groups in Brussels	170
Commercial public affairs consultancies in Brussels	143
EU law firms in Brussels	125
Total	2309

Source: Calculated from data in Greenwood (2003).

As the table shows, business interests are most represented at the
European level. Almost two thirds of the 1450 'formal' EU interest
groups (as recognized by the EU institutions) represent private businesses or industrial interests. In addition there are 250 firms with
public affairs divisions that are geared to influencing the EU policy
process. There are also 143 commercial 'lobbying' firms and 125 law
firms in Brussels. The self-described 'public affairs consultancies' specialize in advising interest groups on EU policy-making and legislation,
and mounting 'advocacy campaigns'. The clients of these commercial
consultancies are mainly individual firms, and these consultancies serve
as an alternative and more a direct route for businesses to influence the
EU institutions, rather than taking action through a European industrial or trade association (Lahusen, 2002, 2003).

In contrast, organizations that represent diffuse interests are less
numerous, but are nevertheless present in significant numbers. There
are well over 300 different interest groups representing public interests
(such as consumer groups, environmental groups and women's
groups), trade unions and the public sector. There are also a large
number of professional associations – representing groups such as
accountants, doctors, lawyers, teachers and journalists – that are
neither clearly on the side of big business nor on the side of 'the little
people'.

Finally, there are a large number of groups that represent territorially
defined interests, in the form of offices of regional or local govern-

ments in Brussels, associations of regions, and interest groups that promote particular national or regional rather than transnational interests.

The formal EU-recognized groups representing business and other interests take a variety of forms. Some bring together groups with the same broad interests throughout the EU, such as the European confederations of industry and trade unions. Others are sectoral (such as the chemicals industry), while others are issue-specific (such as environmental groups and women's groups). With few exceptions, European level groups have corporate rather than individual membership structures, representing a small or intermediate number of organizations rather than many thousands of private citizens. Conflicting interests among the various groups within the umbrella organizations – can often undermine the coherence of a single European voice by a particular industry or group of interests.

With regard to the number of people employed by the EU interest groups, and hence involved in EU 'civil society', estimates range from 10 000 to 30 000 (Greenwood, 2003, p. 9). Concrete indicators of the level of interest group activity in Brussels are the 3 400 annual passes issued by the European Parliament to outside interests (Watson, 2002). If one assumes that these passes are only issued to individuals who are actively involved in monitoring and lobbying the EU institutions (and not to administrative and support staff), then it could be said that there are about as many people trying to influence EU policy from the outside as there are actively making policy on in the inside of the EU institutions.

Business interests: the large firm as a political actor

Lobbying of the political process by private firms only really took off at the national level in the 1970s and 1980s, when governments began to set standards for the marketplace through new forms of economic and social regulation. However, with the European single market these standards are now set almost exclusively at the European level, and business interests are thus naturally drawn to the new political centre.

Business interests have not only responded to the emergence of regulatory competences in Brussels, they have also actively promoted this development. Even if certain European industries have been opposed to global free trade, most sectors of the European economy have been in favour of removing barriers to the free movement of goods, services and capital between the member states. This observation was at the heart of neofunctionalist theories of European integration in the 1950s, when business interests were the first to transfer their loyalties to the European level and promote European competences in sectors that were originally excluded (Haas, 1958, pp. 162–213). The situation was similar with the European single market, when European multinationals urged national governments and the Commission to pursue further market integration to help Europe recover from the recession of the 1970s (Sandholtz and Zysman, 1989).

A survey of over 224 business groups in Brussels in the mid 1990s revealed that the median number of full-time equivalent staff employed by a business group was 3–3.5, and that the majority of these groups had an annual turnover of more than €100 000 (Greenwood, 2002, pp. 12–13). The largest business group in terms of staff is the European Chemical Industry Council (CEFIC), which employs over 80 people.

Many business groups are national associations, offices of individual firms or sector-specific European associations, such the CEFIC and the Confederation of Agricultural Organizations in the EC (COPA), of national farmers associations. However, there are also several powerful cross-sectoral associations: most notably the Union of Industrial and Employers' Confederations (UNICE), the peak association of national business associations; the Association of Chambers of Commerce and Industry (EUROCHAMBRES); the European Round Table of Industrialists (ERT), comprising the chief executives of some of the largest European firms; the EU Committee of the American Chamber of Commerce (AMCHAM-EU), of American firms in Europe; and the European Association of Craft, Small and Medium-Sized Enterprises (UEAPME).

UNICE, for example, is a confederation of 32 national federations of business from 22 European countries – EU and non-EU – that was established in 1958. The UNICE office in Brussels has a permanent staff of 30, but the bulk of its work is in a network of committees and working groups that involve over 1000 officials from the member organizations. UNICE plays a high-profile role in EU policy-making, and its officials meet on an almost daily basis with Commission staff. It also regularly makes formal submissions to the EU institutions such as Commission and Council working groups and EP committees, but these submissions are usually only bland statements of business interests that are designed to include the views of as many member organizations as possible. One problem for UNICE is that member businesses and national associations have several exit options through their own private channels of representation if they think UNICE is not representing their interests effectively enough.

One of these exit options is the ERT which was established in 1983, by a select group of chief executive officers of some of the largest firms in Europe. Membership is by invitation only, and in 2004 it comprised 45 firms in a wide variety of sectors, with a combined turnover of over €850 billion and over four million employees worldwide. The members of ERT are the 'great and the good' of European business (see http://www.ert.be). In the early days its primary focus was the single market project: promoting the removal of technical barriers to trade in Europe while preventing the introduction of high social and environmental standards that would impose large costs on business (Cowles, 1995). Since the establishment of the single market, the members have maintained their personal contacts at the highest political level in national capitals and Brussels, and are therefore uniquely placed to make the case for business at the European level (van Apeldoorn, 2001). From the 1980s the ERT clubbed together with AMCHAM-EU and UNICE in the 'big business troika' (Cowles, 1997, 1998), and in the 1990s it was a central player in the formation of global business networks, such as the Transatlantic Business Dialogue, which brings together CEOs from Europe, the US and Canada (Cowles, 2002).

However this monolithic picture of business interests campaigning together to drive the EU policy process masks the fact that it is individual firms in pursuit of their own private interests that lies at the heart of the Brussels lobbying system. Individual firms, whether national, multinational or non-European, will only participate in umbrella organizations if the benefits are greater than the costs of participating. The growth in the membership of these cross-sectoral organizations suggests that they have been able to produce results, that is, EU policies that promote individual firms' interests. However individual firms have also developed sophisticated lobbying strategies of their own.

To find out where firms go to influence EU policy-making, David Coen (1997, 1998a) conducted a survey of 300 firms to ascertain how they allocated resources to influence the EU policy process. The data revealed that by the mid 1990s firms were allocating approximately equal resources to European and national associations. More significantly, however, individual firms had dramatically increased their private contacts with the Commission, either in addition to or deliberately bypassing the European-level associations. In terms of which strategy produced the highest pay-offs, approaching the Commission directly was the clear winner. Surprisingly, the employment of specialist lobbyists in Brussels was not seen as a rewarding strategy. Instead private consultants were employed to provide specialist information and monitoring services as a supplement to rather than a substitute for direct political action by individual firms.

In summary, business interests and the owners of capital are powerfully represented in the EU policy process. Regulation of the market at the European level provides a strong incentive for firms to spend valuable resources to ensure that policy outcomes do not harm their interests. Moreover individual firms have become increasingly sophisticated in their lobbying strategies, using multiple channels and diversifying their public affairs expenditure. The easy access of these interests to the Commission and the multiplicity of actors involved suggest a pluralist model of intermediation of business interests. But, for pluralism to work, groups with opposing interests to those of the business community must be equally well organized.

Trade unions, public interests and social movements

Groups with interests often diametrically opposed to the owners of business were not well represented in Brussels until the early 1990s. Representatives of a variety of societal interests have been formally represented in the Economic and Social Committee since its establishment following the Treaty of Rome, in an early attempt to inject an element of corporatism into the EU policy process. But, its status is purely consultative. A wide variety of social interests, such as trade unions, environmentalists and consumer groups, then became interested in the Brussels process as a result of the new EU competences in such areas as health and safety at work, environmental policy, consumer protection and social policy, in the wake of the Single European Act and Maastricht Treaty. However it was not until the 1990s that these groups really began to compete on a more equal basis with business groups.

The European Trade Union Confederation (ETUC) was founded in 1972. Like UNICE, ETUC is an umbrella organization, comprising 66 national trade union federations in 28 EU and non-EU states. These national federations together account for more than 60 million individual trade union members (Greenwood, 2003, p. 166). Also like UNICE, the number and diversity of the ETUC members make it difficult to construct a coherent European-level trade union strategy (Visser and Ebbinghaus, 1992; Dølvik and Visser, 2001). Unlike UNICE, ETUC is part of a network of like-minded public interest groups, even though its members have limited resources and few opportunities to pursue alternative lobbying strategies.

However, ETUC has increasingly been able to gain a place at the bargaining table as the legitimate 'social partner' of UNICE and the European Centre of Public Enterprises (CEEP), which represents nationalized industries. In 1984 the president of the Commission, Jacques Delors, announced that no new social policy initiatives would be forthcoming without the prior approval of both sides of industry, as represented by UNICE and ETUC. In the early years of this social dialogue little progress was made since UNICE insisted that its members would not be bound by any agreement reached with ETUC. However persistent Commission sympathy for the ETUC's cause ensured that the social dialogue did not dissolve. Delors launched the Commission's strategy for a European social policy at an ETUC meeting in May 1988, and the Commission supported the ETUC's proposal for a European Social Charter, which was signed in 1989 by all the member states except the UK. As a result of further Commission pressure, in 1990 the social dialogue produced three joint proposals that the Commission duly proposed as legislation (Story, 1996).

A boost for ETUC came with the Maastricht Treaty, which institutionalized the social dialogue in the area of social policy. The Maastricht Social Agreement extended the competences of the EU in the social policy field for all member states except the UK. Under the rules of the agreement, the Commission is now statutorily obliged to consult both business and labour before submitting proposals for social policy legislation (see Chapter 8). In addition, a member state may request that business and labour seek to reach an agreement on the implementation of directives adopted under the Social Agreement. Moreover, and most significantly, if business and labour reach a collective agreement on a particular policy issue, this can serve as a direct substitute for EU legislation. These rules provide the social partners with a considerable degree of agenda-setting power in the area of social policy (Boockmann, 1998). In other words, this is a classic model of corporatism in a central area of EU socioeconomic policy (Obradovic, 1996; Falkner, 1996).

However the social dialogue has not been a complete success from the point of view of labour interests (Falkner, 2000c; Compston and Greenwood, 2001). In practice, institutionalizing corporatism in the social policy area has given business interests a veto over legislation that they may not have been able to block in a centre-left-dominated EU Council or EP (Branch and Greenwood, 2001). The ETUC has also become reliant on the Commission's Directorate-General for Employment and Social Affairs for information, expertise and resources (Dølvik and Visser, 2001). And despite the quasi-corporatist EU decision-making on European-wide labour rights, there are few signs of a genuine transnational industrial relations system developing, with no European-wide collective agreements in particular industrial sectors or even within multinational firms (Martin and Ross, 2001). As a result labour interests are less influential at the European level than they have traditionally been at the national level, and they feel aggrieved by the gradual erosion of national corporatism by the process of EU economic integration and the passing of labour market regulation competences to the European level (Streeck and Schmitter, 1991; Falkner, 2000a).

Nevertheless, other diffuse interests have increased their access to policy-makers as EU integration has opened up new channels that enable interest group to go over the heads of national politicians and bureaucrats. Few public interest groups had a voice in Brussels before the late 1980s, but by the 1990s they were playing a central part in many EU policy debates.

In the environment field, eight groups make up the so-called 'G8 environmental NGOs': the European Environmental Bureau (EEB), the World Wide Fund for Nature (WWF), the Friends of the Earth Europe (FoEE), Greenpeace, the European Federation for Transport and Environment (T&E), Birdlife International, Climate Network Europe (CNE) and Friends of Nature International (IFN). Together these groups employ over 70 full-time staff and claim to have 20 million individual members between them. The individual membership basis of these groups enables the leaderships in Brussels to act cohesively, and their scientific and resource base means that these groups have acted as crucial monitors of the enforcement of EU environmental law (Harlow and Rawling, 1992; Webster, 1998).

In the area of consumers interests, the main interest group is the European Consumers' Organization (BEUC), which was founded in 1962, employs nine full-time staff and has a corporate membership structure, involving 34 national consumer organizations (Greenwood, 2003, p. 203). There is also a number of smaller groups: the European Association for the Coordination of Consumer Representation in Standardization (ANEC), the Association of European Consumers (AEC), the Confederation of Family Organizations in the European Union (COFACE) and the European Community of Consumer Cooperatives (EUROCOOP). Unlike the environmental groups, these groups are all umbrella organizations of various national consumer associations.

A large number of 'social NGOs' represent a wide variety of other public interests. For example there are at least 12 groups that bring together individual NGOs with similar interests: the Association of Voluntary Service Organizations (AVSO), the European Council for Voluntary Organizations (CEDAG), the Centre for Non-Profit Organizations (CENPO), the Combined European Bureau for Social Development (CEBSD), the European Citizen Action Service (ECAS), the European Foundation Centre (EFC), the European Platform of Social NGOs, the European Round Table of Charitable Social Welfare Associations (ETWELFARE), the European Social Action Network (ESAN), the International Council on Social Welfare (ICSW), SOLIDAR, and Voloneurope. Many of these organizations are themselves federations of federations. For example the European Platform of Social NGOs brings together 39 European-level public interest federations, networks and councils.

As with the labour movement, the key source of power and influence for these public interests is the Commission. Virtually all environmental, consumer and other public interest groups in Brussels derive their main source of funding from the EU budget, via the various directorates-general of the Commission. For example in 2002 environmental groups received a total of €6.5 million per year from the Commission, and consumer groups received €1.6 million (Greenwood,

2003, p. 199). One example of funding social NGOs was the €7 million the Commission spent in 1999 on anti-racist activists, most of which was channelled through European-level interest groups (Guiraudon, 2001).

The Commission has also been instrumental in setting up fora that provide these groups with access to the EU policy process. For example the EEB has often been invited to attend meetings of the Environment Council, and has even been a member of the Commission's delegation to the Earth Summits. In the area of consumer interests, the Consumers Contact Committee (CCC) was set up by the Commission in 1961, but was plagued by a lack of commitment on the part of the Commission and the rival interests of the various European-level consumer associations. In 1995 the Commission transformed its Consumer Policy Service into a proper directorate-general (DG), and reorganized the CCC into the Consumers' Committee (CC). The CC has a more streamlined structure, consisting of a small number of representatives (one from each of the five European-level consumer associations) and chaired by a Commission official (Young, 1997, 1998).

A similar process is taking place with the social NGOs. There has been much talk of a 'civil dialogue'. Several groups, including the Employment and Social Affairs DG and the Social Affairs Committee in the European Parliament, lobbied unsuccessfully for a legal reference to civil dialogue in the Amsterdam Treaty, in line with the model for the social dialogue. But even without a formal reference in the treaty, the European Platform of Social NGOs has emerged as the *de facto* forum for bringing together social NGOs and Commission officials on a regular and structured basis (Geyer, 2001).

One unfortunate consequence of these corporatist and neo-pluralist strategies by the Commission has been the cooptation of public interest groups. The practice of state officials proactively choosing partners has created a distinction between 'insider' and 'outsider' groups. The ETUC, BEUC and the EEB are clearly insiders in the EU policy process. Other groups are not sufficiently represented by the formal structures of representation in the EU or in the network of European associations with links to the Commission, while some NGOs have failed to socialize their members into acting inside rather than outside the emerging European-level organizational structures (Warleigh, 2001).

One result of the exclusion of some interests from the elitist structure of interest group representation in the EU is the increased use of more direct forms of collective action against the EU institutions, for example in the form of demonstrations in Brussels and other types of protest against the EU institutions (Tarrow, 1995; Imig and Tarrow, 2001). For instance farmers from several member states have often taken to the streets of Brussels to protest against the reform of the

Common Agricultural Policy or other farming issues, often against the explicit instructions of COPA, their European association (Bush and Simi, 2001). Numerous other groups have protested on the streets of Brussels or outside the EP in Strasbourg, ranging from bikers protesting against limits on the size of motorbike engines to animal rights campaigners protesting against the transportation of live animals. However the Europeanization of social protest through non-formal channels of representation is dependent on the pan-European politicization of an issue as well as the resources of the groups concerned. As a consequence, compared with the growing participation by insider groups such as the ETUC, the ability of outsider groups to mobilize in Brussels varies enormously (Marks and McAdam, 1996).

Territorial interests: at the heart of multilevel governance

Another set of non-business interests that has established an important role in the EU policy process is subnational regions. Table 7.2 shows the number of offices of substate authorities in Brussels. These include the offices of the state governments of the German, Belgian and Austrian federal systems; regional councils and other official organs of the decentralized unitary states of Italy, France and Spain; local government bodies of the unitary states of the UK, Ireland, Denmark, the Netherlands, Sweden, Greece, Portugal and Finland; and various intermediary associations of local authorities, communities, municipalities, towns, cities, regions and subnational units.

Some of these subnational groups have been represented in Brussels since the start of the 1970s, but the majority only began to mobilize in the late 1980s following the reform of EU regional policies. The 1988 reform of the structural funds led to the conscious 'outflanking' of national governments by the Commission and the regions (Pollack, 1995b) (see Chapter 9). On the one hand, the Commission consciously sought the involvement of regional interests in the initiation, adoption and implementation of regional policy. On the other hand, regional interests made the most of the opportunity to bypass national governments, many of which were of opposing political hues or were cutting back on national regional spending. 'Partnership' between the Commission and regional government became the guiding principle in this policy area. Regional bodies were invited to submit funding applications directly to the Commission, and funds were forwarded directly to regional authorities rather than passing through central government treasuries. In addition, regional bodies were responsible for implementing their own framework programmes, monitored by Commission officials.

The formal involvement of regions in EU policy-making was further institutionalized by the creation of the Committee of the Regions

Table 7.2   *Regions and localities with offices in Brussels, 2004*

Member state	No. of substate offices in Brussels
United Kingdom	25
France	23
Germany	21
Spain	20
Italy	19
Netherlands	15
Austria	12
Poland	12
Sweden	10
Denmark	9
Finland	9
Belgium	5
Greece	3
Slovakia	3
Ireland	2
Czech Republic	1
Estonia	1
Hungary	1
Norway	1
Total	192

Source: The Brussels European Liaison Office (http://www.blbe.irisnet.be).

(CoR) by the Maastricht Treaty (Hooghe, 1995). The CoR replaced the Consultative Council of Regional and Local Authorities (CCLRA) which had been set up by the Commission in 1988 as part of the new regional policy regime. The members of the CCLRA had been appointed by two European-wide subnational associations: the Assembly of European Regions (AER) and the Council for European Municipalities and Regions (CEMR). In the new CoR, these transnational associations were replaced by representatives of regional and local governments in each member state. Some of these were nominated by the central government, as in the UK, but most were independently nominated by subnational bodies, such as the French regional assemblies and the German states. The Maastricht Treaty specified that the CoR had the right to be consulted not only in the adoption and implementation of EU regional policies but also in all policy areas that had implications for European economic and social cohesion. This included all policies that affect the level of economic and social disparities in Europe, such as the Common Agricultural Policy and the Common Transport Policy.

The existence of EU competences in the area of regional policy, and the deliberate funding and promotion of regional representation by the Commission are not the only explanations of the different levels of regional mobilization. Another important factor is whether the member state of which a region is part has a tradition of private/pluralist or state-funded/corporatist interest representation (Marks *et al.*, 1996; Jeffrey, 2000). In other words regions tend to establish offices in Brussels not because of the competences of the EU, but because of their own competences *vis-à-vis* national governments. As a result those subnational governments with the broadest range of policy competences, such as the German and Belgian states, all have offices in Brussels. Furthermore, backed by constitutional statutes the German and Belgian states have forced their national governments formally to include them in the German and Belgian delegations in the Council when the agenda touches on subnational competences. Nevertheless, as Table 7.2 shows, there are more regional interest groups in Brussels from the UK and France, two of the most centralized states in Europe, than from Germany, Spain or Italy.

The consequence, many claim, is a system of 'multilevel governance', whereby policies are made through interaction between regional, national and European-level authorities. Because of the role of regional authorities in the operation of the structural funds, the multilevel governance approach was developed first in research on EU regional policy (Marks, 1993). However as regional interests have been incorporated into other EU policies, and as EU policy deliberation and implementation has involved a growing number of participants at the regional and local levels, the multilevel governance conception has gradual evolved into a general model of EU decision-making (Hooghe and Marks, 1996).

However, it is difficult to extrapolate a general theory of the EU from the structure of interest intermediation in the area of regional policy-making. And because the CoR has remained marginalized in the EU policy process, regions are considerably less influential in most other policy areas than are the various business, labour or social interests (Hooghe, 2002). In response, proponents of multilevel governance have argued that this concept refers to the emergence of multiple levels of bargaining outside the dominance of the national governments, and not only to the notion that the EU is a three-level system (Marks *et al.*, 1996; Kohler-Koch, 1996).

In summary, since the start of the single market project Brussels has become more like Washington, DC than most national European capitals in terms of the volume and intensity of private lobbying of the political process. The bulk of this activity is by individual firms and national and European associations that represent business interests. However, fostered by the EU institutions, public interests, old and new social movements and subnational governmental bodies have begun to fight back. The result is a sophisticated and complex system with elements of pluralism, corporatism and neopluralism.

National Interests and the Consociational Cartel

The informal and semiformal systems of transnational interest representation compete in the EU policy process with a highly institutionalized system of national interest representation. The EU is a multinational political system, and the structure of the policy process is deliberately designed to accommodate most, if not all, national preferences, cultures, styles and traditions. This relates not only to the adoption of EU law, where national governments are formal participants in the central legislative and executive organs (the Council and European Council), but also to the policy initiation and policy implementation stages of the EU policy process.

At the policy initiation stage, the Commission has a formal monopoly on legislative initiative in most areas of social and economic policy. However in practice the Commission develops policy proposals in cooperation with representatives from national administrations. This operates through a network of working groups composed of national representatives and chaired by a Commission official. Most of these representatives are civil servants, but national administrations also use officials from domestic interest groups to represent their views in the policy process. The national civil servants in these committees are more likely to be influenced by interest groups from their own particular state than by the European level groups.

At a more informal level, the Commission is highly understaffed and relies on officials and representatives from national constituencies – such as national peak associations of business or professional groups – to supply knowledge and information about existing national policy regimes and interests. Furthermore the Commission itself is a multinational bureaucracy, with senior officials linked to specific national constituencies and interest groups. The result is an ongoing bargaining process between the Commission and the representatives of state and non-state national interests. At the policy initiation stage the Commission aims to discover policy ideas that accommodate as many national preferences as possible in the hope that excluded interests can be incorporated at a later stage: the formal legislative bargaining stage in the Committee of Permanent Representatives and the Council.

The same process of privileging national interest groups exists at the implementation stage. EU directives have to be transposed into law through national instruments. This gives a specific role to national administrations in the implementation of EU policies. In terms of the incorporation of interests, moreover, this allows different national legal and administrative traditions to be reconciled with EU action. The implementation process is overseen by a network of supervisory and regulatory committees in the 'comitology' system (see Chapter 2). These committees are composed of delegates from national administrations. Many come directly from national interest groups, or are seconded from interest groups because of their particular policy expertise.

In other words the EU policy process possesses all the classic features of the consociational model of interest intermediation (cf. Taylor, 1991, 1996; Chryssochoou, 1994; Gabel, 1998c). As discussed in Chapter 5, society in the EU is primarily divided along territorial–cultural rather than transnational–socioeconomic lines. The elites of these national segments – national governments, public administrations and representatives of national interest groups – are the main participants in the EU policy process. In this sense the national administrations in the EU, who incorporate the views of national interest groups before coming to the EU bargaining table, are the functional equivalent of the ethnic, linguistic and religious political parties in the Dutch, Belgian and Swiss consociational systems.

These elites are able to present and defend their perceived 'national interests' above all other types of political conflict at the European level. This facilitates the calculation of winners and losers of policy proposals along national rather than transnational–socioeconomic lines. The need to secure cross-class support in national elections ensures that national governments defend the interests of all their constituents over interests in other member states that may be closer ideologically. For example, a British Labour government would be more inclined to listen to and defend the interests of British business than the interests of the working class across Europe.

European level interest groups, which are themselves associations of national groups, try to coordinate the positions taken by their national members, so that a common message is transmitted at both the national and European levels. European level interest groups often urge their national members to persuade reluctant governments to support their proposals. For example in battles on several social policy directives – such as the Works Council Directive or the series of directives regulating working hours – the British Trade Union Congress supported the position taken by the ETUC and lobbied the British Labour government, which was generally opposed to the legislation, to support the Commission's proposals.

However the cohesion of the European-level interest groups often breaks down, and national interest groups often decide to line up with their national governments and officials at the various stages of the EU policy-making process. When this happens the European-level associations have few sanctions to impose on their members, and the EU system seems less pluralist or corporatist and more consociational.

But, whether private or public interests benefit from this shift to national-based conflicts depends on which national groups have access to national decision-makers. It does not always hold that national-based interest representation is more protective of public interests than European-level interest representation. For example Schneider and Baltz (2003) find that concentrated special interests tend to be more influential than public interests in shaping national bargaining positions in pre-legislative negotiations on legislative proposals from the Commission.

Explaining the Pattern of Interest Representation

This complex system of European-level interest articulation and inter-mediation has evolved through an interaction between the growing demand for participation by non-state actors in the EU policy process, and the supply of access by supranational governmental officials. The goals of these actors have remained stable: for interest groups, policy outcomes close to their interests; and for EU governmental actors, more power in the EU decision-making process. However, the strategies of the actors have evolved in response to the changing structure of opportunities in the EU.

Demand for representation: globalization and Europeanization

On the demand side, public and private interests in Europe have faced a transformation of economic and political institutions since the 1960s. First, the globalization of the economy – through the expansion of cross-border trade and capital movements – has challenged the traditional patterns of capital–labour relations in Europe. The removal of tariff barriers, and the resultant globalization of product markets, has forced individual firms that compete in international markets to pursue new competitive strategies. Freed from restraints on capital mobility, these strategies have included cross-border relocation, merger, joint ventures, specialization and diversification. As a result, companies have had to become multinational to survive.

This has produced new relationships between economic and governmental actors. Multinational firms are less interested in securing national protection of their products and markets than in securing transnational policies that will enable them to increase productivity. Instead of lobbying for national protection, companies are increasingly lobbying politicians and regulators to secure neoliberal and deregulatory policies. From an individual firm's point of view, the rewards from national corporatist bargaining with governmental and labour actors, and even from membership of national business associations, have receded as the benefits of private action have increased. As discussed above, in the last ten years individual companies in Europe have become less interested in national policy processes and national business associations are more interested in approaching market regulators privately and directly, whether at the regional, national, European or international levels and even in other national systems.

Hence European integration and globalization have undermined the ability of national state officials to incorporate business actors into consensual models of interest intermediation in the national system (Streeck and Schmitter, 1991; Crouch and Menon, 1997). Once business interests exit, there is little incentive for governments to talk to the other side. Moreover, whereas individual companies possess the resources to organize at new levels of politics, labour and other public interests need collective organizations to secure resources.

Second, the opportunity structure for social and economic interests in Europe has been transformed by the accumulation and concentration of market regulation functions at the European level, most notably in the Commission. Firms are not interested in the large public spending priorities, such as health, education and welfare, which are still controlled by national governments. What they are interested in, and why they began to take interest in politics at the domestic level in the first few decades of the postwar period, are rules governing the production, distribution and exchange of goods, products and services in the marketplace (Coen, 1998a, 1998b). Multinational corporations were quick to realize that the centralization of market regulation in the EU institutions would significantly reduce the transaction costs of doing business in Europe. Consequently individual companies were some of the most vocal proponents of the single market, and since the establishment of the single market, Brussels' position at the centre of multinational lobbying strategies has been confirmed.

However the incentive for business interests to seek European-level regulations varies by industrial sector (Weber and Hallerberg, 2001). Firms' preferences for European-level market regulation depend on the size of the threat of competition from firms outside the EU, and on the transaction costs of moving assets and changing production levels in their particular industry. Industries with strong competition and high transaction costs, such as the car and aerospace industries, were the first to mobilise to persuade EU policy-makers to introduce European-wide market integration and regulation in their sectors.

On the other side, with a single political centre regulating the European market, the cost of mobilizing non-business interests has also reduced. Instead of trying to prevent industry-wide cost-cutting in several EU states, public interests with a coordinated transnational plan of action can go straight to Brussels to campaign for their causes. For example, in response to the deregulatory policies of the British

Conservative governments in the 1980s the British trade union movement became one of the strongest financial sponsors and political backers of the activities of the ETUC. Similarly it is much cheaper for environmental and consumer groups to defend their interests in Brussels than in each national capital.

Similar factors explain the desire of private and public interests to organize at the European level (cf. Jordan, 1998). Driven by economic globalization, private companies have abandoned national interest intermediation in favour of direct action at the European level to promote market liberalization. Driven by political Europeanization, diffuse interests have turned to Brussels as the new political centre in which to pursue European-wide social interests as an adjunct to and sometimes substitute for national structures of interest intermediation (Warleigh, 2000; Geddes, 2000a; Imig and Tarrow, 2001).

And once there are incentives to mobilize at the European level, the rules of the game of EU policy-making provide plenty of opportunities for private or public interests to influence EU policies. The EU legislative procedures (as we saw in Chapter 4) grant agenda-setting, amendment and veto powers to multiple actors. Hence interest groups are likely to find someone somewhere in the EU system who will listen to their arguments or want to receive information they can use to shape policy outcomes (Crombez, 2002). Contrast this with policy-making at the domestic level in Europe, where majority support for governing parties in parliaments usually means there are few opportunities to change legislation or budgets dramatically once they have been proposed. Hence, at the domestic level, interest groups are forced to focus their efforts on the prelegislative stage of policy-making. At the EU level, in contrast, interest groups have the opportunity to change the direction of policy at any point in the legislative process, from prelegislative preparation through amendment during legislative adoption, and even post-adoption implementation.

Supply of access: policy expertise and legislative bargaining

Without adequate response by EU decision-makers, the new interest group strategies would have been ineffectual and short-lived. The fact that all forms of EU lobbying have increased suggests that the demand for representation has been met with a concomitant supply of access to the policy process by political actors in the EU institutions (Pollack, 1997b; Cram, 1998, Bouwen, 2002).

As discussed throughout, the key institution in the supply of access to non-state interests is the Commission, which has an incentive to grant private interest groups with access in exchange for specialized information and expertise (Broscheid and Coen, 2003). Given the size and complexity of the task of regulating a single market of over 450 million people and 25 national regulatory systems, the Commission is an extremely small bureaucracy. 'Not surprisingly, officials often lack the necessary detailed expertise and knowledge of sectoral practices and problems' (Mazey and Richardson, 1997, p. 198). The Commission has even sought to formalize this process. As a guide to Commission staff, the Commission has drawn up directories listing all known national and European-level interest groups by policy area as part of a 'procedural ambition' to maximize consultation with European civil society. In addition, when the Commission identifies an unoccupied niche for a European-level group, it attempts to create and sustain one. The Commission has also adopted the British practice of publishing 'green papers' – preliminary legislative proposals – as a means of opening up the debate on EU policy to a wider audience. The Commission refers to this overall strategy as an 'open and structured dialogue with special interest groups' (European Commission, 1992; McLaughlin and Greenwood, 1995).

The European Parliament has pursued a similar strategy to the Commission. Although it is not responsible for policy initiation its powers have increased, making it an increasingly popular target for interest groups (Earnshaw and Judge, 2002). From the EP's point of view, more power means a greater need for detailed policy expertise to enable it to compete effectively with the Council and the Commission in the legislative process. Whereas the Council has national public administrations to supply information, individual MEPs have limited research budgets. Consequently, when writing reports and proposals for EP resolutions, *rapporteurs* seek out key interest groups to canvass their views. Indeed it is often rumoured that representatives from European interest associations have written significant portions of some EP reports.

Table 7.3 shows the results of a survey of MEPs in 2000 about their links with interest groups (cf. Kohler-Koch, 1997). Over 90 per cent of MEPs stated that they had contacts with interest groups at least once a month. Interestingly, MEPs are more likely to be in contact with national interest groups than with European-level associations. For example 51 per cent had contacts at least once a month with national environmental groups, but only 36 per cent had similar contacts with such groups at the European level. This is not surprising if one considers that MEPs are elected on national party lists in national constituencies (see Chapter 6), and are hence more eager to speak to national groups than European-level groups.

Moreover, and contrary to Austen-Smith's theory of 'counteractive lobbying' (as discussed in the introduction), the survey also revealed that MEPs are more likely to be in contact with groups with similar policy preferences than groups with divergent preferences. MEPs on the centre-right (in the EPP) are more likely to be in contact with

Table 7.3   *MEPs' contacts with interest groups, by party group, 2000*

| | All MEPs | By party group (left to right) | | | | |
		EUL/NGL	G/EFA	PES	ELDR	EPP
		Percentage of MEPs who had contact with a particular type of interest group at least once a month				
Any interest group	91	100	92	90	94	94
National groups						
Consumer groups	42	31	54	42	42	42
Environmental groups	51	64	85	48	58	43
Trade unions	39	62	38	54	26	28
Professional associations	47	46	31	51	37	54
Agriculture/fisheries groups	33	23	23	22	47	41
Industry organizations	45	25	38	38	58	54
Trade/commerce associations	32	7	15	25	47	44
Banking/insurance groups	24	0	8	23	28	31
European-level groups						
Consumer groups	36	23	31	43	42	33
Environmental groups	36	31	46	37	47	32
Trade unions	25	23	15	42	21	17
Professional associations	17	0	0	16	28	23
Agriculture/fisheries groups	18	8	0	12	32	26
Industry organizations	29	8	23	27	47	34
Trade/commerce associations	15	0	0	12	22	23
Banking/insurance groups	12	0	0	14	6	17
Human rights groups	35	43	46	42	32	30
No. of MEPs responding to the survey	193	14	13	61	19	72

Notes: EUL/NGL European United Left/Nordic Green Left, G/EFA Greens/European Free Alliance, PES Party of European Socialists, ELDR European Liberal, Democrat and Reform Party, EPP European People's Party. Not enough MEPs from the other party groups (the UEN and EDD) answered the survey questions to produce reliable results for these groups.

Source: European Parliament Research Group 'MEP Survey 2000' (field research conducted in November 1999 to February 2000, see: http://www.lse.ac.uk/depts/eprg).

groups representing industry, trade/commerce, banking/insurance and agriculture/fisheries than are MEPs on the left (in the PES, G/EFA and EUL/NGL), who are more likely to be in contact with groups representing trade unions, environmental interests and human rights (cf. Wessels, 1999).

The primary motivation for the supply of representation by the Commission and the EP is the ongoing power game in the EU legislative process (cf. Cram, 1998). In other words information and expertise matter, but only as a way of increasing the chance of Commission officials and MEPs securing what they want from the EU legislative process. Interest groups possess what Greenwood (1997, pp. 18–23) calls 'bargaining chips', which they offer actors in the EU political process. In addition to information and expertise, these include the ability to influence the national member organizations of a European association and the ability to help in the implementation of policy. Both of these can be used by the Commission and the EP to undermine opposition to a proposal in the Council. For example the German government would be reluctant to oppose a legislative initiative if the Commission or EP could demonstrate that key German interest groups supported the initiative and were willing to facilitate the transposition of the policy into national practice.

Whereas the mobilization of national loyalties and interests strengthens the position of national governments in the Council, the mobilization and incorporation of transnational interests strengthens the hand of the supranational institutions. As a result the institutional structure of the EU system provides an incentive for the Commission and the EP to supply negotiating space and resources to groups that represent transnational socioeconomic constituencies, including the labour movement, environmentalists, consumers and social NGOs as well as individual companies and business organizations.

Conclusion: a Mix of Representational Styles

The system of interest representation at the European level is complex and dense. Business interests, which have more incentives and substantially more financial and political resources than public interests, are particularly capable of playing the Brussels game. At face value this makes interest group politics at the European level look like primitive pluralism, in which there is little countervailing power to block manipulation of the political process by the owners of capital. Without cohesive European political parties to promote wider public interests, diffuse interests will always struggle to compete with the more highly organized and resourced business lobby. This vision of a Europe dominated by an alliance of big business against the people of Europe was a common criticism by left-wing parties and Marxist scholars in the 1970s and early 1980s (for example Holland, 1980).

However national interests are also privileged as a result of the institutionalization of consociational practices, such as committees of national experts and bargaining in the Council. Policies are never adopted without the consent of a broad alliance of national groups. Consequently, when these national constituencies are close to labour or public interests, business groups cannot monopolize the policy process. For example, viewed from the UK, where business interests dominated in the 1980s, the EU policy process appears to replicate the continental corporatist model. Viewed from Scandinavia, in contrast, where public interests have managed to secure high levels of labour, environmental and consumer protection, the EU appears to work like Anglo-Saxon pluralism.

A further brake on pluralism is the increasing organization and participation of public interests at the European level. On the one hand, the centralization of market regulation in Brussels provides a focus for social movements at the European level. On the other hand, institutional competition provides an incentive for the Commission and EP to formalize neo-pluralist and corporatist practices. The promotion of transnational alliances spanning both sides of a policy debate strengthens the information capacity and the credibility of these supra-national actors against the Council in the day-to-day legislative process. Also, by fostering the emergence of socioeconomic allegiances that cut across national divisions, these strategies increase the public support bases for the Commission and the EP.

The constant interaction between consociational accommodation of national interests and pluralist, neo-pluralist and corporatist intermediation of transnational socioeconomic interests is slow, opaque and unpredictable. Without a dominant executive actor, such as a president or governing political party, to serve as the ultimate arbiter, any well-connected group of interests can block a policy initiative. Despite this the EU has been able to incorporate a wide variety of interests in the policy process and still produce significant policy outputs (see Chapters 8–12).

Finally, at the national level interest representation exists side by side with the formal channels of representative government, via party competition and elections. As the previous chapter has shown, the EU does not have a real system of competitive party government. Some scholars and activists believe that a vibrant civil society in Brussels may be a way of bringing the EU closer to the citizens (for example Schmitter, 2000). However, as discussed in Chapter 5, public support for the EU has declined while the volume and density of interest group activity in Brussels has increased. Clearly citizens are not convinced. Hence, as at the domestic level in Europe – where for decades the decline of parties and the rise of interest groups has been predicted but has never materialized – interest groups are unlikely ever to be more than lubricants of the policy-making machine, albeit essential lubricants.

Part III

Policy-Making

Chapter 8

Regulation of the Single Market

Modern studies of public policy differentiate between three basic types of economic policy: regulatory policies, expenditure policies and macroeconomic policies (Musgrave, 1959; Lowi, 1964). The EU supplies all three of these policy types: this chapter considers EU regulation, Chapter 9 studies EU expenditure and Chapter 10 looks at the macroeconomic issues involved in economic and monetary union.

With the increased delegation of economic, social and environmental regulatory policy competences to the European level, the EU has been described as a 'regulatory state' (see especially Majone, 1996; Egan, 2001). This chapter analyzes the regulations produced by the EU, how they are made, and why the EU regulates some areas more than others. We shall first look at some general political science explanations of regulation and regulatory policy-making.

Theories of Regulation

Economic policies have two possible effects: redistribution and efficiency. The difference between these effects is illustrated in Figure 8.1. In this hypothetical society there are two citizens, A and B, and the current government policy, X, produces benefits of AX and BX for the citizens. The government considers two possible policy changes: Y and Z. A move to policy Y would have a 'redistributive' effect, making citizen A better off (by $AY - AX$) but citizen B worse off (by $BY - BX$). In fact any policy change along the line that goes through X and Y would mean a redistribution of benefits from one citizen to the other. In contrast a move to policy Z would benefit both citizens (by $AZ - AX$ and $BZ - BX$ respectively). In fact, any policy change from X to somewhere in the shaded area would make one citizen better off without making the other worse off. This is known as a 'pareto-efficient' outcome (after the Italian sociologist Vilfredo Pareto).

235

Figure 8.1   *Difference between redistributive and efficient policies*

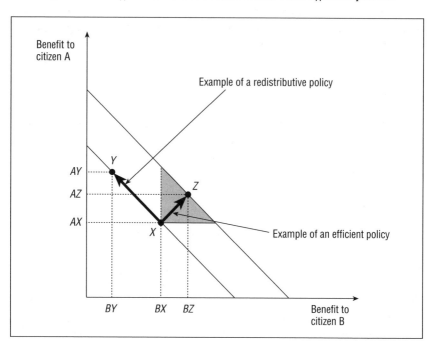

Producing outcomes that are in the interests of everyone – the 'public interest' – is the traditional aim of regulatory policies (Mitnick, 1980; Sunstein, 1990). In neoclassical economic theory, free markets are naturally pareto-efficient, but in the real world there are numerous 'market failures'. Regulation can be used to correct these failures:

- *Technical standards* and *consumer protection standards* enable consumers to acquire information about the quality of products that would otherwise not be publicly available.
- *Health and safety standards* and *environmental standards* reduce the adverse effects (negative externalities) of market transactions on individuals who do not participate in the transactions.
- *Competition policies* prevent the emergence of monopolistic markets, market distortions (through state subsidies) and anticompetitive practices (such as price collusion).
- *Industry regulators*, through such instruments as price controls, ensure that natural monopolies operate according to market practices.

However if economic policies are made by traditional democratic (majoritarian) institutions such as parliaments or governments, they will tend to be redistributive rather than efficient. Parliaments and governments are controlled by political parties, which will try to achieve policy outputs that benefit their supporters (see Chapter 6). Democratic government consequently tends to lead to policies that redistribute resources from the losing minority to the winning majority in a particular electoral contest (Lijphart, 1994; Majone, 1998b). For example in the case of expenditure policies, governments on the left usually raise the taxes imposed on the wealthiest members of society and increase public spending on social benefits, whereas governments on the right tend to reduce taxes and cut benefits. If democratic majorities are allowed to govern regulatory policies, similar redistributive outcomes will result: for example the left will use regulation to improve the rights of workers and protect the environment, thus imposing costs on business, and the right will do the opposite.

Consequently, a central argument in the regulatory politics literature is that if regulatory policies are meant only to correct market failures, with pareto-efficient rather than redistributive outcomes, these policies should be made by 'non-majoritarian', or independent, institutions (Majone, 1996). As early as the 1880s the US government established independent agencies to regulate the US market (Skowronek, 1982), and European governments began to take similar steps in the 1980s (Majone, 1994). At the domestic level in Europe, independent agencies have been set up to regulate industries that were previously publicly owned, and at the EU level the Commission has been delegated the responsibility for regulating the single market.

However, this traditional 'public interest' justification of regulation is essentially normative (Joskow and Noll, 1981). Contemporary political science also analyzes policy outputs using positive theories, which seek to explain policy outcomes through deductive reasoning. The first positive approach to regulation was Stigler's (1971) 'economic theory of regulation', in which regulation is demanded by private interests and supplied by politicians. On the demand side, applying Olson's (1965) theory of interest-group organization, certain interests groups are more able than others to mobilize to influence regulators (see Chapter 7). For example the cost to a monopolistic firm of a price control is large (selective), whereas the benefit to an individual consumer or taxpayer is small (diffuse). Consequently producer groups (business interests) are more able to exert influence on regulators than diffuse public interests, such as consumers, taxpayers, environmentalists and employees.

On the supply side, using Downs' (1957) theory of electoral politics, Stigler assumes that politicians primarily seek re-election. They recognize that regulations impose costs on some voters and provide benefits to others, and that groups that are the subject of regulation tend to have more available resources to finance politicians' campaigns. The general voter tends to be 'rationally ignorant' about the details of specific regulatory policy proposals, and as a result politicians have an incentive to supply regulatory policies to producers. Stigler (1971, p.

94) consequently concludes that 'as a rule, regulation is acquired by the industry and is designed and operated primarily for its benefit'.

This positive theory leads to opposite conclusions from the traditional normative approach about how regulations should be made: independent regulators are unlikely to produce pareto-efficient policies and are more easily 'captured' than democratic/majoritarian institutions such as parliaments and elected governments. But the reality tends to lie somewhere between these perspectives (Peltzman, 1989). In practice no single producer, industry or profession is ever able to capture a regulatory agency completely, and regulations invariably provide at least some benefits to consumers and other diffuse interests (Stigler and Friedland, 1962; Jordan, 1972). In fact, as the losses to consumers increase their incentive to mobilize to prevent regulatory capture grows (Peltzman, 1976; Becker, 1983).

The normative theory of regulation also ignores the part played by institutions in shaping the way in which regulators behave. Regulation is made in a complex institutional environment, involving legislatures, courts, executives and competing regulatory agencies on multiple levels of government. For example in multilevel political systems such as those in the US and EU, regulations can be produced at several levels of government (Kelemen, 2000). Given a choice, producers would prefer market regulations to be produced at the highest level of government. First, because it is more expensive to organize at a higher level it will be harder for diffuse interests to mobilize against producers at that level (cf. Cawson and Saunders, 1983; Dunleavy, 1997). Second, at the higher level there may be competition between different local regulatory regimes and this enables footloose capital to choose the least regulated regions and force governments to introduce deregulatory policies to attract capital (Scharpf, 1997a).

The discretion of regulatory agencies can also be limited by institutional controls (as we saw in Chapter 2): a legislature can use a variety of institutional mechanisms to ensure that a regulator does not supply policies that are solely for the benefit of the subject producer. For example a parliament can specify the public interest criteria in a regulator's contract, choose a new head of the agency every few years, and require the regulator to consult diffuse interests and report to a parliamentary committee and the media (cf. Fiorina, 1982; Weingast and Moran, 1983; Moe, 1987; Horn, 1995). Nevertheless, if a regulatory agency is tightly controlled by a legislative majority we are back to where we started: with a parliamentary majority using regulation as a means to redistribute benefits to a particular electoral majority rather than to society as a whole.

In sum, regulatory policy-making is a struggle. Normative analysis tells us that if regulatory policies are to be efficient (in their attempt to overcome market failures), they should be delegated to non-majoritarian institutions such as the European Commission. However positive theory tells us that once regulatory powers have been delegated, the subjects of regulation (producer groups) are more likely to be able to influence regulators than are public interest groups. In addition, business interests will tend to demand institutional configurations that allow them to 'capture' the regulator, such as regulatory agencies at the highest political level. Faced with this situation, politicians can introduce mechanisms to limit regulatory discretion. However politicians like to provide policies that cater to supporters' interests, and as a result might wish to allow regulatory capture by a particular sector of the economy, such as the French agricultural sector or the British financial services sector. Alternatively politicians could simply capture the regulatory authority themselves, for example by limiting the independence of the Commission.

Deregulation via Negative Integration: the Single Market and Competition Policies

The EU produces two types of regulatory policy: negative integration policies, which involve the removal of barriers to international trade and competition; and positive integration policies, which involve the establishment of new EU-wide regulations (Tinbergen, 1965; Scharpf, 1996). Negative integration policies include the establishment of the single market and competition policies. Because these policies involve the abolition of national rules and the liberalization of national markets, and because neoliberals are generally in favour of such policies, they are often seen as deregulatory rather than regulatory.

The single market

At the Milan European Council in June 1985 the EU heads of government adopted the Single European Act (SEA) and the Commission's white paper *Completing the Internal Market* (European Commission, 1985). The SEA set the deadline of 31 December 1992 for the implementation of the Commission's proposals, and introduced new institutional mechanisms to achieve this goal: qualified-majority voting in the Council and the cooperation procedure with the EP (see Chapter 3). The Commission's white paper set out approximately 280 pieces of legislation that would be necessary to complete the single market. This legislation covered three main areas: physical barriers, technical barriers and fiscal barriers (cf. Pelkmans and Winters, 1988).

First, with regard to physical barriers the Commission proposed lifting controls on the movement of goods and persons. By the end of 1991 the Council had agreed to abolish customs formalities, paperwork and inspections at borders between member states (amounting to approximately 60 million documents a year). In October 1992 the Commission issued the Common Customs Code, and customs barriers were finally abolished on 31 December 1992. By the end of 1992 81 measures had been adopted on issues relating to the movement of agricultural produce and the compensation of farmers at borders under the Common Agricultural Policy. However less progress was made on barriers to the movement of persons: the UK, Ireland and Denmark refused to agree to the abolition of passport controls and the introduction of common visa requirements. Nonetheless the other member states signed the Schengen Accord, and the EU gained new institutional mechanisms and legal instruments to take action in this area with the justice and home affairs 'pillar' of the Maastricht Treaty and the subsequent reforms to this pillar in the Amsterdam Treaty (see Chapter 11).

Second, the Commission used the heading 'technical barriers' as a catch-all category. In the case of product standards, in 1979, in the *Cassis de Dijon* judgment (see Chapter 4), the European Court of Justice had ruled that any product that met the standards of one member state could be legally sold in another. Building on this principle of 'mutual recognition', the Commission proposed a 'new approach to technical harmonization' (Pelkmans, 1990). This involved establishing mutual recognition as a basic principle in the single market: restricting harmonization to minimum technical and health and safety standards; contracting with pan-European standards organizations – such as the CEN (European Standardization Committee) and CENELEC (European Electrotechnical Standardization Committee) – to develop voluntary European standards; and introducing the 'CE mark' for products that met the required standards.

On public procurement, governments were prevented from favouring domestic companies in government contracts. On the free movement of persons, residency rights were extended to non-workers (such as students and retirees), non-nationals gained access to state subsidies and social benefits, and rules were established for comparing educational and professional qualifications. In the area of services, a host of directives were passed on the liberalization of financial services, air, water and road transport, and the opening-up of national telecommunications and television markets. On the movement of capital, controls on the free flow of capital between the member states were abolished. Finally, on company law, various rules governing cross-border company activities were harmonized (although a European Company Statute was not adopted until 2001), and common rules on the protection of intellectual property were agreed.

Third, to remove fiscal barriers the Commission proposed the harmonization of value added tax (VAT, or sales tax) and excise duties on goods such as alcohol and tobacco. After protracted negotiations, the

Council adopted a framework for harmonizing VAT in October 1992. This included a standard minimum VAT rate of 15 per cent in each member state, the abolition of luxury rates (and lower rates on special items for a transition period), and rules on where VAT should be paid – in the case of cross-border trade, for example, VAT would be paid in the country of destination. In the same month the Council agreed a harmonized structure for excise duties, with the elimination of restrictions on cross-border purchases of goods such as alcoholic drinks and tobacco (for personal use), and the eventual abolition of duty-free sales on planes and boats (in 1999).

However the single market programme did not stop at the end of 1992. The implementation and transposition of the legislative programme was still under way, and many pieces of single market legislation needed reforming and updating. In March 1992 the Commission consequently set up the High Level Group on the Operation of the Internal Market, chaired by Peter Sutherland (a former commissioner). The group's report, the so-called Sutherland Report, proposed greater consultation with the actors affected by single market regulation, greater access to the EU decision-making process, and better cooperation between the Commission and national administrations to ensure that uneven implementation of legislation would not create barriers to trade (Sutherland *et al.*, 1992). Acting on these recommendations the Commission drafted an action plan for the single market, which was adopted at the Amsterdam European Council in June 1997. The action plan promised progress on two levels: a rolling programme of simplification of single market legislation (the SLIM programme) and a coordinated effort by the Commission and the member states to ensure the implementation of existing legislation.

Also, to shame the member states into action, in November 1997 the Commission launched a 'single market scoreboard'. This was a record of the member states' efforts to implement single market legislation and the frequency of single market infringements by each member state. Table 8.1 shows the results of the first scoreboard report in November 1997 and the twelfth report in May 2003. The data reveal three things. First, there was a considerable improvement in implementation rates in this six-year period: from an average of 6.3 pieces of legislation not transposed per member state in 1997 to an average of 2.4 in 2003. Second, the number of infringement proceedings launched by the Commission continued to rise, with almost 1600 proceedings still being 'open' in 2003 (although the measures reported in the two reports are quite different). Third, there was considerable variation in implementation rates among the member states. On average the richer/Protestant states in Northern Europe (Denmark, Finland, Sweden, the Netherlands) were more efficient than the poorer/Catholic states Southern Europe in transposing EU

Table 8.1   *The single market scoreboard, 1997 and 2003*

| | Percentage of single market legislation not transposed into national law | | Infringement proceedings | |
	1/11/97 (Rank)	15/4/03 (Rank)	New proceedings opened, 1/9/96– 1/9/97(Rank)	Total open proceedings, 15/4/03 (Rank)
Denmark	3.2 (1)	0.6 (1)	6 (2)	36 (3)
Finland	4.3 (3)	1.0 (2)	7 (3)	47 (4)
Sweden	6.2 (8)	1.0 (3)	5 (1)	32 (1)
Netherlands	3.5 (2)	2.0 (7)	12 (7)	68 (6)
Luxembourg	6.5 (9)	3.2 (9)	9 (5)	34 (2)
United Kingdom	4.6 (4)	1.5 (5)	24 (13)	121 (8)
Spain	4.7 (5)	1.2 (4)	17 (10)	153 (13)
Ireland	5.4 (6)	3.5 (13)	12 (8)	132 (9)
Portugal	5.9 (7)	3.7 (14)	21 (11)	57 (5)
Greece	7.5 (11)	3.3 (11)	7 (4)	144 (12)
Belgium	8.5 (13)	1.8 (6)	14 (9)	138 (11)
Austria	10.1 (15)	3.4 (12)	11 (6)	79 (7)
Germany	8.5 (14)	3.0 (8)	22 (12)	136 (10)
France	7.4 (10)	3.3 (10)	35 (14)	220 (15)
Italy	7.6 (12)	3.9 (15)	40 (15)	200 (14)
EU average/total	6.3	2.4	242	1597

Note: The two reports used different measures of infringements: in the 1997 report the Commission used the number of proceedings that had been opened between September 1996 and September 1997, and in 2003 it used the total number of proceedings that were still 'open' (had not been resolved).

Sources: European Commission (1997, 2003).

regulations into domestic law. Also, in 2003 two member states (Italy and France) accounted for 26 per cent of all outstanding infringement proceedings.

Competition policies

Article 3(g) of the EC Treaty states that the EU shall include 'a system ensuring that competition in the internal market is not distorted'. To achieve this goal, the treaty includes a chapter on 'rules applying to competition'. These articles endow the Commission with powerful policy tools to prevent anti-competitive practices from undermining free trade and competition in the single market, including the ability to impose fines. These primary laws have been supplemented with a series of secondary regulations. The result is three main strands of EU competition policy:

- *Antitrust regulations*: Articles 81 to 86 of the EC Treaty establish a series of rules that outlaw a variety of agreements between companies that would restrict competition (such as cartels, price fixing or predatory pricing agreements, exclusive sales agreements and discrimination on the grounds of nationality by a firm in a 'dominant position' in a national market) and ensure that publicly owned industries abide by the EU competition rules.
- *Regulation of state aids*: Articles 87–9 of the treaty outlaw government subsidies to industry that threaten competition and trade between the member states, unless the subsidies promote the interests of the EU as a whole or specific sectoral or regional objectives.
- *Merger control*: in December 1989 the Council adopted the first Merger Regulation (which took effect in December 2000), and amended this regulation in January 2004 (which took effect in May 2004).

This competition policy is very much based on the US model of antitrust regulation. In fact US competition lawyers helped to draft the competition articles in the Treaty of Rome, and were eager to prevent European cartels that would be protected in competition with US companies. However, unlike US competition policy, which is concerned with preventing anti-competitive practices in the private sector, EU competition policy also deals with anti-competitive practices by government-owned and government-subsidized businesses.

Nevertheless, for a variety of reasons the Directorate-General for Competition has not always pursued a policy of 'perfect competition', particularly in the regulation of public sector industries. First, the directorate-general is constrained by the Commission's lack of political power against certain member states, especially in the face of potentially high economic and sectoral costs of competition policy decisions. Second, until the mid 1980s most commissioners responsible for competition policy were ideologically in favour of promoting 'Euro-champions'.

However the Commission's status in competition policy was enhanced as a result of the political commitment behind the liberalizing aspects of the single market programme. Also, a series of commissioners responsible for competition policy – Peter Sutherland (1985–89), Leon Brittan (1989–93), Karel Van Miert (1993–99) and Mario Monti (2000–4) – sought to apply antitrust principles more strictly and were not afraid to confront member states and multinationals. As a result the competition policy portfolio has become one of the most powerful and prized positions in the Commission.

Responding to the rise in cross-border mergers in anticipation of the single market and to heavy lobbying by multinational firms, the member states finally adopted the Merger Regulation in 1989, after over 15 years of negotiations. The Merger Regulation created a so-called 'one-stop shop'. First, the Commission was given the power to assess and veto mergers between companies that would have a combined worldwide turnover of €5 billion and an EU-wide turnover of €250 million. Second, the regulation set up a procedure and timetable for reviewing mergers. In the first stage the Commission would have one month to decide either that the merger was within the scope of the regulation, to approve the merger or to initiate proceedings. The Commission would then undertake a detailed appraisal and (within four months) decide whether to approve a merger, conditionally approve the merger, or prohibit a merger. If the Commission blocked a merger the companies concerned had two months to appeal against the decision at the European Court of Justice.

In general this merger procedure worked well. Between September 1990 and February 2004, of the 2430 merger cases reviewed by the Merger Task Force in the directorate-general for Competition, only 18 mergers were blocked by the Commission (one by Brittan, 10 by Van Miert and seven by Monti).

However it became increasingly clear that reform was needed (Wilks and McGowan, 1995; McGowan and Cini, 1999). First, as the number of cross-border mergers in Europe grew, the workload of the Merger Task Force increased dramatically: from approximately 60 cases per year in the early 1990s to over 300 per year between 1999 and 2004.

Second, companies on the receiving end of negative decisions became increasingly vocal in their criticism of the Commission. The procedures were regarded as less transparent than the equivalent procedures of the US Federal Trade Commission. The Commission was also accused of not giving sufficient economic justification for its decisions. Moreover the mechanism for appealing to the European Court of Justice after a merger had been blocked was anachronistic, since an appeal to the court could take several years, by which time the conditions for the original merger would have passed, and one or more of the companies might have even ceased to exist. This mechanism also compared unfavourably with the US merger control system, whereby the US Federal Trade Commission had to seek *a priori* court approval for a decision to block a merger.

Third, smaller member states argued that market concentration should be treated differently in their case as their companies were really competing in European-wide markets. Fourth, unlike the division of powers between the US Justice Department and the Federal

Trade Commission, or between the German Industry Ministry and Federal Cartel Office (Bundeskartellamt), there was no clear separation of powers in the application of EU merger controls, with the Merger Task Force acting as 'policeman, judge and jury' (McGowan and Cini, 1999, p. 193).

Finally, the political stakes rose as the extraterritorial impact of the Commission's merger decisions grew (Damro, 2001). Two of the 18 vetoes by the Commission involved mergers between two US companies whose economic activities were mainly conducted in the US market: the merger between Boeing and McDonnell-Douglas, which the Commission blocked in 1997; and the merger between General Electric and Honeywell, which was blocked in 2001. Both these mergers had been approved by the US Federal Trade Commission, and in both cases the US federal government intervened at the highest political level to try to persuade the Commission to give. However the Commission stood firm, much to fury of the US government and the powerful US industrial interests involved.

The amended merger regulation and reforms of the Merger Task Force addressed some of these problems. First, to improve the possibility of companies responding to Commission concerns, some flexibility was introduced into the time frames. This was accompanied by a new code of practice for the Merger Task Force, which the Commission introduced to increase the transparency of Commission decision-making. Second, to reduce uncertainty about how the Commission would decide in each case, a new set of guidelines was introduced, specifying in greater detail the criteria by which the Commission would approve or reject a proposed merger. Third, to increase the credibility of veto decisions the Commission appointed a chief competition economist and set up an independent a panel to scrutinize the Merger Task Force's conclusions.

However two concerns remained: the new system did not introduce *a priori* judicial review of Commission decisions against a proposed merger, and there was still no clear separation of powers between the politicians (the competition commissioner and the other members of the Commission) and the antitrust regulators (in the Merger Task Force).

New liberalization methods: the open method of coordination and the Lamfalussy process

Despite the completion of the single market and the EU's new deregulatory policy framework, large segments of the economies of the member states remained highly regulated and beyond the direct harmonization efforts of EU regulatory legislation or the indirect liberalization effects of the single market and EU competition policies. Two such examples were national labour markets and the financial services sector. National labour markets in most member states were still highly regulated and inflexible, for example there were rules governing how firms should hire and fire employees and whether temporary and part-time contracts were allowed. Similarly, despite the fact that the white paper on the single market proposed a number of directives for the integration and liberalization of the European financial services sector, little progress had been made in this area by the late 1990s.

At the start of the new millennium the Commission and the member states decided to take action in these two areas. Competences and procedures existed within the treaties for the usual 'Community method' to be applied in both areas. For example, the competences on social policy (see below) could be used to pass a directive liberalizing hiring and firing rules for small and medium-sized enterprises in all member states. Similarly directives harmonizing financial services rules could be initiated under the main single market article (Article 94), using qualified-majority voting in the Council and co-decision with the EP.

However the member state governments and the Commission decided against using the standard method, and instead developed new methods for both these areas. In fact the methods they chose were diametrically opposed: an even weaker version of the intergovernmental method for the liberalization of national labour markets; and an even stronger version of the supranational method for the integration of financial services markets.

In both cases the story began at the Lisbon European Council in March 2000. Conscious of the fact that the EU's economic performance had lagged behind that of the US throughout the 1990s and there were no signs that the EU would catch up in the next decade, the heads of government signed up to an ambitious reform agenda. The aim of the new 'Lisbon Agenda' was to make the EU 'the most competitive and dynamic knowledge-based economy in the world'. The governments highlighted three main means of achieving this goal:

- Better policies at the European and national levels for the information society, including investment in the 'knowledge-economy' and completing and depending the internal market in the services sector.
- Modernizing the European social model, by structural reform of domestic labour markets and welfare states in parallel with policies to tackle social exclusion and increased investment in education and training.
- Macroeconomic policies to secure sustainable growth while undertaking the necessary structural reforms to the domestic economy.

The vagueness of these goals reflected a political compromise. The governments on the centre-right, plus the British Labour government, wanted to concentrate on structural, labour market and welfare state reforms, while the governments on the left, led by the French and German administrations, wanted to emphasize investment in human capital, education and the new knowledge economy. With such competing views on how structural changes in the EU economy should be achieved, and because many of the reforms would be highly sensitive – for example the liberalization of domestic labour markets – the governments accepted that it would be difficult to agree a coherent package of legislation to promote structural reform through the normal EU legislative method.

The Commission was also reluctant to initiate controversial new legislation that might provoke a backlash from some of the large member state governments. Ironically, by weakening the Commission's power to initiate legislation in the Maastricht and Amsterdam Treaties, and by choosing an amenable Commission President in Romano Prodi, the governments were no longer able to use the Commission to force each other to honour the collective commitments they had made – as they had done with the Delors Commissions and the single market programme and Economic and Monetary Union. Consequently the governments and the Commission decided to by-pass the normal method of EU legislation and try a new mode of policy cooperation, known as the 'open method of coordination' (OMC) (see Chapter 2).

OMC involves essentially two things (Hodson and Maher, 2001; de la Porte and Pochet, 2002; Scharpf, 2002). The first is the agreement of a common set of goals, which the member state governments have promised to achieve independently and without recourse to EU legal instruments. The second involves 'naming and shaming', whereby the governments regularly monitor each other's progress towards the agreed goals, and publicly congratulate or admonish each other accordingly. This has some force, as governments do not like to be embarrassed for failing to honour commitments made to their EU colleagues. However if voters or powerful vested interests (such as organized labour) oppose a reform, governments have proven reluctant to enforce the agreement. As a result, and in the absence of recourse to the usual channels of enforcement via the Commission and the European Court of Justice, the record of OMC in the area of structural economic reform is mixed, with some governments (such and Denmark and Finland) undertaking quite radical reforms while others (notably France, Germany and Italy) lagging behind in many areas (Mosher and Trubek, 2003; Murray, 2004).

In contrast to the progress in the area of labour market liberalization, to promote faster integration and liberalization of European financial markets, in July 2000 the EU set up a 'committee of wise men', chaired by Alexandre Lamfalussy, a former president of the European Monetary Institute (the precursor of the European Central

Bank). The committee concluded its deliberations in February 2001 and proposed a list of legislative and regulatory measures (for example a directive on financial prospectuses), and a new legislative procedure for adopting these measures and regulating European financial markets. The procedure works as follows:

- A directive or regulation is adopted through the usual co-decision procedure, but only setting out the 'framework principles' in a given area.
- A new regulatory committee – the European Securities Committee (ESC) – then fills in the legislative details in cooperation with the Commission; and the EP is 'kept fully informed';
- After this a second new committee – the Committee of European Securities Regulators (CESR) is responsible for the technical implementation, monitoring and application of a measure.
- The Commission then enforces the regulatory rules in the usual way, that is, by issuing warnings and taking member states to the European Court of Justice when required.

The Commission duly established the two committees in June 2001. The first meeting of the ESC was held in September 2001, and since then has met almost every month. However it was not until February 2002 that the EP agreed to the use of the new Lamfalussy process. The EP was initially concerned about the lack of transparency and control of the new process, but accepted an assurance by the Commission that in any referrals back for new legislation for political approval the EP would be treated equally with the Council.

Under the Lamfalussy process, politicians in the Council and EP are only able to agree broad policy guidelines, while the legislative details are delegated to policy expects. This isolation of a large part of the EU legislative process from elected politicians is the opposite of the open method of coordination, in which elected politicians are given ultimate freedom to change, block or renege on commitments.

At face value this may seem contradictory, but it follows the 'normative' difference between efficient and redistributive regulatory policies. Because the regulation of financial services is primarily concerned with addressing issues of market failure (such as asymmetric information in the trading of financial products), the long-term collective interest is best guaranteed by isolating these policies from majoritarian political processes (rather like the isolation of monetary policy from the political business cycle – see Chapter 9). In contrast the deregulation of labour markets involves the removal of rights for particular sections of society (employed semiskilled labour) and promoting the interests of other sections of society (business and consumers). Hence these policies are highly politicized and need to be made through the normal channels of majoritarian parliamentary and electoral politics.

Against this normative perspective, a 'positive' theoretical explanation would be that the difference between the two policy areas derives from the power of the social interests that are most affected by them. The interests of the financial services industry, which has substantial political resources and a common European-wide interest, is best served by a regulatory process that allows technical experts to make regulations in the interests of this sector, beyond the enquiring eyes of consumers, parliaments and the media. In contrast unskilled labour, which is well organized in most member states and benefits from the current restrictive labour market rules, is best served by allowing each member state to decide how to regulate its labour markets.

The impact of deregulatory policies: liberalization and regulatory competition

The single market programme and EU competition policies have both a direct and an indirect impact on national sectors and industrial policies (Helm and Smith, 1989). On the direct side, having taken over the responsibility for regulating capital, goods and services from the member states, the EU has liberalized both trade between the member states and competition within several national markets. On the indirect side, through competition policies and regulations and directives that supplement the operation of the single market, the EU has forced member state governments to reduce their intervention in the economy. For example the directorate general for Competition has pursued a policy of 'contestable competition' , whereby national markets do not have to be perfect, but firms (either domestically located or from other member states) must be free to enter and leave the market without significant costs.

The result has been the deregulation of a large number of sectors (Kassim and Menon, 1996), including:

- *Air transport*: liberalization packages were adopted in 1987, 1990 and 1992, domestic air markets were opened to any EU-based airline from April 1997, and through competition policy the Commission has prevented consolidation where it would have created monopolies on certain routes and has forced governments to reduce the state subsidies provided to their airlines.
- *Telecommunications*: open competition in telecommunication equipment was agreed in 1988, competition in voice telephony and telex services was established from 1993, and open competition for the supply of infrastructure and the provision of all telecommunication services in both fixed and mobile telephony (open networks provision) began in January 1998.

- *Electricity supply*: a directive was adopted in 1996 to liberalize national electricity markets over a nine-year period, leading to separation of production, transmission and distribution, which in most cases has meant the privatization of electricity production and supply.
- *Financial services*: the banking, securities and insurance markets have been opened to competition from other member states, which includes a 'single passport' for financial firms to operate anywhere in the EU and reciprocal access to the EU market for services from non-EU states.

Furthermore, the introduction of mutual recognition of national standards raised the possibility of competition between national rules and regulators (Siebert, 1990; Neven, 1992; Hosli, 1995a). With open access to any national market in the single market, firms could choose to be registered in the member state with the lowest regulatory costs. The effect could be a 'race to the bottom' or 'social dumping', in that member states could be forced to reduce the regulatory burden on firms by lowering labour standards and tax rates to attract capital (Joerges, 1997). In the US the deregulatory effect of regulatory competition is known as the 'Delaware effect', named after the East Coast state that has successfully used its lack of regulation to attract investment (Carey, 1974).

However there has been little evidence of a Delaware effect in the EU (Woolcock, 1994; Sun and Pelkmans, 1995). For most companies the cost of regulation is a marginal consideration when deciding where to locate. Far more important are proximity to markets, labour quality and the financial incentives offered by regional or central governments (Goodhart, 1998). In fact economic integration and regulatory competition can push up the level of regulation. High standards can help domestic producers to gain access to foreign markets, resulting in a 'race to the top'. For example California became the leader in environmental standards both nationally and globally (Vogel, 1995). The same is true in sectors where there is international cooperation between the EU and the US, such as financial services, where higher standards have become the norm (Genschel and Plümper, 1997).

It is too early to tell whether the Delaware or the California effect is most prevalent in the EU. What is certain is that economic and monetary union will facilitate further regulatory competition as a result of the reduction in transaction costs that comes from exchange-rate stability and greater price transparency in regulatory costs (see Chapter 10). Consequently the single market, combined with monetary union, is likely to have a broad impact on national macroeconomic policies, forcing member states to hold down tax rates on capital and non-wage labour costs (Krugman, 1987; Scharpf, 1997a).

In summary, the single market was set up with a pareto-efficient policy aim, whereby every member state, industry, consumer and citizen would benefit from economies of scale in the larger market and the efficiency effects of trade and market liberalization (Cecchini, 1988; Smith and Wanke, 1993). Also, the single market and EU competition policies were established to tackle market failures, in that harmonized standards for goods and services would reduce information asymmetries, and public procurement rules, state-aid regulations and merger controls would address the problem of market power (Gatsios and Seabright, 1989; Pelkmans, 1990). Moving these issues to the European level reduced the ability of national administrations to use rules and goods and services to achieve value-allocative goals, such as the protection of a particular industry, high labour and other process standards, and culturally specific product standards. Hence as Dehousse (1992, p. 399) argues, 'it is difficult to avoid the conclusion that the combined effect of market integration and power fragmentation is to make government intervention more difficult'.

Reregulation via Positive Integration: Environmental and Social Policies

The EU has also developed a series of 'positive integration' policies to supplement the single market programme, the most significant of which are environmental policy and social policy. Because these policies have replaced national rules with common EU rules they can be seen as reregulatory policies. But, unlike competition policies and rules designed to integrate the single market, EU environmental and social regulation is not intended primarily to secure pareto-efficient outcomes. These policies involve choosing values that are preferred by some citizens but not others. As Easton (1965, p. 50) explains:

> An allocation may deprive a person of a valued thing already possessed, it may obstruct the attainment of values which would otherwise have been attained, or it main give some persons access to values and deny them to others.

That is, EU environmental and social policies do not redistribute resources directly, but they do lead to a 'reallocation of values' in European society: with some citizens' values being promoted at the expense of others'.

Environmental policy

Although this was not covered in the Treaty of Rome, in 1972 the heads of government agreed to launch a series of environmental action programmes. These culminated in the sixth action programme for the environment, which set out the priorities for the EU up to 2010 and highlighted four areas: climate change, nature and biodiversity, environment and health, and the management of natural resources and waste.

Environmental policy became a full competence of the EU with the implementation of the Single European Act, and was strengthened and extended by the Maastricht Treaty, which introduced qualified-majority voting in the Council on environmental legislation and the principle of sustainable development as a central aim of the EU. While allowing member states to apply higher environmental protection standards if they wished, the treaty required the EU to develop a common environmental policy to achieve 'a high level of protection', and rectify environmental damage at source, based on the 'polluter pays' principle.

To this end, the main EU actions in the environment field have been as follows:

- *Air and noise pollution*: since 1970 the EU has adopted ever-stricter directives on air pollution by vehicles, large combustion plants and power stations, the Commission has proposed measures to phase out chlorofluorocarbons and introduce an energy tax on carbon dioxide emissions, and EU rules have been laid down on noise pollution by motor vehicles, aircraft, lawnmowers, household equipment and building-site machinery. The EU is also a strong supporter of the 1997 Kyoto Protocol to the UN Framework Convention on Climate Change.
- *Waste disposal*: since 1975 a series of directives have established EU regulations on toxic and dangerous waste, the transborder shipment of hazardous waste, and the disposal of specific types of waste and manufactured products (for example the End-of-Life Vehicle Directive, adopted in September 2000).
- *Water pollution*: since 1976 a number of directives have established common standards for surface and underground water, bathing water, drinking water, fresh water and the discharge of toxic substances, and the EU has signed several international conventions to reduce pollution in international waterways.
- *Chemical products*: after the industrial disaster in Seveso in 1977 the EU adopted a series of directives regulating the use, storage, handling, packaging and labelling of a wide variety of dangerous chemicals, and providing for a European inventory of all chemical substances on the market.
- *Nature protection and biodiversity*: between 1982 and 1992 the EU adopted directives relating to the International Convention on Trade in Endangered Species (CITES), which established rules on the conservation of wild birds, the protection of natural habitats, and scien-

tific experiments on animals. The EU also offers financial support for projects to conserve natural habitats.

- *Environmental impact assessment*: in 1985 the Council adopted a directive, which has subsequently been extended, requiring environmental impact assessments of all public and private industrial and infrastructure projects above a certain size. The directive also requires that the public be consulted.
- *Eco-labelling and eco-audits*: in 1992 the Council adopted a regulation that lays down rules for granting EU eco-labels to environmentally friendly products, and in 1993 the Council adopted a regulation that established a voluntary environmental auditing scheme.
- *European Environment Agency* (EEA): the EEA, which was set up in 1994 in Copenhagen, is responsible for collecting data and supplying information for new environmental legislation, developing forecasting techniques to enable preventative measures to be taken, and ensuring that EU environmental data are incorporated into international environmental programmes.
- *Natural and technological hazards*: the EU adopted an action programme on civil protection in 1998, is a signatory of the UN Convention on the Transboundary Impacts of Industrial Accidents, has adopted measures on the prevention of major industrial accidents, protection against radiation and the management of radioactive waste, and has issued two directives on the potential impact of genetically modified organisms (GMOs) – one on the release of GMOs into the environment and the other regulating the use of GMOs.

As is clear from this list, the EU uses a variety of instruments to promote environmental protection. In addition to the EU-level environmental regulations, these instruments include an expenditure programme (the LIFE programme), participation in international treaties and cooperating with third countries, and the provision of incentives for public and private actors to protect the environment, ranging from voluntary systems such as eco-labelling and the EU system of environmental auditing to compulsory systems such as the environmental impact assessment of public and private projects.

There is more EU legislation in the area of environmental policy than in almost any other policy area, and environmental legislation tends to be adopted more quickly than legislation in most other areas (Jordan *et al.*, 1999). However there is some variation in the effectiveness with which environmental legislation is implemented by the member states (Bailey, 1999; Knill and Lenschow, 2000, 2001; Grant *et al.*, 2000). Börzel (2000) argues that the existing level of environmental protection in a state is not what determines how effective it is in implementing the

EU legislation, rather its institutional structure and the power exerted by industrial interests tend to be more important (cf. Knill and Lenschow, 1998). This contrasts with EU social regulation, where the existing national welfare regime and variety of capitalism influences how much discretion a state exercises when implementing EU rules.

From the normative perspective, the reason why the EU is able to act so easily and effectively in this policy area is that most EU environmental regulations address market failures arising from the integration of the single market, and so are pareto-efficient in their goals (Gatsios and Seabright, 1989; Malone, 1996; Eichener, 1997). First, environmental pollution is an unwanted side effect (negative externality) of most economic activities, affecting many persons who are not involved in the transactions that produce the pollution. Second, without environmental standards and environmental labelling, consumers lack the necessary information to make judgements about the quality and environmental friendliness of the goods they buy. To limit these two types of market failure, the EU has established environmental standards at all stages of the economic process: from production (such as chemical emissions), to distribution (such as eco-labelling), consumption (such as vehicle emissions) and disposal (such as waste management).

However there are several aspects of EU environmental policy that do not fit this pareto-efficiency justification for regulation (Weale, 1996; Lee, 1997; Marín, 1997; McCormick, 2001). For example EU environmental regulation covers far more than cross-border pollution. The EU sets standards for both the national and the European level, EU environmental regulations have almost universally been based on the high standards of the most environmentally advanced member states such as Denmark, Germany and the Netherlands, rather than on the lower standards of the UK, Ireland and southern Europe, even though the lower standards, in most cases, would have been sufficient to protect against negative externalities and provide a degree of information to consumers.

Environmental policy at the EU level is driven primarily by the desire to prevent a distortion of competition in the single market – an ideological argument that is disguised as the need to address a market failure. The Commission and the member states with strong environmental movements and green parties have continually argued that the single market has forced them to lower their environmental standards in order to remain competitive. Their efforts have been supported by a highly developed environmental movement at the European level (including such organizations as the European Environmental Bureau and Greenpeace), whose lobbying activities are heavily subsidized from the EU budget (see Chapter 7). Hence in this policy area diffuse interests have the same access to regulators as private sectoral and industrial interests (Pollack, 1997b; Webster, 1998; Zito, 1998).

In addition, in most cases the member states with lower environmental standards have been willing to accept higher standards. This is because they are aware that their citizens support environmental issues being tackled at the European level, and that their industries will have to meet high environmental standards if they are to gain access to markets in North America and Japan. The result, as Sbragia (1996, p. 253) points out, is that 'rather than "environmental dumping", the Union's policy-making process has led to "up-market environmentalism"'. In other words, in the area of environmental regulation, particularly in the case of product standards (such as packaging, labelling and waste-disposal rules), the EU has experienced a California effect rather than a Delaware effect (Vogel, 1997).

Social policy

The Treaty of Rome provided for an EU social policy through:

- Its general objective of promoting 'social progress and a high level of employment'.
- A section allowing for closer cooperation (by unanimity in the Council) in the improvement of living and working conditions.
- A requirement that the member states ensure equal pay for men and women.
- A European Social Fund to help occupational and geographic mobility.
- The free movement of workers, with rights to residence, social security and non-discrimination in employment.

Little progress was made on these issues in the 1960s and 1970s, except in respect of the coordination of social security systems for migrant workers and equal pay for women.

However EU social policy received a new impetus in the 1980s. Fearing that the single market would primarily benefit capital rather than labour, the French socialists François Mitterrand (the French president) and Jacques Delors (the Commission president) argued for a 'social dimension' of European integration. As a result the Single European Act provided for the harmonization of health and safety standards at work using qualified-majority voting in the Council. Then in December 1989, 11 member states (excluding the UK) signed the Commission's proposed Charter on the Fundamental Rights of Workers (the Social Charter), which listed 47 actions for the establishment of a social dimension of the single market programme: the Commission turned these into legislative proposals in the subsequent Social Action Programme. During the negotiations on the Maastricht Treaty in 1992, a majority of member states proposed incorporating the aims of the Social Charter into the EU treaty and using qualified-majority voting in the Council on most social policy issues. However the British Conservative government vetoed this proposal. The solution was a separate agreement on social policy between the other 11 member states. This Social Protocol provided for qualified-majority voting in areas such as working conditions and workers' consultation, and unanimity voting in more sensitive areas such as social security.

The Maastricht Social Protocol also strengthened the social dialogue between European level representatives, management and labour: the European Trade Union Confederation (ETUC), the Union of Industrial and Employers' Confederations of Europe (UNICE) and the European Centre of Enterprises with Public Participation (CEEP) (Compston and Greenwood, 2001). First, the protocol made it mandatory for the Commission to consult the 'social partners' before initiating legislation in the social policy field. Second, the Protocol allowed the social partners to initiate their own agreements (so-called 'Euro-agreements'), which could either be implemented in the member states by the member associations of the social partners or be turned into formal EU legislation by a decision of the Council, on the basis of a proposal to do so by the Commission.

Nevertheless, in December 1997 the British Labour government agreed to the Amsterdam Treaty, which incorporated the Social Protocol into a new Social Chapter of the EU Treaty, including the provisions related to the social dialogue. The Amsterdam Treaty also included provisions for cooperation between the member states to combat unemployment (Articles 125–30). The treaty bases and decision-making procedures for passing EU social legislation following the reforms of the Amsterdam Treaty are shown in Table 8.2.

Despite the new legislative provisions, examples of EU social legislation have been few and far between compared with environmental legislation. The main recent developments in EU social policy are as follows:

- *Free movement of workers*: the right to reside has been extended to students, retirees, ex-employers and the self-employed, but there have been repeated problems with the application of freedom of movement of persons, particularly in the case of nationals from third countries, and migrant workers from other EU member states still do not have fully equal social rights throughout the EU (see Chapter 11).
- *Health and safety at work*: directives have been passed to establish a general health and safety framework covering all the main sectors, specialized rules for particular industries, and health and safety protection for part-time workers. Two action programmes have been undertaken in this area (1996–2000 and 2002–6).

Table 8.2   *Treaty bases and decision procedures for EU social legislation*

Treaty Article	Policy issue	Council Voting	Role of EP
Social policy			
137	Health and safety at work	QMV	Co-decision
	Working conditions		
	Information and consultation of workers		
	Integration of persons excluded from the labour market		
	Equal opportunities and treatment of men and women		
	Combating social exclusion		
	Modernization of social protection systems		
137	Social security		
	Protection of workers when their contracts are terminated	Unanimity	Consultation
	Representation of workers, including codetermination		
	Conditions of employment for third-country nationals		
139	'Social dialogue' between management and labour:		
	– issues requiring QMV under Article 139	QMV	None
	– issues requiring unanimity under Article 139	Unanimity	None
141	Equal pay, treatment and opportunities for men and women	QMV	Co-decision
Other provisions related to social policy:			
13	Non-discrimination on the basis of sex, race, ethnic origin, religion or belief, disability, age, or sexual orientation	Unanimity	Consultation
37	Safeguard of employment and living standards of farmers	QMV	Consultation
40	Free movement of workers	QMV	Co-decision
42	Social security (necessary for freedom of movement)	Unanimity	Co-decision
44	Freedom of establishment	QMV	Co-decision
47	Mutual recognition of diplomas	QMV	Co-decision
71	Transport safety	QMV	Co-decision
94	Harmonization of laws in the single market	Unanimity	Consultation
95	Harmonization of laws in the single market	QMV	Co-decision
128	Annual employment guidelines for the member states	QMV	Consultation
129	Incentive measures for cooperation on employment policy	QMV	Co-decision
308	New policy competences for the EU	Unanimity	Consultation

Note:
Social policy chapter (Title XI, Chapter 1). QMV = qualified-majority voting (see Chapter 3). The operation of the consultation and co-decision procedures is analyzed in Chapter 3.

- *Working conditions*: the series of measures adopted in this area include directives on the protection of pregnant women at work (1991), the provision of proof on an employment contract (1992), working time (1993), parental leave (1996), equal rights for temporary workers (1997) and fixed-term work (1999).
- *Worker consultation*: despite repeated proposals by the Commission since the 1970s on the right of workers to be consulted and participate in company decisions, the works councils directive was not adopted until 1994 (1997 in the UK). A directive establishing a general framework for informing and consulting employees was then passed in 2002.
- *Equality between men and women*: little new legislation has been adopted on sexual equality since the mid 1980s, but the main piece of legislation governing equal pay and treatment in the work place (adopted in 1976) was amended in 2002, significantly shifting the burden of proof from the employee to the employer.
- *Anti-discrimination*: after the addition of the so-called 'general non-discrimination clause' (Article 13) in the Amsterdam Treaty, the EU adopted some of the most advanced pieces of legislation anywhere in the world on equality in the workplace: in June 2000 a directive on equal treatment irrespective of racial or ethnic origin, and in December 2000 a directive establishing a general framework for equal treatment, covering non-discrimination on the grounds of religion, disability, age, and sexual orientation.
- *Employment*: based on the employment chapter in the treaty, EU action in this area involves each member state presenting a national action plan for employment, on the basis of which the Commission and the Council issue a series of non-binding recommendations in the form of a joint employment report, and the establishment of the European Employment Services (EURES) – a network of public employment agencies, trade unions and employers organizations, to promote the cross-border recruitment of employees.

As the above list shows, social legislation at the European level is far from the traditional social policy of domestic welfare states, in which the state is responsibile for supplying social goods such as social insurance, health care, welfare services, education and housing (Titmus, 1974). These core redistributive powers remain firmly in the hands of national administrations (although the EU has authority over certain direct redistributive policies in other areas, see Chapter 9). As Giandomenico Majone (1993a) argues, social policy at the EU level is predominantly 'social regulation', designed to address market failures rather than to redistribute resources between employers and workers or between rich and poor.

The most developed areas of EU social policy are social security rights for migrant workers, health and safety standards and product safety standards (Eichener, 1992, 1997; Leibfried and Pierson, 1996). The provision of social security to migrant workers increases the efficiency of the labour market as part of the general single market goal, whereas health and safety and product standards reduce information costs to consumers and the effects of production processes on the health of workers. The costs of these standards are spread among all producers and consumers, and the benefits are received by all consumers and industrial workers. Hence both the costs and the benefits are diffuse.

The EU has been much less successful in adopting common rules on working conditions and industrial relations, and in pursuing labour market policies. In the case of working conditions some EU-wide standards have been agreed, for example on working time, rights for part-time and temporary employees, maternity and paternity leave, and fixed-term contracts. But in contrast to health and safety standards, these rules tend not to conform to the standards that prevail in the most advanced member states; rather they set out minimum basic requirements and there is a high degree of flexibility in terms of how the member states apply the rules (Streeck, 1995, 1996; Armstrong and Bulmer, 1998, pp. 226–54; Bastian, 1998). With regard to industrial relations, the rules on workers' consultation and information only apply to large multinational firms and allows a high degree of flexibility in their application (Rhodes, 1995; Falkner, 1996; Streeck, 1997). Finally, despite the employment chapter in the EU Treaty, the EU does not have the power to force member states to adopt common labour market policies.

Again, this fits the 'social regulation' theory of EU social policy. Policies on workers' rights, working conditions and industrial relations are less about addressing market standards than about applying particular ideological preferences for the operation of capitalism (Teague, 1994; Jackman, 1998). National policies on these issues reflect the different levels of support for socialist parties, the varying power of national trade union movements, the historical development of compromises between capital and labour, and the nature of specialization in national economies (Esping-Anderson, 1990; Hall and Soskice, 2001). On the question of adopting common policies in these areas, all the member states prefer there to be no common standards than to accept harmonized rules that would dramatically change their existing practices. For example successive British governments have opposed rules that would impose new costs on British employers, such as the rule on workers' consultation. Similarly the French and German governments have opposed rules that would liberalize national labour markets, such as regulations on fixed-term contracts. As a result, agreements in these contentious areas have tended to establish basic minimum standards and give a large degree of discretion to the member states. Consequently they have each found the easiest way of 'fitting' the new EU rules into their existing structure of labour market rules and capital–labour relations (Menz, 2003). The result is considerable variation in the extent to which the rules have penetrated domestic systems.

The only areas in which the EU has made progress well beyond Majone's pareto-efficient notion of 'social regulation' and imposed a set of European-wide social values are equality and non-discrimination (Ostner and Lewis, 1995; Mazey, 1998). First, in the area of gender equality the EU legislation of the 1970s was far more advanced than that prevailing in most member states at the time. Second, the new general non-discrimination legislation covers more sources of discrimination than were previously covered in any EU member state (gender, race, ethnicity, religion and beliefs, disability, age, and sexual orientation), and goes much further than most laws in these areas by imposing the burden of proof on the employer rather than the employee. The European Court of Justice has played a considerable part in the expansion of gender equality rights (see Chapter 4).

The EU reregulatory regime: between harmonization and voluntarism

The result of this mix of environmental and social policies is a particular EU reregulatory regime (cf. Scharpf, 1999, pp. 84–120; Majone, 1996; Kassim and Hine, 1998; Young and Wallace, 2000; Thatcher, 2002a). First, in a number of areas EU reregulatory policies have led to the harmonization of existing national regulations (or the establishment of regulations where no national rules existed) into a single, integrated European regulatory framework. This is particularly so in the case of product standards, such as technical specifications, environmental protection and labelling, and other consumer protection rules. The single European-wide regulatory framework also covers health and safety at work. Many of these areas fit the normative view of regulation as the redressing of market failures.

Second, in several other areas EU reregulatory policies have led to the setting of common European norms and values that go well beyond the narrow market failure justification. For example in environmental policy EU rules have established some of the highest standards in the world and in social policy the EU has begun to regulate 'process standards, such as workers' rights, industrial relations practices and non-discrimination in the workplace.

But, in these issues the EU reregulatory regime tends to be 'voluntarist' (Streeck, 1995, 1996). As Streeck (1996, pp. 424–31) explains:

Neovoluntarism stands for a type of social policy that tries to do with a minimum of compulsory modification of both market outcomes and national policy choices, presenting itself as an alternative to hard regulation as well as to no regulation at all. In particular, neovoluntarism allows countries to exit from common standards... Neovoluntarism would represent a break with the practice of European welfare states, which is to create hard, legally enforceable status rights and obligations for individual citizens and organised collectivities.

The only area of proactive EU social policy that does not fit the neovoluntarism argument is equal pay, treatment and opportunities, first for men and women and more recently for other social groups, where EU rules and norms have been at the vanguard of developments in the member states.

However, even reregulatory policies that are primarily designed to address market failures have a strong indirect redistributive effect, and are therefore a form of 'welfare state' at the European level (Leibfreid, 1992; Leibfried and Pierson, 1995; Montanari, 1995; Gomà, 1996; Scharpf, 1997a; Kleinman, 2002). The EU does not have the direct redistributive capacity of national welfare states (see Chapter 9), but the emerging reregulatory regime reflects a particular welfare compromise at the European level that constrains existing welfare compromises and choices at the domestic level. This places downward pressure on member states with high labour market standards (such as Germany and Scandinavia), and upward pressure on states with low labour market standards (such as the UK and states in Southern Europe). Moreover the constraints on domestic redistributive and value-allocative choices have been reinforced by attempts to harmonize national fiscal policies in economic and monetary union (see Chapter 10).

Explaining EU Regulatory Policies

Three developments in EU regulatory policies need explaining:

- Why has the EU been more able to adopt deregulatory (negative integration) than reregulatory (positive integration) policies?
- Why has the EU been more able to adopt product standards (such as environmental standards) than process standards (such as labour market regulations)?
- Why has the EU been more able to adopt gender equality and general non-discrimination legislation than legislation governing working conditions or workers' rights?

When answering these questions, scholars of the EU have focused on four aspects of the EU policy-making process: (1) the demand for EU deregulation and reregulation by national governments; (2) the demand for EU deregulation and reregulation by private interests; (3) the supply of regulatory policies and policy ideas by the Commission; and (4) the institutional constraints on this demand and supply in the EU legislative process.

The demand for regulation: intergovernmental bargaining

With the Single European Act, the member state governments unanimously agreed to the creation of the single market. This consensus for a deregulatory project at the European level arose from an ideological compromise that emerged in the mid 1980s (Cameron, 1992; Garrett, 1992). On one side, the British Conservative government, led by Margaret Thatcher, saw the single market as a way of exporting the British deregulatory model to the Continent. On the other side, following the failure of Mitterrand's 'socialism in one country' experiment in the early 1980s, the French socialist government saw the single market as a means of developing Europe's industrial competitiveness and capacity *vis-à-vis* the US and Japan. For the French and the other socialist governments, liberalization of intra-EU trade and deregulation of national markets were necessary evils to achieve the long-term benefits of lower transaction costs and higher economies of scale. In other words, once the single market project was perceived as pareto-efficient, the benefits of collective action were viewed as outweighing the costs (cf. Moravcsik, 1991, 1993). The EU governments consequently agreed to delegate to the Commission the task of proposing a plan to complete the single market.

Parallel to the deregulatory project of the single market, the socialist governments argued the case for EU environmental and social policies, and attempted to include provisions in the Single European Act to secure these ends. But as Scharpf (1996, 1997b) explains, consensus is more easily achieved on *product*-related regulations than on *process*-related standards. Product regulations are standards governing how a good or service is packaged, labelled and marketed (such as environmental packaging rules, technical standards and product safety codes), while process regulations are standards governing how goods and services are produced (such as working conditions and industrial relations rules). Richer countries (such as Scandinavia) tend to have higher product and process standards, while poorer countries (such as those in Southern Europe) tend to have lower product and process standards. How rich and poor states order their preferences regarding common EU product and process standards is illustrated in Figure 8.2.

Figure 8.2 *Intergovernmental bargaining on product and process regulations*

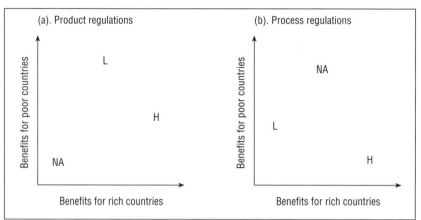

Note: NA = non-agreement, L = common EU low standards, H = common EU high standards.

Source: Adapted from Scharpf (1996).

Where product regulations are concerned, both rich and poor countries would ideally like the EU to adopt the standards they already have domestically: so rich states would like common high standards, while poor states would like common low standards. However both rich and poor states would prefer an EU agreement on any standard (either high or low) to no common standards at all (shown as 'non-agreement' in the figure). If no standards were agreed, different national rules would continue to exist, which would prevent the functioning of a single market in the product concerned, as each state would exclude the products of the other state for not meeting the required domestic standards (Majone, 1993a, 1996). In this situation, governments can agree to delegate agenda-setting powers to the Commission, to propose the most appropriate standards for the EU as a whole, and to introduce qualified-majority voting in the Council to facilitate an agreement and solve this particular coordination problem. Consequently the Commission has proposed comparatively high consumer protection and environmental packaging and labelling standards for the single market, which countries with lower standards have been prepared to accept as they are preferable to no common product standards at all (Egan, 2001). On these issues therefore, the 'leaders' have been able to drag the 'laggards' along (Héritier, 1994; Héritier *et al.*, 1996; Sbragia, 1996; Liefferink and Andersen, 1998).

On process regulations, in contrast, rich and poor states have conflicting preferences. Rich states, which tend to have high process standards (such as labour market rules that protect workers in the event of redundancy), would ideally like these rules to be extended to the EU as a whole. Without an agreement on common rules, states with lower standards would be able to offer cheaper unit labour costs and therefore attract investment away from richer states. The result of such regulatory competition, as many socialist parties in richer states have claimed, would be 'social dumping', as the richer states would be forced to lower their standards to those of the poorer states in order to remain competitive. But, rich states would prefer that no agreement be reached on common process standards rather than accept the imposition of common low standards, as the absence of an agreement would allow them to maintain their high standards and compete over productivity. Meanwhile poor countries with comparatively low labour market standards would ideally prefer no agreement to either the imposition of common high standards or common low standards. Common high standards would force these states to raise their production costs without also raising their productivity levels, leading to higher unemployment, and common low standards would undermine their competitive advantage, the absence of common process standards would enable them to offer cheaper production costs to footloose capital. Hence, the optimal outcome on process standards for both rich and poor states is non-agreement: acceptance of existing national 'regulatory diversity' on workers' rights, and resistance by most states to the extension of qualified-majority voting in the Council in this area (Lange, 1993; Golub, 1996b, 1996c; Héritier, 1996).

The demand for regulation: private interests and Euro-pluralism

In opposition to this 'intergovernmentalist' account, other scholars emphasize the role of private (non-state) interests in promoting European integration and influencing the EU policy process (Sandholtz and Stone Sweet, 1997). According to this view, variations in the development of EU regulatory policies stem from the different degrees of influence of business interests and public interests in the EU policy process. As discussed in Chapter 7, business interests are more organized at the European level than are environmentalists, consumer groups and trade unions. There are three main reasons for this. First, because of the 'logic of collection action', business interests (which can reap specific benefits from the EU policy process) are more able to secure from their members the resources needed to lobby the EU than are public interests (which can only obtain diffuse benefits from the EU policy process). Second, as positive theories of regulation predict (see above), in multilevel political systems business interests have a particular incentive to promote regulatory policies at the higher level because they are more able than their opponents to influence the policy process at that level. However business interests would also like to promote regulatory competition between the different lower regimes in order to facilitate downward pressure on domestic regulations (Dunleavy, 1997). Third, in the EU system business interests have a particular incentive to remove regulatory policy-making from the national level, where corporatism is the prevalent style of regulatory policy-making (Streeck and Schmitter, 1991).

In accordance with this thinking, business interests, via the European Round-Table of Industrialists (ERT) and other transnational business associations, lobbied strongly for the single market programme to be promoted by the Commission and adopted by national governments (Sandholtz and Zysman, 1989; Cowles, 1995). Moreover, business interests were willing to tolerate common high product standards, as these are less costly than process standards, they reduce market distortions and they enable European products to be sold in the North American and Japanese markets. In the case of process standards, businesses in richer states want standards to be lowered as this would increase their competitiveness, while businesses in poorer states fear that EU rules in this area will impose new production costs. As a result, the ERT and the Union of Industrial and Employers Confederations of Europe (UNICE) have only been willing to allow voluntaristic process regulations, as in the working time and works councils directives.

But, this Stiglerian capture of the EU regulatory process by business interests is not complete. The Commission is a multiparty institution (see Chapter 6), and socialist commissioners (particular those with the social affairs and environment portfolios) have been eager to involve the trade union movement and environmental and consumer groups in the EU policy process, and have even funded their activities from the EU budget (see Chapter 7). Likewise socialist governments in the Council (particularly from states with high product standards) have continually supported the Commission's attempts to produce directives aimed at harmonizing product standards, as in the Social Charter. The consequence is the involvement of the European Trade Union Confederation in prelegislative bargaining with UNICE under the Agreement on Social Policy. Without this element of corporatism at the European level it is unlikely that the Commission would have proposed and the member states agreed to several key process-related directives in the post-Maastricht era: those on parental leave, working time and works councils (Falkner, 1996, 1997; Pollack, 1997b).

The supply of regulation: policy entrepreneurship, ideas and decision framing

Policy outcomes are not only the result of demands by governments and interest groups, they are also determined by variations in the supply of policies – through the initiation of policy ideas by the Commission and the shaping of policy choices in the Brussels policy process. For a number of reasons the supply of policies does not always match the demand. First, the Commission's institutional interests are different from those of the member state governments. Like all bureaucracies it has an incentive to increase its own power and prestige in the policy process, and once powers have been delegated to it (for example to initiate regulatory policies), the Commission has a degree of discretion in how it exercises these powers (see Chapter 2). Second, the way in which a policy issue is framed can determine how actors order, update and act on their policy preferences (Tversky and Kahneman, 1981; Riker, 1986; Majone, 1989). By controlling the initiation of policy the Commission is free to frame policy issues in the way it perceives is most likely to secure support in the legislative process. Putting these two together, the Commission is a 'policy entrepreneur' (Kingdon, 1984): selecting the policies that promote its interests; restricting the available choices for governments; continually pressing and negotiating until it gets what it wants; and involving other actors in the policy process to force reluctant governments to accept its proposals (cf. Peters, 1992, 1994; Richardson, 1996; Cram, 1997; Majone, 1996, pp. 74–8; Young and Wallace, 2000).

For example in its white paper *Completing the Internal Market* the Commission proposed the new approach to harmonization. This was a particular 'cultural frame', with a new method of harmonizing rules of exchange (including in export-oriented industries), mutual recognition of the establishment of property rights (applying to only a few industries, such as financial services and the professions), and enforcement of these rules by national administrations (Fligstein and Mara-Drita, 1996). Moreover, in the 1988 report on the *Cost of Non-Europe*, the Commission made it clear that the proposals contained in the white paper would benefit all member states, and therefore was a pareto-efficient project. As a result, the Commission was able to overcome the deadlock in the Council over the achievement of one of the original goals of the Treaty of Rome (cf. Garrett and Weingast, 1993; Dehousse and Majone, 1994; Pierson, 1996). Likewise, in policing the operation of the single market the Commission has been highly activist in extending EU competition rules to cover a wide variety of public utilities (Schmidt, 1998).

A similar story can be told about advances in reregulatory policies, where intergovernmental bargaining or business interest lobbying would not have produced EU policies without the agenda-setting role and strategies of the Commission (cf. Cram, 1993). In the case of environmental issues, the Commission proposed high standards and involved environmental interest groups in EU decision-making to increase its prestige amongst the 'green' member states and to gain the support of the majority in the EP (cf. Eichener, 1997; Héritier, 1997; Lenschow, 1997; Pollack, 1997b), and was instrumental in constructing a new policy frame at the European level around the notions of 'sustainability' and 'conditionality' (Lenschow and Zito, 1998). On workers' rights and worker consultation, the Commission proposed the 'social dialogue' as a conscious way of circumventing a lack of consensus in the Council (Rhodes, 1995; Falkner, 1996; Strøby-Jensen, 2000). In the area of health and safety at work, the Commission deliberately promoted the use of scientific expertise through the comitology system. This gave particular credibility to proposals that many member states and business interests would otherwise have been reluctant to accept (Eichener, 1997), And, in the area of non-discrimination the Commission chose an opportune time to push for agreement on the general non-discrimination directive (just as the extreme-right Austrian Freedom Party became part of a coalition government in Austria), which forced the other member states to support the legislation or face being compared unfavourably to the new Austrian administration, which agreed to support the measure.

All in all, by promoting innovative policy networks and mechanisms of interest accommodation, and by controlling the supply of expertise and information to national governments, the Commission has found ways of forcing the hand of a reluctant Council. Héritier (1997) consequently calls this 'policy-making by subterfuge'.

Institutional constraints: legislative rules and political structure

The demand for and supply of EU regulation policies does not go on in an institution-free environment. Contemporary 'new institutional' theories of political science explain policy outcomes by focusing on how institutions constrain, shape and channel political behaviour (cf. March and Olsen, 1989). These approaches tend to fall into two camps: 'institutional rational choice' (see for example Shepsle, 1989; Tsebelis, 1994) and 'historical institutionalism' (see for example Thelen and Steinmo, 1992). However these two camps share many assumptions about the interaction between institutions and actors' preferences, and about institutional choice, and are hence much closer to each other than traditional rational choice and structural-functionalist theories (Hall and Taylor, 1996). In line with the general political science vogue, a growing number of scholars of the EU use these two new institutional theories to explain EU policy outputs (cf. Pollack, 1996; Jupille, 2004).

From an institutional rational choice perspective, variations in the rules of the EU legislative process produce variations in policy outcomes (see Chapter 3). Where unanimity is required in the Council, as in the consultation procedure, any member state can veto a policy proposal it dislikes. But the agenda-setting power resides with the Commission, and even the least pro-integration member states are often willing to consider policy changes that are marginally more integrationist than the *status quo* (of no EU regulation). Consequently if the Commission proposes a policy that the least pro-integration member states prefer to the *status quo*, unanimity voting will not lead to 'lowest common denominator' outcomes (Garrett, 1992, 1995b; Tsebelis and Garrett, 1996). Furthermore under the cooperation procedure, and now the co-decision procedure, whereby there is qualified-majority voting in the Council and the EP has a powerful role in the legislative process, the Commission or the EP can be 'conditional agenda-setters' (Tsebelis, 1994). As long as a majority in the Council prefers a Commission or EP proposal to the *status quo* the minority will not be able to block it. This goes some way towards explaining why the EU has been able to adopt reregulatory policies in health and safety and process-related environmental standards that would not have been accepted under unanimity rules (cf. Golub, 1996b, 1996c; Weale, 1996; Gehring, 1997; Pollack, 1997a; Andersen and Rasmussen, 1998).

Historical institutionalists, on the other hand, tend to focus on the structural properties of the EU system and the resulting path dependency. For example in Pierson's (1996) account, because governments have to be reelected every few years they tend to have short 'time horizons'. The Commission, in contrast, can take a longer-term view. Also, because different political parties win national elections, national governments in the Council do not have stable policy preferences, so when designing decision rules and delegating powers to the Commission, the Council tends not to think about the long-term implications. This explains why governments were unable to predict that the Commission and the EP would use qualified-majority voting rules to achieve outcomes that were not intended when the governments adopted the Single European Act. Based on a similar logic, Bulmer argues that different policy areas have different 'policy logics' (Bulmer 1994; Armstrong and Bulmer, 1998, pp. 43–64). For example different normative programmes are associated with different policy issues: the single market project is a 'collective good', and environmental standards should be as rigorous as possible (cf. Jachtenfuchs, 1995). Also, in an argument similar to the early neofunctionalists' theory of policy spillover, once the EU became responsible for regulation of process standards it became the focus of societal expectations and lobbying for the expansion of regulation into product standards.

Conclusion: Neoliberalism Meets the Social Market

The single market has fundamentally changed the process of governance in Europe. Rules on the production, distribution and exchange of goods, services and capital are now predominantly set at the European level and this has produced a particular regulatory regime that combines neoliberal deregulation and social-market reregulation.

The single market programme has had a powerful deregulatory effect. Mutual recognition and the new approach to harmonization combined with EU competition policies have led to the removal of tariff barriers between member states and to the liberalization of most sectors of the European economy. National governments are no longer free to use trade barriers, state aid or special operating licences to protect their industries from competition from firms in other EU member states. As a result, for some on the left (particularly in Scandinavia and France) the single market programme constitutes a victory for the neoliberal project (Grahl and Teague, 1990).

Nevertheless there are important reregulatory elements in the single market regime. First, the harmonization of national product standards is meant to achieve efficient policy outcomes in the European public interest. Instead of reducing the rules applying to goods and services, the EU has been particularly successful in establishing new EU-wide product standards (such as vehicle emissions), and in most cases these new standards are at higher levels than was the case in most member states.

Second, the harmonization of process standards is meant to achieve redistributive policy outcomes. These regulations have not redistributed resources directly by taking them from one group (through taxation) and giving them to another (through public expenditure). However they have had an indirect redistributional effect by imposing costs on producers and protecting the values and interests of environmentalists, consumers, workers and other diffuse interests. The redistributional impact of these rules has meant that producer groups and centre-right political parties have mobilized to prevent their harmonization at the EU level. But where qualified-majority voting has existed in the legislative process, and because the Commission has been supported by a centre-left majority in the EP, these anti-regulation forces have been unable to prevent redistributive coalitions from being reestablished at the European level. This has been the case in the area of health and safety at work and in numerous process-related environmental regulations.

In contrast, when unanimity has been required in the Council, centre-right governments and business interests have been able to block the adoption of EU-wide process standards (as in the case of workers' rights and industrial relations). However the Commission has used entrepreneurial strategies – such as encouraging voluntary agreements between labour and business interests at the EU level – to unblock legislative vetoes. The final legislation has had to be 'neovoluntarist' (rather than strict harmonization) to pass the Council. Nonetheless these rules have begun to define a regulatory regime at the EU level that is fundamentally different from neoliberalism and establishes new rights and powers for diffuse interests, as well as imposing additional costs on European industries, particularly multinational ones.

Although social democracy entered the doldrums in the mid to late 1980s, social democrats and the interests they represent have remained a powerful force in Europe, and they have become increasingly institutionalized at the EU level (see Chapter 6). Contrary to Stigler's theory, the Commission has supplied regulation for both producer groups and diffuse interests. Whereas some of the Commission's directorate-generals have strong links with transnational business interests, others have been 'captured' by EU-level environmental, consumer and trade union groups. Also, as the EP has gained more power in the EU legislative process these groups have been able to pursue their interests more effectively. Finally, at the end of the 1990s electorates across the EU voted for governments that promised to mediate the effects of trade liberalization on national welfare states.

The EU regulatory regime is a powerful constraint on domestic welfare coalitions. But reports either of Brussels imposing 'socialism through the back door' or of the EU promoting the demise of the European 'social market' model are grossly exaggerated.

Chapter 9

Expenditure Policies

Compared with national political systems, the capacity of the EU to distribute resources between individuals and states through taxation and public spending is limited. The EU budget constitutes about one per cent of total EU GDP. However for member states, farmers, regions, private organizations, or individual citizens who receive money from the EU budget, the absolute sums involved are quite considerable, and someone somewhere in the EU has to pay for this. To help understand how EU expenditure policies are made, and who gets what and why, we shall first look at some general theories of public finances and redistribution.

Theories of Public Expenditure and Redistribution

A common starting point for the analysis of public finances is Musgrave's (1959) famous threefold typology of the goals of public expenditure:

- *Allocation (or efficiency)*: public expenditure is used to address market failures (see Chapter 8), and in so doing is meant to promote the public interest rather than to produce 'winners' and 'losers'.
- *Redistribution*: in direct contrast to the allocation goal, government expenditure is used to redistribute resources from one group of citizens or localities to another, for example through progressive taxation, social security spending and subsidies to poor regions.
- *Stabilization*: public expenditure is used to achieve macroeconomic goals, such as lower unemployment, lower inflation and higher productivity, either from the demand side (by increasing welfare

271

Table 9.1   *Wealth and government expenditure in the EU and elsewhere,*
1994–2004

	GDP per head (€, PPS)			General government expenditure as percentage of national GDP		
	1994	2004	Increase (%)	1994	2004	Change
Austria	19 660	27 580	40.3	57.4	51.0	−6.4
Belgium	18 510	26 570	43.5	53.3	49.7	−3.6
Cyprus	13 130	19 690	50.0	n/a	n/a	−
Czech Republic	n/a	15 880	−	44.8	46.1	+1.3
Denmark	19 210	27 700	44.2	61.6	56.4	−5.2
Estonia	5 260	11 020	109.5	n/a	n/a	−
Finland	16 149	24 910	54.3	62.9	50.8	−12.2
France	17 890	25 770	44.0	54.9	54.1	−0.8
Germany	18 520	24 940	34.7	49.0	48.6	−0.4
Greece	11 340	18 700	64.9	49.9	46.6	−3.3
Hungary	7 900	13 970	76.8	60.3	48.2	−12.1
Ireland	14 350	30 590	113.2	44.3	35.1	−9.2
Italy	17 670	23 960	35.6	54.5	47.9	−6.6
Latvia	4 530	9 530	110.4	45.8	44.9	−0.9
Lithuania	4 740	10 800	127.8	37.3	35.0	−2.3
Luxembourg	28 120	46 560	65.6	44.5	46.3	+1.8
Malta	n/a	17 450	−	n/a	n/a	−
Netherlands	18 460	26 900	45.7	53.6	48.2	−5.3
Poland	n/a	10 920	−	54.9	47.2	−7.7
Portugal	11 070	17 100	54.5	46.0	46.1	+0.1
Slovakia	7 740	11 970	54.7	59.0	45.2	−13.8
Slovenia	10 670	17 420	63.3	n/a	n/a	−
Spain	13 420	21 770	62.2	47.3	39.1	−8.2
Sweden	17 980	25 700	42.9	70.9	58.6	−12.3
United Kingdom	16 960	27 080	59.7	45.0	43.0	−2.0
EU15	17 060	25 210	47.8	51.3	48.0	−3.2
EU25	−	22 940	−	n/a	n/a	−
United States	25 080	34 650	38.2	36.5	35.7	−0.8
Norway	20 090	32 940	64.0	54.1	48.7	−5.4
Canada	19 630	30 510	55.4	49.7	40.1	−9.6
Switzerland	22 970	29 410	28.0	n/a	n/a	—
Japan	20 370	25 580	25.6	35.2	38.1	+2.9
Romania	n/a	7 460	−	n/a	n/a	−
Bulgaria	4 540	7 450	64.1	n/a	n/a	−
Turkey	n/a	6 230	−	n/a	n/a	−

Note: PPS = purchasing power standard (accounts for differences in national price
levels), n/a = data not available.

Sources: Eurostat for GDP per head at PPS; OECD for government expenditure.

spending) or from the supply side (by increasing spending on education, training, research and infrastructure).

As can be seen in Table 9.1, public expenditure accounts for a major part of GDP throughout the Western world and almost 50 per cent in the EU. Public expenditure as a percentage of GDP is generally higher in the EU than in other OECD countries, including the US and Japan. However, there is considerable variation within the EU: the difference between the lowest proportion of GDP spent by a government (Ireland) and the highest (Sweden) is almost 16 per cent. In general, richer states tend to spend a larger proportion of GDP in the public sector than do poorer states. Although, during the past decade public expenditure as a percentage of GDP has declined throughout the EU (with the exception of Portugal and Luxembourg) as governments have sought to constrain public spending, either to meet the macroeconomic criteria related to Economic and Monetary Union (see Chapter 10) or as part of reforms of the welfare state. In most states public expenditure has risen in absolute terms, but at a slower rate than the growth of GDP. As a result, public expenditure is not significantly lower in the accession states than in the 15 existing EU states.

The traditional explanation for the development of the redistributive powers of the state, through the growth of public expenditure, is normative: to achieve greater equality (see Marshall, 1950; Rawls, 1971). As Esping-Andersen (1990) famously observed, different normative projects have created three different 'worlds of welfare capitalism':

- A *liberal regime*, where means testing is used to determine whether individuals qualify for benefits and entitlements are stigmatized (as in the US).
- A *corporatist (or Christian democratic) regime*, where the state provides social insurance, benefits are primarily geared towards the family and the overall redistributive impact is small (as in Germany, France and Italy).
- A *social democratic regime*, where benefits are generally universal, the state replaces the market in many spheres and the redistributive impact is large (as in Scandinavia).

In each of these models, redistribution is justified on the ground of reducing inequality (Wilensky, 1975; Heidenheimer *et al.*,1990), but they differ in terms of the degree of equality they aim to achieve.

The theory of 'fiscal federalism' is also primarily normative (Oates, 1972, 1999). According to this theory, because the lower levels of government are constrained in respect of macroeconomic policy-making (since monetary policy is centralized), the central (federal) government should have basic responsibility for macroeconomic stabilization, for example by using the central budget to alleviate demand shocks (see Chapter 10). Local governments, in contrast, should be responsible for providing public services and redistributing incomes within their juris-diction, according to the particular political preferences of their con-stituents. If the central government were to take over redistributive functions from the local governments, the general level of welfare would be reduced as the central government would replace tailor-made policies with a single, uniform level of expenditure (cf. Weingast, 1995). Nevertheless decentralized public expenditure can lead to nega-tive externalities (such as the consumption of public goods in one locality by people living in another locality) and tax competition between welfare regimes (to attract investment) (Break, 1967). Fiscal decentralization also means that the burden of providing universal public services (from which everyone benefits regardless of income) will fall disproportionality on poorer localities. Consequently, in most federal systems, funds from the central government budget are used to reduce regional inequality.

However, the growth of redistributive policies can also be explained by positive theories (cf. Mueller, 1989, pp. 445–65). Majority decision-making in a democracy results in the transfer of resources from the minority to the majority. One might expect that because there are more citizens on low incomes than on high incomes, governments would pursue progressive taxation and welfare programmes for the poor (Meltzer and Richard, 1981). Because the median voter in a democratic system is considerably poorer than the average member of the wealthy elite in a non-democratic system, democratic systems tend to have higher taxes and higher levels of public spending than do non-democratic polities (Acemoglu and Robinson, 2001; Boix, 2003). Nevertheless, because the pivotal voter (in the key electoral constituen-cies) is often considerably better off than the person with the median level of income – particularly in countries where voter turnout is low – political parties often advocate expenditure programmes that will dis-proportionately benefit the middle class (Stigler, 1970; Tullock, 1971).

Furthermore, when voting on budgetary packages it is easier for leg-islators to increase the size of government spending than to reduce it. If government spending remains stable, a change in the structure of public expenditure will mean that some social groups will gain at the expense of others. However if the budget is increased, benefits can be distributed in such a way that everyone gains at least something (see Figure 8.1 in the previous chapter). For example legislators from rural constituencies can vote for welfare programmes for the urban poor, in return for legislators from inner cities voting for welfare programmes for farmers. This 'vote trading' consequently leads to the expansion of public expenditure, and an increase in public deficits (cf. Weingast *et al.*, 1981).

However budgetary expansion can be restricted by institutional mechanisms. First, a balanced-budget rule, such as the proposed 'balanced budget amendment' in the US and the expenditure ceiling in the EU, prevents expenditure from being increased without simultaneously raising revenue (Akrill, 2000a). If revenue cannot be increased, changes in the budget can only occur by removing expenditure from one programme (group of citizens) and giving it to another. Second, if the budget has to be adopted by unanimity, as is the case with multiannual budgetary packages in the EU, any decision-maker can veto a proposed change that redistributes resources away from their supporters. As a result of these two institutional constraints, all legislators can demand that contributions made by her or his supporters to the budget are exactly equal to the compensation they receive. This compensation (side-payment) can take two forms: direct benefits from expenditure programmes, or indirect benefits from non-expenditure programmes, such as other policy areas.

According to Olson's (1965) theory of collective action (see Chapter 7), different interest groups have different incentives to organize to secure benefits from government. The benefits of a welfare programme tend to be concentrated, whereas the costs are diffuse. For example the benefits of agricultural subsidies to each individual farmer are much larger than the costs to each individual consumer or taxpayer. As a result farmers are more likely to lobby governments and fund political campaigns to secure farm subsidies than consumer groups are to try to prevent these subsidies. Also some groups find it harder to organize than others. Because of their lack of resources and information, low-income citizens tend to be underrepresented in the policy process, whereas doctors and pensioners tend to be more powerful. Hence public expenditure programmes tend to benefit highly organized or concentrated minorities at the expense of unorganized minorities and the diffuse majority.

In sum, public expenditure is a core responsibility of government, and is primarily used to redistribute resources from one social group to another. At face value, redistributive policies aim to reduce inequalities in society, but the reality is often very different. Who gains from expenditure policies depends on the interests of political decision-makers, the power of organized interests, and the institutional rules of budgetary decision-making.

The Budget of the European Union

Since the Treaty of Rome the EU has operated under five budgetary rules (Begg and Grimwade, 1998, pp. 59–60):

- *Unity*: all revenues and expenditures must be included in a single budget.
- *Annuity*: revenues and expenditures must be drawn up and adopted on an annual basis.
- *Equilibrium*: revenue must always equal expenditure (the balanced budget rule).
- *Universality*: budgetary revenues must not be allocated to particular expenditure items.
- *Specification*: each expenditure item must have a specific objective.

Since 1988 the Council has adopted the EU budget through multiannual 'financial perspectives'. These packages set the general levels of expenditure for each main budgetary category as well as the overall ceiling of the budget relative to the GNP of the EU member states and the structure of revenues. Within these multiannual frameworks, the precise amounts of revenue and expenditure are agreed in an annual budgetary cycle.

Revenue and the own-resources system

The EU budget is funded through the four 'own resources' of the EU:

- *Agriculture levies*: under the Common Agricultural Policy (CAP), these are charges on imports of agricultural products from non-EU countries.
- *Customs duties*: common customs tariffs and other duties are levied on imports from non-EU countries.
- *Value added tax (VAT)*: a harmonized rate is applied in all member states, and this should not exceed 1 per cent of EU GNP.
- *GNP-based own resource*: based on the GNP of the member states, this covers the difference between planned expenditure and the amount yielded from the other three resources.

As Figure 9.1 shows, the balance between these sources of income changed between 1980 and 2001, with the GNP-based resource contributing almost 50 per cent of the revenue in the 2001 budget. The Council established the first three resources in 1970 to replace the old system of financing the EU by direct contributions from the member states, based on their relative GNP. The member states expected that import levies and VAT would be sufficient to cover EU expenditure, but two factors made this impossible. First, as the EU became a net exporter in the 1980s, revenues from agricultural and other import duties fell. Second, in the early 1990s the EU budget grew as a percentage of EU GNP (see below). Consequently the Commission proposed the reintroduction of GNP-based contributions by national

Figure 9.1 *Relative composition of the EU's own resources, 1980–2001 (per cent)*

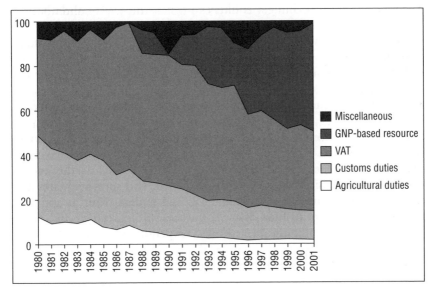

Source: European Commission (2000a).

governments (a 'fourth own resource'). This is calculated on an annual basis to cover the shortfall in revenues from import levies and the VAT levy.

Expenditure

The expenditure of the EU has grown as its policy competences have expanded and in response to internal and external developments. Following the plan for the single market and the new competences established by the Single European Act, a new budget package was adopted in February 1988 for the period 1988–92 – the so-called 'Delors I' plan. After the signing of the Maastricht Treaty, and in line with the preparations for Economic and Monetary Union and the prospective enlargement of the EU to include Austria, Finland, Sweden and Norway, a budget package for the period 1993–9 was agreed in December 1992 (the 'Delors II' plan); which was revised when Norway decided against membership and only Austria, Finland and Sweden joined in January 1995. Following the Amsterdam Treaty, the launch of Economic and Monetary Union, the prospect of a new world trade agreement and the anticipated accession of Central and Eastern European countries, a budget package for the 2000–6 period was adopted at the Berlin European Council in March 1999 (the 'Agenda

2000' plan). Table 9.2 shows the breakdown of expenditure for the 2000–6 package at the time of its adoption, at 1999 prices. At current prices the annual EU budget is likely to break the €100 billion barrier for the first time in 2005 or 2006.

The composition of EU expenditure has changed considerably since the 1980s. The two main expenditure categories are the CAP and the structural funds. The Delors I package doubled expenditure on the structural funds to pursue the goal of economic and social cohesion, and reformed expenditure under the CAP. The Delors II package continued this strategy with the addition of a new Cohesion Fund as part of the social and economic cohesion budget and a further scaling down of expenditure on the CAP. The Agenda 2000 package furthered the relative reduction of expenditure on the CAP, although at a slower rate than the Commission had originally proposed, and stabilized cohesion spending at the same level as in the 1993–9 budget plan (at approximately 0.46 per cent of EU GNP)

As a result, as Figure 9.2 shows, expenditure under the CAP declined from almost 70 per cent of the EU budget in 1980 to 47 per cent in 2001, while expenditure on structural and cohesion policies increased from 11 per cent of the budget to 34 per cent. In the 2000–6 budget, expenditure on agriculture and the cohesion policies accounts for 79 per cent. The remainder is allotted as follows: approximately 7 per cent for other internal policies (mostly research and development), 5 per cent for external policies (mostly humanitarian and development aid), 5 per cent for running the EU institutions (mostly the Commission), 3 per cent for pre-accession aid (to the Central and South-East European countries), and 1 per cent for the EU's budgetary reserves.

The annual budget procedure: 'the power of the purse'

A traditional function of parliaments is to control the purse strings, and the European Parliament acquired a limited budgetary role through reforms to the annual budgetary procedure in 1970 and 1975. This procedure is set out in Article 272 of the treaty. However, as Table 9.3 shows, the 1993 inter-institutional agreement between the Council, the EP and the Commission determines how the procedure operates in practice.

The Council has the final say on 'compulsory expenditure'– that is, expenditure that is necessary under the treaties. This is mostly expenditure on the CAP and the small amount of expenditure arising from international agreements. In combination the Council and the EP have the final say on non-compulsory expenditure, which includes the annual expenditure on economic and social cohesion and most expenditure on other internal policies, such as research, education and finan-

Table 9.2   *EU budget, financial perspective, 2000–6 (€ million)**

	2000	2001	2002	2003	2004	2005	2006
Common Agricultural Policy	40 920	42 800	43 900	43 770	42 760	41 930	41 660
Structural funds	32 045	31 455	30 865	30 285	29 595	29 595	29 170
Other internal policies	5 900	5 950	6 000	6 050	6 100	6 150	6 200
External policies	4 550	4 560	4 570	4 580	4 590	4 600	4 610
EU administration	4 560	4 600	4 700	4 800	4 900	5 000	5 100
Reserves	900	900	650	400	400	400	400
Compensations	–	–	–	–	–	–	–
Pre-accession aid	3 120	3 120	3 120	3 120	3 120	3 120	3 120
Total	91 995	93 385	93 805	93 005	91 465	90 795	90 260
Expenditure as % of EU GNP	1.13	1.12	1.13	1.11	1.05	1.00	0.97
Expenditure ceiling as % of EU GNP	1.13	1.12	1.18	1.19	1.15	1.13	1.13

* 1999 prices.

Source: European Commission (2000a).

Figure 9.2   *Relative composition of EU expenditure, 1980–2001 (per cent)*

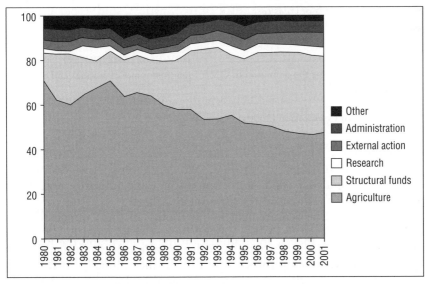

Source: European Commission (2000a).

Table 9.3   *The annual budget cycle*

Stage of budget procedure	Treaty deadlines Art. 272)	1993 inter-institutional Agreement timetable (of preceding year)
EP–Council–Commission dialogue on budget priorities	–	Early April
Commission submits preliminary draft budget to Council	1 September	15 June
EP–Council conciliation meeting on compulsory expenditure	–	Late July
EP–Council conciliation meeting before Council's first reading	–	June/July
Council's first reading – establishment of draft budget by QMV	31 July	July
Draft budget and Council's position sent to EP	5 October	Early September
EP's first reading – *amend non-compulsory expenditure by an absolute majority*	19 November	End October
EP-Council conciliation meeting	–	Mid November
Council's second reading – *reject or amend the EP amendments by QMV*	4 December	End November
EP's second reading – *adopt budget by an absolute majority + 3/5ths of votes cast* – *reject budget by an absolute majority + 2/3rds of votes cast*	within 15 days	Mid December
Deadline for new budget	1 January (of budget year)	1 January (of budget year)

Note: See Chapter 3 for the definition of QMV (qualified-majority voting) and absolute majority voting

Source: European Commission (2000a).

cial support for European level interest groups (see Chapter 7). The proposed constitution, if ratified, would abolish the distinction between compulsory and non-compulsory expenditure, and thus increase the EP's influence over the annual budget.

In contrast to the requirement of unanimity in the Council for the multiannual package deals, the annual budget is adopted by QMV in the Council and by an absolute majority of all members in the EP (see Chapter 3 for the voting rules in the EP and the Council). At the final stage it is easier for the EP to accept the final budget than to reject it, as adoption requires an absolute majority of MEPs plus three-fifths of votes cast, while rejection requires an absolute majority and two-thirds of votes cast.

The budget is prepared by the Directorate-General for the Budget of the Commission, and is negotiated by the members of the Budget Committee in the EP, the Budget Committee of the Committee of Permanent Representatives (COREPER) and the Budget Council (consisting of junior ministers from the national finance ministries).

In this procedure each institution has its own interests: the Commission to promote further European integration and defend its support groups; the Council to promote national interests and national constituencies; and the EP to promote integration and policies that will increase its power in the EU system (see Chapters 2 and 3). Conflicts between these interests are resolved by an EP–Commission–Council trialogue and an EP–Council conciliation procedure.

The EP has used its limited veto power to extract concessions from the Commission and the Council by adding budget lines as a substitute for its lack of legislative initiation power (see Chapter 3). For example in the adoption of the 1995 budget it forced the Council to accept increased expenditure on education and training, which the Council had cut in both the first and second readings (Laffan, 1997, pp. 80–1). However the EP is constrained by its exclusion from the multiannual package deals, its inability to alter compulsory expenditure and the limited overall size of the EU budget relative to national expenditure. Consequently, the absolute redistributive capacity of the EP is weak compared with that of national parliaments in Europe and the US Congress.

The Common Agricultural Policy

Agriculture may seem a minor issue compared with foreign affairs or the state of the economy. But the CAP is the largest item of EU expenditure, it was the first genuinely supranational policy of the EU, several member states maintain a romantic attachment to rural society, and the EU public is increasingly concerned about food safety and animal rights. As a result the political stakes are high when it comes to the making and reform of the CAP.

Objectives and operation of the CAP

The Treaty of Rome established the CAP as a central policy of the European Economic Community. Article 33 of the treaty sets out its objectives as follows:

(a) to increase agricultural productivity, by promoting technical progress and ensuring rational development of agricultural production and the optimum utilization of the factors of production, particularly labour;

(b)   to ensure a fair standard of living for the agricultural community, in particular by increasing the individual earnings of persons engaged in agriculture;

(c)   to stabilize markets;

(d)   to ensure the availability of supply; and

(e)   to ensure that supplies reach consumers at reasonable prices.

These goals encompass all three of Musgrave's (1959) public expenditure goals: (d) and (e) are about the *allocation* of resources to ensure the supply of food at a price the market could not achieve by itself in 1960s Europe; (b) is about the *redistribution* of resources – a welfare policy for farmers; and (a) and (c) are about market *stabilization* – using demand-side and supply-side management to control inflation, secure agricultural employment and increase productivity in the agriculture sector.

In June 1960 the Commission put forward a proposal for achieving these goals through three 'guiding principles':

- A *single market*: the removal of barriers to the free movement of agricultural products between the member states.
- *Community preference*: priority should be given to produce from the EC member states.
- *Financial solidarity*: the cost of the policy should be borne by the Community as a whole rather than by the individual member states.

After protracted negotiations, in 1962 the member states agreed to turn these principles into practice through three mechanisms to protect the price of agricultural goods supplied by farmers in the member states:

- Protection against low internal prices: by buying surplus goods from farmers – paid out of the European Agricultural Guidance and Guarantee Fund (EAGGF) – when prices fall below an agreed guarantee price in the European market.
- Protection against low import prices: through import quotas and levies (paid into the EAGGF) on imported agricultural goods when the world price falls below an agreed price.
- Subsidies to achieve a low export price: through refunds (paid out of the EAGGF) for the export of agricultural goods when the world price falls below an agreed price.

The result is a system of indirect income support for farmers, paid for by European taxpayers through the EU budget, and by European consumers through the extra prices charged on imported agricultural goods.

Problems with the CAP

When the CAP was set up Europe was not self-sufficient in most agricultural goods. However as agricultural production stabilized and Europe became a net exporter of agricultural goods the CAP price-support mechanism created some intractable problems:

- Guaranteed prices encouraged overproduction and production grew faster than demand, resulting in 'wine lakes' and 'grain mountains'.
- These surpluses had to be stored thus imposing an additional cost on the CAP budget.
- Environmental destruction resulted from overintensive farming and excessive use of herbicides, pesticides and artificial fertilizers.
- The bulk of revenues went to larger farmers (who earned more because they produced more), but it was smaller farmers who were in need of the most support.
- Import quotas and levies created numerous trade disputes and prevented the development of global free trade in agricultural goods.
- Export subsidies depressed world prices, distorting agriculture markets in the Third World, thus contributing to global development problems.

The original goals of the CAP had been fulfilled, and the allocation function was no longer necessary as goods could be supplied by the open market at cheap prices. The redistribution of resources to farmers had made some farmers better off than others, and better off than many other sections of society. Moreover, the markets no longer needed to be stabilized and although the CAP consumed ever-greater resources, its utility to EU taxpayers and small farmers had fallen and its distortion of global agriculture markets increased. Consequently by the early 1990s the CAP was no longer sustainable in its original form. Consumer and environmental groups, several member state governments and a number of foreign governments demanded reform.

Reform of the CAP: towards a new type of (welfare) policy

In 1992 the EU member states agreed the first major reform of the CAP, which had been drafted and negotiated through the Agriculture Council by Ray MacSharry, the Irish agriculture commissioner. The MacSharry Plan included four main changes to the policy:

- Price cuts in certain sectors: the guaranteed prices for cereals and beef were reduced over a three-year period (29 per cent and 15 per cent respectively), to levels that were closer to world market prices (price cuts were later introduced for fruit and vegetables).

- Direct income support for farmers: a system of direct payments to farmers was introduced (in addition to the price support schemes) to compensate for price reductions in particular farm sectors.
- Set-aside scheme: a system was introduced in which farmers in certain sectors (particularly cereals) and specific regions are paid to leave their land fallow ('set aside') instead of growing crops that would have to be bought by the EU.
- Accompanying measures: new aid programmes were introduced to promote rural development, environmentally friendly agriculture, the replacement of agricultural land with forests, and early retirement for farmers.

In July 1997 the EU agriculture commissioner, Franz Fischler, unveiled proposals for further CAP reforms, as part of the Commission's Agenda 2000 budget package to prepare for EU enlargement. Fischler proposed extending the MacSharry reforms by increasing the price cuts on cereals and beef and introducing price cuts for milk, olive oil and wine. He also proposed that the CAP be transformed from a policy of price support to one of income support. Fischler also proposed to strengthen the non-welfare objectives of the policy – that is, environmental protection, food safety (following the 'mad cow disease' [BSE] crisis), and animal welfare (following public protests about the transportation of live animals).

At the Berlin European Council in March 1999 the agreement reached by the agriculture ministers and the Commission was significantly watered down by a Franco-German deal on the new budget framework (Akrill, 2000b; Galloway, 2000). While the basic element of the Fischer Plan remained intact, namely the gradual replacement of price support by income support, the new agreement, at the behest of France, ensured that price support would continue for key producers (such as dairy and cereal farmers) and would be reduced at a slower rate than the Commission had proposed.

Nevertheless, as a result of the CAP reforms the prices of agricultural goods in the EU are increasingly set by the free market. Hence the CAP is no longer about allocation or market stabilization. Instead it fulfils two other purposes. First, through the shift to direct income support the redistributive function has become paramount. In other words the CAP is becoming a liberal welfare state regime (in Esping-Andersen's typology): public programmes are funded via taxation instead of charging higher prices to consumers, and means testing is used to establish who qualifies for welfare subsidies – in this case low-income farmers.

Second, the 'new CAP' aims to redress market failures resulting from agricultural production (see Chapter 8). For example environmental destruction and rural underdevelopment are negative externalities of transactions in the agriculture market, and in the supply of agricultural goods there is information asymmetry in respect of food quality and safety – that is, the consumer has less information than the producer. By addressing environmental protection, rural development and food safety, the CAP aims to recreate the allocative efficiency of the market, making it in the general European public interest rather than the narrow interest of farmers.

Nevertheless, as with the establishment of the CAP and the MacSharry reforms, further CAP reform will only be achieved if the necessary ideas, interests and circumstances coincide in the EU policy process.

Making agricultural policy: can the iron triangle be broken?

Agricultural policy is made by an 'iron triangle' of agriculture ministers, agriculture officials in the Commission, and European-level farming interests (cf. Daugbjerg, 1999; Pappi and Henning, 1999).

First, the Agriculture Council, which meets at least every month, is the central decision-making body – the part played by the EP is limited as CAP legislation is passed under the consultation procedure (see Chapter 3). Agriculture ministers are often from political parties that are supported by farmers (such as the Irish Fianna Fail, the French Gaullists, the Italian Christian Democrats, and the Bavarian Christian Social Union) and/or represent rural regions (such as Bavaria, rural France and Spain, East Anglia in the UK and Jutland in Denmark). Moreover the work of the Agriculture Council is supported by the Special Committee of Agriculture (SCA) rather than the usual Committee of Permanent Representatives (COREPER); the SCA is staffed by officials from national agriculture ministries, whereas the members of COREPER tend to be career diplomats.

Finance ministers, who are generally more in favour than agriculture ministers of reining-in agricultural subsidies, only intervene whenever there are major questions on the financing of the CAP, and the heads of government (in the European Council) are usually only called into play to negotiate the major reform packages. Also, there are often disputes between agriculture and finance ministers. For example on several occasions in the 1980s the German agriculture minister (from the Bavarian Christian Social Union) opposed proposals by the German finance minister to scale down the CAP subsidies.

Second, agricultural interests are protected by the fact that the CAP is managed by the Commission. The agriculture commissioner, who is responsible for initiating reform proposals and changes to the CAP regime, has always come from a farming state, and usually from a political party with close links to farming interests. The Agriculture Directorate-General (DG) is the largest DG in the Commission (see Chapter 2) and is staffed predominantly by officials from the main farming member states (for example France and Germany) and as a result is rarely prepared to listen to the views of the Consumer, Environment and Economic Affairs DGs. Also, the day-to-day management of the CAP is undertaken by the network of agriculture, veterinary and food safety committees around the Commission, and these committees are staffed by 'national experts', most of whom are nominated by and answerable to national agriculture ministries.

Third, farming interests are strongly represented at the national and European levels (Keeler, 1996). In most member states the 'corporatist' relationship between national farmers' associations and agriculture ministries ensures that farmers play a central role in the making of national agriculture policies. At the European level, the Confederation of Professional Agricultural Organizations (COPA) is the most well-resourced, well-staffed and highly-organized of all the supranational sectoral associations (see Chapter 7).

Each element of this triangle has a vested interest in defending the interests of the others: subsidies to farmers; the centrality of the CAP in the EU decision-making process for agriculture commissioners and the Agriculture Directorate-General; and the independence of the Agriculture Council and the protection of domestic supporters of the agriculture ministers. In contrast, there are few incentives for consumers to mobilize to attempt to break the iron triangle, as the cost of the CAP to each individual consumer or taxpayer is less than the cost of organizing an anti-CAP campaign (Nedergaard, 1995).

Nevertheless the iron triangle has been undermined by two developments. First, social, economic and political changes in Europe have reduced the power of agricultural interests. As Table 9.4 shows, there has been a dramatic change in the status of agriculture in national economies since the 1970s. Between 1970 and 2000 the share of agriculture as a percentage of the labour force of the member states declined from over 20 per cent in seven member states and 10–20 per cent in three of the other states to less than 10 per cent in all member states but two (Greece and Portugal), with an average of just 4.3 per cent across the EU. Moreover income from agriculture accounted for only 1.7 per cent of EU GDP in 2001.

Active farmers comprise less than 5 per cent of the electorate in most member states. This has forced many agricultural parties, and parties with traditional support in rural areas, such as Christian democrats, to appeal to urban middle-class voters, who are the ones paying for the CAP. Voters with a 'strong agricultural attribute' – including farmers, retired farmers, spouses of farmers, voting-age children of farmers, and former farmers in other occupations – may still constitute as much as

Table 9.4   *The changing status of agriculture in the member states, 1970–2000/1*

| | Share of agriculture as percentage of labour force | | | Share of agriculture as percent of national GDP | Average size of agricultural holding (hectares) |
	1970	2000	Change	2001	2001
Austria	18.7	6.1	–12.6	1.3	17.0
Belgium	5.0	1.9	–3.1	1.1	22.6
Denmark	11.5	3.7	–7.8	2.3	45.7
Finland	24.4	6.2	–18.2	0.9	27.3
France	13.5	4.2	–9.3	2.2	42.0
Germany	8.6	2.6	–6.0	0.9	36.3
Greece	40.8	17.0	–23.8	6.7	4.4
Ireland	27.1	7.9	–19.2	2.5	31.4
Italy	20.2	5.2	–15.0	2.4	6.1
Luxembourg	9.7	3.3	–6.4	0.6	45.4
Netherlands	4.9*	3.3	–1.6	2.2	20.0
Portugal	28.6*	12.5	–16.1	2.4	9.3
Spain	29.5	6.9	–22.6	3.6	20.3
Sweden	24.4	6.2	–18.2	0.6	37.7
United Kingdom	2.4*	1.5	–0.9	0.6	67.7
EU15	–	4.3	–	1.7	18.7
Cyprus	–	5.4	–	3.9	–
Czech Republic	–	5.2	–	1.7	–
Estonia	–	7.0	–	3.2	–
Hungary	–	6.5	–	3.8	–
Latvia	–	14.4	–	3.0	–
Lithuania	–	18.4	–	3.1	–
Malta	–	1.4	–	2.2	–
Poland	–	18.7	–	3.1	–
Slovakia	–	6.9	–	1.9	–
Slovenia	–	9.6	–	2.0	–
Accession states	–	13.3	–	3.1	–
United States	–	2.4	–	–	176.8
Japan	–	4.2	–	–	2.0

* 1980

Source: European Commission (2002b).

17 per cent of the electorate in some member states (Keeler, 1996, p. 129). Placed between the middle class and the urban working class, this constituency can be pivotal in determining electoral outcomes. But in the 1990s socialist parties swept to power throughout the EU (in coalition with green parties in many member states) and socialists

made up 50 per cent of the Santer Commission. For the first time, with socialists and even greens in a large number of agriculture ministries, the issue of agricultural subsidies started to be wrapped up with broader issues of food production, such as the environmental sustainability of farming and the quality of produce. Nevertheless, with the focus on restraining public spending to qualify for economic and monetary union, reform of the CAP was not at the top of the political agenda of most centre-left governments in the 1990s.

Second, external pressures have created new incentives for the CAP to be reformed. These began with the negotiations in the Uruguay Round of the General Agreement on Tariffs and Trade (GATT) in 1987 and 1988. Without reform of the subsidies on European agriculture a ground-breaking agreement on global trade liberalization could not be achieved. Many of the non-EU signatories of GATT were not prepared to support the EU's trade liberalization agenda while the EU continued to subsidise the export of agricultural products to their domestic markets. Nevertheless, the GATT agreement was finally signed when the EU trade ministers and heads of state promised to reform the CAP as part of the deal (Patterson, 1997). The MacSharry reform plan was immediately proposed, with strong pressure being put on agriculture ministers to approve the reform package.

A similar situation existed at the end of the 1990s, with the prospective enlargement of the EU to include Central and East European countries. One consequence of the enlargement would be a 50 per cent increase in agricultural land in the EU and a 100 per cent increase in agricultural labour. Even with a move towards direct income support rather than price support, there would be a dramatic increase in the cost of the CAP as a result of the enlargement (Daugbjerg and Swinbank, 2004). As Table 9.4 shows, in three of the accession states – Poland, Lithuania and Latvia – up to 19 per cent of the workforce are involved in agriculture. However the new member states are unlikely to stand as a single bloc on agricultural issues – against reform of the CAP for example – because the structure of agriculture and the relationship between agricultural interests, political parties and bureaucrats vary among these states (Sharman, 2003).

As with the GATT agreement, agriculture ministers and COPA may have preferred to delay enlargement in order to protect their interests, but this decision was out of their hands. Also, once international trade issues and enlargement became associated with reform of the CAP, an 'issue linkage' was established, which created specific incentives for non-agricultural industrial interests to lobby against the CAP (Coleman and Tangermann, 1999). For many industrial sectors, the benefits reaped from the GATT agreement and EU enlargement would be greater than the costs of mobilizing to break the grip of the farming lobby at the national and European levels. Hence the socioeconomic interests that supported the CAP were outnumbered by socioeconomic interests that recognized that failing to reform the CAP would jeopardize their policy goals elsewhere.

Cohesion Policy

Under the EU treaty, one of the central aims of the EU is to promote 'economic and social cohesion' – that is, to reduce disparities between different regions and social groups in the EU. This is a classic normative redistributive goal. To this end an ever-larger proportion of the EU budget has been transferred to less-developed regions. However the extent to which cohesion policy is a genuine welfare policy and how much it has been able to reduce social and economic disparities in Europe are open to question.

Operation of the policy

The EU has four structural funds:

- The European Regional Development Fund (ERDF), which was set up in 1975 and is managed by the Regional Policy Directorate-General.
- The European Social Fund (ESF), which was set up in 1960 and is managed by the Employment and Social Affairs Directorate-General.
- The Guidance Section of the EAGGF, which was set up as part of the CAP in 1962 and is managed by the Agriculture Directorate-General.
- The Financial Instrument for Fisheries (FIFG), which was set up in 1994 and is managed by the Fisheries Directorate-General.

The 1988 reform of the structural funds introduced four key principles for the management of social and economic cohesion policies:

- *Additionality*: the member states cannot use EU resources to reduce national spending on regional development, so EU resources go directly to regions or managing authorities rather than to national treasuries.
- *Partnership*: the policy operates through close cooperation between the Commission, national governments and regional authorities (which in some states had to be created for the purpose) in the process that runs from the preparation of projects to the implementation and monitoring of expenditure.
- *Programming*: funding is delivered through multiannual development programmes.

- *Concentration*: EU assistance measures are concentrated in a series of priority objectives.

The structural funds were then reformed again in 1999 as part of the Agenda 2000 package. One aspect of the reforms was a reduction and streamlining of the objectives, down to three:

- *Objective 1*: to promote development and structural adjustment in regions that lag behind, defined as having a per capita GDP of below 75 per cent of the EU average.
- *Objective 2*: to combat structural adjustment in regions with industrial, service or fisheries sectors facing major change, rural areas in serious decline, and deprived urban areas.
- *Objective 3*: (for regions not covered by Objectives 1 and 2) to modernize 'human resources' infrastructure, such as education and training systems.

The Commission also set up separate 'community initiatives', to be funded by the structural funds. In 1999 these were reduced to just four: planning and cooperation between border regions (Interreg); rural development (Leader); urban regeneration (Urban); and transnational cooperation to combat all forms of discrimination and inequality in the labour market (Equal).

In addition to the structural funds, a cohesion fund was established in 1994 as part of the implementation of the Maastricht Treaty, and linked to the specific goal of economic and monetary union (EMU). Because qualification for EMU involved meeting strict budgetary and fiscal criteria (see Chapter 10), the cohesion fund was geared to increasing the growth capacity of the four poorest member states: Greece, Ireland, Portugal and Spain. Two types of project are supported by the fund: environmental protection, and transport and other infrastructure networks.

Table 9.5 shows how much each member state receives under the 2000–6 cohesion policy budget. The main beneficiaries of the policy are the four 'cohesion countries': Greece, Portugal, Spain, and Ireland, in descending order of receipts per capita. The other main beneficiaries are southern Italy, the new German Länder, Northern Ireland and the north of England, the industrial north and rural south of France, and the rural areas of Finland.

As with the CAP, the Commission proposed a more radical reform of the cohesion policies than the member states eventually agreed to at the Berlin European Council meeting that adopted the 2000–6 budget package. The Commission feared that the existing policies would not be sustainable with the addition to the EU of a large number of comparatively poor regions. Consequently in the draft Agenda 2000

Table 9.5 Member state receipts from cohesion policy, 2000–6 (€million 1999 prices)

	Structural funds							Community initiatives				Total (€m)	Total per capita (€)
	Objective 1	Objective 1 – transition*	Objective 2	Objective 2 and 5b – transitional*	Objective 3	FIFG	Cohesion	Interreg	Urban	Equal	Leader		
Greece	20 961	–	–	–	–	–	3 060	568	24	98	172	24 883	2370
Portugal	16 124	2905	–	–	–	–	3 300	394	18	107	152	23 000	2300
Spain	37 744	352	2 553	98	2 140	200	11 160	900	106	485	467	56 205	1423
Ireland	1 315	1773	–	–	–	–	720	84	5	32	45	3 974	1046
Italy	21 935	187	2 145	377	3 744	96	–	426	108	371	267	29 656	518
Finland	913	–	459	30	403	3	–	129	5	68	52	2 062	397
Germany	19 229	729	2 984	526	4 581	107	–	737	140	484	247	29 764	363
United Kingdom	5 085	1166	3 989	706	4 568	121	–	362	117	376	106	16 596	278
France	3 254	551	5 437	613	4 540	225	–	397	96	301	252	15 666	266
Sweden	722	–	354	52	720	60	–	154	5	81	38	2 186	246
Luxembourg	–	–	34	6	38	–	–	7	–	4	2	91	228
Austria	261	–	578	102	528	4	–	183	8	96	71	1 831	226
Netherlands	–	123	676	119	1 686	31	–	349	28	196	78	3 286	207
Belgium	–	625	368	65	737	34	–	104	20	70	15	2 038	198
Denmark	–	–	156	27	365	197	–	34	5	28	16	828	156
Total	127 543	8411	19 733	2721	24 050	1078	18 240	4828	685	2797	1980	212 066	564

* Transitional support is provided to certain regions that by 1999 had attained an economic and social position that no longer justified the provision of such a high level of Community regional assistance in 2000–6 as before.

Source: European Commission (2001).

package proposed that the EU population presently covered by the structural funds should be reduced to 35–40 per cent (rather than the 51 per cent covered under the 1988–99 framework), that Objective 1 should be geared to improving competitiveness, that Objective 2 should be geared to economic diversification, and that spending under the social fund should be integrated with the EU's employment strategy.

The member state governments accepted some of these proposals, but in the case of the multiannual package deal, states whose regions would no longer qualify for support under the proposed reforms – particularly Ireland – sought and secured significant funds for the transition period. As Table 9.5 shows, the package deal ensured that every member state would gain something from the structural policies. In the subsequent reform of the rules governing the structural funds, in June 1999, the governments decided to rein in some of the autonomous implementing powers of the Commission in the area of cohesion policies – which some scholars have described as 'creeping renationalization' of this policy area (for example Sutcliffe, 2000).

Impact: a supply-side policy with uncertain convergence implications

The result of the reforms is a policy that combines elements of redistribution and allocation (cf. Behrens and Smyrl, 1999; De Rynck and McAleavey, 2001). Under the cohesion policies there are significant fiscal transfers via the EU budget from taxpayers in the wealthier region (Belgium, the Netherlands, Luxembourg, Austria, northern Italy, the Paris basin, southern Germany, the south of England and southern Scandinavia) to the four 'cohesion countries' (Ireland, Portugal, Greece and Spain) and the poorer regions in the wealthier states (particularly southern Italy and eastern Germany). For the main recipient regions, revenues from the structural funds and the cohesion fund amount to 3–5 per cent of regional GDP. In other words there is a certain amount of 'fiscal federalism', whereby fiscal transfers are made between territorial units through a central budget.

It is not only the poor member states that benefit from the cohesion policies. In fact over 50 per cent of EU citizens live in regions covered by the regional-based objectives. This is a product of the design of the EU cohesion policy. The policy is a regional policy, whereby transfers are made at the substate level, rather than pure fiscal federalism, whereby transfers would be made between member states. Also, the per capita GDP and industrial decline criteria are designed in such a way that every member state can claim to have a poor or backward region. When measured at the level of the member states, EU cohesion policy is as much about subsidies for the 'middle-income' member states as it is about improving the living standards of low-income member states (as is the case with many domestic welfare programmes).

In addition, EU cohesion policy is more about supply-side macroeconomic stabilization than demand-side income support. If it were a classic (Keynesian) welfare policy, subsidies would be given directly to low-income regions, families or individuals, to spend as they saw fit. Such a policy would increase the spending power of low-income groups, and hence the demand for goods and services in the single market. In contrast cohesion resources are primarily spent on infrastructure projects, such as improving transport and telecommunications networks and education facilities. Such a policy increases the efficient supply of the factors of production (land, labour and capital), and as a result improves the competitiveness (and comparative advantage) of recipient regions in the single market (Leonardi, 1993; Martin and Rogers, 1996). In other words the basic aim of the cohesion policies is convergence between regional economies rather than between regional incomes (Anderson, 1995, Bufacchi and Garmise, 1995).

The extent to which the cohesion policies have reduced social and economic disparities is uncertain. At a theoretical level there is a basic difference between convergence and divergence theories (Leonardi, 1993). On the one hand, convergence in incomes and economies may occur naturally in a free market, as capital flows to where land and labour are cheapest (see for example Krugman, 1991). On the other hand, economic integration in a free market could lead to divergence as capital flows from the periphery, where infrastructure is weak and demand is low, to the core, where infrastructure is plentiful and there is a high return on investment (Myrdal, 1957).

At an empirical level, in terms of per capita GDP, the gap between the EU's richest and poorest regions narrowed by only 2 per cent between 1980 and 1992 (cf. Helgadottir, 1994). At this rate the six poorest regions would not reach the EU average until 300 years' time! (Cole and Cole, 1998, p. 296.) However Leonardi (1993, 1995) finds that if convergence is measured as the average deviation from the mean for all regions, between 1960 and 1992 there was considerable convergence in terms of per capita GDP. Because Leonardi accepts the divergence theory, he concludes that this convergence must have been due to the cohesion policies. As discussed, cohesion is not purely about per capita GDP, it is also about reducing other socioeconomic disparities. For example some of the regions with the highest par capita GDP, such as Hamburg and Bremen, have considerable socioeconomic, infrastructural and unemployment problems (Keating, 1995). Steinle (1992) finds that the most competitive EU regions are those with intermediate levels of economic development, and Fagerberg and Verspagen (1996) have found that the cohesion policies may have actually increased disparities in certain important economic variables, such as access to research and development resources. Finally, Rodriguez-Pose (1998) claims that variations in social conditions and social infrastructure are key factors in determining variations in regional economic performance, and hence whether regions can effectively use EU resources to foster economic growth.

Making cohesion policy: Commission, governments and regions

As with the CAP, EU cohesion policy is made through a triangular interaction between the main legislative body (the Council), the main executive actors in the Commission, and private interests (the regional authorities). However unlike the CAP, these three actors do not have mutually reinforcing interests. This produces two competing policy logics rather than a unified iron-triangle: intergovernmental bargaining in the Council on the basis of national costs and benefits; versus strategic behaviour by the Commission and the regions to undermine the autonomy of the national governments (Hooghe and Keating, 1994).

The volume of resources available through the structural funds, plus which member states should gain the most and which regions qualify for support, are decided by the member state governments in the Council. Also, in the implementation of the cohesion policies 90 per cent of funds are spent on 'national initiatives'. At the beginning of each programme period, each member state submits a proposal to the Commission in the form of a regional development plan or a single programming document, on the basis of which two- to six-year regional development programmes are negotiated between the Commission and the member state governments, with significant input by the regional authorities concerned. Implementation of the programmes is supervized by monitoring committees which are made up of representatives of the regions, the member state governments and the Commission.

However, the member states are not in full control of cohesion policy as the Commission has introduced four principles, each of which constrains the autonomy of national governments. For example the principle of 'additionality' has forced several member states to alter their accounting practices for managing the distribution of regional funds, and the principle of 'partnership' has enabled the Commission to bypass national governments and negotiate directly with representatives from the regions on the preparation and implementation of projects and encouraged several member states to set up new regional authorities. The Commission has also deliberately developed expenditure and programmes under the community initiatives scheme, whereby projects to address European-wide concerns are initiated by the Commission rather than the member states.

Linked to the principle of partnership, representatives of subnational authorities have sought to influence EU cohesion policies directly. There are more than 200 offices of regions and local authorities in Brussels (see Chapter 7), many of which have established direct informal contacts with the Regional Policy Directorate-General of the Commission. Senior officials in the this directorate-general tend to come from regions that receive substantial resources under the structural funds, such as the Spanish Basque region, and are consequently connected to networks of subnational elites (cf. Ansell *et al.*, 1997). Moreover the Maastricht Treaty established the Committee of the Regions, which provides the representatives of subnational authorities and assemblies with a formal consultation role in the making and implementation of regional policy (much like that of the EP under the consultation procedure) and has institutionalized transnational contacts between governmental authorities below the level of the state (Loughlin, 1996).

The access to and influence of regions in the EU policy process varies considerably among the member states. In general the regions in federal states such as Germany and Belgium, and regions with strong identities, as in parts of Spain, Italy, France and the UK, tend to have the most influence in Brussels (cf. Conzelmann, 1995; Marks *et al.*, 1996). Nevertheless, several authors claim that the EU regional policies have contributed to decentralization and devolution in states where there were no previously regional authorities, as in France, the UK, Portugal, Ireland and Greece (Jones and Keating, 1995; Balme and Jouve, 1996; Ioakimidis, 1996; Hooghe, 1996b; Nanetti, 1996).

The EU may be some way from being a 'Europe of regions', where regions replace nation-states as the main territorial unit of the EU political system (Anderson, 1990; Borras-Alomar *et al.*, 1994). But cohesion policies have pushed the EU towards a 'Europe *with* the regions'. Regions are active players in the EU policy-making process, alongside national governments and the Commission, and the redistribution of resources directly to subnational territorial units is an integral part of the EU political system (Hooghe, 1996a; Marks *et al.*, 1996).

Other internal policies

As noted earlier, approximately 7 per cent of the EU budget is spent on other internal policies – Table 9.6 shows the breakdown of this in the 2004 budget. The largest proportion was spent on investment in scientific research and development, with the remainder being evenly split between two areas: programmes to improve infrastructure and industrial competitiveness in the EU, and projects to foster a civil society at the European level and social integration in the EU.

Research and development

EU expenditure on research and development took off in the 1980s, primarily because of concern that Europe was falling behind the level of technological development in the US and Japan. In 1982 the Commission and the 'big-twelve' European high-technology firms (including Philips, Siemens, Thomson and Olivetti) persuaded the member states to agree to the ESPRIT programme (European Strategic Programme for Research and Development in Information Technologies) (cf. Sandholtz, 1992). The success of ESPRIT enabled the Commission to secure funding for a number of parallel programmes and the first multiannual framework programme for 1984–87, with a budget of €3.8 billion. This was followed by the second framework programme (1987–91, €5.4 billion), the third framework programme (1990–94, €5.7 billion – a reduction in real terms), the fourth framework programme (1994–98, €13.1 billion), the fifth framework programme (1998–2002, €15 billion), and the sixth framework programme (2002–6, €16.3 billion).

The funds for these programmes go to an agreed set of research categories and academic and private researchers bid for funding. In terms of the disciplines covered, the Sixth Framework Programme provided resources in the following areas:

- Information society technologies (€3625 million).
- Life sciences, genomics and biotechnology (€2255 million).
- Sustainable development and ecosystems (€2120 million).
- Nanotechnologies and nanosciences (€1300 million).
- Aeronautics and space (€1075 million).
- Food quality and safety (€685 million).
- Social sciences (€225 million).

The total amount of resources spent on research and the amount for each category is set by means of Commission–Council–EP negotiations. Since the Maastricht Treaty the framework programmes have been adopted through the co-decision procedure between the Council and the EP. In the Council the member state governments seek to ensure funding for areas of research in which their own universities, public institutions and firms have a particular interest. For example the UK and Germany, which are home to Europe's leading biotechnology firms, have consistently argued that investment in biotechnology research is essential if Europe is to catch up with Japan and the US. Nevertheless, the member states are also careful to restrain the EU budget in this area, and usually reduce the amounts proposed by the Commission. The EP, in contrast, usually reinstates the amounts proposed by the Commission.

Table 9.6   *Expenditure on other internal policies, 2004*

Policy area	Amount (€ million)	Percentage of expenditure on other internal policies	Percentage of total EU expenditure
Research and technological development	4312.5	61.2	4.33
Infrastructure	1159.2	16.4	1.16
Trans-European Networks	716.7	10.2	0.72
Internal market	180.9	2.6	0.18
Other fisheries and sea-related measures	74.3	1.1	0.07
Transport	59.1	0.8	0.06
Energy	50.9	0.7	0.05
Other agricultural operations	43.0	0.6	0.04
Euratom nuclear safeguards	19.3	0.3	0.02
Other regional operations	15.0	0.2	0.02
Social integration and civil society	1248.4	17.7	1.25
Education, vocational training and youth	565.3	8.0	0.57
Environment	241.9	3.4	0.24
Social dimension and employment	191.3	2.7	0.19
Culture and audiovisual media	117.6	1.7	0.12
Labour market and technological innovation	114.3	1.6	0.11
Consumer policy	18.0	0.3	0.02
Other areas	330.7	4.7	0.33
Area of freedom, security and justice	180.5	2.6	0.18
Information and communication	98.8	1.4	0.10
Statistical information	37.3	0.5	0.04
Measures to combat fraud	9.9	0.1	0.01
Performance facility reserve	3.9	0.1	0.00
Aid for reconstruction	0.3	0.0	0.00
Total	7050.8	100.0	7.08

Source: European Commission (2004).

Nevertheless, the Commission, in collaboration with the public and private sector elites in the pan-European research community, controls the setting of the overall research policy agenda, for example by determining which types of research should be funded by the EU (Cram, 1997). The Commission also decides which individual projects should receive funds. As Peterson (1995a, p. 408) notes:

Every five years, intergovernmental bargaining between the Council and the other institutions eventually produces a budget and agreement on the broad institutional parameters of the Framework

Programme. But the institutional framework for EU research policy does not change much or suddenly over time, thus empowering a technocrocy that is well-entrenched after ten years of the Framework Programme's existence ... [and] the Commission ... can be counted on to remain the 'ringleader' of the EU research policy networks that correspond to individual EU initiatives.

Infrastructure

Some of the EU budget is devoted to investment in infrastructure, in the broadest meaning of the word. The largest of the areas covered is the Trans-European Networks programme (TENs), which was established in 1993 to upgrade infrastructure and foster infrastructural links between the member states in terms of:

- *Information networks,* particularly telecommunications networks.
- *Transportation networks,* particularly high-speed train links.
- *Energy networks,* such as electricity supplies.

Other related areas are the promotion of information exchange between small firms (under 'internal market'), and the promotion of energy efficiency and renewable energy resources (under 'energy'). Many of the projects funded from this part of the EU budget are also supported by loans from the European Investment Bank.

On these issues, the member states again have the ultimate sanction. However the amount of resources devoted to each individual programme is small, and bargaining between the member states on budgetary issues tends to concentrate on the larger budgetary items, such as the CAP, the cohesion funds and research. As a result the Commission has been relatively free to experiment with new infrastructure project ideas, and once a project is set up it tends to remain an item in future budgets. However the member states did block a Commission proposal, linked to the TENs programme, for a new financial instrument (a 'Union bond'), which would have enabled the EU to raise funds for infrastructure projects on the international capital markets. Most of the member state governments felt that this would give the Commission access to funds that would not be subject to the same fiscal restraint as the rest of the EU budget, and that the Commission was trying to bypass the European Investment Bank.

Social integration and a European civil society

Since the 1970s a portion of the EU budget has been devoted to promoting social integration in Europe. For example the EU spends more than €500 million each year on educational exchanges, cross-border vocational training schemes and cooperation on youth policies. A major part of this funding goes to the ERASMUS programme, which has enabled a significant proportion of university students (the future European intellectual and professional elite) to spend six months or more studying in another member state. In addition the EU runs the European City of Culture project and helps with the production and distribution of European-made television programmes and films throughout the EU under the MEDIA programme (this comes under the heaing of 'culture and audiovisual policy').

Finally, as Laffan (1997, pp. 129–30) points out, 'many obscure budgetary lines are used to create an embryonic civil society that is transnational in nature and to counteract the excessive representation of producer groups in the Union's governance structures'. For example, the EU funds the 'social dialogue' between European-level labour and employers' peak associations (listed under 'other social operations'), and the activities of the peak association representing consumers at the European level (listed under 'consumer protection') (see Chapter 7).

Several member states have questioned this use of EU resources, but the Commission argues that the funds are essential to establish a 'neopluralist' policy community in Brussels, where public and private interests have equal access to decision-makers. Similarly the EP has used its power over non-compulsory expenditure to secure funding for groups with close ideological or organizational links to the EP party groups or with ties to individual MEPs. For example the EP proposed the establishment of the European Migrants Forum (representing minorities living in the EU member states), and secured funding for the Forum through a special line in the EU budget.

In summary, the primary justification for EU expenditure on research and infrastructure is not the redistribution of resources from rich to poor. In Musgrave's terms, these policies are supply-side measures to foster macroeconomic stabilization in the EU (Sharp and Pavitt, 1993). On the one hand they enable resources to be used more productively within the EU, and hence complement the macroeconomic goals of cohesion policy. On the other hand they aim to increase EU competitiveness *vis-à-vis* the US and Japan. However a by-product of EU expenditure on research is the creation of a supranational technocracy around the Commission. As a result EU research policy is in fact redistributive: from EU taxpayers to the elite scientific community, and especially to technocrats with links to the Commission. Similarly expenditure on civil society measures and social integration is explicitly political: to take from EU taxpayers and give to the not-for-profit community in Brussels and the pro-European cultural and social interests in the member states.

Explaining EU Expenditure Policies

There are three interrelated questions about EU expenditure policies that need to be addressed:

- Why does the EU tax and spend to the amount that it does – in other words, why is the EU budget so small?
- Why is the bulk of expenditure in two main areas – agriculture and cohesion policy – and what explains the decline of agriculture and the rise of cohesion spending?
- Why are some individuals, regions and member states net winners, while others are net losers?

When answering these questions, academic analyses has focused on four aspects of the making of EU expenditure policies: (1) member state bargaining over the national costs and benefits, (2) the power of particular interest groups, (3) strategic behaviour by the Commission to promote its own institutional interests, and (4) the institutional rules of the expenditure game.

Intergovernmental bargaining: national cost–benefit calculations

The design of the EU budget is a product of a series of intergovernmental bargains between the member state governments (see for example Carrubba, 1997; Webber, 1999; cf. Mattila, 2002; Rodden, 2002). One way of thinking about this is that the EU budget is an equilibrium outcome of a bargaining game between the governments, in which each government is willing to pay into/take out of the EU budget exactly how much it believes it will gain/lose from the EU's non-fiscal policies (such as the single market and monetary union). As a result, changes in the expenditure policies of the EU, and particularly expansions of the budget and increased spending on the main policy areas, occur because the losers from the process of economic integration and regulation demand fiscal compensation (Pollack, 1995b, pp. 363–73; cf. Moravcsik, 1993, 1998). Equally, cuts in EU expenditure, particularly on the CAP, proceed only if those states which benefit most from the budget – such as France in the case of the CAP – can be 'bought off' with other policies. If other policy benefits are not available, reform is virtually impossible (cf. Meunier, 1998; Akrill, 2000b; Sheingate, 2000).

In this regard the CAP was originally set up to support French farmers in return for German access to French industrial markets. Similarly the ERDF was established as part of the package that secured British and Irish accession to the EU. In the Single European Act, the doubling of the structural funds was explicitly linked to the completion of the single market, which Spain, Ireland, Greece and Portugal argued would primarily benefit the core economies of the EU at the expense of those on the periphery. Finally, in the Maastricht Treaty the cohesion fund was Spain's price for supporting the German-oriented design of economic and monetary union (EMU).

When bargaining over the budget, member states calculate how much they will gain or lose from other EU policies, such as trade liberalization in the single market. If a member state is a net exporter to the rest of the EU, its industries will be able to secure new markets as a result of the single market and EMU (cf. Frieden, 1991). Conversely if a state is net importer from the other member states, its production will be predominantly for the national market and its industries will suffer under competitive pressure from importers as a result of trade liberalization. Figure 9.3a consequently shows that the more a member state was a net importer from the rest of the EU in 1995, the more it received from the EU budget in 1995–2000, while the more a member state was a net exporter to the rest of the EU in 1995, the more it paid in 1995–2000 – with the notable exception of Ireland, which is a large net exporter and a large budget recipient. Furthermore, as Figure 9.3b shows, this cost–benefit calculation does as well as the traditional equity-based explanation of who gets what under the EU budget – whereby richer member states (in terms of per capita GDP) pay in and poorer member states take out (cf. De La Fuente and Domenech, 2001).

However there are two important subtleties within this general rule. First, Denmark appears to be an anomaly: a wealthy state that has an export-based economy, but is a net recipient under the EU budget (particularly from the CAP). But this can also be explained in the intergovernmental logic (Carrubba, 1997). The governments of the member states are primarily concerned with re-election: in wealthy states whose citizens support European integration, the median voter is willing to allow contributions into the budget in return for benefits to the national economy (from the single market, for example). However in states where the citizens are anti-European (see Chapter 5), governments will demand more from the EU in return for their continued participation in European integration. As a result, Denmark has been able to remain a net recipient and in the early 1980s the UK government negotiated a budget rebate when Thatcher demanded 'our money back'.

Second, the benefits to individual net recipient states are higher (on average 5 per cent of national government revenue in the case of the four cohesion states) than the costs to individual net contributor states (on average less than 1 per cent of national government revenue). This leads to a particular type of bargaining situation once the redistributive bargain has been struck, in which the benefits are concentrated but the

Figure 9.3   Two explanations of net fiscal transfers between the member states

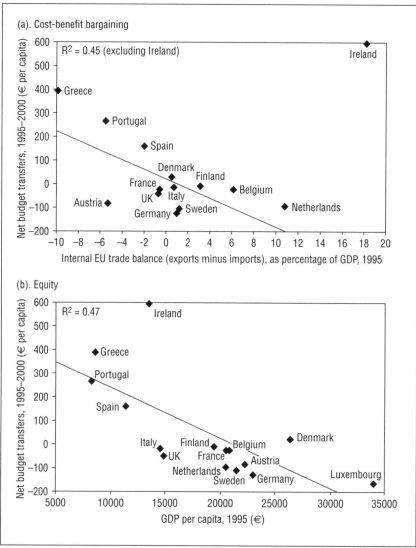

Sources: Mattila (2002); Eurostat.

costs are diffuse. As a result recipient states have more at stake than contributor states in negotiations over increases or decreases in the EU budget. As net contributions for individual states rise, so do the political costs of EU integration. For example in the negotiations on Agenda 2000, Germany (the largest net contributor in all definitions of the meaning) and the Netherlands (which had moved from being a net recipient to a contributor) demanded UK-style rebates from the EU budget (Laffan, 1997, pp. 47–60). However, because of the amounts involved these states are more likely to continue paying in than Spain, Greece, Ireland and Portugal are to give up their considerable EU hand-outs. Hence despite Ireland's dramatic increase in per capita GDP in the 1990s, which should have made it a net contributor rather than a recipient in the 2000–6 budget, Ireland was able to maintain many of its subsidies in the negotiations in Berlin in 1999.

Private interests: farmers, regions, scientists and 'Euro-pork'

The benefits of EU expenditure policies are also reaped at the individual level or by groups at a substate level. For example a country's receipts from the CAP are felt by farmers and not by the country's consumers. Also, in the majority of member states there are regions that are net contributors to the EU budget while other regions are net recipients, and in research policy money is targeted at specific scientific communities at the expense of EU taxpayers.

It could be said that the EU gives out 'pork' from the Euro-barrel to those individuals and groups that ask loudest. As discussed at the start of this chapter, Olson's (1965) 'logic of collective action' tells us that groups that can secure concentrated and selective benefits (enjoyed only by the members of the group) tend to be more able than groups with diffuse interests to organize to influence the policy process. The benefits accruing to individual farmers under the CAP, individual recipient regions under cohesion policies, and individual scientists under EU research policy are far greater than the costs to individual taxpayers in the EU. As a result, farmers have a powerful lobbying voice in Brussels (through COPA), and have campaigned continuously against reform of the CAP (Keeler, 1996). Similarly, a key determinant of whether a regional authority sets up an office in Brussels is whether it comes under Objective 1, 2, 3 (cf. Keating and Jones, 1995, pp. 100-8; Marks *et al.*, 1996;). However some of the poorer and peripheral regions lack the bureaucratic capacity to lobby effectively in Brussels, and hence make the most of their opportunities to form 'partnerships' with the Commission (Bailey and De Propris, 2002).

Non-European multinational firms have been able to secure participation in ESPRIT and other research and development programmes through continued lobbying of the Commission and member state governments (Wyatt-Walker, 1995). Moreover private consultants and lobbying firms in Brussels sell advice to numerous private and public interest groups on securing a grant from the EU budget (Laffan, 1997, pp. 90–3). In fact, Laffan estimates that every day the Commission awards approximately three grants, usually in exchange for advice, research or representation.

In this explanation the equilibrium level of redistribution is different from that in the intergovernmental approach. Taxpayers do not pay into the EU budget in direct relation to what they benefit from European integration. Instead redistribution occurs at the level at which the diffuse costs to taxpayers are equal to the individual costs of mobilizing to reduce the tax burden: in other words they are indifferent between paying into the EU budget and organizing to reform the CAP or cohesion policies (cf. Becker, 1983).

However this equilibrium can be unsettled by issue linkage, which creates selective incentives for particular interests that are net contributors to the EU budget. For example when the success of the GATT negotiations was linked to reform of the CAP, multinational firms had a vested interest in pressuring the Commission and member state governments to agree to such a reform.

Commission entrepreneurship: promoting multilevel governance

The expenditure game is not simply a battle between competing member states or rival interest groups. As the referee of this game, the Commission can use its agenda-setting powers to shape policy outcomes and promote its institutional interests (Peters, 1992, 1994; Tsebelis and Garrett, 1996; Cram, 1997; Pollack, 1997a). First, the Commission has an interest in promoting European integration in the expectation that this will lead to the delegation of more executive power from the Council to the Commission and greater Commission influence in a larger number of policy domains. Second, in the everyday bargaining process of EU politics, to secure the approval of its policy proposals by the Council and the EP, the Commission has an incentive to support key member states and influential societal groups and private interests.

For example the Agriculture Directorate-General obstructed CAP reforms in the 1970s and 1980s to protect its position and the interests of its support group (COPA). Similarly the College of Commissioners promoted CAP reforms in the 1990s to protect the policy credibility of the Commission in other areas, and particularly in trade negotiations (Grant, 1997, pp. 147–60). Also, by persuading the member states to accept the first package of CAP reforms in 1992 the Commission brought about a 'paradigm shift' in the definition of the CAP, from which there was no turning back in the second package of reforms in 1999 (Coleman, 1998; Skogstad, 1998; Daugbjerg, 2003).

In the case of cohesion policies, the Commission's introduction of the principles of additionality, partnership and concentration in the 1988 reform of the structural funds was a deliberate attempt to bypass member state governments in the implementation of policy and to promote decentralization and federalization within the member states (see Marks, 1992, 1993). And during the 1993 talks on reform of the structural funds the Commission successfully negotiated a more substantial package of funds for the regions than most member states has had in mind at the beginning of the negotiations. The Commission achieved this by carefully securing a unilateral commitment by each member state and enlisting the support of regional authorities against reluctant governments (Marks, 1996; Hooghe, 1996a).

With regard to research policy, the Commission has promoted projects that result in transnational cooperation between national firms and the creation of 'Euro-champions', often against national governments' policy of protecting 'national champions' (Peterson, 1991, 1995a; Pollack, 1995b), and has resisted any move away from the established 'framework programme' method of distributing funds allocated for scientific research (Banchoff, 2002).

Hence Commission activism has facilitated expenditure policies that do more to undermine national government interests than to protect them. There is a strong correlation between an individual's attitude towards European integration and whether or not the individual is a member of a group, region or member state that receives funds from the EU budget (Whitten *et al.*, 1998). In a sense, by targeting funds at groups below the level of the state, the Commission can hope to 'divide and rule' the member state governments. Similarly, by providing financial support to public interest groups, such as non-governmental organizations and consumer groups, the Commission can weaken the influence of powerful private interests, such as farmers (Pollack, 1997b).

In other words the Commission has attempted to use expenditure policies to promote the development of multilevel rather than state-centric governance (Marks, 1993; Jachtenfuchs, 1995; Marks *et al.*, 1996; Kohler-Koch, 1996). First, the Commission has promoted participation by private interests and subnational authorities alongside national authorities. Second, the Commission has manipulated this 'policy-centric' and non-hierarchical structure of policy-making to maximize its influence over policy outcomes.

Institutional rules: unanimity, majority, agenda-setting, and the balanced-budget rule

Nevertheless, the interactions between governments, private interests and the Commission are shaped by the institutional rules of expenditure policy-making. The multiannual budgetary bargains, which determine the overall size of the EU budget and the relative increases or reductions in the various expenditure policies, are decided by unanimity between national governments in the Council. These rules produce a particular type of policy outcome. If all member states have a veto they can demand that their receipts from the EU budget are exactly equivalent to the amount they can expect to gain from non-fiscal EU policies (such as the single market). Moreover by exchanging support for each other's projects, all states can be accommodated in a budgetary bargain.

In other words, by using the unanimity rule the overall policy impact must be allocative rather than redistributive: everyone must win, otherwise an individual member will exercise a veto (Mueller, 1989, pp. 43–9). This is similar to the type of distributive bargain found in a consociational system, where the state supplies finances each societal segment regardless of their specific welfare needs (Lijphart, 1968). However, once the budgetary ceiling and the relative weight of the expenditure policies are set by the multiannual budgetary deals, a qualified-majority voting is used to determine policy changes and implementation issues within the budgetary constraints, and these decisions can have significant redistributive implications. For example at this lower level of bargaining the EU reaches decisions on issues such as appropriation and expenditure in the annual budgetary cycle, which types of crop will be supported under the CAP, which regions qualify for support under the cohesion policy, which projects will be funded under the research policy, and which interest groups will receive funds to support their organization in Brussels.

The move from unanimity to majority voting has two implications. First, as discussed in Chapter 1 majority voting enables the majority to redistribute resources from the minority. For example the large recipients of EU funds and the indifferent states can outvote the large net contributors. Second, majority voting gives agenda-setting power to the actor responsible for policy initiation. Under the EU's decision-making rules, the Council only requires a qualified-majority to support a Commission proposal but there must be unanimity to overrule the Commission (see Chapter 3). For example, during the redesign of the structural funds in 1993 the French and British governments were opposed to the Commission's plan but were unable to block majority support for the reforms (Marks, 1996). Similarly, under the annual budgetary procedure the EP has used its agenda-setting power to force the Council to accept the provision of funds to the main EP party groups' pet schemes and interest groups.

And once these redistributive bargains are struck they are difficult to undo because of the requirement for unanimity for larger bargains. For example the CAP may originally have been an allocative pay off, but because of the changes in the structure of agriculture, the influence of the Agriculture Directorate-General, the power of the agricultural lobby and the interests of farm ministers, the CAP has become a redistributive policy: from taxpayers and consumers to farmers. Any major reform of the CAP will require a new budgetary package deal to be passed by unanimously in the Council. Under this rule the farming states can veto the reform or demand some form of compensation.

Finally, the strict 'balanced-budget' rule – whereby EU expenditure must not exceed EU income – places a significant institutional constraint on the evolution of EU budgetary policies. Having to reach an agreement without such a rule would probably lead to a rapid expansion of the EU budget, as each member state would come to the table with a separate demand – rather like every cabinet ministers asking the finance minister for funds for their particular projects, which has led to budgetary expansion in many countries. When there is a tight fiscal constraint, competing budgetary claims have to be balanced in some way. For example Akrill (2000a) points out that the balanced-budget rule and the expenditure ceiling of 1.27 per cent of EU GNP forced the member states to accept CAP reform in the early 1990s. Without the budgetary ceiling it would have been easier for the member states to allow agriculture spending to continue to rise than to face up to the need for reform.

Conclusion: a Set of Linked Welfare Bargains

The absolute volume of funds channelled through the EU budget is small relative to those at the national level in Europe or the federal level in the US. Nevertheless EU expenditure policies aim to achieve all the classic goals of public finance: allocation, stabilization, and redistribution. For example allocation was one of the original goals of the CAP and is a central dynamic of multiannual budgetary packages, in that it is designed to offset losses incurred by certain member states in non-fiscal policy areas. Meanwhile stabilization, through supply-side measures, is a core goal of the cohesion, science and infrastructure policies.

However, as in other political systems, the dominant outcome of EU public expenditure policies is redistribution. First, this is an inevitable product of political bargaining in a democratic society. Certain groups, such as farmers, are more able to organize to secure or protect benefits than are the contributors to the EU budget, namely the EU taxpayers. The size of the EU budget may be small, but the resources received from the EU by individual farmers, regions, scientists and non-governmental organizations are substantial.

Second, redistribution is a deliberate strategy of the Commission. The Commission has used its agenda-setting powers to produce winners from the EU budget at the expense of European taxpayers and net contributor member states. Through this strategy the Commission targets resources at non-state actors that can undermine the dominance of the member state governments in the EU policy process. However the Commission has also promoted redistribution to certain groups to 'buy' support for European integration, such as backward regions and anti-integration member states.

Third, once redistributive policies are in place they are very difficult to reform. Redistribution creates entrenched interests that are willing to spend resources to protect their subsidies. The CAP would be easier to reform if it were purely an allocative policy, as would cohesion policy if it were purely a stabilization policy. The fact that these have become welfare policies for farmers and regions, respectively, means that it is unlikely that the net contributor states and EU taxpayers will be able to secure a fundamental reform of these policies without a major external shock.

The result is a redistributive equilibrium: between the amount the Commission and recipient groups can gain, and how much contributor states and EU taxpayers are willing to lose. But two such external shocks are now working their way through the system: EMU and the expansion of the EU to Central and Eastern Europe. These developments are likely to unbalance the delicate equilibrium of EU expenditure policies and prompt new redistributive bargains.

Chapter 10

Economic and Monetary Union

The Political Economy of Monetary Union
Development of Economic and Monetary Union in Europe
Explaining Economic and Monetary Union
Monetary and Economic Policy in EMU
Conclusion: the Need for Policy Coordination

Economic and monetary union (EMU) was launched on 1 January 1999 and euro notes and coins were introduced in 12 EU states on 1 January 2002. This chapter seeks to answer two questions about this project. Why did twelve EU governments decide to replace their national currencies with the euro? And, how does EMU work? To help answer these questions we shall first look at some general theories of monetary union.

The Political Economy of Monetary Union

The Nobel laureate Robert Mundell (1961) pioneered the theory of optimal currency areas (OCA). According to this theory, independent states will form a monetary union if the benefits of joining exceed the costs (see also McKinnon, 1963; Kenen, 1969). The main cost of monetary union is the loss of a major macroeconomic policy tool: an independent exchange rate. In classical economic theory, this tool is used to protect economies from varying economic conditions between states. One of the basic laws of economics is the existence of economic cycles, in which economic growth ('boom') is followed by recession ('bust'), which is followed by growth and so on. If there is growing demand in one state and falling demand in another, the governments of the two states are likely to pursue different monetary policies. The government facing a recession will cut interest rates to stimulate demand, while the government at the top of the economic cycle will raise interest rates to prevent the economy from overheating. But this is impossible in a monetary union as exchange rates are fixed and there is a 'one size fits all' interest rate policy.

However, asymmetries in economic cycles or asymmetric economic shocks can be addressed by other means, including:

- *Labour mobility*: the unemployed in the state where there is recession could move to take up jobs in the state where there is high growth.
- *Wage flexibility/capital mobility*: workers in the state where there is low demand could reduce their wages (thus increasing the supply of labour at a given price), and thereby attract capital from the high demand state to the state in recession (assuming that capital is mobile).
- *Fiscal transfers*: the state with the booming economy could increase taxes in order to reduce demand, and transfer these tax revenues to the state in recession, where they can be spent to increase demand.
- *Budget deficits*: the state in recession can run a budgetary surplus and spend the extra resources to increase demand.

But economic theory suggests that fiscal transfers and the use of budgetary deficits are only temporary solutions to an asymmetric shock. If the demand shock is more permanent than simply a cyclical downturn, governments will either run up significant public deficits or become reliant on fiscal transfers. Moreover if fiscal transfers and budget deficits become a permanent feature, they can be a substitute for wage and price changes and prevent labour from moving to obtain jobs.

Consequently, in his original formulation of the OCA theory, Mundell (1961) argued that a state faced with asymmetric shocks should weigh up two possible strategies: (1) reducing the exchange rate; and (2) stable exchange rates combined with wage reductions and labour mobility. If the economic and social costs of the second strategy are more painful than the first, then Mundell concluded that a state should not join a monetary union.

However, there are three main problems with this original formulation of the OCA theory. First, there are other benefits of a single currency, which may outweigh the costs of giving up floating exchange rates. Second, more recent economic theory has raised doubts about the benefits of using exchange rate reductions as a macroeconomic tool. Third, the theory ignores the part played by political calculations in the making of macroeconomic policy decisions.

Starting with the first of these issues, the main economic benefits of a single currency are as follows (Eichengreen, 1990; De Grauwe, 2003):

- *Lower transaction costs*: by removing the cost of exchanging currencies, firms involved in trade between states do not have to pay exchange rate commissions or insure themselves against currency fluctuations.
- *A more efficient market*: a common currency reduces the possibility of price discrimination, eliminates the information costs of con-

suming goods and locating businesses across borders, and hence promotes market integration and market efficiency.

- *Greater economic certainty*: exchange-rate stability increases the certainty of prices and revenues, which improves the quality of production, investment and consumption decisions (which in turn increases collective welfare).
- *Lower interest rates*: greater economic certainty also reduces the risk premium on interest rates, and so interest rates are likely to be lower in a larger economy and in an economy that is less exposed to trade in a foreign currency.
- *Higher economic growth*: 'new growth' theorists argue that larger and more integrated economies with greater productivity, more capital accumulation, better information, more economies of scale and lower interest rates can produce permanently higher levels of economic growth.

Some of these benefits are disputed by economists. The potential for lower interest rates and higher growth rates tend to be overemphasized by supporters of monetary union in Europe. Indeed one economic theory predicts that reducing uncertainty about exchange rates does not necessarily reduce systematic risk in the economy, as political decision-makers will tend to compensate for the loss of exchange-rate manipulation by increased use of other macroeconomic tools, such as the money supply (Poole, 1970). Also the empirical evidence backing new-growth theory is weak in both Europe and the US, and the theoretical arguments have come under increasing attack (Krugman, 1998). The market efficiency gains are unlikely to take effect in the short term, and even the transaction-cost benefits of the elimination of currency exchange must be weighed against the loss to the banking industry of revenues from service charges on currency exchange, which were estimated to account for 5 per cent of European banks' total revenues before the launch of EMU.

Nevertheless most commentators accept that even if the non-certain benefits are discounted, certain direct transaction-cost benefits will result from the removal of currency speculation and exchange for firms involved in cross-border trade in a currency union. For example the European Commission estimates that these benefits could amount to savings of 0.25–0.5 per cent of EU GDP (European Commission, 1990).

Turning to the second of the problems in the OCA theory, there are limitations on the use of the exchange rate as a shock absorber. In the short term devaluation will increase the demand for exported goods by lowering their price in other markets. However in the longer term devaluation will raise the price of imported goods, which will in turn raise the costs of production and provoke higher wage demands.

Consequently the long-term effects of manipulating exchange rates are higher prices and lower output. In other words, if states are experiencing different economic situations the exchange rate is a relatively ineffective way of adjusting to these differences. Hence if the long-term benefits of floating exchange rates are less than the OCA theory assumes, then the costs of joining a single currency will be smaller.

As for the third weakness of the OCA theory, political considerations often override economic calculations. Voters and elites have different preferences about inflation, unemployment, welfare protection and government debt. A centre-left electoral majority may be in favour of maintaining a high level of employment and welfare protection, and be willing to finance this by means of high taxes or a large public debt. In this situation the government is unlikely to be able to enforce wage reductions or labour market reforms to attract capital investment. Thus a government in a high-wage/low-growth state may decide that the political costs of the structural adjustment needed for monetary union are too high to pay, and therefore decide to retain a separate currency.

Alternatively, the public may support economic and political union for non-economic reasons. A public can have a high level of 'affective' support for political integration even if they perceive that it may make them economically worse off in the short term (see Chapter 5). This support may enable a government in a low-demand state to use the promise of economic and political integration to implement structural adjustment programmes. Conversely in a high-growth state, public support for currency union may enable a government to sanction fiscal transfers to other states to maintain the currency union.

Finally, there are two other political implications of currency union that must be placed alongside the potential economic costs and benefits:

- *A single voice in the global economy*: a single currency has external political implications, for example in the case of the EU the euro may rival the US dollar as the dominant global currency, which will give the EU political clout on global economic issues.
- *A step towards political union*: a single currency is likely to facilitate further political integration, through pressures for fiscal transfers and tax harmonization, demands for political government over monetary policy, or the emergence of new allegiances towards the EU institutions.

Citizens who favour further political integration may view these as potential benefits of monetary union, but citizens who oppose further political integration will view them as costs. These mass political preferences will influence the elite's calculations when deciding whether to establish or join a monetary union.

In summary, the main cost of monetary union is the inability to reduce the exchange-rate to absorb a demand shock. However, this cost must be weighed against the long-term ineffectiveness of exchange-rate policies and the potential economic benefits of a single currency, particularly lower transaction costs. In addition, these economic calculations are often constrained by publics' and governments' political preferences concerning inflation, unemployment, wage levels, labour market policies and the desirability of further political integration.

Development of Economic and Monetary Union in Europe

While the Maastricht Treaty set out the plan for EMU, the idea of such a union had been discussed as far back as 1956 during the negotiations on the Treaty of Rome. Also, two precursors to the Maastricht plan were important for the eventual preparation and design of EMU (Dyson, 1994). The first of these was the Werner Report of 1971, which proposed that EMU be introduced by 1980, but this was never achieved because Europe plunged into recession in the mid 1970s. The second was the Economic and Monetary System (EMS), set up in 1979. The EMS had two main elements: a basket of currencies (the ecu), weighted according to the strengths of the participating currencies; and an exchange-rate mechanism (ERM), with a permissible band of fluctuation around the central ecu rate and a system of buying and selling currencies to ensure that they remained within this band. The initial band was set at ±2.25 per cent. This was sustainable until the international currency crises of 1992, when the Italian and British currencies were unceremoniously expelled from the EMS and a new ±15 per cent band was set up for the remaining members' currencies.

The Delors Report

The 1985 Single European Act proposed that EMU should be an eventual goal of the EU, but did not set out how this could be achieved. Then at the 1988 Hanover European Council the governments set up a committee chaired by Commission President Jacques Delors to prepare a report on the best way to launch EMU. The committee was composed of two commissioners, the central bank governors of the then 12 member states, and three independent experts. The final report of the committee – the so-called Delors Report, which was delivered to the European Council in June 1989 – set out a plan for EMU (Committee for the Study of Economic and Monetary Union, 1989).

First, the report argued that monetary union should involve the irrevocable fixing of exchange rates (not necessarily with a single set of notes and coins), complete liberalization of capital transactions and integration of the banking and financial markets. Second, the report proposed that economic union should involve a single market, competition policies to strengthen market mechanisms, common policies aimed at structural change and regional development (with the possibility of significant fiscal transfers), and macroeconomic policy coordination, with binding rules on budget deficits. Third, the report set out a three-stage plan:

- Stage I: the introduction of free capital movement and the start of macroeconomic coordination between the member state governments (by 1 July 1990).
- Stage II: reform of the treaties to establish the institutional structure of EMU, which would include a European system of central banks and restricted fluctuation margins for national currencies.
- Stage III: the fixing of exchange rates and the establishment of an independent European Central Bank, with the single goal of maintaining price stability.

Like the Werner Report the Delors Report suggested a phased approach, but was careful not to define this too precisely. Based on the experience of the EMS, the committee emphasized the importance of economic coordination and convergence as a precondition for monetary union. The plan also reflected a compromise. On the one side, Delors' aim was to design a project that would be irreversible: 'the decision to enter upon the first stage should be a decision to embark on the entire process' (ibid., p. 31). On the other side, the governor of the German Bundesbank, Karl Otto Pöhl, wanted to be certain that the single currency would be as stable as the Deutschmark, and so argued for constraints on national deficits and a fully independent European central bank.

The Delors Committee made no comment on whether or not the project was desirable. But under the direction of Delors, the Commission soon made clear where it stood. It published a report in October 1990 entitled 'One Market, One Money', which argued that the full benefits of the single market could not be realized without a single currency (European Commission, 1990).

The Maastricht Treaty design

Meanwhile, in June 1990 the Dublin European Council decided to convene an intergovernmental conference (IGC) to prepare the treaty reforms needed to implement Delors' proposals. At the Rome

European Council in October 1990 the heads of government agreed by a majority (with Margaret Thatcher voting against) that the IGC would propose a fixed timetable for Stage III. The IGC was duly launched at the second Rome European Council, in December 1990, and was completed at the Maastricht European Council in December 1991 with the agreement on the Treaty on European Union (the Maastricht Treaty).

The Maastricht Treaty provided the legal framework for implementation of the Delors Report's proposals through four key provisions. First, the treaty set out the timetable. Stage II was set for January 1994, when the European Monetary Institute would be established to prepare the ground for Stage III. Stage III would then start in one of two ways: either by choice (in January 1997) if a majority of EU states met a set of required economic conditions; or automatically (on 1 January 1999), with participation by those EU states which met the required criteria. The Maastricht Treaty indicated that EMU could not be cancelled or postponed without breach of the EU treaty.

Second, the treaty set out four convergence criteria for qualifying for membership of EMU:

- *Price stability*: an average inflation rate no greater than 1.5 per cent above the inflation rates of the three best-performing member states.
- *Interest rates*: an average nominal long-term interest rate no greater than 2 per cent above the interest rates of the three best-performing member states.
- *Government budgetary position*: an annual current account deficit not exceeding 3 per cent of GDP and a gross public debt ratio not exceeding 60 per cent of GDP.
- *Currency stability*: membership of the narrow band of the ERM (with fluctuations of less than 2.5 per cent around the central rate) for at least two years, with no devaluations.

Third, the treaty set out the institutional structure of the European Central Bank (ECB) and the European System of Central Banks (ESCB). The ECB would include an executive board and a governing council. The European Council would appoint the six members of the executive board for non-renewable eight-year terms (with staggered terms of office), subject to the approval of the EP. The governing board would comprise the six executive board members plus the governors of the national banks participating in the ESCB (EMU member states only), who would be appointed by the member state governments for renewable five-year terms.

Fourth, the treaty set out how monetary policy would operate in EMU:

- *An independent Central Bank*: 'neither the ECB, nor a national central bank, nor any member of the decision-making bodies shall seek or take instructions from Community institutions or bodies, from any government of a member state or from any other body' (Article 108).

- *A main goal of price stability*: 'the primary objective of the ESCB shall be to maintain price stability. Without prejudice to the objective of price stability, the ESCB shall support the economic policies in the Community with a view to contributing to the achievement of the objectives of the Community' (Article 105) (although the 'objectives of the Community' set out in Article 2 of the treaty include 'economic progress' and 'a high level of employment').

- *The role of the ECB in monetary policy*: the basic tasks of the ECB and ESCB would be to define and implement monetary policy, conduct foreign exchange operations, hold and manage the official reserves of the member states, and promote the smooth operation of payments systems.

- *The role of the Council in monetary policy*: the Council of Economic and Finance Ministers (EcoFin) would have the final say on interventions in foreign exchange markets (by unanimity), could conclude monetary agreements with third countries (by qualified-majority voting), and would decide the position of the EU in international relations on issues relating to EMU (by qualified-majority voting).

- *The role of the Council in economic policy*: EcoFin would also conduct 'multilateral surveillance' through the adoption of common economic policy guidelines (drafted in cooperation with the Commission) and collective scrutiny of how the governments implemented these guidelines; EcoFin would be responsible for imposing fines on member states with excessive budget deficits.

Who qualifies? Fudging the convergence criteria

Before the Maastricht Treaty came into effect in November 1993 the EMS was hit by an international currency crisis that threatened to disrupt the carefully laid plans. It soon became clear that a majority of member states would not meet the convergence criteria by the 1997 deadline. As a result, in 1996 a 'two-speed EMU' appeared to be the most likely outcome, with a small set of states whose currencies were closely linked to the Deutschmark (Germany, France, the Netherlands, Luxembourg, Austria and Belgium) going ahead in 1999, and states with weaker currencies (Spain, Italy, Portugal, Ireland, Greece and Finland) joining at a later date. In the meantime the Swedish, Danish and British governments indicated that they were unlikely to join due to concerns about national sovereignty and anti-European feeling amongst their citizens. Denmark and the UK had negotiated 'opt-outs' from the EMU provisions of the Maastricht Treaty.

However the currency crisis had the opposite effect, in that it strengthened the belief amongst many member states' political and administrative elites that fixed exchange rates and the delegation of monetary policy to a supranational central bank were essential if the EU economy was to be isolated from the vagaries of international currency speculation (Henning, 1998). Moreover, rather than abandon the project the likely second-tier governments were more determined than ever to join EMU in order to constrain the power of international currency speculators (Cobham, 1996; Sandholtz, 1996; Jones *et al.*, 1998).

Consequently the Spanish, Portuguese and Italian governments made huge budgetary cuts. The Italian government re-entered the ERM in November 1996 and introduced a one-off 'Europe tax' to reduce its budget deficit to below the 3 per cent target, the Finnish government joined the ERM and introduced a series of macroeconomic reforms, and Ireland became the fastest growing economy in Europe, which allowed the government to reduce its public debt and revalue the currency in the ERM.

Consequently, at the Brussels European Council in May 1988, the heads of government supported the Commission's proposal that EMU should be launched between 11 member states. As Table 10.1 shows, only three states met all the convergence criteria, if interpreted strictly. However the Commission argued that the gross public debt criterion was less important than the annual deficit criterion, and that it was more important for the gross public debt figures to be 'moving in the right direction', in other words falling. This was clearly not the case in Belgium and Italy. Belgium, however, was already in a currency union with Luxembourg, and this would have to be broken up if Belgium could not join EMU. Moreover the Belgium economy was relatively small compared with the size of the eurozone.

Italy constituted a bigger problem. Opinion in the German Bundesbank and the German government was divided over whether Italy should be allowed to join, with several leading figures arguing that Italian entry would undermine the stability of the new currency and defeat the object of the convergence criteria. Nonetheless, backed by the Commission and the French government, which feared a devaluation of the lira if Italy remained outside EMU, Italian Prime Minister Romano Prodi managed to persuade the other governments that he could implement a budgetary plan that would significantly reduce Italy's debt by 2002. The admittance of Italy to EMU was clearly a political compromise. Greece was the only member state that wished to join in 1997 but was excluded for not meeting the convergence criteria. It eventually managed to join on 1 January 2001.

Table 10.1   *Qualification for economic and monetary union, by*
*convergence criterion**

| | Inflation Rate, 1997 (%) | Interest Rate, 1997 (%) | government budgetary position | | Change from 1995 | Exchange rate (in ERM, March 1998) |
			Deficit, 1997 (% of GDP)	Debt (% 1997 of GDP)		
Target	2.7	7.8	≤3.0	≤60.0		Yes
Founder members of EMU						
Luxembourg	1.4	5.6	−1.7	6.7	+1.0	Yes
Finland	1.3	5.9	0.9	55.8	−3.7	Yes
France	1.2	5.5	3.0	58.0	+9.5	Yes
Germany	1.4	5.6	2.7	*61.3*	+11.0	Yes
Portugal	1.8	6.2	2.5	62.0	−1.8	Yes
Austria	1.1	5.6	2.5	*66.1*	+0.7	Yes
Ireland	1.2	6.2	−0.9	66.3	−22.8	Yes
Spain	1.8	6.3	2.6	68.8	+6.2	Yes
Netherlands	1.8	5.5	1.4	*72.1*	−5.7	Yes
Italy	1.8	6.7	2.7	*121.6*	−3.3	Yes
Belgium	1.4	5.7	2.1	*122.2*	−11.2	Yes
Did not qualify for EMU						
Greece	*5.2*	*9.8*	*4.0*	*108.7*	−0.7	Yes
Political decision not to join EMU						
United Kingdom	1.8	7.0	1.9	53.4	+3.0	*No*
Denmark	1.9	6.2	−0.7	65.1	−13.1	Yes
Sweden	1.9	6.5	0.8	*76.6*	−2.4	*No*

* The figures in italics indicate that a member state did not meet the convergence criteria as set out in the Maastricht Treaty.

Source: European Commission (1998b).

Three other states – Denmark, Sweden and the UK – made a political decision not to join EMU at its launch. Denmark and the UK invoked their opt-outs under the Maastricht Treaty, while Sweden simply decided not to join. Denmark and Sweden later held referendums on joining EMU (in May 2000 and September 2003 respectively), but membership was rejected by the electorates in both states, despite vigorous campaigns in favour by the two governments (see Chapter 6). Meanwhile in the UK, in 1997 the newly elected Labour government promised to hold a referendum on the issue. But, it soon became clear that the chancellor of the exchequer, Gordon Brown, was considerably less enthusiastic about membership than was the prime minister, Tony Blair. By 2004 the prospect of a referendum had receded, following a negative assessment of the economic case for membership EMU by Gordon Brown, the Swedish referendum result and the shift of the focus of the European debate in the UK to the proposed EU constitution.

Resolving other issues: appeasing the unhappy French government

That was not the end of the story, as a number of other issues remained to be resolved. First, now that more member states would be joining EMU than the German government had expected, German Finance Minister Theo Waigel proposed a 'Stability Pact' to prevent governments from running large public deficits once EMU was launched. This was immediately opposed by the French socialist government, which had recently been elected on a platform that was broadly critical of the monetarist design of EMU. A compromise was reached at the Amsterdam European Council in June 1997. In return for agreeing to the imposition of fines on wayward governments, France secured a condition that they could only be imposed following agreement by a qualified-majority of member states, and that for cosmetic reasons the agreement should be called the 'Stability and Growth Pact'.

Second, the French government managed to secure support for a measure that would introduce a political element to EMU. In 1997 the French finance minister Dominique Strauss-Kahn proposed that a special 'Euro-X Committee' be established (consisting of only the finance ministers of the EMU member states) to oversee the management of the single currency (this eventually became the Euro-11 committee when 11 states joined EMU at its inception). His intentions were made obvious when he described this arrangement as the 'economic government of the euro'. However the German government insisted that such a committee should not compromise the independence of the ECB, and the British government feared that it would gradually replace EcoFin as the main economic policy organ of the EU. As a compromise the governments agreed that the committee would focus on technical issues and policy questions specific to the eurozone states (such as international monetary cooperation), and that EcoFin would remain the main forum for macroeconomic policy coordination. Unlike the solution on the Stability and Growth Pact, this was seen as a victory for the French government as it was clear that the committee would become the main macroeconomic policy arena in EMU.

With regard to the question of who should serve as the first president of the ECB, until late 1997 most member states accepted that Wim

Duisenberg, a former governor of the Dutch central bank and president of the EMI, would be given the job. But then the French Gaullist president, Jacques Chirac, and the socialist prime minister, Lionel Jospin, jointly proposed Jean-Claude Trichet, the French central bank governor, as a rival candidate. They claimed that there had been an informal agreement between Mitterrand and Kohl that in return for the ECB being located in Frankfurt the first president of the bank would be French. However the German government disputed this and the French government threatened to veto Duisenberg. A deal was finally struck in May 1998, when Chirac accepted the appointment of Duisenberg in return for an informal agreement from Duisenberg that he would retire half-way through his tenure to give way to Trichet. Trichet eventually took over as president of the ECB in November 2003.

Explaining Economic and Monetary Union

Several aspects of the story so far need to be explained. Why was monetary union launched at the time it was? Why was it designed in the way it was – that is, with three stages, convergence criteria, an independent central bank, the goal of price stability, and the Stability and Growth Pact? And why did certain states join but not others? Scholars of the EU have proposed four main explanations: (1) economic rationality, (2) interstate bargaining, (3) agenda-setting by non-state interests, and (4) the dominance of neoliberal ideas about monetary policy.

Economic rationality: economic integration and a core optimal currency area

The costs and benefits of forming a single currency union vary according to the degree of economic integration of the states involved (cf. Krugman, 1990). The benefits of monetary union increase as trade between the states increases (Cameron, 1997, 1998). More economic integration means removal of the transaction costs of currency exchange. Moreover as trade increases the cost of surrendering the exchange rate as an instrument of national macroeconomic policy falls. As the structural conditions of the economies level out, with the more efficient allocation of resources due to the single currency and the gradual synchronization of economic cycles, the likelihood of asymmetric shocks declines. Thus as trade integration increases, the need to use an independent exchange rate recedes.

As Figure 10.1 shows, when the expected benefits increase and the expected costs fall, the lines intercept at a certain level of trade integration. At this point (T) it makes rational economic sense to form or join a currency union, as doing so at any time after this point will mean

Figure 10.1   *Costs and benefits of monetary union*

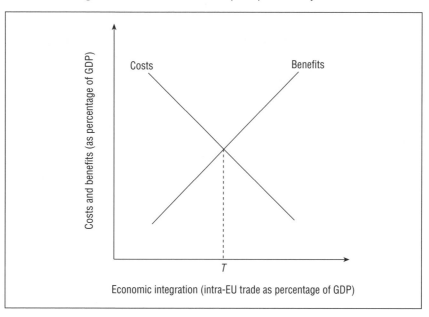

more benefits than costs for the member states concerned. It is difficult to tell when this point was reached by the EU member states. In the mid 1990s the level of imports and exports of goods (excluding services) between the member states varied considerably (Table 10.2). For the larger economies intra-EU trade accounted for less than a quarter of total GDP, while for many of the smaller economies intra-EU trade accounted for more than half of total GDP. Moreover for Germany, the core economy of the EU, trade with the rest of the world was almost as large as trade with the rest of the EU. In other words when the decision was taken to launch EMU, on the basis of simple economic cost-benefit calculations the smaller states were more likely to benefit than the larger states.

The data also suggest that between 1994 and 2001 trade integration in the EU proceeded faster for the eurozone states than for the non-eurozone states, and in the case of the UK there was even a decline in trade with the rest of the EU as a percentage of UK GDP. This suggests that the economic benefits of EMU membership might be endogenous to the creation of EMU. In other words, once a political decision has been made to join EMU the economics will follow, as trade integration will increase as a result of adopting the single currency.

Empirical analyses of the EU economy suggest that the EU is not an optimal currency area, particularly compared with the US

Table 10.2   *Trade integration in the EU and openness to the world economy, 1994–2001*

| | Intra-EU trade (value of imports plus exports as % of GDP) | | Non-EU trade (value of imports plus exports as % of GDP) | |
	1994	2001	1994	2001
Euro12				
Belgium	83.6*	113.5	29.3*	44.5
Luxembourg	–	94.5	–	20.0
Ireland	80.2	83.0	34.1	46.8
Netherlands	65.0	75.3	27.7	39.0
Austria	33.7	49.6	16.8	26.8
Portugal	39.6	44.8	12.5	13.4
Finland	30.4	36.2	24.0	26.3
Spain	22.8	31.9	11.5	14.4
Germany	23.1	31.8	16.3	25.5
France	23.6	31.1	13.5	18.2
Italy	20.9	23.9	14.5	19.4
Greece	20.8	16.5	11.4	16.2
Other EU states				
Denmark	35.4	40.9	17.3	20.2
Sweden	33.6	37.7	23.8	25.6
United Kingdom	24.1	22.6	18.7	19.7

* Belgium and Luxembourg combined. Intra-EU trade in 2001.

(Eichengreen, 1990; Feldstein, 1992; Caporale, 1993; De Grauwe and Vanhaverbeke, 1993). First, the economic performances of the member states differ markedly, so asymmetric economic cycles are likely to be frequent and persistent. Second, there is a relatively low degree of labour market flexibility in the European economy, both in terms of labour mobility between states, and in terms of the flexibility of wages and employment regulations (see below). Hence in the presence of an asymmetric shock, labour is unlikely to move or allow wages to be reduced to attract capital.

Nevertheless an optimal currency area may exist between the core EU economies (Dornbusch, 1990). As Figure 10.2 shows, although the labour market may not be flexible, the economic cycles of Germany, France and the Benelux countries (the EU5) are closely linked. The situation for the 12 members of the Eurozone (Euro12 in the figure) is less clear-cut: the labour markets are as rigid as in the five core states, but the economies are more divergent.

In summary, economic logic may be able to explain why EMU was launched in the 1990s, but it only offers a partial explanation of why certain states joined and others did not. Economics suggests that EMU

Figure 10.2 *is the EU an optimal currency area?*

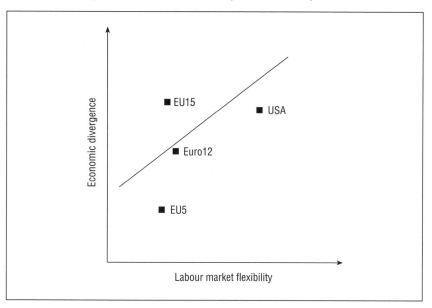

Source: Adapted from De Grauwe (2003), p. 82, by permission of Oxford University Press.

should have been launched only between the core member states. Economics cannot explain why Italy and Spain joined when they had comparatively low levels of trade integration and potentially divergent economic cycles, but Denmark did not despite its comparatively high level of trade integration. Most economists also accept that economics cannot explain the chosen design of EMU, with three stages, convergence criteria and a specific institutional structure (Artis, 1996; Crowley, 1996). These questions are more convincingly answered by politics than by economics.

Interstate bargaining: a Franco-German deal

The institutional design of EMU was the product of bargaining among the member state governments during the intergovernmental conference that agreed the Maastricht Treaty (Moravcsik, 1998; Hosli, 2000; Eichengreen and Frieden, 2001). Two inherently contradictory forces operate in this strategic context. First, the government that has the least to lose from non-agreement on a policy is most likely to secure an outcome closest to its ideal preferences. With nothing to lose from a failure to reach agreement, this government does not need to compromise. In contrast a government that has a lot to lose from non-agreement will be willing to make significant concessions to achieve a successful bargain. Second, because agreement has to be reached by unanimity between the governments the result is a package deal (or 'log-roll'). This involves adding other issues to the agenda, so that each government can get something from the final agreement. In this situation the government with the least to lose may be forced to compromise to secure its interests in other areas.

Both of these dynamics were important in the politics of EMU (Sandholtz, 1993). First, the design of EMU was essentially a German plan (Moravcsik, 1993, 1998): the adoption of convergence criteria, the creation of a European central bank independent from political control, and the central goal of price stability were all demanded by the German government as conditions for its approval of EMU. By these means the German government hoped that EMU would be an optimal currency area, as only a few states would be likely to meet the conditions and therefore the euro would be as stable as the Deutschmark. The German government, backed by the Bundesbank, was prepared to veto the whole project and continue with the EMS, which was effectively run by the Bundesbank. The hegemony of Germany in the system was illustrated in the ERM crisis of 1992–93, when the Bundesbank dictated which states should leave the ERM and the price to be paid by the remaining members (Cameron, 1993; Smith and Sandholtz, 1995). Meanwhile the other member states were prepared to pay the German price to regain some say over monetary policy. In EMU, the common interest rate would be set for the European economy as a whole rather than just Germany, and all the member states' central bank governors would have an equal say in this.

However certain aspects of the package deal, and the final decision of EMU when it was launched in 1999, were not completely to Germany's liking. The French government extracted painful concessions from Germany. In the matter of institutional design, Germany accepted the establishment of an ECB Governing Council, where the ECB Executive Board could potentially be out-voted by national central bank governors, and a political role for EcoFin in the management of external exchange rate policy (Garrett, 1994). Also, while the German government got its way with the Stability and Growth Pact, the French government secured the creation of the Euro-11 Committee and successfully politicized the choice of the ECB president.

Germany also had little to gain from monetary union with high inflation countries such as Italy, Spain and even France. But cross-border investors in and exporters of sophisticated manufactured goods (and the trade unions that work in this sector) – both of which are powerful economic interests in Germany – gain considerably from fixed exchange rates with their main export or investment markets and therefore strove to persuade the German government to support the EMU project (Josselin, 2001; Frieden, 2002). In addition many scholars contend that Germany was willing to make concessions on the precise design of EMU because it had a broad political interest in maintaining the pace of political integration in Europe following German reunification and the collapse of the Soviet Union (Dyson *et al.*, 1994; Woolley, 1994; McKay, 1996, pp. 84–95; Kaltenthaler, 2002). In this view, EMU was part of a broad historic package-deal between France and Germany, with France supporting German reunification in return for Germany giving up the Deutschmark and the Bundesbank relinquishing control of the European economy.

Agenda-setting by non-state interests: the Commission and central bankers

An alternative view is that the timing and institutional design of EMU were the result of agenda-setting by non-state actors, beyond the control of intergovernmental bargaining. The most influential non-state actor in setting the agenda of EMU was the European Commission (Sandholtz, 1993; Dyson, 1994, pp. 114–48; Smith and Sandholtz, 1995; Dyson and Featherstone, 1999, pp. 691–745). Since the 1960s, several Commissioners and prominent figures in the Commission's administration had argued for monetary union, but it was not until the presidency of Jacques Delors that the Commission openly pursued a strategy to promote and secure EMU. Delors had considerable experience in the field of monetary policy – in his capacity as French finance minister he had engineered the U-turn in French monetary policy in the early 1980s. He was also ideologically committed to the goal of monetary union, which he advocated at every opportunity. He successfully argued that the member states should set up a committee under his leadership to prepare a plan for EMU, and he duly presented the resultant strategy at the intergovernmental conference on the Maastricht Treaty. The Commission's strategic use of expertise and information was crucial in changing the perceptions of EMU held by and the institutional preferences of central bankers, employers' organizations and trade unions (Jabko, 1999; Verdun, 2000).

One concrete example of Delors' influence was acceptance of his idea that EMU should progress in a series of stages, with economic convergence being pursued in parallel to the technical and institutional preparations for the launch of the single currency. Once each stage had been completed it would be politically very difficult to take a step backwards – as this would have a negative impact on the credibility of the EU as a whole. Most economists argued that Delors' strategy did not make economic sense (for example Eichengreen, 1993), and few member states supported the idea at its inception. However, due to Delors' persistence of and the absence of a coherent alternative plan, his model was institutionalized as the collective strategy for EMU.

The other main non-state actors to play an important role in EMU were the member states' central bank governors, who shared common strategic interests in the project (Verdun, 1999). EMU would guarantee their independence from political interference by national finance ministers, and they would each participate in making EU monetary policy in the ECB Governing Council. These actors also shared similar ideas about how monetary policy should be managed (see below), and were able to offer considerable expertise on numerous technical issues in the transition to EMU, such as how a payments system should be designed and run. Their national governments delegated particular responsibilities to them. All the central bank governors sat on the Delors Committee, and the Committee of Central Bank Governors proposed the draft statute of the European System of Central Banks, which was incorporated without amendment into a Protocol annexed to the Maastricht Treaty. It was in the interest of governments to secure credible technical advice and ensure that EMU was supported by the people who would be running EU monetary policy. However once the governments had delegated important design issues to the governors they were unable to control the actions of the central bankers and the ideas they put forward.

The power of ideas: the monetarist policy consensus

Kathleen McNamara (1998, 2001) argues that a key factor in the almost unanimous agreement between the member state governments and the various non-state actors on the goal and design of EMU was the emergence of a 'monetarist policy consensus' in Europe by the end of the 1980s. The main reason for this consensus was that most of the governments had experienced policy failure in the 1970s, when Keynesian demand management policies had proved inadequate for coping with slow growth, high unemployment and high inflation. Monetarism emerged as an alternative economic paradigm that was both theoretically coherent and an empirical success. At a theoretical level, among other things monetarism offered a convincing critique of why there was no inherent trade-off between unemployment and inflation, as had been predicted by the Phillips curve (Friedman, 1968). At an empirical level there was the highly successful example of German economic growth in the 1970s and early 1980s as a result of monetarist policies. Centre-right parties now had a 'big idea' against the Keynesian hegemony of the 1960s and 1970s. As Keynesian policies failed, monetarist policies were increasingly accepted by mainstream parties and international organizations such as the OECD (see for example McCracken, 1977), and as centre-right parties won elections across Europe in the early and mid 1980s, centre-left parties began to reject their old policies and accept the new economic orthodoxy.

Figure 10.3   *Monetarist and Keynesian views of monetary union*

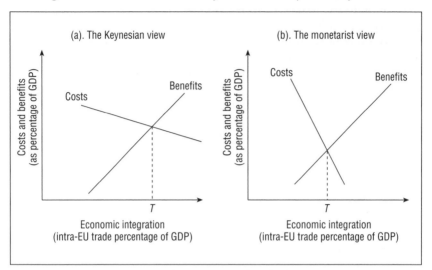

Source: De Grauwe (2003, p. 79), by permission of Oxford University Press.

Monetarism had a particular policy prescription for exchange rates. Monetarist economists argued that manipulating exchange rates (much like Keynesian demand management) would only bring short-term benefits, and that the long-term effects would be wage and price inflation. They insisted that stable or even fixed exchange rates, combined with wage flexibility and labour market reforms, offered the only long-term cure for low productivity.

To understand what this meant for EMU, consider the Keynesian and monetarist interpretations in Figure 10.3 of the costs and benefits of monetary union. The Keynesian view (Figure 10.3a) is that the world is full of rigidities – wages and prices are stable, labour is immobile – so the exchange rate is a powerful tool for macroeconomic management. In this interpretation the cost of fixing exchange rates falls slowly as trade integration increases (cf. Minford, 1996). In contrast, in the monetarist view (Figure 10.3b) the exchange rate is an ineffective tool, and the costs of losing this tool fall rapidly as trade integration increases. Hence monetarists supported fixed exchange rates in a monetary union at considerably lower levels of economic and trade integration than were accepted by Keynesians (cf. Bofinger, 1994).

These ideas gradually gained force from the end of the 1970s and prevailed until the 1990s. As early as 1975 *The Economist* published an 'All Saint's Day Manifesto', which was written by several prominent monetarist economists and called for a revival of the idea of EMU (*The Economist*, 1 November 1975, p. 33). The German government, supported by the Bundesbank, used similar ideas to justify the EMS. In the 1980s the Commission directorate-general in charge of economic and monetary affairs was full of modified monetarists who prepared the Commission's strategy for the Delors Committee and wrote the 'One Market, One Money' report (European Commission, 1990).

In the 1980s and early 1990s governments across Europe introduced 'sound money' policies and made the central banks responsible for maintaining the stability of exchange rates. Once this orthodoxy had been accepted it was a small step to fixing exchange rates and delegating monetary policy to an independent supranational central bank. This made sense both on economic grounds, in terms of increased individual and collective welfare, and on political grounds, in terms of limiting macroeconomic policy uncertainty for national decision-makers (Østrup, 1995; Cameron, 1997).

Monetary and Economic Policy in EMU

So far we have focused on understanding how and why EMU was established. The rest of the chapter looks at how monetary and economic policy is made in EMU. Essentially, will the design of EMU produce a stable currency? How will EMU work in the face of asymmetric economic cycles? How will European level monetary policies affect national fiscal and labour market policies? And, how will EMU change the role of the EU in the global economy?

Independence of the ECB: establishing credibility and reputation

There is a natural inflationary bias in the making of monetary policy by elected politicians (Nordhaus, 1975; Barro and Gordon, 1983; Lohmann, 1999). Even if the main goal is price stability, finance ministers can gain from 'surprise inflation'. If governments can produce an inflation rate that is higher than expected by businesses and trade unions (when borrowing money and negotiating wages) there will be a short-term increase in output and employment. Growth and higher employment win votes, so in the run-up to an election there is an incentive for the government to 'pump up' the economy by cutting interest rates. Private actors will be aware that the government is supplying this surprise inflation, and that the long-term effect will be an increase in interest rates to curb inflation. However, to pre-empt this strategic behaviour, a government can supply a surprise rate of inflation that is beyond the expectation of firms. Hence the long-term effect of allowing elected politicians to set interest rates is an economic cycle driven by political incentives rather than economic logic (a 'political business cycle'), a higher rate of inflation than is optimal for the economy, and a government policy that is not credible with national and international currency consumers.

A widely accepted solution is to delegate the making of monetary policy to an independent central bank. By isolating interest rates from electoral politics, governments can make a credible commitment to reducing inflation. Central bank independence can be achieved through several mechanisms (cf. Grilli *et al.*, 1991; Cukierman *et al.*, 1993):

- The central bank can be made responsible for setting interest rates.
- The central bank can be made responsible for setting inflation and/or money supply targets.
- The goal of price stability can be set out in a constitution, rather than simply in a legislative act, to avoid alteration of the goal by a future electoral majority.
- The terms of office of the central bank officials can be made longer than the terms of office of the political representatives who appoint them (usually four or five years).
- Sanctions can be used if the central bank fails to achieve price stability (for example automatic dismissal of the president of the bank if an inflation target is missed).

Empirical research shows that there is a significant correlation between the level of central bank independence and the average long-term inflation rate, with the most independent banks producing the lowest inflation rates (Cukierman, 1992; Alesina and Summers, 1993; Franzese, 1999).

The design of the ECB meets most of these criteria (Kaufmann, 1995). The ECB is solely responsible for implementing monetary policy, without interference from the Council or national governments. The goal of price stability is set out in the treaty, so it is very difficult for governments to revoke it. The ECB is relatively free to decide monetary policy goals, such as an inflation target or a money supply target. The term of office for ECB officials is eight years. Finally, because the political authority of EMU – the EU Council – requires unanimity to change the institutional design of the delegation to the ECB, the independence of the ECB is highly credible (Keefer and Stasavage, 2003).

However credibility is not enough to ensure stable monetary policy. A central bank also needs to be legitimate – to possess what economists call 'reputation' (Winkler, 1996). Reputation enables markets and the public to accept monetary policy decisions that might be unpopular in the short term. In the absence of a history of currency stability and economic growth as a result of a central bank's decisions, the markets and the public may be fickle in the face of inflation or recession. Consequently there is a particular problem for the ECB as a new institution managing a new currency. Without an established reputation, public opinion in states that suffer asymmetric shocks is likely to turn against the ECB quicker than it would against a national central bank with a history of independence, such as the Bundesbank.

Several scholars have consequently argued that the ECB's reputation would be enhanced if the ECB was more transparent, for example if the minutes of its meetings were made public and its inflation forecasts and assumptions were published (Verdun, 1998; Buiter, 1999; cf. de Haan and Eijffinger, 2000). Without transparent decision-making it is difficult for economic interests and the public to determine whether the central bank is responsible for a downturn in the economy or whether this is the result of unexpected economic shocks (Keefer and Stasavage, 2002). Hence central banks that are transparent usually establish a reputation for sound monetary policies faster than central banks that act in secret (Stasavage, 2003).

In its defence the ECB argues that publishing voting records would undermine the collective responsibility of the ECB and encourage political interference in its decision-making (Issing, 1999). Also, under Duisenberg, the ECB contended that because the inflation target was set out in the treaty (the goal of price stability), the basic goal is transparent and the ECB does not have much discretion in interpreting its mandate (see below).

Furthermore, the claim that central bank independence is the best way of guaranteeing long-term economic benefits is not universally accepted (McNamara, 2002). The delegation of monetary policy to a central bank can suffer from the same problems as other principal–agent relations in politics (see Chapter 2). Central bankers, who tend to be 'hawks' in the making of monetary policy, can have long-term policy preferences that diverge from the preferences of the politicians or the public. In the short term this is precisely the aim of delegation: to prevent politicians from promoting growth today that citizens will have to pay for tomorrow. But locking in a hawkish monetary policy via central bank independence may not be in the long-term interests of large sections of society, and so may undermine the legitimacy of the EU as a whole.

The separation of monetary policy and fiscal policy can also cause coordination problems (Bini Smaghi and Casini, 2000; Way, 2000; Buti *et al.*, 2001). If the central bank pursues a restrictive monetary policy, politicians will be tempted to increase public debt to reflate the economy, which will prompt the central bank to raise interest rates further and politicians to borrow more money, and so on. Failure to coordinate fiscal and monetary policies can result in what happened in the US in the 1980s, when the Federal Reserve Bank kept raising interest rates and federal government debt spiralled out of control.

Hence delegating monetary policy to an independent central bank may only be credible if there is a parallel agreement on how politicians should manage fiscal policy and public borrowing (Stasavage and Guillaume, 2002). Hence, the convergence criteria in Stage II of EMU and the Stability and Growth Pact at the start of Stage III can be interpreted as 'contracts' between European level monetary policy and national fiscal policies (Winkler, 1999). But without a binding commitment by and clear incentives for governments to abide by these contracts, the credibility of these coordination efforts is questionable.

ECB decision-making in the setting of interest rates

The decisions taken by the ECB Executive Board are carefully scrutinized. First, the ECB president presents an annual report to EcoFin and the Economic and Monetary Affairs Committee of the EP, and the EP committee can ask to hear evidence from the ECB president as often as it likes (the EP modelled the operating procedures of this committee on the US Senate committee hearings of the US Federal Reserve chairman). Second, the European press carefully watch the weekly meetings of the ECB and analyze every word in the statements and speeches by the ECB president and the other members of the Executive Board.

As mentioned earlier, however, the minutes of Executive Board and Governing Council meetings are not available to the public. Moreover under the rules of the treaty, member state governments cannot instruct their central bank governors to pursue a particular monetary policy. Nevertheless governments can influence the ECB through their choice of central bank governors. When the term of office of a national central bank governor ends (after five years), a government may appoint someone whose views are more representative of those of the national public. Also, with staggered terms of office in the ECB Executive Board, the governments may collectively decide to appoint inflation-averse persons to the board and gradually remove 'hawkish' monetarists.

Political scrutiny of ECB decisions is unlikely to conflict with the policy of the ECB if the national economic cycles are synchronized. In this situation the ECB Governing Council will have little difficulty agreeing to a 'one size fits all' interest rate. However if there are asymmetric economic cycles, when some national economies are growing while others are declining, a common ECB position is more problematic. In this situation it is reasonable to assume that the six members of the Executive Board will propose an interest rate that is considered ideal for the EMU economy as a whole, or slightly above that rate to establish a hawkish reputation. However, under pressure from their national public and governments, those central bank governors whose economies are in recession will probably vote for lower interest rates, while those whose economies are booming will probably vote for higher interest rates. This was often the case in the early years of the US Federal Reserve, when state central banks sought different monetary policies from the Federal Reserve Board (Eichengreen, 1991).

Under the design of the Maastricht Treaty, in the ECB Governing Council there is one vote per central bank governor and member of the ECB Executive Board, and decisions are taken by a simple majority. With this voting rule we can assume that the Governing Council agrees on the interest-rate preference of the median member of the council, as this member's vote can turn the preferences on either side of his or hers into a winning majority. The members of the Executive Board are likely to be pivotal if the interest rate preferences of the central bank governors are split more or less evenly either side of the preferences of the board. However if there is public pressure in a large number of states for lower interest rates, the six members of the Executive Board can be outvoted by the 12 central bank governors. In contrast, the Federal Open Market Committee of the US Federal Reserve has 12 members, of whom seven are members of the Federal Reserve Board and five are presidents of the regional banks in the US.

The practice of 'one member, one vote' in the ECB Executive Board also causes problems if economic cycles are unevenly distributed between the large and small economies (Bindseil, 2001). For example in 2002–3 Germany, France and Italy had growth rates of 1–2 per cent, while most of the smaller states (Ireland, Greece, Finland, Luxembourg and Belgium) had growth rates of 2–4.5 per cent. The central bank governors from the three largest economies all preferred lower interest rates, but were easily outvoted by a coalition of small states and the ECB Executive Board. The design of the voting rules inside the ECB was consequently one of the reasons why the German and French governments had to run public deficits in this period, and hence break the rules of the Stability and Growth Pact (see below).

In the run-up to the 2004 enlargement, and with the prospect of several of the new member states joining the EU, in December 2003 the ECB proposed a reform of the voting rules. Under the new system the number of central bank governors with voting rights will be limited to 15, and the members of the Executive Board will retain their voting rights. If the number of member states in EMU exceeds 15, the voting rights will rotate between states. This rotation will be based on the size of the states' economies. For example if there are 22 member states in EMU, the governors from the largest economies will have voting rights in four years out of every five (80 per cent of the time), the governors from the medium-sized economies will have voting rights in four years out of seven (57 per cent of the time) and the governors from the smallest economies will have voting rights in three years out of eight (37.5 per cent of the time). This system will alleviate the problem of larger states being outvoted by smaller states, but it might be politically damaging for a state that suffers an economic shock in a year when it does not have voting rights on the Governing Council (cf. Baldwin *et al.*, 2001a).

Inflation targets: ECB–EcoFin relations

There is some room for political interpretation of the division of labour between the ECB and EcoFin (De Grauwe, 2002a). The treaty states that the aim of the ECB is to maintain price stability. Formally speaking, price stability means zero inflation. But, quite reasonably the ECB has interpreted price stability to mean an annual inflation of 0–2 per cent. There has been much criticism of this interpretation. For example this target is asymmetric because it assumes that inflation above 2 per cent is worse than inflation below 2 per cent. As discussed above, part of the reason why the ECB has been so conservative in interpreting its mandate is its desire to establish a good reputation with the markets. However such a low and asymmetric target is potentially dangerous, since it is much harder for central banks to deal with deflation (in which prices start falling) than with inflation above 2 per cent – as experienced by Japan in much of the 1990s, when even negative interest rates had little effect on economic growth.

An alternative interpretation of the treaty, based on a division of labour between the ECB and EcoFin, is advocated by several central bankers and finance ministers, including Gordon Brown in the UK (cf. Buiter, 1999). According to this interpretation EcoFin can set the inflation target – for example a 2 per cent target with symmetric assumptions about inflation above or below that level – and the ECB could then set interest rates to achieve this target. This would increase the transparency and accountability of monetary policy, and would allow some political control of interest rate policy.

Critics of this alternative approach argue that separating inflation targets and interest rate decisions would defeat the purpose of an independent central bank, as politicians would have an incentive to set the inflation target at a high level to achieve high growth, and thereby increase their votes in the short term. However the danger of this happening would be lower under a separation of inflation targets and interest rates than under a system where these two policy tools are both held by politicians. In a divided regime, to pump up the European economy the politicians would have to set the inflation target at an unreasonably high level, which would then be heavily criticized by economic interests and the public. The danger of a political business cycle is also smaller in the EU context than in most political systems, because the finance ministers in EcoFin have different electoral timetables. Hence at a time when some governments would want to raise inflation (in the build up to an election) others would want to keep it down (immediately after an election).

National fiscal policies: the Stability and Growth Pact

Political pressures on the ECB also result from the constraints on national fiscal policies in EMU. A negative demand shock in one state will increase a government's budget deficit, as there will be a reduction in tax revenues and an increase in unemployment and social security expenditure. However experiences in the 1970s and 1980s suggest that large budget deficits lead to unsustainable long-term debts, as occurred in Italy, Belgium and Greece. Furthermore, within EMU there is the possibility that a government will attempt to 'free ride' on the sound monetary policies of other states by running a high public deficit with only a moderate threat to the value of the common currency, and hence to the value of its bonds (Horstmann and Schneider, 1994). Consequently the convergence criteria are designed to ensure that budget deficits are minimized before entry to EMU, and to give credibility to these constraints the treaty includes provisions to combat excessive deficits. Evidence suggests that these fiscal constraints constitute a 'decisive structural break' in the development of European governments' fiscal policies (Freitag and Sciarini, 2001), although many European governments, both left and right, converged on sound fiscal policies prior to the Maastricht Treaty (Cusack, 2001; Clark *et al.*, 2002).

The constraints imposed on national fiscal autonomy by the Maastricht Treaty have been significantly strengthened by the Stability and Growth Pact. Two Council Resolutions in July 1997 specified how the excessive deficits procedure under the Stability and Growth Pact would operate:

- *Decision*: on the basis of a report from the Commission and the Economic and Finance Committee of the Council (the Euro Committee), the EcoFin Council judges that a member state has an 'excessive deficit' if its annual government deficit exceeds 3 per cent of GDP, unless there has been a severe economic downturn (an annual fall of real GDP of at least 2 per cent) or an unusual event has occurred outside the control of a member state.
- *Recommendations*: the Ecofin Council then makes recommendations to the member state concerned and establishes a deadline of four months for effective corrective action to be taken, which normally means that the deficit is corrected in the year after its identification. If after a progressive notice procedure the member state fails to comply, the Council can decide (by a qualified-majority) to impose sanctions, at the latest ten months after the reporting of an excessive deficit.

- *Sanctions*: these take the form of a non-interest-bearing deposit with the Commission. The deposit comprises a fixed component equal to 0.2 per cent of GDP and a variable component linked to the size of the deficit. Each subsequent year the Council may decide to intensify the sanction by requiring an additional deposit, although the annual amount must not exceed the upper limit of 0.5 per cent of GDP. A deposit may be converted into a fine if the excessive deficit has not been corrected after two years.
- *Abrogation of sanctions*: the EcoFin Council may decide to abrogate some or all of a sanction, depending on the progress made by the member state concerned in correcting the excessive deficit, but any fines already imposed are not reimbursable.

In other words the Stability and Growth Pact places a severe constraint on a member state running a large enough deficit to threaten the stability of the euro. However, a political decision is needed to impose sanctions.

Because of the Stability and Growth Pact, expansion of the welfare state can only be financed by raising revenues through taxation. This presents a problem in the event of an asymmetric shock, when instead of running a budget deficit the government has to find a way to cut other expenditure programmes or to raise taxes (Buiter *et al.*, 1993; Eichengreen and Von Hagen, 1996). Raising taxes, however, increases production and wage costs, and therefore reduces the competitiveness of the economy. Raising taxes at the bottom of an economic cycle is also pro-cyclical as it takes money out of circulation at precisely the time it is needed.

The main problem with the Stability and Growth Pact is that it locks in a particular mix of monetary and fiscal policies, whereby the ECB pursues a restrictive monetary policy (as defined by the price stability goal in the treaty), while national governments are forced to pursue restrictive fiscal policies (government budgets must be close to balance or in surplus). While this policy mix is certainly anti-inflationary, if there are asymmetric economic cycles it is likely to be very unpopular in member states with the lowest levels of growth. With divergent cycles, the interest rates set by the ECB will be higher than those needed for a state at the bottom of an economic cycle, but the state will not be able to borrow money to get the economy moving again.

Also, with a policy mix of tight monetary policies at the European level and constraints on national government budget deficits, states are unlikely to introduce structural reforms. EMU would work more efficiently if states reformed their labour markets and welfare states (see below). However such structural reforms would produce higher unemployment in the short term. Consequently the public would be unlikely to support such structural reforms unless they were balanced with monetary and fiscal policies to stimulate economic growth.

The contradictions of this policy mix in EMU came to a head in 2002 and 2003. At that time the one-size-fits-all interest rate was higher than was needed for the French and German economies. The French and German governments chose to borrow money to tackle the problem of rising unemployment and a sluggish economy, knowing that raising taxes or introducing labour market reforms at the bottom of an economic cycle were politically unfeasible. As these governments increased their borrowing they exceeded the 3 per cent annual deficit criterion in the Stability and Growth Pact. Ironically Germany, which had insisted on the pact in the first place because it feared that France and Italy would run high deficits, now found itself in the position of being one of the first member states to face the prospect of sanctions.

But in November 2003 France and Germany were able to secure the support of enough other member states to suspend the excessive deficits procedure. The Commission was so infuriated by the decision of the governments effectively to abandon the Stability and Growth Pact that it decided to take a case to the European Court of Justice, on the ground that the governments had breached the rules of the July 1997 resolutions (although only a few months earlier the president of the Commission, Romano Prodi, had described the rules as a 'stupidity pact'!) This incident illustrated that in practice the pact was not a credible way of coordinating national fiscal policies and European level monetary policies in a monetary union with divergent economic cycles, as governments would always respond to their voters' preferences first.

If the Stability and Growth Pact was to be completely abandoned, it might seriously damage the credibility of the whole EMU project. If the governments were to abolish one of the central institutional structures of the project, what would there be to stop them fundamentally altering other institutional arrangements, such as the independence of the ECB? Also, the desire to prevent 'bad' governments from free-riding on the 'good' governments would remain. Hence the pact is likely to be reformed rather than completely replaced. One possible reform to address the problem of asymmetric economic cycles would be to apply different rules at different points in the cycle, with governments being allowed to borrow more when the economy was in recession in return for running a surplus when the economy was booming (Artis and Buti, 2000; Buti and Giudice, 2002; De Grauwe, 2002b; Hughes Hallett and McAdam, 2003).

European fiscal policies: budget transfers and tax harmonization

If asymmetric economic cycles persist, and the EU maintains a restrictive set of constraints on national fiscal policies, there is likely to be a growing demand for interstate fiscal transfers linked to the macroeconomic consequences of EMU (Sala-i-Martin and Sachs, 1991; Eichengreen, 1994; McKay, 1999; Crowley, 2001; Wildasin, 2002). With a budget of only 1.27 per cent of EU GDP, the redistributive capacity of the EU is small (see Chapter 9), and in the 1970s it was widely felt that EMU would not be possible without a significant increase in the budget – as argued in the McDougall Report (McDougall, 1977). Also, in most currency unions an asymmetric economic performance among the regions has been tackled by the greater centralization of budgets, as in the US in the 1930s and at the state level in Europe since 1945 (for example after the reunification of Germany in 1990).

In the event of a demand shock in EMU, member states in recession might demand an increase in expenditure under the EU's structural funds, and a gearing of this expenditure to short-term EMU-related shocks. However the decision on this would have to be taken by unanimity, and the net contributor member states might not wish the EU budget to be enlarged. However if there were a threat of EMU collapsing as a result of the political implications of downward pressure on a particular member state's welfare expenditure, the publics in the net contributor states might agree to pay more into the EU budget to preserve the stability of the single currency.

Alternatively the states in recession could demand that tax rates be harmonized (Radaelli, 1996). With varying rates of tax on capital and labour among the EMU states, governments could choose to cut taxes to attract investment, and this would put pressure on other governments to do the some. The effect would be an overall reduction of tax revenues, and under the Stability and Growth Pact this would have to be met by a similar reduction in welfare expenditure. Again, in the event of an asymmetric shock the recession-hit states would be likely to demand that the other states maintain high tax rates to enable them to raise taxes to meet their own budget shortfalls.

In December 1997, on the eve of the launch of EMU, the new German socialist government raised the issue of tax harmonization and policies to prevent 'tax competition'. On the initiative of Oskar Lafontaine, the German finance minister, the issue was debated at the Vienna European Council. The EU heads of government concluded that:

> The European Council . . . emphasises the need to combat harmful tax competition. Cooperation in the tax policy area is not aiming at uniform tax rates and is not inconsistent with fair tax competition but is called for to reduce the continuing distortions in the single market, to prevent excessive losses of tax revenue or to get tax structures to develop in a more employment-friendly way.

The treaty already has provisions for the harmonization of tax rates. But as with budgetary reforms, to be passed tax harmonization requires unanimity in the Council. This is unlikely as Denmark and the UK, which have comparatively low corporate tax rates, are vigorously opposed to it. However these two states are outside the euro, and if the members of EMU are determined to harmonize their corporate tax rates they might try to invoke the 'flexible integration' provisions in the treaty, which allow a group of member states unilaterally to agree to new policy instruments. Although Ireland, which is a member of EMU but has a comparatively low corporate tax rate (16 per cent in 2002, compared with the EU average of 33 per cent), would no doubt try to block any move to harmonize corporate taxes in the eurozone.

Labour market flexibility: mobility, structural reforms and wage agreements

According to the optimal currency area theory, a monetary union should be able to adapt to asymmetric economic cycles either through labour movement from states in recession to states in high growth, or through reductions in wage and labour costs in states in recession (to attract capital investment).

There is far less labour movement across borders in the EU than in the US (see Chapter 11). In certain sectors – such as the building industry, the service sector and the informal economy – migrant workers do follow capital investments, for example Irish, British and Portuguese workers have sought employment in the fast-growing building sector in Berlin (Eichengreen, 1993b). However it is hard to imagine that the EU will experience a similar situation to that in the US in the 1930s and 1940s, when there was a mass movement of unemployed and underemployed people from the southern states to the north-eastern states and the rapidly expanding car industry in Detroit.

Nevertheless, there is less labour mobility *within* existing European nation-states than in the US. Political upheaval is avoided because European states have been able to manage internal demand and supply shocks through mechanisms other than labour movement, such as lower wages in low-demand regions and fiscal transfers from high-demand to low-demand regions (as in Germany following reunification in 1990) (Eichengreen, 1993a).

Also, the issue of labour mobility varies from state to state in the EU. For example the success of the Irish economy in the 1990s was attributed to its open labour market, with high levels of immigration and emigration by workers in both low-wage and high-wage job categories – more like a regional economy in the US than a national economy in Europe (Krugman, 1997). Thus, although Ireland is a peripheral economy in EMU, and was already out of synch with the core economies at the start of monetary union, it is likely to be able to adapt to an asymmetric shock. The situation is more problematic for

Table 10.3 *Productivity, labour costs and unemployment in the EU*

	Labour productivity per person employed, 2003 (EU25 = 100)	Hourly labour costs, 2000 (euros)	Unemployment, 2003 (%)
Luxembourg	139.5	24.2	3.7
Ireland	129.5	17.3	4.6
Belgium	127.4	–	8.1
France	122.2	24.4	9.4
Italy	114.1	–	8.6
Finland	107.1	22.2	9.0
Austria	105.3	23.6	4.4
Spain	103.0	14.2	11.3
Netherlands	102.8	23.0	3.8
Germany	102.7	26.5	9.3
Greece	98.8	10.4	9.3
Portugal	68.7	8.1	6.4
Euro12	108.4	–	8.8
Denmark	105.7	27.1	5.6
United Kingdom	104.5	23.4	5.0
Sweden	103.4	28.6	5.6
Malta	96.9	–	8.2
Cyprus	85.6	10.7	4.4
Slovenia	74.7	9.0	6.5
Hungary	69.0	3.8	5.8
Slovakia	61.9	3.1	17.1
Czech Republic	58.8	3.9	7.8
Poland	54.1	4.5	19.2
Lithuania	46.9	2.7	12.7
Estonia	46.7	3.0	10.1
Latvia	41.6	2.4	10.5
EU25	100.0	–	9.0

Note: Table sorted by the unemployment rate in each group of states.

Source: Eurostat.

Portugal. It too is a peripheral economy and was growing faster than the core economies when EMU was launched. But unlike Ireland, Portugal has many unemployed skilled workers because they tend not to emigrate, and a shortage of low-skilled workers because such workers have not immigrated from elsewhere in the EU (Munchau, 1998; Torres, 1998).

With regard to wage flexibility, the EU is unlikely to be able to use wage flexibility to tackle an asymmetric shock. As Table 10.3 shows, there is considerable variation in the level of labour costs among the EMU member states, with labour being much cheaper in the peripheral economies than in the core ones. However, the table also shows that labour costs are generally more a reflection of productivity rates than of demand and supply shocks. For example Spain has high unemployment despite the fact that its labour costs are relatively low. To resolve this situation, either Spanish productivity would need to rise or labour costs would need to be reduced relative to the European average.

To make wages flexible, wage bargaining negotiations could be decentralized, at least to the member state level, and perhaps lower – to the regional or even the enterprise level. This would allow trade unions in different economic situations to accept different wage settlements. However decentralized wage bargaining can lead to inflationary pressures, as high settlements in one region or sector prompt demands for high settlements in other regions/sectors. Empirical research suggests that economies perform best (in terms of relatively high growth with low inflation and low unemployment) when there is centralized wage bargaining, which allows for wage negotiations to respond directly to the centralized monetary and fiscal policies to balance inflation and employment objectives (Iversen, 1998a, 1999). Indeed the danger for EMU is that the ECB will raise interest rates to pre-empt the inflationary pressures that could arise from separate wage settlements in each of the member states, which would then prompt trade unions to demand higher wages, and so on (Iversen, 1998b; Hall and Franzese, 1998). But, despite efforts to establish European-wide collective agreements within some sectors and some multinational companies, different national industrial relations traditions and competing trade union interests undermine the prospect of a genuine coordination of wage demands at the European level (Marginson and Sisson, 1998).

Increasing labour market flexibility comes down to political commitment to EMU by governments and the public. If there is a high degree of public support for EMU, governments will be able to introduce labour market reforms, such as liberalizing the rules that govern the hiring and firing of employees by small businesses, and trade unions will be able to negotiate flexible wage rates. As discussed in Chapter 5, public support for the EU is high in Portugal, Ireland, Spain and Italy, lower in France and Germany, and quite 'soft' in several of the other states, including the Netherlands. The problem for most governments is that deregulation of the labour market might be in the long-term interests of the eurozone as a whole, but it is against the short-term interests of large sections of the electorate. Moreover the allocation of policy competences in the EU – whereby labour market policies are decided at the national level and monetary policy and fiscal policy constraints are imposed from the EU level – prevents an easy solution to the problem.

The external impact of EMU

Finally, the euro is likely to challenge the US dollar as the dominant global reserve currency. As Table 10.4 shows, the size of the EU economy is comparable to that of the US in terms of share of world GDP and global trade. However the US dollar is used far more than the euro in global foreign exchange holdings and transactions. With the newness of the ECB compared with the reputation and stability of the US Federal Reserve, it may take some time for non-European companies and governments to choose to hold and trade in the euro rather than the dollar. However the emergence of the euro as a major world currency may be faster than expected (Kenen, 1995, pp. 108-23; Portes and Rey, 1998). If the euro is more stable than the dollar, it will be attractive as a store of value. The emergence of the euro will also make European financial markets more liquid, which will make the euro cheaper to hold in reserve than any other European currency. And for political reasons, some developing countries may prefer to hold their debts in a European currency rather than US dollars, and the euro will give them the first opportunity to do so without incurring significant transaction costs.

This change in the global currency balance has political ramifications for the EU, both internal and externally. On the internal side, the euro-zone, like the US, is less open to the world economy than the European national economies were before EMU. As a result, currency fluctuations between the euro and the dollar will not have such large inflationary or deflationary effects on the European economy as they did before.

On the external side, in the medium term the euro may enable the US and Europe to cooperate in managing the global economy (Henning and Padoan, 2000; see also Chapter 12). For example, with the two

Table 10.4   *The Euro in the global economy*

	Economic size		*Use of currencies*	
	Share of world GDP, 2003 (%)	*Share of world trade, excl. intra-EU, 2003 (%)*	*Share of global foreign exchange reserves, 2002 (%)*	*Foreign exchange transactions, 2001 (%)*
Euro12	16.2	17.6	14.6	18.8
US	21.5	15.6	64.8	45.8
Japan	7.6	6.5	4.5	11.3

Sources: Organisation for Economic Cooperation and Development, Bank for International Settlements (2001), International Monetary Fund (2003).

dominant global reserve currencies the US and EU may be more able to agree common strategies to manage Third World debt. Also, in the face of global recession, the US Federal Reserve and the ECB can coordinate a joint reduction in interest rates to boost global economic growth, as they did immediately after the terrorist attacks on New York and Washington on 11 September 2001.

Conclusion: the Need for Policy Coordination

With an independent central bank pursuing the primary goal of price stability, and with the transaction-cost benefits and potential growth impact of the single currency, the euro is likely to be a stable currency with a favourable interest rate. However, there is significant economic divergence among the 12 EMU member states, and this divergence will increase if some of the new member states in Central and Eastern Europe join the euro. EMU's real test will be to manage these differences, especially in the face of continued divergence in economic cycles, a major asymmetric demand shock or a European-wide recession.

Labour mobility in the EU is low and there is insufficient wage flexibility. Consequently the EMU member states do not constitute an optimal currency area (OCA). However, according to the strict interpretation of the term, neither the US nor most domestic economies in the EU are OCAs. In a world of global trade and global financial markets, the benefits of an independent exchange rate, and hence the costs of joining a monetary union, are lower than the OCA theory suggests. Moreover other policy tools can be used to overcome asymmetric economic cycles. Governments can introduce labour market reforms to enable wage and price flexibility in the single currency area, or the EU budget can be increased to allow for more fiscal transfers in the event of a demand shock. Also, an OCA may in fact develop endogenously, as the existence of a single currency increases trade integration and encourages the convergence of economic cycles, although the empirical evidence on the synchronization of business cycles in monetary unions is mixed (de Haan *et al.*, 2002).

However, labour market flexibility, moderate wage settlements and sound public finances will not come about automatically; they will rely on political commitment to EMU by governments and the public. Member state governments must be willing to abide by the fiscal rules, reform their labour markets, not interfere in ECB decisions and agree to supranational fiscal transfers when necessary. Citizens must support structural reforms, be prepared to negotiate flexible wage rates, and be willing to cross borders to take up jobs. But given the widespread opposition to such policies by the citizens of most member states, it is unlikely that many governments will make much of an effort to rein in public spending or deregulate labour markets.

In the event of a major economic recession in Europe, and if the political costs of tight monetary policy become too high for governments and the public to bear, the system has some safety valves. The ECB is not immune to outside pressure. Without an established reputation, the ECB is sensitive to public opinion, and its decisions can be influenced through the strategic appointment of Executive Board members and national central bank governors. In addition, EcoFin has the power to change the way in which monetary policy is made within EMU, to reform the Stability and Growth Pact, to overhaul the EU budget, to harmonize taxation rates, and to intervene in international exchange markets to adjust the value of the euro in the global economy. However political control of the ECB would risk price stability, and Council decisions on most of these issues require unanimity, which is difficult to achieve, especially in an EU of 25 states.

With the continued existence of divergent economies, perhaps the only way to make EMU work is to improve the coordination of European level monetary policies and national fiscal and labour market policies (for an opposing view see Issing, 2002). The ECB is unlikely to cut interest rates if member state governments do not pursue sound public finances and labour market reforms, and governments facing an economic downturn will not be able to bring about a balanced budget or structural reforms if the EU interest rates are too high. Unless these conflicting objectives can be resolved – perhaps by means of a reformed Stability and Growth Pact and EcoFin setting inflation targets for the ECB – a battle between the politicians and the central bankers is likely be a central feature of EMU.

Chapter 11

Citizen Freedom and Security Policies

Theories of Citizenship and the State
EU Freedom and Security Policies
Explaining EU Freedom and Security Policies
Conclusion: Skeleton of a Pan-European State

One of the central aims of the modern state is to grant and protect citizens' rights and freedoms. In a similar way, the Amsterdam Treaty commits the EU to 'maintain and develop an area of freedom, security and justice'. This chapter seeks to analyse and explain how far the EU has been able to establish European-wide citizenship rights while protecting existing rights and freedoms as the borders between the member states have gradually dissolved. To help in this task we shall first look at general theories of the relationship between citizens and the state.

Theories of citizenship and the state

In liberal democracies, citizens are entitled to a variety of rights and freedoms. These fall into four main categories (cf. Berlin, 1969; Rawls, 1971; Walzer, 1983):

- *Civil rights*: freedom of movement, the right to privacy, freedom of religion, and freedom from torture.
- *Political rights*: right of association, freedom of speech, the right to vote in elections and the right to stand as a candidate and be elected.
- *Economic rights*: the right to private property, freedom to work, the right to trade and the right to provide or receive services.
- *Social rights*: the right to equality (of opportunity and/or outcomes), the right to education and health care, and the right to employment.

The traditional liberal (or enlightenment) view is that these rights and freedoms are inextricably linked to the emergence of the modern *state*. For example, according to Tilly (1990) the development of European states followed one of two 'trajectories': either they emerged to protect the economic rights and interests of the bourgeoisie; or they emerged

344

to promote and protect the rights of the monarchy, the landed aristocracy and the administrative elites (cf. Moore, 1967). In both cases, citizenship rights were initially the preserve of the privileged classes, and they were guaranteed and protected by means of the state's 'monopoly of the legitimate use of physical force' (Weber, 1946 [1919], p. 78). The expansion of citizenship went hand in hand with expansion of the power of the state. Modern constitutions, courts, police forces and border controls emerged in the nineteenth century in response to middle-class demands for the protection of private property from the state, criminal activity and immigration.

In the same vein, the *nation* is traditionally viewed as a vehicle for the establishment and protection of political and social rights. Democratic rights and freedoms cannot exist without a single national identity because a democratic 'will' (public opinion) requires a single language and mass media, and majority rule is not legitimate without a single national culture (Smith, 1991). Also, social citizenship requires cross-class social solidarity, with a common national destiny and a ruling class that is willing to allow economic redistribution and grant social rights to the working class (Marshall, 1950). As a result, in most European countries the welfare state only developed once the nation had been established as the dominant focus of political identification (Flora and Heidenheimer, 1981).

Consequently, this traditional connection between the nation-state and citizenship suggests that 'transnational citizenship' in the EU – which is neither a state nor a nation – is impossible (Aaron, 1974; cf. Meehan, 1993). However this is not the case. At a theoretical level, the connection between the nation-state and citizenship is a particular geographical and historical ideal type. First, the classic, homogeneous nation-state only developed in a few countries in north-western Europe (such as France and Sweden) and the fully democratic welfare state only emerged in the middle of the twentieth century (Birnbaum and Badie, 1983). However citizenship rights existed in non-state, non-national settings well before this period. For example in city-state Europe, economic rights, such as the right to trade, were granted to non-residents well before the nation-state was established, and in multi-ethnic polities, such as Belgium and Switzerland, redistributive welfare states were founded without strong sociocultural solidarity bonds.

Second, with regard to the issue of democracy and democratic political and civil rights, it is not clear which came first: the nation-state or democracy. In most European systems and the US the practice of democracy preceded the nation-state. In other words national identity and the institutions of the nation-state were products of the development of universal democratic citizenship rights, and not *vice versa* (Rokkan, 1973; Skowronek, 1982).

At an empirical level, citizens' rights today are very different from those in the mid-nineteenth century and even the immediate postwar period. The growth of political and economic migration in the late 1980s and throughout the 1990s has forced Western nation-states to reconfigure their traditional citizenship policies (Brubaker, 1992; Habermas, 1992; Hollifield, 1992; Favell, 1997a). For example, as a result of global free trade and capital flows, economic rights have been extended to non-residents and residents who are not nationals, such as guest workers. Also, the boundary of political rights has become increasingly blurred with the emergence of dual nationality and the extension of voting rights to first- and even second-generation expatriots. Finally, Western societies are no longer homogeneous nations. Successive waves of immigration have produced multicultural polities and forced states to develop new definitions of citizenship and new social and political rights, such as racial equality and minority representation (Kymlicka, 1995).

In other words there is a tension in citizenship politics. On the one hand citizenship requires the institutions of a state to guarantee positive freedoms (through the courts) and to secure and protect negative freedoms (through the police and security forces). For example markets, including the European single market, cannot exist without the existence and protection of property rights. On the other hand, in the world of global capitalism, global labour movements and multiethnic societies:

> the classical formal order of the nation-state and its membership is not in place. The state is no longer an autonomous and independent organization closed over a nationally defined population ... Rights, participation, and representation in the polity, are increasingly matters beyond the vocabulary of national citizenship. (Soysal, 1994, pp. 163–4)

This tension is central to the politics of citizenship in the EU: by establishing transnational citizenship rights the EU has undermined the traditional nation-state; and to define and secure transnational citizenship, new state powers and security mechanisms are being reinvented at the European level, in cooperation with the state powers at the national level (Bauböck, 1994; Martiniello, 1995).

EU Freedom and Security Policies

EU policies on citizens' rights and internal security fall into four main categories:

- *The free movement of persons* between the EU member states, ranging from work and residency rights to the removal of border controls between the member states.

- *Fundamental rights* for EU nationals in other member states, such as equal economic, political and civil rights.
- *Immigration and asylum policies,* involving cooperation on refugee policies and common policies towards third-country nationals.
- *Police and judicial cooperation,* to combat drug-trafficking, terrorist activities, cross-border crime, and illegal immigration.

The first two of these confer rights on EU citizens who move between and/or live in other EU member states; the second two relate to how the member states and the EU institutions decide who has access to national and EU citizenship rights, and how these rights should be guaranteed and protected.

From free movement of workers to 'an area of freedom, security and justice'

The Treaty of Rome established a basic citizenship right: the right for citizens of one member state to seek and take up work in any other member state. The Single European Act built on this foundation, with the aim of removing all physical barriers to the movement of services and labour as part of the single market. The Maastricht Treaty then added a 'justice and home affairs' pillar (the so-called 'third pillar' of the EU), which covered free movement, immigration policies and police and judicial cooperation. A major change came with the Amsterdam Treaty, which was signed in June 1997 and entered into force in May 1999. The treaty added a new Title (IV) to the EU treaty with the aim of creating 'an area of freedom, security and justice'.

Subsequently, at the Vienna and Tampere European Councils (in December 1998 and October 1999 respectively) the member state governments approved and revised an action plan to bring about the area of freedom, security and justice. In the plan an 'area of freedom' was defined as covering the free movement of persons, as well as protecting fundamental rights and combating all forms of discrimination. An 'area of security' was defined as common policies to combat crime, particularly terrorism, trade in human beings, arms and drug trafficking, and corruption and fraud. An 'area of justice' was defined as equal access to justice for all EU citizens, cooperation between the member states' authorities on civil matters, and the establishment of minimum common rules covering criminal acts, procedures and penalties. The plan also listed a series of concrete policy issues that the EU would tackle in each of these areas, and a provisional timetable for agreeing the associated policies.

Responding to the action plan, in March 2000 the European

Commission set up a 'scoreboard', which aimed to inform EU citizens of developments in this policy area and to embarrass the member state governments into action by setting out what measures had been taken by what date and what still needed to be done. As the scoreboard revealed, by mid 2004 progress towards a genuine area of freedom, security and justice was mixed.

Free movement of persons

The Treaty of Rome established the free movement of persons as a fundamental objective of the European Economic Community, but this provision originally applied only to cross-border economic activity. Nationals of one EU member state have the right to seek work, reside and provide or receive a service in another member state. Secondary legislation and ECJ judgements have extended entry, residency and working rights to non-EU nationals who are dependants of EU citizens (spouses and children of EU citizens) and to some economically independent non-EU citizens (people who have sufficient funds and resources not to be a burden on the recipient state, such as students, company employees and the self-employed). However there are two limitations on these rights. First, these rights do not apply fully to third-country nationals, even if they are married to EU citizens (cf. Barrett, 2003). Second, the Treaty of Rome allowed any member state to deny the entry of another EU national if she or he posed a potential threat to national security, public health or public policy. On the basis of these provisions the member states retained their intra-EU border controls.

Subsequently the removal of physical barriers to the free movement of goods and persons became a central part of the single market programme. The white paper *Completing the Internal Market* (European Commission, 1985) suggested that this implied the complete elimination of internal frontier controls and borders by 31 December 1992 (see Chapter 8). The Council adopted several measures to remove controls on the free movement of goods by that date, but little progress was made on removing the controls on the free movement of persons. Most member states were reluctant to remove these internal controls without harmonized rules on the crossing of the EU's external borders, such as common visa requirements and asylum policies, but due to domestic sensitivities and the requirement for unanimity the Council failed to reach agreement on such rules by the date in question (see the section on immigration policies below).

In the meantime, in 1985 France, Germany and the three Benelux countries signed the Schengen Accord. This was an intergovernmental agreement, outside the EU treaty, for the complete elimination of border controls between the signatory states. An implementation convention was eventually adopted in 1990. Italy, Spain, Portugal and Greece signed the accord in 1992, and the members of the Nordic passport union – Denmark, Sweden, Finland and Norway (although not in the EU) – joined in 1995. On 26 March 1995 the Schengen Convention entered into force, with only France refusing to remove all its border controls on the ground that Belgium and the Netherlands had not formally undertaken policies to prevent drug trafficking.

The Amsterdam Treaty introduced two major changes to the free movement of persons. First, Article 62(1) of the treaty committed the Council to removing 'controls on persons, be they citizens of the Union or nationals of third countries, crossing internal borders' within five years of the entry into force of the treaty. Second, through a protocol attached to the EU Treaty, the Amsterdam Treaty incorporated the 3000 pages of the Schengen *acquis* into the legal framework of the EU. The Council, acting by unanimity, became the main executive body under the Schengen rules, and the Schengen secretariat became part of the Council's general secretariat. While the ECJ was granted jurisdiction over some decisions, decision-making in this area remains highly secretive. The EP has no formal right of consultation, and the Schengen protocol explicitly excludes the ECJ from exercising jurisdiction on matters of law and order or internal security arising from the Schengen Convention.

In addition the provisions do not apply to all the member states. Through a series of protocols attached to the Amsterdam Treaty, the UK, Ireland and Denmark negotiated a series of 'opt-outs'. The UK and Ireland chose to be excluded from all aspects of the new Title IV and from the Schengen *acquis*, although they may choose to opt in to individual proposals on an *ad hoc* basis. In a separate provision of the treaty, Ireland declared that it intended to participate as fully as possible while remaining in the passport union with the UK. Denmark, on the other hand, opted out from Title IV with no possibility of opting in to individual proposals. Nonetheless Denmark is a member of Schengen (but reserves the right to opt out on any new policy proposal) and participates in the provisions on common visa policies (see below).

After their countries joined the EU in May 2004 the citizens of the 10 new member states did not immediately gain full freedom of movement throughout the EU (Jileva, 2002). During the accession negotiations several member states, particularly Germany and Austria, voiced their fear that they would be subjected to a huge influx of immigrants from Central and Eastern Europe, so the applicant states were required to accept a transition period in which movement would be restricted. Until 2006 the EU-15 are free to apply their own national rules to the citizens of the new member states. These measures will then be reviewed and can be extended until 2009, or 2011 in the case of member states that experience serious labour market disruptions as a result of EU enlargement.

A similar transition period was imposed when Spain and Portugal acceded to the EU in the mid 1980s, but was quickly abandoned when the other member states realized that the number of Spanish and Portuguese workers seeking jobs elsewhere in the EU actually declined. There were two reasons for this decline. First, most of those in Spain and Portugal who wished to emigrate to the EU had done so in the years immediately prior to their countries' accession. Second, as the per capita GDP gap between Spain and Portugal and the rest of the EU declined, the incentive to emigrate declined. The situation will probably be similar for the new member states, as large numbers of migrants from Central and Eastern Europe had already moved to Western Europe prior to accession, and the per capita GDP of most of the new states is likely to grow at a faster rate than in the rest of the EU (Krause and Schwager, 2003).

Thus despite media fears of a 'flood of migrants' from the new member states, most migration experts put the number at about 100 000 per year for the whole of the EU, with that number declining rapidly. Also, with the growing burden imposed on public finances by the ageing population, and with skills shortages in key jobs in the service sector (such as computer engineering and health care), the governments of many of the EU-15 states are actively trying to attract skilled migrant workers (Favell and Hansen, 2002). As a result the transition measures are likely to be abandoned in 2006, if not before. Indeed Sweden, Denmark, Ireland, the Netherlands, the UK, France and Spain have either applied relatively liberal access measures or announced that their transition measures will be removed in 2006.

Fundamental rights and freedoms

In addition to freedom of movement, the Treaty of Rome established several economic rights for citizens of the EU member states. Through its rules on state aid, the common market and competition policy, the treaty placed limits on the extent to which the state could intervene in private economic interactions. The treaty also outlawed economic discrimination (such as in the granting of contracts and in pay and conditions) on the grounds of nationality and gender. Everson (1995) argues that in combination with the establishment of the 'direct effect' of EU law (see Chapter 4), these provisions turned EU nationals into 'market citizens', not only in other member states but also in their own.

However citizens' identification with the EU could not be guaranteed by offering economic rights alone. In 1974 the Paris Summit first discussed the idea of adding political and civil rights to the economic rights. During the preparation of the Single European Act in 1984, the

Adonnino Report argued that a 'People's Europe' – via cultural, educational and identity policies – should be pursued in parallel to the completion of the single market. Then in 1990 at the Rome European Council that launched the Intergovernmental Conference (IGC) that negotiated the Maastricht Treaty, the Spanish prime minister, Felipé González, secured the agreement of the other EU heads of government that the EU treaty should establish EU citizenship. Part Two of the treaty defines 'Citizenship of the Union' as follows:

- EU citizens are nationals of the EU member states ('Citizenship of the Union shall complement not replace national citizenship').
- EU citizens have the right to reside anywhere in the EU.
- EU citizens have the right to vote or stand as a candidate in local and EP elections wherever they reside in the EU.
- EU citizens in third countries have the right to consular protection by the embassy of any EU member state.
- EU citizens have the right to petition the EP, to complain to the EU ombudsman, and to write to any EU institution in any of the official languages of the EU.

Despite the symbolic value of declaring 'EU citizenship', these provisions are limited. First, they do not mean that all EU citizens have the same rights in every member state: each member state has its own set of civil, economic, political and social rights and these are selectively granted to people from other member states. For example EU nationals residing in another state cannot vote in national elections, and an ethnic minority EU citizen who resides in another member state does not have the same racial equality rights as minorities who are nationals of that state.

Second, EU citizenship rights only apply fully to EU nationals. One implication of this is that the member states retain the right to decide who is an EU citizen, and hence who has access to the economic and political rights granted under the EU treaty. Moreover by restricting the rights to EU nationals, millions of legal residents in the territories of the EU are specifically excluded from receiving these rights. A third-country national who has the right to reside and work in one member state does not have the same right in other member states.

Third, the citizenship provisions in no way define a set of fundamental rights for EU nationals or residents in the EU (O'Leary, 1995, pp. 303–14). During the Amsterdam Treaty negotiations several member states proposed that the EU should accede to the European Convention on Human Rights (ECHR). However the ECJ ruled in March 1996 (Opinion 2/94) that the EU did not have the authority to take such an action – the treaty would have to be reformed to mandate the EU to sign the ECHR. Instead, the Amsterdam Treaty established respect for liberty, democracy, and human and fundamental rights as basic principles of the EU; granted the ECJ the power to ensure that the EU institutions adhered to these principles; provided for sanctions against member states that breached human rights; and provided the EU with the competence to pass legislation to combat discrimination on the grounds of sex, race or ethnic origin, religion or belief, disability, age, and sexual orientation (Article 12). But this was not a mandate to sign-up to the ECHR or the equivalent of a genuine bill of rights.

In June 1999 the Cologne European Council set up a convention of representatives from the member states and the EU institutions to prepare a charter of rights for the EU. The convention reported in October 2000, and the Charter of Fundamental Rights of the EU was approved unanimously by the governments, the EP and the Commission in December 2000. The Nice Treaty, which was adopted in December 2001 and entered into force in February 2003, did not make any reference to the charter, but it did introduce a mechanism for expelling a member state (by a four-fifths majority in the Council) from the EU for breach of fundamental rights, (Article 7). Then in June 2004 the charter became an integral part of the proposed EU constitution.

The Charter of Fundamental Rights of the EU brings together in a single text all the main personal, civil, political, economic and social rights contained in the ECHR, the constitutions of the EU member states, and various other international conventions on fundamental rights. The charter adds some provisions that are specific to the EU, namely the rights set out in Part Two of the EU treaty (such as freedom of movement, the right of petition and so on). The charter also adds several new rights that reflect changes in society since 1950 (when the ECHR was adopted). For example, the Charter introduces a right to 'good administration', protection of personal data and rules governing bioethics, and recognizes arrangements other than marriage for founding a family (it deliberately does not refer to marriage as a union between a man and a woman).

As the charter is not part of the EU treaties (until the Constitution is ratified), the articles in it do not have the same legal basis as the primary articles in the treaties (see Chapter 4). Nevertheless the symbolic value of the Charter has important policy implications as it will establish the highest legal norms for the ECJ, the Commission and the Council when applying the articles in the treaty (Menéndez, 2002). For example the ECJ has already defined a body of rights for EU citizens (such as the right to a fair trial, privacy, free association and property), and ruled that all EU institutions must respect fundamental rights, as must the member state authorities when implementing EU law (see Chapter 4). When defining these rights, the ECJ referred to the ECHR and national constitutions as the sources of fundamental rights and freedoms. From now on, though, if a question before the ECJ touches on fundamental rights issues it may choose to refer to and apply the articles of the Charter especially now that the member states have agreed to insert the Charter in the Constitution. Similarly, if a member state is in breach of human rights, the Commission and the Council are likely to refer to the Charter to decide whether sanctions should be applied (under Article 7).

In sum, EU citizenship is not exactly the same as national citizenship in that it does not establish full and equal economic, political, civil and social rights for all individuals regardless of where they reside in the EU. Nevertheless it is the first step towards a genuine 'post-national citizenship' of Europe, where the right to reside, seek work, receive welfare benefits, pursue educational opportunities, participate in society and politics, and have one's identity and culture protected, is no longer the independent preserve of the European nation-states but the subject of collective agreement between the member states and policy-making by the supranational EU institutions (Shaw, 1997; Wiener, 1997).

Immigration and asylum policies

Without internal borders, any person who was granted entry to or citizenship of one member state could conceivably move freely within the territory of the EU. Consequently the goal of removing physical barriers to the movement of persons inside the single market forced the member states to address the issue of the movement of persons across the external borders of the EU. In 1986 the member state governments set up an Ad Hoc Working Group on Immigration (AWGI). This was an intergovernmental body of officials from interior ministries outside the EU institutional structure, and through this informal cooperation the governments agreed two conventions on immigration policy: the Dublin Convention on Asylum in 1990, and the External Frontiers Convention in 1991.

The Dublin Convention aimed to prevent multiple asylum applications by mutual recognition of all states' asylum regulations and ensuring that asylum applications would only be processed by the member state in which the asylum seeker first arrived in the EU. The External Frontiers Convention provided for the mutual recognition of visas for non-EU nationals, and abolished the need for third-country nationals residing legally in one member state to obtain a visa to travel to another EU state for a period of less than three months. However these conventions had to be transposed into national legislation in all EU member states before they could enter into force. Several member states refused to ratify the Dublin Convention, and the UK and Spain refused to sign the External Frontiers Convention due to their ongoing disagreement over Gibraltar.

Nevertheless the Maastricht Treaty brought the work of the AWGI into the framework of the EU through its provisions for cooperation in the fields of justice and home affairs (JHA) – the third pillar of the EU. The JHA pillar established asylum policy, the crossing of external frontiers, immigration policy and policy towards third-country nationals as areas of common interest to the member states. However this development was more an institutionalization of the existing intergovernmental provisions than a new supranational competence: the AWGI simply became a subcommittee of the Council committee responsible for JHA issues (the K.4 Committee), decision-making remained by unanimity, the Commission still had no right of initiative, and there was no role for the EP or the ECJ. Also, the Maastricht Treaty lumped together immigration policies and police and judicial cooperation, which ensured that these issues continued to be addressed as security questions rather than as issues of citizens' rights and freedoms.

Under the JHA provisions, justice and home affairs ministers began to meet on a more regular basis and to adopt more common policies. However these policies tended to be non-binding resolutions and recommendations rather than directly effective joint actions or decisions (Niessen and Guild 1996). The few joint actions of note covered the easing of travel restrictions on third-country nationals studying in the EU, a system of common transit visas in all member states, a uniform format for residence permits, and burden-sharing with regard to the admission and residence of refugees. However several of the member states refused to be bound by joint actions. Also, decisions tended to be restricted to information-exchange issues, such as the decision in November 1992 to set up two clearing houses for data exchange on asylum rules, asylum applications and immigration developments: the Centre for Information, Discussion and Exchange on Asylum (CIREA), and the Centre for Information, Discussion and Exchange on the Crossing of External Borders and Immigration (CIREFI).

Nevertheless, the Amsterdam Treaty brought immigration and asylum issues into the EC section of the EU treaty, and in so doing combined them with the provisions for the removal of internal borders and separated them from the provisions on police and judicial cooperation on criminal matters. The new Title (IV) commits the Council to adopt common policies in the following areas:

- Standards and procedures for checking on persons crossing the EU's external borders.
- Rules on visas for stays of longer than three months, including a single list of countries whose citizens require visas to visit the EU.
- The conditions under which third-country nationals shall have freedom to travel in the EU for up to three months.
- standards and procedures for granting and withdrawing asylum and

refugee status, including minimum standards for the reception of asylum seekers and refugees;

- Minimum standards for the temporary protection of displaced persons (*de facto* refugees rather than asylum seekers);
- Measures on immigration policy, including common conditions of entry and residence and common rules on illegal immigration and repatriation.
- Measures defining the rights and conditions under which third-country nationals can work and reside anywhere in the EU.

The Amsterdam Treaty specified that for the first five years after the treaty's entry into force (up to May 2004) these policies would be adopted through a mix of intergovernmental and supranational procedures. On the intergovernmental side, the Council was to act by unanimity, and legislation was to be initiated by the member state governments. On the supranational side, the Commission was given a right of legislative initiative, the Council could adopt legally binding and directly effective directives or regulations, the EP would have to consulted, and the ECJ was granted jurisdiction (but only if all national legal remedies had been exhausted). The Nice Treaty then reinforced the supranational procedures: legislation on checks at external borders, visas, third-country nationals, asylum and the temporary protection of refugees would now have to be passed by the co-decision procedure, in which the EP has equal power with the Council (see Chapter 3); and from May 2004 the Council would decide by qualified-majority voting rather than unanimity on many of these policy issues.

In the meantime, in line with the Amsterdam Treaty goals, in October 1999 the Tampere European Council set out the basic elements of EU immigration policy:

- There should be a comprehensive approach to the management of migration (the policy should cover immigration for the economic needs of the European economy as well as asylum protection).
- Third-country nationals should, as far as possible, have comparable rights to the nationals of the member state in which they lived.
- There should be partnerships with countries of origin, including policies of codevelopment.
- There must be a common policy for asylum that fully respects the terms of the Geneva Convention and the member states' obligations under international treaties.

In 2000 and 2001 the Commission issued a series of communications setting out how it thought these goals could be achieved, in terms of legislation that would have to be adopted and by what date. This resulted in a raft of legislative proposals, covering *inter alia* common rules for non-EU nationals working in the EU; the right of third-country nationals to family reunification; an EU long-term residence status for third-country nationals who have resided in a member state for five years; the admission of third-country nationals as students, vocational trainees or volunteers; and a programme for financial and technical assistance to third countries relating to migration and asylum.

A series of measures were also proposed and adopted in the specific area of asylum. In July 2001 the Council adopted a directive setting out minimum standards for the temporary protection of persons displaced by economic, political or environmental disasters, and therefore not eligible for asylum status (granted to individuals who had suffered political persecution). In January 2003 the Council adopted a directive establishing minimum standards for the reception of asylum applicants. This requires member states to provide asylum-seekers with health care, accommodation, schooling and access to the labour market. Then in February and September 2003 the Council adopted two regulations establishing the criteria and mechanisms for determining which member state is responsible for examining an asylum application (in other words, incorporating part of the Dublin Convention into the EU legal *aquis*).

In summary, the EU now defines how the member states grant asylum, visas, and temporary protection for third-country nationals, and the Commission and EP have played a role in shaping these policies. The member states still control most aspects of immigration policy, such as who can be given citizenship, which third-country nationals have the right to reside permanently in the EU and which workers should be given access to the national labour market to fill skills shortages. However the EU now has policy competences in most areas of immigration policy, and there is growing pressure for common EU immigration policies, particularly to address labour market shortages and the problem of the aging population, where many member states need to increase the number of people paying into the state pensions system.

Police and judicial cooperation

In 1975 the European Council set up a forum for cooperation between interior ministries and police agencies to combat terrorism. This new intergovernmental group, the Trevi group (cryptically named after its first chairman, A. R. Fonteijn, and the fountain in Rome, where it first met), was not formally part of the EU institutions. Its main activities involved information exchanges about terrorist activities, the security aspects of air traffic systems, nuclear plants and other vulnerable targets, and cooperation in the development of tactics and equipment to fight terrorism. In the 1980s Trevi's mandate was widened to include cooperation in fighting football hooliganism and serious international organized crime such as drug trafficking, arms trafficking and bank robbery, and in 1988 the Trevi 1992 project was launched to study the consequences of the single market programme on cross-border security issues.

With the creation of the third pillar, the Maastricht Treaty brought the Trevi framework formally into the EU structure in the justice and home affairs provisions. In addition to the immigration and asylum provisions discussed above, the provisions covered judicial cooperation on civil matters, judicial cooperation on criminal matters, customs cooperation, police cooperation to prevent terrorism, drug trafficking and other forms of serious international crime, and the creation of the European Police Office (EUROPOL). As with the immigration and asylum issues, this was essentially the institutionalization of existing intergovernmental practices. The committees around the Trevi ministers meetings (such as the Ad Hoc Group on Organized Crime) simply became working groups of COREPER, under the K.4 Committee. Also, decision-making remained by unanimity, and the Commission, the EP and the ECJ were excluded.

As with the immigration policies, progress in the area of police and judicial cooperation was slow and conducted through non-binding instruments. Justice and home affairs ministers adopted action plans to fight drug addiction, organized crime, trafficking in human beings, the exploitation of children, and the control of large groups of people who posed a threat to law and order (in other words, football hooligans). In most areas the action plans did not lead to the establishment of common European-wide practices. In December 1991 the Council passed the EUROPOL Convention, but this was not signed by all member states until July 1995, and due to ratification problems EUROPOL only came into operation (in The Hague) in 1998.

Despite this slow progress, and unlike with the immigration and asylum policies, the member states did not move police and judicial cooperation policies to the first pillar. Instead these policies were left in a revamped third pillar: Title VI of the treaty, on 'police and judicial cooperation in criminal matters'. Under these provisions the member states are committed to adopting common policies in the following areas:

- The prevention, detection and investigation of criminal offences.
- The collection, storage, processing, analysis and exchange of information on criminal offences, subject to appropriate protection of personal data.
- Enabling EUROPOL to support cross-border investigations, to

undertake investigations in specific cases and to establish a database on cross-border crime.

- Facilitating extradition between the member states.
- Preventing conflicts of jurisdiction between the member states.
- The approximation of rules on criminal matters.

Council decision-making is still by unanimity, but the Commission shares the right of policy initiation with the Council, and the EP must be consulted before the Council can act. Also, the old joint action of the third pillar was replaced by two new legal instruments: decisions, and framework decisions. Decisions are similar to regulations in the EC pillar, and framework decisions are similar to directives in that they apply to the approximation of laws.

Moreover, and perhaps most significantly, the ECJ has some limited jurisdiction. The ECJ cannot review the validity of acts conducted by national police and administrative agencies when carrying out the objectives of the new third pillar. However, the ECJ has the power of judicial review over decisions and framework decisions, and can also rule on a disputes between member states over the interpretation of acts under the third pillar. Finally, and most contentiously, member states can voluntarily accept the jurisdiction of the ECJ to make pre-liminary rulings. However this means that once a member state has accepted an ECJ jurisdiction and referred an issue to it, the ECJ's sub-sequent ruling is binding on all courts in all member states. It is unlikely that most of the governments were aware of this implication when signing the Amsterdam Treaty.

Progress was slow, but the events of 11 September 2001 spurred the EU into action. For example in the area of police cooperation, in December 2002 the Council established a European Police College (CEPOL) for training police officers at the European level; in June 2002 a Council decision set up a European network to capture persons responsible for genocide, crimes against humanity and war crimes; in November 2002 a Council decision established a mecha-nism for evaluating the legal systems of the member states for fighting terrorism; and in December 2002 a Council decision introduced a series of measures to promote police and judicial cooperation in the combating of terrorism. Similarly in the area of judicial cooperation, in February 2002 a Council decision set up the European Justice Office (EUROJUST) in The Hague to improve cooperation between the member states in investigating and prosecuting people suspected of serious cross-border crime; in June 2002 the Council adopted a frame-work decision establishing a European arrest warrant for serious cross-border crimes; in February 2003 a Council decision established a simplified extradition procedure between the member states; and in July 2003 the EU signed an agreement with the US on mutual legal assistance in the fight against terrorism and international organized crime.

In sum, compared with EU socioeconomic policies, and even asylum and immigration policies, the internal security powers of the EU are relatively limited. The EU is a long way from possessing a monopoly on the legitimate use of physical force. For example EUROPOL is not a European FBI with independent powers of investigation, and EURO-JUST is not a European justice department with independent powers of prosecution and enforcement (although the proposed constitution would replace EUROJUST with a European public prosecutor, albeit with fairly limited powers). Nonetheless the interior ministries and police forces of the member states have been active promoters of European level policies in this area to increase their own ability to investigate, capture and prosecute individuals involved in cross-border crimes.

Explaining EU Freedom and Security Policies

There are several issues in the development of EU freedom and security policies that need to be explained:

- Why are policies to promote the free movement of persons less advanced than policies to promote the free movement of goods, services and capital?
- Why (until the Amsterdam Treaty) were immigration and asylum policies dealt with under the same decision-making mechanisms as police and judicial cooperation?
- Why in the Amsterdam Treaty was a major integrationist step taken in the area of asylum and immigration policy, with agenda-setting powers being delegated to the Commission and the introduction of binding policy instruments?

The research in political science and sociology has produced four main types of explanation of the development of EU citizenship and security policies: (1) exogenous changes in European and global society; (2) strategic behaviour by EU governments; (3) strategic behaviour by administrative elites; and (4) the interests and strategies of supranational actors.

Exogenous pressure: growing international migration and crime

It is often claimed that one of the side-effects of globalization is that states are less able to control the global movement of persons (Cornelius *et al.*, 1994; Sassen, 1996; Bhagwati, 2003; cf. Joppke,

1999; Guiraudon and Lahav, 2000). Even if the most extreme versions of this thesis exaggerate the openness of borders, since the mid 1980s most states in Western Europe have found it difficult to prevent the arrival and settlement of asylum seekers, refugees fleeing states suffering from economic or political collapse, family members of previous migrants and undocumented immigrants.

One consequence of this is that Europe is now a multiethnic continent. As Table 11.1 shows, by the mid 1990s almost 6 per cent of EU residents were racial, ethnic or religious minorities, and by 2000 more than 6 per cent of EU residents had been born in a different country from the one in which they were residing. France, the UK, Belgium and the Netherlands, which once had colonial empires, had had significant minority populations since the 1950s, and Germany had welcomed successive generations of guest workers in the 1960s and 1970s (mostly from Turkey). By the 1990s it had become clear that these guest workers were permanent immigrants. Their children (and children's children) had been born in Germany but did not have German citizenship. Moreover in the 1990s many other EU states became net-immigration states for the first time, including Italy, Spain, Portugal, Greece and Ireland.

The 1990s also saw a new wave of refugees to Western Europe from Central and Eastern Europe, former Yugoslavia, North Africa, the Horn of Africa (Ethiopia and Somalia), the Great Lakes region of Africa (especially Rwanda and Burundi), and Afghanistan. Some of these persons were able to claim asylum status under the 1951 UN Convention on Asylum, but many were not as they could not prove personal persecution. Nonetheless they were *de facto* refugees, in flight from economic deprivation, environmental destruction, civil wars or collapsed states, and therefore had to be offered some form of protection, either permanent or temporary. As can be seen in the table, the EU states were not equal recipients of these *de jure* and *de facto* refugees. For example in the early 1990s Germany (with about 20 per cent of the EU population) received almost 60 per cent of asylum applications, and in the early 2000s the UK (with about 13 per cent of the EU population) received over 20 per cent.

In response to the changing patterns of global migration, European governments introduced new immigration, societal integration and asylum policies (Baldwin-Edwards and Schain, 1994; Papademetriou and Hamilton, 1996; Joppke, 1998). Throughout Europe, attacks on immigrants began to rise, as did support for anti-immigration parties and public demand for a stop to further immigration and asylum (European Parliament, 1985, 1991; Lahav, 1997, 2004). Despite their differing philosophies on citizenship and society, most of the governments adopted a similar two-pronged strategy: policies to promote the social integration of existing minority populations through equal opportunity and other race relations policies; and greater controls on immigration and asylum (Cornelius *et al.*, 1994; Migration Policy Group, 1996; Favell, 1997a).

Nevertheless, the variation in the burden of asylum applications can only be partially explained by government policies (Thielemann, 2003b, 2004; Vink and Meijerink, 2003). Government policies did have some effect. After the German government introduced more restrictive asylum procedures in the mid 1990s the number of asylum applications declined. Several other states followed the German lead (notably France and Denmark), whereupon the UK seemed to be a comparatively 'soft touch' for asylum seekers. Despite this, other factors played a much larger part in refugees' choice of destination, such as their country of origin, the size of the existing community of fellow nationals and the second language of the refugee. For example most asylum seekers in the early 1990s were from former Yugoslavia and preferred to go to Germany because it had a large Yugoslav population and was physically not too far from the Balkans. Similarly, in the late 1990s there was an explosion of asylum seekers from Afghanistan, who preferred to go to the UK. Because they either had family connections in the UK or spoke English as second language, the relative distance of Afghanistan from the UK was not a determining factor.

The 1990s also saw a rise in international organized crime, that is, 'crimes perpetrated by groups and organizations moving across the various national jurisdictions in which they are defined as a violation of the criminal code' (Anderson *et al.*, 1995, p. 14). This category of crime covers a variety of activities, ranging from serious crimes such as terrorism, drug trafficking, money laundering, Mafia activities, arms trafficking and fraud against private corporations and governmental (national and EU) budgets, to lesser crimes such as football hooliganism, the smuggling of tax-free goods and national cultural treasures, and the distribution of banned racist and pornographic publications (cf. Martin and Romano, 1992). It is difficult to ascertain the exact extent to which international crime has increased, but the limited statistics that do exist suggest a moderate increase in all member states (Alvazzi del Frate *et al.*, 1993).

The removal of border controls in the single market has not necessarily facilitated the rise in migration and organized crime. Rather migration rose after the collapse of communism, conflicts in the Balkans and central Asia, and crises in northern, eastern and central Africa. Similarly organized crime in Europe is a part of global criminal activities and is connected to the globalization of capital flows and national policies unrelated to the EU, for example the liberalization of laws on soft drugs such as cannabis.

Nevertheless the removal of physical controls on the movement of goods, services and persons has made it difficult for national govern-

Table 11.1 *Minorities and migrants in the EU*

	Ethnic minorities as % of pop'n, 1994	Foreign born population as % of pop'n, 2001	Residents from other EU15 states as % of pop'n, 2001	Asylum applications, 2002 Total	% of EU25	Total pop'n as % of EU25 pop'n, 2003
Austria	5.1	11.0	2.7	39 354	10.0	1.8
Belgium	9.8	8.2	5.4	18 798	4.8	2.3
Cyprus	n/a	n/a	–	950	0.2	0.2
Czech Republic	n/a	2.0	–	8 483	2.2	2.2
Denmark	5.0	6.0	1.0	5 946	1.5	1.2
Estonia	n/a	n/a	–	9	0.0	0.3
Finland	0.8	2.8	0.3	3 443	0.9	1.1
France	8.3	10.0	2.0	51 087	13.0	13.1
Germany	7.4	8.9	2.3	71 127	18.2	18.2
Greece	8.2	7.0	0.4	5 664	1.4	2.4
Hungary	n/a	3.0	–	6 412	1.6	2.2
Ireland	1.1	3.9	2.6	11 634	3.0	0.9
Italy	2.6	2.4	0.3	7 300	1.9	12.6
Latvia	n/a	n/a	–	24	0.0	0.5
Lithuania	n/a	n/a	–	367	0.1	0.8
Luxembourg	11.5	37.5	29.3	1 042	0.3	0.1

Malta	n/a	n/a	–	350	0.1	0.1
Netherlands	6.4	10.4	1.2	18 667	4.8	3.6
Poland	n/a	0.1	–	5 169	1.3	8.4
Portugal	1.7	2.2	0.5	244	0.1	2.3
Slovakia	n/a	0.5	–	9 743	2.5	1.2
Slovenia	n/a	n/a	–	650	0.2	0.4
Spain	2.9	2.7	0.4	6 309	1.6	9.0
Sweden	2.5	11.5	2.0	33 016	8.4	2.0
United Kingdom	6.3	4.4	1.4	85 866	21.9	13.1
Total EU15	5.9	6.4	1.6	359 497	–	–
Total EU25	–	–	–	391 654	100.0	100.0

Sources: Minority Rights Group (1997); Eurostat; OECD (2003).

ments to pursue independent policies to control migration or international crime. Open internal borders means that one government's immigration policy has a potential impact on the number of migrants to other EU states. Such negative externalities of separate national immigration policies have forced the member state governments to accept that migration should be tackled collectively at the European level through some form of 'burden-sharing' – with the costs of common initiatives and public goods being shared by the member states (Thielemann, 2003a). The situation is not so clear in the case of cross-border crime, as reducing crime in one state will not automatically increase criminal activity in a neighbouring state. Nonetheless failure to tackle this issue at the European level would enable international criminals to make the most of the new open borders in Europe.

Government interests: from high politics to regulatory failure and voters' demands

While the changing nature of European society and cross-border crime have provided governments with an incentive to tackle these issues at the European level. However, there are also significant countervailing forces. In the historical development of European integration, member state governments have often differentiated between 'high politics' and 'low politics' (Hoffmann, 1966). High politics covers issues that touch on the fundamental definition, identity and security of the nation-state. Low politics covers issues that are not as threatening to the viability of the nation-state, such as European economic integration, the single market programme, and EU social and environmental regulation. Therefore governments are more likely to allow supranational policy competences on low-politics issues than on high-politics ones. The free movement of persons and the related issues of immigration and policing are high-politics issues. These policies are central to the definition of the nation-state, relating to who is part of the social contract between state and citizens, who has the rights and freedoms of national citizenship, and who has the right to be protected by the forces of the state.

Consequently, as part of the single market programme the member state governments were less willing to remove physical borders on the movement of persons than those against the movement of goods, services and capital. However the time came when they could no longer resist the pressure for common action, at which point they chose to cooperate through informal intergovernmental measures – first through informal mechanisms and then in a separate intergovernmental pillar in the EU. Under these arrangements national sovereignty is preserved in two ways: decisions are taken by unanimity, which allows any government to veto a measure that threatens a vital national interest; and decisions do not have direct effect in domestic law – they need to be transposed into domestic law by parliaments and are justiciable only in domestic courts.

However, in the mid 1990s the political calculations of the member state governments changed for two reasons. First, they were forced to face up to the failure of intergovernmental regulation of migration and policing issues. As already noted the single market produced negative externalities on immigration, asylum and policing policies as governments were affected by each other's policies on refugees, border controls and immigration. As a result the governments had a collective interest in developing frameworks to discuss each other's policies and develop common strategies, despite this being an area of high politics, and they duly established institutions for collective decision-making with the Trevi framework, the Schengen Accord and the Justice home affairs provisions of the Maastricht Treaty.

However the intergovernmental nature of these institutions obstructed coherent policy development. In addition to the unanimity requirement, there was no independent agenda-setter; the governments had to rely on each other to come up with legislative proposals, and these inevitably tended to promote the individual interests of the government currently holding the Council presidency, rather than the collective interests of the EU. Also, once a policy had been adopted there was no guarantee that non-binding actions (such as conventions) would ever be enforced. Each member state had an incentive not to implement agreements once they had been adopted as they were costly to force on an unwilling publics, and their citizens could free-ride on the liberal policies of other states. The result was a classic collective action problem (a 'joint-decision trap') with a sub optimal outcome: few collective policies and a low level of implementation (Ireland, 1995; Ugar, 1995). Put this way, the issue facing governments in the area of migration policies in the mid 1990s was similar to the issue they had faced market regulation policies in the mid 1980s: there was a growing public and elite perception of regulatory failure, and the easiest way of tackling this crisis was to delegate agenda-setting to an independent agent – the Commission (Stetter, 2000; Alink *et al.*, 2001).

Second, governments were forced to respond to new voter concerns. In democratic systems the primary goal of governments is to be re-elected (Downs, 1957). In other words, a reason for governments not to delegate high-politics issues to the supranational level is that voters might be opposed to external interference in these areas. However, voters can change their minds and concede to the erosion of national sovereignty in order to secure individual and collective goals, such as personal freedom, reduced immigration or the control of crime. In the mid 1990s this is exactly what happened in the area of migration policy. For the first time a majority of Europe's voters were in favour of more cooperation at the European level to stem migration flows (Turnbull and Sandholtz, 2001; Lahav, 2004, pp. 69–112). Rather than complaining about interference from Brussels, voters recognized the ineffectiveness of national immigration policies and demanded collective action. As they shared the voters' (negative) attitude towards immigration, the political elites at both the national and European levels were eager to oblige.

With the growth in international criminal activity and the shock of the terrorist attacks in the US on 11 September 2001, voters also started to favour EU action on cross-border crime. The Eurobarometer survey in spring 2003 revealed majority support in all member states for EU policies on terrorism, human trafficking, drug trafficking, and other organized crime (Table 11.2). There was also majority support across the EU, albeit with a majority opposed in some states, for EU asylum, refugee and immigration policies. The respondents who opposed EU action in these areas either lived in countries with low levels of immigration (such as Finland) or feared that common EU policies would result in their country being subjected to a large influx of migrants from Central and Eastern Europe (such as Austria). Finally, a majority of respondents thought that domestic crime, justice and policing should be tackled at the national rather than the EU level. Not surprisingly, despite competences in the treaties on police cooperation and judicial cooperation in civil matters, EU policies on these issues were underdeveloped compared with EU migration policies and policies on judicial cooperation to fight cross-border crime.

Consequently in the Amsterdam and Nice Treaties the member state governments took a decisive step towards supranational decision-making on free movement and internal security issues by delegating agenda-setting powers to the Commission, establishing some provisions for the adoption of policies by qualified-majority voting, and granting monitoring and enforcement powers to the Commission and the ECJ. The UK and Ireland chose to opt out from these provisions because as island states they were more able to impose *de facto* controls at borders than were the continental states, and hence did not suffer the same negative externalities of the single market. However unanimity was kept as the main decision rule. This reflected the deep seated concern of most governments (including those of Germany and the UK) that in a policy area that was central to the definition of the nation-state, governments were unlikely to be able to enforce an agreement if they were outvoted (Moravcsik and Nicolaïdis, 1998, pp. 28–31; Geddes, 2000b, pp. 110–30; Givens and Luedtke, 2004). By the time of the Tampere European Council and the Nice Treaty, however, the German and British governments had chosen to support the adoption of asylum policies by a qualified-majority in the Council.

Table 11.2 *Survey on whether freedom and security policies should be decided at the national or the EU level*

	Percentage responding 'national'	Percentage responding 'EU'	Most pro-EU public (% of 'EU' respondents)	Least pro-EU public (% of 'EU' respondents)
Majority pro-EU level in all states				
Terrorism	13	85	Sweden (90)	Austria (70)
Exploiting human beings	17	80	Netherlands (86)	Austria (67)
Organized crime	25	72	Netherlands (82)	UK (52)
Drugs	29	68	Greece (77)	UK (55)
EU majority pro-EU level, but some states pronational				
Political asylum	41	54	Italy (71)	Austria (31)
Accepting refugees	42	54	Italy (68)	Finland (15)
Immigration	44	52	Italy (73)	Finland (16)
EU majority pro-national level, but some states pro-EU				
Juvenile crime	59	37	Greece (72)	UK (20)
Urban crime	64	33	Greece (70)	UK (20)
Majority pro-national level in all states				
Justice	66	31	Italy (44)	Denmark (14)
Police	71	27	Greece (38)	Finland (11)

Note: The survey question was: 'For each of the following areas do you think that decision should be made by the government, or jointly within the European Union?'

Source: *Eurobarometer*, no. 59 (Spring 2003).

In effect these governments were consciously seeking to 'Europeanize' domestic issues as a way of diffusing voters' concerns (Monar, 2001, pp. 756–8).

Bureaucrats' strategies: bureau-shaping and the control paradigm

Governments are not unitary actors, and within governments politicians and bureaucrats have different interests. Whereas politicians seek re-election, bureaucrats seek more influence over policy outcomes, for example through larger budgets (Niskanen, 1971) or greater freedom to shape their own organizational structures and policy choices (Dunleavy, 1991; see also Chapter 2). Consequently senior administrative elites in the immigration and internal security fields, national justice, interior home affairs, and customs and excise – have been eager to collaborate on the development of common policies on monitoring and controlling the movement of people and preventing cross-border crime (Bigo, 1994; Guiraudon, 2003).

The single market programme posed a major threat to the status and resources of interior and justice ministries in Europe. The removal of border controls on the movement of goods, services, capital and labour implied that fewer resources would need to be spent in interior and justice ministries. Also, without customs and excise duties, these departments would receive fewer revenues. As mentioned earlier, the statistical evidence reveals only a moderate increase in cross-border crime and the movement of persons as a result of the single market, but interior and justice ministers across the EU produced reports designed to scare politicians into dedicating resources to their ministries to fight the spectre of 'Euro-crime' (Clutterbuck, 1990; Latter, 1991; Heidensohn and Farrell, 1993).

As part of their response to these alleged threats, administrative elites in interior ministries sought to develop new networks and decision-making mechanisms at the European level. One of their motivations was the opportunity to share policy ideas with officials facing similar problems. Another motivation, was that cooperation at the European level would to some extent free them from domestic political pressures, the attention of interest groups that were opposed to restrictive migration or security policies, competition from other ministries for resources and space in the policy agenda, and parliamentary and judicial scrutiny. Virginie Guiraudon (2000) has called this 'venue shopping', whereby interior ministry officials looked for the forum that offered them the greatest freedom to devise and implement policies that best suited their collective policy interests. The *ad hoc* intergovernmental settings at the European level were perfect for this, with no official records of meetings and beyond the attention of parliaments and publics. Bigo (1994, pp. 164–5) concurs, arguing that this 'freed senior civil servants ... from national and/or political constraints which often make it difficult to deal with controversial matters which nonetheless have to be settled speedily'.

The domination of agenda-setting by interior ministry officials rather than justice ministry officials or interest groups representing migrants or business interests was one of the main reasons why the debate on migration was framed in terms of security or control rather rights or freedoms (Huysmans, 2000; Kostakopoulou, 2000). Whereas 'freedom of movement' implies a reduction of the state's role in regulating the movements of persons, 'controlled migration' implies a legitimate role for the state and state officials in monitoring the movement of persons and preventing activities that threaten state security. For example, at the domestic level most interior ministries consistently argued that social integration is best achieved through controls on immigration and asylum rather than the promotion of race relations or anti-racism policies (King, 1994; Geddes, 1995; Baldwin-Edwards, 1997). Not surprisingly, this perspective was transferred wholesale to the European level. Whereas at the domestic level, other ministries, social groups and political parties could present countervailing view, these views are not effectively represented at the European level. As a result EU immigration and asylum policies became a subset of security policies in the Trevi, Schengen and Maastricht frameworks.

Through their interactions at the European level a new policy paradigm emerged amongst interior ministry officials: 'controlling population rather than territory' (Chalmers, 1998). Traditionally the state has maintained internal security through controls on who enters its territory. In a single market with open borders this is no longer feasible. However security forces can also control populations regardless of where they reside, through information exchange on criminal activities and asylum seekers, common strategies on identity cards and police stop-and-search policies, and cooperation between civil and judicial authorities (cf. den Boer, 1994; Anderson *et al.*, 1995, pp. 131–40). These 'compensatory measures' were first discussed in the context of Trevi and Schengen and form the basis of EUROPOL. As result of this new policy idea, justice and interior ministries and securities agencies were able to maintain the levels of their funding despite the removal of border controls.

However not all bureaucratic interests have benefited from the Europeanization of control. As Bigo (1994, p. 172) argues, 'Those most favourable to Europe are inside ministerial cabinets or in the informal coordination structures between major services; their role gives them power over the services which they coordinate, and they have their own correspondents, interests, and political outlook.' Agencies that are disconnected from national security elites and are not involved in inter-agency and European-wide collaboration, such as the British Customs and Excise Department and Immigration Service, the French Gendarmerie and the Spanish Guardia Civil, tend to be opposed to common EU internal security policies. Agencies that are in favour of common policies, such as British and French drugs police, have consistently argued for cuts to be made to the budgets of anti-European agencies, which they claim do not fit in with the new security environment in Europe.

Supranational entrepreneurship: supplying credibility and accountability

The institutional outcome in the Amsterdam Treaty and the development of policies since then are also products of deliberate strategies by supranational actors, outside the control of national governments and administrative elites. As a result of the activities and policy ideas promoted by the EU institutions and non-governmental organizations, the member state governments were persuaded that replacing inter-governmental procedures with supranational mechanisms would improve the credibility and accountability of policy-making, particularly in the case of immigration and asylum policies. And once the new agenda-setting powers were delegated to the Commission, supranational agents at the European level have been eager to use them to their maximum extent.

The most influential of the supranational interests was the Commission. Under the Maastricht Treaty the Commission was virtually excluded from influencing policy-making in the justice and home affairs (JHA) field. But following the ratification of the treaty, the Commission strengthened its ability to develop JHA policy ideas, with a new division in the secretariat-general to monitor and support the third pillar, and a JHA policy portfolio with one of the commissioners (Anita Gradin). This was a long-term strategy. Despite the absence of formal agenda-setting powers, the Commission sought to develop credible policy ideas in the expectation that this would tempt the member state governments to delegate this function to the Commission in the next round of institutional reform. As a result, between 1994 and 1996 the Commission undertook a series of policy initiatives, such as 'think papers' on a variety of JHA issues, several policy proposals (for example on the issue of trafficking in persons), the funding of independent research on national immigration and social integration policies, and negotiations with the US State Department on possible US–European cooperation on international migration and crime issues (for example, on a transatlantic temporary protection regime for refugees from the former Yugoslavia). The Commission also argued in the IGC that a central reason for the lack of policy development in this area was because it did not have an agenda-setting role (European Commission, 1996b).

This strategy paid off. Seeing that the Commission had developed expertise in these areas and could present credible policy ideas, the member state governments agreed (in the Amsterdam Treaty) to share the right of initiative with the Commission. Once this power had been delegated the new directorate-general for JHA set to work on legislative proposals across the full range of policy areas covered by the fields of freedom, security and justice (Uçarer, 2001). One example of the Commission's entrepreneurship in this field was its freedom, security and justice scoreboard, which listed over 50 issues upon which the member states had promised to act (either in the treaties or in the Vienna and Tampere European Councils), and for each issue set out what action the Commission thought was needed and the timetable either the member states had alluded to or the Commission thought was necessary. This raised the profile of EU policies amongst interest groups and the media, and focused the minds of decision-makers in national ministries.

The second supranational actor with a vested interest in further policy integration in this area was the EP. Since the establishment of the Trevi and Schengen groups, the EP had been critical of the secretive nature of intergovernmental cooperation on migration and security issues. It was also critical of the Maastricht Treaty provisions, despite its new right to question the Council presidency about JHA developments. The EP argued that the decision procedures removed policy-making accountability from national parliaments without replacing it with effective powers of scrutiny for the EP (cf. Monar, 1995). In its report to the 1996 intergovernmental conference, and through the two EP representatives in the Conference Reflection Group, the EP argued that legislation in this policy domain should be adopted using the consultation procedure (European Parliament, 1995b). This was a minimalist strategy as the EP did not demand full legislative rights, simply the right to issue an opinion on policy proposals, which would give it a limited power of delay (see Chapter 3). The member state governments agreed – it seemed a small price to pay to satisfy domestic and European-level demands for greater transparency and accountability in policy-making, which the EU heads of government had established as one of the main aims of the intergovernmental conference in all policy areas.

Third, in its submission to the intergovernmental conference, the ECJ was careful not to propose any concrete measures for reform. However, the ECJ argued that there was a clear clash of jurisdictions in the Maastricht design. Under the citizenship provisions in the first pillar the ECJ had to protect the fundamental rights of EU citizens, but although the policy areas tackled under the third pillar touched on this issue, neither it nor national courts had jurisdiction over Council decisions on justice and home affairs. The ECJ consequently argued that:

> judicial protection ... especially in the context of cooperation in the field of Justice and Home Affairs, must be guaranteed and structured in such a way as to ensure consistent interpretation and application of both Community law and of the provisions adopted within the framework of such cooperation. (Ibid., p. 5)

The ECJ went on to suggest that the intergovernmental conference should determine the limits of EU action in the JHA field, and establish proper instruments and mechanisms for legal oversight of Council decisions (cf. Neuwahl, 1995). A few months later, in March 1996, the ECJ issued Opinion (2/94) on a request from the Council, arguing that Article 235 was an insufficient basis for the accession of the EU to the European Convention on Human Rights. This opinion was against the views of a number of pro-integrationist member states, such as the Benelux countries. The ECJ's mixed strategy – critical analysis accompanied by moderation – paid off in the Amsterdam Treaty, which extended the ECJ's jurisdiction to all migration and security issues.

Finally, during the intergovernmental conference a number of non-governmental organizations (NGOs) and quasi-governmental organizations lobbied for more supranational policy-making on migration and security issues (cf. Ireland, 1991; Favell, 1997b; Niessen, 2000). These included Brussels-based groups such as the European Council of Refugees and Exiles, Migrants Forum, the Churches' Commission for Migrants in Europe, Migration Policy Group, and the Starting Line Group (which brought together national NGOs to campaign for a general anti-racism clause in the EU Treaty). They also included national groups such as the Dutch Standing Committee of Experts on International Immigration, Refugee and Criminal Law, and the British Commission for Racial Equality (CRE) and the Federal Trust. Despite their differing perspectives, these groups were unanimous in their criticism of the secretive nature of intergovernmental decision-making, the lack of judicial and parliamentary control, and the subordination of migration issues to crime policies (Hix, 1995b; Federal Trust, 1996; Hix and Niessen, 1996; Meijers *et al.*, 1997; Chopin and Niessen, 1998). Their demands were particularly effective in the case of centre-left governments, which were part of the same social milieu as the leaders of these NGOs. For example, under pressure from the CRE the new UK Labour government dropped its opposition to a general anti-racism clause in the treaty and accepted the idea of the other member states integrating their immigration policies, to which Britain could then chose to opt in.

Conclusion: Skeleton of a Pan-European State

Through the development of EU policies on citizens' freedoms and security, a social contract is emerging between EU citizens and the EU-polity. Unlike a traditional state, the EU does not have the exclusive right to decide who can be an EU citizen. However with the completion of the single market, the EU institutions have established and are responsible for governing a set of common economic rights for nationals of the member states, based on the freedom to move between countries, seek employment, trade, and provide and consume services. Furthermore, with the establishment of EU citizenship in the Maastricht Treaty and the extension of these provisions in the Amsterdam Treaty, the member states are no longer independent from the EU polity in determining who may receive social, civil and political rights in the domestic system.

Also unlike a traditional state, the EU does not have a legitimate monopoly on the use of force to guarantee, protect and secure individual and collective rights. However, through the development of EU competences on immigration and asylum and on police and judicial cooperation, the member state governments have chosen to cooperate in deciding how domestic security forces operate to secure these goals. Furthermore, through the delegation of agenda-setting powers to the Commission, the right of consultation and co-decision for the EP and the right of judicial review by the ECJ, the Amsterdam and Nice Treaties established a new policy regime in which the EU institutions have a say in fighting cross-border crime and directing those domestic security agencies which make asylum and immigration decisions.

This novel development is the result of a number of factors. The growth of multiethnic societies in Europe, the increase in global migration, the globalization of capital, and the single market programme, all undermine not only the ability of member state governments to pursue independent migration and policing policies, but also the administrative capacity and funding of bureaucrats in justice and interior ministries. In response the governments and administrative elites established intergovernmental mechanisms to facilitate information sharing and the development of collective migration and security strategies – first through mechanisms outside the EU framework (such as the Trevi group and the Schengen Accord) and then in the third pillar of the EU (in the Maastricht Treaty).

However this does not explain why member state governments agreed in the Amsterdam Treaty to inject a major dose of supranational agenda-setting, scrutiny, adoption and enforcement into this policy area, and why a significant number of legislative decisions were passed under these new procedures. The explanation lies in a common response by the governments to several forces. First, growing demand by the European electorates for action to fight cross-border crime and control immigration gave the governments a window of opportunity to adopt common policies in a traditional area of high politics. Second, the establishment of policy expertise by the Commission gave the governments the opportunity to delegate agenda-setting and enforcement powers to this independent and credible institution – and in so doing to overcome policy failure in this area. Finally, NGOs, the EP and the ECJ lobbied the governments to address the transparency and accountability of decision-making, and eagerly supported the Commission's legislative proposals under the new decision-making rules.

Chapter 12

Foreign Policies

Theories of International Relations and Political Economy
External Economic Policies: Free Trade, Not 'Fortress Europe'
External political relations: an EU foreign policy
Explaining the Foreign Policies of the EU
Conclusion: a 'Soft Superpower'?

The EU pursues two main types of policy towards the rest of the world: economic policy, through trade agreements and development and humanitarian aid; and foreign and security policy, through the Common Foreign and Security Policy (CFSP) and the European Security and Defence Policy (ESDP). This chapter seeks to understand and explain why the EU is able to act with a single voice on the global stage on some issues but not others. To aid this task we shall first consider some theoretical issues in the fields of international relations and international political economy.

Theories of International Relations and Political Economy

There are three dominant theoretical frameworks in the contemporary field of international relations: realism, liberalism and constructivism (cf. Woods, 1996).

Realism views international relations as a continuous struggle for power and domination between states in a system of anarchy – what Bismarck called Realpolitik (Morgenthau, 1948, Waltz, 2000). In the contemporary neorealist version, this approach has three core assumptions:

- States are unitary actors, and the political elite and the mass public have a single conception of the national interest.
- This interest is primarily defined in geopolitical/security terms, such as the territorial integrity of the state and the structure of the political order, rather than in economic terms.
- The state acts upon this interest in a rational manner by seeking to maximize its security given the relative balance of power between states (Waltz, 1979; Keohane, 1986).

Realists consequently argue that because states have stable territorial and sociopolitical structures, their geopolitical and security preferences are also stable. As a result, each of the rival actors in the international system can predict how the others are likely to behave. Moreover, because security interests are perceived to be in conflict rather than complementary, interstate politics tends to be a zero-sum game – that is, if one state wins, another must lose. Therefore cooperation between states is unlikely as there is little opportunity for the provision of a common public good, and there are no credible enforcing agents in a system of anarchy. Hence once created, international institutions (such as the United Nations and the EU) are instruments of states' preferences and powers, rather than constraints on their powers.

Liberalism, on the other hand, sees international relations as driven by global economic interdependence. This approach starts from a different set of assumptions about state preferences and behaviour:

- States are not unitary actors, as state preferences are formed through competition between domestic interests and ideologies, where social groups seek to capture the state to promote their private interests ('rent seeking') and elites seek to protect their positions of power by trading-off the international and domestic systems in a two-level game (Evans *et al.*, 1993; Milner, 1997).
- In this competition between societal actors and elites, individual preferences are driven by economic interests rather than geopolitical concerns (Rosecrance, 1986).
- In the international system state officials act rationally to pursue their economic preferences, but these preferences are shaped by developments in other systems (interdependence) and the behaviour of international and supranational institutions (Keohane and Nye, 1989).

As a result, in contrast to realists, liberals predict that states' preferences are not stable. States' interests in the international system change as a result of two factors (Frieden, 1991; Moravcsik, 1997). First, preferences change if different societal actors win in domestic competition, for example when different political parties are elected. Second, preferences change when individuals' economic interests and opportunities are redefined in the face of changes in the global system.

Liberals also predict more interstate cooperation and international institution formation than do realists. Because states' interests are defined economically and economic interdependence increases with globalization, they have an incentive to create institutions to help solve collective action problems, for example to coordinate product standards or enforce international trade rules (Krasner, 1983; Keohane, 1984; Greico, 1990). This results in international regimes (rather than anarchy) and the delegation of enforcement functions to international institutions such as the World Trade Organization.

The realist–liberal divide has specific application in the field of international political economy (cf. Frieden and Lake, 1995). In global economic relations, realists assert the primacy of politics over economics. International economic policies are pursued to achieve geopolitical goals, such as state security and political hegemony. Consequently realists assume that states will sacrifice economic gain to strengthen their position in the global balance of power. For example trade protection often reduces a state's long-term welfare, but may increase its leverage in the international system. Although free trade agreements do emerge, realists consider that this is usually a result of 'hegemonic stability', in which a single dominant actor has the power to construct an economic regime to suit its own political interests at the expense of those of its partners.

Liberals, on the other hand, assert the primacy of economics and societal economic interests over politics and power relations. Most liberals accept the assumption of neoclassical economics that the free market is the most efficient way of allocating resources. For example, rather than competing in the production of the same goods, welfare will be maximized if states specialize in the production of goods in which they have a comparative advantage. Consequently liberals argue that in a world where individual economic interests drive politics, states should recognize the potential 'gains from trade', and pursue free trade rather than protectionist policies. Nevertheless liberals do accept that government is important for the provision of public goods – goods and services that would not be supplied in sufficient quantity by the market (see Chapter 8). As a result global governance institutions are necessary to provide the necessary conditions for free trade and competitive global markets, such as stable property rights and rules against protectionism and unfair competition.

Liberals also think that domestic government institutions produce particular external economic policy outcomes. For example free trade policies historically developed as a result of trade policies being locked into a constitution (as in the case of the interstate commerce clause in the US constitutions) or the establishment of a parliamentary majority in favour of trade liberalization (as in the battle over the Corn Laws in the mid nineteenth century in Britain – McGillivray *et al.*, 2001). Similarly, by forcing leaders to promote the interests of the median voter rather than a particular special interest, democratic regimes tend to promote free trade policies and the enforcement of international trade agreements (Mansfield *et al.*, 2002).

Finally, constructivism, in contrast to the rationalist/utilitarian foundations of both neorealism and liberalism, sees international relations as dominated by cultural, ideological and ideational forces. Despite the fact that the constructivist research programme is rather heteroge-neous, most scholars in this approach share three main assumptions about the social construction of international politics (see especially Ruggie, 1998a):

- The preferences of actors cannot be explained without recourse to the ideological and/or cultural norms behind their positions – as Ruggie (1998b, p. 863) puts it: '*American* hegemony was every bit as important as American *hegemony* in shaping the postwar order' (cf. Finnemore, 1996).
- Actors are not strictly 'rational', in the narrow instrumentalist sense of the term used by realists or liberals, as they are bound by psy-chological or normative constraints and are often forced to take symbolic or historically determined actions (cf. Hill, 2003, pp. 98–126).
- The preferences and behaviour of actors evolve as a result of social interaction and socialization – as opposed to the realist view that preferences are fixed, and the liberal view that preferences change instrumentally (Finnemore and Sikkink, 1998; Risse *et al.*, 1999).

As a result, constructivists argue that international institutions can have profound and unexpected consequences. Actors are forced to adapt their preferences and behaviour to the 'constitutive' norms of institutional organizations and society, such as the human rights clauses of the United Nations charter. International norms can also be constructed and promoted by non-state actors (for example non-gov-ernmental organizations) as well as by states (Keck and Sikkink, 1998). Hence like liberals, constructivists do not think that states are the only actors in international politics. Furthermore, through regular interac-tions in international institutions, the preferences of foreign policy elites and the normative justifications for their actions are likely to converge. The result, which is not dissimilar from the early neofunc-tionalist view of European integration (see Chapter 1), is that interna-tional institutions create new identities amongst elites, which then gradually percolate down into society.

Obviously these three approaches predict different things about the EU's foreign policies. From the neorealist perspective, because the EU is not a state it will not have a clear and indivisible national interest. Instead EU foreign policies will be dominated by the geopolitical and security concerns of the member states. From a liberal perspective, in contrast, the battle between the member states will be between rival economic interests rather than geopolitical interests. While liberal theory predicts that EU external economic policies will determine how the EU acts in foreign and security policies, realist theory predicts the opposite. Also, while realists expect member states' foreign policy preferences to be stable, liberals and constructivists expect them to change. For liberals, states' policies will change as the power of domestic economic interests changes. But for constructivists, EU diplomats' and negotiators' preferences will change as a result of their interaction in and adaptation to the institutional and normative environment of EU foreign policy-making. Finally, whereas realists predict that the institutional rules of EU foreign policies will be largely irrelevant, liberals and constructivists both think that institutions matter: liberals because the allocation of agenda-setting and decision-making powers determines policy outcomes; and constructivists because the design of the rules determines the values and identities that emerge.

External Economic Policies: Free Trade, Not 'Fortress Europe'

The EU has developed common external economic policies in parallel to the development of internal economic integration. Part of this has been out of the necessity to preserve the coherence of the single market. However it has also been out of the choice to promote EU economic interests in the global economy. The result is three types of external economic policy:

- A single set of rules on the importation of goods.
- Bilateral and multilateral trade agreements between the EU and other states or blocs.
- Trade, aid and cooperation policies with developing countries.

Before discussing these policies it is important to understand the pattern of EU trade.

The pattern of EU trade

With a population of over 450 million the EU is the world's largest market. Even before the 2004 enlargement, the EU of 15 member states (EU15) and the US were easily the two largest traders in the world. In 2002, total exports to and imports from the EU15 (excluding trade between the EU member states) accounted for approximately 18 per cent of total world trade, whereas exports to and imports from the US accounted for 20 per cent, to/from Japan for 7 per cent and to/from China for 6 per cent (World Trade Organization, 2003). Moreover since the 1960s EU external trade has grown faster than EU GDP, with the result that in 2002 external trade contributed 21 per cent of the total GDP of the 15 member states, compared with 18 per cent of US GDP.

As Table 12.1 shows, the US is the EU's largest trading partner, accounting for almost 20 per cent of total EU trade (equally about 20 per cent of US trade is with the EU). While a large proportion of the rest of the EU's trade is with other developed countries, such as Japan and the members of the European Free Trade Area (EFTA), an increasing proportion is with emerging economies: China and Russia are now the EU's fourth and fifth largest trading partners respectively; and 8 per cent of EU trade is with the 'dynamic Asian economies' (Hong Kong, South Korea, Malaysia, Singapore, Thailand and Taiwan). Until the mid 1990s the EU ran a small trade deficit (with imports exceeding exports) with the rest of the world, after which it managed a modest surplus. In contrast the US has experienced a growing trade deficit since the early 1990s.

In terms of the composition of EU trade, the bulk is intra-industry trade (in which the same products are imported as exported) in the manufacturing sector, for example machinery, chemicals and other manufacturing goods. Although services have been excluded from the statistics on commodities trade in Table 12.1, EU trade in services such as financial services, tourism and transport has risen to almost one third of total EU trade in commodities. In terms of the trade balance by sector, like other advanced industrial economies the EU is a net importer of raw materials for manufacturing (such as minerals and fuels, and crude materials, oils and fats) and a net exporter of finished products, although the trade surplus in some manufacturing sectors (for example steel and textiles) has declined since the 1980s. As a result of the CAP the EU is almost self-sufficient in agricultural products, and consequently exports almost as large a volume of food products, beverages and tobacco as it imports.

Of course the overall trade figures for the EU conceal significant differences between the member states. For example in terms of the geographic orientation of trade, the UK, Ireland and the Netherlands export more to the US than the EU average. A similar situation exists between Germany and Austria and Central and Eastern Europe (prior to EU enlargement), and between the UK, France and Spain and the developing world. In terms of the product orientation of trade, the structure of trade for Portugal and Greece is similar to developing countries, whereas Germany accounts for almost 30 per cent of EU exports of manufactured goods, and the UK is the main exporter of financial services.

The Common Commercial Policy

Articles 131–4 of the EU treaty set out that the EU has a single external trade policy, known as the Common Commercial Policy (CCP). The CCP has an underlying liberal objective: to promote 'the

Table 12.1   *External trade of the EU*

	Imports to EU15, 2003 (€bn)	Exports from EU15, 2003 (€bn)	Proportion of total external EU15 trade, 2003 (%)	Trade balance (exports–imports), 2003 (€bn)
With individual states (top 10 states)				
US	151.2	220.5	19.0	+69.3
Switzerland	56.0	68.4	6.3	+12.5
Japan	66.8	40.1	5.4	−26.7
China	75.9	30.1	5.4	−45.8
Russia	51.8	33.1	4.3	−18.8
Norway	48.7	25.8	3.8	−22.9
Poland	31.3	38.3	3.6	+7.0
Czech Republic	29.7	30.2	3.1	+0.5
Hungary	26.0	26.1	2.7	+0.1
Turkey	24.0	28.1	2.7	+4.2
With other trading blocs				
European Free Trade Association (EFTA)	107.2	96.5	10.4	−10.7
Dynamic Asian economies (DAEs)	91.0	73.2	8.4	−17.8
Organization of Petroleum Exporting Countries (OPEC)	71.3	66.5	7.0	−4.8
African, Caribbean and Pacific countries (ACP)	43.3	40.3	4.3	−3.0
By commodity				
Machinery and equipment	358.4	445.0	41.0	+86.5
Other manufactured goods	273.2	259.0	27.1	−14.2
Chemicals	80.5	154.4	12.0	+73.9
Minerals and fuels	144.7	26.3	8.7	−118.4
Crude materials, oils and fats	72.7	37.6	5.6	−35.2
Food products, beverages and tobacco	58.1	50.7	5.6	−7.4
Total external EU trade	987.7	972.9	100.0	−14.8

Notes: The members of EFTA are Switzerland, Iceland, Liechtenstein and Norway, the DAEs are Hong Kong, South Korea, Malaysia, Singapore, Thailand and Taiwan.

Source: Eurostat.

harmonious development of world trade, the progressive abolition of restrictions on international trade and the lowering of customs barriers' (Article 131). Nonetheless the CCP operates through several protectionist policy instruments, the four main ones being as follows:

- *The Common External Tariff.* With the establishment of the common market, the EU states agreed to apply the same tariffs on goods entering their country from any state outside the EU. As part of the multilateral General Agreement on Tariffs and Trade, in 2000 the EU reduced tariffs by approximately one-third, to an average of 18 percent on agricultural goods and zero percent on many manufactured goods.
- *Import quotas.* Because of the single market the member states were obliged to replace their national quotas with EU-wide restrictions on the importation of certain goods (as monitoring national quotas is impossible without border controls on goods). These quotas currently apply to a wide variety of products, including textiles, agricultural products, iron and steel, but as a result of the multilateral multifibre agreement, by 2005 quotas will be phased out on textiles and clothing.
- *Anti-dumping measures.* The Commission has the power to impose import tariffs and minimum price levels if exporters to the EU sell at discriminatory prices that are likely to harm domestic producers. According to the World Trade Organization, the EU is the most frequent user of anti-dumping measures, issuing about 150 measures per year.
- *Voluntary Export Restraints (VERs).* VERs are agreements between an exporter state and an importer state, whereby the exporter agrees to limit the volume of goods consigned to the importer. VERs usually result from political pressure, such as the threat of antidumping action by an importer. However they can also be established to protect the interests of both exporters and import-competing domestic producers (by allowing an increase in price), at the expense of consumers in the importing country.

In addition to these instruments, the EU uses several minor measures to restrict free trade: (1) export promotion measures, where the Commission organizes EU trade fairs and coordinates national initiatives; (2) trade sanctions, which are usually imposed for political reasons and are based on decisions by the UN Security Council; (3) countervailing duties, which the EU imposes if there is evidence of export subsidies in third countries; (4) safeguard clauses, which allow the members of the WTO to suspend normal rules to protect a vital interest; and (5) rules of origin, which determine the proportion of a product that must be added locally for a product to qualify as originating from the EU or from a state covered by a preferential trade agreement.

Under the decision-making rules of the CCP, only the Commission has a monopoly of legislative initiative, and is also responsible for managing the execution of the CCP. The Commission negotiates all external trade agreements related to goods and in areas where the EU has competence, on behalf of the Council (rather like the US president's 'fast track' mandate from the US Congress). Moreover, the Commission has the power of executive decree: to adopt anti-dumping measures, countervailing duties and other import restrictions, which have to be reviewed by the Council after a set time.

The Council, on the other hand, is the main legislative body and acts by a qualified-majority to issue negotiating mandates to the Commission or approve agreements negotiated by the Commission (except for the adoption of association agreements, which require unanimity). The Council scrutinizes legislative initiatives and oversees the Commission's actions in a special committee of COREPER, which is known as the Article 133 Committee and is composed of senior national trade officials.

The EP has no formal role in the day-to-day adoption of legislation under the CCP. But the assent of the EP (by a simple majority) is required for the adoption of multilateral or bilateral trade agreements (Article 300), or if a trade agreement necessitates the amendment of EU legislation adopted by the co-decision procedure. Also, the EP's External Economic Relations Committee holds hearings of Commission officials, receives regular reports from the Commission and the Council, and adopts resolutions that signal the EP's position on trade issues.

Multilateral trade agreements: GATT and the WTO

The EU has been one of the key players in the negotiation and establishment of the multilateral global trading regime that has gradually led to the liberalization of world trade. The General Agreement on Tariffs and Trade (GATT) was first agreed in 1948 and since the Dillon Round in 1960–62 the EU has attempted to coordinate a common stance in successive negotiations to reform the GATT. With the Commission as the EU's negotiator, the EU acted with a single voice in each of the subsequent negotiations: the Kennedy Round in 1964–67, the Tokyo Round in 1973–79, the Uruguay Round in 1986–94, and the Doha Round from 2001 to onwards. The Uruguay Round culminated with the establishment of the World Trade Organization (WTO), based in Geneva.

The Uruguay Round covered a number of sensitive areas for the EU, including services, intellectual property, agriculture and textiles. The

EU was also a central cause of the negotiations continuing beyond the 1990 deadline: the problem was a protracted disagreement between the EU, the US and the Cairns Group (a group of states in favour of agricultural free trade, led by Australia) over the liberalization of trade in agricultural products, which included limits on domestic export subsidies. Without the support of the EU, the largest trade bloc, the WTO could not function. With this powerful veto threat, the EU was able to extract some important concessions from the US in the area of farming subsidies, in return for a promise of a modest reform of the CAP (see Chapter 9).

Nevertheless, since the establishment of the WTO the EU has been one of its strongest defenders. Successive EU trade commissioners have argued to their colleagues in the Commission and to the member state governments that because the EU is the largest trader it has the most to gain from the liberalization of world trade. Moreover if the EU does not abide by the WTO rules there will be little incentive for the US to do the same. This has been a growing concern for the EU, as the US has progressively become isolationist on trade policy issues since the mid 1990s. The US still supports multilateral trade bargaining, and repeatedly criticizes the EU for various anti-free-trade policies, such as export subsidies on agricultural products under the CAP. However the Bush administration has been more keen than most recent US governments to protect particular US industrial sectors from external competition (for example agriculture and steel). Moreover when the WTO has ruled against US protectionist measures and authorized the EU to introduce tariffs on US goods as compensation, US trade negotiators have deliberately challenged other EU policies before the WTO to strengthen their hand in bilateral EU–US negotiations.

One prominent example of this sort of game between the US, the EU and the WTO is the story of the US Foreign Sales Corporation (FSC) scheme. In November 1997 the EU challenged the legality of the FSC before the WTO. The Disputes Settlement Body and the Appellate Body of the WTO ruled that the FSC constituted an illegal export subsidy and gave the US until 1 November 2000 to end the scheme. On 15 November 2000 President Clinton signed the Extra Territorial Income Act (ETI) to replace the FSC. But in January 2002, the WTO ruled that the ETI did not modify the substance of the export subsidy scheme and was therefore in breach of WTO rules. Then in May 2003 the WTO endorsed the EU's request to introduce tariffs against the US to the value of US$4 billion, which was roughly equal to the annual subsidy under the FSC–ETI scheme. The EU delayed the introduction of the countermeasures in the hope of resolving the dispute, but having failed to reach an agreement, on 1 March 2004 it imposed an additional customs duty of 5 per cent on a list of US products, to increase by 1 per cent per month to a maximum of 17 per cent. The products covered by the tariff were strategically chosen by the EU to target industrial sectors in pivotal electoral constituencies, thus maximizing the pressure on the US government. In June 2004 the US Congress passed an act that finally repealed the FSC–ETI.

While the EU was able to use its trade muscle to force the US to abide by the multilateral trade rules, the dispute provoked the US into challenging EU rules in a number of areas, such as on the permitted percentage of genetically modified organisms (GMOs) in foodstuffs and the geographical origin of foodstuffs. It is not clear whether the EU is in breach of the WTO rules in either of these areas. However, these US actions signalled the fact that the US does not like to be defeated by the EU while the EU is equally as willing as the US to protect certain industrial sectors (namely agriculture) and to use consumer preferences (on GMOs for example) as non-tariff barriers against free trade with the US. Fearing US retaliation, or that the US might turn against the multilateral trading system, when the WTO has looked set to rule against the EU on a high-profile issue the Commission has generally urged the Council to reform the offending policy or law before the WTO has a chance to act.

Bilateral preferential trade agreements

The EU has many different types of preferential trade agreements with a wide range of countries and regions of the world. In terms of the degree of access to the single market granted by these agreements, the hierarchy is as follows (with the most privileged at the top):

- The European Economic Area (EEA) with Norway, Iceland and Liechtenstein.
- Europe Agreements with the Central and Eastern European states that subsequently joined the EU or will join soon (Bulgaria and Romania).
- Stabilization and Association Agreements with Croatia and the Former Yugoslav Republic of Macedonia.
- Free trade agreements with Switzerland, Turkey, Israel, Egypt, Jordan, Morocco, Tunisia, Algeria, Lebanon and Syria.
- Partnership Agreements with 78 African, Caribbean and Pacific former colonies of European Countries (see below).
- The Generalized System of Preferences, which gives privileged access to the single market for certain products from 145 developing countries.
- Mutual recognition agreements with the US and Canada.
- Partnership and Cooperation Agreements with the 10 members of the Commonwealth of Independent States.
- Inter-Regional Association Agreements with the Andean Pact,

Mercosur, the Central American Customs Union, the Gulf Cooperation Council and the Association of Southeast Asian Nations.
- A variety of trade agreements with other countries, including China, Australia, New Zealand, South Africa, Argentina, Brazil, India, Pakistan, Mexico, and South Korea.

The different degrees of access to the single market provided by these agreements reflect the political priorities of the EU. For example the EEA allows states that would be eligible to join the EU but have chosen to remain outside to be part of the EU single market – a similar relationship to that between a 'commonwealth' of the US (such as Puerto Rico) and the US market. The Europe Agreements were tailored for those Central and Eastern European states which were in the process of negotiating membership of the EU. The Commission has argued that the agreements with the US and Canada for the 'mutual recognition' of product standards in a number of product areas (based on the same principles as in the EU single market) could be the basis for a general free trade agreement between the EU and the North American Free Trade Area (NAFTA). Lower down in the hierarchy of access are the general members of the WTO (such as Japan), and at the bottom are non-members of the WTO (for example Iran).

Development policies: aid and trade in 'everything but arms'

The EU uses its external economic policies to promote political and economic progress in the developing world. All the member states are also members of the Organisation for Economic Cooperation and Development's (OECD) Development Assistance Committee (DAC), which coordinates national aid and development policies. The member states have delegated responsibility to the Commission to participate in the activities of the DAC and coordinate the positions of the EU states in this committee. Together the member states provide just over 50 per cent of all global development aid, compared with 22 per cent by the US and 17 per cent by Japan. This amounts to an average of 0.4 per cent of EU GDP, with Denmark and Sweden being the highest donors (around 1 per cent). In addition approximately 3 per cent of the EU budget is spent on development assistance.

The EU's main development activity is the agreement between the EU and the former colonies of EU member states in Africa, the Caribbean and the Pacific – the so-called ACP countries (Holland, 2002, pp. 196–219). The first agreement between the EU and the ACP states was the Lomé Convention, signed in 1975; the most recent was the ACP–EU Partnership Agreement, which was signed in June 2000 in Cotonou (Benin) and expires in 2020. The agreement involves 78 countries (48 in Africa, 15 in the Caribbean and 15 in the Pacific), including 41 of the 49 least developed countries in the world. It combines preferential trade with grants and loans (worth €862 million in the 2001–3 period).

In addition to development assistance, the EU has an active humanitarian aid policy. This policy is coordinated by the European Community Humanitarian Aid Office (ECHO) of the Commission, established in 1992. ECHO manages three different types of humanitarian aid: emergency aid, food aid and refugee aid. The amount it spends on humanitarian aid is much smaller than the amount the EU spends on development assistance. For example the total budget of ECHO in 2004 (excluding funds earmarked for unforeseen emergences) was €377 million, of which €70 million was to be spent in central Africa, €42 million in Afghanistan and €21 in Iraq.

The EU also uses its trade policies to promote economic development. The most prominent example of this is the so-called 'Everything But Arms' initiative. In February 2001 the Council adopted a regulation granting tariff-free access to the EU for imports of all products from the 49 least developed countries (as defined by the United Nations) without any quantitative restrictions (apart from arms and munitions) for an unlimited period of time. Duties on bananas, rice and sugar were not removed immediately, but will be removed in January 2006, July 2009 and September 2009 respectively. This initiative means that the EU provides more open access to its market for products from the poorest states than does any other developed state or group of states. However the Everything But Arms programme can also be interpreted as a strategic decision by the EU – in the middle of the latest round of trade liberalization negotiations – to deflect criticism by the poorest states of the EU's agricultural export subsidies under the CAP.

In sum, the EU's external economic policies are inconsistent. A central aim of the single market, the CCP and some of the internal policies (most notably the CAP) is to favour domestic producers over producers in third countries. Also, through preferential trade agreements the EU has consciously tried to distort international trade to favour certain exporters, such as former colonies and prospective member states. However the assertion that the EU is a 'fortress Europe', which was a widespread view outside the EU in the 1980s (cf. Schuknecht, 1992), is not wholly true. The EU imports and exports more goods and services than any other market in the world. In most sectors the import duties are low relative to some of the EU's competitors, and the EU is also an active promoter of the liberalization of free trade through its activities in the successive GATT negotiations, the WTO and the EU's various bilateral free trade agreements.

Nevertheless, a major blight on the EU's claim to promote global free trade is the subsidy of agricultural exports under the CAP (see Chapter 9). These subsidies suppress global market prices in numerous agricultural products, and have a disproportionate impact on the economies of the world's poorest countries. Many poor countries would have a comparative advantage in the global economy in one or several agricultural products, but are not able to sustain production of these products at the current global market prices. However there is hope. Given a choice between the successful conclusion of the Doha Round of world trade negotiations and reform of the CAP, the EU is likely to be able to force the French government to accept reform of the CAP, as happened at the end of the Uruguay Round. Hence when push comes to shove, the EU's instinct is for free trade.

External Political Relations: Towards an EU Foreign Policy

The Maastricht Treaty introduced a new aim for the EU:

> to assert its identity on the international scene, in particular through the implementation of a common foreign and security policy including the eventual framing of a common defence policy, which might in time lead to a common defence (Article 2).

However a common European foreign, security and defence policy has been considerably more difficult to achieve than a common external economic policy.

Development of foreign policy cooperation and decision-making

The West European Union (WEU) was set up in 1948 between the European members of the North Atlantic Treaty Organization (NATO), including the UK, which was not a signatory of the Treaty of Rome. The six founding states subsequently agreed a plan for a European Defence Community (EDC) in 1952. However the French National Assembly rejected the latter because of concerns about national sovereignty.

It was not until the attempt to relaunch European integration at the Hague Summit in 1969 that the EC member states sought to add a political dimension to the process of economic integration. The Hague Summit set up European Political Cooperation (EPC) outside the legal structure of the EC treaties. EPC enabled EC foreign ministers and heads of government to debate broader political and security issues in the General Affairs Council, alongside their regular meetings in the

European Council. The day-to-day business of EPC was managed by a network of committees composed of national bureaucrats and headed by 'political directors' – senior officials from the member states' foreign ministries.

EPC actions were taken through 'common positions' of the EC foreign ministers or heads of government. These were not binding, but the governments agreed that they would try not to undertake national actions that would contradict a common position. In 1981, in the London Report, the governments strengthened this structure by providing a new role for the rotating presidency of the Council, formalizing a 'troika' system (of the previous, current and next presidencies of the Council), establishing a consultation role for the Commission, and allowing common positions to be adopted in a number of new areas (such as economic and trade sanctions).

The institutionalization of foreign policy cooperation was further enhanced when EPC was brought into the EC treaty framework in the 1987 Single European Act (SEA). While EPC remained separate from the institutions and policies of the EC, linking it to the treaty framework provided a legal framework for EPC actions, formalized the relationship between EPC and the General Affairs Council, and gave more freedom to the EP to scrutinize the actions of national officials and foreign ministers. Also the member states introduced a new decision-making norm for foreign policy: that decisions should be by consensus, and that if a consensus could be reached, governments in the minority should abstain rather than veto an agreement. This became known as 'constructive abstention' and has remained a central decision-making norm in the area of foreign policy cooperation.

However, at the beginning of the 1990s foreign and security policy issues were pushed to the top of the agenda with the revolutions in Central and Eastern Europe, the collapse of the Soviet empire and the sudden end of the Cold War. The inadequacy of the EPC structure, even within the SEA framework, was further highlighted by the outbreak of the Gulf crisis in August 1990 and the civil war in Yugoslavia in June 1991. In response Europe's leaders agreed in June 1990 that an intergovernmental conference (IGC) on political union should be convened in parallel to the one preparing institutional reforms for economic and monetary union. The political union IGC, which concluded in December 1991 with the Maastricht Treaty, transformed EPC into the Common Foreign and Security Policy (CFSP): the so-called 'second pillar' of the EU. The Maastricht Treaty set out five CFSP objectives:

- To strengthen the common values, fundamental interests and independence of the EU.
- To strengthen the security of the EU and its member states in all ways.

- To preserve peace and strengthen international security, in accordance with the principles of the United Nations Charter.
- To promote international cooperation.
- To develop and consolidate democracy and the rule of law, including human rights.

To achieve these goals the decision-making procedures and instruments of foreign policy cooperation were reformed. Foreign policy issues became a normal part of Council business: the EPC meetings of foreign ministers were subsumed within the General Affairs Council; the Political Committee (of the political directors) became part of the Committee of Permanent Representatives (COREPER); and the EPC secretariat joined the Council secretariat. The Commission became fully associated with the work carried out under the CFSP. The Commission was not granted a formal right of initiative, but was made responsible for implementing some of the Council's foreign policy decisions (for example if a foreign policy decision has implications for the EU budget) and was allowed to generate policy ideas. The Commission consequently created a new Directorate-General for External Political Affairs to manage these responsibilities.

The EP was not given a role in CFSP decision-making, but the presidency of the Council is required to consult the EP on the main aspects of the CFSP to ensure that the EP's views are taken into account, and to answer all EP questions relating to the CFSP. In addition the EP's Committee on Foreign Affairs, Security and Defence Policy set up special colloquia four times a year with the chairman of the Political Committee (the political director from the member state holding the Council presidency).

The Maastricht Treaty also established two CFSP policy instruments:

- *Common positions*: these are adopted in the Council by unanimity (but with the informal constructive abstention rule applying) and require the member states to implement national policies that comply with the position defined by the EU on a particular issue, for example in international organizations (such as the UN Security Council). However there are no legal sanctions for failing to comply with common positions.
- *Joint actions*: these are operating actions to implement common positions, are adopted by the Council after the European Council has agreed that a matter should be the subject of a joint action, and may be adopted by a qualified-majority (following a decision by unanimity that a qualified-majority can be used). This was the first time that a treaty provided for the use of qualified-majority voting in the foreign policy field. Also, joint actions are more binding than common positions. As with common positions, the member states

are required to change their policies in accordance with a joint action, but under joint actions they must also inform and consult the Council on how joint actions have been implemented. If a member state is unable or unwilling to implement a joint action, it must justify its position to the other member states.

In addition the Maastricht Treaty brought the issue of defence policy into the EU framework for the first time. Here there was a compromise between the 'Atlanticists', who favoured strong ties with the US (for example the UK and the Netherlands), the 'Europeanists', who favoured a European defence policy independent of NATO (mainly France), and the neutral member states (Ireland at that time). The treaty recognized the West European Union as 'an integral part of the development of the EU' and provided for the foreign and defence ministers of the WEU member states to discuss defence issues within the framework of the EU Council. But to address the fears of the Atlanticists the treaty asserted that the aim was to 'strengthen the European pillar of the Atlantic Alliance'.

Having accepted this bargain, the EU heads of government decided that the reform of the CFSP should be a central issue for the 1996–97 IGC. The resulting Amsterdam Treaty made seven significant changes:

- *Common strategies.* A new foreign policy instrument was established: the 'common strategy', whereby the European Council sets out a particular issue's objectives, duration and means, to be made available by the EU and the member states. These goals are then implemented through common positions, joint actions (in the CFSP) or legislation (in other EU policies). The intention is to give a clearer focus to EU foreign policy, and to combine all the external policies of the EU into a single framework.
- *Distinction between common positions and joint actions.* Joint actions are supposed to be used when specific operational action is required, while common positions are meant for less clearly definable situations 'of a geographic or thematic nature' (Article 15).
- *Constructive abstention.* The use of 'constructive abstention' was formalized in the treaty: all CFSP decisions are taken by unanimity, but abstentions do not count as votes against. Also, to encourage member state governments to abstain rather than veto, governments are allowed to explain an abstention in a formal declaration, and governments that abstain are not bound to participate in the implementation of a decision, although they must still refrain from taking an action directly contrary to the decision.
- *Qualified-majority voting.* The Treaty formalized the use of qualified-majority voting in two areas: for common positions or joint actions to implement a common strategy adopted (by unanimity) in

the European Council; and for any decisions to implement a joint action or common position already adopted by the Council. However if a member state objects to the use qualified-majority voting for 'important and stated reasons of national policy', it can request that the matter be referred to the European Council for a decision by unanimity.

- *High representative for the CFSP ('Mr/Ms CFSP').* The treaty established a new post: high representative for the CFSP, fused with the office of the secretary-general of the Council. The treaty prescribes that the high representative will 'assist the Council in matters coming within the scope of the CFSP, in particular through contributing to the formulation, preparation and implementation of policy decisions, and, when appropriate and acting on behalf of the Council at the request of the Presidency, through conducting political dialogue with third countries'. A new Troika was also established between the high representative for the CFSP, the commissioner for external relations, and the foreign minister of the member state holding the Council presidency.

- *Enhanced strategic planning.* A new planning and early-warning unit, the Policy Unit, was established in the secretariat-general of the Council (under the direction of the high representative for the CFSP), and the Council presidency was granted several new powers: to convene an extraordinary Council meeting with 48 hours' notice (or shorter in an emergency); the possibility of being mandated to negotiate on behalf of the EU in international negotiations; and enhanced responsibility for ensuring the implementation of EU actions.

- *European Security and Defence Policy (ESDP).* The Amsterdam Treaty strengthened defence policy cooperation, by granting the European Council the competence to elaborate and implement common defence policies, particularly with regard to armaments. However, the treaty explicitly stated that these policies must not jeopardize NATO, and it granted the right to remain neutral, as demanded by Sweden, Austria, Finland and Ireland. However no decision was taken as to what to do with the WEU once the WEU Treaty expired in 1998.

Since the Amsterdam Treaty entered into force in May 1999 the EU has been very active in the area of foreign policy. Indeed the General Affairs Council has become so dominated by foreign policy business that it rarely has time to resolve disputes in other policy areas, which was its original purpose at the pinnacle of the Council hierarchy (see Chapter 2). The European Council agreed three common strategies in quick succession: on Russia in June 1999, Ukraine in December 1999, and the Mediterranean in June 2000. However frustration with the vagueness of common strategies has meant that no new common strategies have been adopted since 2000.

Nevertheless the post of high representative has generally been considered to be a success. The first holder of the post, Javier Solana, a former Spanish foreign minister, quickly established a high profile on the international stage. He played an active part in the Middle East peace process and in the resolution of the conflict in former Yugoslavia. He also drafted and negotiated a 'European Security Strategy', which was unanimously approved by the EU foreign ministers in 2003 and set out how and why EU security policies differ from the Bush administration's 'pre-emptive strike' security doctrine. However confusion about and conflict between the responsibilities of the high representative and the external relations commissioner led the member state governments to agree in the proposed Constitution that these two posts should be merged into a single EU foreign minister.

There has also been significant development in the area of defence policy (Howorth, 2001; Deighton, 2002). Even before the implementation of the Amsterdam Treaty, in December 1998 the French and British governments (the two European nuclear powers and members of the UN Security Council) agreed on the St Malo defence initiative. This Franco-British initiative aimed to create an operational defence capacity for the EU. This would be done by merging the WEU into the EU structure to become the 'European pillar' of the NATO alliance. The EU would have access to national assets committed to NATO, and it would be able to act without US participation.

These aims were adopted almost wholesale by the EU at the Cologne European Council, in June 1999. Frustrated with the failure of the EU in the Yugoslav region and the fact that NATO was the primary actor in the 1999 Kosovo crisis, all the member states, including the neutrals, agreed that the core features of the defence capability of the EU should be humanitarian and rescue operations, peacekeeping and military crisis management – the so-called 'Petersberg tasks'. In December 1999 the Helsinki European Council set 2003 as the deadline by which the ESDP would be fully operational – meaning that the EU would be able to deploy a force of up to 60 000 persons within 60 days. To ensure that this deadline could be met, the member states made specific commitments on personnel (in November 2000), and equipment and other resources (in November 2001).

In December 2000 the Nice European Council then established new military decision-making structures. The Political and Security Committee (PSC) replaced the Political Committee. The PSC is assisted by a politico-military working group, a committee for civilian aspects of crisis management, a military committee (EUMC), and a military staff (EUMS). The EUMC gives military advice to the PSC and the high representative, while the EUMS is responsible for early warning, strategic planning and situation assessment. For the first time military uniforms can be seen in the corridors of the EU Council building in

Brussels. In April 2003 the first ever EU military operation was conducted, when an EU force took over all peacekeeping responsibilities from NATO in the Former Yugoslav Republic of Macedonia.

Hence there has been a gradual establishment of foreign and defence policy competences at the European level and progressive movement towards supranational decision-making, with a limited agenda-setting role for the Commission, increased policy initiative and coordination by the Council presidency and the high representative for the CFSP, the possibility of majority voting (or at least for policy implementation); and instruments to ensure that the EU acts as a united force in world affairs. Nevertheless the CFSP remains essentially an intergovernmental policy area: the General Affairs Council is the dominant executive and legislative body, and 'governance by consensus' is the decision-making norm.

Policy success and failure: haunted by the capability-expectations gap

Despite this institutional integration, the record of EU action in the area of foreign and security policy is far from consistent. There were some early policy successes under the EPC. For example the EC first presented a common front in the negotiations at the Conference on Security and Cooperation in Europe in the early 1970s. However the inadequacy of EPC became obvious when the EC attempted to negotiate a broad political and economic agreement with the US through EPC. First, EPC was insufficiently flexible to enable the US to take part in the intra-European negotiations on the future of Western European security. Henry Kissinger, the US secretary of state, claimed that this was antithetical to a basic assumption of the Atlantic Alliance: that in return for providing military protection the US had the right to participate in European security decision-making. The problem with EPC was that it tended to facilitate positions that were then presented to the US as *faits accomplis* (Featherstone and Ginsberg, 1996, p. 85). Second, and related to this issue, EPC prevented the EC from negotiating with its partners with a single voice. Following a series of visits to Washington by different foreign ministers and EC officials, Kissinger made his now legendary remark: 'Who speaks for Europe?' (Dinan, 1994, p. 85).

Another area in which initial success was replaced by policy intransigence was economic sanctions against the apartheid regime in South Africa (Holland, 1988). In 1977 the EC adopted a code of conduct to regulate the employment practices of European firms with subsidiaries in South Africa. In 1985 and 1986 this was reinforced with a series of sanctions on trade between the EC member states and South Africa in oil, iron and steel, paramilitary goods and sensitive technologies, and the banning of cultural, sporting and scientific contacts and military and nuclear cooperation. However towards the end of the 1980s internal disputes over how best to tackle the South African regime undermined Europe's status as the leader of the global anti-apartheid movement.

Within a few months of the implementation of the Maastricht Treaty the Council agreed to the adoption of a series of joint actions. However this was less the result of a new institutional capacity than the consensual nature of the issues involved. For example, one of the actions related to South Africa, where common action was now possible because the member states were united in their support for democracy, whereas before they had been divided over how best to bring down apartheid (Holland, 1995). Most of the other joint actions addressed 'soft' foreign policy issues, such as support for the Middle East peace process, dispatching a team of observers to the parliamentary elections in Russia, and providing humanitarian aid to the Great Lakes region of Africa.

However when it came to 'hard' issues the EU was patently incapable of acting in a clear and decisive manner. For example in the case of former Yugoslavia, whereas the member states were in agreement about sending humanitarian aid, they were divided over when to recognize the sovereignty of Croatia, whether to maintain a blockade on the provision of arms to the Bosnian Muslims, and whether to act against Serbian oppression and ethnic cleansing. Part of the problem was that the CFSP could be used to prevent a member state from using military force if this was in breach of a common EU policy, but it could not be used to agree a common military strategy and direct the use of force. Consequently the EU found itself in the embarrassing position of initially telling the US to keep out of Europe's 'back yard', and then relying on the US to force the sides in the conflict to sit down in a small town in the US Midwest to negotiate a peace agreement. However the EU was instrumental in securing the peaceful accession of Slovenia from Yugoslavia, and made an important contribution to the eventual peace settlement in Bosnia (the Owen plan).

An even clearer example of EU incapacity occurred during the 2002–4 Iraq crisis. After the events of 11 September 2001 the member states took the unprecedented step of declaring their solidarity with the US by invoking the self-defence clause of the NATO charter: in other words they declared that the attack on the US was also an attack on Europe. While the semblance of a common European position just about held together during the US-led military offensive to oust the Taliban regime in Afghanistan, this united front collapsed when the Bush administration turned its attention to regime change in Iraq and seemed set to use military force to oust Saddam Hussein. On one side the UK, Spain, Italy, Poland, Portugal and Denmark were prepared to support US military action, even without full UN endorsement. On the other side, France, Germany and Belgium – which Donald Rumsfeld infamously described as 'Old Europe' – insisted that the proposed war was illegal under international law.

Following the rapid takeover of Iraq and the later capture of Saddam Hussein it appeared that the 'hawks' had been vindicated. However by 2004, as Iraq descended into chaos, and as the US seemed unwilling to hand over authority for the stabilization and management of Iraq to the United Nations, the pro-US coalition was starting to collapse in the face of strong public opposition to the military occupation and the policies of the Bush administration. The clearest illustration of this was the dramatic electoral removal of the right-wing Spanish government in March 2004, just days after a major terrorist bombing by Al-Qaeda in Madrid. Also British and Italian governments' support for Bush eroded as they feared that they too would be punished by their voters in forthcoming elections.

The fundamental problem for the EU in the area of external political and security relations is what Christopher Hill (1988) calls the 'capability–expectations gap'. On the one hand the EU public and the EU's partners (notably the US) are demanding that the EU take a more active role in world affairs – as a pacifier of regional conflicts, an intervener and mediator in global conflicts, a facilitator of North–South cooperation and a joint supervisor of the world economy. On many of these issues the EU is regarded as 'a panacea, a cross between Father Christmas and the Seventh Cavalry' (ibid., p. 322). On the other hand the EU does not have the institutional resources or the political legitimacy to take on these roles. The reforms contained in the Maastricht and Amsterdam Treaties may have reduced the institutional constraints on the capacity for common action, but the rival historical and political interests of the member states prevent the definition of a common European security identity, and undermine any possibility of acting upon this identity in a united front.

However, the EU is not alone in having a capability–expectations gap. The management and implementation of foreign policy is more complex today than in the bipolar world of the 1950s to 1980s. Without an overarching global balance-of-power or security architecture, and with the new security threat posed by global terrorism, the definition of policy goals is more complex and the result of policy actions is less predictable. For example even the US has a gap between its military capacity as the sole military superpower, and the use of this 'awesome power' to achieve major US foreign policy objectives, such as the spread of democracy in the Middle East and the building of a stable and democratic state in Iraq.

Explaining the Foreign Policies of the EU

Among a number of questions arising from this survey of EU foreign policies, several stand out:

- Why has the EU been more successful in pursuing common economic policies than common foreign and security policies?
- Why has the EU pursued a relatively liberal global economic policy despite pressures for and fear of a 'fortress Europe'?
- Why has the EU been able to adopt and implement common foreign and defence policies on some issues but not others?

The extensive literature on the EU's external relations offers four main perspectives on these questions: (1) the importance of global economic and geopolitical relations in driving the EU's agenda and decision-making; (2) the dominance and intransigence of European nation-states' geopolitical interests; (3) the role of domestic economic interests in the EU; and (4) the influence of the institutional rules on EU foreign policy outcomes.

Global economic and geopolitical (inter)dependence

Europe is more a responder to global economic and geopolitical developments than a shaper of these developments. Global developments beyond the EU's control determine the agenda and timetable of its global policies and the options available to EU policy-makers. For example in recent decades the EU has been forced to react to two major exogenous developments: economic globalization, and the end of the Cold War.

With regard to economic globalization, since the mid 1970s there has been a dramatic increase in cross-border trade and capital movements. First, import volumes as a percentage of the GDP of advanced industrial countries, which remained steady at 10–16 per cent between 1880 and 1972, rose to almost 22 per cent between 1973 and 1987 (McKeown, 1991, p. 158). Also, whereas internal demand grew at approximately 2 per cent per year, international trade grew at almost 5 per cent per year. In other words, between the 1970s and 1990s trade grew at a rate that was about 66 per cent greaterer than the growth in domestic demand. Second, cross-border capital flows have increased faster than the domestic demand for capital. For example international capital flows to the advanced industrial countries rose from an annual average of $99 billion in 1975–77 to $463 billion in 1985–89 (Turner, 1991; p. 23). Also, total net lending in world markets grew from $100 billion per year in the late 1970s to $342 billion in 1990, and foreign exchange trading more than quadrupled between 1982 and 1992 to $1000 billion per day, or 40 times the average daily volume of world trade.

This economic globalization has had two main effects (Milner and Keohane, 1996; Garrett and Lange, 1996). First, globalization has facilitated global convergence in the price of goods, services and capital. This has put pressure on the EU to reform its internal policies to allow convergence with its global competitors. Second, globalization has benefited some domestic interests but disadvantaged others; that is, financial services, importing firms and firms producing for global markets have benefited at the expense of the producers of goods for the domestic market (Frieden, 1991; Frieden and Rogowski, 1996). As trade and capital flows have grown, there has been pressure from organized interests for policies to promote free trade. For example in the Uruguay Round of the GATT negotiations, the linkage between trade liberalization and CAP reform meant that pro-free-trade EU states and domestic economic interests argued for CAP reform as a means of promoting greater trade liberalization (cf. Devuyst, 1995; Patterson, 1997; Meunier, 1998; Hennis, 2001; Landau, 2001; see slso Chapter 9). Similarly the liberalization of world trade meant that the new ACP–EU Partnership Agreement had to be based on free trade rather than preferential trade (Forwood, 2001).

Meanwhile the fall of the Berlin Wall, the democratic revolutions in Central and Eastern Europe, and the collapse of the Soviet Union and its empire created a new strategic environment for Western Europe (Knudsen, 1994; Sperling and Kirchner, 1997). The EU member states were immediately forced to address a series of interrelated security, political and economic issues that previously had been absent from the EU agenda. These included how to incorporate a united Germany into the Western alliance, how to stabilize democracy and the free market in the new democracies in Central and Eastern Europe, how to involve these states in a broader 'European house' without antagonizing Russia, and how to tackle the potentially large influx of economic migrants (Smith, 1996; Heiberg, 1998).

The end of the Cold War has also thrown up new global political and security challenges that were suppressed by the previous balance of power relations. India and Pakistan have been added to the list of countries that possess nuclear weapons, against the terms of the international nuclear weapons treaties, and a number of other 'rogue states' seem intent on developing a nuclear capability, such as Iran and North Korea. Furthermore the new spectre of global terrorism in the name of Islamic fundamentalism has emerged, centred on the Al-Qaeda network and the personality cult of Osama bin Laden. The number of terrorist attacks on Western targets increased dramatically from the mid 1990s onwards, and the attacks on New York and Washington on 11 September 2001 profoundly demonstrated the vulnerability of Western democracies to attacks by well-coordinated, well-funded terrorists who are willing to give up their lives for the cause. The growing perception in both the Muslim world and the West of a 'clash of civilizations' has presented problems for many European societies. For example the UK, France and Spain have sizeable and growing Muslim communities that contain individuals who support or sympathize with the anti-Western movements in the Middle East. As a result the connection between foreign and internal security issues is now much closer than at any time during the Cold War.

In other words, EU foreign policies are essentially reactive rather than proactive: responding to global events rather than shaping them. This is particularly true in comparison to the position of the US, with the EU invariably being forced to follow the lead of whichever administration is in Washington. For example, when developing a policy towards Central and Eastern Europe, the EU had to take account of how many troops the US would pull out of Europe, whether the US Congress would retreat into isolationism, and how fast the US administration wanted to enlarge NATO to the east (Ullrich, 1998). Even in the negotiations on the Maastricht and Amsterdam Treaties the US government was instrumental in determining the shape of the proposed rules on defence cooperation (van Staden, 1994; Duke, 1996).

Intransigent national security identities and interests

However not all issues are of the same political salience and sensitivity for states. As discussed in the previous chapter, Hoffmann (1966) distinguished between two types of issue: 'high politics', which touch on the fundamental definition, identity, security and sovereignty of the nation-state; and 'low politics', which address issues that are not as threatening to the viability of the nation-state, such as European economic integration and regulatory policies. Because foreign and security policies are central to the concept of national identity and security, the EU member states have been less willing to agree to supranational forms of decision-making in this area than in the less politically sensitive area of external economic and trade policies.

As a result the history of the development of the EU's common foreign and defence policies has been one of competition between rival nation-states' interpretations of how best to defend their security (Pfetsch, 1994; Hill, 1996). The West European nation-state remains the sovereign actor in foreign policy issues so, instead of the EU developing an autonomous identity and capacity on the global stage, it is simply a vehicle for the member states to pursue those parts of their foreign policies which coincide. When the interests of the states diverge the EU becomes incapacitated and the member states pursue their interests independently of the EU. In this regard the institutional design of the CFSP is largely irrelevant (Stavridis, 1997). What matters is the political commitment of the member states, which cannot be obtained merely by introducing more effective decision-making procedures. The only hope for the EU is that individual security interests will eventually converge, and that this will be facilitated by continued bargaining over the CFSP and policy coordination through networks and institutions such as the Policy Unit and the Military Staff Unit. However from a realist perspective this is unlikely, as security interests tend not to vary over time.

Moreover there is some evidence that the member states' security identities in the foreign policy field also determine the global economic policies of the EU. The member states allow supranational institutions and common policies in the case of external economic affairs because they share certain common economic interests. However when security interests diverge, external trade policy preferences also diverge. For example states that favour an independent European defence capability are reluctant to allow the European economy to become dependent on transatlantic trade. Conversely states that favour a transatlantic defence community have been at the forefront of attempts to tie the EU economy into a broader transatlantic economic community. In other words the free trade/protectionism cleavage between the member states on trade policies follows the Atlanticist/Europeanist cleavage on security policies.

However the instrumental promotion of national interests can go hand in hand with the establishment of supranational modes of decision-making in foreign policy issues. For example in the case of crisis management the member states were willing to agree to qualified-majority voting because in this area the need to reach a quick decision was more important than the preservation of national sovereignty (Wagner, 2003). More generally, the desire to preserve national sovereignty varies among the member states, and the traditionally weaker states often feel that their national interests can be enhanced by participation in and delegation of powers to the EU level. As a result, 'all else being equal, governments of weaker countries are more likely to support supranational CFSP institutions than governments of stronger countries' (Koenig-Archibugi, 2004b, p. 167). The UK and France have traditionally been most eager to preserve the intergovernmental nature of foreign policy decision-making. Some of the larger states prefer to delegate contentious issues to the European level, to promote policy outcomes that would be difficult to bring about domestically. In particular, amongst the big states, executives in coalition-government systems (Germany and Italy) tend to be more in flavour of supranational decision-making on foreign policy issues than are executives in single-party government systems (the UK, France and Spain) (Koenig-Archibugi, 2004a).

Nevertheless there is evidence that member states' foreign policy preferences and objectives have changed as a result of their participation in the making of European level foreign and security policies (Glarbo, 1999; Smith, 2000; Manners and Whitman, 2003; Smith, 2003; Tonra, 2003). As Karen Smith (2003, pp. 197–8) explains:

Once the member states have agreed that the EU should pursue particular objectives, they become involved in a process in which their initial preferences are reshaped, and in which they must make compromises over how these objectives will be achieved.... Declarations and statements create expectations that the EU will act ... and make it difficult to roll back rhetorical commitments to pursue objectives. And, through this process, the EU's international identity thus haltingly, gradually, acquires more substance.

One example of this is the development of EU policies towards Central and Eastern Europe and the decision to allow 10 new states to join at the same time – the so-called 'big bang approach' (Fierke and Wiener, 1999; Schimmelfennig, 2001, 2002, 2003, Sjursen, 2002; K. Smith, 2004, pp. 184–206). In the mid 1990s the existing member states had different attitudes towards enlargement. For example, many of the net recipients from the EU budget feared losing their subsidies, and while Germany was in favour of a limited enlargement, the UK and the Scandinavian states favoured more rapid enlargement and a larger number of new members. Moreover the UK emphasized the market preparedness of the prospective states, whereas France and Germany emphasized the need for political commitment to European integration among the prospective members. Nevertheless, through a gradual process of policy formulation, negotiation and agenda-setting by the Commission, by the end of 1999 the governments of all 15 member states supported the big bang approach, despite opposition to enlargement by the majority of voters in several member states, including France and Germany.

Domestic economic interests: EU governments and multinational firms

From a liberal perspective, however, the determination of policy preferences is the other way round: security interests are derived from economic interests. These interests may be defined at the national level, where governments adjust their preferences to cater to the median voter or the most powerful domestic economic interests (Rogowski, 1990). Alternatively interests may be defined and articulated at the European level by private economic actors that have no specific national allegiance, such as multinational corporations and sectoral associations (Junne, 1994). In either case, EU global policies change as the balance of power shifts among domestic economic interests, or the latter change their preferences in light of exogenous developments, such as globalization and the emergence of new markets (for example in Central and Eastern Europe and the Mediterranean region).

Economic interests have played a vital part in shaping the external economic policies of the EU (Ugar, 1998; Hofhansel, 1999). For example multinational corporations, not only from the EU member states but also from non-EU states in Europe (such as Sweden), did much to shape the EU's agenda in the Uruguay Round of the GATT negotiations. The European Round-Table of Industrialists and the EU Committee of the American Chamber of Commerce have campaigned exensively to persuade anti-free-trade EU governments to support trade liberalization, and supplied the Commission with arguments to strengthen its position in Council bargaining. Similarly a group of European and American multinational corporations formed the Trans-Atlantic Business Dialogue (TABD) in 1994 to campaign for greater transatlantic free trade. In a series of meetings the TABD drew up detailed proposals for the mutual recognition of standards in a number of product areas. The Commission and the US government subsequently adopted these proposals almost in their entirety.

Economic interests are also a key factor in explaining the EU's external political and security policies (cf. Praet, 1987). For example German businesses were the largest investors in Central and Eastern Europe following the collapse of communism, so Germany had both an economic and a strategic interest in promoting the development of stable markets in its neighbours. In this instance, economic interest went hand in hand with security interests. In other situations, however, collective economic interest has overridden security concerns. For example the need to defend the credibility of GATT and the WTO is forcing the French and British governments to redefine and reform their historical relations with their former colonies, many of whish relations have been maintained for security and military reasons. Administrative elites may oppose any perceived threat to national identity and security interests, but domestic economic groups are less interested in these concerns than in their own material well-being, and governments are ultimately accountable to the median voter. Hence in the liberal interpretation, if a state is faced with a choice between free trade and protecting a security interest, and if a large proportion of the electorate is employed in globally competitive industries, the government will choose free trade.

In almost direct contrast to claims of the determinacy of security interests, from this perspective the external economic implications of the single market and the EU's interest in promoting global free trade have been a major determinants of the pace of institutional integration and the nature of policy outcomes in the foreign and security policy field. Part of the reason for this is that trade policy is managed in the first pillar through a division of competences along regional lines in the Commission and in the agenda of trade ministers, such as EU–US relations, EU–Asia relations and EU–Mediterranean relations. When external economic issues touch on political and security concerns they are passed on to foreign ministers. However, this forces governments to tackle many political/security issues on an agenda and timetable that is set by the EU's single market and external economic policy agenda (M. Smith, 1998).

Institutional rules: decision-making procedures and Commission agenda-setting

Finally, and related to this perspective is the argument that the EU's global policies are determined by the institutional context at the EU level. Against the scepticism of realists, liberal-institutionalists maintain that the supranational institutional framework shapes EU global policies in three ways: (1) through the existence of a supranational actor (the Commission) with certain agenda-setting powers and a vested interest in promoting political integration and collective EU policy outcomes; (2) through the institutional design of trade policy-making, which limits the ability of anti-free-trade states to block a liberal policy outcome; and (3) through the decision-making rules and institutional norms in the CFSP field, which have promoted policy movement despite conflicting security interests.

First, the Commission has particular policy preferences in the field of EU global policies (Smith, 1997a; Nugent and Saurugger, 2002). On the one hand, the Commission has institutional interests: further economic and political integration in treaty reforms, and rules that grant it significant agenda-setting power and policy discretion (see Chapter 2). On the other hand, the Commission has political preferences: there has tended to be a free-trade majority in the College of Commissioners, but the Commission is also in favour of the EU playing a greater (interventionist) role in global political and economic affairs.

In the making of EU trade policy the Commission has used its agenda-setting and policy-implementation powers to maximum effect. The Commission has successfully promoted multilateral and bilateral free trade agreements against the preferences of important member states (notably France), and has been able to place new issues on the agenda, such as the mutual recognition agreements with the US and the organization and promotion of the EU–Asia summits. In some respects the Commission has successfully captured the external trade policy of the EU (Bilal, 1998).

However there has been a backlash from the member states. Recognizing the ability of the Commission to shape trade policy outcomes, during the Amsterdam Treaty negotiations the member states refused to agree to the Commission's request to delegate negotiating authority to the Commission in the 'new trade issues' of services and intellectual property, preferring instead to allow the Council to decide (by unanimity) whether and when to delegate this authority (Meunier and Nicolaïdis, 1999).

In the making of foreign and security policies the Commission does not have the same agenda-setting capabilities as in trade policies. Nevertheless the Commission has been able to influence policy outcomes through informal agenda-setting, such as the generation of policy ideas (Nuttall, 1997). The Commission has also used its powers in external trade policy to promote explicitly political goals, as in the development of the EU's policy towards the Mediterranean (Piening, 1997; Gomez, 1998). The Commission's potential for activism in such a sensitive policy area is one of the main reasons why the member state governments have been reluctant to delegate full agenda-setting powers to the Commission (Nuttall, 1996).

Second, in the field of external economic policies, Hanson (1998, p. 81) argues 'that [EU] trade policy liberalization is largely the result of changes in the institutional context of trade policy-making' (cf. Ugar, 1998; Young, 2000). By delegating trade policy-making to the EU level and trade policy negotiations to the Commission, the member states have consciously chosen to constrain the range of possible policy options available to them and effectively locked-in a liberal trade policy (Nicolaidis, 1995; Meunier and Nicolaïdis, 1999). Related to this, the rules for adopting trade policy deals make it difficult for protectionist member states to reject international agreements negotiated by the Commission. As the Commission is able to make a take-it-or-leave-it proposal to the Council, which the Council cannot amend, the only choice for the member states is either to accept a proposed package or veto a carefully negotiated international deal (which itself requires unanimity). Faced with this choice, even the most protectionist member states are forced to accept global free trade deals negotiated by the Commission on the member states' behalf (cf. Jupille, 1999; Meunier, 2000).

Third, the design of decision-making in foreign and security policies has promoted policy convergence and consensus and restricted competition and divergence. For example Bulmer (1991) argues that even the limited institutional structure of European political cooperation has created a relationship between the member states that is akin to 'cooperative federalism', whereby the member states recognize that foreign policy-making should be 'shared' between the European and the national level. Similarly the establishment of a new institutional framework for the CFSP immediately produced several policy changes, such as an increase in the number of common positions agreed, use of the new joint action policy instrument, and the integration of CFSP issues into the general EU timetable (Cameron, 1998). Indeed, Michael E. Smith (1998, p. 332) argues that the development of the EU's foreign policy shows that 'intergovernmental systems can still be altered with rules that are more powerful than analysts appreciate, and that neither the ECJ nor the Commission are necessarily needed to develop and reinforce them'. Moreover when the member states learned that using supranational modes of decision-making – such as qualified-majority voting and agenda-setting by the Commission – did not present a fundamental threat to national security they were willing to accept the development of these rules in the Amsterdam Treaty (M.E. Smith, 2004a, 2004b).

Conclusion: a 'Soft Superpower'?

The EU has the potential to be a major force in shaping global events. But the EU has exploited this potential more in the economic sphere than in the political and security spheres. The EU is the world's largest trader, and through the Common Commercial Policy it has used its power to promote global free trade. The single market has been opened to the world through multiple trade agreements with almost every region of the world. Moreover the EU has played a crucial role in the WTO and worked to promote and defend its legitimacy.

However the EU has been less capable of speaking with a single and consistent voice on global political and security issues. The member state governments have progressively strengthened the institutional capacity of the EU to agree and implement foreign policy actions, and this has facilitated the definition of collective interests, the adoption of policy compromises, the prevention of national actions that could undermine common policies, and the presentation of common views in a coherent manner to the outside world. While EU has taken action on a number of non-sensitive issues, such as political and economic support of the new democracies in Central and Eastern Europe, it has been incapable of acting coherently and decisively when faced with fundamental challenges to EU security, as demonstrated by the EU's response to the conflict in Yugoslavia and its failure to agree a common position during the Iraq crisis.

Why does this dichotomy exist? The answer lies in a mixture of the liberal, realist and constructivist theories of international relations. The liberal theory appears to explain EU global economic policies. In this area, policies have been driven more by economic than by security interests. As the world's largest trader, global free trade is in the EU's economic interest although free trade advances are partly due to the organizational power of multinational businesses, which are more able to organize at the EU level than are the producers of goods or services for domestic markets. Supranational institutions have also played a part. The Commission has had an institutional incentive to facilitate global free trade institutions as a means of increasing its negotiating mandate and policy freedom from the member states governments.

However, realist theory is more helpful in explaining EU foreign and security policies. The deep historical and cultural roots of the member states' security interests have undermined the ability of the EU to define and promote a single European foreign policy. In fact, Piner Tank (1998) argues that the loss of economic sovereignty as a result of economic integration and common trade policies has strengthened the resolve of the member states to maintain their sovereignty over foreign and security policies. Consequently the mix of supranational and inter-governmental decision rules, as set up by the Maastricht and Amsterdam Treaties, may enable common policies to be adopted, but they are not sufficient to produce decisive actions.

Finally, constructivist theory helps explain why, even when they are deeply divided over a key issue, the member states endeavour to reconcile their national interests with the collective interests of the EU as a whole. For example in the midst of the Iraq crisis, the battle between the Franco-German axis and the British–Spanish–Italian axis was fought out around the table of a series of foreign ministers' and European Council meetings with both sides arguing that their position was most suitable for the long-term interests of Europe as a whole (Hill, 2004).

Overall, what is remarkable given the deep historical legacy of the nation-states of Europe, is that they have agreed to enact common foreign policies at all – against what many realists would have predicted. Also, if the liberals and constructivists are right, in the new realities of post Cold War world the 'soft power' that the EU projects through its trade, aid, human rights, crisis management and peace-keeping policies may turn out to be just as influential in shaping the preferences of the EU member states and the destiny of the world as the more obvious 'hard' military power of the US (Moravcsik, 2002b).

Chapter 13

Conclusion: Rethinking the European Union

What Political Science Teaches Us About the EU
What the EU Teaches Us about Political Science

This book has looked at the EU in a different way from the traditional approaches to European integration and EU studies. It has not proposed a new integration theory, nor has it provided a detailed description of particular events or developments in Brussels. Instead it has argued that we can improve our understanding of how the EU works by applying to the EU our general understanding of the main processes in modern political systems. The key underlying assumption, then, is that the EU is a fully functioning political system. Because of this, political science has a lot to teach us about the EU. Conversely studying the EU helps us to reevaluate our general theories of political organization and behaviour.

What Political Science Teaches Us About the EU

Operation of government, politics and policy-making in the EU

Political science tells us a considerable amount about each of the processes analyzed in this book. In the area of executive politics, the Council delegates agenda-setting and policy implementation tasks to the Commission, primarily to reduce transaction costs and facilitate policy credibility. However the Commission is not a neutral actor. Like all political executives, commissioners have their own career and partisan/ideological goals; and like all bureaucracies the Commission administration has incentives to expand its fiscal resources, political and regulatory powers, and autonomy from political control. But, the EU governments can predict this. To preempt this 'bureaucratic drift' the Council has established mechanisms to constrain the Commission, such as control over the appointment of commissioners and the comitology system.

With regard to legislative politics, both the Council and the EP have established internal institutions to improve legislative decision-making: the Council presidency and the EP leadership structures improve agenda organization; and sectoral Councils and EP committees facilitate bargaining on an issue-by-issue basis. As expected, different legislative coalitions have formed on different policy dimensions (such as pro-/anti-integration and left-right), and actors have different powers under the various legislative rules (qualified-majority/unanimity and co-decision/consultation).

In the field of judicial politics, the member state governments established the ECJ to overcome a collective action problem: the lack of incentive for each member state to implement market liberalization without an external threat. However several actors had incentives to promote the subsequent 'constitutionalization' of the treaties: the ECJ developed doctrines to increase its institutional autonomy and influence over policy outcomes; national courts accepted EU law to strengthen their powers against national parliaments and governments; and private litigants sought EU norms to further their private interests. Moreover the institutional design of the EU made it difficult for anti-integrationist forces to rein in the ECJ.

In the area of public opinion, EU society is primarily divided along national lines. However citizens form their attitudes towards the EU on the basis of personal economic interests and political values. As a result individuals from the same social group in different member states share similar views on European integration. The result is a complex political environment for the EU political elites. The structure of attitudes towards European integration, with both the working class and the middle class being internally divided over the question, means that parties on both left and right in different member states often have different attitudes towards the EU.

Turning to democratic processes in the EU system, EP elections do not allow voters to throw out the EU executive or choose the EU policy agenda. This is not because the EP lacks the power over the Commission or in the legislative process. Rather, EP elections are not about choosing rival policy agendas for the EU because national parties have an incentive to use these contests as part of their battle for domestic government office. Nevertheless, as the powers of the EP have grown the incentive for MEPs with similar policy preferences to cooperate and organize together has lead to growing organizational power and cohesion in the main party groups in the EP. As a result, despite the failure of EP elections to lead to the mobilization of pan-European political forces, the party system in the EP would be familiar to any European citizen with some cursory understanding of his or her national party system.

With regard to interest representation, groups that can secure selective benefits from the EU (such as businesses and farmers) have more of an incentive to organize at the EU level than do groups for whom the benefits and costs of EU policies are diffuse (such as consumers, taxpayers, workers and environmentalists). Nevertheless the Commission and the EP provide access and subsidies to under-represented groups, to increase their policy expertise, secure the adoption of legislation in the Council and develop a wide support base for their actions.

On regulatory policies, the single market is a classic regulatory project: its aim is positive-sum rather than zero-sum. However EU regulatory policies do have indirect redistributive consequences. The deregulation of national rules favours producer groups, whereas the harmonization of process standards protects workers, environmentalists and consumers. Nevertheless, on some regulatory issues the member state governments prefer any EU regulation to none (the *status quo*), and as a result the EU is more able to adopt deregulatory policies and common product standards (such as environmental labelling) than common process standards (such as workers' rights).

As regards expenditure policies, the member states that benefit most from the single market and EMU are willing to grant 'side payments' to those who benefit least. However, because receipts are concentrated whereas payments are diffuse, social groups that benefit from EU programmes have more of an incentive to mobilize to protect their subsidies than do groups that pay into the budget. Also, expenditure policies tend to cause executive officials (such as the Agriculture Directorate-General in the Commission), legislators (such as agriculture ministers) and private interests (such as the farm lobby) to join forces to promote and protect expenditure in their policy area.

In the operation of economic and monetary union the EU is not an optimum currency area, and as a result the eurozone is likely to experience asymmetric shocks. However the EU is ill-equipped to address such shocks: there is little labour movement between the states, fiscal transfers through the EU budget are small, and under the rules of the Stability and Growth Pact governments must not run fiscal deficits. But, the institutional design of EMU allows for policy flexibility. The member states can implement labour market reforms, the ECB is not completely immune from political pressure, and finance ministers can introduce tax harmonization, reform the fiscal rules, allow more fiscal transfers and devalue the euro.

In the area of citizen freedom and security policies, member state governments have responded to voters' demands for action to combat the perceived threat of cross-border crime and illegal immigration that can result from the free movement of persons in the single market. Bureaucrats in interior ministries have also sought to increase their capacity to control the movement of persons. Meanwhile the EU institutions have demanded institutional reforms to improve policy accountability and increase their influence over policy outcomes, and as a result the member state governments have instituted qualified-majority voting, established new EP and ECJ powers, and delegated agenda-setting powers to the Commission.

Finally, the member states have found it easier to agree common external economic policies than common political and security policies. On economic issues, policies tend to be driven by economic interests. As the world's largest trader, global free trade is in the EU's collective economic interest, and multinational firms, which benefit from free trade, and are more able to lobby the EU than are domestic producers, who gain from protectionist policies. On political and security issues, in contrast, the member states have competing geopolitical interests, and therefore have been reluctant to delegate agenda-setting power to the Commission or introduce qualified-majority voting in this policy area.

Connections between government, politics and policy-making in the EU

Political science teaches us about how the processes of government (interactions within and between the executive, legislative and judicial institutions), politics (the strategies by individuals and groups to influence government) and policy-making (policy processes and outputs) are interconnected in the EU. With regard to the *connection between politics and government*, EU member state governments are composed of national political parties whose primary goal is to be re-elected. This has two effects. First, governments seek EU policies that are in line with their electoral commitments, accord with domestic public opinion, or directly benefit their voters and supporting interest groups. Second, governments have limited time horizons as the long-term impact of EU decisions is less important than their short-term political salience and impact.

In contrast the supranational institutions – the Commission, the EP and the ECJ – are relatively isolated from short-term electoral considerations. Individual commissioners may wish to have their terms renewed, which encourages them to remain connected to their domestic governing and party elites. However their future in this respect is unpredictable as governments and party elites change. Similarly, because European elections are fought as national contests the re-election of MEPs depends on the electoral success of their domestic party rather than their individual or party group performance in the EP. Nevertheless the supranational institutions are not completely isolated from public opinion – if the member state governments are to grant them more powers they need the support and confidence of the EU citizens. Consequently the Commission has often proposed populist measures, the ECJ became less activist after the rise of

Euroscepticism in the mid 1990s, and the EP tries to raise its profile in the run-up to EP elections.

With regard to the *connection between politics and policy-making*, public opinion and party competition shape the preferences and strategies of actors in the policy-making process. For example member state governments are reluctant to delegate powers to the Commission and the ECJ in areas where their electorates oppose EU action. And on highly salient issues such as key pieces of legislation and the candidacy for the post of Commission president, parties in government put pressure on their MEPs to back their government's position in the Council. Conversely on issues for which there is strong public support for EU action (as in the environmental field) and on low-saliency issues (such as the single market programme), governments are more willing to allow policy outcomes that might strengthen the powers of the EU institutions in the long term.

The structure of interest representation also shapes policy outcomes. Groups that can secure selective or concentrated benefits from the EU policy process have the greatest incentive to mobilize. Thus business interests have lobbied for the single market programme and against high environmental and social regulations, regions lobby to maintain cohesion expenditure, and farmers lobby to maintain the CAP. Nevertheless diffuse interests (such as environmentalists, consumers and trade unions) have secured policies when the Commission has had an incentive to incorporate these groups, when centre-left parties have been powerful in the Council, and when the centre-left in the EP has been able to set the legislative agenda.

In addition, transnational social divisions, domestic party competition and interest group organization have all contributed to the emergence of a new left–right dimension in the EU policy process. The traditional European integration dimension remains: between groups and institutions seeking further integration and groups in favour of maintaining national sovereignty. However on many policy issues (such as macroeconomic questions in EMU and aspects of the governance of the single market that have redistributive or value-allocative implications) the battle lines are between 'regulated capitalism' (supported by parties on the left) and neoliberalism (supported by parties on the right).

With regard to the *connection between government and policy-making* the EU institutional rules facilitate particular policy outcomes. For example the delegation of executive and judicial powers to the Commission and the ECJ has locked in the policy of ever closer union. The Commission and the ECJ have used these powers to protect their own institutional interests in the EU system and to secure the interests of their support groups (the interests organized around the Commission, and national courts and the legal community around the

ECJ). Member state governments failed to predict these outcomes because of lack of information and their short time horizons. And because treaty reform requires unanimity, this delegation has always been 'one-way traffic'.

The legislative rules have also shaped policy outcomes. Qualified-majority voting in the Council has facilitated agreement on deregulatory policies and EU-wide product standards. In contrast unanimity voting has undermined efforts to adopt common process standards, such as workers' rights. Also, the EP has used its powers under the cooperation and co-decision procedures to promote the policies of the main party groups, but this has usually been conditional on the majority of governments in the Council preferring any EU legislation at all to no common regulations.

However as member state governments have come to understand the long-term relationship between institutional rules and policy outcomes they have consciously chosen institutional designs to promote or prevent particular policy outcomes. For example most of the governments have been reluctant to delegate executive and judicial powers in areas of fundamental national sovereignty, such as foreign policy and internal security. Similarly, anti-integration and centre-right governments have fought to maintain the consultation procedure and unanimity voting in policy areas that are likely to result in federalist and left-wing outcomes, such as tax harmonization.

Finally, the *connection between government/policy-making and politics* has generally been weaker than the connections in the opposite direction. Developments at the EU level have only had a limited impact on domestic preference formation and contestation. EU citizens remain ill-informed about EU governance, and domestic political parties remain focused on the battle for domestic government office and policy outputs. As a result, whereas new issues that arise in domestic politics are invariably placed on the EU agenda (such as the need to combat cross-border crime and illegal immigration in the late 1990s), issues at the EU level are rarely debated at the domestic level, as the absence of domestic debate on the proposed EU constitution patently shows.

Nevertheless voters' and interest groups' preferences change as their incentives and the environment change. This has prompted governments and the EU institutions to use EU policy outputs to change the structure of preferences in the domestic system. For example, centre-right governments have promoted EU competition and state-aid policies to produce domestic firms, which have an interest in open markets, and a larger private-sector middle class, which tends to support centre-right political parties. Similarly pro-integration member state governments and the Commission have used EU regional policies to buy support for the EU in peripheral states.

However things are starting to change. The end of permissive consensus, the launch of EMU, the growing use of referendums to decide major EU issues, and the rise of party-political contests over the EU agenda all mean that EU citizens, rank-and-file party members and non-governing party elites are starting to take notice of the governing and policy-making processes at the EU level. The result is increasing restriction on elites' freedom to manoeuvre at the EU level.

What the EU Teaches Us About Political Science

At the *micro level*, research on the EU has produced some important findings on the relationship between actors and their institutional environment. In particular the development and operation of the EU seems to confirm the core assumptions of the 'institutional rational choice' and 'historical-institutionalist' approaches in political science.

As in all systems, in the EU system policy outcomes are the result of strategic interaction between the actors. The location of actors in the EU policy space determines which actors are pivotal in turning minority coalitions into winning coalitions, be this in the Commission, the EP or the least integrationist government in the Council. However the formal and informal institutions of the EU system are also crucially important in shaping political outcomes. The EU is a complex political system with numerous rules and procedures. These determine the order in which decisions are tackled, the time horizons of the actors, the types of payoff that can be achieved in the policy process, who has agenda-setting power (and under what conditions), whether or not actors can exercise a veto, and consequently under which conditions actors are pivotal (independently of their policy preferences). The informal norms of the EU system – such as the need to achieve a broad political consensus – are as important in determining political outcomes as the formal rules. Put another way, equilibria in the EU system are usually 'structure-induced'.

The formal and informal rules of the EU game have not developed randomly. Institutional choices are policy choices by other means. In the recurring institutional reform game that is EU politics, the actors have developed highly sophisticated institutional preferences, such as which policies should be tackled at the EU level, who should have the right to initiate proposals under each of these policies, which internal rules of procedure should be used in each of the EU institutions, which private actors should be included in the policy process, and which procedures should be used to implement policies. In particular strategic and institutional circumstances, actors are able to choose between rules or choose new ones. Actors will try to change rules to secure outcomes that are closer to their ideal preferences. However in a highly complex strategic and institutional setting actors can never be certain of the long-term policy impact of institutional choices. But as they start to learn that the long-term consequences of institutional changes are uncertain, they become more conservative when designing rules, preferring to stick with the institutional *status quo* than risk an undesirable policy outcome. As a result the EU has become harder to reform.

Extrapolating this to the *meso level*, research on the EU tells us something interesting about each of the cross-systemic processes discussed in this book. In the area of government, once executive, legislative or judicial powers have been delegated to independent agents – be they governmental agencies or courts – these powers are very difficult to recind. In the US and at the domestic level in the EU, this has generally led to a strengthening of the power of bureaucrats and judges at the expense of directly elected legislative representatives. However the growing power of the EP in the legislative process and in scrutinizing the activities of the Commission may be an important exception to this general rule.

In the area of politics, the EU tells us that citizens' opinions matter, but not as much as we might like. Governing elites in the EU are only forced to respond to public opinion when issues become highly salient, and as a result they often have an incentive to collude to keep issues off the political agenda. Nonetheless events in the EU illustrate that in complex policy systems there are numerous opportunities for interest groups to become key intermediaries between society and decision-makers. But political parties are never absent for long. When agendas become politicized, party organizations, alliances and interests begin to drive the policy agenda and link the processes of mass politics, governmental bargaining and policy outputs.

In the area of policy-making, the EU shows how regulation has become the key instrument of modern governance. The redistributive bargains of the democratic welfare state were struck in the immediate postwar period. The current policy battles relate to the degree of state regulation of private economic and social interactions, and competing agendas have begun to emerge. Those on the right support freedom from regulatory red-tape and the delegation of regulatory policies to agencies that are independent from political majorities. In opposition, the 'old left' agenda of wealth redistribution is being replaced by a 'new left' agenda of strong protection against social and economic risk, political accountability and control of independent regulators.

Finally, extrapolating to the *macro level*, the EU shows that a highly developed political system can emerge without the full-blown apparatus of the state and/or strong popular support and mass political participation. The key reasons for this are the single market, the single currency, regulatory rather than redistributive policies, and limited encroachment into the traditional areas of state power (internal and external security). The related policies tend to be positive-sum rather than zero-sum: there are few clear losers in the EU political system. If the outcomes were highly redistributive, the EU would require a greater use of force to impose its policies and a greater degree of democratic participation to legitimize redistributive outcomes.

What this means, however, is that if economic and political integration is to proceed much further, the EU will need a greater state capacity as well as genuine democratic contestation to legitimize this state power. Not surprisingly the trade-off between these two elements is the central issue in the debate on the reform of the EU: how to strengthen the leadership and executive capacity of the EU (within and between the Council and Commission) while at the same time increasing the democratic accountability of the holders of executive office in the EU to the EP, national parliaments and citizens. Whether Europe's leaders can sell a major reform such as the proposed constitution to the EU electorate is another question. The allocation of policy powers between the national and European levels that has emerged through successive treaty reforms may prove to be a stable equilibrium that cannot be altered without a dramatic change in voters' preferences. Nevertheless, if the enlargement of the EU from 15 to 25 states prevents the EU from addressing voters' concerns, the European public may start to demand a radical overhaul of the design of the EU.

In summary, the key contention of this book is that to understand how the EU works we need to think about it in a more structured, systematic and scientific way. Only by doing so can we begin to answer the vital theoretical and normative questions that surround the construction of this new and important political system. And along the way we may learn some new things about the world of politics.

Decision-Making Procedures in the European Union

KEY:

Policy areas

CFI	Court of First Instance
ECF	Economic and Financial Committee (of the ECB)
ECSB	European System of Central Banks
EIB	European Investment Bank
ESC	Economic and Social Committee
EMI	European Monetary Institute
ER	Exchange rate
IO	International organizations
MFP	Multiannual framework programme
TCNs	Third-country nationals
TENs	Trans-European networks

Right of initiative

C	Commission
C(Op.)	Commission opinion is required
MS	One member state
8 MS	At least eight member states
1/3 MS	One-third of member states
Pres.	Presidency of Council
ECB	European Central Bank
EP	European Parliament
EP(1/4)	At the request of a quarter of the members of the EP
ECJ	European Court of Justice
CFI	Court of First Instance

Council voting rule

Unan.	Unanimity
QMV	qualified-majority, where votes are weighted according to Article 205 (ex 148)
4/5 of MS	four-fifths of member states
Const. abs.	'constructive abstention', where a decision can be carried, with a member state opposed
Veto + un.	if a m.state claims a threat to a vital national interest, it can request the decision be referred to the European Council, for a decision by unanimity
5ys-QMV	qualified-majority after five years from entry into force of the treaty
W2/3(ex subject)	a decision of two-thirds of votes cast, weighted according to the usual QMV, excluding the votes of the subject member state
Un. (European Council)	unanimity required in the European Council
'To block'	a negative decision by the Council is required to block a request by a member state
None (Com)	Commission exercises legislative power, not the Council

Parliament involvement

Con. (5ys-Cod)	Consultation procedure, then co-decision procedure after five years from entry into force of the treaty
Abs. majority	Requires the support of the majority of all members of the European Parliament, not simply of votes cast
Simple maj.	Requires the support of 50 per cent plus one of those MEPs taking part in the vote
2/3 Majority	Requires the support of two-thirds of votes cast and a majority of all the members of the European Parliament

Title	Issue	Article	Right of initiative	Council voting rule	Parliament involvement
Treaty on European Union					
I Common Provisions	Decide that there is a risk of a breach of EU principles	7(1) EU	C or 1/3 MS or EP	4/5 of MS	Assent
	Suspend rights/revoke suspension	7(2) EU	C or 1/3 MS	Unanimity	Assent
		7(3)/(4) EU	Council	QMV	None
V Common Foreign and Security Policy	Adoption of decisions	23(1) EU	Council	Unanimity/constr.abs.	None
	Implementation /common positions /appointment of special representative	23(2) EU	MS	QMV/veto + un.	None
	Procedural questions	23(3) EU	Council	Simple majority	None
	Agreements with third countries or IOs	24 EU	MS (Pres.)	Unanimity	None
	Agreements with third countries or IOs implementing Joint actions	24 EU	MS (Pres.)	QMV/veto + un.	None
VI Police and Judicial Cooperation in Criminal Matters	Enhanced cooperation in CFSP	27e EU	MS + C(Op.)	QMV/veto + un. (to block)	None
	Expenditure beyond budget or for military	28 EU	Council	Unanimity	None
	Adoption of measures	34(2a,b,di) EU	C or MS	Unanimity	Consultation
	Implementation	34(2c,dii) EU	C or MS	QMV	Consultation
	Authorize enhanced integration	40a EU	8 MS + C(Op.)	QMV	Consultation
	Join enhanced integration	40b EU	MS + C(Op.)	QMV (to block)	None
	Expenditure beyond budget	41 EU	Council	Unanimity	None
	Transfer to EC pillar	42 EU	C or MS	Unanimity	Consultation
VII Enhanced Cooperation	Common expenditure	44(2) EU	Council	Unanimity	None
VIII Final Provisions	Establish an Intergovernmental Conference to amend the Treaties	48 EU	C or MS	Unanimity + Ratification	Consultation
	Acceptance of new member states	49 EU	MS + C(Op.)	Unanimity + Ratification	Assent
Schengen Protocol	Implementation	2(1) Protocol	Council	Unan. (of signatories)	None
	Participation of UK & Ireland	3 Protocol	Council	Unan. (of signatories)	None
	Agreement with Norway and Iceland	5 Protocol	Council	Unan. (of signatories)	None
Treaty Establishing the European Community					
Part One: Principles	Authorization enhanced cooperation	11	C	QMV/veto + un.	Consultation
	Joining enhanced cooperation	11a	MS + C(Op.)	None (Com.)	None
	Discrimination on grounds of nationality	12	C	QMV	Co-decision
	General non-discrimination (e.g. sex, race, ethnicity, religion)	13(1)	C	Unanimity	Consultation
	Incentive measures for non-discrimination	13(2)	C	QMV	Co-decision
	Guidelines for internal market sectors	14	C	QMV	None

Category	Description	Article		Voting	
Part Two: Citizenship	Facilitate free movement and residence	18	C	QMV	Co-decision
	Arrangements for voting rights	19	C	Unanimity	Consultation
	Extension of EU citizens' rights	22	C	Unanimity	Consultation
Part Three: Community Policies					
I Free Movement of Goods	Common customs tariff	26	C	QMV	None
II Agriculture	Operation of the CAP	37(2)	C	QMV	Consultation
	New products covered by CAP	37(3)	C	QMV	None
III Free Movement of Persons, Services and Capital	Workers: establish freedoms, social security rights	40	C	QMV	Co-decision
		42	C.	Unanimity	Co-decision
	Right of Establishment: all provisions, amend rules of professions	44-47	C	QMV	Co-decision
		47(2)	C	Unanimity	Co-decision
	Services: liberalization	52	C	QMV	Consultation
	Capital and payments: direct investments, threat to EMU,	57	C	QMV (unan. to repeal)	None
		59	C	QMV	None
	urgent measures	60	C	QMV	None
IV Visas, Asylum, Immigration and Free Movement of Persons	Internal borders, asylum, immigration, extradition	62(1)	C or MS	Unanimity	Consultation
	Checks at external borders (after agreement on field of application)	62(2a)	C or MS	QMV	Co-decision
	Issue of visas, rules on uniform visa	62(2bii,biv)	C or MS	Unanimity (Sys-QMV)	Con. (Sys-cod)
	Visa list, uniform format for visas	62(2bi,biii)	C or MS	QMV	Consultation
	Movement of TCNs with visa	62(3)	C or MS	Unanimity (QMV from 2004)	Co-decision
	Asylum and temporary prot. of refugees (after framework adopted)	63(1)/(2a)	C	QMV	Co-decision
	Conditions of entry and residence of TCNs	63(3a)	C	Unanimity	Consultation
	Clandestine immigration	63(3b)	C	Unanimity (QMV from 2004)	Co-decision
	Emergency measures on immigration	64	C	QMV	None
	Judicial cooperation in civil matters (if Council acted already)	65	C	QMV	Co-decision
	Administrative cooperation in areas under Title IV	66	C	Unanimity (QMV from 2004)	Consultation
V Transport	Decision after 5 years to move to co-decision	67	C	Unanimity	Consultation
	General transport policy	71	C	QMV	Co-decision
	Abolition of discrimination	75	C	QMV	None
	Sea and air transport	80	C	QMV	Co-decision

Title	Issue	Article	Right of initiative	Council voting rule	Parliament involvement
VI Competition, Taxation And Approximation of Laws	Competition: rules applying to undertakings	83	C	QMV	Consultation
	State aid: new categories of state aid,	87(3)	C	QMV	None
	general state aids policy,	89	C	QMV	Consultation
	Taxation: limited taxes on internal trade,	92	C	QMV	None
	harmonization of indirect taxation	93	C	Unanimity	Consultation
	Approximation of laws: single market regulation (rarely used),	94	C	Unanimity	Consultation
	single market regulation (most areas),	95	C	QMV	Co-decision
	prevent distortion of competition	96	C	QMV	None
VII Economic and Monetary Union	Economic policy: economic policy guidelines,	99(2)(4)	C	QMV	None
	rules for multilateral surveillance,	99(5)	C	QMV	Co-operation
	assistance in event of severe difficulties,	100	C	QMV	None
	privileged access to financial institutions,	102	C	QMV	Co-operation
	guarantees against EC financial liability,	103	C	QMV	Co-operation
	decision of existence of excessive deficit,	104(6)	C	QMV	None
	implementation of excessive deficit rules,	104(13)	Council	W2/3 (ex. subject)	None
	replace Excessive Deficit Protocol,	104(14)	C	Unanimity	Consultation
	rules for application of Ex. Def. Protocol,	104(14)	C	QMV	Consultation
	confer special tasks on the ECB	105(6)	C	Unanimity	Assent
	Monetary policy: amendment of ECSB statutes (part),	107(5)	ECB/C	QMV/unanimity	Assent
	ER system with non-EU currencies,	107(6)	C or ECB	QMV	Consultation
	abandon central rates in such a system,	111(1)	C or ECB	Unanimity	Consultation
	general orientations for ER policy,	111(1)	C or ECB	QMV	None
	international agreements and policy	111(2)	C or ECB	QMV	None
		111(3)(4)	C	QMV	None
	Institutional provisions: appointment of ECB officials,	112	Council	Un. (European Council)	Consultation
	provisions for composition of EFC	114	C	QMV	None
	Transition Provisions: appointment of EMI president,	117(1)	C	Un. (European Council)	Consultation
	confer extra tasks to EMI,	117(7)	C	Unanimity	Consultation
	assistance in balance of payments crisis,	119	Council	QMV	None
	which states qualify for EMU,	121	C	QMV (European Council)	Consultation
	derogation for a state from EMU	122	C	QMV	None
	set single currency conversion rates	123(4a)	C	Unanimity	None
	measures for intro. of single currency	123(4b)	C	QMV	None
VIII Employment	Annual employment policy guidelines	128(2)	C	QMV	Consultation
	Recommendations to member states	128(4)	C	QMV	None

Policy Area	Description	Article	Body	Voting	Procedure
	Incentive measures for cooperation	129	C	QMV	Co-decision
	Establishment of employment committee	130	Council	QMV	Consultation
IX Common Commercial Policy	Harmonize rules on aid for exports	132	C	QMV	None
	General CCP provisions	133(4)	C	QMV	None
	Int'l agreements in trade in services and intellectual property	133(5)	C	QMV	None
	Int'l agreements under CCP if internal policies require unanimity	133(5)	C	Unanimity	None
	Int'l agreements under CCP on culture, education, health etc.	133(6)	C	Unanimity	None
	Extend CCP to intellectual property and services	133(7)	C	Unanimity	Consultation
X Customs Cooperation	strengthen customs cooperation	135	C	QMV	Co-decision
XI Social Policy, Education, Vocational Training and Youth	Social Provisions: health and safety, equality, exclusion etc.,	137(1a,b,e,h,I,j,k)	C	QMV	Co-decision
	social security, termination, TCNs etc.,	137(1c,d,f,g)	C	Unanimity	Consultation
	implementing social agreements,	139(2)	C	QMV	None
	impl. social agreements in unan. areas,	139(2)	C	Unanimity	None
	equality pay for men and women,	141	C	QMV	Co-decision
	social security for migrant workers,	144	Council	QMV	None
	European Social Fund: implementation	148	C	QMV	Co-decision
	Education, Vocational training and youth: incentive measures for education, recommendations for education,	149(4)	C	QMV	Co-decision
	vocational training	149(4)	C	QMV	None
	Incentive measures for culture	150	C	QMV	Co-decision
XII Culture	Incentive measures for culture	151(5)	C	Unanimity	Co-decision
	Recommendations for culture	151(5)	C	Unanimity	None
XIII Public Health	Safety standards on organs etc.	152(4)	C	QMV	Co-decision
	Recommendations for public health	152(4)	C	QMV	Co-decision
XIV Consumer Protection	General measures	153	C	QMV	Co-decision
XV Trans-Euro. Networks	Guidelines and other measures on TENs policy	156	C	QMV	Co-decision
XVI Industry	Specific support measures for industry	157	C	QMV	Co-decision
XVII Economic and Social Cohesion	Specific actions outside Structural Funds	159	C	QMV	Co-decision
	Define tasks, objectives and organisation of Funds (from 2007)	161	C	QMV	Assent
	Implementation decisions	162	C	QMV	Co-decision
XVIII Research and Technological Development	Adoption of MFP	166(1)	C	QMV	Co-decision
	Adoption of specific programmes in MFP	166(4)	C	QMV	Consultation
	Set up joint undertakings	172	C	QMV	Consultation
	Implementation of MFP	172	C	QMV	Co-decision
XIX Environment	General environment policies	175(1)	C	QMV	Co-decision
	Taxes, development plans, etc.	175(2)	C	Unanimity	Consultation
	Environmental action programmes	175(3)	C	QMV	Co-decision
XX Development Coop.	General measures covering development cooperation	179	C	QMV	Co-decision
XXI Econ, Fin &Tech Coop	General measures covering economic, financial and technical coop.	181a	C	QMV	Consultation

Title	Issue	Article	Right of initiative	Council voting rule	Parliament involvement
Part Four: Association of Overseas Countries and Territories					
	Rules for association with EU	187	Council	Unanimity	None
Part Five: Institutions of the Community					
I.1(1) European Parliament	Adoption of uniform electoral procedure	190(4)	EP	Unanimity	Abs. majority
	Rules on performance of the duties of MEPs	190(5)	EP	QMV	Simple maj.
	Rules on performance of the duties of MEPs if related to taxes	190(5)	EP	Unanimity	Simple maj.
	Statute governing political parties at the European level	191	C	QMV	Co-decision
	Own initiative proposals	192	EP	None	Abs. majority
	Establishment of committee of enquiry	193	EP(1/4)	None	Abs. majority
	Regulation of duties of ombudsman	195(4)	EP	QMV	Abs. majority
	Censure of the Commission	201	EP	None	2/3 majority
I.1(2). Council	Confer implementation powers	202	C	Unanimity	Consultation
	Determine order of presidency	203	Council	Unanimity	None
	Appointment of secretary-general and deputy sec-gen of Council	207	Council	QMV	None
	Pay of Commissioners, ECJ and Court of First Instance	210	Council	QMV	None
I.1(3) Commission	Alter the number of commissioners	213	Council	Unanimity	None
	Appointment of Commission president	214	Council	QMV (European Council)	Assent
	Appointment of members of the Commission	214	Council	QMV (European Council)	Assent
	Fill a commissioner vacancy	215	Council	QMV	None
	Decide not to fill a commissioner vacancy	215	Council	Unanimity	None
I.1(4) Court of Justice	Increase number of advocates general	222	ECJ	Unanimity	None
	Approve the ECJ's rules of procedure	223	ECJ	QMV	None
	Approve the CFI's rules of procedure	224	CFI and ECJ	QMV	None
	Creation of judicial panels	225a	C or ECJ	Unanimity	Consultation
	Confer jurisdiction on the ECJ in area of industrial property rights	229a	C	Unanimity	Consultation
I.1(5) Court of Auditors	Amend statute of ECJ	245	ECJ or C	Unanimity	Consultation
	Appointment of members of the COA	247(3)	Council	QMV	Consultation
	Employment conditions of COA members	247(8)	Council	QMV	None
	Approve the COA rules of procedure	248(4)	COA	QMV	None
I.2 Common instit'l prov's	Principles for access to documents	255	C	QMV	Co-decision
I.3 Economic and social committee	Determine allowances of members of the ESC	258	Council	QMV	None
	Appointment of members of the ESC	259	Council	QMV	None

I.4 Committee of the regions	Appointment of members of the Committee of the Regions	263	Council	QMV	None
I.5 Europ. Investment Bank	Amend articles 4, 11, 12 or 18(5) of the Statute of the EIB	266	EIB or C	QMV	Consultation
II Financial Provisions	Provisions for own resources	269	C	Unanimity	Consultation
	Adoption of the budget	272	C	QMV	Budgetary
	Authorize expenditure if no budget	273	C	QMV	Assent
	Examine budget implementation	276	Council	QMV	Assent
	Rules on responsibility of financial controllers and auditors	279(1)	C	Unanimity (QMV from 2007)	Consultation
	Rules for Commission access to EU own resources	279(2)	C	Unanimity	Consultation
	Measures countering fraud	280	C	QMV	Co-decision

Part Six. General and Financial Provisions

Staff Regulations for EC officials	283	C	QMV	Consultation
Measures for production of statistics	285	C	QMV	Co-decision
Set up data protection supervisory body	286	C	QMV	Co-decision
Rules governing the languages of the EU institutions	290	Council	Unanimity	None
Amend list of 'essential interests of security'	296	C	Unanimity	None
Application of treaty to remote regions	299	C	QMV	Consultation
Negotiation of international agreements by Commission	300(1)	C	QMV	None
Conclusion of international agreements	300(2)(3)	C	Unanimity	Consultation
Conclusion of association agreements	300(3)	C	Unanimity	Assent
Adoption of any measure not covered in the treaty	308	C	Unanimity	Consultation
Suspension of voting rights/revoke suspension	309	C	QMV	None

Bibliography

Aaron, R. (1974) 'Is Multinational Citizenship Possible', *Social Research*, 41(4): 638–56.

Abélès, M., Bellier, I. and McDonald, M. (1993) *Approche anthropologique de la commission européenne: Executive Summary* (Brussels: European Commission).

Acemoglu, D. and Robinson, J. A. (2001) 'A Theory of Political Transitions', *American Economic Review*, 91: 938–63.

Akrill, R. W. (2000a) 'The European Union Budget, the Balanced Budget Rule and the Development of Common European Policies', *Journal of Public Policy*, 20(1): 1–19.

Akrill, R. W. (2000b) 'CAP Reform 1999: A Crisis in the Making?', *Journal of Common Market Studies*, 38(2): 343–53.

Albert-Roulhac, C. (1998) 'The Influence of EU Membership on Methods and Processes of Budgeting in Britain and France, 1970–1995', *Governance*, 11(2): 209–30.

Aldrich, J. H. (1995) *Why Parties? The Origin and Transformation of Political Parties in America* (Chicago, Ill.: University of Chicago Press).

Alesina, A., Angeloni, I. and Schuknecht, L. (2002) 'What Does the European Union Do?', unpublished mimeo.

Alesina, A. and Summers, L. (1993) 'Central Bank Independence and Macroeconomic Performance: Some Comparative Evidence', *Journal of Money, Credit and Banking*, 25.

Aleskerov, F., Avci, G., Iakouba, V. and Türem, Z.U. (2002) 'European Union Enlargement: Power Distribution Implications of the New Institutional Arrangements', *European Journal of Political Research*, 41: 379–94.

Alink, F., Boin, A. and t'Hart, P. (2001) 'Institutional Crisis and Reforms in Policy Sectors: The Case of Asylum Policy in Europe', *Journal of European Public Policy*, 8(2): 286–306.

Almond, G. A. (1956) 'Comparing Political Systems', *Journal of Politics*, 18(2): 391–409.

Almond, G. A. (1996) 'Political Science: The History of the Discipline', in R. E. Goodin and H.-D. Klingemann (eds), *A New Handbook of Political Science* (Oxford: Oxford University Press).

Almond, G. A. and Verba, S. (1963) *The Civic Culture* (Boston, Mass.: Little, Brown).

Alter, K. J. (1996) 'The European Court's Political Power', *West European Politics*, 19(3): 458–87.

Alter, K. J. (1998a) 'Explaining National Court Acceptance of European Court Jurisprudence: A Critical Evaluation of Theories of Legal Integration', in A.-M. Slaughter, A. Stone Sweet and J. H. H. Weiler (eds), *The European Court and National Courts – Doctrine and Jurisprudence: Legal Change in Its Social Context* (Oxford: Hart).

Alter, K. J. (1998b) 'Who Are the "Masters of the Treaty?": European Governments and the European Court of Justice', *International Organization*, 52(1): 121–47.

Alter, K. J. (2000) 'The European Union's Legal System and Domestic Policy: Spillover or Backlash?', *International Organization*, 54(3): 489–518.

Alter, K. J. (2001) *Establishing the Supremacy of European Law: The Making of an International Rule of Law in Europe* (Oxford: Oxford University Press).

Alter, K. J. and Meunier-Aitsahalia, S. (1994) 'Judicial Politics in the European Community: European Integration and the Pathbreaking *Cassis de Dijon* Decision', *Comparative Political Studies*, 26(4): 535–61.

Alvazzi del Frate, A., Zvekic, U. and Dijk, J. M. van (eds) (1993) *Understanding Crime:*

Experiences of Crime and Crime Control (Rome: United Nations Interregional Crime and Justice Research Institute).

Andersen, M. A. and Rasmussen, L. N. (1998) 'The Making of Environmental Policy in the European Council', *Journal of Common Market Studies*, 36(4): 585–97.

Andersen, S. S. and Burns, T. (1996) 'The European Union and the Erosion of Parliamentary Democracy: A Study of Post-parliamentary Governance', in S. S. Andersen and K. A. Eliassen (eds), *The European Union: How Democratic Is It?* (London: Sage).

Andersen, S. S. and Eliassen, K. A. (1993) 'The EC as a Political System', in S. S. Andersen and K. A. Eliassen (eds), *Making Policy in Europe: The Europeification of National Policy-Making* (London: Sage).

Anderson, C. (1995) 'Economic Uncertainty and European Solidarity Revisited: Trends in Public Support for European Integration', in C. Rhodes and S. Mazey (eds), *The State of the European Union*, 3 (London: Longman).

Anderson, C. (1998) 'When in Doubt, Use Proxies: Attitudes Towards Domestic Politics and Support for European Integration', *Comparative Political Studies*, 31(5): 569–601.

Anderson, C. and Kaltenthaler, K. (1996) 'The Dynamics of Public Opinion Toward European Integration, 1973–93', *European Journal of International Relations*, 2(2): 175–99.

Anderson, C. and Reichert, M. S. (1996) 'Economic Benefits and Support for Membership in the E.U.: A Cross-National Analysis', *Journal of Public Policy*, 15(3): 231–49.

Anderson, J. J. (1990) 'Skeptical Reflections on a Europe of Regions: Britain, Germany and the ERDF', *Journal of Public Policy*, 10(4): 417–48.

Anderson, J. J. (1995) 'Structural Funds and the Social Dimension of EU Policy: Springboard or Stumbling Block?', in S. Leibfried and P. Pierson (eds), *European Social Policy: Between Fragmentation and Integration* (Washington, DC: The Brookings Institution).

Anderson, M, den Boer, M., Cullen, P., Gilmore, W., Raab, C. and Walker, N. (1995) *Policing the European Union* (Oxford: Clarendon Press).

Ansell, C. K., Parsons, C. A. and Darden, K. A. (1997) 'Dual Networks in European Regional Development Policy', *Journal of Common Market Studies*, 35(3): 347–76.

Apeldoorn, B. van (2002) 'The European Round Table of Industrialists: Still a Unique Player?', in J. Greenwood (ed.), *The Effectiveness of EU Business Associations* (London Palgrave).

Armstrong, K. A. and Bulmer, S. J. (1998) *The Governance of the Single European Market* (Manchester: Manchester University Press).

Artis, M. (1996) 'Alternative Transitions to EMU', *Economic Journal*, 106: 1005–15

Artis, M. and Buti, M. (2000) '"Close-to-Surplus": A Policy-Maker's Guide to the Implementation of the Growth and Stability Pact', *Journal of Common Market Studies*, 38(4): 563–91.

Aspinwall, M. (2002) 'The Dimensionality of the EU Policy Space', *European Union Politics*, 3(2): 81–111.

Aspinwall, M. and Schneider, G. (2000) 'Same Menu, Separate Tables: The Institutionalist Turn in Political Science and the Study of European Integration', *European Journal of Political Research*, 38(1): 1–36.

Attinà, F. (1990) 'The Voting Behaviour of the European Parliament Members and the Problem of Europarties', *European Journal of Political Research*, 18(3): 557–79.

Attinà, F. (1992) *Il Sistema Politico della Communità Europea* (Milan: Giuffrè).

Austen-Smith, D. (1993) 'Information and Influence: Lobbying for Agendas and Votes', *American Journal of Political Science*, 37(3): 799–833.

Austen-Smith, D. and Wright, J. R. (1994) 'Counteractive Lobbying', *American Journal of Political Science*, 38(1): 25–44.

Axelrod, R. (1970) *Conflict of Interest: A Theory of Divergent Goals with Application to Politics* (Chicago, Ill.: Markham).

Aylott, N. (2002) 'Let's Discuss this Later: Party Responses to Euro-Division in Scandinavia', *Party Politics*, 8(4): 441–61.

Bagehot, W. (1963 [1865]) *The English Constitution* (London: Fontana).

Bailey, D. and De Propris, L. (2002) 'The 1988 Reform of the European Structural Funds: Entitlement or Empowerment', *Journal of European Public Policy*, 9(3): 408–28.

Bailey, I. (1999) 'Flexibility and Harmonization in EU Environmental Policy', *Journal of Common Market Studies*, 37(4): 549–71.

Baldwin, R., Berglöf, E., Giavazzi, F. and Widgrén, J. (2001a) 'Eastern Enlargement and ECB Reform', *Swedish Economic Policy Review*, 89(1): 15–50.

Baldwin, R., Berglöf, E., Giavazzi, F. and Widgrén, J. (2001b) *Nice Try: Should the Nice Treaty by Ratified?* (London: Centre for Economic Policy Research).

Baldwin-Edwards, M. (1997) 'The Emerging European Immigration Regime: Some Reflections on Implications for Southern Europe', *Journal of Common Market Studies*, 35(4): 497–520.

Baldwin-Edwards, M. and Schain, M. (eds) (1994) *The Politics of Immigration in Western Europe* (London: Frank Cass).

Balme, R. and Jouve, B. (1996) 'Building the Regional State: Europe and Territorial Organization in France', in L. Hooghe (ed.), *Cohesion Policy and European Integration: Building Multi-Level Governance* (Oxford: Oxford University Press).

Banchoff, T. (2002) 'Institutions, Inertia and European Union Research Policy', *Journal of Common Market Studies*, 40(1): 1–21.

Bank for International Settlements (2002) *Triennial Central Bank Survey of Foreign Exchange and Derivatives Market Activity 2001* (Basle: Bank for International Settlements).

Banzhaf, J. F. (1965) 'Weighted Voting Doesn't Work: A Mathematical Analysis', *Rutgers Law Review*, 19: 317–43.

Bardi, L. (1996) 'Transnational Trends in European Parties and the 1994 Elections of the European Parliament', *Party Politics*, 2(1): 99–114.

Baron, D. and Ferejohn, J. A. (1989) 'Bargaining in Legislatures', *American Political Science Review*, 83(4, 1181–206.

Barrett, G. (2003) 'Family Matters', *Common Market Law Review*, 40(2): 369–421.

Barro, R. J. and Gordon, D. B. (1983) 'A Positive Theory of Monetary Policy in a Natural Rate Model', *Journal of Political Economy*, 91(4): 585–610.

Bartolini, S. and Mair, P. (1990) *Identity, Competition, and Electoral Availability: The Stability of European Electorates, 1885–1985* (Cambridge: Cambridge University Press).

Bastian, J. (1998) 'Putting the Cart Before the Horse? Labour market challenges ahead of monetary union in Europe', in D. Hine and Kassim (eds), *Beyond the Market: The EU and National Social Policy* (London: Routledge).

Bauböck, R. (1994) *Transnational Citizenship: Membership and Rights in International Migration* (Aldershot: Edward Elgar).

Baumgartner, F. R. and Leech, B. L. (1996) 'The Multiple Ambiguities of "Counter-active Lobbying"', *American Journal of Political Science*, 40(2): 521–42.

Becker, G. S. (1983) 'A Theory of Competition Among Pressure Groups for Political Influence', *Quarterly Journal of Economics*, 98(3): 371–400.

Begg, I. and Grimwade, N. (1998) *Paying for Europe* (Sheffield: Sheffield Academic Press).

Behrens, P. and Smyrl, M. (1999) 'A Conflict of Rationalities: EU Regional Policy and the Single Market', *Journal of European Public Policy*, 6(3): 419–35.

Bell, D. (1960) *The End of Ideology* (New York: Free Press).

Bentley, A. (1967) *The Process of Government* (Chicago, Ill.: University of Chicago Press).

Bergman, T. (1997) 'National Parliaments and EU Affairs Committees: Notes on Empirical Variation and Competing Explanations', *Journal of European Public Policy*, 4(3): 373–87.

Berlin, I. (1969) *Four Essays on Liberty* (Oxford: Oxford University Press).

Bermann, G. (1994) 'Taking Subsidiarity Seriously: Federalism in the EC and the US', *Columbia Law Review*, 94(2): 331–456.

Bernitz, U. (2001) 'Sweden and the European Union: On Sweden's Implementation and Application of European Law', *Common Market Law Review*, 38: 903–934.

Beyers, J. (1998) 'Where Does Supranationalism Come From? Ideas Floating Through the Working Groups of the Council of the European Union', *European Integration On-line Papers*, 2(9, http://eiop.or.at/eiop/texte/1998–009a.htm,.

Beyers, J. and Dierickx, G. (1998) 'The Working Groups of the Council of the European Union: Supranational of Intergovernmental Negotiations?', *Journal of Common Market Studies*, 36(3): 289–317.

Bhagwati, J. (2003) 'Borders Beyond Control', *Foreign Affairs*, 82(1): 98–101.

Bigo, D. (1994) 'The European Security Field: Stakes and Rivalries in a Newly Developing Area of Policy Intervention', in M. Anderson and M. den Boer (eds), *Policing Across National Boundaries* (London: Pinter).

Bilal, S. (1998) 'Political Economy Considerations on the Supply of Trade Protection in Regional Integration Agreements', *Journal of Common Market Studies*, 36(1): 1–32.

Bindseil, U. (2001) 'A Coalition-Form Analysis of the "One Country – One Vote" Rule in the Governing Council of the European Central Bank', *International Economic Journal*, 15(1): 141–64.

Bini Smaghi, L. and Casini, C. (2000) 'Monetary and Fiscal Policy Co-operation in EMU', *Journal of Common Market Studies*, 38(3): 375–91.

Birnbaum, P. and Badie, P. (1983) *The Sociology of the State* (Chicago, Ill.: University of Chicago Press).

Blondel, J. (1984) 'Dual Leadership in the Contemporary World: A Step Towards Executive and Regime Stability?', in D. Kavanagh and G. Peele (eds), *Comparative Government and Politics: Essays in Honour of S. E. Finer* (London: Heinemann).

Blondel, J., Sinnott, S. and Svensson, P. (1997) 'Representation and Voter Turnout', *European Journal of Political Research*, 32(2): 243–72.

Blondel, J., Sinnott, S. and Svensson, P. (1998) *People and Parliament in the European Union: Participation, Democracy and Legitimacy* (Oxford: Clarendon Press).

Bobbio, N. (1996) *Left and Right: The Significance of a Political Distinction*, trans. A. Cameron (Cambridge: Polity).

Boer, M. den (1994) 'The Quest for European Policing: Rhetoric and Justification in a Disorderly Debate', in M. Anderson and M. den Boer (eds), *Policing Across National Boundaries* (London: Pinter).

Bofinger, P. (1994) 'Is Europe an Optimum Currency Area', Discussion Paper no. 915 (London: Centre for Economic Policy Research).

Bogdandy, A. V. and Bast, J. (2002) 'The European Union's Vertical Order of Competences: The Current Law and Proposals for Its Reform', *Common Market Law Review*, 39: 227–68.

Bogdanor, V. (1986) 'The Future of the European Community: Two Models of Democracy', *Government and Opposition*, 22(2): 344–70.

Boix, C. (2003) *Democracy and Redistribution* (Cambridge: Cambridge University Press).

Boockmann, B. (1998) 'Agenda Control by Interest Groups in EU Social Policy', *Journal of Theoretical Politics*, 10(2): 215–36.

Borras-Alomar, S., Christiansen, T. and Rodriguez-Pose, A. (1994) 'Towards a "Europe of the Regions"? Visions and Realities from a Critical Perspective', *Regional Politics and Policy*, 4(2): 1–27.

Börzel, T. (1999) 'Transnational Adaptation to Europeanization in Germany and Spain', *Journal of Common Market Studies*, 37(4): 573–96.

Börzel, T. (2000) 'Why there is no "Southern Problem": on Environmental Leaders and Laggards in the European Union', *Journal of European Public Policy*, 7(1): 141–62.

Börzel, T. (2001) 'Non-Compliance in the European Union: Pathology or Statistical Artefact?', *Journal of European Public Policy*, 8(5): 803–24.

Börzel, T. (2002) *States and Regions in the European Union: Institutional Adaptation in Germany and Spain* (Cambridge: Cambridge University Press).

Bosch, A. and Newton, K. (1995) 'Economic Calculus or Familiarity Breeds Content?', in O. Niedermayer and R. Sinnott (eds), *Public Opinion and Internationalized Governance* (Oxford: Oxford University Press).

Bouwen, P. (2002) 'Corporate Lobbying in the European Union: the Logic of Access', *Journal of European Public Policy*, 9(3): 365–90.

Bowler, S. and Farrell, D. (1993) 'Legislator Shirking and Voter Monitoring: Impact of European Parliament Electoral Systems upon Legislator-Voter Relationships', *Journal of Common Market Studies*, 31(1): 45–69.

Bowler, S. and Farrell, D. (1995) 'The Organization of the European Parliament: Committees, Specialization and Co-ordination', *British Journal of Political Science*, 25(2): 219–43.

Bradley, K. St. C. (1997) 'The European Parliament and Comitology: On the Road to Nowhere?', *European Law Journal*, 3(3): 230–54.

Brams, S. J. and Affuso, P. J. (1985) 'New Paradoxes of Voting Power in the EC Council of Ministers', *Electoral Studies*, 4(1): 135–9.

Branch, A. and Greenwood, J. (2001) 'European Employers: Social Partners?', in H. Compston and J. Greenwood (eds), *Social Partnership in the European Union* (London: Palgrave).

Bräuninger, T., Cornelius, T., König, T. and Schuster, T. (2001) 'The Dynamics of European Integration: A Constitutional Analysis of the Amsterdam Treaty', in G. Schneider and M. Aspinwall (eds), *The Rules of Integration: Institutionalist Approaches to the Study of Europe* (Manchester: Manchester University Press).

Bräuninger, T. and König, T. (2001) *Indices of Power IOP 2.0* (computer program). (Konstanz: University of Konstanz, [http://www.uni-konstanz.de/FuF/Verwiss/koenig/IOP.html]).

Break, G. (1967) *Intergovernmental Fiscal Relations in the United States* (Washington, DC: The Brookings Institution).

Bribosia, H. (1998) 'Report on Belgium', in A.-M. Slaughter, A. Stone Sweet and J. H. H. Weiler (eds), *The European Court and National Courts – Doctrine and Jurisprudence: Legal Change in Its Social Context* (Oxford: Hart).

Brinegar, A., Jolly, S. and Kitschelt, H. (2002) 'Varieties of Capitalism and Political Divides over European Integration', in G. Marks and M. Steenbergen (eds), *European Integration and Political Conflict* (Cambridge: Cambridge University Press).

Broscheid, A. and Coen, D. (2003) 'Insider and Outsider Lobbying of the European Commission: An Informational Model of Forum Politics', *European Union Politics*, 4(2): 165–89.

Brown, C. C. and Oates, W. E. (1987) 'Assistance to the Poor in a Federal System', *Journal of Public Economics*, 32: 307–30.

Brubaker, R. (1992) *Citizenship and Nationhood in France and Germany* (Cambridge, Mass.: Harvard University Press).

Bruter, M. (2004) 'Winning Hearts and Minds for Europe: The Impact of News and Symbols on Civic and Cultural European Identity', *Comparative Political Studies*, 36(10): 1148–79.

Brzinski, J. B. (1995) 'Political Group Cohesion in the European Parliament, 1989–1994', in C. Rhodes and S. Mazey (eds), *The State of the European Union*, 3 (London: Longman).

Buchanan, J. M. and Tullock, G. (1962) *The Calculus of Consent* (Ann Arbor, Mich.: Michigan University Press).

Budden, P. (2002) 'Observations on the Single European Act and "Relaunch of Europe": A Less "Intergovernmental" Reading of the 1985 Intergovernmental Conference', *Journal of European Public Policy*, 9(1): 76–97.

Bufacchi, V. and Garmise, S. (1995) 'Social Justice in Europe: An Evaluation of European Regional Policy', *Government and Opposition*, 30(2): 179–97.

Buiter, W. (1999) 'Alice in Euroland', *Journal of Common Market Studies*, 37(2): 181–209.

Buiter, W., Corsetti, G. and Roubini, N. (1993) 'Maastricht's Fiscal Rules', *Economic Policy*, April 1993.

Bulmer, S. (1991) 'Analysing European Political Co-operation: The Case for Two-Tier Analysis', in M. Holland (ed.), *The Future of European Political Cooperation: Essays on Theory and Practice* (London: Macmillan).

Bulmer, S. (1994) 'The Governance of the European Union: A New Institutionalist Approach', *Journal of Public Policy*, 13(4): 351–80.

Bulmer, S. and Wessels, W. (1987) *The European Council: Decision-Making in European Politics* (London: Macmillan).

Burley, A.-M. and Mattli, W. (1993) 'Europe Before the Court: A Political Theory of Legal Integration', *International Organization*, 47(1): 41–76.

Bush, E. and Simi, P. (2001) 'European Farmers and Their Protest', in D. Imig and S. Tarrow (eds), *Contentious Europeans: Protest and Politics in an Emerging Polity* (Lanham, MD: Rowman and Littlefield).

Buti, M. and Guidice, G. (2002) 'Maastricht's Fiscal Rules at Ten: An Assessment', *Journal of Common Market Studies*, 40(5): 823–48.

Buti, M., Roeger, W. and in't Veld, J. (2001) 'Stabilizing Output and Inflation: Policy Constraints and Co-operation under a Stability Pact', *Journal of Common Market Studies*, 39(5): 801–28.

Butler, D. and Ranney, D. (eds) (1994) *Referendums Around the World: The Growing Use of Direct Democracy* (London: Macmillan).

Butt Philip, A. (1985) *Pressure Groups in the European Community* (London: Universities Association of Contemporary European Studies).

Caldeira, G. A. and Gibson, J. L. (1995) 'The Legitimacy of the Court of Justice in the European Union: Models of Institutional Support', *American Political Science Review*, 89(2): 356–76.

Cameron, C. (2000) *Veto Bargaining: Presidents and the Politics of Negative Power* (Cambridge: Cambridge University Press).

Cameron, D. (1992) 'The 1992 Initiative: Causes and Consequences', in A. M. Sbragia (ed.), *Euro-Politics: Institutions and Policymaking in the "New" Europe* (Washington, DC: The Brookings Institution).

Cameron, D. (1993) 'British Exit, German Voice, French Loyalty: Defection, Domination, and Cooperation in the 1992–93 ERM Crisis', paper presented at the annual meeting of the American Political Science Association, Washington, DC, September.

Cameron, D. (1997) 'Economic and Monetary Union: Underlying Imperatives and Third-Stage Dilemmas', *Journal of European Public Policy*, 4(3): 455–85.

Cameron, D. (1998) 'Creating Supranational Authority in Monetary and Exchange-Rate Policy: The Sources and Effects of EMU', in W. Sandholtz and A. Stone Sweet (eds), *European Integration and Supranational Governance* (Oxford: Oxford University Press).

Cameron, F. (1998) 'Building a Common Foreign Policy: Do Institutions Matter?', in J. Peterson and H. Sjursen (eds), *A Common Foreign Policy for Europe? Competing Visions of the CFSP* (London: Routledge).

Caporale, G. M. (1993) 'Is Europe an Optimum Currency Area? Symmetric Versus Asymmetric Shocks in the EC', *National Institute Economic Review*(144): 95–103.

Cappelletti, M., Seccombe, M. and Weiler, J. H. H. (eds) (1986) *Integration Through Law*, vols 1 and 2 (Berlin: De Gruyter).

Carey, S. (2002a) *The Impact of Political Parties on Public Support for European Integration*, unpublished doctoral thesis, University of Essex.

Carey, S. (2002b) 'Undivided Loyalties: Is National Identity an Obstacle to European Integration?', *European Union Politics*, 3(4): 387–413.

Carey, W. L. (1974) 'Federalism and Corporate Law: Reflections upon Delaware', *Yale Law Review*, 83(4): 663–705.

Carrubba, C. J. (1997) 'Net Financial Transfers in the European Union: Who Gets What and Why?', *The Journal of Politics*, 59(2): 469–96.

Carrubba, C. J. (2001) 'The Electoral Connection in European Union Politics', *Journal of Politics*, 63(1): 141–58.

Carrubba, C. J. and Volden, C. (2001) 'Explaining Institutional Change in the European Union: What Determines the Voting Rule in the Council of Ministers', *European Union Politics*, 2(1): 5–30.

Catabia, M. (1998) 'The Italian Constitutional Court and the Relationship Between the Italian Legal System and the European Union', in A.-M. Slaughter, A. Stone Sweet and J. H. H. Weiler (eds), *The European Court and National Courts – Doctrine and Jurisprudence: Legal Change in Its Social Context* (Oxford: Hart).

Cawson, A. and Saunders, P. (1983) 'Corporatism, Competitive Politics and Class Struggle', in R. King (ed.), *Capital and Politics* (London: Routledge).

Cecchini, P. (1988) *The European Challenge, 1992: The Benefits of a Single Market* (Aldershot: Gower).

Chalmers, D. (1995) 'The Single Market: From Prima Donna to Journeyman', in J. Shaw and G. More (eds), *New Legal Dynamics of European Union* (Oxford: Clarendon Press).

Chalmers, D. (1997) 'Judicial Preferences and the Community Legal Order', *Modern Law Review*, 60(2): 164–99.

Chalmers, D. (1998) 'Bureaucratic Europe: From Regulatory Communities to Securitising Unions', paper presented at the annual conference of the Council for European Studies, Baltimore, 28 February.

Chalmers, D. (2001) 'The Positioning of EU Judicial Politics Within the United Kingdom', in K. H. Goetz and S. Hix (eds), *Europeanised Politics? European Integration and National Political Systems* (London: Frank Cass).

Chopin, I. and Niessen, J. (eds) (1998) *Proposals for Legislative Measures to Combat Racism and to Promote Equal Rights in the European Union* (Brussels and London: Starting Line Group and Commission for Racial Equality).

Christiansen, T. (2001) 'Intra-Institutional Politics and Inter-Institutional Relations in the EU: Towards Coherent Governance?', *Journal of European Public Policy*, 8(5): 747–69.

Christiansen, T. (2002) 'The Role of Supranational Actors in EU Treaty Reform', *Journal of European Public Policy*, 9(1): 33–53.

Christiansen, T., Falkner, G. and Jørgensen, K. E. (2002) 'Theorizing EU Treaty Reform: Beyond Diplomacy and Bargaining', *Journal of European Public Policy*, 9(1): 12–32.

Christin, T. and Hug, S. (2002) 'Referendums and Citizen Support for European Integration', *Comparative Political Studies*, 35(5): 586–617.

Chryssochoou, D. (1994) 'Democracy and Symbiosis in the European Union: Towards a Confederal Consociation?', *West European Politics*, 17(1): 1–14.

Cichowski, R. A. (2000) 'Western Dreams, Eastern Realities: Support for the European Union in Central and Eastern Europe', *Comparative Political Studies*, 33(10): 1243–78.

Cini, M. (1996) *The European Commission: Leadership, Organisation and Culture in the EU Administration* (Manchester: Manchester University Press).

Cini, M. (1997) 'Administrative Culture in the European Commission: The Cases of Competition and Environment', in N. Nugent (ed.), *At the Heart of the Union: Studies of the European Commission* (London: Macmillan).

Claes, M. and de Witte, B. (1998) 'Report on the Netherlands', in A.-M. Slaughter, A. Stone Sweet and J. H. H. Weiler (eds), *The European Court and National Courts – Doctrine and Jurisprudence: Legal Change in Its Social Context* (Oxford: Hart).

Clark, W. R., Golder, M. and Golder, S. N. (2002) 'Fiscal Policy and the Democratic Process in the European Union', *European Union Politics*, 3(2): 205–30.

Clutterbuck, R. (1990) *Terrorism, Drugs and Crime in Europe after 1992* (London: Routledge).

Cobham, D. (1996) 'Causes and Effects of the European Monetary Crisis of 1992–93', *Journal of Common Market Studies*, 34(4): 585–604.

Coen, D. (1997) 'The Evolution of the Large Firm as a Political Actor in the European Union', *Journal of European Public Policy*, 4(1): 91–108.

Coen, D. (1998a) *The Large Firm as a Political Actor in the European Union* (London: Routledge).

Coen, D. (1998b) 'The European Business Interest and the Nation-State: Large-Firm Lobbying in the European Union and the Member States', *Journal of Public Policy*, 18(1): 75–100.

Cohen, M. A. (1992) 'The Motives of Judges: Empirical Evidence from Antitrust Sentencing', *International Review of Law and Economics*, 12(1): 13–30.

Cole, A. (2001) 'National and Partisan Contexts of Europeanization: The Case of the French Socialists', *Journal of Common Market Studies*, 39(1): 15–36.

Cole, J. and Cole, F. (1997) *A Geography of the European Union*, 2nd edn (London: Routledge).

Coleman, W. D. (1998) 'From Protected Development to Market Liberalism: Paradigm Change in Agriculture', *Journal of European Public Policy*, 5(4): 632–51.

Coleman, W. D. and Tangermann, S. (1999) 'The 1992 CAP Reform, the Uruguay Round and the Commission', *Journal of Common Market Studies*, 37(3): 385–405.

Colomer, J. M. (1999) 'On the Geometry of Unanimity Rule', *Journal of Theoretical Politics*, 11(4): 543–53.

Committee for the Study of Economic and Monetary Union (1989) *Report on Economic and Monetary Union in Europe* (the Delors Report) (Luxembourg: Office for Official Publications of the European Union).

Compston, H. and Greenwood, J. (eds) (2001) *Social Partnership in the European Union* (London: Palgrave).

Conant, L. (2002) *Justice Contained: Law and Politics in the European Union* (Ithaca, NY: Cornell University Press).

Conzelmann, T. (1995) 'Networking and the Politics of EU Regional Policy: Lessons from North Rhine-Westphalia, Nord-Pas de Calais and North West England', *Regional and Federal Studies*, 5(2): 134–72.

Coombes, D. (1970) *Politics and Bureaucracy in the European Community: A Portrait of the Commission of the E.E.C.* (London: Allen & Unwin).

Cooter, R. and Drexl, J. (1994) 'The Logic of Power in the Emerging European Constitution: Game Theory and the Division of Powers', *International Review of Law and Economics*, 14(2): 307–26.

Cooter, R. and Ginsburg, T. (1997) 'Comparative Judicial Discretion: An Empirical Test of Economic Models', in D. Schmidtchen and R. Cooter (eds), *Constitutional Law and Economics of the European Union* (Cheltenham: Edward Elgar).

Corbett, R., Jacobs, F. and Shackleton, M. (1995) *The European Parliament*, 3rd edn (London: Catermill).

Corbett, R., Jacobs, F. and Shackleton, M. (2000) *The European Parliament*, 4th edn (London: Catermill).

Cornelius, W. A., Martin, P. L. and Hollifield, J. F. (1994) 'Introduction: The Ambivalent Quest for Immigration Control', in W. A. Cornelius, P. L. Martin and J. F. Hollifield (eds), *Controlling Immigration: A Global Perspective* (Stanford, CA: Stanford University Press).

Council of the European Communities (1990) *The Council of the European Community* (Luxembourg: Office of Official Publications of the European Communities).

Council of the European Union (1995) *Draft Report of the Council on the Functioning of the Treaty on European Union* (Brussels: Council of Ministers).

Court of Justice (1995) *Report of the Court of Justice on Certain Aspects of the Application of the Treaty on European Union* (Luxembourg: Court of Justice of the European Union, 22 May 1995).

Court of Justice (1999) *The Future of the Judicial System of the European Union (Proposals and Reflections)* (Luxembourg: Court of Justice of the European Union, May 1999).

Cowles, M. Green (1995) 'Setting the Agenda for a New Europe: The ERT and EC 1992', *Journal of Common Market Studies*, 33(4): 501–26.

Cowles, M. Green (1997) 'Organizing Industrial Coalitions: A Challenge for the Future?', in H. Wallace and A. R. Young (eds), *Participation and Policy-Making in the European Union* (Oxford: Clarendon Press).

Cowles, M. Green (1998) 'The Changing Architecture of Big Business', in J. Greenwood and M. Aspinwall (eds), *Collective Action in the European Union* (London: Routledge).

Cowles, M. Green (2002) 'Large Firms and the Transformation of EU Business Associations: A Historical Perspective', in J. Greenwood (ed.), *The Effectiveness of EU Business Associations* (London: Palgrave).

Cowles, M. Green and Risse, T. (2001) 'Europeanization and Domestic Change: Conclusions', in M. Green Cowles, J. Caporaso and T. Risse (eds), *Europeanization and Domestic Change* (Ithaca, NY: Cornell University Press).

Cox, G. W. (1987) *The Efficient Secret: The Cabinet and the Development of Political Parties in Victorian England* (Cambridge: Cambridge University Press).

Cox, G. W. and McCubbins, M. (1993) *Legislative Leviathan: Party Government in the House* (Berkeley, CA: University of California Press).

Craig, P. (1998) 'Report on the United Kingdom', in A.-M. Slaughter, A. Stone Sweet and J. H. H. Weiler (eds), *The European Court and National Courts – Doctrine and Jurisprudence: Legal Change in Its Social Context* (Oxford: Hart).

Craig, P. (2001) 'The Jurisdiction of the Community Courts Reconsidered', in G. de Búrca and J. H. H. Weiler (eds), *The European Court of Justice* (Oxford: Oxford University Press).

Cram, L. (1993) 'Calling the Tune Without Paying the Piper? Social Policy Regulation: the Role of the Commission in European Union Social Policy', *Policy and Politics*, 21(1): 135–46.

Cram, L (1994) 'The European Commission as a Multi-Organization: Social Policy and IT Policy in the EU', *Journal of European Public Policy*, 1(2): 195–217.

Cram, L. (1997) *Policy-Making in the EU: Conceptual Lenses and the Integration Process* (London: Routledge).

Cram, L. (1998) 'The EU Institutions and Collective Action: Constructing a European Interest?', in J. Greenwood and M. Aspinwall (eds), *Collective Action in the European Union* (London: Routledge).

Crombez, C. (1996) 'Legislative Procedures in the European Community', *British Journal of Political Science*, 26(2): 199–218.

Crombez, C. (1997a) 'The Co-Decision Procedure in the European Union', *Legislative Studies Quarterly*, 22(1): 97–119.

Crombez, C. (1997b) 'Policy Making and Commission Appointment in the European Union', *Aussenwirtschaft*, 52, (1–2): 63–82.

Crombez, C. (2000) 'The Treaty of Amsterdam and the co-decision procedure', in G. Schneider and M. Aspinwall (eds), *The Rules of Integration: Institutional Approaches to the Study of Europe* (Manchester: Manchester University Press).

Crombez, C. (2001) 'Institutional Reform and Co-Decision in the European Union', *Constitutional Political Economy*, 11(1): 41–57.

Crombez, C. (2002) 'Information, Lobbying and the Legislative Process in the European Union', *European Union Politics*, 3(1): 7–32.

Crouch, C. and Menon, A. (1997) 'Organised Interests and the State', in M. Rhodes, P. Heywood and V. Wright (eds), *Developments in West European Politics* (London: Macmillan).

Crowley, P. (1996) 'EMU, Maastricht and the 1996 Intergovernmental Conference', *Contemporary Economic Policy*, 14): 41–55.

Crowley, P. (2001) 'The Institutional Implications of EMU', *Journal of Common Market Studies*, 39(3): 385–404.

Cukierman, A. (1992) *Central Bank Strategy, Credibility and Independence: Theory and Evidence* (Cambridge, Mass.: Massachusetts Institute of Technology Press).

Cukierman, A., Webb, S. B. and Neyapti, B. (1993) 'The Measurement of Central Bank Independence and its Effect on Policy Outcomes', *The World Bank Economic Review*, 6: 353–98.

Cusack, T. R. (2001) 'Partisanship in the Setting and Coordination of Fiscal and Monetary Policies', *European Journal of Political Research*, 40: 93–115.

Dahrendorf, R. (1959) *Class and Class Conflict in Industrial Society* (London: Routledge).

Dalton, R. J. (1988) *Citizen Politics in Western Democracies: Public Opinion and Political Parties in the United States Great Britain, West Germany and France* (Chatham: Chatham House).

Dalton, R. J., Kuechler, M. and Bürklin, W. (1990) 'The Challenge of New Movements', in R. J. Dalton and M. Kuechler (eds), *Challenging the Political Order: New Social and Political Movements in Western Democracies* (Oxford: Oxford University Press).

Damro, C. (2001) 'Building an External Identity: The EU and Extraterritorial Competition Policy', *Journal of European Public Policy*, 8(2): 208–26.

Daugbjerg, C. (1999) 'Reforming the CAP', *Journal of Common Market Studies*, 39(3): 407–28.

Daugbjerg, C. (2003) 'Policy Feedback and Paradigm Shift in EU Agricultural Policy: The Effects of the MacSharry Reform on Future Reform', *Journal of European Public Policy*, 10(3): 421–37.

Daugbjerg, C. and Swinbank, A. (2004) 'The CAP and EU Enlargement: Prospects for an Alternative Strategy to Avoid the Lock-in of CAP Support', *Journal of Common Market Studies*, 42(1): 99–119.

De Grauwe, P. (2002a) 'Challenges for Monetary Policy in Euroland', *Journal of Common Market Studies*, 40(4): 683–718.

De Grauwe, P. (2002b) 'Europe's Instability Pact', *Financial Times*, 25 July 2002, p. 17.

De Grauwe, P. (2003) *The Economics of Monetary Integration*, 5th edn (Oxford: Oxford University Press).

De Grauwe, P. and Vanhaverbeke, W. (1993) 'Is Europe and Optimum Currency Area? Evidence From Regional Data', in P. R. Masson and M. P. Taylor (eds), *Policy Issues in the Operation of Currency Unions* (Cambridge: Cambridge University Press).

De La Fuente, A. and Domenech, R. (2001) 'The Redistributive Effects of the EU Budget: An Analysis and Proposal for Reform', *Journal of Common Market Studies*, 39(2): 307–30.

De Rynck, S. and McAleavey, P. (2001) 'The Cohesion Deficit in Structural Fund Policy', *Journal of European Public Policy*, 8(4): 541–57.

De Winter, L. and Swyngedouw, M. (1999) 'The Scope of EU Government', in H. Schmitt and J. Thomassen (eds), *Political Representation and Legitimacy in the European Union* (Oxford: Oxford University Press).

Decker, F. (2002) 'Governance Beyond the Nation-State: Reflections on the Democratic Deficit in the European Union', *Journal of European Public Policy*, 9(2): 256–72.

Dedman, M. (1996) *The Origins and Development of the European Union, 1945–1995* (London: Routledge).

Dehousse, R. (1992) 'Integration v. Regulation? On the Dynamics of Regulation in the European Community', *Journal of Common Market Studies*, 30(4): 383–402.

Dehousse, R. (1995) 'Constitutional Reform in the European Community: Are there Alternatives to the Majoritarian Avenue?', in J. Hayward (ed.), *The Crisis of Representation in Europe* (London: Frank Cass).

Dehousse, R. (1997) 'Regulation by Networks in the European Community: The Role of European Agencies', *Journal of European Public Policy*, 4(2): 246–61.

Dehousse, R. and Majone, G. (1994) 'The Institutional Dynamics of European Integration: From the Single Act to the Maastricht Treaty', in S. Martin (ed.), *The Construction of Europe – Essays in Honour of Emile Noël* (Dordrecht: Kluwer).

Deighton, A. (2002) 'The European Security and Defence Policy', *Journal of Common Market Studies*, 40(4): 719–41.

Devuyst, Y. (1995) "The European Community and the Conclusion of the Uruguay Round', in C. Rhodes and S. Mazey (eds), *The State and the European Union*, 3 (London: Longman).

Dicey, A. V. (1939 [1885]) *Introduction Study of the Law of the Constitution* (London: Macmillan).

Diez Medrano, J. and P. Gutiérrez (2001) 'Nested Identities: National and European Identity in Spain', *Ethnic and Racial Studies*, 24: 753–78.

Dimitrova, A. and Steunenberg, B. (2000) 'The Search for Convergence of National Policies in the European Union: An Impossible Quest?', *European Union Politics*, 1(2): 201–26.

Dinan, D. (1994) *Ever Closer Union? An Introduction to the European Community* (London: Macmillan).

Docksey, C. and Williams, K. (1997) 'The Commission and the Execution of Community Policy', in G. Edwards and D. Spence (eds), *The European Commission*, 2nd edn (London: Catermill).

Dogan, R. (1997) 'Comitology: Little Procedures with Big Implications', *West European Politics*, 20(3): 31–60.

Dogan, R. (2001) 'A Cross-Sectional View of Comitology: Incidence, Issues and Implications', in T. Christiansen and E. Kirchner (eds), *Committee Governance in the European Union* (Manchester: Manchester University Press).

Dølvik, J. E. and Visser, J. (2001) 'ETUC and European Social Partnership: A Third Turning-Point?', in H. Compston and J. Greenwoods (eds), *Social Partnership in the European Union* (London: Palgrave).

Donnelly, M. and Ritchie, E. (1997) 'The College of Commissioners and the Cabinets', in G. Edwards and D. Spence (eds), *The European Commission*, 2nd edn (London: Catermill).

Donohue, J. D. and Pollack, M. A. (2001) 'Centralization and Its Discontents: The Rhythms of Federalism in the United States and the European Union', in K. Nicolaïdis and R. Howse (eds), The Federal Vision: Legitimacy and Levels of Governance in the United States and the European Union (Oxford: Oxford University Press).

Dornbusch, R. (1990) 'Two-Track EMU, Now!', in K. O. Pöhl *et al.*, *Britain and EMU* (London: Centre for Economic Performance).

Downs, A. (1957) *An Economic Theory of Democracy* (New York: Harper and Row).

Downs, W. M. (2001) 'Denmark's Referendum on the Euro: The Mouse that Roared ... Again', *West European Politics*, 24(1): 222–6.

Drake, H. (1995) 'Political Leadership and European Integration: The Case of Jacques Delors', *West European Politics*, 18(1): 140–60.

Drewry, G. (1993) 'Judicial Politics in Britain: Patrolling the Boundaries', in M. L. Volcansek (ed.), *Judicial Politics and Policy-Making in Western Europe* (London: Frank Cass).

Duke, S. (1996) 'The Second Death (or Second Coming?) of the WEU', *Journal of Common Market Studies*, 34(2): 167–90.

Dunleavy, P. (1979) 'The Urban Basis of Political Alignment: Social Class, Domestic Property Ownership and State Intervention in Consumer Processes', *British Journal of Political Science*, 9(3): 409–43.

Dunleavy, P. (1990) *Democracy, Bureaucracy and Public Choice: Economic Explanations in Political Science* (London: Harvester Wheatsheaf).

Dunleavy, P. (1997) 'Explaining the Centralization of the European Union: A Public Choice Analysis', *Aussenwirtschaft*, 52, (1–2): 183–212.

Dunleavy, P. and O'Duffy, B. (1998) 'The Organizational Structure of the European Commission: A Bureau-Shaping Analysis', unpublished mimeo (London: London School of Economics and Political Science).

Dunleavy, P. and O'Leary, B. (1987) *Theories of the State: The Politics of Liberal Democracy* (London: Macmillan).

Dyson, K. (1994) *Elusive Union: The Process of Economic and Monetary Integration in Europe* (London: Longman).

Dyson, K. (2000) *The Politics of the Euro-Zone: Stability or Breakdown?* (Oxford: Oxford University Press).

Dyson, K. and Featherstone, K. (1999) *The Road to Maastricht: Negotiating Economic and Monetary Union* (Oxford: Oxford University Press).

Dyson, K., Featherstone, K. and Michalopoulis, G. (1994) 'The Politics of EMU: The Maastricht Treaty and the Relevance of Bargaining Models', paper presented at the annual meeting of the American Political Science Association, New York, September.

Earnshaw, D. and Judge, D. (1995) 'Early Days: the European Parliament, Co-Decision and the European Union Legislative Process Post-Maastricht', *Journal of European Public Policy*, 2(4): 624–49.

Earnshaw, D. and Judge, D. (1997) 'The Life and Times of the European Union's Co-operation Procedure', *Journal of Common Market Studies*, 35(4): 543–64.

Earnshaw, D. and Judge, D. (2002) 'No Simple Dichotomies: Lobbyists and the European Parliament', *Journal of Legislative Studies*, 8(4): 62–79.

Easton, D. (1957) 'An Approach to the Study of Political Systems', *World Politics*, 9(5): 383–400.

Easton, D. (1965) *A Framework for Political Analysis* (Englewood Cliffs, NJ: Prentice-Hall).

Easton, D. (1975) 'A Reassessment of the Concept of Political Support', *British Journal of Political Science*, 5: 435–57.

Edwards, G. and Spence, D. (eds) (1997) *The European Commission*, 2nd edn (London: Catermill).

Egan, M. P. (2001) *Constructing a European Market* (Oxford: Oxford University Press).

Ehin, P. (2001) 'Determinants of Public Support for EU Membership: Data from the Baltic States', *European Journal of Political Research*, 40: 31–56.

Ehlermann, C.-D. and Hancher, L. (1995) 'Comments on Streit and Mussler', *European Law Journal*, 1(1): 84–8.

Eichenberg, R. C. and Dalton, R. J. (1993) 'Europeans and the European Community: The Dynamics of Public Support for European Integration', *International Organization*, 47(4): 507–34.

Eichener, V. (1992) *Social Dumping or Innovative Regulation? Processes and Outcomes of European Decision-Making in the Sector of Health and Safety at Work Harmonization*, EUI Working Paper SPS no. 92/28 (Florence: European University Institute).

Eichener, V. (1997) 'Effective European Problem-Solving: Lessons from the Regulation of Occupational Safety and Environmental Protection', *Journal of European Public Policy*, 4(4): 591–608.

Eichengreen, B. (1990) 'Costs and Benefits of European Monetary Unification', Discussion Paper no. 453 (London: Centre for Economic Policy Research).

Eichengreen, B. (1991) 'Designing a Central Bank for Europe: A Cautionary Tale from the Early Years of the Federal Reserve System', Discussion Paper no. 585 (London: Centre for Economic Policy Research).

Eichengreen, B. (1993a) 'Labor Markets and European Monetary Unification', in P. Masson and M. Taylor (eds), *Policy Issues in the Operation of Currency Unions* (Cambridge: Cambridge University Press).

Eichengreen, B. (1993b) 'Thinking About Migration: Notes on European Migration Pressures at the Dawn of the Next Millennium', in H. Siebert (ed.), *Migration: A Challenge for Europe* (Ann Arbor, Mich.: University of Michigan Press).

Eichengreen, B. (1994) 'Fiscal Policy in EMU', in B. Eichengreen and J. Frieden (eds), *The Political Economy of European Monetary Unification* (Boulder, CO: Westview).

Eichengreen, B. and Frieden, J. A. (2001) 'The Political Economy of European Monetary Unification: An Analytical Introduction', in B. Eichengreen and J. A. Frieden (eds), *The Political Economy of European Monetary Unification*, 2nd edn (Boulder: Westview).

Eichengreen, B. and Von Hagen, J. (1996) 'Fiscal Policy and Monetary Union: Federalism, Fiscal Restrictions, and the No-Bailout Rule', in H. Siebert (ed.), *Monetary Policy in an Integrated World Economy* (Mohr: Tübingen).

Eijk, C. van der and Franklin, M. (eds) (1996) *Choosing Europe? The European Electorate and National Politics in the Face of Union* (Ann Arbor, Mich.: University of Michigan Press).

Eijk, C. van der, Franklin, M. and van der Burg, W. (2001) 'Policy Preference and Party Choice', in H. Schmitt and J. Thomassen (eds), *Political Representation and Legitimacy in the European Union* (Oxford: Oxford University Press).

Eijk, C. van der, Franklin, M. and Oppenhuis, E. (1996) 'The Strategic Context: Party Choice', in C. van der Eijk and M. Franklin (eds), *Choosing Europe? The European Electorate and National Politics in the Face of Union* (Ann Arbor, Mich.: University of Michigan Press).

Elazar, D. J. (2001) 'The United States and the European Union: Models for Their Epochs', in K. Nicolaïdis and R. Howse (eds), *The Federal Vision: Legitimacy and Levels of Governance in the United States and the European Union* (Oxford: Oxford University Press).

Epstein, D. and O'Halloran, S. (1999) *Delegating Powers: A Transaction Cost Politics Approach to Policy Making Under Separate Powers* (Cambridge: Cambridge University Press).

Eskridge, W. N. Jr (1991) 'Reneging on History? Playing the Court/Congress/President Civil Rights Game', *California Law Review*, 38: 613–84.

Esping-Andersen, G. (1990) *The Three Worlds of Welfare Capitalism* (Cambridge: Polity Press).

European Commission (1985) *Completing the Internal Market: White Paper of the Commission the European Council*, COM(85) 310 (Luxembourg: Office of Official Publications of the European Communities).

European Commission (1990) 'One Market, One Money: An Evaluation of the Potential Benefits and Costs of Forming an Economic and Monetary Union', *European Economy*, 44.

European Commission (1992) *An Open and Structured Dialogue between the Commission and Special Interest Groups*, SEC(92) 2272 final (Brussels: European Commission, 2 December).

European Commission (1995) *The Agricultural Situation in the Community* (Luxembourg: Office for Official Publications of the European Communities).

European Commission (1997) *Single Market Scoreboard, No. 1* (Luxembourg: Office for Official Publications of the European Union).

European Commission (1998a) *European Union Financial Report, 1996* (Luxembourg: Office for Official Publications of the European Communities).

European Commission (1998b) *Report on Progress Towards Convergence and the Recommendation with a View to the Transition to the Third Stage of Economic and Monetary Union, Part 1: Recommendation* (Luxembourg: Office of Official Publications of the European Communities, 25 March 1998).

European Commission (1998c) *Committee Procedures: Simpler, More Democratic, More Transparent*, IP/98/554 (Brussels: European Commission, 24 June 1998).

European Commission (2000a) *The Community Budget: Facts in Figures* (Luxembourg: Office for Official Publications of the European Communities).

European Commission (2000b) *The European Commission, 2000–2004* (Luxembourg: Office for Official Publications of the European Communities).

European Commission (2001) *Working for the Regions* (Luxembourg: Office for Official Publications of the European Union).

European Commission (2002a) *Report on the Working of the Committees During 2000*, Official Journal No. C 37, 2002, Item 2 (Luxembourg: Office for Official Publications of the European Union).

European Commission (2002b) *Agricultural Situation in the European Union: 2002 Report* (Luxembourg: Office for Official Publications of the European Union).

European Commission (2003) *Internal Market Scoreboard, No 12* (Luxembourg: Office for Official Publications of the European Union).

European Commission (2004) *General Budget of the European Union for the Financial Year 2004* (Luxembourg: Office for Official Publications of the European Union).

European Parliament (1985) *Committee of Inquiry into the Rise of Fascism and Racism in Europe: Report of the Findings of the Inquiry* (Evrigenis Report) (Luxembourg: Office for Official Publications of the European Communities).

European Parliament (1991) *Committee of Inquiry on Racism and Xenophobia: Report on the Findings of the Inquiry* (Ford Report) (Luxembourg: Office for Official Publications of the European Communities).

European Parliament (1995a) *Report on the Functioning of the Treaty on European Union with a View to the 1996 Intergovernmental Conference*, PE 212.450 (Brussels: European Parliament).

European Parliament (1995b) *Resolution on the Functioning of the Treaty on European Union With a View to the 1996 Intergovernmental Conference – Implementation and Development of the Union*, PE 190.440 (Brussels: European Parliament).

European Parliament (1997) *Progress Report, 1 August 1996 to 31 July 1997, on the Delegations to the Conciliation Committee (Fontaine, Imbeni, Verde i Aldea)*, PE 223.209 (Brussels: European Parliament).

Evans, R. B., Jacobson, H. K. and Putnam, R. D. (eds) (1993) *Double-Edged Diplomacy: International Bargaining and Domestic Politics* (Berkeley, CA: University of California Press).

Everson, M. (1995) 'The Legacy of the Market Citizen', in J. Shaw and G. More (eds), *New Legal Dynamics of European Union* (Oxford: Clarendon Press).

Fagerberg, J. and Verspagen, B. (1996) 'Heading for Divergence? Regional Growth in Europe Reconsidered', *Journal of Common Market Studies*, 34(3): 431–48.

Falkner, G. (1996) 'European Works Councils and the Maastricht Social Agreement: Towards a New Policy Style?', *Journal of European Public Policy*, 3(2): 192–208.

Falkner, G. (2000a) 'Effects of EU Membership on a New Member State', *Journal of Common Market Studies*, 38(2): 223–50.

Falkner, G. (2000b) 'Policy Networks in a Multi-Level System: Convergence Towards Moderate Diversity?', *West European Politics*, 23(4): 94–120.

Falkner, G. (2000c) 'The Council and the Social Partners? EC Social Policy Between Diplomacy and Collective Bargaining', *Journal of European Public Policy*, 7(5): 705–24.

Falkner, G. (2002) 'How Intergovernmental and Intergovernmental Conferences? An Example from the Maastricht Treaty Reform', *Journal of European Public Policy*, 9(1): 98–119.

Favell, A. (1997a) *Philosophies of Integration: Immigration and the Idea of Citizenship in France and Britain* (London: Macmillan).

Favell, A. (1997b) 'European Citizenship and the Incorporation of Migrants and Minorities in Europe: Emergence, Transformation and Effects of a New Political Field', paper presented at the annual conference of the European Sociological Association, Essex, 27–30 August.

Favell, A. and Hansen, R. (2002) 'Markets Against Politics: Migration, EU Enlargement, and the Idea of Europe', *Journal of Ethnic and Migration Studies*, 28(4): 581–601.

Fearon, J. (1999) 'Electoral Accountability and the Control of Politicians: Selecting Good Types Versus Sanctioning Poor Performance', in A. Przeworksi, S. C. Stokes and B. Manin (eds), *Democracy, Accountability and Representation* (Cambridge: Cambridge University Press).

Featherstone, K. and Ginsberg, R. H. (1996) *The United States and the European Union in the 1990s: Partners in Transition*, 2nd edn (London: Macmillan).

Federal Trust (1996) *Justice and Fair Play*, Intergovernmental Conference of the European Union 1996, Federal Trust Papers 6 (London: Federal Trust).

Feldstein, M. (1992) 'Europe's Monetary Union: The Case Against EMU', *The Economist*, 13 June, pp. 19–22.

Felsenthal, D. S. and Machover, M. (1997) 'The Weighted Voting Rule in the EU's Council of Ministers, 1958–95: Intentions and Outcomes', *Electoral Studies*, 16(1): 33–47.

Felsenthal, D. S. and Machover, M. (2001) 'The Treaty of Nice and Qualified Majority Voting', *Social Choice and Welfare*, 18(3): 431–64.

Ferejohn, J. A. and Weingast, B. R. (1992) 'A Positive Theory of Statutory Interpretation', *International Review of Law and Economics*, 12(2): 263–79.

Ferejohn, J. and Weingast, B. R. (eds) (1997) *The New Federalism: Can the States be Trusted?* (Stanford, CA: Hoover Institution Press).

Ferrara, F. and Weishaupt, J. T. (2004) 'Get Your Act Together: Party Performance in European Parliament Elections', *European Union Politics*, 5(3) (forthcoming).

Fierke, K. and Wiener, A. (1999) 'Constructing Institutional Interests: EU and NATO enlargement', *Journal of European Public Policy*, 6(5): 721–42.

Finer, S. E. (1987) 'Left and Right', in V. Bogdanor (ed.), *The Blackwell Encyclopaedia of Political Institutions* (Oxford: Blackwell).

Finnemore, M. (1996) *National Interests in International Society* (Ithaca, NY: Cornell University Press).

Finnemore, M. and Sikkink, K. (1998) 'International Norm Dynamics and Political Change', *International Organization*, 52(4).

Fiorina, M. (1982) 'Legislative Choice of Regulatory Forms: Legal Process or Administrative Process?', *Public Choice*, 39(1): 33–66.

Fitzmaurice, J. (1978) *The European Parliament* (London: Saxon House).

Flanagan, S. C. (1987) 'Value Change in Industrial Societies', *American Political Science Review*, 81(4): 1303–18.

Fligstein, N. and Mara-Drita, I. (1996) 'How to Make a Market: Reflections on the Attempt to Create a Single Market in the European Union', *American Journal of Sociology*, 102(1): 1–33.

Fligstein, N. and McNichol, J. (1998) 'The Institutional Terrain of the European Union', in W. Sandholtz and A. Stone Sweet (eds), *European Integration and Supranational Governance* (Oxford: Oxford University Press).

Flora, P. and Heidenheimer, A. J. (eds) (1981) *The Development of the Welfare State in Europe and America* (New Brunswick: Transaction Books).

Forwood, G. (2001) 'The Road to Cotonou: Negotiating a Successor to Lomé', *Journal of Common Market Studies*, 39(3): 423–42.

Franchino, F. (2000a) 'Control of the Commission's Executive Functions: Uncertainty, Control and Decision Rules', *European Union Politics*, 1(1): 59–88.

Franchino, F. (2000b) 'Statutory Discretion and Procedural Control of the European Commission's Executive Functions', *Journal of Legislative Studies*, 6(1): 28–50.

Franchino, F. (2000c) 'The Commission's Executive Discretion, Information and Comitology', *Journal of Theoretical Politics*, 12(2): 155–81.

Franchino, F. (2001) 'Delegation and Constraints in the National Execution of the EC Policies: A Longitudinal and Qualitative Analysis', *West European Politics*, 24(4): 169–92.

Franchino, F. (2002) 'Efficiency or Credibility? Testing the Two Logics of Delegation to the European Commission', *Journal of European Public Policy*, 9(5): 677–94.

Franchino, F. (2004) 'Delegating Powers in the European Community', *British Journal of Political Science*, 34: 449–76.

Frank, J. (1973) *Courts on Trial: Myth and Reality of American Justice* (Princeton, NJ: Princeton University Press).

Franklin, M. (1992) 'The Decline of Cleavage Politics', in M. Franklin, T. Mackie and H. Valen (eds), *Electoral Change: Responses to Evolving Social and Attitudinal Structures in Western Countries* (Cambridge: Cambridge University Press).

Franklin, M. (2000) 'How Structural Factors Cause Turnout Variations at European Parliament Elections', *European Union Politics*, 2(3): 309–28.

Franklin, M., Mackie, T. and Valen, H. (eds) (1992) *Electoral Change: Responses to Evolving Social and Attitudinal Structures in Western Countries* (Cambridge: Cambridge University Press).

Franklin, M., Marsh, M. and McLaren, L. (1994) 'Uncorking the Bottle: Popular Opposition to European unification in the wake of Maastricht', *Journal of Common Market Studies*, 32(4): 101–17.

Franklin, M., Marsh, M. and Wlezian, C. (1994) 'Attitudes Towards Europe and Referendum Votes: A Response to Siune and Svensson', *Electoral Studies*, 13(2): 117–21.

Franklin, M., van der Eijk, C. and Marsh, M. (1995) 'Referendum Outcomes and Trust in Government: Public Support for Europe in the Wake of Maastricht', in J. Hayward (ed.), *The Crisis of Representation in Europe* (London: Frank Cass).

Franklin, M., van der Eijk, C. and Oppenhuis, E. (1996) 'The Institutional Context: Turnout', in C. van der Eijk and M. Franklin (eds), *Choosing Europe? The European Electorate and National Politics in the Face of Union* (Ann Arbor, Mich.: University of Michigan Press).

Franklin, M. and Wlezien, C. (1997) 'The Responsive Public: Issue Salience, Policy Change, and Preferences for European Unification', *Journal of Theoretical Politics*, 9(3): 347–63.

Franzese, R. J. (1999) 'Partially Independent Central Banks, Political Responsive Governments, and Inflation', *American Journal of Political Science*, 43(3): 681–706.

Freitag, M. and Sciarini, P. (2001) 'The Political Economy of Budget Deficits in the European Union: The Role of International Constraints and Domestic Structure', *European Union Politics*, 2(2): 163–89.

Frieden, J. A. (1991) 'Invested Interests: The Politics of National Economic Policies in a World of Global Finance', *International Organization*, 45(4): 425–51.

Frieden, J. A. (2002) 'Real Sources of European Currency Policy: Sectoral Interests and European Monetary Integration', *International Organization*, 56(4): 831–60.

Frieden, J. A. and Lake, D. A. (1995) 'Introduction: International Politics and International Economics', in J. A. Frieden and D. A. Lake (eds), *International Political Economy: Perspectives on Global Power and Wealth* (London: Routledge).

Frieden, J. A. and Rogowski, R. (1996) 'The Impact of the International Political

Economy on National Policies: An Overview', in R. O. Keohane and H. V. Milner (eds), *Internationalization and Domestic Politics* (Cambridge: Cambridge University Press).

Friedman, M. (1968) 'The Role of Monetary Policy', *American Economic Review*, 58(2): 1–17.

Frowein, J. A. (1986) 'Integration and the Federal Experience in Germany and Switzerland', in M. Cappelletti, M. Seccombe and J. Weiler (eds), *Integration Through Law: European and the American Federal Experience, Volume 1: Methods, Tools and Institutions, Book 1: A Political Legal and Economic Overview* (Berlin: De Gruyter).

Gabel, M. J. (1998a) *Interests and Integration: Market Liberalization, Public Opinion, and European Union* (Ann Arbor, Mich.: University of Michigan Press).

Gabel, M. J. (1998b) 'Public Support for European Integration: An Empirical Test of Five Theories', *Journal of Politics*, 60(2): 333–54.

Gabel, M. J. (1998c) 'The Endurance of Supranational Governance: A Consociational Interpretation of the European Union', *Comparative Politics*, 30(2): 463–75.

Gabel, M. J. (1998d) 'Economic Integration and Mass Politics: Market Liberalization and Public Attitudes in the European Union', *American Journal of Political Science*, 42(3): 936–53.

Gabel, M. J. and Anderson, C. J. (2002) 'The Structure of Citizens Attitudes and the European Political Space', *Comparative Political Studies*, 35(8): 893–913.

Gabel, M. J. and Hix, S. (2002) 'The European Parliament and Executive Politics in the EU: Voting Behaviour and the Commission President Investiture Procedure', in M. Hosli, A. Van Deemen and M. Widgrén (eds), *Institutional Challenges in the European Union* (London: Routledge).

Gabel, M. J. and Hix, S. (2003) 'Defining the EU Political Space: An Empirical Study of the European Elections Manifestos, 1979–1999', *Comparative Political Studies*, 35(8): 934–64.

Gabel, M. J. and Palmer, H. (1995) 'Understanding Variation in Support for European Integration', *European Journal of Political Research*, 27(1): 3–19.

Gabel, M. J. and Whitten, G. (1997) 'Economic Conditions, Economic Perceptions, and Public Support for European Integration', *Political Behaviour*, 19(1): 81–96.

Galbraith, J. K. (1953) *American Capitalism and the Concept of Countervailing Power* (Boston, Mass.: Houghton Mifflin).

Galloway, D. (1999) 'Agenda 2000 – Packaging the Deal', *Journal of Common Market Studies*, 37 (Annual Review): 9–35.

Galloway, D. (2001) *The Treaty of Nice and Beyond: Realities and Illusions of Power in the EU* (Sheffield: Sheffield Academic Press).

Garman, J. and Hilditch, L. (1998) 'Behind the Scenes: An Examination of the Importance of Informal Processes at Work in Conciliation', *Journal of European Public Policy*, 5(2): 271–84.

Garrett, G. (1992) 'International Cooperation and Institutional Choice: The European Community's Internal Market', *International Organization*, 46(2): 533–60.

Garrett, G. (1994) 'The Politics of Maastricht', in B. Eichengreen and J. Frieden (eds), *The Political Economy of European Monetary Unification* (Boulder, CO: Westview).

Garrett, G. (1995a) 'The Politics of Legal Integration in the European Union', *International Organization*, 49(1): 171–81.

Garrett, G. (1995b) 'From the Luxembourg Compromise to Codecision: Decision Making in the European Union', *Electoral Studies*, 14(3): 289–308.

Garrett, G., Kelemen, R. D. and Schulz, H. (1998) 'The European Court of Justice, National Governments, and Legal Integration in the European Union', *International Organization*, 52(1): 149–76.

Garrett, G. and Lange, P. (1996) 'Internationalization, Institutions and Political Change', in R. O. Keohane and H. V. Milner (eds), *Internationalization and Domestic Politics* (Cambridge: Cambridge University Press).

Garrett, G. and McLean, I. (1996) 'On Power Indices and Reading Papers', *British Journal of Political Science*, 26(4): 600.

Garrett, G., McLean, I. and Machover, M. (1995) 'Power, Power Indices and Blocking Power: A Comment on Johnston', *British Journal of Political Science*, 25(4): 563–8.

Garrett, G. and Tsebelis, G. (1996) 'An Institutional Critique of Intergovernmentalism', *International Organization*, 50(2): 269–99.

Garrett, G. and Tsebelis, G. (1999) 'Why Resist the Temptation to Apply Power Indices to the European Union', *Journal of Theoretical Politics*, 11(3): 291–308.

Garrett, G. and Weingast, B. R. (1993) 'Ideas, Interests and Institutions: Constructing the European Community's Internal Market', in J. Goldstein and R. O. Keohane (eds), *Ideas and Foreign Policy: Beliefs, Institutions and Political Change* (Ithaca, NY: Cornell University Press).

Gatsios, K. and Seabright, P. (1989) 'Regulation in the European Community', *Oxford Review of Economic Policy*, 5(2): 37–60.

Geddes, A. (1995) 'Immigration and Ethnic Minorities and the EU's "Democratic Deficit"', *Journal of Common Market Studies*, 33(2): 197–217.

Geddes, A. (2000a) 'Lobbying for Migrant Inclusion in the European Union: New Opportunities for Transnational Advocacy', *Journal of European Public Policy*, 7(4): 632–49.

Geddes, A. (2000b) *Immigration and European Integration: Towards Fortress Europe?* (Manchester: Manchester University Press).

Gehring, T. (1997) 'Governing in Nested Institutions: Environmental Policy in the European Union and the Case of Packaging Waste', *Journal of European Public Policy*, 4(3): 337–54.

Gely, R. and Spillar, P. T. (1992) 'The Political Economy of Supreme Court Constitutional Decisions: The Case of Roosevelt's Court Packing Plan', *International Review of Law and Economics*, 12(1): 45–67.

Genschel, P. and Plümper, T. (1997) 'Regulatory Competition and International Co-operation', *Journal of European Public Policy*, 4(4): 626–42.

Geyer, R. (2001) 'Can EU Social NGOs Co-operate to Promote EU Social Policy?', *Journal of Social Policy*, 7(4): 632–49.

Gibson, J. L. and Caldeira, G. A. (1995) 'The Legitimacy of Transnational Legal Institutions: Compliance, Support, and the European Court of Justice', *American Journal of Political Science*, 39(2): 459–98.

Gibson, J. L. and Caldeira, G. A. (1998) 'Changes in the Legitimacy of the European Court of Justice: A Post-Maastricht Analysis', *British Journal of Political Science*, 28(1): 63–91.

Giddens, A. (1973) *The Class Structure of the Advanced Societies* (London: Hutchinson).

Giddens, A. (1994) *Beyond Left and Right: The Future of Radical Politics* (Cambridge: Polity Press).

Gilardi, F. (2002) 'Policy Credibility and Delegation to Independent Regulatory Agencies: A Comparative Empirical Analysis', *Journal of European Public Policy*, 9(6): 873–93.

Givens, T. and Luedtke, A. (2004) 'The Politics of European Union Immigration Policy: Institutions, Salience, and Harmonization', *The Policy Studies Journal*, 32(1): 145–65.

Glarbo, K. (1999) 'Wide-Awake Diplomacy: Reconstructing the Common Foreign and Security Policy of the European Union', *Journal of European Public Policy*, 6(4): 634–51.

Goetschy, J. (1999) 'The European Employment Strategy: Genesis and Development', *European Journal of Industrial Relations*, 5(2): 117–37.

Goetz, K. H. (1995) 'National Governance and European Integration: Intergovernmental Relations in Germany', *Journal of Common Market Studies*, 33(1): 131–44.

Goetz, K. H. (2000) 'European Integration and National Executives: A Cause in Search of an Effect?', *West European Politics*, 23(4): 211–31.

Golub, J. (1996a) 'The Politics of Judicial Discretion: Rethinking the Interaction Between National Courts and the European Court of Justice', *West European Politics*, 19(2): 360–85.

Golub, J. (1996b) *Why Did They Sign? Explaining EC Environmental Bargaining*, EUI Working Paper RSC no. 96/52 (Florence: European University Institute).

Golub, J. (1996c) 'State Power and Institutional Influence in European Integration: Lessons from the Packaging Waste Directive', *Journal of Common Market Studies*, 34(3): 313–39.

Golub, J. (1996d) 'Modelling Judicial Dialogue in the European Community: The Quantitative Basis of Preliminary References to the ECJ', Robert Schuman Centre Working Paper 96/58 (Florence: European University Institute).

Golub, J. (1999) 'In the Shadow of the Vote? Decision Making in the European Community', *International Organization*, 53(4): 733–64.

Gomà, R. (1996) 'The Social Dimension of the European Union: A New Type of Welfare System?', *Journal of European Public Policy*, 3(2): 209–30.

Gomez, R. (1998) 'The EU's Mediterranean Policy: Common Foreign Policy by the Back Door?', in J. Peterson and H. Sjursen (eds), *A Common Foreign Policy for Europe? Competing Visions of the CFSP* (London: Routledge).

Goodhart, D. (1998) 'Social Dumping Within the EU', in D. Hine and Kassim (eds), *Beyond the Market: The EU and National Social Policy* (London: Routledge).

Gourevitch, P. A. (1989) 'The Politics of Economic Policy Choice in the Post–War Era', in P. Guerrieri and P. C. Padoan (eds), *The Political Economy of European Integration: States, Markets and Institutions* (London: Harvester Wheatsheaf).

Grahl, J. and Teague, P. (1990) *1992 – The Big Market: The Future of the European Community* (London: Lawrence and Wishart).

Grant, W. (1997) *The Common Agricultural Policy* (London: Macmillan).

Grant, W., Matthews, D. and Newell, P. (2000) *The Effectiveness of European Union Environmental Policy* (London: Macmillan).

Green, A. W. (1969) *Political Integration by Jurisprudence* (Leyden: Sijthoff).

Greenwood, J. (1997) *Representing Interests in the European Union* (London: Macmillan).

Greenwood, J. (2002) *Inside the EU Business Associations* (London: Palgrave).

Greenwood, J. (2003) *Interest Representation in the European Union* (London: Palgrave).

Greenwood, J. and Aspinwall, M. (eds) (1998) *Collective Action in the European Union* (London: Routledge).

Greenwood, J., Grote, J. R. and Ronit, K. (eds) (1992) *Organized Interests and the European Community* (London: Sage).

Greico, J. M. (1990) *Cooperation Among Nations: Europe, America and Non-Tariff Barriers to Trade* (Ithaca, NY: Cornell University Press).

Greve, M. F. and Jørgensen, K. E. (2002) 'Treaty Reform as Constitutional Politics: A Longitudinal View', *Journal of European Public Policy*, 9(1): 54–75.

Grilli, V., Masciandro, D. and Tabellini, G. (1991) 'Political and Monetary Institutes and Public Financial Policies in the Industrial Countries', *Economic Policy*, 13): 341–92.

Grimm, D. (1995) 'Does Europe Need a Constitution?', *European Law Review*, 1(3): 282–302.

Guiraudon, V. (2000) 'European Integration and Migration Policy: Vertical Policy-Making as Venue-Shopping', *Journal of Common Market Studies*, 38(2): 251–71.

Guiraudon, V. (2001) 'Weak Weapons of the Weak? Transnational Mobilization around Migration in the European Union', in D. Imig and S. Tarrow (eds), *Contentious Europeans: Protest and Politics in an Emerging Polity* (Lanham, MD: Rowman & Littlefield).

Guiraudon, V. (2003) 'The Constitution of a European Immigration Policy Domain: A Political Sociology Approach', *Journal of European Public Policy*, 10(2): 263–82.

Guiraudon, V. and Lahav, G. (2000) 'A Reappraisal of the State Sovereignty Debate: The Case of Migration Control', *Comparative Political Studies*, 33(2): 163–95.

Haan, J. de and Eijffinger, C. W. (2000) 'The Democratic Accountability of the European Central Bank', *Journal of Common Market Studies*, 38(3): 393–408.

Haan, J. de, Inklaar, R. and Sleijpen, O. (2002) 'Have Business Cycles Become More Synchronized?', *Journal of Common Market Studies*, 40(1): 23–42.

Haas, E. B. (1958) *The Uniting of Europe: Political, Social and Economic Forces 1950–1957* (London: Stevens and Sons).

Haas, E. B. (1961) 'International Integration: The European and the Universal Process', *International Organization*, 15(3): 366–92.

Habermas, J. (1992) 'Citizenship and National Identity: Some Reflections on the Future of Europe', *Praxis International*, 12(1): 1–19.

Habermas, J. (1995) 'Comment on the Paper by Dieter Grimm: "Does Europe Need a Constitution"', *European Law Journal*, 1(3): 303–7.

Hall, P. A. and Franzese, R. J. (1998) 'Mixed Signals: Central Bank Independence, Coordinated Wage-Bargaining, and European Monetary Union', *International Organization*, 52(3): 505–35.

Hall, P. A. and Soskice, D. (eds) (2001) *Varieties of Capitalism: The Institutional Foundations of Competitiveness* (Oxford: Oxford University Press).

Hall, P. A. and Taylor, R. C. R. (1996) 'Political Science and the Three Institutionalism', *Political Studies*, 44(4): 936–57.

Hallstein, W. (1972) *Europe in the Making* (London: Allen and Unwin).

Hanley, D. (2002) 'Christian Democracy and the Paradoxes of Europeanization: Flexibility, Competition and Collusion', *Party Politics*, 8(4): 463–81.

Hanson, B. T. (1998) 'What Happened to Fortress Europe?: Trade Policy Liberalization in the European Union', *International Organization*, 52(1): 55–85.

Hardin, R. (1971) 'Collective Action as an Agreeable N-Person Prisoners' Dilemma', *Behavioral Science*, 16: 472–71.

Harlow, C. and Rawling, R. (1992) *Pressure Through Law* (London: Routledge).

Harmsen, R. (1999) 'The Europeanization of National Administrations: A Comparative Study of France and The Netherlands', *Governance*, 12(1): 81–113.

Hartley, T. C. (1986) 'Federalism, Courts and Legal Systems: The Emerging Constitution of the European Community', *American Journal of Comparative Law*, 34: 229–48.

Hartley, T. C. (2003) *The Foundations of European Community Law*, 5th edn (Oxford: Clarendon Press).

Haverland, M. (2000) 'National Adaptation to European Integration: The Importance of Institutional Veto Points', *Journal of Public Policy*, 20(1): 83–103.

Hayes-Renshaw, F. and Wallace, H. (1995) 'Executive Power in the European Union: the functions and limits of the Council of Ministers', *Journal of European Public Policy*, 2(4): 559–82.

Hayes-Renshaw, F. and Wallace, H. (1997) *The Council of Ministers* (London: Macmillan).

Heath, A., McLean, I., Taylor, B. and Curtice, J. (1999) 'Between First and Second Order: A Comparison of Voting Behaviour in European and Local Elections in Britain', *European Journal of Political Research*, 35: 389–414.

Hees, M. van and Steunenberg, B. (2000) 'The Choice Judges Make: Court Rulings, Personal Values, and Legal Constraints', *Journal of Theoretical Politics*, 12(3): 305–23.

Heiberg, E. O. (1998) 'Security Implications of EU Expansion to the North and East', in K. A. Eliassen (ed.), *Foreign and Security Policy in the European Union* (London: Sage).

Heidenheimer, A. J., Heclo, H. and Adams, C. T. (1990) *Comparative Public Policy: The Politics of Social Choice in America, Europe, and Japan*, 3rd edn (New York: St. Martin's Press).

Heidensohn, F. and Farrell, M. (ed.) (1993) *Crime in Europe*, 2nd edn (London: Routledge).

Helgadottir, H. (1994) 'Rich Get Richer, Poor Get Poorer', *The European*, 4–10 February.

Helm, D. and Smith, S. (1989) 'The Assessment: Economic Integration and the Role of the European Community', *Oxford Review of Economic Policy*, 5(2): 1–19.

Henning, C. R. (1998) 'Systemic Conflict and Regional Monetary Integration: The Case of Europe', *International Organization*, 52(3): 537–73.

Henning, C. R. and P. C. Padoan (2000) *Transatlantic Perspectives on the Euro* (Washington, DC: The Brookings Institution).

Hennis, M. (2001) 'Europeanization and Globalization: The Missing Link', *Journal of Common Market Studies*, 39(5): 829–50.

Héritier, A. (1994) '"Leaders" and "Laggards" in European Policy-Making: Clean Air Policy Changes in Britain and Germany', in F. van Waarden and B. Unger (eds), *Convergence or Diversity: The Pressure of Internationalization on Economic Governance Institutions and Policy Outcomes* (Aldershot: Avebury).

Héritier, A. (1996) 'The Accommodation of Diversity in European Policy-Making and its Outcomes: Regulatory Policy as a Patchwork', *Journal of European Public Policy*, 3(2): 149–67.

Héritier, A. (1997) 'Policy-Making by Subterfuge: Interest Accommodation, Innovation and Substitute Democratic Legitimation in Europe – Perspectives from Distinct Policy Areas', *Journal of European Public Policy*, 4(2): 171–89.

Héritier, A. (2001) 'Differential Europe: National Administrative Responses to Community Policy', in M. Green Cowles, J. Caporaso and T. Risse (eds), *Transforming Europe: Europeanization and Domestic Change* (Ithaca, NY: Cornell University Press).

Héritier, A., Knill, C. and Mingers, S. (1996) *Ringing the Changes in Europe: Regulatory Competition and Redefinition of the State. Britain, France, Germany* (Berlin: De Gruyter).

Hervey, T. (2001) 'Community and National Competence in Health After Tobacco Advertising', *Common Market Law Review*, 38(6): 1421–46.

Heywood, P. and Wright, V. (1997) 'Executives, Bureaucracies and Decision-Making', in M. Rhodes, P. Heywood and V. Wright (eds), *Developments in West European Politics* (London: Macmillan).

Hill, C. (1988) 'The Capability–Expectations Gap, or Conceptualizing Europe's International Role', *Journal of Common Market Studies*, 31(3): 305–28.

Hill, C. (ed.) (1996) *The Actors in Europe's Foreign Policy* (London: Routledge).

Hill, C. (2003) *The Changing Politics of Foreign Policy* (London: Palgrave).

Hill, C. (2004) 'Renationalizing or Regrouping? EU Foreign Policy Since 11 September 2001', *Journal of Common Market Studies*, 42(1): 143–63.

Hinich, H. J. and Munger, M. C. (1997) *Analytical Politics* (Cambridge: Cambridge University Press).

Hix, S. (1994) 'The Study of the European Community: The Challenge to Comparative Politics', *West European Politics*, 17(1): 1–30.

Hix, S. (1995a) 'Political Parties in the European Union System: A 'Comparative Political Approach' to the Development of the Party Federations', unpublished PhD thesis, Florence, European University Institute.

Hix, S. (1995b) *The 1996 Intergovernmental Conference and the Future of the Third Pillar*, Briefing Paper no. 20 (Brussels: Churches' Commission for Migrants in Europe).

Hix, S. (1997) 'Executive Selection in the European Union: Does the Commission

President Investiture Procedure Reduce the Democratic Deficit?', *European Integration On-line Papers*, 1(21), (http://eiop.or.at/eiop/texte/1997–021a.htm).

Hix, S. (1998a) 'The Study of the European Union II: The "New Governance" Agenda and Its Rival', *Journal of European Public Policy*, 5(1): 38–65.

Hix, S. (1998b) 'Elections, Parties and Institutional Design: EU Democracy in Comparative Perspective', *West European Politics*, 21(3): 19–52.

Hix, S. (1999) 'Dimensions and Alignments in European Union Politics: Cognitive Constraints and Partisan Responses', *European Journal of Political Research*, 35: 69–106.

Hix, S. (2001a) 'Parliamentary Oversight of Executive Power: What Role for the European Parliament in Comitology', in T. Christiansen and E. Kirchner (eds), *Committee Governance in the European Union* (Manchester: Manchester University Press).

Hix, S. (2001b) 'Legislative Behaviour and Party Competition in European Parliament: An Application of Nominate to the EU', *Journal of Common Market Studies*, 39(4): 663–88.

Hix, S. (2002a) 'Constitutional Agenda–Setting Through Discretion in Rule Interpretation: Why the European Parliament Won at Amsterdam', *British Journal of Political Science*, 32(2): 259–80.

Hix, S. (2002b) 'Parliamentary Behavior with Two Principals: Preferences, Parties, and Voting in the European Parliament', *American Journal of Political Science*, 46(3): 688–98.

Hix, S. (2002c) *Linking National Politics to Europe* (London: Foreign Policy Centre).

Hix, S. (2004) 'Electoral Systems and Legislative Behavior: Explaining Voting-Defection in the European Parliament', *World Politics*, 56(1): 194–223.

Hix, S. and Goetz, K. H. (2000) 'Introduction: European Integration and National Political Systems', *West European Politics*, 23(4): 1–26.

Hix, S., Kreppel, A. and Noury, A. (2003) 'The Party System in the European Parliament: Collusive or Competitive?', *Journal of Common Market Studies*, 41(2): 309–31.

Hix, S. and Lord, C. (1995) 'The Making of a President: The European Parliament and the Confirmation of Jacques Santer as President of the Commission', *Government and Opposition*, 31(1): 62–76.

Hix, S. and Lord, C. (1997) *Political Parties in the European Union* (London: Macmillan).

Hix, S. and Niessen, J. (1996) *Reconsidering European Migration Policies: The 1996 Intergovernmental Conference and the Reform of the Maastricht Treaty* (Brussels: Migration Policy Group/Churches' Commission for Migrants in Europe/Starting Line Group).

Hix, S., Noury, A. and Roland, G. (2005) 'Power to the Parties: Cohesion and Competition in the European Parliament, 1979–2001', *British Journal of Political Science*, 35(2).

Hodson, D. and Maher, I. (2001) 'The Open Method as a New Mode of Governance', *Journal of Common Market Studies*, 39(4): 719–46.

Hoffmann, S. (1966) 'Obstinate or Obsolete? The Fate of the Nation State and the Case of Western Europe', *Daedalus*, 95(4): 862–915.

Hoffmann, S. (1982) 'Reflections on the Nation-State in Western Europe Today', *Journal of Common Market Studies*, 21(1–2): 21–37.

Hoffmann, S. (1989) 'The European Community and 1992', *Foreign Affairs*, 68(4): 27–47.

Hofhansel, C. (1999) 'The Harmonization of EU Export Control Policies', *International Organization*, 32(2): 229–56.

Holland, M. (1988) 'The European Community and South Africa: In Search for a Policy for the 1990s', *International Affairs*, 64(3): 415–60.

Holland, M. (1995) 'Bridging the Capability–Expectations Gap: A Case Study of the CFSP Joint Action on South Africa', *Journal of Common Market Studies*, 33(4): 555–72.

Holland, M. (2002) *The European Union and the Third World* (London: Palgrave).

Holland, S. (1980) *Uncommon Market* (London: Macmillan).

Holler, M. and Widgrén, J. (1999) 'Why Power Indices for Assessing European Union Decision-Making?', *Journal of Theoretical Politics*, 11(3, pp.321–330.

Hollifield, J. F. (1992) *Immigrants, Markets and the State* (Cambridge, Mass.: Harvard University Press).

Hooghe, L. (1995) 'Subnational Mobilization in the European Union', *West European Politics*, 18(3): 175–98.

Hooghe, L. (1996a) 'Building a Europe With the Regions: The Changing Role of the European Commission', in L. Hooghe (ed.), *Cohesion Policy and European Integration: Building Multi-Level Governance* (Oxford: Oxford University Press).

Hooghe, L. (ed.) (1996b) *Cohesion Policy and European Integration: Building Multi-Level Governance* (Oxford: Oxford University Press).

Hooghe, L. (1999a) 'Images of Europe: Orientations to European Integration among Senior Officials of the Commission', *British Journal of Political Science*, 29(2): 345–67.

Hooghe, L. (1999b) 'Supranational Activists or Intergovernmental Agents? Explaining the Political Orientations of Senior Commission Officials to European Integration', *Comparative Political Studies*, 32(4): 435–63.

Hooghe, L. (2000) 'EU Cohesion Policy and Competing Models of European Capitalism', *Journal of Common Market Studies*, 36(4): 457–77.

Hooghe, L. (2001) *The European Commission and the Integration of Europe: Images of Governance* (Cambridge: Cambridge University Press).

Hooghe, L. (2002) 'The Mobilization of Territorial Interests and Multilevel Governance', in R. Balme, D. Chabanet and V. Wright (eds), *Collective Action in Europe* (Paris: Presses de Sciences Po).

Hooghe, L. and Keating, M. (1994) 'The Politics of European Union Regional Policy', *Journal of European Public Policy*, 1(3): 367–93.

Hooghe, L. and Marks, G. (1996) '"Europe With the Regions": Channels of Regional Representation in the European Union', *Publius*, 26(1): 1–20.

Hooghe, L. and Marks, G. (1998) 'The Making of a Polity: The Struggle over European Integration', in H. Kitschelt, P. Lange, G. Marks and J. Stephens (eds), *The Politics and Political Economy of Advanced Industrial Societies* (Cambridge: Cambridge University Press).

Hooghe, L., Marks, G. and Wilson, C. (2003) 'Does Left/Right Structure Party Positions on European Integration?', *Comparative Political Studies*, 35(8): 965–89.

Horn, M. (1995) *The Political Economy of Public Administration: Institutional Choice in the Public Sector* (Cambridge: Cambridge University Press).

Horstmann, W. and Schneider, F. (1994) 'Deficits, Bailout and Free Riders: Fiscal Elements of a European Constitution', *Kyklos*, 47(3): 355–83.

Hosli, M. O. (1995a) 'The Political Economy of Subsidiarity', in F. Laursen (ed.), *The Political Economy of European Integration* (The Hague: Kluwer).

Hosli, M. O. (1995b) 'The Balance Between Small and Large: Effects of a Double–Majority on Voting Power in the European Union', *International Studies Quarterly*, 39(2): 351–70.

Hosli, M. O. (1996) 'Coalitions and Power: Effects of Qualified Majority Voting in the Council of the European Union', *Journal of Common Market Studies*, 34(2): 255–73.

Hosli, M. O. (1997) 'Voting Strength in the European Parliament: The Influence of National and of Partisan Actors', *European Journal of Political Research*, 31(3): 351–66.

Hosli, M. O. (2000) 'The Creation of the European Economic and Monetary Union

(EMU): Intergovernmental Negotiations and Two-Level Games', *Journal of European Public Policy*, 7(5): 744–66.

Howorth, J. (2001) 'European Defence and the Changing Politics of the EU', *Journal of Common Market Studies*, 39(4): 765–89.

Huber, J. D. (1996a) *Rationalizing Parliament: Legislative Institutions and Party Politics in France* (Cambridge: Cambridge University Press).

Huber, J. D. (1996b) 'The Impact of Confidence Votes on Legislative Politics in Parliamentary Systems', American Political Science Review, 90(2): 269–82.

Huber, J. and Shipan, C. (2002) *Deliberate Discretion? The Institutional Foundations of Bureaucratic Autonomy* (Cambridge: Cambridge University Press).

Hubschmid, C. and Moser, P. (1997) 'The Co-operation Procedure in the EU: Why was the EP Influential in the Decision on Car Emissions Standards?', *Journal of Common Market Studies*, 35(2): 225–42.

Hug, S. (1997) 'Integration Through Referendums?', *Aussenwirtschaft*, 52(1–2): 287–310.

Hug, S. (2002) *Voices of Europe: Citizens, Referendums, and European Integration* (Lanham, MD: Rowman Littlefield).

Hug, S. and Sciarini, P. (2000) 'Referendums on European Integration: Do Institutions Matter in the Voter's Decision', *Comparative Political Studies*, 33(1): 3–36.

Hughes, J. Sasse, G. and Gordon, C. (2002) 'Saying "Maybe" to the "Return to Europe": Elites and the Political Space for Euroscepticism in Central and Eastern Europe', *European Union Politics*, 3(3): 327–55.

Hughes Hallett, A. J. and McAdam, P. (2003) 'Deficit Targeting Strategies: Fiscal Consolidation and the Probability Distribution of Deficits under the Stability Pact', *Journal of Common Market Studies*, 41(3): 421–44.

Huysmans, J. (2000) 'The European Union and the Securitization of Migration', *Journal of Common Market Studies*, 38(5): 751–77.

Imig, D. (2002) 'Contestation in the Streets: European Protest and the Emerging Euro–Polity', *Comparative Political Studies*, 35(8): 914–33.

Imig, D. and Tarrow, S. (eds) (2001) *Contentious Europeans: Protest and Politics in an Emerging Polity* (Lanham, MD: Rowman and Littlefield).

Inglehart, R. (1970a) 'Cognitive Mobilization and European Identity', *Comparative Politics*, 3(1): 45–70.

Inglehart, R. (1970b) 'Public Opinion and Regional Integration', *International Organization*, 24(4): 764–95.

Inglehart, R. (1977a) *The Silent Revolution: Changing Values and Political Styles Among Western Publics* (Princeton, NJ: Princeton University Press).

Inglehart, R. (1977b) 'Long Term Trends in Mass Support for European Unification', *Government and Opposition*, 12(2): 150–77.

Inglehart, R. (1991) 'Trust Between Nations: Primordial Ties, Societal Learning and Economic Development', in K. Reif and R. Inglehart (eds), *Eurobarometer: The Dynamics of European Public Opinion – Essays in Honour of Jacques–René Rabier* (London: Macmillan).

Inglehart, R. and Rabier, J.-R. (1978) 'Economic Uncertainty and European Solidarity: Public Opinion Trends', *Annals of the American Academy of Political and Economic Science*, 440: 66–97.

Inglehart, R. and Reif, K. (1991) 'Analyzing Trends in Western European Opinion: The Role of the Eurobarometer Surveys', in K. Reif and R. Inglehart (eds), *Eurobarometer: The Dynamics of European Public Opinion – Essays in Honour of Jacques-René Rabier* (London: Macmillan).

International Monetary Fund (2003) *Annual Report 2003* (Washington, DC: International Monetary Fund).

Ioakimidis, P. C. (1996) 'EU Cohesion Policy in Greece: The Tensions Between Bureaucratic Centralism and Regionalism', in L. Hooghe (ed.), *Cohesion Policy and*

European Integration: Building Multi-Level Governance (Oxford: Oxford University Press).

Ireland, P. (1991) 'Facing the True "Fortress Europe": Immigrant Politics in the EC', *Journal of Common Market Studies*, 29(5): 457–80.

Ireland, P. (1995) 'Migration, Free Movement, and Immigrant Integration in the EU: A Bifurcated Policy Response', in S. Leibfried and P. Pierson (eds), *European Social Policy: Between Fragmentation and Integration* (Washington, DC: The Brookings Institution).

Irwin, G. (1995) 'Second-Order or Third-Rate: Issues in the Campaign for the Elections for the European Parliament', *Electoral Studies*, 14(2): 183–98.

Issing, O. (1999) 'The Eurosystem: Transparent and Accountable, or "Willem in Euroland"', *Journal of Common Market Studies*, 37(3): 503–19.

Issing, O. (2002) 'On Macroeconomic Policy Co-ordination in EMU', *Journal of Common Market Studies*, 40(2): 345–58.

Iversen, T. (1998a) 'Wage Bargaining, Hard Money and Economic Performance: Theory and Evidence for Organized Market Economies', *British Journal of Political Science*, 28: 31–61.

Iversen, T. (1998b) 'Wage Bargaining, Central Bank Independence, and the Real Effects of Money', *International Organization*, 52(3): 469–504.

Iverson, T. (1999) *Contested Economic Institutions: The Politics of Macroeconomics and Wage Bargaining in Advanced Democracies* (Cambridge: Cambridge University Press).

Jabko, N. (1999) 'In the Name of the Market: How the Commission Paved the Way for Monetary Union', *Journal of European Public Policy*, 6(3): 475–95.

Jachtenfuchs, M. (1995) 'Theoretical Perspectives on European Governance', *European Law Journal*, 1(2): 115–33.

Jachtenfuchs, M. (2001) 'The Governance Approach to European Integration', *Journal of Common Market Studes*, 39(2): 245–64.

Jackman, R. (1998) 'The Impact of the European Union on Unemployment and Unemployment Policy', in D. Hine and Kassim (eds), *Beyond the Market: The EU and National Social Policy* (London: Routledge).

Jacobs, F. (1997) 'Legislative Co-Decision: A Real Step Forward?', paper presented at the Fifth Biennial Conference of the European Community Studies Association, Seattle, 29 May–1 June.

Janssen, J. I. H. (1991) 'Postmaterialism, Cognitive Mobilization and Public Support for European Integration', *British Journal of Political Science*, 21: 443–68.

Jeffery, C. (2000) 'Sub–National Mobilization and European Integration', *Journal of Common Market Studies*, 38(1): 1–23.

Jileva, E. (2002) 'Visa and Free Movement of Labour: the Uneven Imposition of the EU *Acquis* on the Accession States', *Journal of Ethnic and Migration Studies*, 28(4): 683–700.

Joerges, C. (1994) 'European Economic Law, the Nation–State and the Maastricht Treaty', in R. Dehousse (ed.), *Europe After Maastricht: An Ever Closer Union?* (Munich: Law Books on Europe).

Joerges, C. (1997) 'The Market without a State? The "Economic Constitution" of the European Community and the Rebirth of Regulatory Politics', *European Integration On-line Papers*, 1(19) (http://eiop.or.at/eiop/texte/1997–019a.htm).

Joerges, C. and Neyer, J. (1997) 'From Intergovernmental Bargaining to Deliberative Political Process: The Constitutionalisation of Comitology', *European Law Journal*, 3(3): 273–99.

Johansson, K. M. (2002) 'Party Elites in Multilevel Europe: The Christian Democrats and the Single European Act', *Party Politics*, 8(4): 423–39.

Johansson, K. M. and Raunio, T. (2001) 'Partisan Responses to Europe: Comparing Finnish and Swedish Political Parties', *European Journal of Political Research*, 39: 225–49.

Johnston, A. (2001) 'Judicial Review and the Treaty of Nice', *Common Market Law Review*, 38: 499–523.

Johnston, M. J. (1994) *The European Council: Gatekeeper of the European Community* (Boulder, CO: Westview).

Johnston, R. J. (1995) 'The Conflict Over Majority Voting in the EU Council of Ministers: An Analysis of the UK Negotiating Stance Using Power Indices', *British Journal of Political Science*, 25: 245–54.

Johnston, R. J. (1996) 'On Keeping Touch with Reality and Failing to be Befuddled by Mathematics', *British Journal of Political Science*, 26: 598–99.

Jones, B. and Keating, M. (eds) (1995) *The European Union and the Regions* (Oxford: Clarendon Press).

Jones, E., Frieden, J. and Torres, F. (eds) (1998) *Joining Europe's Monetary Club: The Challenges for Smaller Member States* (London: Macmillan).

Jones, G. (ed.) (1991) *West European Prime Ministers* (London: Frank Cass).

Joppke, C. (ed.) (1998) *Challenge to the Nation-State: Immigration in Western Europe and the United States* (Oxford: Oxford University Press).

Joppke, C. (1999) *Immigration and the Nation-State: The United States, Germany, and Great Britain* (Oxford: Oxford University Press).

Jordan, A., Brouwer, R. and Noble, E. (1999) 'Innovative and Responsive? A Longitudinal Analysis of the Speed of EU Environmental Policy-Making, 1967–1997', *Journal of European Public Policy*, 6(3): 376–98.

Jordan, G. (1998) 'What Drives Associability at the European Level? The Limits of the Utilitarian Explanation', in J. Greenwood and M. Aspinwall (eds), *Collective Action in the European Union* (London: Routledge).

Jordan, W. A. (1972) 'Producer Protection, Prior Market Structure and the Effects of Government Regulation', *Journal of Law and Economics*, 15(2): 151–76.

Joskow, P. L. and Noll, R. G. (1981) 'Regulation in Theory and Practice: An Overview', in G. Fromm (ed.), *Studies in Public Regulation*, Cambridge, Mass.; Massachusetts Institute of Technology Press).

Josselin, D. (2001) 'Trade Unions and EMU: Sectoral Preferences and Political Opportunities', *West European Politics*, 24(1): 55–74.

Judge, D. (1993) '"Predestined to Save the Earth": The Environment Committee of the European Parliament', in D. Judge (ed.), *A Green Dimension for the European Community* (London: Frank Cass).

Judge, D. and Earnshaw, D. (1994) 'Weak European Parliament Influence? A Study of the Environment Committee of the EP', *Government and Opposition*, 29(2): 262–76.

Judge, D., Earnshaw, D. and Cowan, N. (1994) 'Ripples and Waves: The European Parliament in the European Community Policy Process', *Journal of European Public Policy*, 1(1): 27–52.

Junne, G. (1994) 'Multinational Enterprises as Actors', in W. Carlsnaes and S. Smith (eds), *European Foreign Policy: The EC and Changing Perspectives in Europe* (London: Sage).

Jupille, J. (1999) 'The European Union and International Outcomes', *International Organization*, 53(2): 409–25.

Jupille, J. (2004) *Procedural Politics: Isues, Influence and Institutional Choice in the European Union* (Cambridge: Cambridge University Press).

Kaltenthaler, K. (2002) 'German Interests in European Monetary Integration', *Journal of Common Market Studies*, 40(1): 69–87.

Kaltenthaler, K. and Anderson, C. (2001) 'Europeans and Their Money: Explaining Public Support for the Common European Currency', *European Journal of Political Research*, 40: 139–70.

Kassim, H. and Hine, D. (1998) 'Conclusion: The European Union, Member States and Social Policy', in D. Hine and H. Kassim (eds), *Beyond the Market: The EU and National Social Policy* (London: Routledge).

Kassim, H. and Menon, A. (eds) (1996) *The European Union and National Industrial Policy* (London: Routledge).

Kassim, H., Menon, A., Peters, B. G. and Wright, V. (eds) (2001a) *The National Coordination of EU Policy: The European Level* (Oxford: Oxford University Press).

Kassim, H., Peters, B. G. and Wright, V. (eds) (2001b) *The National Coordination of EU Policy: The Domestic Level* (Oxford: Oxford University Press).

Katz, R. S. (2001) 'Models of Democracy: Elite Attitudes and the Democratic Deficit in the European Union', *European Union Politics*, 2(1): 53–79.

Kaufmann, H. M. (1995) 'The Importance of Being Independent: Central Bank Independence and the European System of Central Banks', in C. Rhodes and S. Mazey (eds), *The State of the European Union*, vol. 3 (London: Longman).

Keating, M. (1995) 'A Comment on Robert Leonardi, "Cohesion in the European Community: Illusion or Reality?"', *West European Politics*, 18(2): 408–12.

Keating, M. and Jones, B. (1995) 'Nations, Regions, and Europe: The UK Experience', in B. Jones and M. Keating (eds), *The European Union and the Regions* (Oxford: Clarendon Press).

Keefer, P. and Stasavage, D. (2002) 'Checks and Balances, Private Information, and the Credibility of Monetary Policy Commitments', *International Organization*, 56(4): 751–74.

Keefer, P. and Stasavage, D. (2003) 'The Limits of Delegation: Veto Players, Central Bank Independence, and the Credibility of Monetary Policy', *American Political Science Review*, 97(3): 407–23.

Keeler, J. T. S. (1996) 'Agricultural Power in the European Community: Explaining the Fate of CAP and GATT Negotiations', *Comparative Politics*, 28(2): 127–49.

Keesbergen, C. van (2000) 'Political Allegiance and European Integration', *European Journal of Political Research*, 37(1): 1–17.

Keck, M. and Sikkink, K. (1998) *Activists Beyond Borders: Advocacy Networks in International Politics* (Ithaca, NY: Cornell University Press).

Kelemen, R. D. (2000) 'Regulatory Federalism: EU Environmental Regulation in Comparative Perspective', *Journal of Public Policy*, 20(3): 133–67.

Kelemen, R. D. (2001) 'The Limits of Judicial Power: Trade–Environment Disputes in the GATT/WTO and the EU', *Comparative Political Studies*, 34(6): 622–50.

Kelemen, R. D. (2002) 'The Politics of "Eurocratic" Structure and the new European Agencies', *West European Politics*, 25(4): 93–118.

Kenen, P. B. (1969) 'The Optimum Currency Area: An Eclectic View', in R. Mundell and A. Swoboda (eds), *Monetary Problems of the International Economy* (Chicago, Ill.: University of Chicago Press).

Kenen, P. B. (1995) *Economic and Monetary Union in Europe: Moving Beyond Maastricht* (Cambridge: Cambridge University Press).

Keohane, R. O. (1984) *After Hegemony: Cooperation and Discord in the World Political Economy* (Princeton, NJ: Princeton University Press).

Keohane, R. O. (ed.) (1986) *Neo-Realism and Its Critics* (New York: Columbia University Press).

Keohane, R. O. and Nye, J. S. (1989) *Power and Interdependence: World Politics in Transition*, 2nd edn (Boston, Mass.: Little, Brown).

Key, V. O. (1961) *Public Opinion and American Democracy* (New York: Knopf).

Kiewiet, D. R. and McCubbins, M. (1991) *The Logic of Delegation: Congressional Parties and the Appropriations Process* (Chicago, Ill.: University of Chicago Press).

King, A. (1981) 'What do Elections Decide?', in D. Butler, H. R. Penniman and A. Ranney (eds), *Democracy at the Polls* (Washington, DC: American Enterprise Institute).

King, M. (1994) 'Policing Refugees and Asylum Seekers in "Greater Europe": Towards a Reconceptualisation of Control', in M. Anderson and M. den Boer (eds), *Policing Across National Boundaries* (London: Pinter).

Kingdon, J. W. (1984) *Agendas, Alternatives, and Public Policies* (Boston, Mass.: Little, Brown).

Kirchner, E. (1992) *Decision-Making in the European Community: The Council Presidency and European Integration* (Manchester: Manchester University Press).

Kitschelt, H. (1993) 'Class Structure and Social Democratic Party Strategy', *British Journal of Political Science*, 23): 299–337.

Kitschelt, H. (1994) *The Transformation of European Social Democracy* (Cambridge: Cambridge University Press).

Kitschelt, H. (1995) *The Radical Right in Western Europe: A Comparative Analysis* (Ann Arbor, Mich.: University of Michigan Press).

Kleinman, M. (2002) *A European Welfare State? European Union Social Policy in Context* (London: Palgrave).

Knill, C. (1998) 'European Policies: The Impact of National Administrative Traditions', *Journal of Public Policy*, 18(1): 1–28.

Knill, C. (2001) *The Europeanisation of National Administrations: Patterns of Institutional Change and Persistence* (Cambridge: Cambridge University Press).

Knill, C. and Lehmkuhl, D. (2002) 'The National Impact of European Union Regulatory Policy: Three Europeanization Mechanisms', *European Journal of Political Research*, 41(2): 255–80.

Knill, C. and Lenschow, A. (1998) 'Coping with Europe: the Impact of British and German Administrations on the Implementation of EU Environmental Policy', *Journal of European Public Policy*, 5(4): 595–614.

Knill, C. and Lenschow, A. (eds) (2000) *Implementing EU Environmental Policy: New Directions and Old Problems* (Manchester: Manchester University Press).

Knill, C. and Lenschow, A. (2001) 'Adjusting to EU Environmental Policy: Change and Persistence of Domestic Administrations', in M. Green Cowles, J. Caporaso and T. Risse (eds), *Transforming Europe: Europeanization and Domestic Change* (Ithaca, NY: Cornell University Press).

Knudsen, O. F. (1994) 'Context and Action in the Collapse of the Cold War European System', in W. Carlsnaes and S. Smith (eds), *European Foreign Policy: The EC and Changing Perspectives in Europe* (London: Sage).

Koenig-Archibugi, M. (2004a) 'International Governance as New *Raison d'État*? The Case of the EU Common Foreign and Security Policy', *European Journal of International Relations*, 10(2): 147–88.

Koenig-Archibugi, M. (2004b) 'Explaining Government Preferences for Institutional Change in EU Foreign and Security Policy', *International Organization*, 58(4): 137–74.

Kohler-Koch, B. (1996) 'Catching Up with Change: The Transformation of Governance in Europe', *Journal of European Public Policy*, 3(3): 359–80.

Kohler-Koch, B. (1997) 'Organized Interests in the EC and European Parliament', *European Integration On-line Papers*, 1(9), (http://eiop.or.at/eiop/texte/1997-009a. htm).

Kohler-Koch, B. (1999) 'The Evolution and Transformation of European Governance', in B. Kohler-Koch and R. Eising (eds), *The Transformation of Governance in the European Union* (London: Routledge).

Kokott, J. (1998) 'Report on Germany', in A.-M. Slaughter, A. Stone Sweet and J. H. H. Weiler (eds), *The European Court and National Courts – Doctrine and Jurisprudence: Legal Change in Its Social Context* (Oxford: Hart).

König, T. and Hug, S. (2000) 'Ratifying Maastricht: Parliamentary Votes on International Treaties and Theoretical Solution Concepts', *European Union Politics*, 1(1): 93–124.

König, T. and Pöter, M. (2001) 'Examining the EU Legislative Process: The Relative Importance of Agenda and Veto Power', *European Union Politics*, 2(3): 329–51.

Koole, R. and Mair, P. (eds) (1995) *Political Data Yearbook 1995, European Journal of Political Research*, 28(3–4).

Kopecky, P. and Mudde, C. (2002) 'Two Sides of Euroscepticism: Party Positions on European Integration in East Central Europe', *European Union Politics*, 3(3): 297–326.

Kostakopoulou, T. (2000) 'The "Protective Union": Change and Continuity in Migration Law and Policy in Post-Amsterdam Europe', *Journal of Common Market Studies*, 38(3): 497–518.

Krasner, S. (ed.) (1983) *International Regimes* (Ithaca, NY: Cornell University Press).

Kraus, M. and Schwager, R. (2003) 'EU Enlargement and Immigration', *Journal of Common Market Studies*, 42(2): 165–81.

Krehbiel, K. (1991) *Information and Legislative Organization* (Ann Arbor, Mich.: University of Michigan Press).

Kreher, A. (1997) 'Agencies in the European Community: A Step Towards Administrative Integration in Europe', *Journal of European Public Policy*, 4(2): 225–45.

Kreppel, A. (1999) 'What Affects the European Parliament's Legislative Influence?', *Journal of Common Market Studies*, 37(3): 521–38.

Kreppel, A. (2000) 'Rules, Ideology and Coalition Formation in the European Parliament: Past, Present and Future', *European Union Politics*, 1(3): 340–62.

Kreppel, A. (2002a) *The European Parliament and Supranational Party System* (Cambridge: Cambridge University Press).

Kreppel, A. (2002b) 'Moving Beyond Procedure: An Empirical Analysis of European Parliament Legislative Influence', *Comparative Political Studies*, 35(7): 784–813.

Kreppel, A. and Tsebelis, G. (1999) 'Coalition Formation in the European Parliament', *Comparative Political Studies*, 32: 933–66.

Krugman, P. (1987) 'Economic Integration in Europe: Some Conceptual Issues', in T. Padoa-Schioppa (ed.), *Efficiency, Stability, Equity* (Oxford: Oxford University Press).

Krugman, P. (1990) 'Policy Problems of a Monetary Union', in P. De Grauwe and L. Papademos (eds), *The European Monetary System in the 1990s* (London: Longman).

Krugman, P. (1991) *Geography and Trade* (Cambridge, Mass.: Massachusetts Institute of Technology Press).

Krugman, P. (1997) 'Good News from Ireland: A Geographic Perspective', in A. W. Gray (ed.), *International Perspectives on the Irish Economy* (Dublin: Indecon Economic Consultants).

Krugman, P. (1998) *The Accidental Theorist and Other Dispatches from the Dismal Science* (London: Norton).

Kucia, M. (1999) 'Public Opinion in Central Europe on EU Accession: the Czech Republic and Poland', *Journal of Common Market Studies*, 37(1): 143–52.

Kymlicka, W. (1995) *Multicultural Citizenship: A Liberal Theory of Minority Rights* (Oxford: Clarendon Press).

Laderchi, F. P. R. (1998) 'Report on Italy', in A.-M. Slaughter, A. Stone Sweet and J. H. H. Weiler (eds), *The European Court and National Courts – Doctrine and Jurisprudence: Legal Change in Its Social Context* (Oxford: Hart).

Laffan, B. (1997) *The Finances of the European Union* (London: Macmillan).

Lahav, G. (1997) 'Ideology and Party Constraints on Immigration Attitudes in Europe', *Journal of Common Market Studies*, 35(3): 377–406.

Lahav, G. (2004) *Immigration and Politics in the New Europe: Reinventing Borders* (Cambridge: Cambridge University Press).

Lahusen, C. (2002) 'Commercial Consultancies in the European Union: the Shape and Structure of Professional Interest Intermediation', *Journal of European Public Policy*, 9(5): 695–714.

Lahusen, C. (2003) 'Moving Into the European Orbit: Commercial Consultancies in the European Union', *European Union Politics*, 4(2): 191–218.

Laitin, D. (2002) 'Culture and National Identity: "The East" and European Integration', *West European Politics*, 25(2): 55–79.

Landau, A. (2001) 'The Agricultural Negotiations in the WTO: The Same Old Story?', *Journal of Common Market Studies*, 39(5): 913–25.

Lane, J.-E., and Berg, S. (1999) 'Relevance of Voting Power', *Journal of Theoretical Politics*, 11(3): 309–20.

Lane, J.-E., and Maeland, R. (1995) 'Research Note: Voting Power under the EU Constitution', *Journal of Theoretical Politics*, 7(2): 223–30.

Lane, J.-E., Maeland, R. and Berg, S. (1995) 'The EU Parliament: Seats, States and Political Parties', *Journal of Theoretical Politics*, 7(3): 395–400.

Lange, P. (1993) 'Maastricht and the Social Protocol: Why Did They Do It?', *Politics and Society*, 21(1): 5–36.

Lange, P. and Meadwell, H. (1991) 'Typologies of Democratic Systems: From Political Inputs to Political Economy', in. H. J. Wiarda (ed.), *New Directions in Comparative Politics*, 2nd edn (Boulder, CO: Westview).

Lasswell, H. D. (1936) *Politics: Who Gets What, When and How* (New York: McGraw–Hill).

Latter, R. (1991) *Crime and the European Community after 1992* (London: HMSO).

Laver, M. J. and Budge, I. (1992) 'Measuring Policy Distances and Modelling Coalition Formation', in M. J. Laver and I. Budge (eds), *Party Policy and Government Coalitions* (New York: St Martin's Press).

Laver, M. J., Gallagher, M., Marsh, M., Singh, R. and Tonra, B. (1995) *Electing the President of the European Commission*, Trinity Blue Papers in Public Policy, 1 (Dublin: Trinity College).

Laver, M. J. and Hunt, W. B. (1992) *Policy and Party Competition* (London: Routledge).

Lee, N. (1997) 'Environmental Policy', in M. Artis and N. Lee (eds), *The Economics of the European Union*, 2nd edn (Oxford: Oxford University Press).

Lehmbruch, G. (1967) *Proporzdemokratie: Politisches System und politische Kultur in der Schweiz und in Österreich* (Tübingen: Mohr).

Leibfried, S. (1992) 'Towards a European Welfare State? On Integrating Poverty Regimes into the European Community', in Z. Ferge and J. E. Kolberg (eds), *Social Policy in a Changing Europe* (Boulder, CO: Westview).

Leibfried, S. and Pierson, P. (1995) 'Semisovereign Welfare States: Social Policy in a Multitiered Europe', in S. Leibfried and P. Pierson (eds), *European Social Policy: Between Fragmentation and Integration* (Washington, DC: The Brookings Institution).

Leibfried, S. and Pierson, P. (1996) 'Social Policy', in H. Wallace and W. Wallace (eds), *Policy–Making in the European Union*, 3rd edn (Oxford: Oxford University Press).

Lenaerts, K. (1991) 'Some Reflections on the Separation of Powers in the European Community', *Common Market Law Review*, 28(1): 11–35.

Lenschow, A. (1997) 'Variation in EC Environmental Policy Integration: Agency Push Within Complex Institutional Structures', *Journal of European Public Policy*, 4(1): 109–27.

Lenschow, A. and Zito, A. (1998) 'Blurring or Shifting of Policy Frames?: The Institutionalization of the Economic–Environmental Policy Linkage in the European Community', *Governance*, 11(4): 415–41.

Leonardi, R. (1993) 'Cohesion in the European Community: Illusion or Reality?', *West European Politics*, 16(4): 492–517.

Leonardi, R. (1995) *Convergence, Cohesion and Integration in the European Union* (London: Macmillan).

Lewis, J. (1998) 'Is the "Hard Bargaining" Image of the Council Misleading? The Committee of Permanent Representatives and the Local Elections Directive', *Journal of Common Market Studies*, 36(4): 479–504.

Liebert, U. (2000) 'Gender Politics in the European Union: The Return of the Public', *Electoral Studies*, 1(2): 197–239.

Liefferink, D. and Andersen, M. S. (1998) 'Strategies of "Green" Member States in EU Environmental Policy-Making', *Journal of Common Market Studies*, 5(2): 254–70.

Lijphart, A. (1968) *The Politics of Accommodation: Pluralism and Democracy in the Netherlands* (Berkeley, CA: University of California Press).

Lijphart, A. (1977) *Democracy in Plural Societies: A Comparative Exploration* (New Haven, CT: Yale University Press).

Lijphart, A. (1981) 'Political Parties: Ideologies and Programs', in D. Butler, H. R. Penniman and D. Ranney (eds), *Democracy at the Polls: A Comparative Study of Competitive National Elections* (Washington, DC: American Enterprise Institute).

Lijphart, A. (1984) *Democracies: Patterns of Majoritarian and Consensus Government in Twenty-One Countries* (New Haven, CT: Yale University Press).

Lijphart, A. (ed.) (1992) *Parliamentary Versus Presidential Government* (Oxford: Oxford University Press).

Lijphart, A. (1994) 'Democracies: Forms, Performance, and Constitutional Engineering', *European Journal of Political Research*, 25(1): 1–17.

Lindberg, L. N. (1963) *The Political Dynamics of Economic Integration* (Oxford: Oxford University Press).

Lindberg, L. and Scheingold, S. (1970) *Europe's Would-Be Polity: Patterns of Change in the European Community* (Cambridge, Mass.: Harvard University Press).

Lindberg, L. N. and Scheingold, S. A. (eds) (1971) *Regional Integration: Theory and Research* (Cambridge, Mass.: Harvard University Press).

Lindblom, C. (1977) *Politics and Markets* (New York: Basic Books).

Lipset, S. M. (1959) *Political Man* (London: Heinemann).

Lipset, S. M. and Rokkan, S. (1967) 'Cleavage Structures, Party Systems and Voter Alignments: An Introduction', in S. M. Lipset and S. Rokkan (eds), *Party Systems and Voter Alignments: Cross-national Perspectives* (New York: Free Press).

Lodge, J. (1994) 'The European Parliament and the Authority-Democracy Crisis', *Annals of the American Academy of Political and Social Science*, 531): 69–83.

Lodge, J. (ed.) (1996) *The 1994 Elections to the European Parliament* (London: Pinter).

Lohmann, S. (1998) 'An Information Rationale for the Power of Special Interests', *American Political Science Review*, 92(4): 809–27.

Lohmann, S. (1999) 'What Price Accountability? The Lucas Island Model and the Politics of Monetary Policy', *American Journal of Political Science*, 43(2): 396–430.

Loughlin, J, (1996) 'Representing Regions in Europe: The Committee of the Regions', *Regional and Federal Studies*, 6(2): 147–65.

Lowi, T. J. (1964) 'American Business, Public Policy, Case Studies, and Political Theory', *World Politics*, 16(4): 677–715.

Lowi, T. J. (1969) *The End of Liberalism* (New York: Knopf).

Luce, D. R. and Raiffa, H. (1957) *Games and Decisions* (New York: Wiley).

Ludlow, P. (1991) 'The European Commission', in R. O. Keohane and S. Hoffmann (eds), *The New European Community: Decisionmaking and Institutional Change* (Boulder, CO: Westview).

Mackie, T. and Rose, R. (1991) *The International Almanac of Electoral History* (London: CQ Press).

MacMullen, A. (1997) 'European Commissioners 1952–1995: National Routes to a European Elite', in N. Nugent (ed.), *At the Heart of the Union: Studies of the European Commission* (London: Macmillan).

Madison, J., Hamilton, A. and Jay, J. (1987 [1788]) *The Federalist Papers* (London: Penguin).

Maduro, M. P. (1997) 'Reforming the Market or the State? Article 30 and the European Constitution: Economic Freedom and Political Rights', *European Law Journal*, 3(1): 55–82.

Magnette, P. (2001) 'Appointing and Censuring the European Commission: The Adaptation of Parliamentary Institutions to the Community Context', *European Law Journal*, 7(3): 292–310.

Maher, I. (1998) 'Community Law in the National Legal Order: A Systems Analysis', *Journal of Common Market Studies*, 36(2): 237–54.

Mair, P. (2000) 'The Limited Impact of Europe on National Party Systems', *West European Politics*, 23(4): 27–51.

Majone, G. (1989) *Evidence, Argument and Persuasion in the Policy Process* (New Haven, CT: Yale University Press).

Majone, G. (1991) 'Cross-National Sources of Regulatory Policy-making in Europe and the United States', *Journal of Public Policy*, 11(1): 79–106.

Majone, G. (1993a) 'The European Community Between Social Policy and Social Regulation', *Journal of Common Market Studies*, 31(2): 153–70.

Majone, G. (1993b) 'The European Community: An "Independent Fourth Branch of Government"?', EUI Working Paper SPS no. 94/17 (Florence: European University Institute).

Majone, G. (1994) 'The Rise of the Regulatory State in Europe', *West European Politics*, 17(3): 78–102.

Majone, G. (1996) *Regulating Europe* (London: Routledge).

Majone, G. (1997) 'The New European Agencies: Regulation by Information', *Journal of European Public Policy*, 4(2): 262–75.

Majone, G. (1998a) 'Europe's "Democratic Deficit": The Question of Standards', *European Law Journal*, 4(1): 5–28.

Majone, G. (1998b) 'From the Positive to the Regulatory State: Causes and Consequences of Changes in the Mode of Governance', *Journal of Public Policy*, 17(2): 139–67.

Majone, G. (2000) 'The Credibility Crisis of Community Regulation', *Journal of Common Market Studies*, 38(2): 273–302.

Majone, G. (2001) 'Two Logics of Delegation: Agency and Fiduciary Relations in EU Governance', *European Union Politics*, 2(1): 103–22.

Majone, G. (2002a) 'Functional Interests: European Agencies', in J. Peterson and M. Shackleton (eds), *The Institutions of the European Union* (Oxford: Oxford University Press).

Majone, G. (2002b) 'The European Commission: The Limits of Centralization and the Perils of Parliamentarization', *Governance*, 15(3): 375–92.

Majone, G. (2002c) 'Delegation of Regulatory Powers in a Mixed Polity', *European Law Journal*, 8(3): 319–39.

Mancini, F. (1989) 'The Making of a Constitution for Europe', *Common Market Law Review*, 26(4): 595–614.

Manners, I. and Whitman, R. G. (2003) 'The "Difference Engine": Constructing and Representing the International Identity of the European Union', *Journal of European Public Policy*, 10(3): 380–404.

Mansfield, E. D., Milner, H. V. and Rosendorff, B. P. (2002) 'Why Democracies Cooperate More: Electoral Controls and International Trade Agreements', *International Organization*, 56(3): 477–513.

March, J. G. and Olsen, J. P. (1989) *Rediscovering Institutions* (New York: Free Press).

Marginson, P. and Sisson, K. (1998) 'European Collective Bargaining: A Virtual Prospect?', *Journal of Common Market Studies*, 36(4): 505–28.

Marín, A. (1997) 'EC Environment Policy', in S. Stavridis, E. Mossialos, R. Morgan and H. Machin (eds), *New Challenges to the European Union: Policies and Policy-Making* (Aldershot: Gower).

Marks, G. (1992) 'Structural Policy in the European Community', in A. M. Sbragia (ed.), *Euro-Politics: Institutions and Policymaking in the 'New' European Community* (Washington, DC: The Brookings Institution).

Marks, G. (1993) 'Structural Policy and Multilevel Governance in the EC', in A. W. Cafruny and G. G. Rosenthal (eds), *The State of the European Community*, 2 (London: Longman).

Marks, G. (1996) 'Decision-Making in Cohesion Policy: Describing and Explaining Variation', in L. Hooghe (ed.), *Cohesion Policy and European Integration: Building Multi-Level Governance* (Oxford: Oxford University Press).

Marks, G. and Hooghe, L. (2003) 'National Identity and European Integration: A Multi-Level Analysis of Public Opinion', mimeo (Chapel Hill, NC: University of North Carolina).

Marks, G., Hooghe, L. and Blank, K. (1996) 'European Integration from the 1980s: State-Centric v. Multi-Level Governance', *Journal of Common Market Studies*, 34(3): 341–78.

Marks, G. and McAdam, D. (1996) 'Social Movements and the Changing Structure of Political Opportunity in the European Union', in G. Marks, F. W. Scharpf, P. C. Schmitter and W. Streeck (eds), *Governance in the European Union* (London: Sage).

Marks, G. and McAdam, D. (1999) 'On the Relationship of Political Opportunities to the Form of Collective Action: The Case of the European Union', in D. della Porta, H. Kriesi and D. Rucht (eds), *Social Movements in a Globalizing World* (London: Routledge).

Marks, G., Nielsen, F., Ray, L. and Salk, J. (1996) 'Competencies, Cracks and Conflicts: Regional Mobilization in the European Union', in G. Marks, F. W. Scharpf, P. C. Schmitter and W. Streeck (eds), *Governance in the European Union* (London: Sage).

Marks, G, and Wilson, C. (2000) 'The Past in the Present: A Cleavage Theory of Party Response to European Integration', *British Journal of Political Science*, 30): 433–59.

Marks, G, Wilson, C. and Ray, L. (2002) 'National Political Parties and European Integration', *American Journal of Political Science*, 46(3): 585–94.

Marquand, D. (1978) 'Towards a Europe of Parties', *Political Quarterly*, 49(4): 425–45.

Marsh, M. (1998) 'Testing the Second-Order Election Model after Four European Elections', *British Journal of Political Science*, 28(4): 591–607.

Marshall, T. H. (1950) *Citizenship and Social Class* (Cambridge: Cambridge University Press).

Martin, A. and Ross, G. (2001) 'Trade Union Organizing at the European Level: The Dilemma of Borrowed Resources', in D. Imig and S. Tarrow (eds), *Contentious Europeans: Protest and Politics in an Emerging Polity* (Lanham, MD: Rowman and Littlefield).

Martin, J. M. and Romano, A. T. (1992) *Multinational Crime, Terrorism, Espionage, Drug and Arms Trafficking* (London: Sage).

Martin, P. and Rogers, C. A. (1996) 'Trade Effects of Regional Aid', in R. Baldwin, P. Haaparanta and J. Kiander (eds), *Expanding the Membership of the European Union* (Cambridge: Cambridge University Press).

Martiniello, M. (ed.) (1995) *Migration, Citizenship and Ethno–National Identity in the European Union* (Aldershot: Avebury).

Martinotti, G. and Stefanizzi, S. (1995) 'Europeans and the Nation State', in O. Niedermayer and R. Sinnott (eds), *Public Opinion and Internationalized Governance* (Oxford: Oxford University Press).

Mattila, M. (2002) 'Redistribution in the European Union and the Enlargement', working paper (Helsinki: University of Helsinki).

Mattila, M. (2004) 'Contested Decisions: Empirical Analysis of Voting in the European Union Council of Ministers', *European Journal of Political Research*, 43(1): 29–50.

Mattila, M. and Lane, J.-E. (2001) 'Why Unanimity in the Council? A Roll Call Analysis of Council Voting', *European Union Politics*, 2(1): 31–52.

Mattli, W. and Slaughter, A.-M. (1995) 'Law and Politics in the European Union: A Reply to Garrett', *International Organization*, 49(1): 183–90.

Mattli, W. and Slaughter, A.-M. (1998a) 'The Role of National Courts in the Process of European Integration: Accounting for Judicial Preferences and Constraints', in A.-M. Slaughter, A. Stone Sweet and J. H. H. Weiler (eds), *The European Court and National Courts – Doctrine and Jurisprudence: Legal Change in Its Social Context* (Oxford: Hart).

Mattli, W. and Slaughter, A.-M. (1998b) 'Revisiting the European Court of Justice', *International Organization*, 52(1): 177–209.

Maurer, A. (1999) *(Co-)Governing after Maastricht: The European Parliament's institutional performance 1994–1999*, POLI 104/rev.EN (Brussels: European Parliament Directorate-General for Research).

Mayhew, D. (1974) *Congress: The Electoral Connection* (New Haven, CT: Yale University Press).

Mazey, S. (1998) 'The European Union and Women's Rights: From the Europeanisation of National Agendas to the Nationalisation of a European Agenda?', in D. Hine and H. Kassim (eds), *Beyond the Market: The EU and National Social Policy* (London: Routledge).

Mazey, S. and Richardson, J. (eds) (1993) *Lobbying in the European Community* (Oxford: Oxford University Press).

Mazey, S. and Richardson, J. (1997) 'The Commission and the Lobby', in G. Edwards and D. Spence (eds), *The European Commission*, 2nd edn (London: Catermill).

Mbaye, H. A. D. (2001) 'Why National States Comply with Supranational Law', *European Union Politics*, 2(3): 259–281.

McAllister, R. (1997) *From EC to EU: An Historical and Political Survey* (London: Macmillan).

McCarthy, N. (2000) 'Proposal Rights, Veto Rights, and Political Bargaining', *American Journal of Political Science*, 44(3): 506–22.

McCormick, J. (2001) *Environmental Policy in the European Union* (Basingstoke: Palgrave).

McCracken, P. (1977) *Towards Full Employment and Price Stability* (McCracken Report) (Paris: Organisation for Economic Cooperation and Development).

McCubbins, M. D., Noll, R. G. and Weingast, B. R. (1990) 'Positive and Normative Models of Procedural Rights: An Integrative Approach to Administrative Procedures', *Journal of Law, Economics, and Organization*, 6): 307–32.

McCubbins, M. D. and Schwartz, T. (1984) 'Congressional Oversight Overlooked: Police Patrols versus Fire Alarms', *American Journal of Political Science*, 28(1): 165–79.

McDonagh, B. (1998) *Original Sin in a Brave New World: An Account of the Negotiation of the Treaty of Amsterdam* (Dublin: Institute of European Affairs).

McDougall, D. (1977) *Report of the Study Group on the Role of Public Finance in European Integration*, vols 1 and 2 (Brussels: European Commission).

McGillivray, F., McLean, I., Pahre, R. and Schonhardt-Bailey, C. (2001) *International Trade and Political Institutions: Instituting Trade in the Long Nineteenth Century* (Cheltenham: Edward Elgar).

McGowan, L. and Cini, M. (1999) 'Discretion and Politicization in EU Competition Policy: The Case of Merger Control', *Governance*, 12(2): 175–200.

McKay, D. (1996) *Rush to Union: Understanding the European Federal Bargain* (Oxford: Clarendon Press).

McKay, D. (1999) 'The Political Sustainability of European Monetary Union', *British Journal of Political Science*, 29: 463–85.

McKay, D. (2001) *Designing Europe: Comparative Lessons from the Federal Experience* (Oxford: Oxford University Press).

McKelvey, R. (1976) 'Intransitivities in Multidimensional Voting Models and Some Implications for Agenda-Control', *Journal of Economic Theory*, 12(3): 472–82.

McKeown, T. J. (1991) 'A Liberal Trade Order: The Long-Run Pattern of Imports to the Advanced Capitalist States', *International Studies Quarterly*, 35(2): 151–72.

McKinnon, R. (1963) 'Optimum Currency Areas', *American Economic Review*, 53: 717–25.

McLaren, L. (2002) 'Public Support for the European Union: Cost/Benefit Analysis or Perceived Cultural Threat?', *Journal of Politics*, 64(2): 551–66.

McLaughlin, A. M. and Greenwood, J. (1995) 'The Management of Interest Representation in the European Union', *Journal of Common Market Studies*, 33(1): 143–56.

McNamara, K. R. (1998) *The Currency of Ideas: Monetary Politics in the European Union* (Ithaca, NY: Cornell University Press).

McNamara, K. R. (2001) 'Where do the Rules Come From? The Creation of the European Central Bank', A. Stone Sweet, W. Sandholtz and N. Fligstein (eds), *The Institutionalization of Europe* (Oxford: Oxford University Press).

McNamara, K. R. (2002) 'Rational Fictions: Central Bank Independence and the Social Logic of Delegation', *West European Politics*, 25(1): 47–76.

Meehan, E. (1993) *Citizenship and the European Community* (London: Sage).

Meijers, H. *et al.* (1997) *Democracy, Migrants and Police in the European Union: The 1996 IGC and Beyond* (Utrecht: Standing Committee of Experts in International Immigration, Refugee and Criminal Law).

Meltzer, A. H. and Richard, S. F. (1981) 'A Rational Theory of the Size of Government', *Journal of Political Economy*, 89: 914–27.

Menéndez, A. (2002) 'Chartering Europe: Legal Status and Policy Implications of the Charter of Fundamental Rights of the European Union', *Journal of Common Market Studies*, 40(3): 471–90.

Menz, G. (2003) 'Re-regulating the Single Market: National Varieties of Capitalism and their responses to Europeanization', *Journal of European Public Policy*, 10(4): 532–55.

Meunier, S. (1998) 'Divided but United: European Trade Policy Integration and EU–U.S. Agricultural Negotiations in the Uruguay Round', in C. Rhodes (ed.), *The European Community in the World Community* (Boulder, CO: Lynne Rienner).

Meunier, S. (2000) 'What Single Voice? European Institutions and EU–U.S. Trade Negotiations', *International Organization*, 54(1): 103–35.

Meunier, S. and Nicolaïdis, S. (1999) 'Who Speaks for Europe? The Delegation of Trade Authority in the EU', *Journal of Common Market Studies*, 37(3): 477–501.

Migration Policy Group (1996) *The Comparative Approaches to Societal Integration Project: Final Report* (Brussels: Migration Policy Group).

Miller, G. (1995) 'Post-Maastricht Legislative Procedures: Is the Council "Institutionally Challenged?"', paper presented at the fourth bennial conference of the European Community Studies Association, Charleston, April.

Miller, G. J. and Hammond, T. H. (1989) 'Stability and Efficiency in a Separation-of-Powers Constitutional System', in B. Grofman and D. Wittman (eds), *The Federalist Papers and the New Institutionalism* (New York: Agathon).

Milner, H. V. (1997) *Interests, Institutions, and Information: Domestic Politics and International Relations* (Princeton, NJ: Princeton University Press).

Milner, H. V. and Keohane, R. O. (1996) 'Internationalization and Domestic Politics: An Introduction', in R. O. Keohane and H. V. Milner (eds), *Internationalization and Domestic Politics* (Cambridge: Cambridge University Press).

Minford, P. (1996) 'The Price of Monetary Unification', in M. Holmes (ed.), *The Eurosceptical Reader* (London: Macmillan).

Minority Rights Group (ed.) (1997) *World Directory of Minorities* (London: Minority Rights Group).

Mitnick, B. M. (1980) *The Political Economy of Regulation: Creating, Designing and Removing Regulatory Forms* (New York: Columbia University Press).

Moberg A. (2002) 'The Nice Treaty and Voting Rules in the Council', *Journal of Common Market Studies*, 40(2): 259–82.

Moe, T. (1987) 'Interests, Institutions and Positive Theory: The Politics of the NLRB', *Studies in American Political Development*, 2: 236–99.

Moe, T. (1989) 'The Politics of Bureaucratic Structure', in J. Chubb and P. Peterson (eds), *Can Government Govern?* (Washington, DC: The Brookings Institution).

Moe, T. (1990) 'The Politics of Structural Choice: Towards a Theory of Public Bureaucracy', in O. E. Williamson (ed.), *Organizational Theory: From Chester Barnard to the Present and Beyond* (Oxford: Oxford University Press).

Monar, J. (1995) 'Democratic Control of Justice and Home Affairs: The European Parliament and National Parliaments', in R. Bieber and J. Monar (eds), *Justice and Home Affairs in the European Union: The Development of the Third Pillar* (Brussels: Interuniversity Press).

Monar, J. (2001) 'The Dynamics of Justice and Home Affairs', *Journal of Common Market Studies*, 39(4): 747–64.

Monnet, J. (1978) *Memoirs* (Garden City: Doubleday).

Montanari, I. J. (1995) 'Harmonization of Social Policies and Social Regulation in the European Community', *European Journal of Political Research*, 27(1): 21–45.

Moore, B. (1967) *Social Origins of Dictatorship and Democracy: Lord and Peasant in the Making of the Modern World* (Harmondsworth: Penguin).

Moravcsik, A. (1991) 'Negotiating the Single European Act: National Interests and Conventional Statecraft in the European Community', *International Organization*, 45(1): 19–56.

Moravcsik, A. (1993) 'Preferences and Power in the European Community: A Liberal Intergovernmentalist Approach', *Journal of Common Market Studies*, 31(4): 473–524.

Moravcsik, A. (1997) 'Taking Preferences Seriously: A Liberal Theory of International Politics', *International Organization*, 51(4): 513–53.

Moravcsik, A. (1998) *The Choice for Europe: Social Purpose and State Power from Messina to Maastricht* (Ithaca, NY: Cornell University Press).

Moravcsik, A. (1999) 'A New Statecraft? Supranational Entrepreneurs and International Cooperation', *International Organization*, 53(2): 267–306.

Moravcsik, A. (2002a) 'In Defense of the "Democratic Deficit": Reassessing the Legitimacy of the European Union', *Journal of Common Market Studies*, 40(4): 603–34.

Moravcsik, A. (2002b) 'The Quiet Superpower', *Newsweek*, 17 June 2002.

Moravcsik, A. (2003) 'The EU Ain't Broke', *Prospect*, March: 38–45.

Moravcsik, A. and Nicolaïdis, K. (1998) 'Keynote Article: Federal Ideals and Constitutional Realities in the Treaty of Amsterdam', *Journal of Common Market Studies: Annual Review*, 36: 13–38.

Moravcsik, A. and Nicolaïdis, K. (1999) 'Explaining the Treaty of Amsterdam: Interests, Influence, Institutions', *Journal of Common Market Studies*, 37(1): 59–85.

Morgenthau, H. J. (1948) *Politics Among Nations: The Struggle for Power and Peace* (New York: Knopf).

Morriss, P. (1996) 'QMV and Power Indices: A Further Comment to Johnston', *British Journal of Political Science*, 26: 595–97.

Moser P. (1996) 'The European Parliament as a Conditional Agenda–Setter: What Are the Conditions? A Critique of Tsebelis (1994)', *American Political Science Review*, 90(4): 834–8.

Moser, P. (1997) 'The Benefits of the Conciliation Procedure for the European Parliament: Comment to George Tsebelis', *Aussenwirtschaft*, 52(1–2): 57–62.

Moser, P. (2000) *The Political Economy of Democratic Institutions* (Cheltenham: Edward Elgar).

Mosher, J. S. and Trubek, D. M. (2003) 'Alternative Approaches to Governance in the EU: EU Social Policy and the European Employment Strategy', *Journal of Common Market Studies*, 41(1): 63–88.

Mueller, D. C. (1989) *Public Choice II* (Cambridge: Cambridge University Press).

Munchau, W. (1998) 'Emu's First Boom and Bust', *Financial Times*, 8 October.

Mundell, R. (1961) 'A Theory of Optimal Currency Areas', *American Economic Review*, 51: 657–65.

Murray, A. (2004) *The Lisbon Scorecard IV: The Status of Economic Reform in an Enlarged EU* (London: Centre for European Reform).

Musgrave, R. A. (1959) *Public Finance in Theory and Practice* (New York: McGraw-Hill).

Myrdal, G. (1957) *Economic Theory and the Underdeveloped Regions* (London: Duckworth).

Nanetti, R. Y. (1996) 'EU Cohesion and Territorial Restructuring in the Member States', in L. Hooghe (ed.), *Cohesion Policy and European Integration: Building Multi-Level Governance* (Oxford: Oxford University Press).

Nedergaard, P. (1995) 'The Political Economy of CAP Reform', in F. Laursen (ed.), *The Political Economy of European Integration* (The Hague: Kluwer).

Nelson, B. F. and Guth, J. L. (2000) 'Exploring the Gender Gap: Women, Men, and Public Attitudes towards European Integration', *European Union Politics*, 35(3): 377–406.

Nelson, B. F. and Guth, J. L. (2003) 'Religion and Youth Support for the European Union', *Journal of Common Market Studies*, 41(1): 89–112.

Nelson, B. F., Guth, J. L. and Fraser, C. R. (2001) 'Does Religion Matter? Christianity and Public Support for the European Union', *European Union Politics*, 2(2): 191–217.

Neuwahl, N. A. E. M. (1995) 'Judicial Control in Matters of Justice and Home Affairs: What Role for the Court of Justice?', in R. Bieber and J. Monar (eds), *Justice and Home Affairs in the European Union: The Development of the Third Pillar* (Brussels: Interuniversity Press).

Neven, D. J. (1992) 'Regulatory Reform in the European Community', *American Economic Review*, 82: 98–108.

Nicolaidis, P. (1995) 'The Effect of Regional Integration on Trade Policy: Lessons from the European Community', in F. Laursen (ed.), *The Political Economy of European Integration* (The Hague: Kluwer).

Niedermayer, O. (1991) 'Public Opinion and the European Parliament', in K. Reif and R. Inglehart (eds), *Eurobarometer: The Dynamics of European Public Opinion – Essays in Honour of Jacques-René Rabier* (London: Macmillan).

Niedermayer, O. (1995a) 'Trends and Contrasts', in O. Niedermayer and R. Sinnott (eds), *Public Opinion and Internationalized Governance* (Oxford: Oxford University Press).

Niedermayer, O. (1995b) 'Trust and Sense of Community', in O. Niedermayer and R. Sinnott (eds), *Public Opinion and Internationalized Governance* (Oxford: Oxford University Press).

Niedermayer, O. and Sinnott, R. (1995) 'Democratic Legitimacy and the European Parliament', in O. Niedermayer and R. Sinnott (eds), *Public Opinion and Internationalized Governance* (Oxford: Oxford University Press).

Niessen, J. (2000) 'The Amsterdam Treaty and NGO Responses', *European Journal of Migration Law*, 2: 203–14.

Niessen, J. and Guild, E. (1996) *The Developing Immigration and Asylum Policies of the European Union: Adopted Conventions, Resolutions, Recommendations, Decisions and Conclusion* (The Hague: Kluwer).

Niskanen, W. A. (1971) *Bureaucracy and Representative Government* (Chicago, Ill.: Aldine, Atherton).

Nordhaus, W. D. (1975) 'The Political Business Cycle', *Review of Economic Studies*, 42: 169–90.

Norris, P. and Franklin, M. (1997) 'Social Representation', in M. Marsh and P. Norris (eds), *Political Representation in the European Parliament*, special issue of *European Journal of Political Research*, 32(2).

North, D. C. (1990) *Institutions, Institutional Change and Economic Performance* (Cambridge: Cambridge University Press).

Norton, P. (ed.) (1996) *National Parliaments and the European Union* (London: Frank Cass).

Noury, A. (2002) 'Ideology, Nationality and Euro–Parliamentarians', *European Union Politics*, 3(1): 33–58.

Nugent, N. (2001) *The European Commission* (London: Palgrave).

Nugent, N. and Saurugger, S. (2002) 'Organizational Structuring: The Case of the European Commission and its External Policy Responsibilities', *Journal of European Public Policy*, 9(3): 345–64.

Nurmi, H. (1997) 'The Representation of Voter Groups in the European Parliament: A Penrose-Banzhaf Index Analysis', *Electoral Studies*, 16(3): 317–27.

Nuttall. S. (1996) 'The Commission: The Struggle for Legitimacy', in C. Hill (ed.), *The Actors in Europe's Foreign Policy* (London: Routledge).

Nuttall, S. (1997) 'The Commission and Foreign Policy–Making', in G. Edwards and D. Spence (eds), *The European Commission*, 2nd edn (London: Catermill).

Oates, W. E. (1972) *Fiscal Federalism* (New York: Harcourt Brace Jovanovich).

Oates, W. E. (1999) 'An Essay on Fiscal Federalism', *Journal of Economic Literature*, 37(4): 1120–49.

Obradovic, D. (1996) 'Prospects for Corporatist Decision-Making in the European Union: the Social Policy Agreement', *Journal of European Public Policy*, 2(2): 261–83.

OECD (2003) *Trends in International Migration* (Paris: Organisation for Economic Cooperation and Development).

O'Leary, S. (1995) *The Evolving Concept of Community Citizenship: From the Free Movement of Persons to Union Citizenship* (The Hague: Kluwer).

Olson, M. (1965) *The Logic of Collective Action* (Cambridge, Mass.: Harvard University Press).

O'Nuallain, C. (ed.) (1985) *The Presidency of the European Council of Ministers* (London: Croom Helm).

Oppenhuis, E, van der Eijk, C. and Franklin, M. (1996) 'The Party Context: Outcomes', in C. van der Eijk and M. Franklin (eds), *Choosing Europe? The European Electorate and National Politics in the Face of Union* (Ann Arbor, Mich.: University of Michigan Press).

Ordeshook, P. C. (1992) *A Political Theory Primer* (London: Routledge).

Ostner, I. and Lewis, J. (1995) 'Gender and the Evolution of European Social Policies', in S. Leibfried and P. Pierson (eds), *European Social Policy: Between Fragmentation and Integration* (Washington, DC: The Brookings Institution).

Ostrom, E. (1990) *Governing the Commons: The Evolution of Institutions of Collective Action* (Cambridge: Cambridge University Press).

Østrup, F. (1995) 'Economic and Monetary Union', in F. Laursen (ed.), *The Political Economy of European Integration* (The Hague: Kluwer).

Oudenhave, G. van (1965) *Political Parties in the European Parliament: The First Ten Years, September 1952–September 1962* (Leyden: A. W. Sijthoff).

Page, E. (1997) *People Who Run Europe* (Oxford: Clarendon Press).

Papademetriou, D. G. and Hamilton, K. A. (1996) *Converging Paths to Restriction: French, Italian, and British Responses to Immigration*, International Migration Policy Program 3 (Washington, DC: Carnegie Endowment for International Peace).

Pappi, F. U. and Henning, C. H. C. A. (1999) 'The Organization of Influence on the EC's Common Agricultural Policy: A Network Approach', *European Journal of Political Research*, 36: 257–81.

Parsons, C. (2002) 'Showing Ideas as Causes: The Origins of the European Union', *International Organization*, 56(1): 47–84.

Patterson, L. A. (1997) 'Agricultural Policy Reform in the European Community: A Three-Level Game Analysis', *International Organization*, 51(1): 135–65.

Pedlar, R. (ed.) (2002) *European Union Lobbying: Changes in the Arena* (London: Palgrave).

Pedlar, R. and Van Schendelen, M. P. C. M. (eds) (1994) *Lobbying the European Union: Companies, Trade Associations and Interest Groups* (Aldershot: Dartmouth).

Pelkmans, J. (1990) 'Regulation and the Single Market: An Economic Perspective', in H. Siebert (ed.), *The Completion of the Internal Market* (Tübingen: Mohr).

Pelkmans, J. and Winters, L. A. (1988) *Europe's Domestic Market* (London: Royal Institute of International Affairs).

Peltzman, S. (1976) 'Toward a More General Theory of Regulation', *Journal of Law and Economics*, 19(2): 211–40.

Peltzman, S. (1989) 'The Theory of Economic Regulation after a Decade of Deregulation', *Brookings Papers on Economic Activity – Microeconomics* (Washington, DC: The Brookings Institution).

Pennings, P. (2002) 'The Dimensionality of the EU Policy Space: The European Elections of 1999', *European Union Politics*, 3(1): 59–80.

Peters, B. G. (1992) 'Bureaucratic Politics and the Institutions of the European Community', in A. M. Sbragia (ed.), *Euro-Politics: Institutions and Policymaking in the "New" Europe* (Washington, DC: The Brookings Institution).

Peters, B. G. (1994) 'Agenda-Setting in the European Community', *Journal of European Public Policy*, 1(1): 9–26.

Peterson, J. (1991) 'Technology Policy in Europe: Explaining the Framework Programme and Eureka in Theory and Practice', *Journal of Common Market Studies*, 29(3): 269–90.

Peterson, J. (1995a) 'EU Research Policy: The Politics of Expertise', in C. Rhodes and S. Mazey (eds), *The State of the European Union*, 3 (London: Longman).

Peterson, J. (1995b) 'Playing the Transparency Game: Consultation and Policy–Making in the European Commission', *Public Administration*, 73(3): 473–92.

Peterson, J. (2001) 'The Choice for EU Theorists: Establishing a Common Framework for Analysis', *European Journal of Political Research*, 39(3): 289–318.

Petracca, M. P. (ed.) (1994) *The Politics of Interests: Interest Groups Transformed* (Boulder, CO: Westview).

Pfetsch, F. (1994) 'Tensions in Sovereignty: Foreign Policies of the EC Members Compared', in W. Carlsnaes and S. Smith (eds), *European Foreign Policy: The EC and Changing Perspectives in Europe* (London: Sage).

Piening, C. (1997) *Global Europe: The European Union in World Affairs* (Boulder, CO: Lynne Rienner).

Pierson, P. (1996) 'The Path to European Integration: A Historical Institutionalist Analysis', *Comparative Political Studies*, 29(2): 123–63.

Pierson, P. (2000) 'Increasing Returns, Path Dependence, and the Study of Politics', *American Political Science Review*, 94(2): 251–67.

Piner Tank, G. (1998) 'The CFSP and the nation-state', in K. A. Eliassen (ed.), *Foreign and Security Policy in the European Union* (London: Sage).

Plötner, J. (1998) 'Report on France', in A.-M. Slaughter, A. Stone Sweet and J. H. H. Weiler (eds), *The European Court and National Courts – Doctrine and Jurisprudence: Legal Change in Its Social Context* (Oxford: Hart).

Pollack, M. A. (1995a) 'Creeping Competence: The Expanding Agenda of the European Community', *Journal of Public Policy*, 14(1): 97–143.

Pollack, M. A. (1995b) 'Regional Actors in an Intergovernmental Play: The Making and Implementation of EC Structural Policy', in C. Rhodes and S. Mazey (eds), *The State of the European Union*, vol. 3 (London: Longman).

Pollack, M. A. (1996) 'The New Institutionalism and EC Governance: The Promise and Limits of Institutional Analysis', *Governance*, 9(4): 429–58.

Pollack, M. A. (1997a) 'Delegation, Agency and Agenda Setting in the European Community', *International Organization*, 51(1): 99–134.

Pollack, M. A. (1997b) 'Representing Diffuse Interests in EC Policy-Making', *Journal of European Public Policy*, 4(4): 572–90.

Pollack, M. A. (1997c) 'The Commission as an Agent', in N. Nugent (ed.), *At the Heart of the Union: Studies of the European Commission* (London: Macmillan).

Pollack, M. A. (1998) 'The Engines of Integration? Supranational Autonomy and Influence in the European Union', in W. Sandholtz and A. Stone Sweet (eds), *European Integration and Supranational Governance* (Oxford: Oxford University Press).

Pollack, M. A. (2001) 'International Relations Theory and European Integration', *Journal of Common Market Studies*, 39(2): 221–44.

Pollack, M. A. (2003) *The Engines of Integration: Delegation, Agency, and Agency Setting in the European Union* (Oxford: Oxford University Press).

Poole, W. (1990) 'Optimal Choice of Monetary Policy Instruments in a Simple Stochastic Macro Model', *Quarterly Journal of Economics*, 85.

Porte, C. de la and Pochet, P. (eds) (2002) *Building Social Europe Through the Open Method of Coordination* (Brussels: Peter Lang).

Portes, R. and Rey, H. (1998) 'The Emergence of the Euro as an International Currency', in D. Begg (eds), *EMU: Prospects and Challenges for the Euro* (Oxford: Blackwell).

Powell, G. B. (2000) *Elections as Instruments of Democracy: Majoritarian or Proportional Visions* (New Haven, CT: Yale University Press).

Praet, P. (1987) 'Economic Objectives in European Foreign Policy Making', in J. K. de Vree, P. Coffey and R. H. Lauwaars (eds), *Towards a European Foreign Policy: Legal, Economic and Political Dimensions* (Dordrecht: Martinus Nijhoff).

Pridham, G. and Pridham, P. (1979) 'The New Party Federations and Direct Elections', *The World Today*, 35(2): 62–70.

Quanjel, M. and Wolters, M. (1993) 'Growing Cohesion in the European Parliament', paper presented at the annual joint sessions of the European Consortium for Political Research, Leiden, April.

Quermonne, J. (1994) *La Système politique de l'Union européene* (Paris: Montchrétien).

Quin, Y. and Weingast, B. R. (1997) 'Federalism as a Commitment to Preserving Market Incentives', *Journal of Economic Perspectives*, 11(4): 83–92.

Radaelli, C. M. (1996) 'Fiscal Federalism as a Catalyst for Policy Development? In Search of a Framework for European Direct Tax Harmonisation', *Journal of European Public Policy*, 3(3): 402–20.

Rasmussen, H. (1986) *On Law and Policy in the European Court of Justice* (Dordrecht: Martinus Nijhoff).

Raunio, T. (1996) 'Parliamentary Questions in the European Parliament: Representation, Information and Control', *Journal of Legislative Studies*, 2(4): 356–82.

Raunio, T. (1997) *The European Perspective: Transnational Party Groups in the 1989–1994 European Parliament* (London: Ashgate).

Raunio, T. (1999) 'Always One Step Behind? National Legislatures and the European Union', *Government and Opposition*, 34(2): 180–202.

Raunio, T. and Hix, S. (2000) 'Backbenchers Learn to Fight Back: European Integration and Parliamentary Government', *West European Politics*, 23(4): 142–68.

Raunio T. and Wiberg, M. (1998) 'Winners and Losers in the Council: Voting Power Consequences of EU Enlargements', *Journal of Common Market Studies*, 36(4): 549–562.

Rawls, J. (1971) *A Theory of Justice* (Cambridge: Harvard University Press).

Ray, L. (1999) 'Measuring Party Orientations Towards European Integration: Results from an Expert Survey', *European Journal of Political Research*, 36: 283–306.

Reif, K. (1984) 'National Election Cycles and European Elections, 1979 and 1984', *Electoral Studies*, 3(3): 244–55.

Reif, K. (1997) 'Reflections: European Elections as Member State Second-Order Elections Revisited', *European Journal of Political Research*, 31(1): 115–24.

Reif, K. and Schmitt, H. (1980) 'Nine Second-Order National Elections: A Conceptual Framework for the Analysis of European Election Results', *European Journal of Political Research*, 8(1): 3–45.

Rhinard, M. (2002) 'The Democratic Legitimacy of the European Union Committee System', *Governance*, 15(2): 185–210.

Rhodes, M. (1995) 'A Regulatory Conundrum: Industrial Relations and the Social Dimension', in S. Leibfried and P. Pierson (eds), *European Social Policy: Between Fragmentation and Integration* (Washington, DC: The Brookings Institution).

Rhodes, R. A. W. and Dunleavy, P. (eds) (1995) *Prime Minister, Cabinet and Core Executive* (London: Macmillan).

Rhodes, M. and van Apeldoorn, B. (1997) 'Capitalism versus Capitalism in Western Europe', in M. Rhodes, P. Heywood and V. Wright (eds), *Developments in West European Politics* (London: Macmillan).

Richardson, J. (1996) 'Actor-Based Models of National and EU Policy Making', in H. Kassim and A. Menon (eds), *The EU and National Industrial Policy* (London: Routledge).

Riker, W. H. (1962) *The Theory of Political Coalitions* (New Haven, CT: Yale University Press).

Riker, W. H. (1975) 'Federalism', in F. I. Greenstein and N. W. Polsby (eds), *Handbook of Political Science*, vol. 5 (Reading, Mass.: Addison-Wesley).

Riker, W. H. (1980) 'Implications from the Disequilibrium of Majority Rule for the Study of Institutions', *American Political Science Review*, 74(2): 432–46.

Riker, W. H. (1986) *The Art of Political Manipulation* (New Haven, CT: Yale University Press).

Riker, W. H. (1992) 'The Merits of Bicameralism', *International Review of Law and Economics*, 12(2): 166–68.

Risse, T., Cowles, M. Green and Caporaso, J. (2001) 'Europeanization and Domestic Change: Introduction', in M. Green Cowles, J. Caporaso and T. Risse (eds), *Transforming Europe: Europeanization and Domestic Change* (Ithaca, NY: Cornell University Press).

Risse, T., Ropp, S. and Sikkink, K. (eds) (1999) *The Power of Human Rights: International Norms and Domestic Change* (Cambridge: Cambridge University Press).

Rittberger, B. (2000) 'Impatient Legislators and New Issue-Dimensions: A Critique of the Garrett-Tsebelis "Standard Version" of Legislative Politics', *Journal of European Public Policy*, 7(4): 554–75.

Rittberger, B. (2001) 'Which Institutions for Post-War Europe? Explaining the Institutional Design of Europe's First Community', *Journal of European Public Policy*, 8(5): 673–708.

Rodden, J. (2002) 'Strength in Numbers? Representation and Redistribution in the European Union', *European Union Politics*, 3(2): 151–75.

Rodriguez-Pose, A. (1998) *Dynamics of Regional Growth in Europe: Social and Political Factors* (Oxford: Oxford University Press).

Rogers, J. R. (2001) 'Information and Judicial Review: A Signaling Game of Legislative–Judicial Interaction', *American Journal of Political Science*, 45(1): 84–99.

Rogers, J. R. and Vanberg, G. (2002) 'Judicial Advisory Opinions and Legislative Outcomes in Comparative Perspective', *American Journal of Political Science*, 46(2): 379–97.

Rogowksi, R. (1990) *Commerce and Coalitions: How Trade Affects Domestic Political Alignments* (Princeton, NJ: Princeton University Press).

Rohrschneider, R. (2002) 'The Democratic Deficit and Mass Support for an EU–Wide Government', *American Journal of Political Science*, 46(2): 463–75.

Rokkan, S. (1973) 'Cities, States, and Nations: A Dimensional Model for the Study of Contrasts in Development', in S. N. Eisenstadt and S. Rokkan (eds), *Building States and Nations: Models and Data Resources*, vol. 1 (London: Sage).

Rokkan, S. (1999) *State Formation, Nation-Building, and Mass Politics in Europe: The Theory of Stein Rokkan*, selected and rearranged by P. Flora, S. Kuhnle and D. Urwin (Oxford: Oxford University Press).

Romer, T. and Rosenthal, H. (1978) 'Political Resource Allocation, Controlled Agendas, and the Status Quo', *Public Choice*, 33(1): 27–44.

Rosamond, B. (2000) *Theories of European Integration* (London: Macmillan).

Rosecrance, R. (1986) *The Rise of the Trading State* (New York: Basic Books).

Ross, G. (1994) *Jacques Delors and European Integration* (Cambridge: Polity Press).

Ruggie, J. G. (1998a) *Constructing the World Polity: Essays on International Institutionalization* (London: Routledge).

Ruggie, J. G. (1998b) 'What Makes the World Hang Together? Neo-utilitarianism and the Social Constructivist Challenge', *International Organization*, 52(4): 855–85.

Saalfeld, T. (2000) 'Members of Parliament and Governments in Western Europe: Agency Relations and Problems of Oversight', *European Journal of Political Research*, 37(3): 353–76.

Saglie, J. (2000) 'Values, Perceptions and European Integration: The Case of the Norwegian 1994 Referendum', *European Union Politics*, 1(2): 227–49.

Sala-i-Martin, X. and Sachs, J. (1991) 'Fiscal Federalism and Optimum Currency Areas: Evidence for Europe from the United States', NBER Working Paper no. 3855 (Cambridge: National Bureau of Economic Research).

Sánchez-Cuenca, I. (2000) 'The Political Basis of Support for European Integration', *European Union Politics*, 1(2): 147–71.

Sandholtz, W. (1992) 'ESPRIT and the Politics of International Collective Action', *Journal of Common Market Studies*, 30(1): 1–39.

Sandholtz, W. (1993) 'Choosing Union: Monetary Politics and Maastricht', *International Organization*, 47(1): 1–39.

Sandholtz, W. (1996) 'Money Troubles: Europe's Rough Road to Monetary Union', *Journal of European Public Policy*, 3(1): 84–101.

Sandholtz, W. and Stone Sweet, A. (1997) 'European Integration and Supranational Governance', *Journal of European Public Policy*, 4(3): 297–317.

Sandholtz, W. and Stone Sweet, A. (eds) (1998) *European Integration and Supranational Governance* (Oxford: Oxford University Press).

Sandholtz, W. and Zysman, J. (1989) '1992: Recasting the European Bargain', *World Politics*, 42(1): 95–128.

Sassen, S. (1996) *Losing Control* (New York: Columbia University Press).

Sbragia, A. M. (ed.) (1992) *Euro-Politics: Institutions and Policymaking in the 'New' European Community* (Washington, DC: The Brookings Institution).

Sbragia, A. M. (1996) 'Environment Policy', in H. Wallace and W. Wallace (eds), *Policy-Making in the European Union*, 3rd edn (Oxford: Oxford University Press).

Scarrow, S. (1997) 'Political Career Paths and the European Parliament', *Legislative Studies Quarterly*, 22(2): 253–63.

Scharpf, F. W. (1988) 'The Joint-Decision Trap: Lessons from German Federalism and European Integration', *Public Administration*, 66(3): 277–304.

Scharpf, F. W. (1996) 'Negative and Positive Integration in the Political Economy of European Welfare States', in G. Marks, F. W. Scharpf, P. C. Schmitter and W. Streeck (eds), *Governance in the European Union* (London: Sage).

Scharpf, F. W. (1997a) 'Economic Integration, Democracy and the Welfare State', *Journal of European Public Policy*, 4(1): 18–36.

Scharpf, F. W. (1997b) 'Introduction: The Problem-Solving Capacity of Multi-Level Governance', *Journal of European Public Policy*, 4(4): 520–38.

Scharpf, F. W. (1999) *Governing in Europe: Effective and Democratic?* (Oxford: Oxford University Press).

Scharpf, F. W. (2002) 'The European Social Model: Coping with the Challenges of Diversity', *Journal of Common Market Studies*, 40(4): 645–70.

Schattschneider, E. E. (1942) *Party Government* (New York: Holt, Rinehart and Winston).

Schattschneider, E. E. (1960) *The Semi–Sovereign People: A Realist's View of Democracy in America* (New York: Holt, Rinehart and Winston).

Schendelen, M. P. C. M. van (1996) '"The Council Decides": Does the Council Decide?', *Journal of Common Market Studies*, 34(4): 531–48.

Schild, J. (2001) 'National v. European Identities: French and Germans in the European Multi-Level System', *Journal of Common Market Studies*, 39(2): 331–51.

Schimmelfennig, F. (2001) 'The Community Trap: Liberal Norms, Rhetorical Action, and the Eastern Enlargement of the European Union', *International Organization*, 55(1): 47–80.

Schimmelfennig, F. (2002) 'Liberal Community and Enlargement: An Event History Analysis', *Journal of European Public Policy*, 9(4): 598–26.

Schimmelfennig, F. (2003) *The EU, NATO and the Integration of Europe: Rules and Rhetoric* (Cambridge: Cambridge University Press).

Schmidt, S. K. (1998) 'Commission Activism: Subsuming Telecommunications and Electricity under European Competition Law', *Journal of European Public Policy*, 5(1): 169–84.

Schmidt, S. K. (2000) 'Only an Agenda Setter? The European Commission's Power over the Council of Ministers', *European Union Politics*, 1(1): 37–61.

Schmidt, S. K. (2001) 'A Constrained Commission: Informal Practices of Agenda-Setting in the Council', in G. Schneider and M. Aspinwall (eds), *The Rules of Integration: Institutionalist Approaches to the Study of Europe* (Manchester: Manchester University Press).

Schmidt, V. (1999) 'National Patterns of Governance Under Siege: The Impact of European Integration', in B. Kohler-Koch and R. Eising (eds), *The Transformation of Governance in the European Union* (London: Routledge).

Schmitter, P. C. (1974) 'Still the Century of Corporatism?', *Review of Politics*, 36(1): 85–131.

Schmitter, P. C. (1996) 'Imagining the Future of the Euro–Polity with the Help of New Concepts', in G. Marks, F. W. Scharpf, P. C. Schmitter and W. Streeck (eds), *Governance in the European Union* (London: Sage).

Schmitter, P. C. (2000) *How to Democratize the European Union . . . and Why Bother?* (Lanham, MD: Rowman & Littlefield).

Schmitter, P. C. and Lehmbruch, G. (eds) (1979) *Trends Towards Corporatist Intermediation* (London: Sage).

Schneider, G. and Baltz, K. (2003) 'The Power of Specialization: How Interest Groups Influence EU Legislation', *Rivista di Politica Economica*, 93(1): 253–87.

Schneider, G. and Cederman, L.-E. (1994) 'The Change of Tide in Political Cooperation: A Limited Information Model of European Integration', *International Organization*, 48(4): 633–62.

Schneider, G. and Weitsman, P. A. (1996) 'The Punishment Trap: Integration Referendums as Popularity Contests', *Comparative Political Studies*, 28(4): 582–607.

Schuknecht, L. (1992) *Trade Protection in the European Community* (Reading: Harwood).

Schulz, H. and König, T. (2000) 'Institutional Reform and Decision-Making Efficiency in the European Union', *American Political Science Review*, 44(4): 653–66.

Schumpeter, J. (1943) *Capitalism, Socialism and Democracy* (London: Allen and Unwin).

Scully, R. M. (1997a) 'Policy Influence and Participation in the European Parliament', *Legislative Studies Quarterly*, 22(2): 233–52.

Scully, R. M. (1997b) 'The EP and the Co-Decision Procedure: A Reassessment', *Journal of Legislative Studies*, 3(3): 58–73.

Scully, R. M. (1997c) 'The EP and Co-Decision: A Rejoinder to Tsebelis and Garrett', *Journal of Legislative Studies*, 3(3): 93–103.

Scully, R. M. (1997d) 'Positively My Last Words on Co-Decision', *Journal of Legislative Studies*, 3(4): 144–6.

Shackleton, M. (2000) 'The Politics of Codecision', *Journal of Common Market Studies*, 38(2): 325–42.

Shapiro, M. J. (1981) *Courts: A Comparative and Political Analysis* (Chicago, Ill.: University of Chicago Press).

Shapiro, M. J. (1992) 'The European Court of Justice', in A. M. Sbragia (ed.), *Euro-Politics: Institutions and Policymaking in the 'New' European Community* (Washington, DC: The Brookings Institution).

Shapiro, M. J. and Stone, A. (eds) (1994) *The New Constitutional Politics of Europe*, special issue of *Comparative Political Studies*, 26(4).

Shapiro, M. J. and Stone Sweet, A. (2001) *On Law, Politics and Judicialization* (Oxford: Oxford University Press).

Shapley, L. S. and Shubik, M. (1954) 'A Method for Evaluating the Distribution of Power in a Committee System', *American Political Science Review*, 48(4): 787–92.

Sharman, J. C. (2003) 'Agrarian Politics in Eastern Europe in the Shadow of EU Accession', *European Union Politics*, 4(4): 447–71.

Sharp, M. and Pavitt, K. (1993) 'Technology Policy in the 1990s: Old Trends and New Realities', *Journal of Common Market Studies*, 31(2): 131–51.

Shaw, J. (1996) *Law of the European Union*, 2nd edn (London: Macmillan).

Shaw, J. (1997) 'Citizenship of the Union: Towards Post-National Membership?', Harvard Law School Jean Monnet Working Paper Series no. 6/97 (Cambridge, Mass:).

Sheingate, A. D. (2000) 'Agricultural Retrenchment Revisited: Issue Definition and Venue Change in the United States and European Union', *Governance*, 13(3): 335–63.

Shepsle, K. A. (1979) 'Institutional Arrangements and Equilibria in Multidimensional Voting Models', *American Journal of Political Science*, 23(1): 27–59.

Shepsle, K. A. (1986) 'Institutional Equilibrium and Equilibrium Institutions', in H. F. Weinberg (ed.), *Political Science: The Science of Politics* (New York: Agathon).

Shepsle, K. A. (1989) 'Studying Institutions: Some Lessons from the Rational Choice Approach', *Journal of Theoretical Politics*, 1: 131–47.

Shepsle, K. A. and Weingast, B. (1987) 'Why are Congressional Committees Powerful?', *American Political Science Review*, 81(4): 935–45.

Shepsle, K. A. and Weingast, B. (1994) 'Positive Theories of Congressional Institutions', *Legislative Studies Quarterly*, 19(2): 149–79.

Shipan, C. R. (2000) 'The Legislative Design of Judicial Review: A Formal Analysis', *Journal of Theoretical Politics*, 12(3): 269–304.

Shonfield, S. (1973) *Europe: Journey to an Unknown Destination* (London: Allen Lane).

Siebert, H. (1990) 'The Harmonization Issue in Europe: Prior Arrangement or a Competitive Process?', in H. Siebert (ed.), *The Completion of the Internal Market* (Tübingen: Mohr).

Siedentop, L. (2000) *Democracy in Europe* (London: Allen Lane).

Sinnott, R. (1995) 'Policy, Subsidiarity, and Legitimacy', in O. Niedermayer and R. Sinnott (eds), *Public Opinion and Internationalized Governance* (Oxford: Oxford University Press).

Sinnott, R. (2002) 'Attitudes and Behaviour of the Irish Electorate in the Referendum on the Treaty of Nice', unpublished mimeo, University College Dublin.

Sitter, N. (2001) 'The Politics of Opposition and European Integration in Scandinavia:

Is Euro-Scepticism a Government-Opposition Dynamic?', *West European Politics*, 24(4): 22–39.

Siune, K. and Svensson, P. (1993) 'The Danes and the Maastricht Treaty: The Danish EC Referendum of June 1992', *Electoral Studies*, 12(2): 117–21.

Siune, K., Svensson, P. and Tongsgaard, O. (1994) 'The European Union: The Danes Said "No" in 1992 but "Yes" in 1993: How and Why?', *Electoral Studies*, 13(2): 107–16.

Sjursen, H. (2002) 'Why Expand? The Question of Legitimacy and the Justification in the EU's Enlargement Policy', *Journal of Common Market Studies*, 40(3): 491–513.

Skogstad, G. (1998) 'Ideas, Paradigms and Institutions: Agricultural Exceptionalism in the European Union and the United States', *Governance*, 11(4): 463–90.

Skowronek, S. (1982) *Building a New American State: The Expansion of National Administrative Capacities* (Cambridge: Cambridge University Press).

Slater, M. (1982) 'Political Elites, Popular Indifference and Community Building', *Journal of Common Market Studies*, 21(1/2): 69–87.

Smith, A. D. (1991) *National Identity* (London: Penguin).

Smith, D. L. and Wanke, J. (1993) 'Completing the Single European Market: An Analysis of the Impact on the Member States', *American Journal of Political Science*, 37(2): 529–54.

Smith, K. (2003) *European Union Foreign Policy in a Changing World* (Cambridge: Polity Press).

Smith, K. (2004) *The Making of EU Foreign Policy: The Case of Eastern Europe*, 2nd edn (London: Palgrave).

Smith, M. (1996) 'The European Union and a Changing Europe: Establishing the Boundaries of Order', *Journal of Common Market Studies*, 34(1): 5–28.

Smith, M. (1997a) 'The Commission and External Relations', in G. Edwards and D. Spence (eds), *The European Commission*, 2nd edn (London: Catermill).

Smith, M. (1997b) 'The Commission Made Me Do It: The European Commission as a Strategic Asset in Domestic Politics', in N. Nugent (ed.), *At the Heart of the Union: Studies of the European Commission* (London: Macmillan).

Smith, M. (1998) 'Does the Flag Follow Trade?: "Politicisation" and the Emergence of a European Foreign Policy', in J. Peterson and H. Sjursen (eds), *A Common Foreign Policy for Europe? Competing Visions of the CFSP* (London: Routledge).

Smith, M. (2003) 'The Framing of European Foreign and Security Policy: Towards a Post-Modern Policy Framework?', *Journal of European Public Policy*, 10(4): 556–75.

Smith, M. E. (1998) 'Rules, Transgovernmentalism, and the Expansion of European Political Co-operation', in W. Sandholtz and A. Stone Sweet (eds), *European Integration and Supranational Governance* (Oxford: Oxford University Press).

Smith, M. E. (2000) 'Conforming to Europe: The Domestic Impact of EU Foreign Policy Co–operation', *Journal of European Public Policy*, 7(4): 613–31.

Smith, M. E. (2004a) *Europe's Foreign and Security Policy: The Institutionalization of Cooperation* (Cambridge: Cambridge University Press).

Smith, M. E. (2004b) 'Institutionalization, Policy Adaptation and European Foreign Policy Cooperation', *European Journal of International Relations*, 10(1): 95–136.

Smith, M. E. and Sandholtz, W. (1995) 'Institutions and Leadership: Germany, Maastricht and the ERM Crisis', in C. Rhodes and S. Mazey (eds), *The State of the European Union*, vol. 3 (London: Longman).

Smyrl, M. (1998) 'When (and How) Do the Commission's Preferences Matter', *Journal of Common Market Studies*, 36(1): 79–99.

Soysal, Y. (1994) *Limits of Citizenship: Migrants and Postnational Membership in Europe* (Chicago, Ill.: University of Chicago Press).

Spence, D. (1997) 'Staff and Personnel Policy in the Commission', in G. Edwards and D. Spence (eds), *The European Commission*, 2nd edn (London: Catermill).

Sperling, J. and Kirchner, E. (1997) 'The Security Architectures and Institutional Features of Post–1989 Europe', *Journal of European Public Policy*, 4(2): 155–70.

Staden, A. van (1994) 'After Maastricht: Explaining the Movement towards a Common European Defence Policy', in W. Carlsnaes and S. Smith (eds), *European Foreign Policy: The EC and Changing Perspectives in Europe* (London: Sage).

Stasavage, D. (2003) 'Transparency, Democratic Accountability, and the Economic Consequences of Monetary Institutions', *American Journal of Political Science*, 47(3): 389–402.

Stasavage, D. and Guillaume, D. (2002) 'When are Monetary Commitments Credible? Parallel Agreements and the Sustainability of Currency Unions', *British Journal of Political Science*, 32: 119–46.

Stavridis, S. (1997) 'The Common Security Policy of the European Union: Why Institutional Arrangements Are Not Enough', in S. Stavridis, E. Mossialos, R. Morgan and H. Machin (eds), *New Challenges to the European Union: Policies and Policy-Making* (Aldershot: Dartmouth).

Stein, E. (1981) 'Lawyers, Judges and the Making of a Transnational Constitution', *American Journal of International Law*, 75(1): 1–27.

Steinle, W. J. (1992) 'Regional Competitiveness in the Single Market', *Regional Studies*, 26(4): 307–18.

Stetter, S. (2000) 'Regulating Migration: Authority Delegation in Justice and Home Affairs', *Journal of European Public Policy*, 7(1): 80–103.

Steunenberg, B. (1994) 'Decision-making under different institutional arrangements: Legislation by the European Community', *Journal of Institutional and Theoretical Economics*, 150(4): 642–69.

Steunenberg, B. (1997a) 'Codecision and its Reform: A Comparative Analysis of Decision-Making Rules in the European Union', in B. Steunenberg and F. van Vught (eds), *Political Institutions and Public Policy* (Amsterdam: Kluwer).

Steunenberg, B. (1997b) 'Courts, Cabinet, and Coalition Parties: The Politics of Euthanasia in a Parliamentary Setting', *British Journal of Political Science*, 27: 551–71.

Stigler, G. J. (1970) 'Director's Law of Public Income Redistribution', *Journal of Law and Economics*, 13(1): 1–10.

Stigler, G. J. (1971) 'The Theory of Economic Regulation', *Bell Journal of Economics and Management Science*, 6(2): 3–21.

Stigler, G. J. and Friedland, C. (1962) 'What Can Regulators Regulate? The Case of Electricity', *Journal of Law and Economics*, 5(1): 1–16.

Stone, A. (1992) *The Birth of Judicial Politics in France: The Constitutional Council in Comparative Perspective* (Oxford: Oxford University Press).

Stone, A. (1993) 'Where Judicial Politics Are Legislative Politics: The French Constitutional Council', in M. L. Volcansek (ed.), *Judicial Politics and Policy-Making in Western Europe* (London: Frank Cass).

Stone Sweet, A. (1998) 'Constitutional Dialogues in the European Community', in A.-M. Slaughter, A. Stone Sweet and J. H. H. Weiler (eds), *The European Court and National Courts – Doctrine and Jurisprudence: Legal Change in Its Social Context* (Oxford: Hart).

Stone Sweet, A. (2002) 'Constitutional Courts and Parliamentary Democracy', *West European Politics*, 25(1): 77–100.

Stone Sweet, A. and Brunell, T. L. (1998a) 'Constructing a Supranational Constitution: Dispute Resolution and Governance in the European Community', *American Political Science Review*, 92(1): 63–81.

Stone Sweet, A. and Brunell, T. L. (1998b) 'The European Court and National Courts: A Statistical Analysis of Preliminary References, 1961–95', *Journal of European Public Policy*, 5(1): 66–97.

Stone Sweet, A. and Brunell, T. L. (1999) *Data Set on Preliminary References in EC Law, 1958–1998* (Florence: European University Institute).

Stone Sweet, A. and Brunell, T. L. (2000) 'The European Court, National Judges, and

Legal Integration: A Researcher's Guide to the Data Set on Preliminary References in EC Law, 1958–98', *European Law Journal*, 6(2): 117–27.

Stone Sweet, A. and Sandholtz, W. (1997) 'European Integration and Supranational Governance', *Journal of European Public Policy*, 4(3): 297–317.

Stone Sweet, A. and Sandholtz, W. (eds) (1998) *European Integration and Supranational Governance* (Oxford: Oxford University Press).

Stone Sweet, A., Sandholtz, W. and Fligstein, N. (eds) (2001) *The Institutionalization of Europe* (Oxford: Oxford University Press).

Story, J. (1996) 'Strategy, Ideology and Politics: The Relaunch of Social Europe, 1987–1989', in O. Cadot, L. Gabel, J. Story and D. Webber (eds), *European Casebook on Industrial and Trade Policy* (Hemel Hempstead: Prentice-Hall).

Streeck, W. (1995) 'From Market Making to State Building? Reflections on the Political Economy of European Social Policy', in S. Leibfried and P. Pierson (eds), *European Social Policy: Between Fragmentation and Integration* (Washington, DC: The Brookings Institution).

Streeck, W. (1996) 'Neo-Voluntarism: A European Social Policy Regime?', in G. Marks, F. W. Scharpf, P. C. Schmitter and W. Streeck (eds), *Governance in the European Union* (London: Sage).

Streeck, W. (1997) 'Industrial Citizenship under Regime Competition: The Case of the European Works Councils', *Journal of European Public Policy*, 4(4): 643–64.

Streeck, W. and Schmitter, P. C. (1991) 'From National Corporatism to Transnational Pluralism: Organized Interests in the Single European Market', *Politics and Society*, 19(2): 133–64.

Streit, M. E. and Mussler, W. (1995) 'The Economic Constitution of the European Community: From "Rome" to "Maastricht"', *European Law Journal*, 1(3): 5–30.

Strøby-Jensen, C. (2000) 'Neofunctionalist Theories and the Development of European Social and Labour Market Policy', *Journal of Common Market Studies*, 38(1): 71–92.

Sun, J.-M. and Pelkmans, J. (1995) 'Regulatory Competition and the Single Market', *Journal of Common Market Studies*, 33(1): 67–89.

Sunstein, C. R. (1990) *After the Rights Revolution: Reconsidering the Regulatory State* (Cambridge: Harvard University Press).

Sutcliffe, J. B. (2000) 'The 1999 Reform of the Structural Fund Regulations: Multi-Level Governance or Renationalization?', *Journal of European Public Policy*, 7(2): 290–309.

Sutherland, P. *et al.* (High Level Group on the Operation of the Internal Market) (1992) *The Internal Market After 1992: Meeting the Challenge* (Luxembourg: Office of Official Publications of the European Communities).

Sutter, M. (2000) 'Fair Allocation and Re-weighting of Votes and Voting Power in the EU Before and After the Next Enlargement', *Journal of Theoretical Politics*, 12(4): 433–449.

Sverdrup, U. (2002) 'An Institutional Perspective on Treaty Reform: Contextualizing the Amsterdam and Nice Treaties', *Journal of European Public Policy*, 9(1): 120–40.

Szczerbiak, A. (2001) 'Polish Public Opinion: Explaining Declining Support for EU Membership', *Journal of Common Market Studies*, 39(1): 105–22.

Taggart, P. (1998) 'A Touchstone of Dissent: Euroscepticism in Contemporary Western European Party Systems', *European Journal of Political Research*, 33: 363–88

Tallberg, J. (2000) 'The Anatomy of Autonomy: An Institutional Account of Variation in Supranational Influence', *Journal of Common Market Studies*, 38(5): 843–64.

Tarrow, S. (1995) 'The Europeanisation of Conflict: Reflections from a Social Movement Perspective', *West European Politics*, 18(2): 223–51.

Taylor, M. (1976) *Anarchy and Cooperation* (New York: Wiley).

Taylor, P. (1982) 'Intergovernmentalism in the European Communities in the 1970s: Patterns and Perspectives', *International Organization*, 36(4): 741–66.

Taylor, P. (1991) 'The European Community and the State: Assumptions, Theories and Propositions', *Review of International Studies*, 17(2): 109–25.

Taylor, P. (1996) *The European Union in the 1990s* (Oxford: Oxford University Press).

Teague, P. (1994) 'Between New Keynesianism and Deregulation: Employment Policy in the European Union', *Journal of European Public Policy*, 1(3): 315–45.

Teasdale, A. L. (1993) 'The Life and Death of the Luxembourg Compromise', *Journal of Common Market Studies*, 31(4): 567–79.

Thatcher, M. (2002a) 'Analysing Regulatory Reform in Europe', *Journal of European Public Policy*, 9(6): 859–72.

Thatcher, M. (2002b) 'Regulation After Delegation: Independent Regulatory Agencies in Europe', *Journal of European Public Policy*, 9(6): 954–72.

Thelen, K. and Steinmo, S. (1992) 'Historical Institutionalism in Comparative Politics', in S. Steinmo, K. Thelen and F. Longstreth (eds), *Structuring Politics: Historical Institutionalism in Comparative Politics* (Cambridge: Cambridge University Press).

Thielemann, E. (2003a) 'Between Interests and Norms: Explaining Burden–Sharing in the European Union', *Journal of Refugee Studies*, 16(3): 253–73.

Thielemann, E. (2003b) 'Does Policy Matter? On Governments' Attempts to Control Unwanted Migrants', European Institute Working Paper (London: London School of Economics and Political Science).

Thielemann, E. (2004) 'Why Asylum Policy Harmonisation Undermines Refugee Burden-Sharing', *European Journal of Migration and Law*, 6(1): 43–61.

Tilly, C. (1990) *Coercion, Capital and European States, 990–1990* (Oxford: Blackwell).

Tinbergen, J. (1965) *International Economic Integration*, 2nd edn (Amsterdam: Elsevier).

Titmus, R. M. (1974) *Social Policy* (London: Allen and Unwin).

Tonra, B. (2003) 'Constructing the Common Foreign and Security Policy: The Utility of a Cognitive Approach', *Journal of Common Market Studies*, 41(4): 731–56.

Torres, F. (1998) 'Portugal Toward EMU: A Political Economy Perspective', in E. Jones, J. Frieden and F. Torres (eds), *Joining Europe's Monetary Club: The Challenges for Smaller Member States* (London: Macmillan).

Truman, D. (1951) *The Process of Government* (New York: Knopf Press).

Tsebelis, G. (1990) *Nested Games: Rational Choice in Comparative Politics* (Berkeley, CA: University of California Press).

Tsebelis, G. (1994) 'The Power of the European Parliament as a Conditional Agenda-Setter', *American Political Science Review*, 88(1): 128–42.

Tsebelis, G. (1995a) 'Conditional Agenda-Setting and Decision-Making Inside the European Parliament', *Journal of Legislative Studies*, 1(1): 65–93.

Tsebelis, G. (1995b) 'Will Maastricht Reduce the "Democratic Deficit?"', *APSA-Comparative Politics Newsletter*, 6(1): 4–6.

Tsebelis, G. (1995c) 'Decision Making in Political Systems: Veto Players in Presidentialism, Parliamentarism, Multicameralism and Multipartyism', *British Journal of Political Science*, 25(2): 289–325.

Tsebelis, G. (1996) 'Maastricht and the Democratic Deficit', *Aussenwirtschaft*, 52(1–2): 29–56.

Tsebelis, G. (1999) 'Veto Players and Law Production in Parliamentary Democracies: An Empirical Analysis', *American Political Science Review*, 93(3): 591–608.

Tsebelis, G. (2000) 'Veto Players and Institutional Analysis', *Governance*, 13(5): 441–74.

Tsebelis, G. (2002) *Veto Players: How Political Institutions Work* (Princeton, NJ: Princeton University Press/Russell Sage Foundation).

Tsebelis, G. and Garrett, G. (1996) 'An Institutional Critique of Intergovernmentalism', *International Organization*, 50(2): 269–99.

Tsebelis, G. and Garrett, G. (1997a) 'Agenda Setting, Vetoes and the European Union's Co-decision Procedure', *Journal of Legislative Studies*, 3(3): 74–92.

Tsebelis, G. and Garrett, G. (1997b) 'More on the Co-Decision Endgame', *Journal of Legislative Studies*, 3(4): 139–43.

Tsebelis, G. and Garrett, G. (2000a) 'Legislative Politics in the European Union', *European Union Politics*, 1(1): 9–36.

Tsebelis, G. and Garrett, G. (2000b) 'The Institutional Foundations of Intergovernmentalism and Supranationalism in the European Union', 55(2): 357–90.

Tsebelis, G., Jensen, C. B., Kalandrakis, A. and Kreppel, A. (2001) 'Legislative Procedures in the European Union: An Empirical Analysis', *British Journal of Political Science*, 31: 573–99.

Tsebelis, G. and Kalandrakis, A. (1999) 'The European Parliament and Environmental Legislation: The Case of Chemicals', *European Journal of Political Research*, 36(1): 119–54.

Tsebelis, G. and Kreppel, A. (1998) 'The History of Conditional Agenda–Setting in European Institutions', *European Journal of Political Research*, 33(1): 41–71.

Tsebelis, G. and Money, J. (1997) *Bicameralism* (Cambridge: Cambridge University Press).

Tsebelis, G. and Yataganas X. (2002) 'Veto Players and Decision–making in the EU After Nice: Policy Stability and Bureaucratic/Judicial Discretion', *Journal of Common Market Studies*, 40(2): 283–307.

Tucker, J. A., Pacek, A. C. and Berinsky, A. J. (2002) 'Transitional Winners and Losers: Attitudes Toward EU Membership in Post-Communist Countries', *American Journal of Political Science*, 46(3): 557–71.

Tullock, G. (1971) 'The Charity of the Uncharitable', *Western Economic Journal*, 9: 379–92.

Turnbull, P. and Sandholtz, W. (2001) 'Policing and Immigration: The Creation of New Policy Spaces', in A. Stone Sweet, W. Sandholtz and N. Fligstein (eds), *The Institutionalization of Europe* (Oxford: Oxford University Press).

Turner, P. (1991) *Capital Flows in the 1980s*, BIS Economic Papers, no. 30 (Basle: Bank of International Settlements).

Turner, C. and Muñoz, R. (2000) 'Revising the Judicial Architecture of the European Union', *Yearbook of European Law*, 19: 1–93.

Tversky, A. and Kahneman, T. (1981) 'The Framing of Decisions', *Science*, 211(3): 453–8.

Uçarer, E. M. (2001) 'From the Sidelines to Center Stage: Sidekick No More? The European Commission in Justice and Home Affairs', *European Integration On-line Papers*, 5(5) (http://eiop.or.at/eiop/texte/2001–005a.htm).

Ugar, M. (1995) 'Freedom of Movement vs. Exclusion: A Reinterpretation of the 'Insider' – 'Outsider' Divide in the European Union', *International Migration Review*, 29(4): 964–99.

Ugar, M. (1998) 'Explaining Protectionism and Liberalization in European Union Trade Policy: The Case of Textiles and Clothing', *Journal of European Public Policy*, 5(4): 652–70.

Ullrich, H. (1998) 'Transatlantic Relations in the Post-Cold War Era', *Journal of European Public Policy*, 5(1): 200–5.

Vanberg, G. (1998) 'Abstract Judicial Review, Legislative Bargaining, and Policy Compromise', *Journal of Theoretical Politics*, 10(3): 299–326.

Vanberg, G. (2001) 'Legislative-Judicial Relations: A Game-Theoretic Approach to Constitutional Review', *American Journal of Political Science*, 45(2): 346–61.

Verdun, A (1998) 'The Institutional Design of EMU: A Democratic Deficit?', *Journal of Public Policy*, 18(2): 107–32.

Verdun, A. (1999) 'The Role of the Delors Committee in Creating EMU: An Epistemic Community?', *Journal of European Public Policy*, 6(2): 308–28.

Verdun, A. (2000) *European Responses to Globalization and Financial Market Integration: Perceptions of Economic and Monetary Union in Britain, France and Germany* (London: Macmillan).

Vink, M. and Meijerink, F. (2003) 'Asylum Applications and Recognition Rates in EU Member States 1982–2001: A Quantitative Analysis', *Journal of Refugee Studies*, 16(3): 297–315.

Visser, J. and Ebbinghaus, B. (1992) 'Making the Most of Diversity? European Integration and Transnational Organization of Labour', in J. Greenwood, J. R. Grote and K. Ronit (eds), *Organized Interests and the European Community* (London: Sage).

Vogel, D. (1995) *Trading Up: Consumer and Environmental Regulation in a Global Economy* (Cambridge, Mass.: Harvard University Press).

Vogel, D. (1997) 'Trading Up and Governing Across: Transnational Governance and Environmental Protection', *Journal of European Public Policy*, 4(4): 556–71.

Volcansek, M. L. (1986) *Judicial Politics in Europe: An Impact Analysis* (New York: Peter Lang).

Volcansek, M. L. (1993a) 'The European Court of Justice: Supranational Policy-Making', in M. L. Volcansek (ed.), *Judicial Politics and Policy-Making in Western Europe* (London: Frank Cass).

Volcansek, M. L. (ed.) (1993b) *Judicial Politics and Policy-Making in Western Europe* (London: Frank Cass).

Vos, E. (1997) 'The Rise of Committees', *European Law Journal*, 3(3): 210–29.

Wagner, W. (2003) 'Why the EU's Common Foreign and Security Policy will Remain Intergovernmental: A Rationalist Institutional Choice Analysis of European Crisis Management Policy', *Journal of European Public Policy*, 10(4): 576–95.

Wallace, W. and Smith, J. (1995) 'Democracy or Technocracy? European Integration and the Problem of Popular Consent', *West European Politics*, 18(3): 137–57.

Waltz, K. N. (1979) *Theory of International Politics* (New York: McGraw-Hill).

Waltz, K. N. (2000) 'Structural Realism after the Cold War', *International Security*, 25(1): 5–41.

Walzer, M. (1983) *Spheres of Justice: A Defense of Pluralism and Equality* (New York: Basic Books).

Warleigh, A. (2000) 'The Hustle: Citizenship Practice, NGOs and "Policy Coalitions" in the European Union – the Cases of Auto Oil, Drinking Water and Unit Pricing', *Journal of European Public Policy*, 7(2): 229–43.

Warleigh, A. (2001) '"Europeanizing" Civil Society', *Journal of Common Market Studies*, 39(4): 619–39.

Watson, R. (2002) 'Knocking on the Parliament's Door', *E!Sharp*, February: 40–2.

Way, C. (2000) 'Central Banks, Partisan Politics, and Macroeconomic Outcomes', *Comparative Political Studies*, 33(2): 196–224.

Weale, A. (1996) 'Environmental Rules and Rule-Making in the European Union', *Journal of European Public Policy*, 3(4): 594–611.

Weatherill, S. and Beaumont, S. (2004) *EU Law: The Essential Guide to the Legal Workings of the European Union*, 4th edn (London: Penguin).

Webber, D. (1999) 'Franco-German Bilateralism and Agricultural Politics in the European Union', *West European Politics*, 22(1): 45–67.

Weber, K. and Hallerberg, M. (2001) 'Explaining Variation in Institution Integration in the European Union: Why Firms May Prefer European Solutions', *Journal of European Public Policy*, 8(2): 171–91.

Weber, M. (1946 [1919]) 'Politics as a Vocation', in H. H. Gerth and C. Wright Mills (eds), *From Max Weber: Essays in Sociology* (New York: Oxford University Press).

Webster, R. (1998) 'Environmental Collective Action: Stable Patterns of Cooperation and Issue Alliances at the European Level', in J. Greenwood and M. Aspinwall (eds), *Collective Action in the European Union* (London: Routledge).

Weiler, J. H. H. (1981) 'The Community System: The Dual Character of Supranationalism', *Yearbook of European Law*, 1: 268–306.

Weiler, J. H. H. (1991) 'The Transformation of Europe', *Yale Law Journal*, 100: 2403–83.

Weiler, J. H. H. (1993) 'Journey to an Unknown Destination: A Retrospective and Prospective of the European Court of Justice in the Area of Political Integration', *Journal of Common Market Studies*, 31(4): 417–46.

Weiler, J. H. H. (1994) 'A Quiet Revolution: The European Court of Justice and Its Interlocutors', *Comparative Political Studies*, 26(4): 510–34.

Weiler, J. H. H. (1995) 'Does Europe Need a Constitution? Reflections on Demos, Telos and the German Maastricht Decision', *European Law Journal*, 1(3): 219–58.

Weiler, J. H. H. (1997a) 'The Reformation of European Constitutionalism', *Journal of Common Market Studies*, 35(1): 97–131.

Weiler, J. H. H. (1997b) 'The European Union Belongs to the Citizens: Three Immodest Proposals', *European Law Review*, 22): 150–6.

Weiler, J. H. H. and Haltern, U. R. (1998) 'Constitutional or International? The Foundations of the Community Legal Order and the Question of Judicial *Kompetenz-Kompetenz*', in A.-M. Slaughter, A. Stone Sweet and J. H. H. Weiler (eds), *The European Court and National Courts – Doctrine and Jurisprudence: Legal Change in Its Social Context* (Oxford: Hart).

Weiler, J. H. H., Haltern, U. R. and Mayer F. (1995) 'European Democracy and its Critique', *West European Politics*, 18(3): 4–39.

Weingast, B. R. (1995) 'The Economic Role of Political Institutions: Market–Preserving Federalism and Economic Development', *Journal of Law and Economic Organization*, 11(1): 1–31.

Weingast, B. R. (1996) 'Political Institutions: Rational Choice Perspectives', in R. E. Goodin and H.-D. Klingeman (eds), *A New Handbook of Political Science* (Oxford: Oxford University Press).

Weingast, B. R. and Moran, M. (1983) 'Bureaucratic Discretion or Congressional Control? Regulatory Policymaking by the Federal Trade Commission', *Journal of Political Economy*, 91(4): 775–800.

Weingast, B. R., Shepsle, K. A. and Johnson, C. (1981) 'The Political Economy of Benefits and Costs: A Neoclassical Approach to Distributive Politics', *Journal of Political Economy*, 89: 642–64.

Werts, J. (1992) *The European Council* (Amsterdam: North Holland).

Wessels, B. (1995a) 'Development of Support: Diffusion or Demographic Replacement?', in O. Niedermayer and R. Sinnott (eds), *Public Opinion and Internationalized Governance* (Oxford: Oxford University Press).

Wessels, B. (1995b) 'Evaluations of the EC: Élite or Mass-Driven?', in O. Niedermayer and R. Sinnott (eds), *Public Opinion and Internationalized Governance* (Oxford: Oxford University Press).

Wessels, B. (1999) 'European Parliament and Interest Groups', in R. S. Katz and B. Wessels (eds), *The European Parliament, National Parliaments, and European Integration* (Oxford: Oxford University Press).

Wessels, W. (1991) 'The EC Council: The Community's Decisionmaking Center', in R. O. Keohane and S. Hoffmann (eds), *The New European Community: Decisionmaking and Institutional Change* (Boulder, CO: Westview).

Wessels, W. (1992) 'Staat und (west-europäische) Integration, Die Fusionsthese', in M. Kreile (ed.), *Die Integration Europas*, PVS Sonderheft no. 23, 36–61.

Wessels, W. (1996) 'German Administration Interaction and European Union: The Fusion of Public Policies', in Y. Mény, P. Muller and J.-L. Quermonne (eds), *Adjusting to Europe: The Impact of the European Union on National Institutions and Policies* (London: Routledge).

Wessels, W. (1997a) 'An Ever Closer Fusion? A Dynamic Macropolitical View on Integration Processes', *Journal of Common Market Studies*, 35(2): 267–99.

Wessels, W. (1997b) 'The Growth and Differentiation of Multi-Level Networks: A Corporatist Mega-Bureaucracy or Open City?', in H. Wallace and A. R. Young (eds), *Participation and Policy-Making in the European Union* (Oxford: Clarendon Press).

Wessels, W., Maurer, A. and Mittag, J. (eds) (2003) *Fifteen Into One? The European Union and its Member States* (Manchester: Manchester University Press).

Wessels, W. and Rometsch, D. (1996) 'Conclusion: European Union and National Institutions', in D. Rometsch and W. Wessels (eds), *The European Union and Member States: Towards Institutional Fusion?* (Manchester: Manchester University Press).

Westlake, M. (1994) *A Modern Guide to the European Parliament* (London: Pinter).

Westlake, M. (1995) *The Council of the European Union* (London: Catermill).

Westlake, M. (1998) 'The European Parliament's Emerging Appointment Powers', *Journal of Common Market Studies*, 36(3): 431–44.

Whitten, G., Gabel, M. and Palmer, H. (1998) '"Euro-Pork": How Fiscal Policy Influences Public Support for European Integration', unpublished mimeo.

Widgrén, M. (1995) 'Probabilistic voting power in the EU Council: The cases of trade policy and social regulation', *Scandinavian Journal of Economics*, 97: 345–56.

Wiener, A. (1997) *Building Institutions: The Developing Practice of European Citizenship* (Boulder, CO: Westview).

Wildasin, D. E. (2002) 'Fiscal Policy in Post-EMU Europe', *European Union Politics*, 3(2): 251–60.

Wilensky, H. (1975) *The Welfare State and Equality* (Berkeley, CA: University of California Press).

Wilks, S. and McGowan, L. (1995) 'Disarming the Commission: The Debate over a European Cartel Office', *Journal of Common Market Studies*, 32(2): 259–73.

Williams, S. (1991) 'Sovereignty and Accountability', in R. O. Keohane and S. Hoffmann (eds), *The New European Community* (Boulder, CO: Westview).

Wilson, J. Q. (1980) *The Politics of Regulation* (New York: Basic Books).

Wincott, D. (1995) 'The Role of Law or the Rule of the Court of Justice? An 'Institutional' Account of Judicial Politics in the European Community', *Journal of European Public Policy*, 2(4): 583–602.

Winkler, B. (1996) 'Towards a Strategic View on EMU: A Critical Survey', *Journal of Public Policy*, 16(1): 1–28.

Winkler, B. (1999) 'Is Maastricht a Good Contract?', *Journal of Common Market Studies*, 37(1): 39–58.

Winkler, G. M. (1998) 'Coalition-Sensitive Voting Power in the Council of Ministers: The Case of Eastern Enlargement', *Journal of Common Market Studies*, 36(2): 391–404.

de Witte, B. (1998) 'Sovereignty and European Integration: The Weight of Legal Tradition', in A.-M. Slaughter, A. Stone Sweet and J. H. H. Weiler (eds), *The European Court and National Courts – Doctrine and Jurisprudence: Legal Change in Its Social Context* (Oxford: Hart).

Wonka, A. (2004) 'Delegation and Abdication? The Appointment of European Commissioners and its Policy Implications', MZES Working Paper (Mannheim: Mannheim Centre for European Studies).

Woods, N. (1996) 'The Use of Theory in the Study of International Relations', in N. Woods (ed.), *Explaining International Relations Since 1945* (Oxford: Oxford University Press).

Woolcock, S. (1994) *The Single European Market: Centralization or Competition Among National Rules?* (London: Royal Institute of International Affairs).

Woolley, J. T. (1994) 'Linking Political and Monetary Union: The Maastricht Agenda and German Domestic Politics', in B. Eichengreen and J. Frieden (eds), *The Political Economy of European Monetary Unification* (Boulder, CO: Westview).

World Trade Organization (2003) *World Trade Statistics 2003* (Geneva: World Trade Organization).

Wright, V. (1996) 'The National Co-ordination of European Policy-Making: Negotiating the Quagmire', in J. Richardson (ed.), *European Union: Power and Policy-Making* (London: Routledge).

Wyatt-Walker, A. (1995) 'Globalization, Corporate Identity and European Technology Policy', *Journal of European Public Policy*, 2(3): 427–46.

Young, A. R. (1997) 'Consumption Without Representation? Consumers in the Single Market', in H. Wallace and A. R. Young (eds), *Participation and Policy-Making in the European Union* (Oxford: Clarendon Press).

Young, A. R. (1998) 'European Consumer Groups: Multiple Levels of Governance and Multiple Logics of Collective Action', in J. Greenwood and M. Aspinwall (eds), *Collective Action in the European Union* (London: Routledge).

Young, A. R. (2000) 'The Adaptation of European Foreign Economic Policy', *Journal of Common Market Studies*, 38(1): 93–116.

Young, A. R. and Wallace, H. (2000) *Regulatory Policies in the Enlarging European Union: Weighing Civic and Producer Interests* (Manchester: Manchester University Press).

Zito, A. R. (1998) 'Comparing Environmental Policy-Making in Transnational Institutions', *Journal of European Public Policy*, 5(4): 671–90.

Zwaan, J. W. de (1995) *The Permanent Representatives Committee* (Amsterdam: Elsvier).

Index